Teachers, Schools, and Society

Fourth Edition

TEACHERS, SCHOOLS, AND SOCIETY

Myra Pollack Sadker

Late Professor
The American University

David Miller Sadker

The American University

The McGraw-Hill Companies, Inc.

New York St. Louis San Francisco Auckland Bogotá Caracas
Lisbon London Madrid Mexico City Milan Montreal New Delhi
San Juan Singapore Sydney Tokyo Toronto

This book was developed by Lane Akers, Inc.

McGraw-Hill

A Division of The **McGraw·Hill** Companies

TEACHERS, SCHOOLS, AND SOCIETY

Photo credits appear on page 620, and on this page by reference.

This book is printed on acid-free paper.

1 2 3 4 5 6 7 8 9 0 DOW DOW 9 0 9 8 7 6

ISBN 0-07-057784-6

This book was set in Garamond Light by GTS Graphics.
The editor was Lane Akers.
The production supervisor was Denise L. Puryear.
The photo editor was Inge King.
The design manager was Joseph A. Piliero.
The text was designed by Joan Greenfield.
The cover was designed by Wanda Kossak; photo by André Baranowski.
Project supervision was done by The Total Book.
R. R. Donnelley & Sons Company was printer and binder.

Library of Congress Cataloging-in-Publication Data

Sadker, Myra Pollack, (Date)
    Teachers, schools, and society / Myra Pollack Sadker, David Miller
Sadker. — 4th ed.
        p.   cm.
    Includes bibliographical references and index.
    ISBN 0-07-057784-6
    1. Teaching. 2. Education—United States—History. 3. Educational sociology—United
States. 4. Education—Study and teaching—United States. 5. Teachers—Training of—United
States. I. Sadker, David, II. Title.
LB1775.S27   1997
371.1′02—dc20
                                                                                    96-26269

http://www.mhcollege.com

ABOUT THE AUTHORS

MYRA POLLACK SADKER was Professor of Education and Dean of the School of Education at American University until 1995. **DAVID MILLER SADKER** is currently Professor of Education and Director of the Master of Arts in Teaching Program at American University. They have coauthored five books, including *Teachers, Schools, and Society* (McGraw-Hill) and *Failing at Fairness: How Our Schools Cheat Girls* (Touchstone Press, 1995). More than fifty of their articles have appeared in *Phi Delta Kappan, Harvard Educational Review, Educational Leadership,* and other professional journals. Their research interests have focused on foundations of education, educational equity, teacher preparation, and curriculum. They have codirected numerous grants funded by the U.S. Department of Education. They have conducted teaching and equity workshops for principals, teachers, and professors in over forty states and overseas. Their research and writing efforts have received distinguished achievement awards from the American Educational Research Association, the American Association of University Women, the Educational Press Association of America, the American University, Harvard University, and the University of Massachusetts.

CONTENTS IN BRIEF

CONTENTS

**PART FOUR
ISSUES AND
TRENDS**

PREFACE

Teachers, Schools, and Society is designed for introductory courses in teacher education variously labeled Introduction to Education, Introduction to Teaching, Schools, and Society, or Foundations of Education. The primary intent of such a course, whatever its label, is to provide you with sufficiently broad and detailed exposure to the realities and intellectual context of teaching so that you can answer those all-important questions: Do I want to become a teacher? What do I need to become the best teacher possible? What should a professional in the field of education know? To help you answer these questions, we have produced a text with the following characteristics.

Content Coverage.

First of all, we have tried to give you a panoramic view of education. To accomplish this, we have elected to view the field from several different vantage points. In Part One you will see the world of teachers and teaching from a new perspective—the teacher's side of the desk. In Part Two your field of vision will be widened so that you can examine the history, structure, culture, and curriculum of that complex place called school. Part Three then examines the broad foundational forces (historical, legal, financial, organizational, and philosophical) that underlie and shape the world of teaching and schools. In Part Four you will have a chance to examine and debate current issues and trends in education and to join us in speculating about their future. Finally, the Observation Manual (Appendix 1) offers guidelines and strategies for collecting important information about teaching as you observe in schools.

Style of Presentation.

The trouble with panoramic views is that the observer is often at such a distance from what is being viewed that all richness of detail is lost. Vague outlines devoid of human interaction dominate the scene. To combat this trap, we have at various points throughout the text replaced our wide-angle lens with a narrower telescopic view that captures the human drama that comprises the world of education. For example, in many chapters we introduce traditionally dry, abstract topics with illustrative scenarios that help personalize and dramatize the topic at hand. In a slightly different vein, introductory quizzes that probe your prior knowledge and beliefs are used to introduce and personalize the chapters on governance, law, and philosophy. We hope that these stylistic elements, along with a writing style that is deliberately informal rather than academic, will add spice and human interest to the text.

Changes in this Edition.

This fourth edition of *Teachers, Schools, and Society* is designed to improve an already comprehensive text through the following changes:

- *Heavy updating.* We thoroughly updated the text, especially chapters dealing primarily with contemporary issues and trends: Student Diversity (Chapter 4), The Struggle for Equal Educational Opportunity (Chapter 14), Contemporary Social Problems and Children at Risk (Chapter 15), and Tomorrow's Schools (Chapter 16).

- *New/expanded topics and issues.* Topics receiving increased attention in this edition include student diversity, educational inequality, school reform, cooperative learning, project-based instruction, school choice, privatization, multiple intelligences, and emotional quotient.

- A Question and Answer Guide to the Teaching Profession (Chapter 3) has been added.

- *Diversity/inequality focus.* Special attention is given to the topic of student diversity, which may well be the single most critical issue facing our schools and our society in the decades ahead. Accordingly, we have updated Student Diversity (Chapter 4), and we have continued to emphasize the history, problems, and progress of the major minority groups. We have also expanded our important discussion of women's struggle for educational equality.

- *Reorganization.* To make room for the additions listed above, we have combined former Chapters 8 and 9 into Life in Schools (Chapter 6). Also, our history chapter has been moved back to the Foundations section, Part 3 (see Chapter 9, The History of American Education).

- *Accompanying teaching and learning resources.* This new edition of *Teachers, Schools, and Society* is accompanied by instructor aids that include:
  1. *Instructor's manual and test bank.* For each chapter, the instructor is provided with a brief overview, a list of learning objectives, and a variety of in-class and field activities. The test bank includes over 1,000 matching, true-false, multiple choice, essay, and short-answer questions in written or electronic format.
  2. *Overhead transparencies.* A set of overhead, color transparencies is available free to users of this text. These transparencies include figures from the book as well as outside material prepared especially for this text.

Acknowledgments   In March 1995, Myra died undergoing treatment for breast cancer. She worked on the fourth edition even while undergoing chemotherapy, and she was always the major force behind providing a student-friendly introduction to teaching. She will always be the primary author of this book.

In the fall of 1995, two graduate assistants appeared in my office ready to begin their programs toward the Master of Arts in Teaching. What they did not know was that they would become major players, partners in producing the latest textbook. What I did not know was that they were major talents, able to conceptualize, research, draft ideas, and critique drafts with incredible professionalism and insight. Christine Cozadd and Jane Lonnquist were and are gifts, and I am deeply in their debt. Myra would have been proud of Jane and Chris, both as colleagues and teachers.

In previous editions, others have contributed to this text and their efforts are included in this latest edition. We would like to thank Daniel Spiro, Lynette Long, and Elizabeth Ihle for their superb preparation of Chapter 13, Philosophy of Education. Nancy Gorenberg researched several topics and was particularly helpful in developing Legal Landmarks in Chapters 11, School Law, and 14, The Struggle for Equal Educational Opportunity. Elsie Lindemuth, Mary Donald, June Winter, Kirstin Hill, Kate Volker, Ward Davis, Pat Silverthorn, Jacqueline Sadker, Julia Masterson, Amy Monaghan, and Alicia Ruvolo were indefatigable researchers, uncovering critical and contemporary resources. Jacqueline Sadker prepared the index for both the third and fourth editions of this text. Kathryn McNerney researched and also updated sections of Chapter 16, Tomorrow's Schools, as well as the Observation Manual (Appendix 1).

Thanks and kudos to Shirley Pollack and Robin Carter for their patience and skill in the typing and production of several versions of the manuscript. Our editor, Lane Akers, was a constant source of ideas and encouragement, a partner and friend in shaping and revising this text. We also want to thank the following users of *Teachers, Schools, and Society* for generously sharing with us their experiences in teaching the book: Elwyn Abrams, University of Louisville; Gordon Bachus, Richard McKinnis, and Audrey Wright, Central Missouri State University; Elden Barrett, Baylor University; Louise Baucom, University of North Carolina, Charlotte; Donald A. Bennett, Paul Freeburn, and J. David Reid, Metropolitan State College; Barry Berman, SUNY Oneonta; Lisa Coleman, Nebraska Wesleyan University; Nora Hernandez Hendrix, Miami Dade Community College; A. B. Henry, Richard Klahn, and Joye Norris, Bemedji State University; Oliver Hofmann, Joseph Hurst, and Renee Martin, University of Toledo; John Maddaus, University of Maine; Gregory Maltby, New Mexico State University; John Mikula, East Stroudsburg University; Sylvia Moon and Paul Plath, University of Evansville; Marshall Parker, Coastal Carolina College; James Pusch and Jane Van Galen, Youngstown State University; Robert Reed, Bowling Green State University; Donald D. Schaffer and Penny Luken, Broward Community College; John Shaughnessy, Spalding University; Lisa Spiegel, University of South Dakota; Howard Swonigan, Central State University; Beverly Tillman, University of Dayton; and John R. Zelazek, Central Missouri State University.

Finally, proving that one's physical size is not a measure of one's contributions, we would like to thank our daughters Robin and Jackie for their tolerance, insight, and love. When they were in elementary school (during the first edition of this book) they endured the piles of paper, research notes, and drafts that made our house a literal version of the paper chase. By the time of this fourth edition, Jackie is preparing to graduate from Columbia University and Robin, now Dr. Robin, is beginning her career in internal medicine. The editions that preceded this one all benefited from their ideas and critiques. They are the two most special people in my life, and Myra and I continue to dedicate this book to them.

David Miller Sadker

GUIDE TO SELECTED EDUCATIONAL ISSUES

Teachers, Schools, and Society

TEACHERS

1

BECOMING A TEACHER

In the past, being a teacher meant meager wages, conformity to a strict moral and social code, and relatively little professional autonomy. The struggle of teachers to attain full professional status has been a difficult but increasingly successful one. Your entry into teaching comes at a particularly interesting time, since the whole field of education is once again in a period of ferment and change. There is a growing public realization that teachers, like students, need the three Rs: reward, recognition, and respect.

This chapter will analyze the pros and cons of teaching as a career. It will also outline the process of professional change, from the early days of meekness and subservience to those of militant labor actions to the current quest for recognition as a profession. You will learn more about the two main professional associations, the National Education Association (NEA) and the American Federation of Teachers (AFT). The chapter will conclude with a discussion of the importance of professionalism today and the move toward board certification of teachers.

When you were young you may have learned to skim rocks over water. You probably found that small, flat stones worked best—skipping across the water two, three, four, even five times before sinking. Each time the stone met the water, ripples stretched in ever-widening circles. Like those ripples, or a fragile paper boat set out to sea, or a helium balloon let loose in the sky, the knowledge, wisdom, understanding, and guidance you share with your future students will travel far. Henry Adams said it well: "A teacher affects eternity; he never knows where his influence stops."

You have watched teachers in action for most of your life, but have you ever really tried to empathize with them, to get in touch with what they might be thinking and feeling as they go about their job? This chapter will ask you to ask some hard questions about what it is like to be a teacher.

What Are You Doing for the Rest of Your Life?

In a "Peanuts" cartoon, Linus comments that "No problem is so big or complicated that it can't be run away from." As usual, Charles Schulz succinctly highlights a human frailty shared by most of us—the tendency to put aside our problems or critical questions in favor of familiar day-to-day routine. In fact, it is amazing to think how little care and consideration most of us give to choosing a career. It is always easier to go to the movies or study for the next exam than it is to reflect on and plan for the future. This is probably one reason the question "What are you going to be when you grow up?" is so frequently asked but so infrequently answered with any conviction.

A careful analysis of who you are and where you are going can help you determine the extent of your commitment to teaching and also whether you are well-matched to such a career or whether some other career, in or out of education, may be more suitable. Since we are talking about the next 40 or so years of your life, a little time and care seem justified.

To help you analyze your commitment to and compatibility with a teaching career, the following pages include a series of Teaching Balance Sheets that summarize some of the advantages and disadvantages of a career in teaching. Read and reflect on them by yourself first, and then discuss them with a friend or classmate. This should help you gain greater awareness of the realities of teaching and whether it is the right profession for you.

Teaching Balance Sheet 1
Working with People

The Good News
Among the Very Young at Heart ...

If you enjoy being in contact with others, particularly young people, teaching could be the right job for you. Almost the entire working day is spent in human interaction. Your discussions will include an amazing array of topics—from rules for adding fractions to procedures for feeding pet snakes, from an analysis of *The Catcher in the Rye* to advice on applying to colleges. If you truly enjoy children, the

The Bad News
Stop the Crowd—I Want to Get Away

There is so much involvement with others that sometimes, perhaps right in the middle of a language arts lesson when 15 kids have their hands in the air, you may feel like saying: "Stop, everybody. I feel like being alone for the next 15 minutes. I'm going out for a cup of coffee." However, given the hectic pace of classroom interaction, such announcements are virtually impossible. For

(Balance Sheet 1 continues on next page.)

pleasure of these interactions will be heightened because young people are so often funny, fresh, and spontaneous. They will make you laugh, they will make you cry, but always they will make you feel needed.

As one Denver high school teacher says: "I think that for the first time in my life, I feel useful. I didn't feel that way at the insurance company when I was pushing buttons and managing people. . . . They were machines, the whole outfit was a machine. But [in teaching] you're working with exciting people. I find high school kids exciting. They're doing things, and they're looking for people to help them do things."[1]

When you have free time away from the classroom, you can join friends and colleagues in the faculty room and discuss anything from the movie you saw last night to the effectiveness of the new curricular materials your school has just purchased. Of course, if you want some quiet time to grade papers, plan lessons, or simply rest, you can usually get that in the faculty room too.

the major part of each day, your job demands that you be involved with people in a fast-paced and intense way—whether you feel like it or not. In fact, according to researchers, you will be involved in as many as 1,000 verbal exchanges in a single day.

Equally as important as the degree of involvement is whom you are involved with—in this case, children. Even if you love young people, there undoubtedly will be times when they will get on your nerves, as when there is one piece of blue chalk and 12 kids want it.

Being surrounded by children all day can have strange effects on adult behavior. One 33-year-old teacher said, "I knew something was wrong when I began to skip out of school."[2] Another woman who taught in a kindergarten tells of the time she warned her 40-year-old brother "to be sure and put on his galoshes. Wow! Did he give me a strange look."[3]

For most teachers, it is just them and a crowd of kids. Funny, but you can feel very alone under these circumstances.

Teaching Balance Sheet 2
Recognition of Your Effort and Competence

The Good News
The Smell of the Chalkboard, the Roar of the Crowd . . .

You have spent several days researching and planning your lesson on social protest literature for your eleventh-grade English class. You have collected and photocopied many fine poems and statements; you have brought records and tapes of social protest songs into the classroom; you have prepared an excellent brief lecture, fine discussion questions, and creative follow-up activities. The lesson is beautifully organized, and you carry it off with dashing style.

The students are spellbound. They ask many questions and make plans for doing their own research on social protest. One group even decides to meet after school to write a social protest song about the destruction of the natural environment. Their animated discussion continues as the bell signals their passage to the next classroom.

The Bad News
Is Anybody There?

After teaching your fantastic lesson on social protest literature, you want to share your elation with your colleagues, so you head for the teachers' room and begin to talk about the lesson. But it is hard to capture the spirit of what went on in the classroom for those magical 45 minutes. You can sense that your description is falling flat. Besides, people are beginning to give you that "What kind of superstar do you think you are?" look. You decide you had better cut your description short and talk about TGIF (Thank God It's Friday) instead.

Positive recognition is infrequent in teaching, since it is rare to have another adult spend even 10 minutes observing you at work in your classroom. Once you have obtained tenure, such observation becomes almost nonexistent. As one teacher said, "I live in my own little world in my classroom. Some-

When you have taught well, your students will let you know it. On rare and special occasions they will come up to you after class or at the end of the year to tell you they appreciate your effort and ability. At younger grade levels, they may write you notes (often anonymous) thanking you for a good class or a good year.

Usually students are not this direct in expressing their appreciation, but you can tell from their behavior when you are doing a good job. Perhaps it is in the excited way they respond to questions or share personal experiences. Or it comes through in their intense efforts to do their very best work for you. If you are a sensitive listener and observer, your students will send you nonverbal messages that translate into "I'm very happy to be in your classroom."

times I think that my children and I share a secret life that is off-limits to anybody else." Consequently, most of your teaching and administrative colleagues will have only a general impression of your teaching competence. (Of course, if you cannot get your students to quiet down, everyone will know about it: Noise is its own advertisement.)

In short, the word may leak out—through students, parents, or even the janitor—if you are doing a really fine job; but on the whole, when you call out, "Hello, I'm here, I'm a teacher. How am I doing?" there will be no cheers from anyone outside your classroom.

Teaching Balance Sheet 3
Intellectual Stimulation

The Good News
As a Teacher, You Are Constantly Involved in Intellectual Matters . . .

Some of you may have become very interested in a particular subject. Perhaps you love literature, or maybe you are intrigued by contemporary social issues. Whatever content excites you, if you decide you want to share this excitement and stimulation with others, then teaching offers a natural channel for doing so.

As a teacher, particularly at the secondary level, you will have the opportunity for continued involvement in the subject area of your choice. In the classroom your interest and enthusiasm can be contagious, in some cases instilling in others your love of the subject. When this happens, the whole process becomes self-rejuvenating, as students offer you new ideas, fresh interpretations. Listen to what high school teachers say about the intellectual stimulation of their subject matter:

"I went into high school teaching because I was excited about science. Even if they never use science in their lives, these kids should know some of what science offers them. They live in a technological age, and I want them to be equipped to understand that age."[4]

The Bad News
The Same Matters Year After Year After Year

Although it is true that you will be continually involved in academic subject matter, the word *continually* is a double-edged sword. Teaching, like most other jobs, entails a lot of repetition. After a while, you may get tired of teaching the same subject matter to a new crop of students every September. If this happens, excitement and interest may be replaced by boredom and a feeling that you are getting intellectually stale.

Also, if you truly love the particular subject you teach, it can be frustrating and disillusioning to work with students who seem unmoved by the ideas that excite you. If this happens, you may turn to your colleagues for intellectual stimulation, only to find that they are more concerned about weed killer and TV shows than the fine character development in *Hamlet* or the intricacies of current government policy.

Since you are just embarking on your teaching career, you may find it difficult to imagine yourself becoming bored with the world of education. However, as you teach class after class on the same subject, you may well become bored after a few years.

(Balance Sheet 3 continues on next page.)

"I guess at some level I want them to be exposed to what I love and what I teach. I want them to know somebody, even if they think I'm crazy, who's genuinely excited about history."[5]

This process of intellectual stimulation and growth can be further advanced by using your extended vacation times to continue your formal education and by maintaining an active dialogue with similarly motivated teachers in your local school district. In short, you will have ready access to the intellectual community if you want it.

Teaching Balance Sheet 4
Creativity

The Good News
Portrait of the Teacher as an Artist . . .

For countless years, there has been an ongoing debate as to whether teaching is a science or an art, and so far no one has come up with a definitive answer. Some writers, however, draw clear parallels between teachers and artists and the creativity that is essential to both:

"I love to teach as a painter loves to paint, as a musician loves to play, as a singer loves to sing, as a strong man rejoices to run a race. Teaching is an art—an art so great and so difficult to master that a man or woman can spend a long life at it without realizing much more than his limitations and mistakes, and his distance from the ideal. But the main aim of my happy days has been to become a good teacher. Just as every architect wishes to be a good architect and every professional poet strives toward perfection."[6]

Unless you are a slavish follower of instructors' guides and mass-produced lesson plans, you will determine and develop what will be taught in the classroom each day and how this instruction will be carried out. You can construct everything from original games to cassette tapes, from slide shows to discussion questions. Even the development of a superb lesson plan is an exercise in creativity, as you strive to meet the needs of the different children who come into your classroom each day. This truly demands creativity.

The Bad News
The Bog of Mindless Routine

Much has been said about the creativity of teaching, but under close inspection, the job breaks down into a lot of mindless routine as well. A large percentage of the day is consumed by clerical work, child control, housekeeping, making announcements, participating in ceremonies. Although there is opportunity for ingenuity and inventiveness, most of the day is spent in the three Rs of ritual, repetition, and routine. As one disgruntled sixth-grade teacher in Los Angeles said:

"Paper work, paper work. The nurse wants the health cards, so you have to stop and get them. Another teacher wants one of your report cards. The principal wants to know how many social science books you have. Somebody else wants to know if you can come to a meeting on such and such a day. Forms to fill out, those crazy forms: Would you please give a breakdown of boys and girls in the class; would you please say how many children you have in reading grade such and such. Forms, messengers—all day long."[7]

Teaching Balance Sheet 5
Social Concern

The Good News
To Touch a Life and Make a Difference . . .

Teaching is not an insignificant, irrelevant, paper-shuffling kind of a job. It has meaning, worth, and value. It gives you the opportunity to touch a young and impressionable life and make it better.

"We were the luckiest class in the school. We had a homeroom teacher who knew the core truth of education: Self-hate destroys, self-esteem saves. This principle guided all her efforts on our behalf. She always minimized our deficiencies, neutralized our rage, and enhanced our natural gifts. She never, so to speak, forced a dancer to sing or a singer to dance. She allowed each of us to light his own lamp. We loved her."[8]

"Mr. Jacobs won our hearts, because he treated us as though we were already what we could only hope to become. Through his eyes we saw ourselves as capable and decent and destined for greatness. . . . Mr. Jacobs introduced us to ourselves. We learned who we were and what we wanted to be. No longer strangers to ourselves, we felt at home in the world."[9]

As a teacher, you will have a rare privilege and responsibility: You can affect and change the lives of children. It is the basic nature of the job to guide academic learning, to help a puzzled and frustrated child finally crack the phonic code or discover pattern and meaning in what were once the lifeless and unrelated facts of history. But the teaching of reading and history and other content areas does not take place in an emotional vacuum.

Each classroom is a composite of the anguish and joy of all its students. Students occupy psychological as well as physical space. There is the child in the fourth seat who seldom volunteers but who always knows the answer. You can feel the pain of her shyness. There is the rambunctious one who spills all over the classroom in a million random ways but is unable to focus on any one task or project. There is the "victim" who inspires taunts and even physical abuse from usually well-mannered classmates. There is the child who barely acknowledges your presence and pencil-taps on the desk in a disturbing and incomprehensible rhythm.

All of these children are struggling for self-esteem and for the discovery of who they are and what they can become. You can become an impor-

The Bad News
The Tarnished Idealist

We all hope to be that special teacher, the one students remember and talk about long after they have left Farrington Elementary School or Monroe High, the one who has reached them in such a personal and intense way that lives are forever enriched.

In reality, it is not so easy to be this kind of teacher. Too often, idealistic goals give way to survival—simply making it through from one day to the next. Teachers are especially vulnerable to feelings of frustration during their first year or two in the classroom. Some find their situations so intolerable that they leave teaching.

One of the key factors leading to depression and dropping out is discipline. All too often, new teachers find themselves judged on their ability to maintain a quiet, orderly room rather than on their ability to reach their students or to achieve instructional objectives. Idealistic young teachers find the worship of control incompatible with their humanistic goals. Likewise, they feel betrayed if a student naively mistakes their offer of friendship as a sign of weakness or vulnerability. They feel hurt and disillusioned when experiments in student self-control result in wild, out-of-control classrooms. As a result, many learn the trade secret—"don't smile until Christmas"—and adopt it quickly.

It is not only the newly initiated who find themselves caught in the ironic war of teacher against student. Long-time veterans also throw up their hands in despair and sometimes throw out their teaching credentials as well.

Teacher-student conflict is not the only source of teachers' lost idealism. In many cases it is in conflict with or disappointment in school administrators who do not do enough to support them and help them with discipline or with a work environment that is so neglected that their classrooms seem to be falling apart around them.

Sometimes teaching means confronting student apathy, or tangling with bureaucratic red tape, or doing without the basic tools of the job. Then trying to make a difference may result in more frustration than satisfaction. Knowing this, can you still say to yourself, "I want to be a teacher"?

(Balance Sheet 5 continues on next page.)

tant part of their sometimes painful and sometimes joyful quest for growth and self-discovery.

If you are drawn to teaching because you want to work with children and in some way make a difference in their lives, you have plenty of company. In fact, most teachers chose their career because it is a helping profession; some people even call it a secular ministry. All other reasons given for becoming a teacher are minor compared to this commitment to making a difference in children's lives. Christa McAuliffe, the teacher who touched all our lives before her tragic death in space, put it well: "I touch the future. I teach."

Teaching Balance Sheet 6
Money Matters and Other Benefits

The Good News
You've Come a Long Way, Teacher . . .

Teachers' salaries have gotten a lot better over the years. If you had taught in 1930, you would have earned approximately $1,000 a year. By 1967–1968, the average yearly salary had increased to more than $7,000 and in 1975–1976 to more than $12,000 a year. Although teachers' salaries dropped in real earning power during the late 1970s, substantial gains were made in the mid-1980s. Between 1980 and 1990 salaries, adjusted for inflation, rose 18 percent. By the end of the 1980s, the average teacher's salary was approaching $30,000. By 1994 it had risen to more than $36,000 a year.

If you decide to teach in Alaska, you will earn a good deal more than if you teach in West Virginia or Arkansas, for salaries vary from state to state and from community to community, often reflecting different costs of living. In most areas, though, salary increases are tied to years of service and academic training.

Besides an improved salary picture, you will enjoy long vacation periods both during the academic year and in the summer. You can use your vacation time for much-needed rest and leisure, for professional and academic study, or for being with friends and family. Sabbatical leaves, often given in the seventh year, provide teachers with an opportunity to study, travel, or engage in other forms of professional improvement. All of these considerations make for a more relaxed and varied lifestyle, one

The Bad News
But Not Far Enough

Although teachers' salaries have improved, they still lag behind what most people would call a good income. When you consider the effects of inflation, the salary gains of the past year are considerably less impressive. Anyone trying to support a family on a teacher's salary will tell you that it is a far cry from wealth and prosperity. Just listen to some teachers talk about trying to make ends meet. A history teacher with a master's degree says: "It's really difficult to maintain a family. . . . I've struggled by doing odd things. I operated the football stadium. I operate the gymnasium for the basketball games, to pick up a few extra dollars. I'm not sure I could have done it then except for a wife who's not demanding or pushy. She's completely comfortable with the things we have, and we don't have a great deal."[10]

A Missouri school teacher who supplements his income by working as a service station attendant says: "You know, it's degrading to serve customers who are the parents of the kids you teach."[11]

And the following comment was overheard in a school that services a well-to-do suburban community: "You can always tell the difference between the teachers' and the students' parking lots. The students' lot is the one with all the new cars in it."[12]

The long periods of vacation are nice—but they are also long periods without income. When a factory worker is put on 2 months' leave with no pay, that gives you time for yourself and your family as well.

If you feel the need for more money, you can turn your vacation time into an opportunity for a second income. Some teachers run summer camps; others teach in summer school; still others write and publish curricular materials. Whether you use your vacation to be with your family, to travel, or to make extra money, time flexibility is a definite plus.

it is called a layoff, not a vacation! The fact is that teachers are among the most active moonlighters, and many hold down two or more jobs in order to make ends meet. In short, your vacations cost you money.

Teaching Balance Sheet 7
The Prestige Factor

The Good News
I'm Proud to Be a Teacher . . .

Fortunately, most people recognize the critical importance of teachers. President John F. Kennedy said, "A child miseducated is a child lost." There are many similar testimonials to the worth and value of teachers. You can even dip back into Roman history and find Cicero acknowledging the importance of the teaching profession: "What nobler employment or more valuable to the state than that of the man who instructs the rising generation?" And Mark Twain, on the lighter side, wryly comments: "To be good is noble, but to teach others how to be good is nobler—and less trouble."

In the past, public opinion polls have confirmed the importance of teachers in our society. A 1967 Louis Harris poll ranked teaching fifth out of a possible 17 professions. Teachers were ranked higher than such professionals as corporate executives, psychiatrists, United States Supreme Court justices, the clergy, reporters and publishers, and members of Congress. A 1970 survey questioned 650 people concerning the prestige rating of more than 500 occupational titles and disclosed that both elementary and secondary teachers were rated above the nineti-eth percentile. Teacher status took a battering from public criticism during the 1970s and early 1980s, but the public is once again acknowledging the importance of teachers. In a 1984 Gallup poll, the public rated the value of teachers' services to society just below those of the clergy and medical doctors, and ahead of school principals, judges, lawyers, business executives, and bankers. According to a 1981 Gallup poll, only 46 percent of parents said they wanted their children to go into teaching. By

The Bad News
I Don't Get No Respect

When you join the ranks of a particular occupation, you will be personally measured and valued according to how society regards that group as a whole. You have no doubt done this yourself. Suppose you walk into a room and are introduced to five people: an assembly-line worker, a college president, a doctor, a garbage collector, and an accountant. Before getting to know these people as individuals, you would probably form some distinct impressions about their intelligence, character, and general worth, based on their occupation. Whether we like it or not, people play status games and value us according to the kind of jobs we have.

Right now when you meet new people, you are probably introduced as a student from a particular university. How will you feel about meeting the world as a teacher? Will that make you feel proud or apologetic?

Ironically, the importance of educating our children is widely recognized, but the key people in this process—teachers—are not always highly valued. There are several reasons for this paradox, one of which is the sexist nature of our society. Almost all occupations with large numbers of women seem to have prestige problems, and teaching is no exception. There may come a day when we will not have to mention this issue, but for the time being, prejudice still exists.

Another reason has to do with the materialistic nature of our society. People's work is frequently measured by the size of the paycheck they bring home, and, as already discussed, the wallets of most teachers are modestly endowed.

(Balance Sheet 7 continues on next page.)

1993 the number had risen to 67 percent. Students also recognize the worth of teachers. According to a 1992 national survey, students gave their teachers a grade of A.[13]

Today's teachers, like doctors and lawyers, are generally considered to be professionals. They are credited with having professional knowledge, are given considerable autonomy in their work, and have developed a professional code of ethics. Like other professionals, they supply a social service that is largely dependent on intellectual abilities. In short, when you become a teacher, society will accord you respect because it values the worth of what you do. You will be considered a professional, someone with specialized training and skills that can be used to benefit others.

Some people question whether teachers should even be considered professionals. In dismissing teachers from the professional ranks, these critics call attention to teachers' relatively short training period (compared with that of doctors or lawyers, for example), and they note that teacher preparation programs are not particularly selective in their admissions procedures. Further, unlike most other professionals, teachers do not choose their clients (students), nor do they have much choice in what they will teach. Their professional autonomy is further limited by school administrators, who hire and fire them and who determine their salaries.

Although there has been a resurgence of support for teachers, when it comes to the game of impressing people, teachers are still not collecting a large pile of status chips.

Profiles in Teaching: Jaime Escalante

Jaime Escalante may be best known for an incident in 1982 involving the Educational Testing Service (ETS) and 14 of his students at Garfield High in East Los Angeles. For 4 years Escalante had been struggling to build a strong advanced placement (AP) calculus program at Garfield, a troubled inner-city school with a poor academic history and an uncertain future. It had been difficult going, but the program finally blossomed that year. Escalante had 18 students in his class, almost double the number from the year before, and they worked so hard that every one of them passed the difficult and prestigious AP examination.

During the summer, however, an unpleasant controversy developed. The ETS, which administers the AP exam, told 14 of the students that a high correspondence in their answers suggested that they may have cheated. They would either have to retake the test or have their scores nullified. Escalante, the students, and others protested. There had been no cheating, they argued. It seemed to be just another example of the experts underestimating the potential of students who are poor and Latino. But the ETS would not budge, and so a retest was arranged. Even after a summer away from the theorems and formulas, all of the students passed the test again, many with higher scores than the first time.

Since then, Escalante's calculus program has taken off, involving hundreds of students every year and

during the summer. And his success encouraged other Garfield teachers to add and expand AP classes in history, English, biology, and other subjects. By 1987, Garfield had become known as one of the best public schools in the country.[a]

How does Escalante account for his achievements? Much of his teaching he sums up as the pursuit of *ganas,* a Spanish word meaning "the will to succeed."

Really it's not just the knowledge of math. Because to have knowledge is one thing, and to use that knowledge is another, and to know how to teach or how to motivate these kids is the combination of both. My skills are really to motivate these kids, to make them learn, to give them *ganas*—desire to do something—to make them believe they can learn.[b]

Escalante's own life story demonstrates much of the persistence and love of hard work that he inspires in his students. When he immigrated to the United States from Bolivia, in 1963, he had already been teaching for 11 years, ever since he was 22 years old, gaining a reputation as one of the finest teachers in La Paz. In Bolivia, he was used to teaching without textbooks or fancy materials, and the low salary required him to teach three sets of classes a day in order to get by.

Anybody, any kid can learn if he or she has the desire to do it. That's what *ganas* is about. The teacher plays an important role in education—we all remember the first teacher who really touched our lives, or gave us some encouragement, or at least appreciated our best. The teacher gives us the desire to learn, the desire to be Somebody.[c]

In class, Escalante is an unpredictable showman as well as a stern father. To get his students' attention and understanding, he will do almost anything, from starting a class with a group cheer to translating a complex question into a play from a basketball game. But while "Kimo," as he is nicknamed, can be a charming, colorful character to those who show sincere effort, latecomers and those with incomplete assignments find themselves interrogated, hounded by calls to parents, and threatened with a transfer to a less effective school a very long bus ride away. Whether he has to resort to rewards, taunts, afternoon study sessions, or even mild bribery, Escalante refuses to allow students to give up.

I use the team approach, I make them believe that we have a team which is going to prepare for the Olympics. And our Olympics is the advanced placement calculus exam. I always talk to them and tell them, "Look, we prepared two years for this competition, and you have to play strong defense. Don't let the test put you down. You're the best." And every time the kids go to take the advanced placement calculus exam, they wear the jacket with a bulldog, which is the school mascot, and the kids go to the testing room yelling "Defense! Defense! Defense!"[d]

Although he has been the subject of the movie *Stand and Deliver,* a biography, and numerous articles, the reasons behind much of Jaime Escalante's success remain a mystery. Many have discussed and argued over whether to view great teaching as an art or a skill, something innate or something learned, but it may be better to just let Escalante be Escalante. In his own words:

The teacher has to have the energy of the hottest volcano, the memory of an elephant, and the diplomacy of an ambassador.... Really, a teacher has to possess love and knowledge and then has to use this combined passion to be able to accomplish something.[e]

[a]Jay Mathews, *Escalante: The Best Teacher in America* (New York: Henry Holt, 1988).

[b]Quoted in Anne Meek, "On Creating Ganas: A Conversation with Jaime Escalante," *Educational Leadership* 46, no. 5 (February 1989): 46–47.

[c]Ibid.

[d]Ibid.

[e]Ibid.

Source: This Profile in Teaching was written by Rafael Heller.

Why Do Teachers Need Professional Organizations?

So you are interested in a teaching position? If you will just agree to the following stipulations and sign the following contract (which dates from the 1920s, when only women needed to apply), we may be able to use you.

Teaching Contract

Miss _____ agrees:

1. Not to get married. This contract becomes null and void immediately if the teacher marries.
2. Not to keep company with men.
3. To be home between the hours of 8 P.M. and 6 A.M. unless in attendance at a school function.
4. Not to loiter downtown in ice-cream parlors.
5. Not to leave town at any time without the permission of the Chairman of the Trustees.
6. Not to smoke cigarettes. This contract becomes null and void immediately if the teacher is found smoking.
7. Not to drink beer, wine, or whiskey. This contract becomes null and void immediately if the teacher is found drinking beer, wine, or whiskey.
8. Not to ride in a carriage or automobile with any man except her brother or father.
9. Not to dress in bright colors.
10. Not to dye her hair.
11. Not to wear less than two petticoats.
12. Not to wear dresses shorter than two inches above the ankles.
13. To keep the schoolroom clean:
    a. To sweep the classroom floor at least once daily.
    b. To scrub the classroom floor at least once weekly with soap and hot water.
    c. To clean the blackboard at least once daily.
    d. To start the fire at 7 A.M. so that the room will be warm by 8 A.M. when the children arrive.
14. Not to wear face powder, mascara, or to paint the lips.

(Reprinted courtesy of the *Chicago Tribune*, September 28, 1975, Section 1.)

Interested? Probably not. But not so long ago, teaching contracts rigidly dictated both the personal and the professional lives of teachers. The reward for this austere dedication was an unimpressive $75 a month.

The fact that such demands upon teachers are now history is due in large part to the strength and influence of teacher organizations. The two principal organizations are the National Education Association (NEA) and the American Federation of Teachers (AFT). During the past few decades, both organizations have successfully promoted the interests of teachers. Through **collective bargaining** (that is, all the teachers in a school system bargaining as one group through a chosen representative), through organized actions (including strikes), and through public relations efforts, they have succeeded in improving both the salaries and the working conditions of teachers.

As you enter the profession, you will find yourself somewhat alone in a new environment and without the protection of tenure. Teacher associations such as the NEA and the AFT can help alleviate the sense of loneliness and vulnerability by providing you with collegial support, opportunities for professional growth, and the security that one derives from participating in a large and influential group.

From Passivity to Power: The Development of Teacher Organizations

In colonial times teachers typically were meek and quiet public servants. In fact, some of them actually were servants, since they had obtained the money to pay for their passage to America by indenturing themselves. As teachers, they obeyed strict rules. They were not allowed to smoke or drink; their courting activities were regulated; churchgoing was compulsory; their pitiful wages were equivalent to those of a farmhand. In order to survive, many teachers were forced to board with a different family each week. (Can you imagine having to eat dinner with a different student's family every week?)[14]

Into the latter part of the nineteenth century, the status and financial position of most teachers remained pathetic. The August 1864 issue of *Illinois Teacher* described the typical teacher as "someone who can parse and cipher; has little brains and less money; is feeble minded, unable to grapple with real men and women in the stirring employments of life, but on that account admirably fitted to associate with childish intellects." In 1874 in Massachusetts, male teachers were paid a monthly salary of $24.51. Women earned less than $8. This lowly status finally began to improve as teachers started to organize.

In 1794 the Society of Associated Teachers of New York City became the first teacher association in this country. Thirty more teacher associations were formed between 1840 and 1861, and in 1857 the first National Teachers' Association was formed. In the 1870s this group merged with the National Association of School Superintendents and the American Normal School Association. This new, enlarged organization became the **National Education Association (NEA).** By 1910 the NEA comprised 6,909 teachers, only about 1 percent of the teachers in the nation.

At first the NEA did not do a great deal to meet the needs of teachers. It did not even admit women. Dominated by college professors and school superintendents, its meetings were devoted to esoteric pursuits rather than such pressing needs as a livable salary. Nevertheless, membership continued to climb. By World War II more than 200,000 teachers belonged to the NEA, while over 30,000 had joined another teacher organization, the AFT.

In 1902 a group of teachers in San Antonio, Texas, became the first to join a labor union, the American Federation of Labor. In 1916, when teachers' unions from Chicago and Gary, Indiana, affiliated with the American Federation of Labor, the **American Federation of Teachers (AFT)** was formed. The AFT's initial membership of 3,000 soon withered to 500, however, owing to the withdrawal of the Chicago Federation of Teachers, whose members were forced to accept a "yellow dog" contract that prohibited union membership. The AFT soon recovered, however, and membership grew to 10,000 by 1920.

The widespread anti-union climate of the 1920s caused the AFT to lose approximately two-thirds of its membership as local leaders were dismissed or threatened with removal from their jobs. Lack of tenure and the resulting job insecurity was a major problem confronting teachers during the great depression of the 1930s. In 27 states teachers either had only 1-year contracts or no contracts at all, and only 4 states had uniform tenure laws. Largely through the work of the AFT, some form of tenure was established in many states by the end of the depression, and AFT membership rose once again.

Following World War II, teacher salaries remained abysmally low, as witnessed by the fact that 26 states still hired teachers for less than $600 a year. The purchasing power of factory workers increased during the 1940s, but teachers' purchasing power declined. Although the states began to adopt minimum salary laws, by 1947 the average teacher's annual salary was only $2,380.

It was not until the late 1950s that teachers' salaries finally reached the point where they were above the national average for all employees. Although it was increasingly obvious that organized effort could have a substantial impact on the financial well-being of teachers, many teachers, especially in rural and suburban areas, felt that militancy and strikes were not appropriate for members of a profession. Unionism made these teachers feel like blue-collar rather than white-collar workers. Many NEA members felt that striking and militant tactics would make teachers lose respect in the eyes of their students—and the community.

The event that established militant labor action as an acceptable tactic for teachers came in 1961. Teacher groups in New York City asked an NEA official in Washington to assist them with collective bargaining. Before the NEA was able to respond, the local AFT affiliate, the United Federation of Teachers (UFT), called a strike; 500 teachers stayed out of work. The board of education agreed to an election to select a bargaining agent, but first the board wanted a committee to study "the most appropriate form" of bargaining. The AFT supported collective bargaining; the NEA came out against it. In a referendum New York City teachers voted for collective bargaining by three to one. The AFT victory in New York City pushed the NEA into a more militant position. By the late 1960s the NEA had conformed to the AFT's more militant style of representation as the two organizations competed fiercely for members.

By 1972, 1,445,392 school personnel were employed under negotiated agreements. During this decade, teacher organizations fought not only for salary but also for teacher rights: the protection of minority and women's rights as well as the assurance of freedom of speech, dress, and other forms of expression. The 1970s also saw teacher organizations becoming more active on the political front as they began making major contributions to political candidates who supported education.

But along with gains attained through militancy came some bitter residue as well. The strikes of the 1960s and 1970s were often marked by terrible acrimony. The public perception of teachers changed from the beloved image of Mr. Chips to that of the self-interest group who closed the schools. Here is how one teacher describes her first strike:

Marked by acrimony and bitterness, strikes changed the traditional image of teachers as meek and passive public servants.

My first strike took place in a determinedly proletarian, mine-scarred community in North Eastern Pennsylvania. Some Scrantonians were amazed to see us come out from behind the shelter of our big wooden desks in neat little rooms and slosh through the streets of dirty snow bearing blatant signs. But that was 1967, long ago. Three more strikes followed in less than a decade and no one is shocked anymore. . . . The original strike shatters innocence; eventually the picket line becomes a biennial habit.[15]

And from another perspective, a first-year superintendent describes the confrontation when the teachers struck:

The entrances to one school were chained and padlocked. Everywhere classroom locks had been jammed with putty. No key or the wrong keys kept us out of supply and medicine closets. Teachers' desk drawers had been emptied and students had been instructed to leave their textbooks at home. Chalk was nonexistent. Even lowly toilet tissue was taken out of the lavatories. In one place we lacked warm hands to accompany our cold, cold hearts, because a boiler had mysteriously broken. Naturally, a "disinterested" citizen filed the lack of hot water as a health hazard. It seems that machines, like plants, missed their familiar masters because a public address system refused to speak and a copying machine to duplicate. The situation was comparable to entering a city after Genghis Khan.[16]

Militant action seemed to fit the 1960s and 1970s, but the 1980s and 1990s brought a climate that was less responsive to unionism and had little tolerance for public employees who go on strike. Today, the AFT focuses as much on professional and education reform as it does on collective bargaining. The NEA, slower to move into a key position on education reform, also faces more conservative communities and has sponsored fewer labor actions in the 1990s.

Today, teaching is one of the most organized occupations in the nation. Nine out of ten teachers belong to either the NEA or the AFT. Six out of ten teachers are represented by one or the other in collective bargaining. It is not too early for you to start thinking about whether you want to join a professional association and which one may best represent you.

Does the National Education Association Speak for You?

Mediumtown Education Association (MEA) Announces
A Reception and Business Meeting
Howard Jackson Hotel 8:00 P.M.
All New Faculty Members Invited

You have been a teacher in Mediumtown for all of 2 weeks, and you know about five faces and three names of other faculty members. You decide to take the MEA up on its offer. It will be a good opportunity to find out about the MEA and to meet some people at the same time.

Before you attend, you decide to do a little research on the MEA's parent organization, the National Education Association. You learn that in the past many people thought that the NEA was not aggressive enough in striving to better teachers' salaries and working conditions. You discover, for example, that the demeaning teacher contract described in the previous section was in force 65 years after the NEA began its work and that the NEA refused to take a stand on segregated education until long after the Supreme Court's 1954

FIGURE 1.1
Milestones in the Birth and Growth of Teacher Associations

1794	The Society of Associated Teachers of New York City becomes the country's first teacher association.
1840–1861	Thirty state teacher associations form.
1857	The first National Teachers' Association is formed. In the late 1870s this group merges with the National Association of School Superintendents and the American Normal School Association to become the National Education Association (NEA).
1902	A group of teachers from San Antonio, Texas, becomes the first to join a labor union, the American Federation of Labor (AFL).
1916	The American Federation of Teachers (AFT) is formed.
1920s	The AFT has more than 10,000 members.
1940s	More than 200,000 teachers belong to the NEA (up from about 7,000 in 1910). More than 30,000 teachers belong to the AFT.
1940s–1950s	More than 100 strike threats are carried out.
1960s–1970s	First the AFT and then the NEA take up militant tactics, including collective bargaining and strikes.
1980s–1990s	Teacher organizations are involved in political action and show growing concern for increased professionalism.

desegregation decision. In view of this history, it does not surprise you that many persons, teachers and nonteachers, used to refer derisively to the NEA as a "tea-and-cookies, do-nothing organization."

One of the reasons for the NEA's historical lack of power, you learn, can be traced to its origin. When the 43 founders of the NEA gathered in the mid-nineteenth century, they intended to form a broad organization that would encompass many different educational interests and groups. Their charter stated the new organization's goals: "To elevate the character and advance the interests of the profession of teaching and to promote the cause of education in the United States." But over the years the NEA's broad and diverse membership has led to internal conflict and even to organizational paralysis.

For example, for many years the NEA was dominated by school administrators, and its policies and actions primarily reflected their interests. Not infrequently, these politics conflicted with the interests of most of its members, who were classroom teachers. By attempting to draw all educators under one great canopy, the NEA so diluted its focus that it became ineffective in representing its diverse interest groups.

During the 1960s and the 1970s, the NEA became a stronger advocate of teachers' rights. During the 1980s and 1990s, the association continued to move into a leadership position in education reform. Most people attribute the more professional and progressive stands of the NEA to the leadership of Mary Hatwood Futrell. President of the organization from 1983 to 1989, Futrell grew up in a female-headed household, attended segregated schools in Lynchburg, Virginia, and taught business courses in high school. From these modest beginnings she became a highly popular and effective leader of the NEA. As a black woman she has served as an important symbol to educators across the nation. Keith Geiger, who followed Futrell as NEA president, continued many of these progressive policies.

Your research tells you that now the NEA is the largest professional and employee organization in the nation. It enrolls 2.2 million members, including elementary and secondary teachers, higher-education faculty, retired educators, and educational support personnel. Fifty-two state-level associations are affiliated with the NEA, as well as approximately 13,000 local associations. An organization that attracts that many people must have something to say, you think to yourself. So, promptly at 8:00 P.M., you settle into your chair at the Howard Jackson Hotel and give the NEA speaker your attention. He begins:

> The NEA has always worked for the best in education. We believe in high educational standards, increased funding from the federal government, and equal educational rights for all our students and for those who educate them. Our policies are determined by our membership through their delegates at the association's annual representative assembly. And the services we provide our members are effective and wide-ranging.

At this point the speaker distributes a well-designed multicolor brochure outlining the association's programs and services. Even a cursory glance shows you that these are impressive. As you flip through the brochure, you see:

- *Publishing.* All members receive a newspaper, *NEA Today,* leaders receive a newsletter, *NEA Now,* and NEA student members receive the annual *Tomorrow's Teachers.*
- *Human and Civil Rights.* The NEA's Human and Civil Rights unit shows the association's dedication to this cause. It offers information and programs on

Professional organizations like NEA have not only made "teacher power" a reality, they have also contributed much to national educational policy.

Christa McAuliffe and Her Testament

A few weeks ago I wrote a piece about school teachers going up in space. I speculated as to what kinds of candidates my own teachers at P.S. 35 would have made if they had applied for the trip. It was a light piece because, like most Americans, I never dreamed anything could happen to the flight of the shuttle *Challenger*.

During the last numbing week, as I watched the television screen, I got to thinking about teachers. Although Christa McAuliffe wasn't a professional astronaut, she did leave behind a wonderful legacy.

Consider this.

For the past 15 or 20 years, America's teachers could not have been held in lower esteem. They were underpaid, underrated and blamed for anything that went wrong with our schools.

It appeared the only time we saw teachers on TV was when they were on strike or arrested for child abuse. The perception was that teachers were people who taught because they couldn't make it in the real world.

Except for covering vandalism and crime in schools, the media ignored what was going on in the classroom. And with reason: If teachers were teaching, and students were learning, it wasn't news—that is, until the destruction of *Challenger*.

Suddenly our schools received more attention than they have ever been given before. Seven brave people died that morning, but it was the death of a school teacher that made our children cry.

When the TV cameras entered the nation's classrooms to record their grief, we saw principals and teachers fighting back their own tears as they tried to comfort the students.

The cameras not only focused on teachers but also panned to the agonized faces of students. They showed teacher to pupil and pupil to teacher—and in that moment of sadness we witnessed the educational process at its best.

When these pictures came into our homes we were reminded of something we tend to take for granted: the role teachers quietly play in the lives of children.

The lesson was not just for grown-ups. You had the feeling that the students had gained a new respect for

teachers as well. It went something like this. "Christa was a teacher, and Christa died in space, but it could have been anybody's teacher—including mine."

So what was Christa McAuliffe's legacy?

When *Sputnik* went up and we realized the Russians were ahead there was a great clamor to educate American children and make our schools second to none. Then after the successes of our own space program, the clamor died down. Education was dropped as our No. 1 priority.

At least it was until last week. After that one horrifying moment in Florida, things changed again. The parent-teacher-pupil bond that had been fraying for a generation seemed to be joined again.

Christa McAuliffe's gift to us is not in the skies but here on earth. From everything you can read, she was a teacher before she went up and she intended to be a teacher when she returned. In death her legacy is to give her fellow professionals new dignity and honor. Thanks to Christa, each one of them can say with pride, "I'm a teacher, too."

Source: Art Buchwald, *The Washington Post*, February 6, 1986.

such topics as women's leadership training, minority involvement, gender equity, affirmative action, desegregation, and academic freedom.

- *Educational Innovation.* NEA's National Center for Innovation (NCI) creates and supports diverse reform projects to seed and support systemic school change. Through its programs, NCI promotes high-quality education, advances the profession, and provides professional development opportunities for association activists.
- *Legal Services.* The Kate Frank/DuShane Legal Services Program offers legal assistance for NEA members in disputes with employers. The program assists by providing counsel and paying other legal expenses such as court costs and filing fees. Through a professional liability insurance policy offered to members, the Educators Employment Liability (EEL) program protects members if they are sued by parents or children for negligence arising out of the member's educational employment.
- *Membership and Affiliates.* This division assists affiliates in leadership training, collective bargaining, grievance procedures, and other projects. Under this program area, the National Education Employee Fund provides interest-free loans to education personnel who are in financial trouble because of strike activity. The Uni-Serv program provides members with staff services at the local level to organize various association programs.
- *Government Relations.* The Government Relations unit organizes and trains NEA members to elect pro-education candidates to federal office. Staff here also work with the federal government to influence the development of legislative proposals, as well as of regulations affecting programs of interest to NEA members. Government Relations is also responsible for advancing the NEA's legislative agenda in Congress.

You begin to read about some of the other special programs NEA provides, such as the Health Information Network, which brings health-related information into schools, when you are jolted to attention by a heated debate. You recognize the angry speaker as the chairman of the history department:

> I think we ought to pay less attention to political education and more attention to education education. NEA-PAC always seems to support losing candidates.

The NEA orientation leader interrupts:

> Let's not get into an argument on this one issue. NEA has been involved politically during the last few years, but the stated position of our organization is that, and I quote, "In our democracy, all citizens have the right—indeed the obligation—to work to elect responsive officials. Thankfully, we live in a country that celebrates such political freedom." But let's get away from politics. As my distinguished colleague from the history department says, we need to discuss the education issues. From tuition tax credits to sex education, NEA is not afraid to face the tough questions. And we put our money where our mouth is. We always keep in mind the old NEA motto, spoken by Horace Mann more than 100 years ago: "Be ashamed to die before you have won some victory for humanity."

You are so impressed with the accomplishments and promise of the NEA and the local MEA that you are about to ask for an application form and write out a check for membership dues. Just then, a man who has been sitting quietly next to you leans over and says:

I belong to the MFT, the Mediumtown Federation of Teachers. It's the local affiliate of the AFT, the American Federation of Teachers. Don't sign anything until you've heard our side.

Does the American Federation of Teachers Speak for You?

The following week you again bump into the quiet, unknown man who attended the MEA meeting. He introduces himself with "just call me Al," and invites you to attend the meeting of the MFT to be held at Union Hall on Friday. He is pretty persuasive, and since you want to know about all of your options before you sign on any dotted line, you agree to go.

You enter the MFT meeting place and take your seat on one of Union Hall's hard-backed chairs. As you glance around the room, you find yourself staring at the podium up front, George Meany's picture on one wall, and the American flag on the other. The very organization of the room gives you an immediate sense of the labor orientation of the AFT and of this local, the MFT. As the speaker begins her talk, your original impressions are confirmed:

When John Dewey became our first member back in 1916, he recognized that teachers need their own organization. Teachers are the backbone of the educational system, and we must speak for ourselves. That is why the AFT will continue to be exclusively of teachers, by teachers, and for teachers.

It was the AFT that backed school desegregation years before the 1954 Supreme Court decision that established the principle that separate is not equal. We ran freedom schools for southern black students, and we have a strong record on academic freedom and civil rights.

It was the AFT that demanded and fought for the teacher's right to bargain collectively.

It was AFT leaders who went to jail to show the nation their determination that teachers would no longer stand for second-class status.

It was the AFT that won New York City teachers their pay increases and other benefits.

And as part of the great labor movement, the AFL-CIO, the AFT continues to show the nation that through the power of the union the voice of America's teachers will be heard.

While you are reading the literature handed out at the MFT meeting, you learn that the AFT, with 885,000 members and more than 2,000 locals, is a good deal smaller than the NEA. The association began gaining impetus in the latter part of the 1950s. By 1961, the AFT had won the right to bargain for New York City teachers, and through collective bargaining and strikes it set precedents by obtaining raises and other benefits for them. As a result of successes in New York, AFT membership began to grow in labor-oriented urban areas where teachers were fed up with low salaries and poor working conditions and were willing to strike as a means of improving things. In Washington, DC, Boston, Cleveland, Chicago, and other cities, the AFT won elections and became the organization to represent teachers. Militancy was bringing the AFT both members and victories, although its successes were usually confined to urban centers.

As you continue reading the literature and listening to the speaker, you find that the AFT's image as a streetwise, scrappy union has begun to shift since the 1970s. In fact, through the ideas and activities of its president, Albert Shanker, the AFT has taken a leadership role in education reform. Shanker supports national exams for students as well as national standards for teachers, as can be seen by the AFT presence on the National Board for Professional Teaching Standards. The AFT also supports both induction programs that enable new teachers to work with master teachers and active recruitment of minorities to the teaching profession.[17]

Your materials point out that the AFT offers a wide array of services, including:

- *The American Teacher,* a monthly newspaper; the *American Educator,* a quarterly professional journal; and *Action,* a weekly newsletter
- Local workshops and national forums on topics such as teacher education, staff development, critical thinking, school finance, and other education reform issues
- Political action in favor of those candidates who support public education

As you weigh the relative merits of the two organizations, you find yourself pondering some basic questions. What should be the role of teachers in our society? What are the best strategies for improving teachers' salaries, status, and working conditions? What approaches will be most effective in improving the quality of American education? Are teacher associations really good for education? While most teachers are members, you are aware that a minority of teachers are opposed to unions. They say that these organizations have put the salaries of teachers above the needs of children. They have pitted administrators against teachers and created needless hostility. And, perhaps worst of all, these critics charge, unions protect incompetent teachers who should be removed from the classroom.

You also cannot help but speculate about a possible merger of these two professional organizations. In fact, many people have suggested that a merger of the NEA and the AFT could form an incredibly powerful force of between 2 and 3 million teachers. Such an organization could wield enormous national leverage and gain significant benefits for education in general and teachers in particular.

Although the NEA and the AFT have a great deal in common, many significant issues still separate the two organizations. Whether or not the NEA and the AFT ever merge, there is no doubt that the next few years will be exciting and challenging ones for teachers and their professional organizations.

Albert Shanker: The Union Leader Goes Professional

In working-class Queens, New York, during the depression, Albert Shanker's mother, a sewing machine operator, would talk with respect about America's professionals—the doctors, the lawyers, the teachers. From his first $38-a-week job as an elementary school teacher in New York City to his current position as head of the 885,000-member American Federation of Teachers, the goal of making teaching a real profession has been a driving force behind Shanker's activities and ambitions.

Yet during his early years in education the word *professional* had a different connotation for Shanker, one with negative overtones. It did not represent a standard of excellence but rather a threat to force teachers to behave in a servile manner and to obey rules, even those that went against their own judgment about good education. Shanker tells the following story:

It is unusual for me to be advocating professionalism. My experience with the way the word professional is used in schools has not been good. . . . I can remember my first exposure to it as a teacher. I started teaching in a very tough elementary school. I had great doubts as to whether I would make it, and after a couple of weeks, the door was opened and the assistant principal stood there. I remember thinking, "Thank God, help is coming." I kept motioning him in, but he continued to stand there, sort of pointing at something, for what seemed like a very long time but was probably only thirty seconds. Finally he said to me, "Mr. Shanker, there are a couple of pieces of paper on the floor over there. It is very unsightly and very unprofessional." Then he left.[a]

Shanker next joined the staff of an East Harlem junior high. As he monitored the cafeteria, supervised the school yard, and checked the bathrooms, life seemed a far cry from his mother's image of the revered professional.

Most teachers refused to tarnish this "professional" image by joining a union, but Shanker saw union-

Why Is Professionalism in Teaching Important?

Many people are certain that teaching is one of the most important occupations in which an individual can serve. In fact, teaching has been imbued with a nobility and dedication of purpose by philosophers, poets, and political leaders since ancient times. What other occupation has inspired such comments as these?

"What noble employment is more valuable to the state than that of the man who instructs the rising generation?" (*Cicero*)

"Education makes a people easy to lead, but difficult to drive; easy to govern but impossible to enslave." (*Lord Brougham*)

"The man who can make hard things easy is the educator." (*Ralph Waldo Emerson*)

ization as the vehicle for true professional status. He joined the United Federation of Teachers (UFT), the AFT local for New York City. In 1959 he became a full-time organizer. By 1964 he was president of the United Federation of Teachers.

In 1968 the UFT became embroiled in a bitter struggle with local community groups. At that time the Ford Foundation had financed a plan to decentralize the New York City system by reorganizing it into smaller systems. The idea was to cut through unresponsive bureaucracy and to improve education by making schools more responsive to community needs. The union did not want local communities to exercise power in removing, hiring, or transferring teachers. Community control became a serious threat to the union's power and to the professional status of teachers.

The union called a strike and closed the city's schools. The confrontation led to ugly incidents of racism and anti-Semitism. Many criticized Shanker's performance as inflaming hostility between blacks and Jews. Although the AFT won the fight and only a weakened decentralization plan went into effect, the New York City struggle left serious scars. In any event, Shanker had moved into the national spotlight.

In 1974 Albert Shanker became president of the American Federation of Teachers. He used all his skill as a communicator and politician to shed the AFT's negative image and bring it into the sunlight of respectability. Shanker's weekly paid advertise- ment in the Sunday *New York Times* became syndicated in major newspapers across the nation. "Where We Stand" appears in numerous newspapers and has foreshadowed many of the major issues and innovations in the current movement for education reform.

Shanker wants to restore dignity to the term *professional* when it is used to describe teaching. He says:

A professional is a person who is an expert, and by view of that expertise is permitted to operate fairly independently, to make decisions, to exercise discretion, to be free of most direct supervision. No one stands over a surgeon at the operating table with direction to cut a little to the left or to the right. . . . If we are to achieve that professional status, we have to take a step beyond collective bargaining—not to abandon it, but to build on it, develop new processes, new institutions, new procedures that will bring us what teachers want in addition to what we get from collective bargaining: status, dignity, a voice in professional matters, the compensation of a professional.[b]

You may agree or disagree with Shanker's ideas, but no critic can charge that he has none. His emphasis on professionalism should give you some thoughts to consider and debate as you think about this important issue.

[a]Albert Shanker, "The Making of a Profession," *American Education* 9, no. 3 (Fall 1985): 10–17, 46, 48.
[b]Shanker, "The Making of a Profession," pp. 10–17.

In his preface to *Goodbye, Mr. Chips,* James Hilton writes that his portrait of the lovable school master is a "tribute to a great profession." But is teaching really a profession? Some experts in the business of defining professions say that it is difficult to determine whether teaching qualifies.

What is a profession anyway? *Educating a Profession,* a publication of the American Association of Colleges for Teacher Education (AACTE), lists 12 characteristics of a profession. Read these carefully and try to determine which criteria the occupation of teaching meets. Then mark your reactions in the appropriate column. You may find it interesting to compare your reactions with those of your classmates.

	Yes	No	Don't Know

1. Professions are occupationally related social institutions established and maintained as a means of providing essential services to the individual and the society.

2. Each profession is concerned with an identified area of need or function (for example, maintenance of physical and emotional health, preservation of rights and freedom, enhancing the opportunity to learn).

3. The profession collectively, and the professional individually, possesses a body of knowledge and a repertoire of behaviors and skills (professional culture) needed in the practice of the profession; such knowledge, behavior, and skills normally are not possessed by the nonprofessional.

4. Members of the profession are involved in decision making in the service of the client, the decisions being made in accordance with the most valid knowledge available, against a background of principles and theories, and within the context of possible impact on other related conditions or decisions.

5. The profession is based on one or more undergirding disciplines from which it builds its own applied knowledge and skills.

6. The profession is organized into one or more professional associations which, within broad limits of social accountability, are granted autonomy in control of the actual work of the profession and the conditions which surround it (admissions, educational standards, examination and licensing, career line, ethical and performance standards).

7. The profession has agreed-upon performance standards for admission to the profession and for continuance within it.

8. Preparation for and induction into the profession is provided through a protracted preparation program, usually in a professional school on a college or university campus.

9. There is a high level of public trust and confidence in the profession and in individual practitioners, based upon the profession's demonstrated capacity to provide service markedly beyond that which would otherwise be available.

10. Individual practitioners are characterized by a strong service motivation and lifetime commitment to competence.

11. Authority to practice in any individual case derives from the client or the employing organization; accountability for the competence of professional practice within the particular case is to the profession itself.   ___   ___   ___

12. There is relative freedom from direct on-the-job supervision and from direct public evaluation of the individual practitioner. The professional accepts responsibility in the name of his or her profession and is accountable through his or her profession to the society.[18]   ___   ___   ___

Do not be surprised if you find some criteria that do not apply to teaching. In fact, even those occupations that spring to mind when you hear the word *professional*—doctors, lawyers, clergy, college professors—do not completely measure up to all these criteria.

The Commission on Education for the Profession of Teaching also listed 12 criteria for semiprofessions. Read these items carefully, and compare them to the characteristics that define a profession. Consider each item separately. Does it accurately describe teaching, or does it sell teaching short? After you have considered all the items and marked your reactions in the appropriate column, decide whether you think teaching is actually a profession, or whether it would more accurately be termed a *semiprofession*.

	Yes	No	Don't Know
1. Lower in occupational status	___	___	___
2. Shorter training periods	___	___	___
3. Lack of societal acceptance that the nature of the service and/or the level of expertise justifies the autonomy which is granted to the professions	___	___	___
4. A less specialized and less highly developed body of knowledge and skills	___	___	___
5. Markedly less emphasis on theoretical and conceptual bases for practice	___	___	___
6. A tendency for the individual to identify with the employment institution more and with the profession less	___	___	___
7. More subject to administrative and supervisory surveillance and control	___	___	___
8. Less autonomy in professional decision making with accountability to superiors rather than to the profession	___	___	___
9. Management of organizations within which semiprofessionals are employed by persons who have themselves been prepared and served in that semiprofession	___	___	___
10. A preponderance of women	___	___	___

11. Absence of the right of privileged communica-
    tion between client and professional
    _____ _____ _____
12. Little or no involvement in matters of life and
    death[19]
    _____ _____ _____

Many people feel that teaching falls somewhere in between professional
and semiprofessional status. For them it might best be thought of as an emerging profession. Where do you place teaching?

Why does all this "profession talk" matter? You may be more concerned
with such questions as: Do I want to work with children? What age level is
best for me? Will I be good at teaching? Will the salary be enough to give me
the quality of life that I want for myself and my family? "Why," you may be
thinking, "should I split hairs over whether I belong to a profession? Who
cares?"

Although the issue of professionalism may not matter to you now or even
during your first year or two of teaching, when classroom survival and performance have top priority, it will eventually become one of the most important issues you face during your career in education. Why?

Here's what Ellen Hogan Steele, a teacher who cares passionately about
the privilege, responsibility, and dignity of belonging to a profession, says:

> I recall a carpenter—he visited my home to discuss a renovation—talking
> about a school strike in a neighboring town. Unaware of my occupation
> he called teachers ignorant, lazy, and lucky to be employed.
>
> "Can you imagine thinking they should make as much as me?" he fumed.
>
> I can imagine that. I presume my work to be as demanding and skilled
> as that of the carpenters I employ. . . . What do teachers want? This teacher
> wants to make a reasonable living, to be recognized as a person who per-
> forms an essential service, to be considered an expert in my small area of
> experience, to be occasionally praised when I do well and to be helped
> to improve when I don't . . . in short, I want someone to know that I'm
> alive, and unless they do, I'll keep on kicking.[20]

Listen to another teacher, Patricia Dombart:

> Take a look at the working world of the insider. You will find that it is
> not an atmosphere that nourishes vision. Though we teachers are numer-
> ous, we are virtually powerless. We affect none of the key elements in our
> working lives. For example, we have no control over class size or the
> length of the school day and class periods. We have almost no input into
> the form and content of report cards. We do not select our schedules,
> grade levels or the buildings in which we teach. Indeed, we do not even
> control the time within our own classrooms, for we are slaves to the P.A.,
> to notes from the nurse, from guidance, the librarian, the main office. We
> are often without the essentials, like paper and pencils and desks. In many
> buildings, janitors and secretaries control these. Acquiring a new pencil
> sharpener may involve stroking three separate egos and forgetting every-
> thing you ever read about reporting sexual harassment. Often, obtaining
> the basics interferes with teaching the basics.[21]

These two teachers speak for most of their colleagues when they call for an adequate salary and the sense of pride and self-worth that comes from doing an important job well and knowing that others respect your competence. Financial well-being and community respect usually go hand in hand with professional status.

Professional status also requires self-determination, power, and the ability to make important decisions about the nature of one's work. Historically, teachers have been relatively powerless. Outside their classrooms they have little say about school policies, procedures, schedules, curriculum, and other matters that have a direct bearing on the quality and effectiveness of their work. But times are changing. You are about to enter a field undergoing significant upheaval.

Tension Point: Professionalism at the Crossroads

"Are You Treated Like a Professional? Or a Tall Child?" This provocative title from *NEA Today* raises questions that educators will grapple with during the decade ahead. When education reform stresses "teacher-proof" education, district central offices and state governments try to exert more control over teaching. An NEA survey, *The Conditions and Resources of Teaching,* makes it clear that teachers resent this kind of deprofessionalization. Says English teacher Carol Davis, "We're told when to get here, when to leave, what to teach, what to want, what not to want, and how to think. . . . I'm trained in how to teach English, but I'm rarely asked for my opinion. If I were to be 'promoted out of my classroom' my opinion would be more respected immediately. The irony would be that I'd no longer be teaching children."[22]

This tendency toward infantalization of teaching is now being radically challenged. The new pride in professionalism takes the perspective that teachers are not slaves to rules and routines established in state education departments and textbook publishing houses. Rather, they are reflective decision makers, selecting objectives and teaching procedures to meet the needs of different learners. They must know their subject matter, learning theory, research on different teaching methodologies, and techniques for curriculum development. This view provides the rationale for transforming teaching into a true profession.[23]

Despite this new vision of professionalism, the United States remains ambivalent about its teachers. Even as interest in teacher empowerment mounts, policies are in effect that threaten to derail teaching's bid for full professional status. For example, many states have alternative certification programs that allow people with limited training to go into classrooms and teach children. One such controversial program is Teach for America. Here highly motivated volunteers undergo very brief teacher training programs and enter some of America's most difficult classrooms. Many educators see such programs as the height of irresponsibility and the opposite of profession building.[24] Can you imagine lawyers or doctors prepared for their professions in this manner? Teaching is the only state-licensed occupation that grants substandard licenses.

While entrance into teaching often includes competency tests (a move toward professionalism), the tests are too simple. "Rather than 'legitimizing complexity' as professions must do when they seek bars to entry, these assessment instruments reinforce conceptions of teaching as simple cookbook-driven work."[25]

Collectively, teachers struggle to empower their profession; individually, they struggle to empower their students.

Growing out of recommendations by the influential Carnegie Forum, a new organization, the National Board for Professional Teaching Standards, has emerged. Its goal is to develop an assessment procedure through which highly competent teachers can become board-certified. This assessment is not to be a quick test for licensure, but rather a complex process to recognize advanced standing in teaching.

Is teaching a full profession? Or is it doomed to semiprofessional status? The case is at a crossroads.

Teacher Education: From Normal Schools to Board-Certified Teachers

Basic to any discussion of a profession is the issue of how its members are prepared. As you read this brief history of teacher preparation, think about whether teachers are prepared in a way commensurate with belonging to a profession.

From colonial America into the twentieth century, the burning question about teacher education was: Why have it? More often than not, most teachers in colonial America received no formal preparation at all. In fact, most elementary teachers never even attended a secondary school. Some learned their craft by serving as apprentices to master teachers, a continuation of the medieval guild system. Others were indentured servants paying for their passage to the New World by teaching for a fixed number of years. Many belonged to the "sink-or-swim" school of teaching, and the education of an untold number of students undoubtedly sank with them.

The smaller number of teachers working at the secondary level—in academies or Latin grammar schools, and as private tutors—had usually received some college education, more often in Europe than in America. Some knowledge of the subject matter was considered desirable, but no particular aptitude for teaching or knowledge of teaching skills was considered necessary.

Teaching was viewed not as a career but as temporary employment. Many of those who entered teaching were teenagers who taught for only a year or two. Others were of dubious character, and early records reveal a number of teachers fired for drinking or stealing.

From this humble beginning there slowly emerged a more professional program for teacher education. In 1823 the Reverend Samuel Hall established a **normal school** (named for its European counterpart) in Concord, Vermont. This private school provided elementary school graduates with formal training in teaching skills. Although quite small, this normal school marked the beginning of teacher education in America. A few years later, in 1839, Horace Mann was instrumental in establishing the first state-supported normal school in Lexington, Massachusetts. Normal schools typically provided a 2-year teacher training program, consisting of academic subjects as well as teaching methodology. Some students came directly from elementary school; others had completed a secondary education. The normal school was the backbone of teacher education well into the twentieth century.

As enrollments in elementary schools climbed and as secondary education became widely accepted, the demand increased for more and better-trained teachers. Many private colleges and universities initiated teacher education programs in the 1900s. The normal schools expanded to 3- and 4-year programs and gradually evolved into state teachers' colleges. As a greater number of students attended these teachers' colleges, they expanded their programs and began offering courses and career preparation in fields other than teaching. By the 1950s many of the state teachers' colleges had evolved into state colleges. In fact, some of today's leading universities were originally chartered as normal schools.

A number of recent education reform reports have fanned the flames of controversy regarding professionalism and teacher preparation. A group of deans from prominent schools of education, called the Holmes group, spent years debating this issue before releasing its 1986 report, entitled *Tomorrow's Teachers*.[26] That same year, the Carnegie Forum also issued a highly publicized report, *A Nation Prepared*.[27] Like the Holmes report, it called for higher standards and increased professionalism for the nation's teachers. The Carnegie report also called for an end to the undergraduate teaching major and the development of master's-level degrees in teaching. While some universities followed this recommendation and created 5-year teacher education programs, others did not. Teacher education remains a hodgepodge of different approaches. Some critics, such as John Goodlad, place much of the blame on universities themselves, for failing to adequately fund and support schools of education.[28]

But not all of the attention has been on initial teacher education. By 1995, 81 teachers from 23 states had reached what may one day be considered a landmark: They became the nation's first "board-certified" teachers. Like medicine, teaching now had not just an entry license—the teaching certificate—but an advanced recognition of a higher level of skills and competencies. These 81 board-certified teachers spent months compiling professional portfolios that included videotaped examples of their teaching. They also scored well on a battery of assessment tests developed by the privately organized National Board for Professional Teaching Standards. Although 289 candidates competed, only 81 teachers were declared board-certified.

How will states and communities recognize, reward, and utilize board-certified teachers? Higher salaries? More release time to develop curriculum or work with less talented teachers? Will these board-certified teachers become leaders—or will the movement become simply another failed attempt to transform what some view as a semiprofession into a true profession?[29]

These and other pivotal questions will likely be answered during your time as a classroom teacher.

SUMMARY

1. When teaching is weighed as to its merits as a profession, both advantages and disadvantages must be considered. On the negative side of the ledger are low income as compared to other professions; lack of respect; mindless routine and repetition; inadequate time for contact with other adults; and the frustration that may result when idealistic goals are sacrificed to behavior problems, student apathy or hostility, and bureaucratic red tape.

2. On the positive side of the ledger are rising salaries; pride in the worth of the profession; the joy of working with children; creative and intellectual stimulation; and the opportunity to affect the lives of the nation's youth. As Christa McAuliffe said, "I touch the future. I teach."

3. In colonial times teachers were treated as meek and docile servants of the public. Their conduct both in and out of school was scrutinized closely, and their income was so meager that many had to board with different families to make ends meet. From these beginnings, those in the field of teaching have struggled for greater income, respect, and professionalism. Professional associations have been key vehicles in attaining these goals.

4. The National Education Association (NEA) is the largest professional and employee association in the nation. Formed during the second half of the 1800s, initially it was slow to work for the needs of its members. (In its early days women were not even admitted.) During the 1960s and 1970s, the NEA became a stronger advocate of teachers' rights. In the 1980s and 1990s, it moved toward a leadership position in education reform.

5. When teachers' unions from the Midwest affiliated with the American Federation of Labor in 1916, the American Federation of Teachers (AFT) was formed. While significantly smaller than the NEA, the AFT has historically taken a more aggressive stance, including strikes, in working for teachers' rights. Under the longtime leadership of Albert Shanker, the AFT has changed its image from that of a scrappy union to that of an important force in education reform.

6. Today both the NEA and the AFT offers a range of services, including magazines, journals, and other professional communications; legal assistance; workshops and conferences; assistance in collective bargaining; and political activism.

7. There is an ongoing debate as to whether teaching is a field that has reached full professional status. Some claim it has not and is, at best, a semiprofession. To support their point of view, these critics note the short preparation time for becoming a teacher; lack of influence over certification and the entry of others into the field; weak policing of the ranks for incompetence; and an inadequate base of specialized knowledge.

8. Those who claim that teaching has full professional status assert that it is one of the most noble occupations in which an individual can serve. Its knowledge and research base is fast becoming more extensive, and teachers' quest for empowerment will be a major movement of the next decade.

9. Initially teaching was considered only temporary employment. In 1823, a private normal school was established to provide future teachers with formal training. In the 1900s, many private universities established teacher education programs. Today reform reports, including *Tomorrow's Teachers* and *A Nation Prepared,* urge higher standards, increased professionalism for teacher preparation, and recognition of superior performance through board certification.

<table>
<tr><td>

DISCUSSION QUESTIONS AND ACTIVITIES

</td><td>

1. The Teaching Balance Sheets have tried to give you both the positive and the negative sides of teaching. You might enjoy reading some fascinating books that will increase your awareness of the pros and cons of teaching:

</td></tr>
</table>

- *Up the Down Staircase,* by Bel Kaufman
- *Teacher,* by Sylvia Ashton-Warner
- *To Sir, with Love,* by Edward Braithwaite
- *The Way It Spozed to Be,* by James Herndon
- *How to Survive in Your Native Land,* by James Herndon
- *36 Children,* by Herbert Kohl
- *The Water Is Wide,* by Patrick Conroy
- *900 Shows a Year,* by Stuart Palonsky
- *Goodbye, Mr. Chips,* by James Hilton
- *Among Schoolchildren,* by Tracy Kidder
- *Amazing Grace,* by Jonathan Kozol

As you read these personal accounts, you may wish to keep an informal checklist of those aspects of teaching to which you react positively and those to which you react negatively. You may also wish to share your reading as well as your checklist with your classmates and your instructor.

2. This chapter emphasized the importance of well-thought-out career decision making. It would be worthwhile for you to read a book by Richard N. Bolles called *What Color Is Your Parachute?* It contains a wide variety of exercises that should help you clarify your commitment to teaching. It will also help you determine what other careers present viable options for you.

3. Interview teachers at different grade levels to determine what they think are the positive and negative aspects of teaching. Share those interview responses with your classmates.

4. Interview students at various grade levels to determine their perceptions of teachers. Ask them to describe a teacher who has been influential in their lives. Share these interview responses with your classmates.

5. Suppose you could write an open letter to students telling them about yourself and why you want to teach. What would you want them to know? When you attempt to explain yourself to others, you often gain greater self-knowledge. On a separate piece of paper, try writing an open letter to students. You might want to share your letter with classmates and to hear what they have to say in their letters. Perhaps your instructor could also try this exercise and share her or his open letter with you.

6. Watch the movie *Stand and Deliver.* What factors do you think make Jaime Escalante a great teacher?

7. What are the similarities and differences between the NEA and the AFT? Write to both organizations to find out more about them. Which do you think will best meet your needs as a teacher?

8. Interview some practicing teachers to determine their opinions of the NEA and the AFT. Interview retired teachers to determine their reactions. Summarize your findings.

9. In your own words, summarize the historical development of the professional associations. You might want to do a research paper on this topic to learn more. Interview teachers who have participated in strikes. What are their reactions? Interview citizens, both those with and those without children in school. What are their opinions about teacher strikes?

10. In your opinion, is teaching a profession? Give reasons for your answer.

NOTES

1. Quoted in Myron Brenton, *What's Happened to Teacher?* (New York: Coward, McCann, & Geoghegan, 1970), p. 24.
2. Quoted in Ann Lieberman and Lynn Miller, *Teachers, Their World and Their Work* (Alexandria, VA: Association for Supervision and Curriculum Development, 1984), p. 45.
3. Ibid., p. 22.
4. Ibid., p. 47.
5. Ibid., p. 47.
6. William Lyon Phelps, quoted in Oliver Ikenberry, *American Education Foundations* (Columbus, OH: Merrill, 1974), p. 389.
7. Quoted in Brenton, *What's Happened to Teacher?*, p. 164.
8. Quoted in Haim Ginott, *Teacher and Child* (New York: Macmillan, 1972), p. 305.
9. Ibid., p. 315.
10. Quoted in Brenton, *What's Happened to Teacher?*, p. 97.
11. Ibid., p. 96.
12. Ibid., p. 94.
13. Mary Jordan, "Pupils Give Their Parents 'D' for School Involvement," *The Washington Post,* May 12, 1992, p. A3.
14. Much of the information in this section was drawn from Marshall O. Donley, Jr.'s excellent article, "The American School Teacher: From Obedient Servant to Militant Professional," *Phi Delta Kappan* 58, no. 1 (September 1976): 112–117.
15. Ellen Hogan Steele, "Reflections on a School Strike II: A Teacher's View," *Phi Delta Kappan* 57, no. 9 (May 1976): 590–592.
16. Ronald J. Perry, "Reflections on a School Strike I: The Superintendent's View," *Phi Delta Kappan* 57, no. 9 (May 1976): 587–590.
17. Albert Shanker, "Where We Stand: Is It Time for National Standards and Exams?" *American Teacher* 76, no. 6 (May/June 1992): 5.
18. Robert Howsam et al., *Educating a Profession,* Report of the Bicentennial Commission of Education for the Profession of Teaching (Washington, DC: American Association of Colleges for Teacher Education, 1976): pp. 6–7.
19. Ibid., pp. 8–9.
20. Steele, "Reflections on a School Strike II," pp. 590–592.
21. Patricia Dombart, "The Vision of a Professional Insider: A Practitioner's View," *Educational Leadership* 43, no. 3 (November 1985): 71–73.
22. Quoted in "Are You Treated Like a Professional? Or a Tall Child?" *NEA Today,* December 1988, p. 4.
23. Ron Brandt, "On Teacher Empowerment: A Conversation with Ann Lieberman," *Educational Leadership* 46, no. 8 (May 1989): 23–24.

NEA Code of Ethics

Preamble

The educator, believing in the worth and dignity of each human being, recognizes the supreme importance of the pursuit of truth, devotion to excellence, and the nurturing of democratic principles. Essential to these goals is the protection of freedom to learn and to teach and the guarantee of equal educational opportunity for all. The educator accepts the responsibility to adhere to the highest ethical standards.

The educator recognizes the magnitude of the responsibility inherent in the teaching process. The desire for the respect and confidence of one's colleagues, of students, of parents, and of the members of the community provides the incentive to attain and maintain the highest possible degree of ethical conduct. The Code of Ethics of the Education Profession indicates the aspiration of all educators and provides standards by which to judge conduct.

The remedies specified by the NEA and/or its affiliates for the violation of any provision of this Code shall be exclusive and no such provision shall be enforceable in any form other than one specifically designated by the NEA or its affiliates.

Principle I—Commitment to the Student

The educator strives to help each student realize his or her potential as a worthy and effective member of society. The educator therefore works to stimulate the spirit of inquiry, the acquisition of knowledge and understanding, and the thoughtful formulation of worthy goals.

In fulfillment of the obligation to the student, the educator—

1. Shall not unreasonably restrain the student from independent action in the pursuit of learning.
2. Shall not unreasonably deny the student access to varying points of view.
3. Shall not deliberately suppress or distort subject matter relevant to the student's progress.
4. Shall make reasonable effort to protect the student from conditions harmful to learning or to health and safety.
5. Shall not intentionally expose the student to embarrassment or disparagement.
6. Shall not on the basis of race, color, creed, sex, national origin, marital status, political or religious beliefs, family, social or cultural background, or sexual orientation, unfairly:

a. Exclude any student from participation in any program;
b. Deny benefits to any student;
c. Grant any advantage to any student.
7. Shall not use professional relationships with students for private advantage.
8. Shall not disclose information about students obtained in the course of professional service, unless disclosure serves a compelling professional purpose or is required by law.

Principle II—Commitment to the Profession

The education profession is vested by the public with a trust and responsibility requiring the highest ideals of professional service.

In the belief that the quality of the services of the education profession directly influences the nation and its citizens, the educator shall exert every effort to raise professional standards, to promote a climate that encourages the exercise of professional judgment, to achieve conditions which attract persons worthy of the trust to careers in education, and to assist in preventing the practice of the profession by unqualified persons.

In fulfillment of the obligation to the profession the educator—

1. Shall not in an application for a professional position deliberately make a false statement or fail to disclose a material fact related to competency and qualifications.
2. Shall not misrepresent his/her professional qualifications.
3. Shall not assist entry into the profession of a person known to be unqualified in respect to character, education, or other relevant attribute.
4. Shall not knowingly make a false statement concerning the qualifications of a candidate for a professional position.
5. Shall not assist a noneducator in the unauthorized practice of teaching.
6. Shall not disclose information about colleagues obtained in the course of professional service unless disclosure serves a compelling professional purpose or is required by law.
7. Shall not knowingly make false or malicious statements about a colleague.
8. Shall not accept any gratuity, gift, or favor that might impair or appear to influence professional decisions or actions.

AFT Bill of Rights

The teacher is entitled to a life of dignity equal to the high standard of service that is justly demanded of that profession. Therefore, we hold these truths to be self-evident:

I. Teachers have the right to think freely and to express themselves openly and without fear. This includes the right to hold views contrary to the majority.

II. They shall be entitled to the free exercise of their religion. No restraint shall be put upon them in the manner, time or place of their worship.

III. They shall have the right to take part in social, civil, and political affairs. They shall have the right, outside the classroom, to participate in political campaigns and to hold office. They may assemble peaceably and may petition any government agency, including their employers, for a redress of grievances. They shall have the same freedom in all things as other citizens.

IV. The right of teachers to live in places of their own choosing, to be free of restraints in their mode of living and the use of their leisure time shall not be abridged.

V. Teaching is a profession, the right to practice which is not subject to the surrender of other human rights. No one shall be deprived of professional status, or the right to practice it, or the practice thereof in any particular position, without due process of law.

VI. The right of teachers to be secure in their jobs, free from political influence or public clamor, shall be established by law. The right to teach after qualification in the manner prescribed by law is a property right, based upon the inalienable rights to life, liberty, and the pursuit of happiness.

VII. In all cases affecting the teacher's employment or professional status a full hearing by an impartial tribunal shall be afforded with the right to full judicial review. No teacher shall be deprived of employment or professional status but for specific causes established by the law having a clear relation to the competence or qualification to teach, proved by the weight of the evidence. In all such cases the teacher shall enjoy the right to a speedy and public trial, to be informed of the nature and cause of the accusation, to be confronted with the accusing witnesses, to subpoena witnesses and papers, and to the assistance of counsel. No teacher shall be called upon to answer any charge affecting his employment or professional status but upon probable cause, supported by oath or affirmation.

VIII. It shall be the duty of the employer to provide culturally adequate salaries, security in illness and adequate retirement income. The teacher has the right to such a salary as will: a) Afford a family standard of living comparable to that enjoyed by other professional people in the community; b) To make possible freely chosen professional study; c) Afford the opportunity for leisure and recreation common to our heritage.

IX. Teachers shall not be required under penalty of reduction of salary to pursue studies beyond those required to obtain professional status. After serving a reasonable probationary period a teacher shall be entitled to permanent tenure terminable only for just cause. They shall be free as in other professions in the use of their own time. They shall not be required to perform extracurricular work against their will or without added compensation.

X. To equip people for modern life requires the most advanced educational methods. Therefore, the teacher is entitled to good classrooms, adequate teaching materials, teachable class size and administrative protection and assistance in maintaining discipline.

XI. These rights are based upon the proposition that the culture of a people can rise only as its teachers improve. A teaching force accorded the highest possible professional dignity is the surest guarantee that blessings of liberty will be preserved. Therefore, the possession of these rights imposes the challenge to be worthy of their enjoyment.

XII. Since teachers must be free in order to teach freedom, the right to be members of organizations of their own choosing must be guaranteed. In all matters pertaining to their salaries and working conditions they shall be entitled to bargain collectively through representatives of their own choosing. They are entitled to have the schools administered by superintendents, boards or committees which function in a democratic manner.

24. Linda Darling-Hammond, "Who Will Speak for the Children?: How 'Teach for America' Hurts Urban Schools and Students," *Phi Delta Kappan* 76, no. 1 (September 1994): 21–34.

25. Linda Darling-Hammond, "The Futures of Teaching," *Educational Leadership* 46, no. 3 (November 1988): 6.

26. *Tomorrow's Teachers: A Report of the Holmes Group* (East Lansing, MI: Holmes Group, 1986).

27. Carnegie Forum on Education and the Economy, Task Force on Teaching as a Profession, *A Nation Prepared: Teachers for the Twenty-First Century* (New York: Forum, 1986).

28. John Goodlad, "A Study of the Education of Educators: One Year Later," *Phi Delta Kappan* 73, no. 4 (December 1991): 311–316.

29. "Board Certification: Here at Last!" *American Teacher* 79 (March 1995): 3; Ann Bradley, "National Board Announces First Teacher Certificates," *Education Week* 14 (January 11, 1995): 9.

EFFECTIVE TEACHING

OBJECTIVES

To recall impressions of good teachers

To consider whether teaching is an art or a science

To analyze research on teacher effectiveness, including academic learning time, classroom management, academic structure, higher- and lower-order questions, wait time, and teacher feedback

To describe models in effective teaching, including direct teaching, cooperative learning, mastery learning, and project-based instruction

To consider new directions in effective teaching

So many inspiring words have been written about the profession of teaching:

"It is the supreme art of the teacher to awaken joy in creative expression and knowledge." (Albert Einstein)

"The teacher is one who made two ideas grow where only one grew before." (Elbert Hubbard)

"The man who can make hard things easy is the educator." (Ralph Waldo Emerson)

Despite such philosophical pronouncements, historically there has been little solid information about the skills that comprise good teaching. New research-based findings, however, now provide a blueprint of teaching skills that enhance student achievement.

This chapter will review current research and new developments in effective teaching. You will have the opportunity to hear how other people describe their best teachers and to learn about classroom management, academic learning time, questioning, wait time, productive feedback, and other approaches relevant to teaching well.

Is Teaching an Art or a Skill?

Think about the best teacher you ever had: Try to evoke a clear mental image of what this teacher was like. Here is what some of today's teachers say about their favorite teachers from the past:

> The teacher I remember was charismatic. Going to his class was like attending a Broadway show. But it wasn't just entertainment. He made me understand things. We went step by step in such a clear way that I never seemed to get confused—even when we discussed the most difficult subject matter.

> I never watched the clock in my English teacher's class. I never counted how many times she said *uh-huh* or *okay* or paused—like I did in some other classes. She made literature come alive—I was always surprised—and sorry—when the bell rang.

> When I had a problem, I felt like I could talk about it with Mrs. Evans. She was my fifth-grade teacher, and she never made me feel dumb or stupid—even when I had so much trouble with math. After I finished talking to her, I felt like I could do anything.

> For most of my life I hated history. Endlessly memorizing those facts, figures, dates. I forgot them as soon as the test was over. One year I even threw my history book in the river. But Mr. Cohen taught history in such a way that I could understand the big picture. He asked such interesting, provocative questions—about our past and the lessons it gave for our future.

The debate has been raging for decades: Is teaching a skill or an art? What do you think?

If you think it is a combination of both, you are in agreement with most people who have seriously considered this question. Some individuals—a rare few—are naturally gifted teachers. Their classrooms are dazzlingly alive. Students are motivated, excited, and their enthusiasm translates into academic achievement. For these truly talented educators, teaching seems to be pure art or magic.

But behind even the most brilliant teaching performance, there is usually hard, honed, practiced skill at work. Look again at those brief descriptions of favorite teachers: Each of those teachers knew how to use proven skills—in motivation, structure and clarity, high expectations, questioning.

> "We went step by step in such a clear way that I never seemed to get confused—even when we discussed the most difficult subject matter." (*structure and clarity*)
> "She made literature come alive." (*motivation*)
> "After I finished talking to her, I felt like I could do anything." (*high expectations*)
> "He asked such interesting, provocative questions—about our past and the lessons it gave for our future." (*questioning*)

Although there is ample room for the gift of artistry, most teaching is based on proven and practiced skills. In the remainder of this chapter, you will be introduced to the research on important skills such as these and will be shown how you can put them to work in the classroom.

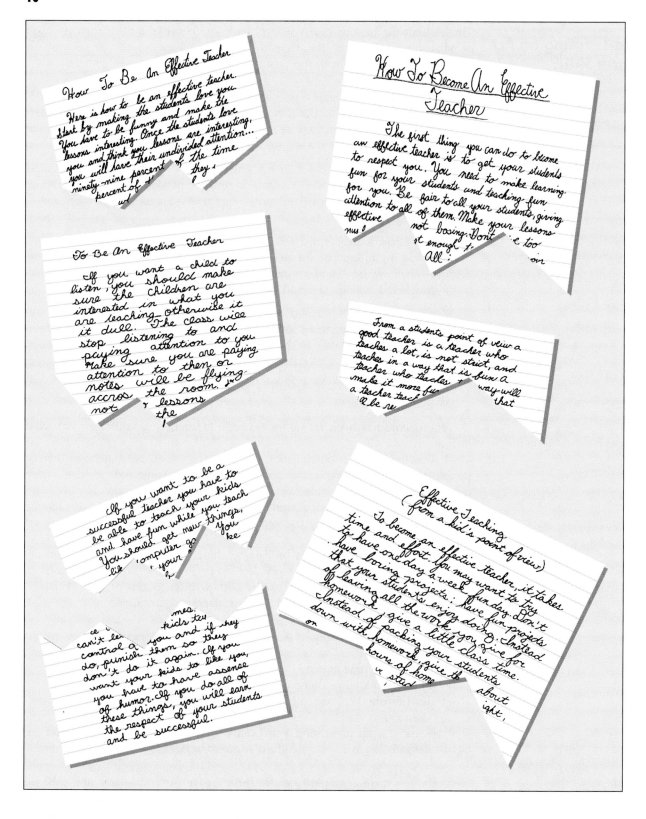

How To Be An Effective Teacher

Here is how to be an effective teacher. Start by making the students love you. You have to be funny and make the lessons interesting. Once the students love you and think your lessons are interesting, you will have their undivided attention... ninety-nine percent of the time... percent of t...   they...

How To Become An Effective Teacher

The first thing you can do to become an effective teacher is to get your students to respect you. You need to make learning fun for your students and teaching fun for you. Be fair to all your students, giving attention to all of them. Make your lessons effective... not boring. Don't... too... st enough t...   ...on All...

To Be An Effective Teacher

If you want a child to listen, you should make sure the children are interested in what you are teaching, otherwise it it dull. The class will stop listening to and paying attention to you. Make sure you are paying attention to then or notes will be flying accros the room. ... not ... lessons ... the

From a students point of view a good teacher is a teacher who teaches a lot, is not strict, and teaches in a way that is fun a teacher who teaches ... way will make it more fun ... that a teacher teac... ...ll be re...

If you want to be a successful teacher you have to be able to teach your kids and have fun while you teach. You should get new things, like 'omputer ga...   ...ke ... your ...

Effective Teaching
(from a kid's point of view)

To become an effective teacher, it takes time and effort. You may want to try to have one day a week fun day. Don't have boring projects; have fun projects that your students enjoy doing. Instead of leaving all the work you give for homework; give a little class time. Instead of packing your class time down with homework; give your students hours of home... ...about ...stud...   ...ight, on

...mes. can't le...   kids to control a... you and if they do, punish them so they don't do it again. If you want your kids to like you, you have to have a sense of humor. If you do all of these things, you will earn the respect of your students and be successful.

The Mysterious Case of Teacher Effectiveness

In 1976 Jere Brophy, one of the country's most respected educational researchers, said:

> Despite seventy-five years of research on the topic relatively little is known about effective teaching. Advances in methodology and conceptualization have begun to make a difference in the last fifteen years or so, but the research is still in its infancy.[1]

In the years since that pronouncement there has been a resurgence, almost a revolution, in teacher education research. New studies, sometimes called *process-product research,* have identified specific teaching skills and behaviors and have analyzed the effects these have on student achievement. Because of this new research, we now have an emerging blueprint of what makes effective teaching—the kind of teaching that enables students to learn and achieve.

The following sections of this chapter will describe numerous teaching skills that have been shown to have a positive effect on student achievement. Some of these research-proven skills are just common sense; they have been part of the folk wisdom of teaching for decades. In other cases, the research findings are surprisingly counterintuitive. Although this chapter will introduce you to these research-based teaching skills, it will be your responsibility to keep up with the burgeoning and sometimes shifting information base as you prepare for and later enter your teaching career.

Some of the research in the following discussion will seem obvious, almost commonsensical. However, common sense is too often taken for granted and consequently is not always applied systematically in the classroom.

Academic Learning Time

Research has shown that students who spend more time pursuing academic content learn more and receive higher achievement scores. Hardly surprising. What is startling is how differently teachers use their classroom time. For example, the Beginning Teacher Evaluation Study[2] showed that one teacher in the Los Angeles school system spent 68 minutes a day on reading, whereas another spent 137 minutes; one elementary school teacher spent only 16 minutes per day on mathematics, whereas another spent over three times that much time. Similarly, John Goodlad's comprehensive research study, *A Place Called School,* found that some schools devote approximately 65 percent of their time to instruction, whereas others devote almost 90 percent.[3] The variation is enormous.

Although it is obviously important to allocate adequate time to academic content, making time on the schedule is not enough. How this allocated time is used in the classroom is the real key to student achievement. In order to study the use of classroom time, researchers have developed the following terms to aid their analysis: allocated time, engaged time, and academic learning time.

Allocated time is the amount of time a teacher schedules for a subject—for example, 30 minutes a day for math. The more time allocated for a subject, the higher student achievement in that subject is likely to be.

Engaged time is that part of allocated time in which students are actively involved with academic subject matter (really listening to a lecture, participating in a class discussion, writing a composition, working on math problems).

Academic learning time is engaged learning time in which students have a high success rate. When working independently, as here, the success rate should be particularly high.

When students are daydreaming, doodling, writing notes to each other, talking with their peers about nonacademic topics, or simply waiting for instructions, they are not involved in engaged time. When there is more engaged time within allocated time, student achievement increases. As with allocated time, there is enormous variation from teacher to teacher and school to school in the amount of time students are actually engaged with the subject matter. In some classes engaged time is 50 percent. In other classes, it is more than 90 percent.

Academic learning time is engaged time with a high success rate. Many researchers suggest that students should get 70 to 80 percent of the answers right when working with a teacher. When working independently, and without a teacher available to make corrections, the success rate should be even higher if students are to learn effectively. Some teachers are skeptical when they hear these percentages; they think that experiencing difficulty "stretches" students and helps them to achieve. However, new studies are demonstrating that a high success rate is positively related to student achievement. How effectively teachers provide for and manage academic learning time in their classrooms is the key in determining student achievement.[4]

In the following sections you will learn about research-based teaching skills that you can use to increase academic learning time and student achievement. Since much time can be frittered away on organizational details and minor student disruptions, we will look first at effective strategies for classroom management. Then those instructional skills that seem consistently to produce higher academic achievement in students will be considered.

Classroom Management

Even before she walked into the room, Lynette could hear the noise of her classmates. So this was going to be her fourth-grade class. Students were running everywhere. Some were drawing on the board, others were playing tag behind the library shelves. A fight seemed to be breaking out in the coat room. "Where is the teacher?" Lynette wondered. School was supposed to have started 5 minutes ago.

• • •

As Alice headed to her fourth-grade classroom, she could see a smiling woman with glasses standing in the doorway and greeting students. "Hello, I'm Mrs. Michaelson," she said. "And you are? . . ."

"Alice Walker."

"I'm so glad you'll be in my class this year. Your seat is in the second row. Go to your desk right now and you'll find a paper that you will need to fill out. It's a special interview form—everyone in the class has one—and it will give us a chance to get to know each other better. Be sure to look at the classroom rules that are posted on the board as you go in. These are very important, and I will explain them to all of you this morning."

As Alice entered the room, she stopped a minute to read the classroom rules:

1. Always raise your hand to talk. Also, raise your hand if you need help.
2. Respect other people's rights and feelings. Avoid teasing and making fun of others.
3. Always walk in the class. Do not run.
4. Respect other people's property.

Walking to her desk, Alice noticed that many students, some unknown and some familiar, were already filling out their forms, and many were quietly chuckling as they did so.

"I wonder what's on that form," thought Alice as she slipped into her seat.

• • •

Two different classrooms on the first day of school—and in that first 5 minutes it becomes obvious that the students will have two very different educational experiences.

Research shows that effective classroom managers are nearly always good planners.[5] They do not enter a room late, after noise and disruption have had a chance to build. They are waiting at the door when the children come in. Starting from the very first day of school, they teach the rules about appropriate student behavior. They do this actively and directly. Sometimes they actually model the procedures for getting assistance, leaving the room, going to the pencil sharpener, and the like. The more important rules of classroom behavior are written down, as are the penalties for not following them.[6]

There are two basic principles for setting class rules: They should be few in number and they should seem fair and reasonable to students. Discussion of class rules can be handled in several ways. Some teachers like to develop the list of rules together with their students; other teachers prefer to present a list of established rules and ask students to give specific examples or to provide reasons for having such a rule. When rules are easily understood and convey a sense of moral fairness, most children will comply.

Good managers also carefully arrange their classrooms to minimize disturbances and make sure that instruction can proceed efficiently. They set up their rooms according to the following principles:

- *Teachers should be able to see all students at all times.* Student desks should be arranged so that the teacher can see everybody from any instructional area where he or she may be working.
- *Teaching materials and supplies should be readily available.* Those that students can take themselves should be clearly marked.

- *High-traffic areas should be free of congestion*. For example, student desks should be placed away from supply cabinets, pencil sharpeners, and so on.
- *Students should be able to see instructional presentations*. Research shows that students who are seated far away from the teacher or the instructional activity are less likely to be involved in class discussions.
- *Procedures and routines should be actively taught in the same way that academic content is taught*. This initial planning and organization reduces time wasted on discipline problems and on establishing classroom routines and procedures.[7] It allows teachers and students more time for involvement in academic learning.

Keeping Instruction Going Smoothly

The observer walked to the back of the room and sat down. It seemed to him that the classroom was a beehive of activity. A reading group was in progress in the front of the room, while the other children were working on math examples at their seats. The classroom was filled with a hum of children working together—but the activity and the noise were organized and not chaotic.

The observer had been in enough schools over the past 20 years to know that this well-managed classroom did not result from magic, but that carefully established and maintained procedures were at work. The observer scrutinized the classroom, searching for the procedures that allowed 33 students and one teacher to work together so industriously, harmoniously, and effectively.

First he examined the reading group, where the teacher was leading a discussion about the meaning of a story. "Why was Maria worried about the trip she was going to take?" the teacher asked. (A few seconds' pause, all the children with eyes on the teacher, several hands raised.) "Sean?"

Modern classrooms are complex environments that require carefully planned rules and routines.

As Sean began his response, the observer's eyes wandered around the rest of the room, where most of the children were busy at work. Two girls, however, were passing notes surreptitiously in the corner of the room.

During a quick sweep of the room, the teacher spotted the misbehavior. The two girls watched the teacher frown and put her finger over her lips. They quickly returned to their work. The exchange had been so rapid and so quiet that the reading group was not interrupted for even a second.

Another student in the math group had his hand raised. The teacher motioned John to come to her side.

"Look for the paragraph in your story that tells how Maria felt after her visit to her grandmother," the teacher instructed the reading group. "When you have found it, raise your hands."

While the reading group looked for the appropriate passage, the teacher quietly assisted John. In less than a minute, John was back at his seat, and the teacher was once again discussing the story with her reading group.

At 10:15 the teacher sent the reading group back to their seats and tapped a bell that was on her desk. "It is now time for social studies. Before you do anything, listen carefully to *all* my instructions. When I tap the bell again, those working on math should put their papers in their desks for now. You may have a chance to finish them later. Then all students should take out their social studies books and turn to page 67. When you hear the sound of the bell, I want you to follow those instructions." After a second's pause, the teacher tapped the bell, and the class was once again a sea of motion, but it was motion that was organized and in control.

The observer made some notes on his forms. There was nothing particularly flashy or dramatic about what he had seen. It was not the type of Broadway performance that teachers sometimes put on to dazzle him. But he was satisfied, because he knew he had been witnessing a well-managed classroom.

• • •

Can you remember from your childhood those activity books in which you had to find the five things wrong in a picture? Let us reverse the game: Try rereading this classroom vignette and look for all the things that are *right* with the picture. What could the observer have noted about the teacher's behavior and her procedures that enabled her students to focus on academic content so effectively? Write down four or five observations on a separate sheet of paper.

In well-managed classes where teachers keep the momentum going, students are more likely to be on task. The teacher in this vignette used several strategies to avoid interruptions and to keep instruction proceeding smoothly.[8]

Did you notice that:

1. The teacher used a questioning technique known as *group alerting* to keep the reading group involved. By asking questions first and then naming the student to respond, she kept all the students awake and on their toes. If she had said, "Sean, why did Maria feel concerned about her trip?" the other students in the group would have been less concerned about paying attention and answering the question. Instead she asked her question first and then called on a student to respond.
2. The teacher seemed to have "eyes in the back of her head." Termed *withitness* by researcher Jacob Kounin, this quality characterizes teachers

Times of Transition

Teachers must manage more than 30 major transitions every day, from one content area to another, through different instructional activities, and through a myriad of housekeeping routines, including having students line up, collecting papers, distributing texts, and the like. During these transitions, discipline problems occur twice as often as in regular classroom instruction. Classroom management expert Jacob Kounin has identified five common patterns that can derail classroom management during times of transition.

- **Flip-flops.** In this negative pattern, the teacher terminates one activity, begins a new one, and then flops back to the original activity. For example, in making a transition from math to spelling, the teacher says, "Please open your spelling books to page 29. By the way, how many of you got all the math problems right?"
- **Overdwelling.** This bad habit includes preaching, nagging, and spending more time than necessary to correct an infraction of classroom rules. "Anna, I told you to stop talking. If I've told you once, I've told you 100 times. I told you yesterday and the day before that. The way things are going I'll be telling it to you all semester, and be-

lieve me, I'm getting pretty tired of it. And another thing, young lady . . ."

- **Fragmentation.** In this bumpy transition, the teacher breaks directions into several choppy steps instead of accomplishing the instructions in one fluid unit. For example, "Put away your reading books. You shouldn't have any spelling books on your desk either. All notes should be off your desk," instead of the simpler and more effective, "Clear your desk of all books and papers."
- **Thrusts.** Classroom momentum is interrupted by nonsequitors and random thoughts that just seem to pop into the teacher's head. For example: The class is busily engaged in independent reading when their quiet concentration is broken by the teacher, who says, "Where's Bob? Wasn't he here earlier this morning?"
- **Dangles.** Similar to the thrust, this move involves starting something only to leave it hanging or dangling. For example, "Richard, would you please read the first paragraph on page 94. Oh, class, did I tell you about the guest speaker we're having today? How could I have forgotten about that?"

Source: Jacob Kounin, *Discipline and Group Management in Classrooms* (New York: Holt, Rinehart & Winston, 1970).

who are aware of student behavior in all parts of the room at all times. While the teacher was conducting the reading group, she was aware of the students passing notes and the one who needed assistance.

3. The teacher was able to attend to interruptions or behavior problems while continuing the lesson. Kounin calls the ability to do several things at once *overlapping*. The teacher reprimanded the students passing notes and helped another child with a math problem without interrupting the flow of her reading lesson.
4. The teacher managed routine misbehavior using the principle of least intervention. Since research shows the time spent disciplining students is negatively related to achievement, teachers should use the simplest intervention that will work. In this case, the teacher did not make a mountain out of a mole hill. She intervened quietly and quickly to stop the students from passing notes. A nonverbal cue was all that was necessary, and the students working on math and reading were not disrupted. The teacher might also have used some other effective strategies. She could have praised the students who were attending to their math ("I'm glad to see so many working well on their math assignments"). If it had been necessary to say more to the girls passing notes, she should have alerted them to what they *should* be doing rather than emphasizing their misbehavior ("Alice and Sarah, please attend to your own work," *not* "Alice and Sarah, stop passing notes").

Good classroom manage-
ment requires constant
monitoring of student
behavior.

5. The teacher managed the transition from one lesson to the next
smoothly and effectively. When students must move from one activity
to another, a gap is created in the fabric of instruction. Chaos can result
when transitions are not handled competently by the instructor. Did you
notice that the teacher in this scene gave her students a clear transition
signal (the bell), gave them thorough instructions so they would know
exactly what they were supposed to do next, and made the transition
all at once for the entire class rather than for separate groups or individuals? These may seem simple, commonsense behaviors, but countless classes have come apart at the seams because transitions were not
handled effectively.

The teacher in this vignette was involved with routine classroom management that included minor rule infractions. Sometimes teachers, of course, must
face more serious misbehavior. When students will not obey a simple reminder,
the teacher should repeat the warning, clearly stating the appropriate behavior. If this fails, the teacher will need to apply punitive consequences, such as
sending the child out of the class or calling the parents. When teachers must
apply such consequences, these should follow the inappropriate behavior
immediately, should be mildly but not severely unpleasant, and should be as
brief as possible.[9] These episodes should communicate the message, "I care
about you, but I will not tolerate inappropriate behavior."

In summary, the major difference between effective and ineffective classroom managers is in planning. Effective managers *prevent* discipline problems
from happening in the first place. As researcher David Berliner says: "In short,
from the opening bell to the end of the day, the better classroom managers
are thinking ahead. While maintaining a pleasant classroom atmosphere, these
teachers keep planning how to organize, manage, and control activities to facilitate instruction."[10]

Effective teachers must be more than good classroom managers, however;
they must also be good organizers of academic content and instruction.

The Pedagogical Cycle

Researcher Arno Bellack has analyzed verbal exchanges between teachers and students and likened them to a pedagogical game.[11] The game is so cyclical and occurs so frequently that many teachers and students do not even know that they are playing. There are four moves:

1. *Structure.* The teacher provides information, provides direction, and introduces the topics.
2. *Question.* The teacher asks a question.
3. *Respond.* The student answers the question, or tries to.
4. *React.* The teacher reacts to the student's answer and provides feedback.

These four steps make up a **pedagogical cycle** diagrammed in Figure 2.1. Teachers initiate about 85 percent of the cycles, which are used over and over again in classroom interaction.

Although these cycles can be found in a majority of classrooms, the quality and effectiveness of the four steps vary widely. When teachers learn to enhance and refine each of the moves of the pedagogical cycle, student achievement is increased.[12]

Clarity and Academic Structure

Have you ever been to a class where the teacher is bombarded with questions?: "I don't understand what we're supposed to do." "Can you explain it again?" "I don't get what you mean." When such complaints are constant in a class, it is a sure sign that the teacher is not making effective use of essential teaching skills: clarity and academic structure. A growing body of research makes it clear that these skills are related to student achievement.

Students need a clear understanding of what they are expected to learn, and they need to be motivated to learn it.[13] Effective structuring sets the stage for learning and typically occurs at the beginning of the lesson. Although the length of structure will vary depending on the age, ability, and background of the students and the difficulty of the subject matter, the following components are usually found in an effective academic structure:

- *Objectives.* Let the students know the objectives of each lesson. They, like the teacher, need a road map of where they are going and why.
- *Review.* Help students review prior learning before presenting new information. If there is confusion, reteach.

FIGURE 2.1
Pedagogical Cycle

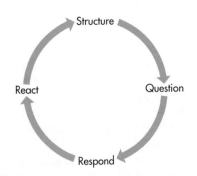

- *Motivation.* Create an "anticipatory set" that motivates students to listen to the presentation. This can be done through an intriguing question, an anecdote, a joke, or interesting teaching materials.
- *Transition.* Relate new information to previously attained student knowledge and experience. Provide ties and connections that will help students integrate old and new information.
- *Clarification.* Break down a large body of information. Do not inundate students with too much too fast. This is particularly true for young children and slower learners, although it also applies to older and faster learners.
- *Examples.* Give several examples and illustrations to explain main points and ideas.
- *Directions.* Give directions distinctly and slowly. If students are confused about what they are supposed to do, repeat or break information into small segments.
- *Enthusiasm.* Demonstrate personal enthusiasm for the academic content. Make it clear why the information is interesting and important.
- *Closure.* Close the lesson with a brief review or summary.

The major activity in academic structuring takes place at the beginning of the lesson, but there may be several points throughout the lesson where substructuring or brief presentations of information are also necessary. Substructures initiate new pedagogical cycles and allow the discussion to continue. A clear summary or review is also important at the close of the lesson.

When teachers are able to motivate and provide a clear introduction, all aspects of the lesson will proceed more smoothly.[14] Through effective and clear structure, as shown in Figure 2.2, the stage is set for the remaining steps of the pedagogical cycle.

FIGURE 2.2
Pedagogical Cycle: Sample Classroom Dialogue

Structure *(teacher)* **(Motivate)**	How many of you have ever stayed up late and felt terribly tired the next day? Being weary dulls your senses, so that you really don't feel much like talking with others. In some ways, nations are like people; they get weary as well.
(Review) **(Transition)**	Yesterday we discussed the horrible battles and terrible casualties of World War I. Today we are going to look at what happens to nations that get weary from war. Like people, nations don't see as clearly or react as quickly when they are war-weary. England and France after World War I were two such war-weary nations.
	Although the signs of a new war were clear and growing, many of the British and French were still recovering from the casualties and physical destruction of World War I. That long and difficult struggle made them blind to new danger signs.
(Objective)	Our objective today is to explore the pre-World War II mentality of the British and French.

(Figure 2.2 continues on next page.)

Question *(teacher)*	What are some of the signs that a new world war was coming?
Respond *(student)*	The growing military buildup in Germany.
React *(teacher)*	Okay.
Question *(teacher)*	Why was this military buildup of particular concern?
Respond *(student)*	Because it was prohibited by the Treaty of Versailles. The Germans were violating the treaty that prohibited them from building an army.
React *(teacher)*	Good.
Question *(teacher)*	Were the Germans involved in any other violations of the peace treaty?
Respond *(student)*	They began to expand, to take over the territory of other countries.
React/Question *(teacher)*	Which countries?
Respond *(student)*	Austria, Czechoslovakia.
React *(teacher)*	Okay.
Substructure *(teacher provides transition, clarification, examples)*	Now we indicated that Europe had undergone a terrible experience in World War I. Millions of lives were lost, property was destroyed, many careers and families were left in shambles, and many Europeans believed that they had seen the last of war. Many people thought that "The Great War," which we called World War I, was the war to end all wars. We described how the French and English were ignoring Germany's military moves because they wanted peace so badly. Yet here were the Germans gearing up for war.
Question *(teacher)*	Why were the Germans gearing up for another war after the pain and suffering they experienced in World War I?
Respond *(student)*	The Treaty of Versailles, the peace treaty, was pretty unfair to Germans. They had to pay reparations. They lost land. Their honor was tarnished. They were unhappy and wanted justice.
React *(teacher)*	Good points.
Question *(teacher)*	Any other reasons?
Respond *(student)*	The depression really hurt Germany. Building industry helped their economy. Also, the Germans blamed the peace treaty for their economic problems. They blamed the Allies and wanted revenge.
React *(teacher)*	Those are terrific points.

Questioning

Good questioning is at the very core of good teaching. As John Dewey said:

> To question well is to teach well. In the skillful use of the question more than anything else lies the fine art of teaching; for in it we have the guide to clear and vivid ideas, and the quick spur to imagination, the stimulus to thought, the incentive to action.[15]

Since questioning is a key element in guiding learning, all students should have equal access to classroom questions and academic interaction. However, research shows that male students are asked more questions than female students are and white students are asked more questions than minorities are. One of the reasons boys get to answer questions and talk more is that they are assertive in grabbing teacher attention. Boys are more likely than girls to call out the answers to the questions. However, when boys call out the answers to questions, teachers are likely to accept their responses. When girls call out the answers to questions, teachers often remind them to raise their hands.[16]

If you want all students, and not just the quickest and most assertive, to answer questions, establish a protocol for participation. For example, make a rule that students must raise their hands and be called on before they may talk. Too many classes offer variations of the following scene:

Teacher: How much is 60 + 4 + 12? (*Many students raise their hands—both girls and boys.*)
Tony: (*Shouts out*) 76!
Teacher: Okay. How much is 50 + 9 + 8?

This scene, repeated again and again in classes across the country, is a typical example of the squeaky wheel—not necessarily the most needy or most deserving—getting the educational oil. Once you make the rule that students should raise their hands before participating, *hold to that rule.* Try to avoid the following:

Teacher: Now it's time for Math Bowl. Remember to raise your hands and wait until I call on you. How much is 60 + 4 +12? (*Several students raise their hands.*)
Teacher: Alice?
Alice: 76.
Teacher: How much is 50 + 9 + 8? (*Several students raise their hands.*)
Teacher: Tom?
Tom: 67.
Teacher: How much is 17 + 14 + 5? (*Several students raise their hands.*)
Tony: (*Shouts out*) 36!
Teacher: How much is 19 + 8 + 4?

Many teachers are well-intentioned about having students raise their hands, but in the rapid pace of classroom interaction, they sometimes forget their own rule. If you hold to that "wait to be recognized" rule, you can make professional decisions about who should answer which questions and why. If you give away this key to classroom participation, you are abandoning an important part of your professional decision making in the classroom.

Many educators differentiate between factual, or lower-order, questions and thought-provoking, or higher-order, questions. One of the most widely used systems for determining the intellectual level of questions is Benjamin Bloom's **taxonomy,** which proceeds from the lowest level of questions, knowledge, to the highest level, evaluation.[17] See Figure 2.3 for a summary of the six levels of the taxonomy along with sample classroom questions at each level. This section will provide more information about the different levels of classroom questions as well as strategies for using them fairly and effectively.[18]

A **lower-order question** is one that can be answered through the processes of memory and recall. For example, "Who was president of the Confederacy during the Civil War?" is a lower-order question. Without consulting outside references, one could respond with the correct answer only by remem-

---

FIGURE 2.3
Bloom's Taxonomy Applied to Questioning Levels

Level I: Knowledge
The student is required to recall or reorganize information. The student must rely on memory or senses to provide the answer.

Sample Questions
What is the meaning of "quixotic"?
List the first 10 presidents of the United States.

Level II: Comprehension
The student is required to go beyond simple recall and demonstrate the ability to arrange and organize information mentally. The student must use previously learned information by putting it in his or her own words and rephrasing it.

Sample Question
In your chapter, the author discusses the causes of World War I. Can you
    summarize these in your own words?

Level III: Application
Students are required to apply previously learned information to answer a problem. At this level students use a rule, a definition, a classification system, directions, or the like in solving a problem with a specific correct answer.

Sample Questions
Applying the law of supply and demand, solve the following problem. *(applying a
    rule)*
Identify the adjectives in the following sentences. *(applying a definition)*
Solve the quadratic equation. *(applying a rule)*

Level IV: Analysis
Students are required to use three kinds of cognitive processes:

1. To identify causes, reasons, or motives (when these have not been provided to
   the student previously).

bering previously learned information. Research indicates that approximately 90 percent of the questions teachers ask are lower-order questions.

A **higher-order question** is one that requires more demanding thought for response. These questions may ask for evaluations, comparisons, causal relationships, problem solving, or divergent, open-ended thinking. Following are examples of higher-order questions:

1. Do you think that Truman was an effective president? Why or why not?
2. What similarities in theme emerge in the three Shakespearean plays *King Lear, Macbeth,* and *Othello?*
3. Considering changes that have taken place in the past decade, what effects might increased student political consciousness have on campus life?
4. Considering what you have learned in this child-care course, how would you go about solving the problem of an infant's persistent crying?
5. What would happen if our shadows came to life?

Despite the fact that higher-order questions have been shown to produce increased student achievement, most teachers ask very few of them.[19]

Sample Question
Why do you think King Lear misjudged his daughter?

2. To analyze information to reach a generalization or conclusion.

Sample Question
What generalizations can you make about the climate of Europe on the eves of World War I and World War II?

3. To find evidence to support a specific opinion, event, or situation.

Sample Question
Many historians think that Abraham Lincoln was our finest president. What evidence can you find to support this statement?

Level V: Synthesis
Students are required to use original and creative thinking in (1) developing original communications, (2) making predictions, and (3) solving problems for which there is no single right answer.

Sample Questions
Write a short story about life on another planet. *(developing an original communication)*

What do you think life would be like if Germany had won World War II? *(making predictions)*

How can our class raise money for the graduation trip? *(solving problems for which there is no single right answer)*

Level VI: Evaluation
Students are required to judge the merits of an aesthetic work, an idea, or the solution to a problem.

Sample Questions
Which U.S. senator do you think is most effective?

Do you think that schools are too hard or not hard enough? Explain your answer.

Many educators think that different questioning levels stimulate different levels of thought. If you ask a fifth-grade student to define an adjective, you are working on lower-level basic skills. If you ask a fifth-grade student to write a short story making effective use of adjectives, you are working on a higher level of student achievement. Both lower-order and higher-order questions are important and should be matched to appropriate instructional goals such as the following:

Ask lower-order questions when:

- Students are being introduced to new information
- Students are working on drill and practice
- Students are reviewing previously learned information

Ask higher-order questions when:

- A content base has been established and you want students to manipulate information in more sophisticated ways
- Students are working on problem-solving skills
- Students are involved in a creative or affective discussion
- Students are asked to make judgments about quality, aesthetics, or ethics

Student Response

If you were to spend a few minutes in a secondary school English class, you might hear a classroom discussion that goes something like this:

Teacher: Who wrote the poem "Stopping by Woods on a Snowy Evening"? Tom?

Tom: Robert Frost.

Teacher: Good. What action takes place in the poem? Sally?

Sally: A man stops his sleigh to watch the woods get filled with snow.

Teacher: Yes. Emma, what thoughts go through the man's mind?

Emma: He thinks how beautiful the woods are. *(Pauses for a second)*

Teacher: What else does he think about? Joe?

Joe: He thinks how he would like to stay and watch. *(Pauses for a second)*

Teacher: Yes—and what else? Rita? *(Waits half a second)* Come on, Rita, you can answer this. *(Waits half a second)* Well, why does he feel he can't stay there indefinitely and watch the woods and the snow?

Rita: He knows he's too busy. He's got too many things to do to stay there for so long.

Teacher: Good. In the poem's last line, the man says that he has miles to go before he sleeps. What might sleep be a symbol for? Sarah?

Sarah: Well, I think it might be . . . *(Pauses for a second)*

Teacher: Think, Sarah. *(Waits for half a second)* All right then—Mike? *(Waits again for half a second)* John? *(Waits half a second)* What's the matter with everyone today? Didn't you do the reading?[20]

There are several instructional skills that this teacher is using effectively. This is a well-managed classroom. The students are on task, engaged in a dis-

Teacher questioning patterns have much to do with the learning climate in classrooms.

cussion appropriate to the academic content. By asking a series of lower-order questions (Who wrote the poem? What action takes place in the poem?), the teacher works with the students to establish an information base. Then the teacher builds to higher-order questions about the poem's theme and meaning.

If you were to give this teacher suggestions on how to improve her teaching skills, you might point out the difficulty students have in answering the more complex questions. You might also note the lightning pace at which this lesson proceeds. The questions are fired so rapidly that the students barely have time to think. This is not so troublesome when they are answering factual questions that require a brief memorized response. However, they begin to flounder when they are required to answer more complex questions with equal speed.

Although it is important to keep classroom discussion moving at a brisk pace, sometimes teachers push forward too rapidly. Slowing down at two key places during classroom discussion can usually improve the effectiveness and equity of classroom responses. In the research on classroom interaction, this slowing down is called **wait time.**[21]

Mary Budd Rowe's research shows that after asking a question, teachers typically wait only 1 second or less for a student response (wait time 1). If the response is not forthcoming in that time, teachers rephrase the question, ask another student to answer it, or answer it themselves. If teachers can learn to increase their wait time from 1 second to 3–5 seconds, significant improvements in the quantity and quality of student response usually will take place.

There is another point in classroom discussion when wait time can be increased. After students complete an answer, teachers often begin their reaction or their next question before a second has passed (wait time 2). Once again it is important for teachers to increase their wait time from 1 second to 3–5 seconds. Based on her research, Mary Budd Rowe has determined that increasing the pause after a student gives an answer is equally as important as increasing wait time 1, the pause after the teacher asks a question. When wait time 1 and wait time 2 are increased from 1 second to 3–5 seconds, classroom interaction is changed in several positive ways.

Changes in Student Behavior

- The length of student response increases dramatically.
- Students are more likely to support their statements with evidence.
- Speculative thinking increases.
- There are more student questions and fewer failures to respond.
- More students voluntarily participate in discussion.
- There are fewer discipline problems.
- Student achievement increases on written tests that measure more complex levels of thinking.

Changes in Teacher Behavior

- Teacher comments are less disjointed and more fluent. Classroom discussion becomes more logical, thoughtful, and coherent.
- Teachers ask more higher-order questions. There is a more cognitively sophisticated pattern of teacher questions and student answers.
- Teachers begin to hold higher expectations for all students.

Research indicates that teachers give more wait time to students for whom they hold higher expectations. A high-achieving student is more likely to get time to think than a low-achieving student. If we do not expect much from our students, we will not get much. High expectations and longer wait time are positively related to achievement. Although more research is needed on this issue, some investigators suggest that white male students, particularly high achievers, are more likely to be given adequate wait time than are females and minorities. Students who are quiet and reserved or who think more slowly may obtain special benefit from increased wait time. In fact, a key benefit of extended wait time is the quality participation of students who were previously silent.

Usually when teachers learn that they are giving students less than a second to think, they are surprised and have every intention of waiting longer. Easier said than done! In the hectic arena of the classroom, it is all too easy to slip into split-second question-and-answer patterns. Teachers who have worked on increasing wait time suggest that some of the following strategies are helpful.

Sometimes teachers fall into a pattern of quickly repeating every answer that students give. Occasionally this repetition can be helpful—if some students may not have heard it or if an answer is so good that the teacher wants to emphasize it. In most cases, however, this repetition, or teacher echo, is counterproductive. It teaches students that they do not need to listen to one another, because the teacher will repeat the answer anyway. It also reduces valuable wait time and cuts down on the pause that allows students to think.

Some teachers adopt self-monitoring cues to slow themselves down at the two key wait-time points. For example, one teacher says that he puts his hand behind his back and counts on his fingers for 3 seconds to slow himself down. Another teacher says that she covers her mouth with her hand (in a thoughtful pose) to keep herself from talking and thereby destroying "the pause that lets them think."

As mentioned previously, wait time is more important in some cases than in others. If you are asking students to repeat previously memorized math facts and you are interested in developing speed, a 3- to 5-second wait time may be counterproductive. However, if you have asked a higher-order question that calls for a complicated answer, be sure that wait times 1 and 2 are ample. Simply put, students, like the rest of us, need time to think.

When teachers allow more wait time, the results can be surprising. As one teacher said, "I never thought Andrea had anything to say. She just used to sit there like a bump on a log. Then I tried calling on her and giving her time to answer. What a difference! She comes up with things that no one else has thought of."

Reaction or Productive Feedback

"Today," the student teacher said, "we are going to hear the story of *The Three Billy Goats Gruff*." A murmur of anticipation rippled through the kindergarten children comfortably seated on the carpet around the flannel board. This student teacher was a favorite, and the children were particularly happy when she told them flannel-board stories.

"Before we begin the story, I want to make sure we know what all the words mean. Who can tell me what a troll is?"

A tow-headed 5-year-old nicknamed B. J. raised his hand. "A troll is someone who walks you home from school."

"Okay," the teacher responded, a slightly puzzled look flickered over her face. "Who else can tell me what a troll is?"

Another student chimed in, "A troll is someone with white hair sticking out of his head."

"Okay," the teacher said.

Another student volunteered, "It hides under bridges and waits for you and scares you."

"Uh-huh," said the teacher.

Warming to the topic, another student gleefully described, "A troll has a long white beard. It loves to eat you up. It especially likes to eat children."

"Okay," the teacher said.

Wide-eyed, B. J. raised his hand again, "I'm sure glad we had this talk about trolls," he said. "I'm not going home with them from school anymore."

"Okay," the teacher said.

● ● ●

This is a classroom in which several good teaching strategies are in operation. The teacher uses effective academic structure, and the students are on task, interested, and involved in the learning activity. The teacher is asking lower-order questions appropriately, to make sure the students know key vocabulary words before the flannel-board story is told. The problem with this classroom lies in the fourth stage of the pedagogical cycle: This teacher does not provide specific reactions and adequate feedback. Did you notice that the teacher reacted with "uh-huh" or "okay" no matter what kind of answer the students gave? Because of this vague feedback and "okay" teaching style, B. J. was left confused about the difference between a troll and a patrol. This real-life incident may seem amusing, but there was nothing funny to B. J., who was genuinely afraid to leave school with the patrol.

Recently attention has been directed not only at how teachers ask questions, but also at how they respond to student answers. A study analyzing classroom interaction in more than 100 classrooms in five states found that teachers generally use four types of reactions.[22]

1. *Praise.* Positive comments about student work, such as "Excellent, good job."
2. *Acceptance.* Comments such as "Uh-huh" and "Okay," which acknowledge that student answers are acceptable. These are not as strong as praise.
3. *Remediation.* Comments that encourage a more accurate student response or encourage students to think more clearly, creatively, logically. Sample remediation comments include "Try again," "Sharpen your answer," "Check your addition."
4. *Criticism.* A clear statement that an answer is inaccurate or a behavior inappropriate. This category includes harsh criticism ("This is a terrible paper") as well as milder comments that simply indicate an answer is not correct ("Your answer to the third question is wrong").

Which of the reactions presented in Figure 2.4 do you think teachers use most frequently? Did you notice that the kindergarten teacher relied heavily on the acceptance, or "okay," reaction? So do most teachers from grade school through graduate school. Here is what the study found.

Acceptance was the most frequent response, accounting for more than half of all teacher reactions. The second most frequent teacher response was remediation, accounting for one-third of teacher reactions. Used infrequently, praise comprised only 11 percent of reactions. The rarest response was criticism. In two-thirds of the classrooms observed, teachers never told a student that an answer was incorrect. In those classrooms where criticism did occur, it accounted for only 5 percent of interaction.

In *A Place Called School,* John Goodlad writes that "learning is enhanced when students understand what is expected of them, get recognition for their work, learn about their errors, and receive guidance in improving their performances."[23] But many students claim that they are not informed or corrected

FIGURE 2.4
Teacher Reactions

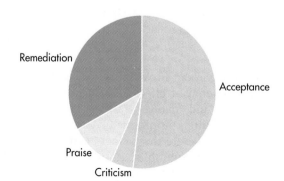

when they make mistakes. Perhaps this is caused by overreliance on the acceptance response, which is the vaguest kind of feedback that teachers can offer. Since there is more acceptance than praise, criticism, and remediation combined, some educators are beginning to wonder: "Is the 'okay' classroom okay?"

Although the acceptance response is legitimate and often appropriate, it is overused. Since achievement is likely to increase when students get clear and specific feedback about their answers, it is important for teachers to reduce the "okay" reaction and to be more varied and specific in the feedback they provide. Following are strategies for providing more specific reactions and clearer feedback to students.

Many educators emphasize the importance of praise as specific feedback in encouraging student achievement, and researcher Jere Brophy has done a thorough analysis of its effects. He found that praise may be particularly important for low-achieving students and those from low socioeconomic backgrounds. He also suggests that praise works best when:[24]

1. *It is contingent upon student performance.* Praise should closely follow student behavior the teacher wants to recognize.
2. *It is specific.* When teachers praise, they should indicate clearly what aspect of the student behavior is noteworthy (for instance, use of topic sentences or ability to substantiate statements with evidence).
3. *It is sincere.* Praise should be varied with the situation and the needs of the individual student. Otherwise it will be dismissed as meaningless and irrelevant.
4. *It lets students know about their competence and the importance of their accomplishments.*
5. *It attributes success to ability or effort.* For example, "Your analysis of the paintings of the impressionists is excellent. I'll bet you spent a long time studying their work in the museum" *(attribution to effort).* Or "This story is fantastic. You've got a real flair for creative writing" *(attribution to ability).* When praise is attributed to abilities or effort, students know that successful performance is under their own control.
6. *It uses past performance as a context for describing present performance.* ("Last week you were really having trouble with your side stroke. Now you've got it together—you've learned to push the water behind you and increase your speed.")

Just as students need to know when they are performing well, they need to know when their answers are inadequate or incorrect. If students do not have information about their weak areas, they will find it difficult to improve. Corrective feedback works best when:

1. *It is specific and contingent upon student performance.* Corrective feedback should closely follow the student behavior the teacher wants to improve.
2. *It focuses on student performance and is not of a personal nature.* Students will accept constructive criticism if it is not personal, hostile, or sarcastic.
3. *It provides a clear blueprint for improvement.* If you tell a student that an answer is wrong and nothing more, the student has clear feedback on level of performance but no strategies for improvement. Effective

feedback suggests an approach for attaining success, such as "Check your addition"; "Use the bold headings as a reading guide"; "Check the definition of an adjective"; "Let's review the vowel sounds."

4. *An environment is established that lets the student know it is acceptable to make mistakes.* We learn from our errors.
5. *It relates eventual success to effort.* "I know you can do it if you try." "If you spend an hour tonight working on this, I'm pretty sure you'll be able to do it. I'll check with you tomorrow."
6. *It recognizes when students have made improvements in their performance.* "Last week you were having trouble identifying topic sentences. Now you've mastered that skill. You've done a good job."

An "okay classroom" allows student error and misunderstanding to go uncorrected; it lets B. J. think that the patrol will eat him up after school. In classrooms where there is appropriate use of remediation and constructive criticism, students not only know when they have made mistakes, but also how to correct them. They also know that this process leads to growth and achievement.

Variety in Process and Content

Variety is the spice of life, the saying goes. The spice of lessons also, variety is related to teaching effectiveness and student achievement.[25]

Have you ever listened to a lecture for an hour and found your initial interest lapsing into daydreams? Have you ever watched a class begin a seatwork assignment with active concentration and found, after 30 minutes, that involvement has turned into passing notes and throwing paper airplanes? When the teacher fails to provide sufficient variety, lessons become monotonous and students get off task.

Effective teachers provide variety in both process and content. In elementary school, variety in content involves moving from one subject area to another. In secondary instruction, the move is from one aspect of a single content area to another, such as the switch from memorizing vocabulary to analyzing symbols in a short story.

A positive classroom atmosphere that includes precise, encouraging feedback helps motivate and guide student effort.

As any smart teacher knows, student interest can be maintained by moving from one activity to another during a single lesson. For example, a 60-minute lesson on the French Revolution might begin with a 10-minute lecture, move into a 15-minute question-and-answer session, then on to a 25-minute movie, and conclude with a 10-minute discussion and closure. Following is a sampler of activities teachers can use to maintain student interest by varying the pattern of the lesson.

discussions	creative writing
lectures	plays
movies, tapes, and other audio-visual presentations	field trips
	boardwork
role plays	participation in learning centers
simulations	music activities
small-group activities	art activities
guest speakers	tutoring
independent seatwork	spot quizzes
guided practice	panel discussions
student presentations	debates
tests	brainstorming sessions
silent reading	students tutoring one another
games	cooperative learning activities
contests	

The preceding sections reviewed research on teaching skills that lead to increased student achievement. However, this provides only a beginning. You will be developing and refining skills in good teaching throughout your teacher preparation program. The final section of this chapter introduces four recent models in effective teaching that you may see implemented in schools and classrooms where you do your field experiences.

Current Models for Effective Instruction

This section describes four models of instruction that have proven successful in enhancing student achievement. Emphasizing high teacher visibility and on-task student behavior, the direct teaching model is particularly effective for subjects that are highly structured, such as mathematics, reading, grammar, and vocabulary. The cooperative learning model yields gains not only in achievement but in interpersonal skills and relationships as well. The mastery learning model is based on the principle that, if given sufficient time, all students in a regular classroom can master academic objectives. Finally, project-based instruction provides students with the opportunity to explore real, not just "academic," issues.

Direct Teaching

The principles on which **direct teaching** is based have emerged from extensive research. In this model, the role of the teacher is that of a strong leader, one who structures the classroom and sequences subject matter to reflect a clear academic focus. Also called *systematic, active,* or *explicit teaching,* the direct teaching model emphasizes the importance of a structured lesson in which presentation of new information is followed by student practice and teacher feedback.

Researchers put forward six principles of direct teaching. They say effective teachers use these principles consistently and systematically most of the time.[26]

1. *Daily review.* At the beginning of the lesson prior learning is reviewed. Frequently, this review focuses on assigned homework, clarifies points of confusion, and provides extra practice for facts and skills that need more attention.
2. *New material.* Effective teachers begin the presentation by letting students know the objectives to be attained. New information is broken down into smaller steps and is covered at a brisk pace. Main points are illustrated by use of concrete examples. The teacher asks questions frequently to check for student understanding and to make sure that students are ready for independent work using new skills and knowledge.
3. *Guided practice.* In this segment of the lesson, students use new skills and knowledge under direct teacher supervision. During guided practice, teachers ask many content questions ("What is the definition of a paragraph?") and many process questions as well ("How do you locate the topic sentence in a paragraph?"). Teachers use student responses as

With direct instruction, teachers carefully explain what students must do to accomplish a task, then present a carefully structured lesson that is usually broken down into small, manageable steps.

a way to check for understanding and evaluate progress. They offer prompts and provide corrective feedback to ensure the accuracy of student skills and information. Guided practice continues until students are answering at a rate of approximately 70 to 80 percent accuracy.

4. *Correctives and feedback.* Correct answers to questions should be acknowledged clearly so that students will understand when their work is accurate. When student answers are hesitant, the teacher provides process feedback ("Yes, Donald, that's correct because. . ."). Inaccurate responses should be corrected immediately, before errors become habitual. Frequent errors are a sign that students are not ready for independent work, and guided practice should continue.

5. *Independent practice.* This stage is similar to guided practice except that students work by themselves at their seats or at home. Independent practice continues until responses are assured, quick, and at a level of approximately 95 percent accuracy. Cooperative learning (see next section) and student tutoring of one another are effective strategies during independent practice.

6. *Weekly and monthly reviews.* Weekly and monthly reviews offer students the opportunity for more practice, a strategy related to high achievement. Barak Rosenshine, a pioneering researcher in developing the principles of direct instruction, recommends a weekly review every Monday, with a monthly review every fourth Monday.

The strategy of direct instruction works well when you are teaching skill subjects, such as grammar or mathematics. It is also useful in helping students master factual material. While there are benefits for all learners, the direct teaching model is most helpful for young children, for slower learners, and during the first stages of learning new and complex information. You may find direct instruction less useful when you are working with mature or gifted learners in areas that call for imaginative responses and student creativity.

Cooperative Learning

Although **cooperative learning** is considered a new development in effective teaching, it has its roots in the 1920s. In a classroom using cooperative learning, students work on activities in small, heterogeneous groups, and they receive rewards or recognition based on the overall group performance.

Cooperative approaches to learning seem startling or new because the classroom environment is so often competitive. For example, when grading is done on a curve, one student's success is necessarily detrimental to others. In this competitive structure, there are clear winners and losers, and only a limited number of A's are possible. Sometimes, classrooms are set up according to an individualistic reward structure, such as independent study or learning contracts. In these cases, students work by themselves to reach learning goals that have no relationship to those of other students. But a cooperative learning structure differs from both of these more traditional approaches in that students depend on one another and work together to reach shared goals.

According to researchers, cooperative learning groups work best when they meet the following criteria.[27] Groups should be heterogeneous, and, at least at the beginning, they should be small, limited to two to six members. Since

In cooperative learning situations, students' individual goals and rewards are tied into group accomplishments.

face-to-face interaction is important, the groups should be circular to permit easy conversation. There must be a genuine feeling of positive interdependence among group members, a sense that the group sinks or swims together. This can be accomplished through a shared group goal, shared division of labor, or shared materials.

Robert Slavin, a pioneer in cooperative learning techniques, developed student team learning methods in which a team's work is not completed until all students on the team understand the material being studied.[28] If student team learning is to succeed, rewards are earned only when the entire team achieves goals set by the teacher. Students tutor one another so that everyone can succeed on individual quizzes, and each member of the group is accountable for learning. Since students contribute to their teams by improving prior scores, it does not matter whether the student is a high, average, or low achiever. Increased achievement by an individual student at any level contributes to the overall performance of the group, resulting in equal opportunity for success.

Research shows that both cognitive and affective growth results from cooperative learning:

- Students taught within this structure make higher achievement gains; this is especially true for math in the elementary grades.
- Students who participate in cooperative learning have higher levels of self-esteem and greater motivation to learn.
- Students have a stronger sense that classmates have positive regard for one another.
- A particularly important finding is that there is greater acceptance of students from different racial and ethnic backgrounds when a cooperative learning structure is implemented in the classroom.[29]

As ability grouping and tracking become more controversial, educators are becoming increasingly interested in cooperative learning as a strategy for working successfully with mixed-ability groups and diverse classroom populations. Consequently, you will be hearing a lot more about cooperative learning throughout the next decade.

Mastery Learning

Based on Benjamin Bloom's Learning for Mastery model developed in 1968, most **mastery learning** programs are committed to the credo that all children can learn. Stemming from an individualized reward structure, these programs are in use from early childhood all the way to graduate school.

Mastery learning programs require specific and carefully sequenced learning objectives. Once the **behavioral objective** is defined, students are taught the skill or material in the objective; then they are given a test to determine if they have met the objective. Those students who complete the test successfully go on for acceleration or enrichment, while those students who fail to demonstrate mastery of the objective participate in corrective instruction. Finally, there is retesting for the group needing additional instruction. The success of mastery learning rests on the *instructional alignment,* which refers to a close match between what is taught and what is tested.[30]

High Success Rate

Many teachers feel that students should be stretched to master challenging material. Research findings challenge this assumption. Such an approach may only frustrate students. Learners are most likely to achieve when they are working at a high level of success.

How can you tell whether students are performing at a high success rate? Researchers offer the following guidelines.[a]

- During classroom discussions, about 70 percent of teacher questions should result in accurate student answers. A high success rate is especially important for younger students and for those who learn more slowly.
- During independent practice, such as homework or seatwork, the success rate should be almost 100 percent.

In theory, a high success rate results in achievement; in reality students are often working at levels of failure instead. One study showed that 14 percent of the time student answers to teacher questions were 100 percent wrong.[b] Researcher Jere Brophy concludes that teachers have a tendency to assign tasks that are too difficult rather than too easy.[c]

[a]Jere Brophy and Carolyn Evertson, *Learning from Teaching: A Developmental Perspective* (Boston: Allyn & Bacon, 1976). See also R. Marliave and J. Filby, "Success Rates: A Measure of Task Appropriateness," in C. W. Fisher and D. Berliner (eds.), *Perspectives on Instructional Time* (New York: Longman, 1986); Gary Borich, *Effective Teaching Methods* (Columbus, OH: Merrill, 1988); Richard Kindsvatter et al., *Dynamics of Effective Teaching* (New York: Longman, 1992).

[b]Gary Davis and Margaret Thomas, *Effective Schools and Effective Teachers* (Boston: Allyn & Bacon, 1989).

[c]Jere Brophy, "Classroom Organization and Management," *The Elementary School Journal* 83, no. 4 (1983).

Typically, students work at their own pace in individualized programs, going on to materials only when mastery of previous work is demonstrated. The teacher merely provides assistance. In contrast, the mastery learning approach is geared to large groups, and the teacher plays a pivotal role in determining the pace of instruction. Since studies have shown that many students, particularly younger ones, find it hard to take charge of their own instruction, mastery learning programs highlight the role of the teacher as instructional leader.

Studies on mastery learning show that it is a powerful tool that has the following effects on teaching and learning:

- Students achieve more and remember what they have learned longer.
- Students at the elementary and junior high levels seem to benefit most.
- Students in language arts and social studies classes benefit more than those in math and science.
- In general, students have more positive attitudes about learning and their ability to learn.
- Teachers have more positive attitudes toward teaching and higher expectations for their students.[31]

Recently, a variation of mastery learning called *outcome-based education* has been receiving a good deal of attention. Focusing on significant outcomes, outcome-based education ensures that both time and learning strategies are flexible to meet the needs of different learners.[32]

Teaching That Works

Good teachers . . .

- Know their subject matter
- Are organized
- Spend the major part of class time on academic activities
- Structure learning experiences carefully
- Clearly present both directions and content information
- Maintain high student interest and engagement
- Actively monitor student progress
- Ensure that students have sufficient time to practice skills
- Involve all students in discussions (not just volunteers)

- Ask both higher- and lower-order questions as appropriate to objectives of the lesson
- Use adequate wait time
- Provide clear academic feedback
- Teach content at a level that ensures a high rate of success
- Vary student activities and procedures
- Hold high expectations for students
- Are enthusiastic about teaching and their subject matter
- Have high regard for students and treat them with respect
- Connect new learning to prior knowledge
- Develop deep rather than shallow knowledge
- Build classroom learning communities

Project-Based Instruction

- What can be done to make elections free of special interest groups?
- How can this school eliminate race and gender bias?

Can you motivate your students to explore these topics? Can you think of other questions or projects to excite youngsters? If you can, you have taken the first step in organizing **project-based instruction (PBI).** Problems that intrigue students are at the heart of this approach, for such questions fuel students' desire to pursue learning. Motivated students do not need prodding from the teacher or the lure of external, artificial rewards.

A second characteristic of PBI is that genuine issues are explored, not artificial ones. Students look beyond the school walls to learn about their world. This emphasis is apparent in the other terms used to describe PBI: *experience-based education, problem-based instruction,* and *anchored instruction* (because it is "anchored" in the real world). PBI is not limited by the boundaries of traditional academic disciplines, such as history or chemistry, because it focuses on real-life problems that cross subject boundaries. What are these problems? The following examples of possible PBI projects and questions concern such real-life problems. Can you add to this list?

- Formulate solutions that might have kept the United States from plunging into a Civil War.
- How can pollution in a local river, bay, or ocean be checked, or even reversed?
- Develop a set of urban policies to halt social deterioration of a central city.
- How can a specific endangered species be saved?

Finding scintillating questions and projects to excite and motivate students is critical, but it is only one aspect of PBI. Other characteristics include:

- *Learner cooperation.* Similar to cooperative learning, PBI depends on small groups or pairs of students collaborating as they explore and investigate various issues. This approach deemphasizes competition and promotes constructive collaboration. For teachers, the challenge is to successfully manage perhaps a dozen such small groups simultaneously. Instructors must guide and challenge these groups, while keeping them on task.
- *Higher-order thinking.* Exploring real and complex issues requires the use of higher-order thinking skills. The very nature of this demanding approach helps students to analyze, synthesize, and evaluate material.
- *Multiple disciplines.* Problems chosen for investigation require students to break with the traditional areas of study and investigate how these areas merge, how different academic subjects shed light on each other. Exploration of ecological issues, for example, requires that students touch upon not only biology and chemistry, but also economics, history, sociology, political science, and other fields.
- *Artifacts and exhibits.* Students involved in PBI are expected to demonstrate what they learn in a very tangible way. Students can produce something as traditional as a report, or work on unique products such as creating a video, a physical model, a computer program, a portfolio of artifacts, or even a presentation, such as a play or a debate. Teachers might organize a class or schoolwide exhibit to display these artifacts and demonstrate the progress made by PBI students.
- *Authentic learning.* While the identification of a problem that excites students is central to project-based instruction, just as crucial is the notion that the problem or issue be a real one, and not an academic exercise. Students are required to pursue an actual unresolved issue, and at least shed some light on our understanding of the problem. They are expected to define the problem, develop a hypothesis, collect information, analyze that information, and suggest a conclusion, one that might work in the real world. The learning is authentic, not artificial or hypothetical.

While project-based instruction is a relatively new approach, many of the elements can be traced to other times and to other educators. Socrates was one of the earliest educators to pursue a project-based approach, with painful results. At the beginning of the twentieth century, the notable American educator John Dewey also promoted many of these ideas, and was a firm believer in having students work with real issues that sparked their curiosity. John Dewey also encountered conservative criticism for many of his ideas. As Socrates, Dewey, and other educators have discovered, exploring real issues can generate real opposition.

While many features of PBI have been around for a long time, in its current form it is both a comprehensive and demanding approach that develops real intellectual skills in students. Moreover, students function as adults in that they explore authentic contemporary issues. Working together, they attempt to solve these problems—in effect, getting a jump on the adult world even before they are adults.[33]

Evaluation of Socrates

TEACHER EVALUATION

Teacher: Socrates

A. Personal Qualifications

	Rating (high to low)	Comments
	1 2 3 4 5	
1. Personal appearance	☐ ☐ ☐ ☐ ☒	*Dresses in an old sheet draped about his body*
2. Self-confidence	☐ ☐ ☐ ☐ ☒	*Not sure of himself—always asking questions*
3. Use of English	☐ ☐ ☐ ☒ ☐	*Speaks with a heavy Greek accent*
4. Adaptability	☐ ☐ ☐ ☒ ☐	*Prone to suicide by poison when under duress*

B. Class Management

	1 2 3 4 5	
1. Organization	☐ ☐ ☐ ☐ ☒	*Does not keep a seating chart*
2. Room appearance	☐ ☐ ☐ ☒ ☐	*Does not have eye-catching bulletin boards*
3. Utilization of supplies	☒ ☐ ☐ ☐ ☐	*Does not use supplies*

C. Teacher–Pupil Relationships

	1 2 3 4 5	
1. Tact and consideration	☐ ☐ ☐ ☐ ☒	*Places student in embarrassing situation by asking questions*
2. Attitude of class	☐ ☒ ☐ ☐ ☐	*Class is friendly*

D. Techniques of Teaching

	1 2 3 4 5	
1. Daily preparation	☐ ☐ ☐ ☐ ☒	*Does not keep daily lesson plans*
2. Attention to course of study	☐ ☐ ☒ ☐ ☐	*Quite flexible—allows students to wander to different topics*
3. Knowledge of subject matter	☐ ☐ ☐ ☐ ☒	*Does not know material—has to question pupils to gain knowledge*

E. Professional Attitude

	1 2 3 4 5	
1. Professional ethics	☐ ☐ ☐ ☐ ☒	*Does not belong to professional association or PTA*
2. In-service training	☐ ☐ ☐ ☐ ☒	*Complete failure here—has not even bothered to attend college*
3. Parent relationships	☐ ☐ ☐ ☐ ☒	*Needs to improve in this area— parents are trying to get rid of him*

Recommendation: Does not have a place in education—should not be rehired.

Source: John Gauss, "Evaluation of Socrates as a Teacher," *Phi Delta Kappan* 63, no. 4 (January 1962), outside back cover. Reprinted by permission of author and publisher.

New Directions for Effective Teaching

Research conducted in the 1980s sought to determine specific teaching behaviors that would result in greater student achievement. The goal was to establish a scientifically based blueprint for effective instruction. However, research in the 1990s is more closely grounded in the principles of how students learn—not as passively receiving information but rather as intentionally constructing their own meaning. Four constructs are fundamental to the new research on effective teaching: multiple forms of knowledge, the significance of "deep" rather than "shallow" teaching, the importance of prior knowledge, and the social nature of learning.

The structure of knowledge varies across the content areas. Each subject—history, literature, science, math—has its own patterns, facts, ideas, notations, and structure. "A map is not like a musical score, which is not like the equation of a function, which in turn differs from an evolutionary tree."[34] The actions a chemistry student goes through to gain knowledge do not look or feel like what a literature student goes through to write a creative story. Given these essential differences, content-specific teaching skills are needed. Effective teaching research of the 1990s asks the question, What teaching skills are most relevant to each of the different academic disciplines?

"Less is more," an aphorism attributed to education reformer Ted Sizer, applies directly to this new approach to teaching and learning. In this vision of effective instruction, good teachers limit the amount of content they introduce but develop it sufficiently for students to gain in-depth understanding. Instead of lecturing to cover superficially a vast body of information—a behavior similar to the "mentioning phenomenon" of bad textbooks—teachers need to organize their content around a limited set of key principles and powerful ideas and then engage students in discussing these concepts. The emphasis is on problem solving and critical thinking rather than on memory.[35]

Through discussion and higher-order inquiry, the teacher's challenge is to elicit the prior knowledge students bring to the classroom. For example, the

The idea of the classroom as a "learning community" conceives of the teacher as someone who helps students activate their prior knowledge of some subject and thereby become intellectually engaged with one another.

Why Is It So Hard to Change the Way Teachers Teach?

After reading about intriguing approaches to teaching, different ways of organizing classes, and the latest research on effective teaching, two questions often pop up in people's minds: Where are all the changes? Why does teaching look so similar year in and year out? Larry Cuban tried to answer these questions in *How Teachers Taught: Constancy and Change in American Classrooms, 1890–1980*. Despite the efforts of waves of educational reformers working hard to increase student-centered instruction, most classrooms have remained teacher-centered over the past century. Why?

Cuban uncovered several reasons that change had been thwarted, including simple, physical reality. Schools were built around teachers, not students, especially in the early part of the century. Classrooms featured desks all facing front, bolted to the floor, physically reinforcing the notion of the teacher as the center of instruction. As if nuts and bolts were not enough, curriculum demands also placed the teacher center stage. To survive instructing 8 or 10 subjects to very large classes, teachers became dependent on reading and dictating assignments directly from the text. This approach also reinforced the idea of the teacher as the focal point of learning, one who molds students into vessels to be filled with information. Uniformity and standardization became important in the twentieth century as principals told teachers what to do, and teachers told students what to do. The organizational climate

did not nurture new teaching techniques, nor did it encourage giving more responsibility to students.

And as if all these in-school barriers were not enough to defeat any notion of change, teacher training all but guaranteed that the status quo would be maintained. New teachers were brought into the profession through a modeling or apprenticeship program, doing their student teaching under the tutelage of veteran, often conservative, older teachers. It was a system geared to the passing down of traditional approaches and conservative attitudes from one generation of teachers to the next.

Cuban believes that the suppression of student-based instruction was no accident. Schools were designed to mold a compliant workforce; student-centered instruction was viewed as rebellious, dangerous, a threat to educational and economic stability.

While Cuban recognizes that classrooms have undergone a few, relatively minor, changes—experiments with open classrooms, greater informality between teacher and student, and yes, even movable chairs—instruction at the close of the century looks strikingly similar to classroom instruction when the twentieth century was new. Do you agree?

Source: Larry Cuban, *How Teachers Taught: Constancy and Change in American Classrooms, 1890–1980* (White Plains, NY: Longman, 1984).

headline "Vikings Cream Dolphins" has a different meaning depending on whether the student is "thinking about eating habits of ancient seafarers or about U.S. football teams."[36] When prior knowledge is made explicit, teachers can help students connect new information to this existing knowledge base or enable them to confront and revise prior knowledge that is inaccurate or distorted.

Finally, this new vision of effective teaching highlights the social nature of learning and of the classroom. As builder of a classroom learning community, the teacher is called upon to be a guide or facilitator, skillful in conducting discussions, group work, debates, and dialogues. In this way the teacher empowers students to talk with one another and rehearse the terminology and concepts involved in each discipline.[37]

To implement this new and challenging vision of effective instruction, teachers must reflect actively and intensely about their own practice; this should not be "passive thought that lolls aimlessly in our minds, but an effort we must approach with rigor, with some purpose in mind, and in some formal way, so as to reveal the wisdom embedded in our experience. . . . In order to tap the rich potential of our past to inform our judgment, we must move backward, reflect on our experiences, then face each new encounter with a broader repertoire of content-specific information, skills, and techniques."[38] When teachers engage in this active and systematic reflection, they ask themselves questions such as:

- What do I do?
- What does this mean?
- How did I come to be this way?
- How might I do things differently?

Going far beyond the rhetorical, these questions are designed to raise consciousness, engender self-scrutiny, and result in effective teaching.[39]

SUMMARY

1. The way in which the teacher allocates time spent on academic content affects student achievement. Allocated time is the amount of time a teacher schedules for a particular subject. Engaged time is the amount of allocated time during which the students are actually involved with the subject matter. Academic learning time is engaged time with a high success rate.

2. Good classroom management is a skill that can lead to high student achievement. It involves planning effectively, establishing rules that are reasonable and not excessive in number, and arranging the classroom so that instruction goes smoothly.

3. Skills that are necessary for maintaining a well-managed classroom include group alerting, withitness, overlapping, using the principle of least intervention, and creating smooth transitions.

4. The pedagogical cycle describes the interaction between the teacher and students. The four steps of the cycle are (1) structure, (2) question, (3) respond, (4) react. The structure must give students a clear understanding of what they are expected to learn. Both higher-order and lower-order questions should be asked by the teacher. Teachers need to remember to wait 3 to 5 seconds after asking a question (wait time 1) and before reacting to a student answer (wait time 2). Teachers also need to be thoughtful in the way in which they react to student comments. Generally teachers react by using either praise, acceptance, remediation, or criticism in responding to the student.

5. Four models of instruction that can lead to high student achievement include (1) direct teaching, (2) cooperative learning, (3) mastery learning, and (4) project-based instruction.

6. The principles of direct teaching include daily review, presentation of new material in a clear manner, guided practice, teacher feedback, independent practice, and weekly and monthly reviews.

7. In a cooperative learning classroom, students work in small groups and rewards are based on the entire group's performance.

8. Mastery learning programs involve specific objectives that must be met, as indicated by assessment. Typically students work at their own pace, going on to new material only when mastery of previous work has been demonstrated. Teachers often play a central role in content and skill mastery.

9. Project-based instruction stimulates students to explore authentic issues. Individually and in small groups, students cross traditional subject boundaries as they investigate real-life problems and demonstrate what they have learned.

10. New research in effective teaching emphasizes multiple forms of knowledge, deep rather than shallow teaching, the importance of prior knowledge, and the social nature of learning.

DISCUSSION QUESTIONS AND ACTIVITIES

1. Do you think education is a science or an art? Debate a classmate who holds the opposite point of view. Interview elementary and secondary teachers and ask them what they think about this question. Do some of them say that it is a combination of both? If so, why? Which part is art, which part science?

2. Why do you think there is so much variation in how different teachers and schools use time for learning? Observe in your own college classrooms to determine how much time is wasted. For each class observed, keep a fairly detailed record of how time is lost (professor 6 minutes late; class ends 15 minutes early, and so on).

3. Research suggests that, in order to achieve, students should be functioning at a very high success rate. Do you agree that this is likely to lead to higher achievement? Or do you think that students need to cope with failure and be "stretched" in order to achieve? Defend your position.

4. Interview teachers at the elementary, secondary, and postsecondary levels and ask them for strategies they use to involve quieter students in classroom discussion. Share the list of strategies with your classmates.

5. Research suggests that less than 10 percent of classroom questions are higher-order, or thought-provoking, questions. Why do you think this is so? How can increasing wait time help teachers ask more higher-order questions?

6. Why do you think classroom discussion at the elementary and secondary levels proceeds at such a rapid pace? Using a watch with a second hand, calculate wait time 1 and wait time 2 in your college classrooms. Is the time split-second, or do your professors provide 3 to 5 seconds of time for thinking?

7. Analyze teacher reactions to student answers in elementary and secondary classrooms where you are an observer and in the college classrooms where you are a student. Are most of these classrooms "okay" classrooms? Why do you think some teacher reactions are vague and diffuse?

8. Think back to your own experiences as an elementary and secondary student. Can you remember a time when you received specific praise concerning some aspect of your performance? How did this make you feel? Describe the incident to your classmates and compare it to their memories. What conclusions can you make about the use of praise in school?

9. Do you think that criticism always has a negative impact? Can you remember any incidents in your own career as a student when criticism was helpful? Harmful? Discuss these incidents with your classmates and listen to their descriptions. What generalizations can you make about criticism and its impact on students?

10. Observe in a classroom that is using direct teaching, cooperative learning, mastery learning, or project-based instruction. Discuss these approaches with your classmates. What are their respective benefits? Do there seem to be disadvantages?

11. Observe social studies, literature, science, and math teachers. What teaching skills seem to be most relevant to each of these academic disciplines?

NOTES

1. Jere E. Brophy, "Reflections on Research in Elementary Schools," *Journal of Teacher Education* 27 (1976): 31–34.

2. N. Filby Fisher, E. Marleave, L. Cahen, M. Dishaw, M. Moore, and D. Berliner, *Teaching Behaviors, Academic Learning Time, and Student Achievement: Final Report of Beginning Teacher Evaluation Study* (San Francisco, CA: Far West Laboratory, 1978).

3. John Goodlad, *A Place Called School* (New York: McGraw-Hill, 1984).

4. David Berliner, "The Half-Full Glass: A Review of Research on Teaching," in P. Hosferd (ed.), *Using What We Know About Teaching* (Alexandria, VA: Association for Supervision and Curriculum Development, 1984).

5. C. M. Evertson, E. T. Emmer, B. S. Clements, J. P. Sanford, and M. E. Worsham, *Classroom Management for Elementary Teachers* (Englewood Cliffs, NJ: Prentice-Hall, 1984). See also Carolyn Evertson and Alene Harris, "What We Know About Managing Classrooms," *Educational Leadership* 49, no. 7 (April 1992): 74–78.

6. Robert Slavin, "Classroom Management and Discipline," in *Educational Psychology: Theory into Practice* (Englewood Cliffs, NJ: Prentice-Hall, 1986).

7. E. T. Emmer, C. M. Evertson, J. P. Sanford, B. S. Clements, and M. E. Worsham, *Classroom Management for Secondary Teachers* (Englewood Cliffs, NJ: Prentice-Hall, 1984).

8. Jacob Kounin, *Discipline and Group Management in Classrooms* (New York: Holt, Rinehart & Winston, 1970).

9. Jere E. Brophy, "Classroom Organization and Management," *The Elementary School Journal* 83, no. 4 (1983): 265–285.

10. David Berliner, "What Do We Know About Well-Managed Classrooms? Putting Research to Work," *Instructor* 94, no. 6 (February 1985): 15.

11. Arno Bellack, *The Language of the Classroom* (New York: Teachers College Press, 1966).

12. Several of the sections on the pedagogical cycle are adopted from Myra and David Sadker, *Principal Effectiveness—Pupil Achievement (PEPA) Training Manual* (Washington, DC: American University, 1986).

13. Donald Cruickshank, "Applying Research on Teacher Clarity," *Journal of Teacher Education* 36 (1985): 44–48.

14. Robert Slavin, "The Lesson," in *Educational Psychology: Theory into Practice*.

15. John Dewey, *How We Think,* rev. ed. (Boston: D. C. Heath, 1933), p. 266.

16. Myra Sadker and David Sadker, "Sexism in the Schoolroom of the 80s," *Psychology Today* 19, (March 1985): 54–57.

17. Benjamin Bloom (ed.), *Taxonomy of Educational Objectives, Handbook I: Cognitive Domain* (New York: David McKay, 1956).

18. This synopsis is adapted from Sadker and Sadker, *Principal Effectiveness—Pupil Achievement (PEPA) Training Manual.*

19. Berliner, "The Half-Full Glass: A Review of Research on Teaching."

20. Myra Sadker and David Sadker, "Questioning Skills," in James Cooper (ed.), *Classroom Teaching Skills,* 4th ed. (Lexington, MA: D. C. Heath, 1990), p. 170.

21. Mary Budd Rowe, "Wait Time: Slowing Down May Be a Way of Speeding Up!" *Journal of Teacher Education* 37 (January/February 1986): 43–50.

22. David Sadker and Myra Sadker, "Is the O.K. Classroom O.K.?" *Phi Delta Kappan* 66, no. 5 (January 1985): 358–361.

23. Goodlad, *A Place Called School.*

24. Jere E. Brophy, "Teacher Praise: A Functional Analysis," *Review of Educational Research* 51 (1981): 5–32.

25. Gary Davis and Margaret Thomas, *Effective Schools and Effective Teachers* (Boston: Allyn & Bacon, 1989).

26. Barak Rosenshine, "Synthesis of Research on Explicit Teaching," *Educational Leadership* 43, no. 4 (May 1986): 60–69. See also Davis and Thomas, *Effective Schools and Effective Teachers.*

27. David Johnson, Roger Johnson, Edythe Johnson Holubee, and Patricia Roy, *Circles of Learning: Cooperation in the Classroom* (Alexandria, VA: Association of Supervision and Curriculum Development, 1984).

28. Robert Slavin, "Cooperative Learning," *Review of Educational Research* 50 (Summer 1980): 315–342. See also Robert Slavin, *Cooperative Learning: Student Teams* (Washington, DC: National Education Association, 1987).

29. Roger Johnson and David Johnson, "Student Interaction: Ignored but Powerful," *Journal of Teacher Education* 36 (July–August 1985): 24. See also Robert Slavin, "Synthesis of Research on Cooperative Learning," *Educational Leadership* 48, no. 5 (February 1991): 71–82.

30. Joan S. Hyman and S. Alan Cohen, "Learning for Mastery: Ten Conclusions After 15 Years and 3000 Schools," *Educational Leadership* 36 (November 1979): 104–109.

31. Thomas Guskey and Sally Gates, "Synthesis of Research on the Effects of Mastery Learning in Elementary and Secondary Classrooms," *Educational Leadership* 43 (May 1986): 73–80.

32. William Spady and Kit Marshall, "Beyond Traditional Outcome-Based Education," *Educational Leadership* 49, no. 2 (October 1991): 67–72.

33. Richard Arends, "Project Based Instruction," in *Classroom Instruction and Management* (New York: McGraw-Hill, 1997).

34. Gaea Leinhardt, "What Research on Learning Tells Us About Teaching," *Educational Leadership* 49, no. 7 (April 1992): 20–25.

35. Jere Brophy, "Probing the Subtleties of Subject-Matter Teaching," *Educational Leadership* 49, no. 7 (April 1992): 4–8.

36. Leinhardt, "What Research on Learning Tells Us About Teaching."

37. Richard Prawat, "From Individual Differences to Learning Communities—Our Changing Focus," *Educational Leadership* 49, no. 7 (April 1992): 9–13.

38. Joellen Killion and Guy Todnem, "A Process for Personal Theory Building," *Educational Leadership* 48, no. 6 (March 1991): 14–16.

39. Bud Wellington, "The Promise of Reflective Practice," *Educational Leadership* 48, no. 6 (March 1991): 4–5.

A QUESTION-AND-ANSWER GUIDE TO THE TEACHING PROFESSION

OBJECTIVES

To evaluate the teaching job market

To compare teacher salaries in public and private schools

To develop a personal plan for entering the teaching profession

To describe the paths to teacher certification

To evaluate the advantages and disadvantages of tenure

To explore education careers available outside the classroom

As you read through this book, you will detect a common thread linking most of the chapters: a specific topic, such as professionalism or student diversity, is the chapter focus. The topic is explored with stunning clarity, and, whenever possible, interesting anecdotes and interactive techniques are included in order to keep you, the reader, spellbound. That's the approach throughout most of the book. The structure of this chapter is different, however. Nonetheless, we trust it will still keep you spellbound.

Beyond the typical, predictable questions concerning the content of any subject, students often have more personal and practical questions, the kind of questions that might be asked during class, but even more likely after class or during office hours. Students considering making education their career want to know everything from what teachers are paid to where the jobs are, from how to land a teaching position to what kinds of education careers are available beyond the classroom. We trust that this chapter will answer at least some of the questions that you want to ask, and even some you never even thought to raise.

Q *What Are My Chances of Finding a Teaching Position?*

A This is a reasonable, practical, and quite natural question for you to be asking at this time. You are about to invest time, energy, money, and talent in preparing yourself to become a teacher, so it makes sense to ask whether you will be able to earn a salary as a teacher when you graduate. While there are few guarantees when it comes to predicting national labor needs, the current teacher job market is encouraging. Several factors suggest that there will be a significant number of teaching positions available into the next decade. This has not always been the case.

Historically, the demand for new teachers has resembled a rollercoaster ride. In the 1950s and 1960s, a teaching shortage meant virtually anyone would be hired as a teacher, with or without the proper credentials. Back then, new graduates of teacher education programs enjoyed the view from the rollercoaster as it soared. By the 1970s, the teacher employment rollercoaster was descending. Shrinking school budgets and the end of the baby boom led to far more teachers than there were positions, and *teacher oversupply* and *teacher unemployment* became new terms in the educational lexicon. By the 1980s, the rollercoaster was back on the ascent as teacher retirements increased and student enrollments began to climb.

A similar level of demand for new teachers continued into the 1990s.[1] In analyzing the job market, it is important to remember that while the national demand for teachers is up, it is not increasing everywhere or in every field. Science and math teachers are in short supply, and science and math continue to be "hot" fields for new teachers. While bilingual, special education, and speech pathology teachers are being recruited by many school districts and states anxious to respond to students with special needs, all states and communities do not respond equally to these special challenges. For example, in the year 1991–1992, over 15 percent of the school-age children in Massachusetts were receiving special educational services for disabilities, but in Louisiana, fewer than 8 percent of the students received such services. Not only do states and local communities differ in their responsiveness to special needs students, they also differ in their employment practices.[2] Communities committed to smaller class sizes need and recruit more teachers than do school districts that routinely schedule large classes, and wealthier districts can sponsor a greater variety of programs and course offerings, all of which directly impact the number of job openings.

Population shifts also affect teacher demand. By the mid-1990s, teacher shortages were felt in the western and southwestern states (Arizona, California, Alaska, and Hawaii), while the need for new teachers was generally lower in the Northeast, Great Lakes, and Middle Atlantic areas. But despite these general trends, there are notable exceptions. Population increases in some communities in New Jersey and New Hampshire created local teacher shortages. Large cities, one of the more challenging classroom environs, also continue to experience a shortage of new teachers. For instance, over half of the administrators in Washington, DC, report difficulty in attracting qualified teacher applicants.[3]

As if all this were not confusing enough, many school districts are committed to hiring a diverse teaching staff. Providing students of all racial and ethnic backgrounds with role models of equally diverse backgrounds sends a clear message that the school district is practicing the lessons of democracy as well as teaching them. But most faculties continue to be populated mainly by white teachers of European ancestry, a fact of life likely to continue into the foreseeable future because relatively few minority members are entering teaching. School personnel officers are also intrigued with the need to correct the gender imbalance in elementary school teachers. Because approximately three out of four elementary teachers are women, schools often hire newly qualified male elementary teachers as soon as they graduate. (School districts appear less motivated to correct the gender imbalance in administration, where the overwhelming number of school principals and superintendents are still men).

By the mid-1990s some local and state governments were experimenting with new methods of school organization, including *privatization* (the movement to turn school management over to private companies) as well as vouchers and even charter schools. These new ways of organizing schools may affect teacher supply and demand in the years ahead. Predicting the impact of all these changes on the teacher job market would be difficult at best. But with student enrollments climbing, a sizable number of teachers moving into their retirement years, and an ever-greater focus being placed on improving schools, education is now a growth industry. In fact, given the role schools play in preparing workers for an increasingly competitive world economic market, it is likely that improving schools will remain high on the national agenda. In terms of employment opportunities, teaching remains a good career choice into the foreseeable future.

Q How Well (or Poorly!) Are Teachers Paid?

A While people are generally drawn to teaching for the personal gratification that comes from working with children and enhancing the quality of life in their communities, most teachers have more than a passing interest in the salary they will receive. While teachers have been underpaid historically, the good news is that, during the recent past, teachers' salaries have been steadily improving. Consider the following:[4]

- Between 1980 and 1994, after adjusting for inflation, the average public school teacher salary increased from $30,528 to $36,495 (in 1994 constant dollars). Elementary and secondary school teacher salaries increased approximately 20 percent.
- The average beginning public school teacher salary increased 17 percent between 1980 and 1994, from $21,028 to $24,661 (in 1994 constant dollars).
- Increases in teacher salaries are greatly influenced by geography. Between 1981 and 1994, teacher salaries increased by nearly 50 percent in New England, but only 7 percent in the Rocky Mountain region.

Figures 3.1 and 3.2 offer insight into the regional differences and state-by-state fluctuations in teacher salaries. But even these ranges don't tell the whole story. Within each state, school districts vary in the salaries they pay teachers, and they may vary *very* dramatically. (We don't have enough pages to illustrate those differences.) You may want to contact specific school districts that you are interested in to request a copy of the salary scale.

FIGURE 3.1

Average Annual Salaries of Teachers by Region and State (In 1994 Constant Dollars)

Region and State	All Teachers, 1993–1994	Region and State	All Teachers, 1993–1994
50 States and Washington, DC	**$36,495**		
New England	41,169	Michigan	*43,135
Connecticut	50,239	Ohio	36,233
Maine	31,459	Wisconsin	37,191
Massachusetts	*39,958	Plains	32,291
New Hampshire	36,915	Iowa	31,219
Rhode Island	39,847	Kansas	34,688
Vermont	*36,581	Minnesota	36,686
Mideast	45,523	Missouri	30,678
Delaware	38,028	Nebraska	30,005
District of Columbia	43,148	North Dakota	25,884
Maryland	40,533	South Dakota	25,575
New Jersey	45,981	Southwest	30,484
New York	47,499	Arizona	*32,153
Pennsylvania	44,340	New Mexico	28,339
Southeast	30,817	Oklahoma	27,148
Alabama	29,134	Texas	30,975
Arkansas	28,289	Rocky Mountains	31,007
Florida	32,498	Colorado	34,331
Georgia	30,911	Idaho	28,223
Kentucky	32,054	Montana	*28,631
Louisiana	*28,934	Utah	28,475
Mississippi	25,612	Wyoming	31,371
North Carolina	30,123	Far West	39,679
South Carolina	30,641	Alaska	*47,195
Tennessee	30,485	California	*40,891
Virginia	*33,623	Hawaii	37,110
West Virginia	31,005	Nevada	34,462
Great Lakes	39,324	Oregon	37,705
Illinois	41,601	Washington	36,395
Indiana	*36,796		

*Estimated by NEA.

Source: National Education Association, *Estimates of State School Statistics, 1993–94.* (Copyright © 1994 by NEA. All rights reserved.) U.S. Department of Commerce, Bureau of the Census, *Statistical Abstract of the United States: 1994*, tables 26, 698, and 699 (Washington, DC: U.S. Department of Commerce, 1994).

Q *Do Private Schools Pay Less Than Public Schools?*

A Yes. Private or independent schools generally pay teachers lower salaries, but they are also more flexible in employing new teachers who are not yet certified. However, private schools vary significantly in their salaries and employment practices, and some are quite competitive with local public schools. Private schools can offer teachers a different set of benefits—small classes, motivated students, a shorter school year, or even housing and meals—so each individual school needs to be contacted in order to determine the entire employment picture. Figure 3.3 compares average public and private school salaries by region.

FIGURE 3.2
Average Annual Salaries of Public School Teachers with Projections to 2005 (in 1992–1993 Constant Dollars)

Source: National Center for Education Statistics, *Projections of Education Statistics to 2005* (Washington, DC: U.S. Department of Education, 1995), p. 81.

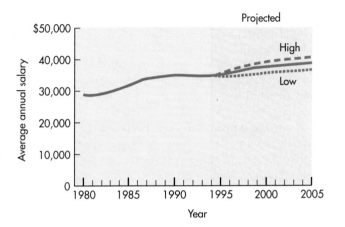

FIGURE 3.3
Average Teacher Salary of Schools with Published Pay Scales

School characteristics	Percent with Salary Schedules	Average Scheduled Salary			
		Bachelor's, No Experience	Master's, No Experience	Master's, 20 Years' Experience	Highest Step on Schedule
Public Districts	**94.4**	**$19,783**	**$21,698**	**$33,199**	**$36,065**
Region					
Northeast	95.2	22,534	24,378	39,797	43,846
Midwest	91.1	18,755	20,598	31,402	33,794
South	98.7	18,903	20,154	28,901	31,382
West	95.0	20,568	22,801	34,809	37,798
Private Schools	**67.7***	**15,141**	**16,511**	**23,253**	**25,499**
Region					
Northeast	72.5	15,101	16,239	23,748	26,208
Midwest	70.2	14,637	15,879	22,821	25,403
South	60.8	14,592	15,961	22,016	23,637
West	67.3	16,565	18,400	24,710	26,880

*Approximately one-third of independent schools do not have a published salary schedule. The average teacher salary in these schools ranges from $12,618 to $19,384.

Source: U.S. Department of Education, National Center for Education Statistics, *School and Staffing Survey, 1990–91 (Private School and Teacher Demand and Shortage Questionnaires)* (Washington, DC: U.S. Department of Education, 1993).

Q *What Steps Can I Take Now to Become an Attractive Teaching Candidate When I Graduate?*

A *Become Informed About the Job Market.* Begin reading current information about the job market and search out those particular content areas and skills that will increase your marketability. This information will help you select appropriate courses and extracurricular activities. There are many sources for obtaining this information, including the two major professional associations: the National Education Association and the American Federation of Teachers. You can write to the NEA at 1201 Sixteenth Street, N.W., Washington, DC 20036, and to the AFT at 555 New Jersey Avenue, N.W., Washington, DC 20001.

For additional sources of information, check with your university's placement office. Also, you may want to begin reading professional education journals that include information about the employment picture. Contact as many sources as possible and stay as current as possible. "Knowledge is power," and knowledge about the employment picture and the kind of candidate who is in demand can give you a powerful start on your teaching career.

▲ *Make Sure Your Coursework Is Planned Carefully.* Once you have analyzed the current and projected job market and have focused on your career goal, begin planning your academic program. Your first concern should be to fulfill your certification requirements. Next, pay special attention to your electives, carefully choosing those courses that will give you employable skills and background experiences. Go beyond minimum requirements and pursue courses that will afford you marketable competencies. Plan to develop a transcript of courses that will reflect a unique and relevant academic background. Upon graduation, that transcript can be an important part of your overall candidacy for a teaching position, so choose your electives with this in mind.

▲ *Do Not Underestimate the Importance of Extracurricular Activities.* Extracurricular activities provide a wide spectrum of experience that can help make you an exceptional teaching candidate. Consider your information about the job market as you choose how to spend your out-of-class time. In addition to participating in student organizations, you may wish to become involved in volunteer work, particularly work that is related to your career goals. Future employers may very well be looking for candidates whose background reflects interest and experience in working with children. Think about offering your services to a local public school or community youth group. Try to make your volunteer situation parallel the future job you would like to have. In this way, you will build an inventory of relevant skills and experiences as well as personal contacts. Later, when you apply for a teaching position, these extracurricular experiences may be the special added attraction that separates you from the crowd and enables you to get the teaching job you want.

These same considerations apply to your part-time or summer employment. Which jobs will provide you with skills and experiences that are most pertinent to future career goals? A day care center or summer camp job may pay less than the local car wash, bank, or restaurant, but these career-related jobs may offer bigger dividends later on. Keep your career in mind as you choose your nonacademic activities.

▲ *Begin Networking.* Through both your coursework and your extracurricular activities, you will come into contact with teachers, administrators, and other school personnel. You should be aware that these people can function as an informal network for information about the local employment picture, as can your professors and even your classmates.

All these people can provide you with current and, frequently, unpublicized information about job openings. Go out of your way to let these people know of your interests, your special skills, and your commitment to teaching. This does not mean that you should become such a nuisance that people will duck behind their desks when they see you coming. It does mean that at the right times and in the right places you can let them know what jobs you are looking for and the skills and experiences you have that qualify you for those jobs. Most professionals like to see new jobs filled by competent people. If they know about you and are impressed with what they know, they will want to help you out.

By the way, you may be in a position to do the same for others. If you hear of job openings in other specialties and you know of competent applicants, be sure to tell them. For you it may be a trivial matter of picking up the telephone. For them there is nothing trivial about such calls—particularly if they get hired.

An incredible number of positions are never announced but are filled via the informal grapevine. Become a part of this informal grapevine by making contacts and keeping them over extended periods of time. The wine that results may be the best job for you.

A *Begin Your Placement Folder Now.* Studies reveal that letters of recommendation greatly influence employment decisions. Do not wait until you are student-teaching to begin gathering these letters. Extracurricular activities, academic coursework, part-time employment, and volunteer work can all provide you with valuable recommendations. Your university placement office can begin a placement folder for you, maintaining these recommendations and forwarding copies to potential employers at the appropriate time.

Ask for letters of recommendation while you are in a job or course or immediately after leaving it. Professors, teachers, and past employers may move to new locations, and tracking them down can be time-consuming and occasionally impossible. Also, over the space of time they may forget just how competent and talented you are (many of us can attest to the ego-crushing blow that can be delivered by the forgetful mind). So collecting letters of recommendation should be a continual process and not one that begins in the last semester of your teacher education program.

Keep in mind that these letters are most useful when they refer to your specific skills and experiences and when these skills and experiences are related to your teaching goals. Encourage individuals writing these letters to be specific, so that their evaluations will provide a complete picture of your competencies.

A *Draft and Continue to Update Your Résumé.* Possibly the most crucial document in your career placement folder is your résumé. Since its purpose is to obtain a job interview, you should write it so that your strengths and competencies are highlighted. The résumé should include standard information that employers need to know about you along with other information that you want them to know. Standard résumé information includes your name, address, and telephone number. You should also note your educational background—your college and university, your major, and your minor if you have one. Also, indicate the location and nature of your student teaching experience. Sometimes candidates choose to write an employment objective at the beginning of their résumé. If you like this approach, you could write an employment objective that reflects the kind of teaching position in which you are interested.

Your résumé should detail any special competencies you have acquired and any activities you have participated in that are relevant to a career in teaching. These might include membership in the student NEA, work in school government, fluency in Spanish, experience with a student newspaper, or leadership positions you have held. You should also indicate honors that you have won, such as Phi Beta Kappa or being listed in *Who's Who in American Colleges and Universities*. Any jobs you have held that are relevant to education—teaching Sunday school, being a camp counselor, working in a day care center, involvement in a recreation program for the elderly—should be described. If you have not worked in areas related to teaching, then list any job experience you have had. If you list professors, supervisors, and cooperating teachers as references, be sure to check with them first. This is not only a basic courtesy but also a way to measure their willingness to recommend you. Figure 3.4 shows a sample résumé that follows these guidelines.

Your résumé should be typed and organized in a clear and readable format so that a prospective employer can scan it quickly for pertinent information. Be sure to proofread your résumé carefully. A typographical error, a spelling mistake, or missing punctuation will turn an otherwise promising résumé into a candidate for the "reject" folder.

A Develop a Portfolio. If you would like to do something a bit more innovative than simply preparing a dynamite résumé, or if your teacher education

---

FIGURE 3.4
Sample Résumé

RÉSUMÉ

Casey Washington
1215 Beech Street
Bethesda, MD
(301) 229-8629

Education

B.A. Elementary Education; minor, Special Education, American University, Washington, DC (1996–2000).

Walt Whitman High School, Bethesda, MD (1992–1996).

Student Teaching Experiences:

Barnard Elementary School, Bethesda, MD, third grade; open classroom–team-teaching situation.

Johnson Elementary School, Washington, DC, sixth grade; self-contained classroom.

Ms. Ellen O'Rouke, cooperating teacher, Barnard Elementary School, (301) 726-0016.

Mr. Peter James, cooperating teacher, Johnson Elementary School, (202) 686-2111.

Ms. Carol Schwartz, college supervisor, (202) 686-2194 (office).

program is promoting more authentic and creative assessment strategies, then you might want to consider developing a *portfolio*. Although the contents vary, a portfolio usually contains more information about you and your skills than a résumé does, and can be a powerful job-seeking tool.

Teacher candidates often include videotapes of their teaching in such portfolios, a very useful item for school personnel trying to assess applicants' teaching skills. Aside from teaching, there may be other talents and accomplishments that can effectively be portrayed on video: athletic skills and musical or dancing talents, perhaps even a school play that you helped to direct or produce. Portfolios can also include written samples of your work, from research papers to sample units that you developed while student teaching. If you created a particularly exciting learning center or school display, perhaps photographs with an accompanying explanation of your effort can help paint a more complete portrait of your skills, talents, and interests. In fact, even if you do not develop an "official" portfolio, you may want to begin to videotape your teaching and collect samples of your work that can supplement your résumé. This will help you to present a more powerful and persuasive application.

Other Experiences

Camp counselor, Camp Hiawatha, Belgrade Lakes, ME (summers, 1992–1993). Taught arts and crafts and swimming.

Swimming instructor, Longly Municipal Pool, Arlington, VA (summer, 1994). Supervised swimming instruction of children ages 5–8.

Classroom aide, Severn Elementary School, fifth- and sixth-grade combination (spring and fall semesters, 1995–1996, unpaid). Helped develop learning centers; assisted in both small- and large-group instruction; tutored students on an individual basis.

Activities

Student adviser (1997–1999). Counseled incoming freshmen and transfer students in course selection and academic preparation.

Resident assistant, Anderson dormitory (1999–2000). Responsible for dormitory administration and for counseling frosh and sophomore students.

Associations

Student NEA, vice president, American University chapter.

Honors

Recipient, Abner Tripleday Scholarship (1996–2000).

References

Personal references are on file at American University and will be supplied upon request.

A Student Teacher's Journal

January 21

Today was my first day of student teaching. It was not quite what I imagined. Ms. Taylor teaches math to three fourth-grade groups and two fifth-grade groups. It's really neat the way it is set up. I basically observed the whole day. It's hard to learn about 150 names. The periods are about 50 minutes long. It's the same schedule every day except that one period is free because that group may have art or library. Also lunch duty is something I'm not quite sure about.

January 29

What a day! Ms. Taylor wasn't here and won't be for another week or more. Ms. Campbell is going to be subbing. She is very nice, but the children in every group went crazy. They were loud, obnoxious, and the fifth graders were especially irritating. This is the first time I've been absolutely aggravated; however, I kept my cool. After lunch it started snowing and Group E just couldn't settle down. Then, of course, the principal came in and said that we were going home an hour early and that really made us lose the class. Finally when 2:00 arrived, kids were screaming and yelling and chaos was born. I've never looked forward to going home more than today.

One final word. About six girls in the fifth-grade class (my homeroom) made me the sweetest card. It said Ms. Koffler we welcome you to our class and if you have any questions please feel free to ask. That made me feel really good, especially after one horrendous day.

January 31

The kids, like myself, were really less motivated today; I guess because it's Friday. They were really good though. During recess the kids in my homeroom gathered around me and made me participate in a game they called MASH. It's a silly fifth-grade game and it reminded me of when I was in elementary school. I felt like I had to be careful of what I said because I didn't want to appear unprofessional. For example, one question was to name two drinks. I almost started to say whiskey sour, but I opted for lemonade and milk instead. It's tough to be a student teacher, because you want to be the children's friend, but you also need to establish the role of teacher.

February 3

I'm still finding it a bit difficult to distinguish the line between friend and teacher. Mark and Jeff asked me if I knew any dirty jokes and of course I said no (I really don't). Then they asked me if I knew any jokes and I had to stop and think. I do know one joke, but it's very inappropriate for fifth graders, I think. Nevertheless, it made me uncomfortable at the thought of not knowing an appropriate joke. Later, when I was laughing along with the kids over something silly, Mark told me that teachers aren't supposed to laugh. I said, "Why not?" He said, "They're just not supposed to." I had to think, "Wait a minute, has Mark got a point?" But I quickly realized that there is no clause in my student teaching handbook that says I can't laugh. Besides you definitely need to have a sense of humor to be a teacher. I feel like I'm slowly but surely learning the ropes.

February 4

Today I had to make a difficult choice. Mary, who has cerebral palsy, got up to leave class at the end of the period and asked two girls if they could carry her books. There was no one left in class but these two girls. Well, both said, "No we can't," and I shot over to them and said, "One of you can surely help Mary carry her books." Erinn finally said okay. The difficult part—should I have carried Mary's books and left the selfish girls alone, or should I have done what I did and confronted the whole situation and demanded that one carry her books? I feel as though I made the right choice, but then again I feel unsure a bit. Teaching is getting more challeng-

A *First, Second, Third, and Fourth Impressions.* In many education courses, you will be asked to participate in local school activities. This participation may take the form of observation or of being a teacher's aide or student teacher. You may want to record and think about your impressions. This can be a useful step in deciding on the kind of position you want. (See "A Student Teacher's Journal.") In each case, you will be making an impression

ing by the moment—especially when it deals with making important decisions and feeling confident after you've made them.

February 11

Teaching is . . .
- fun
- challenging
- hard
- exciting
- frustrating
- choosing
- choosing plan A and feeling good about it
- choosing plan B and wishing you had chosen plan A
- learning
- caring
- growing
- facilitating
- tiresome
- experiencing all walks of life
- showing how biased and unbiased you really are
- making decisions
- broadening
- accepting
- creating
- building
- a natural high
- exhilarating
- rewarding
- disappointing
- role modeling
- helping others feel good about themselves
- organizing, and planning, planning, planning, planning, planning, planning

February 27

In Language Arts I conducted a small reading group. The kids sat on the floor and I sat in the rocker. I had a really good time. I like Language Arts because you can do so much with the students. You can talk and ask tons of questions. It's great. I like Language Arts too because there aren't as many restrictions as in, say, math where there is one answer to problems and it's not as open to creativity.

There are many roles a teacher plays. This placement has taught me so many things about teaching. One thing is that you need to stay in control, even when you get so mad. I love teaching more than ever. I'm so glad that I stuck with it even when I had my doubts. I'm never bored. Things are always happening, changing. . . .

March 4

It's my birthday and the kids in my homeroom threw a surprise party during lunch. They made me a banner and a gingerbread house and cupcakes and they gave me lots of cards. The kids in the other classes gave me cards too. It was wonderful. I felt so good. . . . I really think the kids like me on the whole. They keep asking me when I'm going to teach their class. When I say I'm not, they get upset.

March 12

Today I had lunch duty. I had to talk into a microphone which made me a little uncomfortable. Since I've been student-teaching, cafeteria duty has been my worst fear. But I conquered. I feel like wearing a T-shirt that says "I survived lunch room duty."

March 13

At lunch I sat with the upper team teachers. Gosh, I remember how weird I felt those first weeks. I didn't like being so uncomfortable and not knowing them. Well, now I love them and I've learned a lot from them. I guess I grew on them and they on me. It's a great feeling to have found a niche.

Source: Cayla Koffler, *Student Teaching Journal* (Washington, DC: American University, 1986). Reprinted with permission.

on the school faculty and administration. Good impressions can lead to future employment offers. Poor impressions can result in your name being filed in the *persona non grata* drawer of people's needs.

Consider every visit to a school an informal interview. Dress and act accordingly. Demonstrate your commitment and enthusiasm in ways that are helpful to school personnel. If you are viewed as a valuable and useful prospective member of the school community, you immediately become a candidate for a current or future teaching position. Remember, known quantities are nearly always preferred to unknown quantities.

Q *What Steps Can I Take to Increase My Chances for a Successful Job Interview?*

A Congratulations! Your application was so persuasive that a top-notch school system has called you in for an interview. You will not want to be too nervous about this interview, but you should realize its importance. At this stage, interviewers are checking to see if someone who looks good on paper looks good in real life as well.

The first thing that will strike an interviewer is your appearance. If you have been clever enough to compile the appropriate credentials and to present these effectively in a résumé, you probably do not need to be reminded about anything as basic as good grooming. Blue jeans and a T-shirt may be your campus costume, but they will not suit an interview situation. Your prospective interviewer will be looking not only for appropriate professional attire but also for qualities such as poise, enthusiasm, self-confidence, and an ability to think quickly and effectively on your feet. He or she will be listening as well as looking, so appropriate grammar, a well-developed vocabulary, and clear speech and diction are important. You should also be focused about your teaching philosophy and goals if you want to appear confident and purposeful in the interview.

Before interviewing with a school system, it is wise to find out as much as possible about both the particular school and the community. If you do not have friends in the community who can supply such information, you can try the local library or, better yet, make a preliminary visit to the school to talk with the secretary, scour the bulletin boards, and pick up available literature.

Many studies emphasize the importance of their interview in obtaining a teaching position.

Once you obtain information about a school or school system, you can begin matching your particular interests and skills with the school district's programs and needs.

As important as such preparatory work is, the most important way of learning what an interviewer is looking for is simply by listening carefully throughout the interview. Sometimes interviewers state their needs openly, such as, "We're looking for a teacher who is fluent in both Spanish and English." In other cases, interviewers merely imply their needs, as, for example, "Many of the children who attend our school are Hispanic." In this case you have first to interpret the interviewer's remark and then to check your interpretation with a statement such as, "It appears that you're looking for a teacher who is fluent in both Spanish and English" or "Are you looking for someone who is fluent in both Spanish and English?" or "Are you looking for someone who has had experience in working with Spanish-speaking children?"

Once you have a clear understanding of the interviewer's needs, it is your job to show that you have the interests, skills, and experience that are required. To continue with the above example, you would now show, if you could, that you speak Spanish and that you have had experience in working with Spanish-speaking children. If you do not possess these qualifications, the only thing you can do is to express an interest in working with Latino students, and in the process learning their language and culture.

It is important to be prepared for some of the questions an interviewer is likely to ask. A recent survey of teachers found that common interview topics include strengths, weaknesses, personal philosophy of teaching, future plans, employment history, teaching style, and classroom management. The same survey also listed characteristics that interviewers look for: enthusiasm, warmth, caring, leadership skills, willingness to learn new things, and confidence.[5] You may also want to note what questions cannot legally be asked—for example, questions about your religion or marital or parental status. Such questions do not relate to your qualifications as a teacher. The Office for Civil Rights is one of several agencies that you can contact if you are victimized by such queries.

Having the proper reference materials on hand is another principle of good interviewing. Therefore, if you have developed a portfolio of teaching materials or other information that you are particularly proud of, you should bring it to the interview. It cannot hurt to have it present, and it might help win the day.

Some candidates who look like superstars on paper lose their advantage as a result of ineffective interviewing skills. Conversely, some candidates who have only mediocre paper credentials come out of an interview with a job offer because they knew how to diagnose and respond to the interviewer's needs. An average interview usually lasts 30 minutes to an hour, and 50 percent of teachers in a recent survey were hired after three or fewer interviews.[6] Therefore, it is essential to make your interview count.

After interviewing, it is both courteous and smart to send the interviewer a follow-up note reminding her or him of how your qualifications meet the school system's needs. You should remember that the interviewer may have talked with dozens of candidates, and under such circumstances it is easy to be forgotten in a sea of faces.

One word of caution: When a job offer comes your way, analyze the school system to make sure that you really want to teach there before signing on the dotted line. Try to find out:

- If teachers in the district view it as a good place to work
- If there have been personnel problems recently and, if so, for what reasons
- If teachers negotiate their contract and what the contract is like
- How large the typical class is
- What kind of support services are available.

Not all of these issues may be appropriate for discussion during an initial interview. However, once you have received an offer, you should find out the answers to these questions; if the answers do not please you, the job may not be right for you. It is unwise to accept a position with the notion that you will leave as soon as a better offer is made. That attitude can quickly lead to a job-hopping profile that may stigmatize you as someone who is either irresponsible or unable to work well with others. In short, do not simply jump at the first available job offer. If your credentials are good and you know how to market yourself, you will get other teaching offers.

Q *What Is Teacher Certification and How Is It Obtained?* Project yourself a few years into the future. You have just graduated from college (by the way, the graduation exercises were quite impressive). After you return home, you stop by your local public school office and make a belated inquiry into teacher openings. The school secretary looks up from a cluttered desk, smiles kindly, and says, "We may have an opening this fall. Are you certified?"

Oops! Certified? Are you certified? Or did you forget to plan and apply for certification?

A A teaching certificate is a license to teach. Teaching certificates are not awarded by your college but by each of the 50 states and the District of Columbia. In a similar way, states are involved with licensure of doctors, lawyers, and other professionals. When you meet the state's requirements, you can apply for and receive your teaching certificate.

Simple so far, but there are several problems involved in this process. Probably the most significant problem is that each state differs from the others in its requirements for teacher **certification.** Each state has individual policies concerning the type of certification available and the length of time for which a certificate is valid. You may meet the standards in one state, but if you decide to teach in another, you may find yourself unqualified for its license.

Since the courses and experiences you need may vary from state to state, it is important to have a broad understanding of the major areas of preparation that are relevant to certification. Joseph Cronin, writing in the *Handbook of Teaching and Policy,* suggests the following three categories:

1. Knowledge of subject matter: for elementary school teachers, a breadth of knowledge (mathematics, social studies, science, and language), and for secondary school teachers, some depth of knowledge (a major and possibly a minor in specific subject matter fields)
2. Knowledge of pedagogy, systemic study of the philosophy and methods of teaching, including the evaluation of student needs and accomplishments

3. Actual practice of teaching, generally supervised or coached by one or more experienced teachers in an actual school for a period of weeks or months[7]

One more aspect of this certification process should be mentioned here, because knowing about it now can save you a good deal of concern later. Most states issue more than one kind of certificate in order to differentiate among the applicants' qualifications and career goals. Although the specific names of these certificates vary from state to state, there are four common types:

1. An **initial** or **provisional certificate**—also called a *probationary certificate*—is the type frequently issued to beginning teachers and is generally nonrenewable. If you are awarded a provisional certificate, it means that you have completed most but not all of the state's certification requirements. It may also mean that the state requires you to have several years of teaching experience before you qualify for higher certification. A provisional certificate gives you some breathing room; you will be allowed to teach in the state provided you complete the additional requirements in a specified period of time.

2. The **standard** or **professional certificate** is issued by the state after you have completed all the requirements for full recognition as a teacher. These requirements may include a specified number of courses beyond the bachelor's degree or a specified number of years of teaching experience. You may find yourself first getting a provisional certificate, then completing all of the state's requirements and obtaining a standard or professional certificate.

3. A **special certificate** is a nonteaching license designed for specialized educational careers, including those in administration, counseling, library science, and early childhood education. If after teaching for several years you decide that you want a career in school counseling (or administration, library science, and so forth), you will have to meet the requirements for a different kind of certificate.

4. An **emergency** or **conditional certificate** is a substandard certificate that recognizes teachers who are a good way from meeting the requirements for regular certification. It is issued on a temporary basis to meet the needs of communities that do not have certified teachers available. For example, a small high school in a rural community may not be able to attract a certified teacher in physics. Faced with the unattractive prospect of not offering its students physics courses, the community may petition the state to award an emergency certificate to someone who does not meet current certification standards.

Some time ago, emergency certification was a common practice. The shortage of teachers forced many states to issue large numbers of such certificates, in some cases to persons who had never completed college. During the 1970s, when shortage turned into surplus, substandard certificates became a rarity. However, shortages may make this certificate common again. Some educators charge that large numbers of teachers are working now in areas for which they are not certified, for example, the teacher certified in English who instructs mathematics classes.

Today alternative certification programs seem increasingly popular. These attempt to confront the problem of teacher shortages by allowing college graduates to become teachers with less education training than is required in traditional certification programs. Only eight states offered alternative routes to certification in 1984. By 1990, 33 states had implemented some form of alternative certification, and 15 more were considering it as a possibility.[8] Because these programs are so recent, there is only limited information on their effectiveness. However, many are concerned that they will harm current efforts toward full professionalism for teachers.

A few final notes on certification. Do not assume that your teacher certification will automatically be given to you when you graduate. Remember, state departments of education, not colleges and universities, issue teaching certificates. Some colleges will apply to a designated state department in your name; others will not. Find out if your institution will apply for you, and, if not, apply to your state's teacher certification office yourself. Certification requirements are currently changing in some states, particularly with the concern about declining student test scores and teacher competency. Most states require teacher competency tests, and others are experimenting with additional forms of evaluation, such as supervised internships.

You should keep up to date with certification requirements in states where you would like to teach. Some teacher preparation programs have gone through an **accreditation** process or review by an outside agency that assures the institution meets accepted standards. Two such accrediting agencies are the **National Council for the Accreditation of Teacher Education (NCATE)** and the **National Association of State Directors of Teacher Education and Cer-**

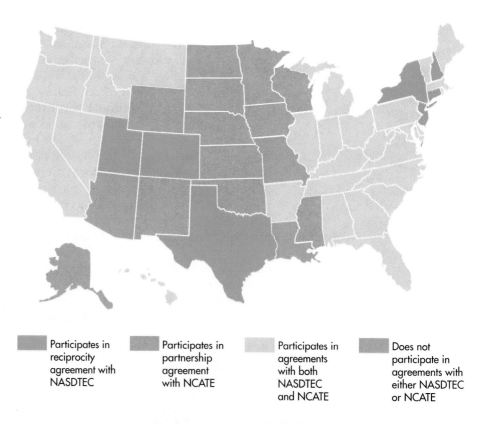

FIGURE 3.5
State Participation with Accrediting Agencies

Source: National Council for the Accreditation of Teacher Education (NCATE) and National Association of State Directors of Teacher Education and Certification (NASDTEC), December 1995.

Participates in reciprocity agreement with NASDTEC

Participates in partnership agreement with NCATE

Participates in agreements with both NASDTEC and NCATE

Does not participate in agreements with either NASDTEC or NCATE

tification (NASDTEC). If your teacher preparation program has been accredited by such an outside agency, you will find that the process of becoming certified in different states is facilitated. (See Figure 3.5.)

If your teacher education program has not been accredited by either NCATE or NASDTEC, your program may still be recognized in your state. State accreditation is fine if you only plan to teach in that state, but less than fine if you are considering other locations. You might want to check to see whether your state has made any *reciprocity agreements* with other states. A number of states have entered such agreements (sometimes referred to as *interstate reciprocity agreements*), in which one state agrees to recognize and license teachers from another state. Your state might have such an agreement or pact with other states; if so, this will increase your professional mobility. Your state department of education can provide you with this information. (See Appendix 3 for the address of the department of education in your state.)

When you have questions about obtaining certification, consult immediately with your college instructor or adviser; or write directly to the appropriate state department of education. Do not depend on hearsay from friends, whose advice may not be accurate.

Although the certification process is sound in principle, it is no guarantee of competency. Unfortunately, we have all been taught by individuals who managed to obtain certification but were not particularly talented or competent as teachers. Conversely, competent teachers are sometimes denied the right to teach because they have not met all the technical requirements of certification. Nevertheless, the intent of certification is to maintain high standards for teachers, and you should be aware of the steps that are needed to get your teaching certificate on schedule.

Q *What Are Teacher Competency Tests?*

A During the last few decades the public became outraged about reports of student achievement decline in standardized tests and high school graduates who could not read or write. Between the 1960s and the 1980s parents watched their children's SAT scores plummet 42 points on the verbal and 26 points on the mathematical sections of the test. In response, many states required elementary and secondary students to pass **minimum competency tests.** Now competency tests for teachers have become commonplace as another step on the road to improving the quality of education. In 5 years, the movement for state-required competency tests spread—or raced—from a handful of states in the Southeast to the overwhelming majority of states across the nation. By 1991, 48 states had begun to use standardized tests for admission into teaching programs, for certification, or for both.[9]

In some states, applicants have been required to write essays on topics related to education and to pass basic skills tests of spelling, grammar, and punctuation. Often states give a battery of tests such as these and also add a component on mathematical skills. In other cases, states or local districts have developed more complex competency-based evaluation systems.

The **National Teacher Examination** (NTE) was initiated in 1940 under the auspices of the American Council on Education (ACE). It came about when a group of superintendents asked for help in teacher selection. With a grant from the Carnegie Foundation, ACE and others formed the Educational Testing Services (ETS), and the exam became its responsibility. By the early 1990s, ETS had determined a new test was needed.

That new test is the Praxis series, a three-part teacher assessment. (See Appendix 2.) At the first level, Praxis I, fundamental literacy skills are assessed by hour-long tests in reading, writing, and mathematics. These three tests apply to teachers in all fields and all grades, and by the mid-1990s, a growing number of states were requiring that these academic skills tests be taken by applicants for teacher certification. Praxis I can be taken in the standard paper-and-pencil format on specified dates around the country, or by means of a more costly computer version with far more flexible timing, widespread availability, and immediate scoring.

Praxis II assesses subject area and professional education knowledge, and includes over 100 exams in subjects ranging from accounting to U.S. history. Praxis II exams are required in approximately half the states. Praxis III, which is a classroom performance assessment, has not gained the widespread popularity of Praxis I and II.

There is enormous controversy among educators as to whether the Praxis series or other competency tests are worthwhile, or even necessary. Those who speak in favor of these exams say that they lend greater credibility and professionalism to the process of becoming a teacher. They claim that such tests identify well-educated applicants who can apply their knowledge in the classroom. They cite examples of teachers who cannot spell, or write, or perform basic mathematical computations, and they plead persuasively that students must be protected from such teachers.

Those who speak out against competency exams claim that they offer a quick fix for improving professional credibility; they treat the symptom, not the problem, and will only have a slight impact on improving education. Furthermore, no evidence supports the idea that teacher testing predicts teacher performance. Others say that the current process of state certification and the period of assessment prior to tenure are sufficient vehicles to weed out incompetent teachers. And still others worry that we do not really know what makes good teachers, and we know even less about how to create tests to spot them. No test can measure enthusiasm, dedication, caring, sensitivity—the qualities that students associate with great teachers.

Another provocative and controversial problem is the impact of standardized competency tests on minority teaching candidates. Earlier, when African-American teachers were systematically paid less, the NTE was used as a vehicle for minorities to attain salary equity with whites. More recently, competency exams have served to block minority candidates from employment. Test results in states across the nation document the problems minority teacher candidates are having in passing such exams. Nevertheless, the courts have ruled that the NTE is an acceptable means of screening teacher candidates.[10]

The problem is that such exams may worsen an already serious situation.

The pipeline of minority candidates for teaching careers, which is only a trickle to begin with, continues to get smaller and is in danger of drying up. This is happening at a time when the minority school population is growing: it is at about 32 percent of K–12 enrollment now, and is a majority in almost all urban districts.

According to 1991 data from the National Center for Education Statistics, 86.8 percent of the nation's public school teachers are white; 88 percent of the principals are white. At the same time, however, black students make up 16.4 percent of the total number of students, but only 8 percent of teachers are black.[11]

Most people—educators and the public alike—agree that testing teachers is hardly the whole answer to raising student achievement. However, with strong public sentiment in favor of testing teachers and with the myriad of competency tests and other evaluation procedures being developed at state and local levels, you had better be prepared to face competency testing when you graduate. The best way to do this is to take all aspects of your education seriously—both the liberal arts and the professional components. If doctors and lawyers have to pass examinations, perhaps you should also.

Q *How Do Teaching Contracts Work?*

A Congratulations, you have been hired by the school system of your choice, and a contract is placed before you. Before you sign it, there are a few things you should know about teacher contracts. This contract represents a binding agreement between you and the school district. It will be signed by you as the teacher being hired and by an agent of the board of education, often the superintendent. The contract usually sets the conditions of your work as well as the salary you will be paid. There may be specific language detailing your instructional duties. If so, this may mean that you will have fewer requirements to participate in activities that are not clearly instructional in nature.

If you do not have tenure (discussed below) and if both you and the school district are willing, you will receive a new contract each year. Once you receive tenure you will be working under a continuing contract and will probably be asked to notify the school district each year as to whether you plan to teach for the district the following year.

Q *What Are Some Advantages of Tenure?*

A A Jewish teacher was once asked to leave his teaching position in Kentucky because he was leading an "un-Christian" personal life.

A second-grade teacher was dismissed from her teaching assignment in Utah because of her dress. She wore miniskirts.

In Massachusetts, a teacher was fired because of his physical appearance. He had grown a beard.

Fortunately, these teachers all had one thing in common: **tenure.** And tenure prevented their school districts from following through on dismissal proceedings.

A vast majority of states currently have tenure laws, and the tenure system works something like this. A newly hired teacher is considered to be in a probationary period. The **probationary teaching period** usually ranges from 2 or 3 years for public school teachers to 6 years for college professors. After demonstrating teaching competence for the specific period, the teacher is awarded tenure, which provides a substantial degree of job security. Generally, a tenured teacher can be fired only for gross incompetence, insubordination, immoral acts, or because of budget cuts stemming from declining enrollments. In practice, public schools rarely fire a tenured teacher.

Since teachers have enjoyed the protection of tenure for many years, it is easy to forget how important this protection is. To get a fresh perspective on tenure, consider what life in schools might be like without it.

Without tenure, hundreds, perhaps thousands, of financially pressed school systems could respond to pressure from taxpayers by firing their experienced teachers and replacing them with lower-paid, less experienced teachers. This would significantly reduce school budgets, usually the largest cost item in the local tax structure. After 2 or 3 more years, these teachers would also face the financial ax. In short, teachers would once again become an itinerant, poorly paid profession. Would anyone really benefit?

Without tenure, the fear of dismissal would cause thousands of teachers to avoid controversial topics, large or small. Many teachers would simply become a mirror of their communities, fearing to stir intellectual debate or to teach unsettling new ideas because job security had become their prime objective. Classrooms would become quiet and mundane places, devoid of the excitement that comes from the open discussion of controversial ideas.

Without tenure, many teachers would have to alter their personal lifestyles. In some communities, they would have to avoid places where liquor is served; in others, their dress or hairstyles would have to be altered. Any behavior that differed from the norms of the community would be potentially dangerous, for such behavior could provide the spark that would trigger public clamor for dismissal. A conformist philosophy would spread from the classroom to teachers' personal lives.

In short, if tenure were to disappear tomorrow, teaching would take a giant step backward. Tenure has provided teachers with the fundamental security that allows them to develop and practice their profession without fear of undue pressure or intimidation. Unfortunately, not all teachers have respected the academic freedom provided by tenure, as we shall see in the next section.

Q *What Are Some Disadvantages of Tenure?*

A   Over the years, it has become apparent that protection of academic freedom through the tenure process has not been without serious drawbacks. One such drawback is the reality that ineffective teachers are protected from dismissal. Many of these ineffective teachers view tenure as a right to job security without a corresponding responsibility to continuing professional growth. Feeling that they are no longer subject to serious scrutiny, such teachers grow "fat and lazy." They fail to keep up with new developments in their field, and each year they drag out old lesson plans and fading lecture notes for yet another outdated performance. Those who pay the price for such ineffective teaching are, of course, the students. Think back a moment. How many ineffective, tenure-protected teachers were you subjected to during your total school experience? How many do you face at present?

As you can see, tenure is a double-edged sword. It serves the extremely important function of preserving academic freedom and protecting teachers from arbitrary and unjust dismissal. But it also provides job security for ineffective teachers and prevents many competent new teachers from entering the profession.

Q *Are Untenured Teachers Protected?*

A   Many students and teachers believe that, until tenure is granted, they are extremely vulnerable, virtually without security. This is not true. During the 1970s, in *Goldberg v. Kelly, Board of Regents v. Roth,* and *Perry v. Sinderman,* the United States Supreme Court outlined several of the rights that are enjoyed by pretenure teachers. In many circumstances, these rights include advance notice of the intention to dismiss a teacher, clearly stated reasons for termination, and a fair and open hearing. In addition, teacher organizations such as the NEA and the AFT provide legal assistance for teachers who might be subjected to the arbitrary and unjust action of a school system.

If, during your probationary years, you feel that you have been unfairly victimized by the school administration, you should seek legal advice. Even nontenured teachers possess rights, but these rights are effective only if they are exercised.

Q *What Kinds of Educational Careers Are Available Beyond the Typical Classroom Experience?*

A The assumption that your education degree has prepared you only for a teaching career is a widespread myth. Actually, there are hundreds of education-related careers, although tunnel vision often keeps them from view. The following list is intended to give you some idea of the nonteaching work options that are available to you.[12]

Day Care Centers   If you want to stay in touch with teaching but do not like the idea of a school classroom, **day care centers** offer a good alternative. You might consider opening your own day care center; in that case, you will need to check out your state's laws regarding operating standards, building restrictions, number of children permitted, and so on.

If you are creative and flexible, you might even devise a position for yourself within a noneducational organization. For example, some department stores advertise a day care service for shopping parents. Why not take off on this idea and market your own "children's center" to other stores, shopping malls, or businesses?

Adult Education   If you prefer to work with a mature population, you might be attracted to **continuing** and **adult education** programs. These are offered through local school systems or nearby colleges and universities. Also, private businesses sometimes sponsor courses that are related to their products—recreation, crafts, cooking, technical training, and so forth. Researching available programs may take time, but you are apt to discover a variety of adult learning programs you did not know existed, and these can be a source of non-traditional teaching opportunities.

Colleges and Universities   A good number of nonteaching jobs exist in colleges and universities. These include academic advisers, who work primarily on a one-to-one basis with students, discussing curricula; admissions officers, who need public relations skills; alumni relations personnel, who conduct fundraising campaigns, organize alumni events, and maintain job placement services; and student services personnel, who do psychological and vocational counseling, advise international students, and administer residential programs. Most colleges offer their employees tuition benefits, so if you want to pursue graduate studies, this may be a good way to gain both experience and a graduate degree.

Community Organizations Churches, synagogues, and nursing homes need creative instructors and program planners. For example, a former English teacher, disturbed by the demeaning, artsy-craftsy programs in a local nursing home, inspired the residents to write their life histories, an experience they found very stimulating. Recreation and community centers hire instructors, program planners, and directors for their numerous programs. Hospitals and health clinics need people to plan and deliver training to their professional and administrative staffs. Some of the large municipal zoos conduct programs to protect endangered animal species and to interact with school groups. Libraries and media centers require personnel to maintain and catalog equipment as well as to train others in their use. Art galleries and museums hire staff to coordinate educational programs for school and civic groups and to conduct tours of their facilities.

The Media The publishing and broadcasting industries hire people with education backgrounds to help write and promote their educational products. For example, large newspapers such as *The Washington Post* maintain staff writers whose job is to cover the education scene, just as other reporters cover the crime, political, and financial scenes. Some newspapers even publish a special edition of their paper for use in schools. Likewise, textbook publishers, educational journals, and television talk shows need people familiar with educational principles to help develop their programs.

Private Industry and Public Utilities Large public and private corporations often use education graduates in their ongoing staff-training programs. Many of these same firms also need people with well-developed instructional skills to demonstrate the use of their sophisticated equipment to potential customers. Likewise, telephone companies hire community service representatives to conduct visitor workshops and to coordinate these workshops with school and civic groups. Some large firms, particularly those with educational products, maintain permanent learning centers and seek persons with educational backgrounds to plan and run them. If you like writing, many large companies spend enormous sums on pamphlets to inform the public about their products; these pamphlets are often written by education graduates.

Computer Software With the dramatic increase in the use of educational software in the classroom, many companies are soliciting people with experience in education as consultants to help develop new programs. Creativity, familiarity with child psychology, and knowledge of the principles of learning are important resources for developing software that will appeal to a diverse and competitive market.

Educational Associations National, state, and regional educational associations hire a diversity of people—many with education backgrounds—as writers, editors, research specialists, administrators, lobbyists, and so on. There are hundreds of these associations, from the NEA to the American Association of Teachers of French. Check the *National Trade and Professional Associations of the United States and Canada* (Columbia Books, Inc.) for listings and descriptions, or contact the associations directly. The *Encyclopedia of Associations* (Gale Research) is another good source for association listings.

Government Agencies   There are a host of local, state, and federal government agencies that hire education graduates for purposes such as training, policy planning, management, research, and so on. Various directories exist to help you through the maze of the federal bureaucracy. Among these is the *United States Government Manual* (Office of the Federal Register, National Archives and Records Service), which describes the various programs within the federal government, including their purposes and top-level staffs. Many of these programs are related directly to the field of education and may offer a rewarding career.

NOTES

1. National Center for Education Statistics, *Projections of Education Statistics to 2005* (Washington, DC: U.S. Department of Education, 1995).
2. Fifteenth Annual Report to Congress on the Implementation of the Individuals with Disabilities Education Act (Washington, DC: U.S. Department of Education, 1993).
3. S. P. Choy, S. A. Bobbitt, R. R. Henke, E. A. Medrich, E. A. Horn, L. J. Lieberman, and J. Lieberman, *America's Teachers: Profiles of a Profession* (Washington, DC: U.S. Department of Education, 1993).
4. Thomas M. Smith, Marianne Perie, Nabeel Alsalam, Rebecca Pratt Mahoney, Yupin Bae, and Beth Aronstamm Young, *The Condition of Education* (Washington, DC: U.S. Department of Education, 1995).
5. Maria Mihalik, "Thirty Minutes to Sell Yourself," *Teacher,* April 1991, p. 32e.
6. Ibid., p. 32d.
7. Joseph Cronin, "State Regulations of Teacher Preparation," in Lee Shulman and Gary Sykes (eds.), *Handbook of Teaching and Policy* (New York: Longman, 1983), p. 174.
8. C. Emily Feistritzer, *Alternative Teacher Certification: A State by State Analysis* (Washington, DC: National Center for Education Information, 1990).
9. Brenda Freeman and Ann Schopen, "Quality Reform in Teacher Education: A Brief Look at the Admissions Testing Movement," *Contemporary Education* 62, no. 4 (Summer 1991): 279.
10. Ibid., p. 280.
11. Anne C. Lewis, "Washington Seen. . ." *Education Digest* 59, no. 5 (January 1994): 60–61.
12. Special thanks to Diana Coleman and Kathryn McNerney for their assistance in writing "The Job Market in Education" and preparing this section.

STUDENT DIVERSITY

OBJECTIVES

To consider differences in individual learning capabilities and styles and their implications for education

To describe and assess the treatment of exceptional learners in school

To analyze the significance of demographic trends for the field of education

To determine effective approaches for teaching that address the rich diversity of our nation's youth

At the beginning of the twenty-first century, approximately one in three students will be a minority group member, and by 2020 almost half of the school population will belong to a minority group. Currently the number of Americans whose native language is other than English is 34.7 million.1 Increasing numbers of school children are identified as exceptional learners—learning disabled, mentally retarded, emotionally disturbed, and gifted. New research on learning styles makes it clear that each and every student learns differently. This chapter will summarize the nature of student differences as well as strategies that will help you get ready to teach children who are more diverse than ever before in our nation's history.

Different Ways of Learning

Consider yourself the newly elected chair of the Teachers' Committee for a More Effective Learning Climate. The committee's responsibility is to offer recommendations to the school board regarding classroom procedures to increase the academic performance of the district's students. It is an awesome responsibility, but you feel up to the task. In fact, you are reviewing the first draft of an eight-recommendation proposal offered by the committee. Take a moment and indicate your reaction to each of the committee's recommendations.[2]

	Strongly Agree	Agree	Disagree
1. Schools and classrooms should be quiet places to promote thinking and learning.	____	____	____
2. All classrooms and libraries should be well-lighted to reduce eye strain.	____	____	____
3. Difficult subjects, such as math, should be offered in the morning when students are fresh and alert.	____	____	____
4. School thermostats should be set at 68 to 72 degrees Fahrenheit to establish a comfortable learning environment.	____	____	____
5. Eating and drinking in classrooms should be prohibited.	____	____	____
6. Classroom periods should run between 45 and 55 minutes to ensure adequate time to investigate significant issues and practice important skills.	____	____	____
7. Students must be provided with adequate work areas, including chairs and desks, where they can sit quietly for the major part of their learning and study.	____	____	____
8. Emphasis should be placed on reading textbooks and listening to lectures, for this is how students learn best.	____	____	____

If you are like most teachers (and like most parents and community members), these recommendations make a lot of good common sense. Perhaps you agree with many of these items, for they reflect the conventional wisdom of our times. And for many students, these recommendations will lead to higher academic achievement. For many—but not all. In fact, for a significant number of students these recommendations can lead to poorer performance and academic failure. The reason: Students have different learning styles—diverse ways of learning, comprehending, knowing.

Did you notice these different approaches to learning in your own elementary and secondary school? Perhaps you see them now in college or graduate school. Some students do their best work late at night, while others set an early alarm because they are most alert in the morning. Many students seek a quiet place in the library to prepare for finals; others learn best in a crowd of people with a radio blaring; yet others study most effectively in a state of perpetual motion, constantly walking in circles to help their concentration. Some students seem unable to study without eating and drinking; simultaneously

FIGURE 4.1
**Factors Contributing to
Learning Styles**

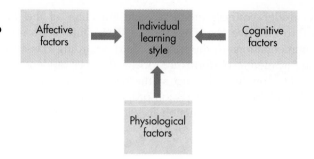

imbibing calories and knowledge, they all but move into the refrigerator when preparing for tests.

We are a population of incredibly diverse learners, and intriguing new research has focused on the different ways students learn. These studies suggest that learning styles may be as unique as handwriting. The challenge for educators is to diagnose these styles and shape instruction to meet individual student needs.

There are at least three areas—described below and diagrammed in Figure 4.1—that contribute to each student's individual learning style:

1. *Cognitive (information processing).* Individuals have different modes of perception, organization, and retention of information. Some students prefer to learn by reading and looking at material, while others need to listen and hear information spoken aloud. Still others learn best kinesthetically, by whole body movement and participation. Some learners focus attention narrowly and with great intensity; others pay attention to many things at once. While some learners are quick to respond, others rely on a slower paced approach. These and other information-processing factors, all part of the **cognitive domain,** contribute to different learning styles.

2. *Affective (attitudes).* Individuals bring different levels of motivation and drive to learning challenges, and the intensity (or lack of intensity) of this motivation is a critical determiner of learning style. Other aspects of the affective dimension include curiosity, the ability to tolerate and overcome frustration, and the willingness to take risks. A fascinating aspect of the **affective domain** is a concept termed *locus of control.* Some learners attribute success or failure to external factors ("Those problems were confusing," "The teacher didn't review the material well," or "My score was high because I made some lucky guesses"). Others attribute performance to internal factors ("I didn't study enough" or "I didn't read the directions carefully"). Those who usually attribute their performance to external factors do not take sufficient responsibility for their behavior. Those who attribute performance to internal factors control their fate and can improve their performance. These and other affective factors contribute to individual learning styles.

3. *Physiology (biology).* Some characteristics of this area are evident. A student who is hungry and tired will not learn as effectively as a well-nourished and rested child. But other factors are less obvious. Different body rhythms cause some students to learn better in the day, while oth-

ers are night owls. Some students can sit still for long periods of time, while others need to get up and move around. Light, sound, and temperature are yet other factors to which students respond differently based on their physiological development.[3]

With this background in learning styles, you now know that the committee's eight recommendations will not create a productive learning climate for all students. The following section paraphrases the original recommendations, explodes myths, and provides research concerning diverse learning styles.[4]

Myth	Fact
Students learn best in quiet surroundings.	Many students learn best when studying to music or other background noise. Some need so much silence that only ear plugs will suffice, but there is no simple sound rule that applies to all.
Students learn best in well-lighted areas.	Some students are actually disturbed by bright light and become hyperactive and less focused in their thinking. For them dimmer light is more effective.
Difficult subjects are best taught in the morning, when students are most alert.	Peak learning times differ. Some students are at their best in the morning, while others function most effectively in the afternoon or evening.

Some students learn best in cooperative learning situations.

Myth	Fact
Room temperature should be maintained at a comfortable 68 to 72 degrees Fahrenheit to promote learning.	Room temperature preferences vary greatly from individual to individual, and no single range pleases all. What chills one learner may provide the perfect climate for another.
Eating or drinking while learning should be prohibited.	Some students learn better and score higher on tests if they are allowed to eat or drink during these times. A blanket ban on such activities may penalize these individuals unfairly.
The most appropriate length of time for a class is 45 to 55 minutes.	This period of time may be too long for some and too brief for others. The comfort time zone of the student rather than a predetermined block of hours or minutes is the factor critical to effective learning.
Students should be provided with appropriate work areas, including chairs and desks, where they spend most of their classroom time.	A substantial number of students need to move about to learn. For these learners, sitting at a desk for long periods of time can actually hinder academic performance.
Reading a textbook or listening to a lecture is the best way to learn.	Diverse students learn through a variety of modes, not only through reading or listening. While these two perceptual modes are relied on by many students, they are not effective means for teaching others. Some learn best through touch (for example, learning to read by tracing sandpaper letters), while others rely on kinesthetic movement, including creative drama, role play, and field-based experiences.

Learning style is not the only area undergoing demystification. Recently, psychologists and educators have been focusing on a related topic, that of multiple forms of intelligence and the meaning of the all-important IQ.

Most of us have some very strong feelings about IQ scores and how accurately or inaccurately they record intellectual abilities. When we find out someone has an IQ of 158, say, we are likely to be impressed. Yet that high-IQ individual may not be able to operate simple equipment or figure out directions for how to get to places. We may also be puzzled when someone who scores poorly on intelligence measures becomes a star on the athletic field or the stage, or creates a beautiful painting in art class.

Multiple Intelligences and Emotional Intelligence

Also puzzled by these contradictions was Harvard professor Howard Gardner. Concerned about the way intelligence was traditionally conceptualized, with so heavy an emphasis on language and mathematical-logical skills, he broadened the concept to define *intelligence* as "the capacity to solve problems or to fashion products that are valued in one or more cultural settings."[5]

As a result of his research, Gardner identified seven different kinds of intelligence, not all of which are commonly recognized in school settings. Yet Gardner believes that his "theory of **multiple intelligences**" more accurately captures the diverse nature of human capability. Gardner's seven intelligences consist of the following:

1. *Logical-mathematical.* Skills related to mathematical manipulations and discerning and solving logical problems (*Related careers:* scientist, mathematician)
2. *Linguistic.* Sensitivity to the meanings, sounds, and rhythms of words as well as to the function of language as a whole (*Related careers:* poet, journalist, author)
3. *Bodily-kinesthetic.* Ability to excel physically and to handle objects skillfully (*Related careers:* athlete, dancer, surgeon)
4. *Musical.* Ability to produce pitch and rhythm as well as appreciate various forms of musical expression (*Related careers:* musician, composer)
5. *Spatial.* Ability to form a mental model of the spatial world and maneuver and operate using that model (*Related careers:* sculptor, navigator, engineer, painter)
6. *Interpersonal.* Ability to analyze and respond to the motivations, moods, and desires of other people (*Related careers:* psychology, sales, teaching)

Recent research indicates that the ability to perform intricate and extended physical maneuvers is a distinct form of intelligence.

7. *Intrapersonal.* Knowledge of one's feelings, needs, strengths, and weaknesses; ability to use this knowledge to guide behavior (*Related benefit:* accurate self-awareness)[6]

Gardner and his colleagues continue to conduct research, and this list is still growing. An eighth intelligence being explored by Gardner concerns appreciating and preserving the environment.

The theory of multiple intelligences goes a long way in explaining why the quality of an individual's performance may differ greatly in different activities rather than reflect a single standard of performance as indicated by an IQ score. Gardner also points out that what is termed *intelligence* may vary depending on cultural values. So, in the Pacific Islands, intelligence is the ability to navigate among the islands. For Muslims, ability to memorize the Koran is a mark of intelligence. Intelligence in Balinese social life is demonstrated by physical grace.

Gardner's theory has sparked the imaginations of many educators, some of whom are redesigning their curricula to respond to differing student intelligences. In addition to the usual concerns about language and math skills, teachers are considering new questions and techniques and are refining their approaches:

- How can I use music to emphasize key points?
- How can I promote hand and body movements and experiences to enhance learning?
- How can I incorporate sharing and interpersonal interactions in my lessons?
- How can I encourage students to retrieve personal experiences, to think more deeply about their internal feelings and memories?
- How can I use visual organizers and visual aids to promote understanding?[7]

As instruction undergoes reexamination, so does evaluation. The old pencil-and-paper tests that were used to assess linguistic, math, and logical intelligences seem much less appropriate for measuring these new areas identified by Gardner.[8] One recent approach being explored in schools involves **portfolios.** Portfolios include student artifacts (papers, projects, videotapes, exhibits) that offer tangible examples of student learning as well as evaluations of student work. Some portfolios attempt to reflect the student's progress in each of the seven intelligences. In music, for example, rather than A's and B's or 80s and 90s, a student's evaluation would consist of descriptions: "The student often listens to music," "She plays the piano with technical competence," "She is able to compose original scores that other students and faculty enjoy," and so on. The concept of multiple intelligences has the potential to radically reshape our current assessment practices.[9]

While the theory of multiple intelligences has made the traditional concept of IQ somewhat antiquated and raised some serious questions about our assessment practices, many consider the concept of EQ to be even more revolutionary. **EQ,** or **emotional intelligence,** is described by Daniel Goleman in his book, *Emotional Intelligence.* Goleman argues that when it comes to predicting success in life, EQ may be a better predictor than IQ. How does EQ work? The "marshmallow story" may help you to understand:

A researcher explains to a four-year-old that he/she needs to run off to do an errand, but there is a marshmallow for the youngster to enjoy. The youngster can choose to eat the marshmallow immediately. But if the four-year-old can wait and *not* eat the marshmallow right away, then two marshmallows will be given when the researcher returns. Eat one now, or hold off and get twice the reward.

What do you think you would have done as a 4-year-old? According to the social scientists who conducted the marshmallow experiment, such decisions are indicative of an emotional disposition that foreshadows critical characteristics of a successful (or less successful) adult. By the time the children in the study reached high school, the now 14-year-olds were described by teachers and parents in a way that suggested their marshmallow behaviors predicted some significant differences. Students who as 4-year-olds were able to delay their gratification, to wait a while and garner a second marshmallow, were reported to be better adjusted, more popular, adventurous, and confident in adolescence. The children who gave in to temptation, who gobbled down the marshmallow and abandoned their chances for a second one, were more likely to be described as stubborn, easily frustrated, and lonely teenagers. In addition to the differences between the gobblers and waiters as described by parents and teachers, there was also a significant SAT scoring gap. Those students who 10 years earlier could wait for the second marshmallow scored 210 points higher than did the gobblers. Reasoning and control, "the regulation of emotion in a way that enhances living,"[10] might be new, and perhaps better, measures of what we call "smart," or "intelligent." The boundaries and definitions of *bright* and *intelligent,* and our notions of how to predict success—these basic concepts are undergoing serious scrutiny and reanalysis, with profound implications for schools in the years ahead. By the way, how would you rate your EQ?

The students you will teach may learn in many different ways, and a single IQ or even EQ score is unlikely to capture the diversity of their abilities and skills. During the last few decades, the range of student diversity has been stretched even further as students with disabilities have been mainstreamed into the regular classroom. Uncovering the special abilities and talents of this new population represents yet another challenge to educators. The next section explores issues and approaches in working with exceptional learners.

Exceptional Learners

In the traditional sixth-grade classroom, teachers may face students whose reading abilities range from fourth- to eighth-grade levels. Integrating **exceptional learners** into the regular classroom adds further challenge to the job of teaching diverse students. When students with disabilities and the gifted are mainstreamed into the classroom, the level may drop to second grade or even lower at one end and rise to a very high level at the upper range limit.

Typically, exceptional learners are categorized as follows:

- Students with mental retardation
- Students with learning disabilities
- Students with emotional disturbance or behavior disorders

- Students with hearing impairments
- Students with visual impairments
- Students with other health and physical impairments
- Students with severe and multiple disabilities
- Gifted and talented students[11]

Today children with disabilities constitute approximately 11 percent of the school-age population, a percentage that includes twice as many males as females. Most of these students who attend public schools are learning disabled (42 percent); another 26 percent have speech and language impairments, and 16 percent are mentally retarded. Almost 90 percent of students receiving special education are considered "mildly handicapped."[12]

The next two sections of this chapter describe issues and developments in teaching students with disabilities as well as gifted and talented learners. Inclusion of each of these populations stretches not only the range of diversity in the classroom but also the range of skills you will need in order to meet the needs of all your students.

Profile in Teaching: Anne Sullivan

Anne Sullivan taught a deaf and blind child to communicate with and inspire the world. Her difficult, trying, and soul-satisfying work with Helen Keller is one answer to the question, Why teach?

When she was 19 months old, Helen Keller suffered a terrible illness. When her fever dropped there was great rejoicing, for no one knew then that Helen would never see or hear again. In her autobiography, Helen Keller writes, "Gradually, I got used to the silence and darkness that surrounded me and for-

The play *The Miracle Worker* tells the story of a brilliant and determined teacher. Anne Sullivan's work with Helen Keller inspired the world.

got that it had ever been different, until she came—my teacher—who was to set my spirit free." It has been said that the genius of Helen's teacher, Miss Sullivan, was hardly less remarkable than that of her pupil. To have another Helen Keller, there would have to be another Anne Sullivan.

Anne Sullivan was born to Irish immigrant parents in Springfield, Massachusetts. Sent at 10 years of age to an almshouse in Tewksbury, she suffered a childhood of abuse, neglect, and illness, which left her half-blind. She studied at the Perkins Institute of the Blind, and she brought her own experience, the teaching methods of the Perkins Institute, and an indomitable will to the challenge of instructing a blind and deaf 7-year-old.

When she first came to the Kellers' home, Anne Sullivan found Helen to be a tireless, unmanageable force. She quickly found that her wild student was not ready to learn language. She needed to learn discipline first. It took time, with teacher and student living by themselves, away from Helen's kind but too indulgent family, before the child became tractable enough to learn. Day after day Miss Sullivan patiently finger-spelled words into Helen's hand while the little girl mimicked the motions of her teacher's fingers. Then came the day when Anne helped Helen unlock the secret of language. Helen describes it in her autobiography, *The Story of My Life*.

> The morning after my teacher came she led me into her room and gave me a doll. The little blind children at the Perkins Institute had sent it and Laura Bridgman had dressed it; but I did not know this until afterward. When I had played with it a little while, Miss Sullivan slowly spelled into my hand the word "d-o-l-l." I was at once interested in this finger play and tried to imitate it. When I finally succeeded in making the letters correctly I was flushed with childish pleasure and pride. Running downstairs to my mother I held up my hand and made the letters for doll. I did not know that I was spelling a word or even that words existed; I was simply making my fingers go in monkey-like imitation. In the days that followed I learned to spell in this uncomprehending way a great many words, among them pin, hat, cup, and a few verbs like sit, stand, and walk. But my teacher had been with me several weeks before I understood that everything has a name. . . .

> We walked down the path to the well-house, attracted by the fragrance of the honeysuckle with which it was covered. Someone was drawing water and my teacher placed my hand under the spout. As the cold stream gushed over one hand she spelled into the other the word water, first slowly, then rapidly. I stood still, my whole attention fixed upon the motions of her fingers. Suddenly I felt a misty consciousness as of something forgotten—a thrill of returning thought; and somehow the mystery of language was revealed to me. I knew then that "w-a-t-e-r" meant the wonderful cold something that was flowing over my hand. That living word awakened my soul, gave it light, hope, joy, set it free! There were barriers still, it is true, but barriers that could in time be swept away.

> I left the well-house eager to learn. Everything had a name, and each name gave birth to a new thought. As we returned to the house every object which I touched seemed to quiver with life. That was because I saw everything with the strange, new sight that had come to me. . . .

I learned a great many new words that day. I do not remember what they all were; but I do know that mother, father, sister, teacher were among them—words that were to make the world blossom for me, "like Aaron's rod, with flowers." It would have been difficult to find a happier child than I was as I lay in my crib at the close of that eventful day and lived over the joys it had brought me, and for the first time longed for a new day to come.[13]

Describing this incident in a letter, Miss Sullivan tells of the remarkable transformation in Helen. She also writes of her own joy as the teacher who worked a miracle:

April 5, 1887

We went out to the pump-house, and I made Helen hold her mug under the spout while I pumped. As the cold water gushed forth, filling the mug, I spelled "w-a-t-e-r" in Helen's free hand. The word coming so close upon the sensation of cold water rushing over her hand seemed to startle her. She dropped the mug and stood as one transfixed. A new light came into her face. She spelled "water" several times. Then she dropped on the ground and asked for its name and pointed to the pump and the trellis, and suddenly turning round she asked for my name. I spelled "Teacher."

P.S. I didn't finish my letter in time to get it posted last night; so I shall add a line. Helen got up this morning like a radiant fairy. She had flitted from object to object, asking the name of everything and kissing me for very gladness. Last night when I got in bed, she stole into my arms of her own accord and kissed me for the first time, and I thought my heart would burst, so full was it of joy.[14]

Special Education: An Exceptional Struggle for Educational Rights

Perhaps you have read the book *Karen*. It is the story of a child with cerebral palsy, a child who continued to persevere despite devastating obstacles. One of these obstacles was an educational system that had no room, no place for children with disabilities. The book was written by Karen's mother, a woman who, like her daughter, refused the rejection of a hostile school and society. She wrote of her attempts to gain educational rights for her daughter and other children with disabilities:

We constantly sought a remedy for this appalling situation which deprived so many of an education, and eventually we found a few doctors and educators who had made strides in developing valid testing methods for handicapped children. On one occasion, when I voiced a plea for the education of the handicapped, a leading state official retorted, "It would be a waste of the state's money. They'll never get jobs." Although he flaunted a number of degrees, apparently he had never encountered Descartes, who said, "I think, therefore I am."

We were frequently discouraged and not a little frightened as many of our "learned" men felt the same way.[15]

Such attitudes were common in our society for years and resulted in inadequate educational programs for millions of exceptional children. Today, the educational rights of these children have been mandated by courts of law and are being put into practice in classrooms across the nation.

In the United States at present, there are several million exceptional children—that is, children who need special educational and related services in order to attain their full potential. They are children who are mentally retarded, learning disabled, emotionally disturbed, physically disabled, or impaired in speech, hearing, or sight. The story of their treatment is one of the bleaker chapters in the history of this country.

Before the Revolutionary War, the most that was offered to exceptional children was protective care in asylums. These asylums made little effort to help these children develop their physical, intellectual, and social skills. Following the American Revolution, however, the ideals of democracy and the development of human potential swept the nation. Within this humanist social context, procedures were devised for teaching the blind and the deaf. Then, in the early 1800s, attempts were made to educate the "idiotic" and the "insane" children who today would be called "mentally retarded" or "emotionally disturbed."

The legal system mirrored society's judgment that the best policy toward the disabled was "out of sight, out of mind." The courts typically saw education as a privilege rather than a right, and they ruled that children with disabilities should be excluded from schools. The notion here was that the majority of children needed to be protected from those with disabilities: from the disruptions they might cause, from the excessive demands they might make, and from the discomfort their presence in classrooms might cause.

The years following World War II brought renewed hope and promise. Pioneers such as Grace Fernald, Marianne Frostig, Alfred Shauss, and Heinz Werner—to name but a few—conducted research, developed programs, and gave a new impetus to the field of **special education.** Their work was aided by the emergence of new disciplines such as psychology, sociology, and social work. Parents also continued their struggle, individually and collectively, to obtain educational opportunities for children with disabilities. They took their cause to both the schools and the courts. As a result of these and other factors, special education has broken away from the isolation and institutionalization that characterized the late nineteenth century and has moved toward an integrated, or "mainstream," position that attempts to provide exceptional children with the least restrictive educational environment.

Recent court decisions have dominated the current movement toward assuring exceptional children of an education appropriate to their individual needs. These rulings have established as law five critical principles of special education:

1. *Zero reject*. The principle of **zero reject** asserts that no child with disabilities may be denied a free, appropriate public education. Using as their basis the Supreme Court's *Brown v. Board of Education* decision regarding racial discrimination, representatives of the disabled have asserted that excluding children with disabilities from public schools violates the *Brown* decision. The courts have responded to this charge with landmark decisions in Pennsylvania *(Pennsylvania Association for Retarded Children v. Commonwealth)* and in Washington, DC, *(Mill v. D.C. Board of Education)* that mandate public schools in those jurisdictions to provide a free, appropriate education to all children with disabilities. For the most part, other federal and state decisions have followed suit.

It is important to recognize that this principle goes beyond simply allowing children with disabilities to pass through the schoolhouse door. It also implies that these children have the right to an education involving accurate diagnosis of individual needs and responsive programs keyed to those needs.

2. *Nondiscriminatory education.* The principle of **nondiscriminatory education,** based on the Fifth and Fourteenth Amendments, assures that children with disabilities will be fairly assessed so that they can be protected from inappropriate classification and tracking. Much of the court activity in this area has centered on the disproportionate number of minority children assigned to special education classes, a situation that some claim is the result of biased testing. In one case, a court ordered that IQ tests could not be used for placing or tracking students. Other courts have forbidden the use of tests that are culturally biased, and still others have ordered that testing take place in the children's native language.

3. *Appropriate education.* The principle of **appropriate education** guarantees all children with disabilities an education most beneficial to their situation and needs. In some cases, this involves placing a child in a regular classroom.

4. *Least-restrictive environment.* The principle of **least-restrictive environment** protects children with disabilities from being inappropriately segregated from their age group peers. Court decisions have emphasized that whenever possible children with disabilities are to be included in regular programs or schools rather than separated in special ones. Special classes and separate schools are not to be used unless a child's disabilities are such that education in a regular classroom with the aid of special materials and supportive services cannot be achieved.

5. *Procedural due process.* The principle of **procedural due process** established the right of the disabled to protest a school's decisions about

Public law 94-142 placed handicapped children into regular classrooms so that they receive the "least restrictive" education possible.

their education. In this case, due process involves the right of children with disabilities and their parents to be notified of school actions and decisions; to challenge those decisions before an impartial tribunal, using counsel and expert witnesses; to examine the school records on which a decision is based; and to appeal whatever decision is reached.

Public Law 94-142

These five principles of special education law are encompassed in a piece of landmark federal legislation called Public Law (PL) 94-142, the Education for All Handicapped Children Act of 1975. This law offers states financial support to make a free and appropriate public education available to every child with disabilities. In 1990, this act was amended and renamed the *Individuals with Disabilities Education Act (IDEA)*, which not only provided a more sensitive description of the act's purpose, but also extended the act's coverage to include disabled learners between the ages of 3 and 21.

PL 94-142 "requires that each handicapped child have access to the program best suited to that child's special needs which is as close as possible to a normal child's educational program."[16] For classroom teachers, this means being aware of the individual needs of all children with disabilities placed in their classrooms and of the specific procedures to be used to meet those needs. The law further states that a specific approach termed an **individualized education program (IEP)** be developed to provide a written record of those needs and procedures.

The law states that an IEP should be written for every child who receives special education services. The IEP must include a statement of the student's current performance as well as the long-term (annual) goals and the short-term objectives. The IEP must also describe the nature and duration of the instructional services designed to meet the prescribed goals. Finally, the IEP must describe the methods of evaluation that will be used to monitor the child's progress and to determine whether the goals and objectives have been met.

There is no specific IEP form that must be used, as long as goals, objectives, services, and evaluation are accurately reflected. In fact, hundreds of different IEP forms are currently in use; some run as long as 20 pages, others are only 2 or 3 pages. What is important is not their format but whether or not they accurately describe the educational needs and the related remedial plans.

Writing these IEPs undoubtedly consumes a lot of time and energy on the part of classroom teachers, but their development leads to better communication among the school staff as well as between teachers and parents. Also, the practice of preparing IEPs should eventually lead to more effective individualization of instruction for all children, not just those with disabilities.

PL 94-142 has been one of the most thoroughly litigated federal laws in history. There has also been controversy about the identification of students eligible for special education services. In particular, confusion revolves around identifying learning-disabled (LD) students, and the educational literature reflects more than 50 terms to describe students with a **learning disability.** Some researchers say that *learning disabled* has become a catchall term for all children whose achievement does not match their IQ potential. Over the past decade, the number of children defined as needing special education services has multiplied, and education costs have climbed as well.[17]

Today most students with mild disabilities go to regular classrooms but leave during the day for special education in a resource room. Recently, these "pullout" programs have been the target of criticism. They are charged with stigmatizing students while failing to improve their academic performance. Many who criticize pulling children out of mainstreamed classes for special education are proponents of what is known as the **regular education initiative.** This initiative endorses placement of the special needs child in a regular class from the start and emphasizes close collaboration between the regular classroom teacher and special educators in order to offer special services *within* the regular classroom. Debate and controversy over the best way to educate students with disabilities will continue throughout the decade.[18]

Regular classroom teachers—those who confront student diversity on a daily basis—often express concerns about their ability to handle a mainstreamed classroom:

> They want us all to be super teachers, but I've got 33 kids in my class and it's really a job to take care of them without also having to deal with special needs kids too. I'm not complaining really—I wouldn't want to do anything other than what I'm doing—but it is demanding.[19]

But when training and support are provided—when attitudes are positive and realistic—teaching in a mainstreamed classroom can be extremely rewarding. Many factors contribute to the success of mainstreamed classrooms. It is important for children with disabilities to have opportunities for success and to participate in both independent and cooperative activities. Most essential, however, is the teacher's ability to understand and accept human differences and to provide an open and supportive environment so that children can discuss these differences in an honest and sensitive manner. In short, if **mainstreaming** is to work, classroom teachers must genuinely care about integrating children with disabilities into their classrooms. They must be committed to exploding stereotypes and must recognize the essential value of helping all children learn to understand and accept differences. Although we have emphasized the legal decisions that prompted the mainstreaming movement, mainstreaming is at its heart a moral issue, one that raises the timeless principles of equality, justice, and the need for all children to learn to live and grow together—not apart.

The Gifted and Talented

Precocious children are among our most neglected students. They too have special needs:[20]

> In Chicago, the school system turned down the request of a 5-year-old boy who wanted to enter school early. While he waits to be allowed to enter kindergarten, the boy spends his time in the public library doing independent research in astronomy and geography. His IQ has been measured at more than 180.

In Westchester County, a suburb of New York City, a 2½-year-old boy already emulates the language abilities of his parents. He speaks and reads English, French, Hebrew, Spanish, and Yiddish, and he has mastered some Danish. He is studying music theory and is conducting scientific experiments. The parents, however, are unable to find any educational facility willing and able to educate their young, gifted child. A member of their local school board told them: "It is not the responsibility or function of public schools to deal with such children." As a result, the parents considered moving to Washington state, where there was an experimental preschool program for the gifted.

If you are like most Americans, you may find it difficult to consider gifted and talented children to be in any way disadvantaged. After all, gifted children are the lucky ones who master subject matter with ease. They are the ones who shout out the solution before most of us have a chance to write down the problem. They exhibit endless curiosity and creativity. The **gifted learner** seems to know everything, answering questions we may not even understand while asking questions we have not even thought of. It is sometimes difficult to find sympathy for these bright students whose intelligence makes the rest of us feel somewhat uncomfortable, inadequate, and sometimes just plain envious.

By definition the gifted are the exception, but there is little agreement regarding the lower limit of giftedness. To some, those with an IQ of 130 or higher should be classified as gifted, whereas others reserve the label for those with a score of 160 or higher. Still others have expanded the concept of gifted to include those with special creative or artistic abilities, even those with outstanding athletic prowess. In short, the matter of who is or is not gifted has not yet been resolved.

Education experts Joseph Renzulli and C. H. Smith define the gifted as those who demonstrate:

1. High ability (including, but not limited to, intelligence)
2. High creativity
3. High task behavior (the drive to initiate and complete a task)[21]

According to this definition, a child who is better than 85 percent of his or her peers in all three aspects of some endeavor and exceeds 98 percent in at least one area can be classified as gifted. The *gifted* part of the phrase *gifted and talented* refers to intellectual ability; the *talented* part is more diverse, encompassing musical, artistic, or other talents. However, talented children may not demonstrate exceptional or gifted abilities in other areas.

Another researcher, Robert Sternberg, has identified "analytic," "synthetic," and "practical" as three major types of giftedness. Students who are gifted analytically are able to dissect problems and understand their parts. They usually do well on conventional tests of intelligence. Synthetic giftedness occurs in people who are creative, intuitive, or insightful. While they may not have the highest IQs, they ultimately may make the greatest contribution to society. Individuals who are practically gifted can go into real-world situations, figure out what needs to be done, and negotiate and work with people to get the task accomplished.[22]

While the definitions of giftedness vary, it is estimated that only a small percentage of our population possesses this high degree of ability, creativity,

FIGURE 4.2
The Way They Were in School

All of these people were considered poor learners in school:

Thomas Edison	Benjamin Franklin	Henry Ford
Paul Gauguin	Pablo Picasso	Abraham Lincoln
William Butler Yeats	Carl Jung	

The following individuals were expelled from school:

Albert Einstein	Edgar Allan Poe	Percy Bysshe Shelley
Salvador Dali	James Whistler	George Bernard Shaw

motivation, or pragmatic talent, making it a very exclusive club. As is often the case with exclusivity, the gifted and talented are frequently the object of hostility. Figure 4.2 illustrates some of the misconceptions people have held about the gifted. Since most people are by definition excluded from this highly selective group, they show little compassion and refuse to believe that the gifted merit any special educational attention. To many Americans it seems downright undemocratic to provide special services to children who already enjoy an intellectual advantage. Even the parents of gifted children have been reluctant to request appropriate educational programs for their children. However, as controversy over tracking and ability grouping escalates, advocates for the gifted are beginning to speak out.

Many gifted students do not make it on their own. Instead of thriving in school, they drop out. Often those who do stay in school become bored and apathetic, and their intellectual talents go unnoticed and unnurtured. The result is that many of our nation's brightest and most competent minds are lost to neglect and apathy.

Research shows that the number of gifted students contemplating suicide continues to increase. Factors contributing to such thoughts include feelings of personal worthlessness, a sense of isolation and loneliness, pressure to achieve, and fear of failure.[23] Talent, giftedness, and creativity set adolescents apart at a time when the push is for conformity and for being "normal." Such differences often result in feelings of "weirdness" instead of positive self-concept. Gifted students most often talk about their feelings of isolation:

> I feel as though I'll never fit in any place, no matter how hard I try.

> Basically, the challenge in my schooling has not been academic, but having to conform—to be just like everyone else in order to be accepted.

> I hate it when people use you. For example, if you have an incredible vocabulary and someone wants your help writing a speech, and then later they tell you to get lost.[24]

The picture is especially dismal for gifted female or minority children. Gifted girls and minority children are identified far less often and less accurately than are gifted white males. Many experts urge the use of multiple data sources that go beyond test scores to facilitate and improve the identification of gifted girls and minority students.

Even in those school districts that do recognize the existence of gifted children, special programs and educational opportunities may not be offered. In

Until recently, schools did little to accommodate the special needs of the gifted and talented.

many districts, the problem is a lack of funds; in others, it is a lack of interest and flexibility, as some schools refuse to adjust their procedures and programs to accommodate the needs and abilities of gifted children.

Currently the regular classroom remains the main vehicle through which most gifted students receive their education. A common format is a combination of mainstreaming for four-fifths of the time and enrollment in a special class for one-fifth of the time. Another approach is to set up resource centers within the regular classroom where gifted students are offered individualized tutoring.[25] Special schools such as the Bronx High School of Science or the North Carolina School for Mathematics and Science provide unique opportunities for those fortunate enough to attend. Qualities of effective gifted programs include a mastery dimension that allows students to move through the curriculum at their own pace; in-depth and independent learning; field study; and an interdisciplinary dimension that allows for the exploration of theories and issues across the curriculum.[26]

What else can public schools do for gifted students? While enrichment provides extra attention, learning experiences, independent study, and advanced reading, an **accelerated program** allows gifted students to skip grades, take **advanced placement** courses and exams, and graduate before their chronological peers. Gifted students in accelerated programs sometimes graduate from college before age 18.

Many Americans accept the notion of enrichment for the gifted, but acceleration runs into strong opposition. Many believe that the negative social consequences of acceleration outweigh the intellectual benefits. This public attitude toward acceleration represents a real obstacle to implementing such programs for the gifted.

Whereas social maladjustment due to acceleration may indeed be a problem for some gifted children, others claim they feel just as comfortable, both academically and socially, with their intellectual peers as they do with their chronological peers. Moreover, failure to accelerate gifted children may lead to boredom, apathy, frustration, and even ridicule. Although social trauma may result from acceleration, it may also result from no acceleration. Several studies confirm the value of acceleration, from early admission to elementary school to early admission to college. Grade-accelerated students surpass their classmates in academic achievement and complete higher levels of education. In most cases grade acceleration does not cause problems in social and emotional adjustment.[27]

Where Do the Mermaids Stand?

Giants, Wizards, and Dwarfs was the game to play.

Being left in charge of about eighty children seven to ten years old, while their parents were off doing parenty things, I mustered my troops in the church social hall and explained the game. It's a large-scale version of Rock, Paper, and Scissors, and involves some intellectual decision making. But the real purpose of the game is to make a lot of noise and run around chasing people until nobody knows which side you are on or who won.

Organizing a roomful of wired-up gradeschoolers into two teams, explaining the rudiments of the game, achieving consensus on group identity—all of this is no mean accomplishment, but we did it with a right good will and were ready to go.

The excitement of the chase had reached a critical mass. I yelled out: "You have to decide *now* which you are—a GIANT, a WIZARD, or a DWARF!"

While the groups huddled in frenzied, whispered consultation, a tug came at my pants leg. A small child stands there looking up, and asks in a small concerned voice, "Where do the Mermaids stand?"

A long pause: A *very* long pause. "Where do the Mermaids stand?" says I.

"Yes. You see, I am a Mermaid."

"There are no such things as Mermaids."

"Oh, yes, I am one!"

She did not relate to being a Giant, a Wizard, or a Dwarf. She knew her category, Mermaid, and was not about to leave the game and go over and stand against the wall where a loser would stand. She intended to participate, wherever Mermaids fit into the scheme of things. Without giving up dignity or identity. She took it for granted that there was a place for Mermaids and that I would know just where.

Well, where DO the Mermaids stand? All the "Mermaids"—all those who are different, who do not fit the norm and who do not accept the available boxes and pigeonholes?

Answer that question and you can build a school, a nation, or a world on it.

What was my answer at the moment? Every once in a while I say the right thing. "The Mermaid stands right here by the King of the Sea!" (Yes, right here by the King's Fool, I thought to myself.)

So we stood there hand in hand, reviewing the troops of Wizards and Giants and Dwarfs as they rolled by in wild disarray.

It is not true, by the way, that Mermaids do not exist. I know at least one personally. I have held her hand.

Source: Robert Fulghum, *All I Really Need to Know I Learned in Kindergarten* (New York: Villard Books, 1989), pp. 81–83.

Recognition of the special needs of the gifted has been slow in coming. However, most states have paid some attention to programs for the gifted. Currently, most school systems provide special gifted services to between 7 and 12 percent of their students. However, with the current trend away from ability grouping, tracking, and special programs, it is possible that fewer resources will be available for the gifted in the years ahead.[28]

When gifted students are placed in appropriate programs, they are often empowered to realize their full potential. One student explains how relieved he was to find that "there are lots of people like me and I'm not a weirdo after all." As one 12-year-old girl said:

> My heart is full of gratitude for my teacher who first wanted to have me tested for the gifted program. I'm not trying to brag, but I'm really glad there's a class for people like me. We may seem peculiar or odd, but at least we have fun and we respect each other's talents.[29]

In the final analysis, it is not only the gifted who have suffered from our national neglect and apathy, it is all of us. How many works of art will never be enjoyed, how many medical breakthroughs and how many inventions have been lost because of our insensitivity to the gifted? We will never know the final cost.

Cultural Diversity

In Los Angeles last week, I saw an elementary school teacher who was teaching a class of 31 children in the third grade, and the 31 children spoke six languages, *none* of which was English. The teacher had one year of Spanish in her collegiate training.[30]

Demographic forecasting, the study of people and their vital statistics, provides fascinating insight into tomorrow's schools. Demographers draw a portrait of a new generation of students far more diverse—by race, ethnicity, and language—than our country has ever known. Changing patterns of immigration and birth rates, the breakdown of the "traditional family," and the graying, or aging, of America are demographic trends that hold far-reaching implications for schools—and the ways that children are taught. Consider the following statistics:[31]

Demographic Patterns

- The 1990 Census shows that the United States now has a greater variety of cultures than at any other time in its history. This increase is due to immigration, mainly from Latin America and Asia but also from the Caribbean, the Middle East, Africa, and Eastern Europe.
- In the 1990s one in four Americans defines himself or herself as Latino or nonwhite. If current birth and immigration rates continue, the Latino population will increase 21 percent, the Asian-American population 22 percent, the African-American population almost 12 percent, and whites only 2 percent by the end of the twentieth century. By 2020, the number of U.S. residents who are nonwhite or Latino will be 115 million, more than double what it is today. In contrast, the white population will not increase.
- During the 1980s, the Latino population grew at a rate five times that of the non-Latino population. More than two-thirds of the Latino population are younger than 35.
- The number of Asians and Pacific Islanders grew by 80 percent between 1980 and 1990. As a result of the war in Southeast Asia, the number of Southeast Asians in the United States skyrocketed from 20,000 in 1960 to more than 1 million in 1990.
- The African-American population increased from 26.5 million in 1980 to approximately 30 million in 1990, a growth rate of 13.2 percent.
- There are approximately 2 million Native Americans and Inuit in the United States. They belong to over 300 federally recognized tribes in the continental United States and over 200 in Alaskan communities. With more than 200 Native American languages still spoken, this is an ethnic group of extraordinary cultural and linguistic diversity.

Patterns of Poverty

- In the 1990s one in five children is living in poverty. Children are six times more likely to be poor than are the elderly. The United States is the first nation in history in which children constitute the poorest segment of society.
- The poorer the child, the younger he or she is likely to be.
- An African-American child is three times more likely to be poor than a white child. However, it is important to note the increasing number of African-American children who have grown up in middle-class families and enjoy income levels that would have been inconceivable in the 1950s. Academically these children perform much like their white counterparts, living proof that, given the right conditions, minority children can realize their potential.
- Nearly two in every five Latino children live in poverty. The unemployment rate for Latinos is 50 percent above the rate for non-Latinos and 60 percent above the rate for whites.
- Twenty-four percent of Native Americans live in poverty. Male unemployment on reservations ranges from 58 percent to more than 80 percent.
- More than half the children living in households headed by women alone are growing up in poverty. Fifty percent of African-American and 30 percent of Latino children live in single-parent families.
- Half of Latino, African-American, and Native American students and one-third of Asian-American students live at or near the poverty level.
- Families make up over one-third of the homeless, and their numbers are growing. Fewer than half of homeless children attend school.

Patterns of Educational Loss

- Blacks, Latinos, and Native Americans repeat grades more often and take longer to complete school than white students do.
- The academic achievement of all minority groups except Asian Americans is lower than that of whites. This is true at all levels of schooling and in every region of the country.
- School failure for minority students crystallizes at about the fourth grade. From that time on, the longer Latino, African-American, Native American, and some Asian-American groups stay in school, the further behind they fall.
- Forty-three percent of Latino students and 36 percent of Native American students drop out of school.
- Asian-American students reflect a polarized pattern of educational achievement. For example, more than 80 percent of Japanese-Americans and Asian-Indian Americans finish high school; however, only 62 percent of Vietnamese-Americans graduate.
- Black students score lowest of any group on both the math and verbal sections of the Scholastic Assessment Test (see Figure 4.3).
- According to several standardized test scores, in the early grades girls are equal to or ahead of boys in academic skills. But by the time students graduate from high school, the pattern has reversed. Some test results, such as SAT scores, show girls behind in both math and verbal skills. No other group starts out ahead and finishes behind.

FIGURE 4.3
1995 SAT Scores by Ethnic Group

Source: College Board, *College Bound Seniors: 1995 Profile of SAT Program Test Takers* (New York: College Board, 1995).

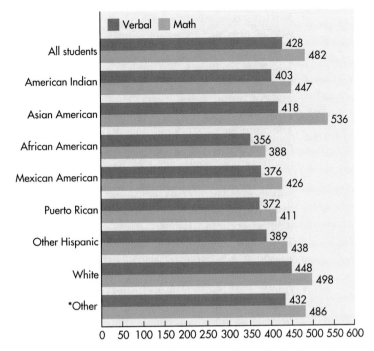

	Verbal	Math
All students	428	482
American Indian	403	447
Asian American	418	536
African American	356	388
Mexican American	376	426
Puerto Rican	372	411
Other Hispanic	389	438
White	448	498
*Other	432	486

*Note: The College Board lists scores for Pacific Islanders and Alaskan Natives under the category of "Other."

Patterns of Crisis

- Violence is an ever more threatening presence in the nation's schools. One in 20 students carries a gun to school.
- In the years 1990–1991, students in New York City, Norfolk, Oklahoma City, Dallas, and Houston have met violent deaths at school. Hundreds of others in school systems across the country have been wounded by school gunfire.

Being a teacher in the years ahead will almost surely mean dealing with a culturally diverse student body and an increased proportion of "at risk" students.

- Much of the wave of violence is related to the epidemic of crack cocaine. Adolescents are experimenting with drugs at younger and younger ages, especially before age 15.
- The typical student has had sex by age 16. One in five students has had four or more partners. For students with four or more partners, only 41 percent report using condoms. Condom use becomes less frequent as students get older.
- The number of students who have already contracted AIDS increased 70 percent between 1990 and 1992. AIDS is now the sixth leading cause of death among youth aged 15 to 24.
- Currently there are more than 1 million pregnancies, almost 500,000 births, and more than 400,000 abortions to women less than 20 years old. Approximately half of these are to unmarried women and half are to women younger than 18.
- The birth rate among 15- to 17-year-olds is increasing. Child rearing among very young adolescents (between the ages of 10 and 14) increased 33 percent during the last decade.
- During the 1980s reported physical abuse against children and adolescents increased 58 percent, and sexual abuse increased 214 percent.
- Mental disorder is the major cause of disability for youngsters between 10 and 18. Suicide has increased at an alarming rate for children.

Behind these statistics and demographic patterns is an explosive human condition, one that could result in a polarized society of haves and have-nots, riots, even revolution. (See Chapter 15 for an in-depth discussion of children at risk.) In the nation's largest school systems, the populations are now from 70 to 96 percent minority. Demographers predict that by the year 2000 one out of three Americans will be a minority group member. Some forecast that by 2020 almost half the school population will be from ethnic minorities. Differing racial and ethnic backgrounds bring language diversity and **limited English proficiency** as well. Demographers say that there will be approximately 5 million students of non-English-speaking background in schools by the year 2000.

Bilingual Education

Before the 1960s, very little attention was paid to students who spoke a language other than English. The attitude of the schools was one of sink or swim—or perhaps, speak or sink. Students either learned to speak English—or failed school. It is not surprising that many students simply failed. This attitude began to change during the 1960s as the American economy became increasingly sophisticated, with English literacy and a high school degree being minimum requirements for participation. For non-English-speaking students to enjoy equal rights, they needed to attain fluency in English. To respond to this need, Congress passed the Bilingual Education Act in 1968. This act required that students be taught in both their native language and English. But passing a law does not always solve the problem.

From the start, the Bilingual Education Act was fraught with problems. The act did not specifically address implementation or standards. Individual school districts and, in some cases, even individual schools experimented with different approaches. The result was a multitude of programs of varying quality and efficacy. In too many cases the act simply was not working.

During the early 1970s parents initiated law suits, and it became apparent that the federal government needed to bring order and standards to bilingual education. In 1974, the Supreme Court heard the case of *Lau v. Nichols*. This class action law suit centered around Kinney Lau and 1,800 other Chinese students from the San Francisco area who were failing their courses because they could not understand English. The Court unanimously affirmed that federally funded schools must "rectify the language deficiency" of these students. Teaching students in a language they did not understand was not an appropriate education. The Court's decision in *Lau v. Nichols* prompted Congress to pass the Equal Educational Opportunities Act (EEOA). Under this law, school districts must take positive steps to provide equal education for language-minority students by eliminating language barriers.

Bilingual education has been the most common approach for enabling language-minority students to become fluent in English. Typically in the bilingual approach, the students learn English as a second language while taking other academic subjects in their native language. The two most widely used approaches to bilingual education are the transitional approach and the maintenance approach. The *transitional approach* emphasizes the use of the native language as a bridge to English-language instruction. As mastery of English increases, use of the native language during instruction is decreased. The *maintenance approach* emphasizes the use of both languages. The goal is to create a student who is truly bilingual, acquiring English while maintaining competence in the native language. Of the two approaches, the transitional is the more common.

In bilingual education programs, English is learned as a second language while the student takes other academic work in his or her native language.

One of the most hotly debated issues surrounding the transitional approach involves the length of time children should stay in native-language programs and the level of proficiency needed for exit. Some maintain that levels should be set low, and entry into English should take place as soon as possible. Others argue that if competence in English is too minimal, students will never develop sophisticated English usage. A recent report has given weight to the late-exit arguments. This report found that when language-minority students spend more time learning in their native language, they are more likely to achieve at levels comparable to majority students.[32]

Bilingual education has always been controversial, with many students continuing to report that it has not lived up to its promise. However, research makes it clear that bilingual education does have a positive effect if correctly implemented. Unfortunately, too many bilingual education programs suffer from faulty administration and inadequate teacher training. Another problem is segregation. Since bilingual classrooms are composed of a single ethnic group, some critics charge that ethnic barriers are created. Finally, many people worry that bilingual education threatens the status of English as the nation's primary vehicle of communication.

The future of bilingual education is uncertain. However, new programs and ideas do hold promise for the future. For example, a San Diego program brings Spanish-speaking and English-speaking students together in the same classroom. At the early grades Spanish is the primary language of instruction, with English used only for a small portion of the day. By the sixth grade, equal time is given to both Spanish and English. Both groups of students gain a second language. However, perhaps the greatest benefit is the enrichment for all students exposed to a diversity of linguistic and cultural experiences.

This demographic portrait of the potential diversity of our nation's children sounds an alarm for our schools. It also poses tough, important, and exciting challenges for teachers in the decades ahead.

Teaching Them All

Imagine this. You have graduated from your teacher preparation program and signed the contract for your first teaching job, and now you stand before your very first class. As you survey your sixth-grade students, you see that 15 boys and 14 girls are present; 7 of your students are Latino, 6 are African American, 4 are Vietnamese, and 12 are white. You know from reading background records that six are learning disabled, and muscular dystrophy has confined another to a wheelchair. One of the children has been identified as exceptionally gifted. About half of your students are from single-parent homes. A third of the children come from middle-class backgrounds, and the remaining two-thirds are from working-class or poor families.

You know from your training, reading, and experience that each of these 29 individuals will have been shaped, in part, by conditions of race, ethnicity, exceptionality, social class, and gender. You understand that these characteristics will influence how these children perceive the world—and how the world views them. You also know that each one is likely to have a learning style as unique as his or her handwriting.

How will you meet the needs of 29 such different schoolchildren? What strategies and approaches will you use to attain equity and excellence in your classroom?

Diversity need not be a threat or a problem—but rather it may be an educational opportunity. The different backgrounds and experiences these students bring to your classroom can enrich the learning environment. You may be required, or you may elect, to take courses in mainstreaming, gender equity, and multicultural education. This chapter provides a beginning, and several others in this book, especially Chapters 14 and 15, offer additional information and strategies. This final section highlights some strategies for dealing with diversity.

Individual and Group Learning Styles

As the student population becomes more diverse, growing numbers of school systems are considering how to provide more varied and responsive learning environments. Here are some of the possibilities:

- *Match style to schedule.* Those students who perform better in the morning would be scheduled to take their more difficult courses early, while secondary schools could extend their course offerings to the evening hours for those who are more effective as night owls. (Colleges do this already; perhaps you are even taking this course at night.)
- *Match style to environment.* Quiet, well-lighted rooms as well as music and "sound-allowed" study areas could be provided. Also, students could be given the option to study independently, with a peer, or in a small group, depending on their preference.
- *Match teaching style to learning style.* Suppose you are a visual learner who relies on seeing material, while your teacher's style is auditory; the teacher lectures exclusively, never writing anything down on the board. Or imagine that you are a kinesthetic learner who must move about; but you are in the classroom of a teacher who cannot tolerate noise or movement of any kind. Problems arising from these kinds of mismatch are obvious, and both researchers and practitioners are exploring the connections between teaching style, learning style, and achievement.

Multicultural Education

According to James Banks, a leading researcher in this area, the major goal of **multicultural education** is to "transform the school so that male and female students, exceptional students, as well as students from diverse cultural, social-class, racial, and ethnic groups will experience an equal opportunity to learn in school."[33] A major assumption of multicultural education is that students from diverse groups will be more likely to achieve if the total **classroom climate** is more consistent with their diverse cultures and learning styles.

We have already discussed individual learning styles, but one frontier of multicultural research is that of cultural learning styles. Some educators posit that, through **enculturation,** particular groups are likely to exhibit characteristic approaches to learning. For example, based on the groundbreaking work of Carol Gilligan, some studies show that women are more likely than men to personalize knowledge; in general, they prefer learning through experience and

School learning environments in the future must accommodate a wide variety of individual and cultural learning styles.

first-hand observation.[34] Other research suggests that the African-American culture emphasizes learning that is aural and participatory. When these children are required to translate their participatory style into formal written tests, they are likely to concentrate so much on the unaccustomed form of expression that they are not able to convey their knowledge of the content.[35] Multicultural educators say that if we can identify and understand cultural learning styles, we can target curriculum and instruction more appropriately. More extensive research in cultural and gender learning styles is needed so that schools can educate our diverse student population most effectively.

A related goal of multicultural education is to help all students develop more positive attitudes toward different racial, ethnic, cultural, and religious groups. According to a 1992 study conducted by People for the American Way, schools have their work cut out for them. In a survey of 1,170 young people between 15 and 24, half described the state of race relations in the United States as generally bad. Fifty-five percent of African-Americans and whites said they were "uneasy" rather than "comfortable" in dealing with members of the other racial group. However, most respondents felt their attitudes toward race relations were healthier than those of their parents.[36]

James Banks says that one way to achieve more positive attitudes toward different groups is to integrate the curriculum and make it more inclusive. He says there are four approaches for accomplishing this.[37]

Multicultural education often begins with the "contributions approach," in which the study of ethnic heroes (for example, Sacajawea or Booker T. Washington) and holidays is included in the curriculum. In the "additive approach," a unit or a course is incorporated (for example, a unit on women in history), but no substantial change is made to the curriculum as a whole. While both approaches represent positive steps, they are more superficial than the "transformation approach," in which the entire Eurocentric nature of the curriculum is changed. The fourth approach, "social action," includes the transformation approach but teaches students how to use political and social action and decision making to achieve multicultural goals. (See Chapter 8 for strategies in assessing multicultural portrayals in textbooks and for analysis of current controversy over multicultural education.)

Cooperative Learning

Picture again that class that faces you in your first teaching job—15 boys, 14 girls, 7 Latino, 6 African-American, 4 Vietnamese, and 12 white students ranging in ability from learning disabled to exceptionally gifted. What other instructional strategies can you employ to teach them all well?

In diverse situations such as these, many teachers have relied on ability grouping—testing students and then grouping them together according to their measured ability. This approach is currently under fire. Critics cite research showing that low-ability groups, hampered by discipline problems, "dumbed-down" instructional materials, and low expectations, continue to lose academic ground. In fact, ability grouping seems to intensify achievement gaps instead of closing them. (See Chapter 6.)

A popular approach to grouping students, called *cooperative learning,* is rapidly becoming a mainstay of the diverse classroom. If you were to use cooperative learning in the class described above, you would not separate your learning-disabled from your gifted students. Just the opposite, in fact. You would carefully create heterogeneous groups. Each group would include boys and girls, high- and low-ability students, children from different races and ethnic backgrounds. These small groups would work together for an extended period of time, several weeks or even months.

Their activities would vary. A frequently used approach is to have students in each group tutor one another for weekly quizzes or tests. For example, you might teach the week's vocabulary words on Monday, let the groups meet and tutor each other from Tuesday through Thursday, and then give the vocabulary test on Friday. While each student still gets an individual grade, the group that makes the most improvement gets some form of group reward: points, a certificate as a Great Group, or a special privilege or opportunity. There are many different forms of cooperative learning—Jigsaw, Student Teams Achievement Division (STAD), Group Inquiry—and you will probably learn how to use many of these during your teacher education program.

Research shows that cooperative learning has a positive effect on achievement as long as it reflects two essential features. The group must work together with positive interdependence to earn rewards, and there must be individual accountability, since the group's success depends on the individual learning of each group member.[38]

Cooperative learning increases not only achievement but also friendships in the classroom. When students of diverse ethnic and racial backgrounds work cooperatively, they learn to like and respect one another. Cooperative learning also helps mainstreamed students with disabilities gain social acceptance by their classmates. These positive outcomes are most likely to occur when students are taught social skills directly.[39]

When you first begin to work with cooperative learning, you may find that your students seem unmanageable and your classroom feels chaotic. The following steps offer some helpful ways to begin:[40]

1. Start with cooperative learning strategies that are short and simple.
2. Make sure students understand how important it is to work cooperatively with other people—not only in the classroom but throughout life.
3. Don't assume that students automatically know how to work in groups in the classroom. Do some direct teaching on social skills and how to talk quietly in groups.
4. Look for opportunities to praise students who are not socially skillful.
5. Use group roles to help students develop social skills. For example, if you have a student who dominates group discussions, assign that person the role of observer.
6. Have enrichment or extension activities available for groups who finish first. Also, those who complete their work early can observe or help other groups.

The Comer Model

The teaching skills discussed in Chapter 2 become even more important when you are working with diverse learners. However, no matter how effective you are or how hard you work, some challenges are so great that you cannot do it alone. Collaboration is essential.

The Song in His Heart

As I look back over a lifetime of teaching, one special student stands out. Kou was the most memorable student I've ever taught. Short, bandy-legged, and incredibly strong for a 13-year-old, he had come from a rural mountain village deep within Laos to my special-education class in the Santa Barbara suburbs. Although he was no bigger than an American nine-year-old, the hormones of puberty had thrown a dark fuzz over his lip. His voice was deep, a shock coming from that small a body. Often, he wore a bemused expression, compounded of amazement and tolerance for the Americans who were so different from his countrymen in pastoral Laos.

On the playground, Kou was king. He could throw farther, higher, and harder than any other child in school. He was unsurpassed at *hack*, a Laotian game played with the head and feet that seemed like a cross between volleyball and soccer. And in soccer, he was the best. He also carved wonderful wooden tops, which served as trade goods for the American treasures the other boys had.

In the classroom, however, Kou had a problem. The letters, numbers, and words that he painfully memorized one week seemed to vanish during the next.

Although I tried every trick in my teaching bag, nothing seemed to work. With my help, Kou attempted all sorts of experiments designed to help him learn: writing in colored chalk, making clay letters, drawing on the playground. Throughout every effort, he remained cheerful and willing. His attitude seemed to be, "Well, this is how it is in America." But his skills did not improve.

Over time, I noticed that Kou often sang to himself as he worked. "Kou, tell me about your song," I said one day. In his halting English, he told me that the song was about a woman whose man had left her all alone.

"Write it down, Mrs. Nolan," demanded La, his friend. And so our song translation project began. As the class chimed in and squabbled over the meaning of different words, Kou sang, thought, then said the words in his fractured English. I wrote the song down on a sheet of paper. When I was finished, the children all read the song aloud, then sang it with Kou. The next day, my students brought tapes of their native music to school. Suddenly, we had a full-fledged language-experience project underway! As we listened, hummed, and made illustrated booklets about the songs and read them back, the legends and stories of Laos and the Hmong people began to tumble from Kou. For the first time, he had a reason to communicate.

Brief, primitive, and loaded with mistakes, Kou's stories became the foundation for his reading, writing, and language instruction. Never a fan of basal readers, I used this experience as an opportunity to leave the textbooks behind.

Kou's quickly improving skills were a source of pride for both of us. When Kou was 15, he left us for junior high. By then he could read at a third-grade level and do survival math. He still had that sweet smile and he still sang softly as he worked. He still longed for the hills of Laos and his old job of herding ducks beside a lake, but he spoke and wrote much better English.

And me? How much I had learned from Kou. Not only did he open the door into a rich and mysterious realm where ghosts walked and crocodiles roamed, but he taught me something about how to be a teacher. From him I learned about the value of starting with a student's interests—and about how powerful a learning tool sharing a culture can be.

Source: Virginia Nolan, "The Song in His Heart," *Instructor* 101, no. 8 (1992): 94.

In fact, collaboration is at the heart of the Comer process, an approach involving parents, mental health specialists, and school faculty and staff working together to improve schools. This process has turned around troubled inner-city schools in New Haven, Connecticut.

After receiving his M.D. from Howard University, James Comer entered the public health service. His analysis of how institutions affect the lives of children and their families led him to the following conclusion: Schools are the only places where children, troubled by poverty, discrimination, and failure, can receive sorely needed support and attention. In 1964 Comer began his psychiatric training at Yale. There he worked with inner-city New Haven schools that were plagued by low attendance and high failure rates. He tried to figure out how the low-income African-American students who attended these schools could be empowered to succeed.

As director of the School Development Program, funded by the Ford Foundation, Comer instituted teams of educational and mental health professionals. He included a social worker, a psychologist, both special education and regular teachers, and administrators. He made special efforts to involve parents in the process. Team members worked together to develop a curriculum that integrated social skills with the academic disciplines. Since the team made decisions based on consensus, they developed a sense of ownership in the project. Avoiding blame fixing, they concentrated instead on how to solve problems. The process worked. School attendance and achievement rose dramatically.

Today the Comer model is used in more than 600 schools in approximately 30 states. Built around a mental health team, a school governance team, and active parent participation, the Comer process is successful at creating schools that offer stability and support and make it possible for low-income African-American children (and other minority children) to succeed.

Since schools alone cannot handle all of the problems children face, many educators, building on Comer's ideas, are calling for a complete overhaul of social services. They view schools as the hub of a carefully coordinated network of youth agencies.[41]

Today, critics charge, our social service system for children does not operate to prevent problems; instead time and attention are consumed by acute emergencies. Too often, programs are redundant and overlapping. Because services are so fragmented, teachers and social service professionals rarely work together; they cannot see the cumulative impact of their work. The school

Collaboration between teachers, parents, and social service providers is becoming more frequent in schools that have a high percentage of "at risk" students.

nurse, drug counselor, special education teacher, and welfare worker seldom make joint evaluations or involve the classroom teacher. Each one has only a limited perspective rather than a comprehensive picture of the child. When each professional provides services in isolation, no one has the responsibility to check the overall condition and well-being of children and families. The result: Some children get the same service over and over again while others get no help at all.

Michael Kirst describes how the system ought to work:

> Only an alliance of parents, social service agencies, and educators can make a big difference for children with multiple needs and dysfunctional families. For example, some schools have become hubs for integrating social services including health care, child care, children's protective services, juvenile justice counseling, and parent education. They stay open from 7 A.M. to 7 P.M. and provide breakfast, snacks, recreation, child care, and a variety of social services.[42]

In the future, as a teacher you may interact on a regular basis not only with children but also with parents and other social service professionals. Working collaboratively, you are much more likely to have the power to make a positive difference in the lives of your students.

SUMMARY

1. Individuals exhibit diverse styles of learning, created by cognitive, affective, and physiological differences among people. Identifying a single preferred educational climate is not possible, since individuals differ so markedly in their learning styles.

2. As some educators challenge the concept of a single appropriate learning style, others have challenged the notion of a single type of intelligence. Gardner's theory of multiple intelligences identifies at least seven kinds of intelligence, ranging from the traditional verbal and mathematical to musical, physical, and interpersonal abilities, and new concepts like emotional intelligence broaden our traditional notions of IQ.

3. Recent legislation and court decisions have required schools to provide students with disabilities with appropriate education in the least restrictive environment.

4. Students with disabilities are guaranteed access to public education under Public Law 94-142, which also requires that an individualized education program be developed to document the school's efforts in meeting the needs of these students.

5. Despite PL 94-142 and the Individuals with Disabilities Education Act controversy exists about the identification of special needs children, the best ways to educate these learners, and the training needed by teachers in order to provide the best possible instruction.

6. Another group of neglected learners consists of gifted and talented students. Few resources are provided for these students in many of the nation's school districts. Without having their needs met, these exceptional learners may become apathetic, bored, isolated, and alienated.

I Taught Them All

In "I Taught Them All," high school teacher Naomi White despaired over her failure to reach all the different kinds of students in her classroom. She wrote:

> I have taught in high school for 10 years. During that time, I have given assignments, among others, to a murderer, an evangelist, a pugilist, a thief, and an imbecile.
>
> The murderer was a quiet little boy who sat on the front seat and regarded me with pale blue eyes; the evangelist, easily the most popular boy in school, had the lead in the junior play; the pugilist lounged by the window and let loose at intervals a raucous laugh that startled even the geraniums; the thief was a gay-hearted Lothario with a song on his lips; and the imbecile, a soft-eyed little animal seeking the shadows.
>
> The murderer awaits death in the state penitentiary; the evangelist has lain a year now in the village churchyard; the pugilist lost an eye in a brawl in Hong Kong; the thief, by standing on tiptoe, can see the windows of my room from the county jail; and the once gentle-eyed little moron beats his head against a padded wall in the state asylum.
>
> All of these pupils once sat in my room, sat and looked at me gravely across worn brown desks. I must have been a great help to those pupils— I taught them the rhyming scheme of the Elizabethan sonnet and how to diagram a complex sentence.[a]

Naomi White wrote "I Taught Them All" in 1937. The frustration, challenges, and disappointments she experienced in the classroom are touching, and many similar situations continue more than half a century later. But as you consider her words, consider also how things have changed. Notice which students pierce her consciousness—the active students, the males. What kinds of issues and problems may have confronted the girls in her class? Because the girls were quieter, were their problems missed? Some of her boys became disappointments as adults, yet none of the girls were even traced and remembered into adulthood. Were their problems as women also seen as quieter, more private, of less concern to society? If Naomi White were teaching today, she might discover additional challenges in responding to the needs of the growing number of minority children in schools.

[a]Naomi White, "I Taught Them All," *Progressive Education* 20 (November 1943): 321.

7. Gifted and talented programs that do exist usually promote one of two strategies: enrichment or grade acceleration. While many people worry that acceleration will lead to social maladjustment, the research indicates that acceleration has a positive impact on gifted students.

8. Changing patterns of immigration and birth rates are demographic trends that will result in classrooms far more diverse in terms of race, ethnicity, and language. Social problems such as poverty, family disruptions, and violence are also affecting American classrooms.

9. By the year 2000, the student population will be approximately one-third minority. Traditionally the schools have not been as successful in teaching minority students, so the years ahead will bring new and difficult challenges.

10. How to move non–English-speaking students into America's classrooms has been both an educational and a legal challenge. In the *Lau v. Nichols* case (1974) the Supreme Court ruled that schools were not doing an adequate job in this area, and Congress subsequently passed the Equal Educational Opportunities Act. Many districts redoubled their efforts in bilingual education. Some teach students in their native language only until they learn English (the transitional approach), while other schools continue to use both languages in the classroom (the maintenance approach). Studies suggest that many bilingual programs continue to fall short of their goals.

11. Strategies successful in working with a diverse student population include a multicultural curriculum, cooperative education, and close collaboration with parents and social service professionals. When effective strategies such as the Comer process are used, cultural pluralism can be viewed not as a threat but as a competitive advantage.

DISCUSSION QUESTIONS AND ACTIVITIES

1. How would you characterize your own learning style? Interview other students in your class to determine how they characterize their learning styles. Based on these interviews, what recommendations could you offer your course instructor about how to meet the needs of different students in your class?
2. What is your opinion of Howard Gardner's theory of multiple intelligences? In which of the intelligences do you feel you are the strongest? Weakest?
3. Can you develop additional intelligences beyond the seven (or eight) that Gardner identifies? (This is often best accomplished in groups!)
4. Review Daniel Goleman's book *Emotional Intelligence* and present a summary of Goleman's findings to your classmates.
5. Would you consider special education a success or a failure? Support your point of view.
6. Observe a mainstreamed classroom in a local school and interview the teacher. What is your assessment of the effectiveness of mainstreaming in this classroom?
7. Given budgetary limitations, do you think schools should provide special resources and programs for gifted students? Why or why not?
8. If you had a gifted child, would you want him or her to be grade accelerated? On what factors would your decision depend?
9. Write a research paper on the education and life experiences of at least one of the new immigrant groups. If possible, interview students and family members who belong to that group about their experiences.
10. Which bilingual approach do you prefer, maintenance or transitional? Why? How can bilingual education be made more effective?
11. Given demographic trends, develop a scenario of a classroom in the year 2020. Describe the students' characteristics and the role of the teacher.
12. If you had the challenge of transforming your school's curriculum so that it would become more multicultural, what changes would you make? Be as specific as possible in your answer.
13. What is your opinion of ability grouping? If you had a gifted daughter or son, would you want your child in a special program?

NOTES

1. Maxine Schwartz Seller, "Immigrants in the Schools—Again: Historical and Contemporary Perspectives on the Education of Post 1965 Immigrants in the United States," *Educational Foundations* 3, no. 1 (Spring 1989): 53–75.

2. Kenneth Dunn and Rita Dunn, "Dispelling Outmoded Beliefs About Student Learning," *Educational Leadership* 45, no. 7 (March 1987): 55–63.

3. James Keefe, *Learning Style Theory and Practice* (Reston, VA: National Association of Secondary School Principals, 1987).

4. Dunn and Dunn, "Dispelling Outmoded Beliefs About Student Learning." See also G. Price, "Which Learning Style Elements Are Stable and Which Tend to Change?" *Learning Styles Network Newsletter* 4, no. 2 (1980): 38–40; J. Vitrostko, *An Analysis of the Relationship Among Academic Achievement in Mathematics and Reading, Assigned Instructional Schedules and the Learning Style Time Preferences of Third-, Fourth-, Fifth-, and Sixth-Grade Students,* unpublished doctoral dissertation, St. John's University, Jamaica, New York, 1983.

5. Howard Gardner and Thomas Hatch, "Multiple Intelligences Go to School: Educational Implications of the Theory of Multiple Intelligences," *Educational Researcher* 18, no. 8 (November 1989): 5.

6. Howard Gardner, "Beyond the I.Q.: Education and Human Development," *Harvard Educational Review* 57, no. 2 (Spring 1987): 187–193.

7. Thomas Armstrong, "Multiple Intelligences: Seven Ways to Approach Curriculum," *Educational Leadership* 52 (November 1994): 26–28.

8. Howard Gardner, "Reflections on Multiple Intelligences: Myths and Messages," *Phi Delta Kappan* 77, no. 3 (November 1995): 200–209.

9. Thomas R. Hoerr, "How the New City School Applies the Multiple Intelligences," *Educational Leadership* 52 (November 1994): 29–33.

10. Nancy Gibbs, "The EQ Factor," *Time* 146, no. 14 (October 2, 1995): 60–68.

11. William Heward and Michael Orlansky, "Educational Equality for Exceptional Students," in James Banks and Cherry Banks (eds.), *Multicultural Education* (Boston: Allyn & Bacon, 1989), pp. 231–250.

12. Heward and Orlansky, "Educational Equality for Exceptional Students."

13. Helen Keller, *The Story of My Life* (Garden City, NY: Doubleday, 1902), pp. 34–37.

14. Letter from Anne Sullivan, quoted in Keller, *The Story of My Life,* p. 257.

15. Marie Killilea, *Karen* (New York: Dell, 1952), p. 171.

16. Ed Martin, quoted in "PL 94-142," *Instructor* 87, no. 9 (1978): 63.

17. Alina Tugend, "Steady Rise in Learning Disabled Spurs Review," *Education Week* 5, no. 11 (November 13, 1985): 1, 18–20. See also Martha McCarthy, "Severely Disabled Children: Who Pays?" *Phi Delta Kappan* 73, no. 1 (September 1991): 66–71.

18. Steven Muir and Jerry Hutton, "Regular Education Initiative: Impact on Service to Handicapped Students," *The Journal of the Association of Teacher Educators* 11, no. 3 (Fall 1989): 7–11. See also "Mainstreaming," *Harvard Education Letter* (January–February 1990): 7; Madeleine Will, *Educating Students with Learning Problems: A Shared Responsibility* (Washington, DC: U.S. Department of Education, 1986).

19. Quoted in David Milofsky, "Schooling the Kid No One Wants," *New York Times Magazine,* January 2, 1977.

20. The anecdotes and many of the quotations in this section were cited in Gene I. Maeroff, "The Unfavored Gifted Few," *New York Times Magazine,* August 21, 1977, reprinted in Celeste Toriero (ed.), *Readings in Education 78/79* (Guilford, CT: Dushkin, 1978).

21. Joseph S. Renzulli and C. H. Smith, "Two Approaches to Identification of Gifted Students," *Exceptional Children* 43 (1977).

22. Robert Sternberg, "Giftedness According to the Triarchic Theory of Human Intelligence," in Nicholas Congelo and Gary Davis (eds.), *Handbook of Gifted Education* (Boston: Allyn & Bacon, 1991).

23. Judy Galbraith, "Gifted Youth and Self-Concept," *Gifted Education* 15, no. 2 (May 1989): 15–17.

24. Quoted in Galbraith, "Gifted Youth and Self-Concept," p. 16.

25. Robert Morris, "Educating Gifted for the 1990s," *Gifted Education* 15, no. 2 (May 1989): 50–52.

26. Joyce Van Tassel-Baska, "Curricular Approaches for Gifted Learners," *Gifted Education* 15, no. 2 (May 1989): 19–34.

27. John Feldhusen, "Synthesis of Research on Gifted Youth," *Educational Leadership* 46, no. 6 (March 1989): 6–11.
28. Lisa Leff, "Gifted, Talented, and Under Siege," *The Washington Post Educational Review,* April 5, 1992, p. 14.
29. Quoted in Galbraith, "Gifted Youth and Self-Concept," p. 17.
30. Harold Hodgkinson, quoted in *Education Week,* May 14, 1986, pp. 14–40.
31. The demographic information in the following section is based on the following: Harold Hodgkinson and Tom Mirga, "Here They Come, Ready or Not: Special Report on the Ways in Which America's Population in Motion Is Changing the Outlook for Schools and Society," *Education Week,* May 14, 1986, pp. 14–40; Harold Hodgkinson, "The Right Schools for the Right Kids," *Educational Leadership* 45, no. 5 (February 1988): 10–14; Alex Molnar, "Turning Children Into Things," *Educational Leadership* 46, no. 8 (May 1989): 68–69; Larry Strong, "The Best Kids They Have," *Educational Leadership* 46, no. 5 (February 1989): 2; John Kellog, "Focus of Change, *Phi Delta Kappan* 70, no. 30 (November 1988): 199–204; Geneva Gay, "Ethnic Minorities and Educational Equality," in Banks and Banks (eds.), *Multicultural Education,* pp. 167–188; Fred Hechinger, *Fateful Choices* (New York: Carnegie Council on Adolescent Development, 1992); The Annie E. Casey Foundation, *KIDS COUNT Data Book* (Washington, DC: Center for the Study of Social Policy, 1992); *Focus on Blacks* (Washington, DC: National Education Association, 1992); *Focus on Asian/Pacific Islanders* (Washington, DC: National Education Association, 1992); *Focus on American Indian/Alaska Natives* (Washington, DC: National Education Association, 1991); *Focus on Hispanics* (Washington, DC: National Education Association, 1991); Andrew Hacker, *Two Nations* (New York: Scribner's, 1992); Mark Roosa, "Adolescent Pregnancy Programs Collection: An Introduction," *Family Relations* 40 (October 1991): 370–372; Donna Harrington-Lueker, "Blown Away," *American School Board Journal* 179, no. 5 (May 1992): 20–26.
32. Gary A. Cziko, "The Evaluation of Bilingual Education: From Necessity and Probability to Possibility," *Educational Researcher* 21, no. 2 (March 1992): 24.
33. James Banks, "Multicultural Education: Characteristics and Goals," in Banks and Banks, *Multicultural Education,* pp. 19–20.
34. Carol Gilligan, *In a Different Voice: Psychological Theory and Women's Development* (Cambridge, MA: Harvard University Press, 1982). See also Mary Field Belenky, Blythe McVicker Clinchy, Nancy Rule Goldberger, and Jill Mattuck Tarule, *Women's Ways of Knowing: The Development of Self, Voice, and Mind* (New York: Basic Books, 1986).
35. Gay, "Ethnic Minorities and Educational Equality."
36. Peter Schmidt, "New Survey Discerns Deep Divisions Among U.S. Youths on Race Relations," *Education Week* 5, no. 27 (March 25, 1992): 5.
37. James Banks, "Integrating the Curriculum with Ethnic Content," in Banks and Banks, *Multicultural Education,* pp. 189–207.
38. Robert Slavin, "Research on Cooperative Learning: Consensus and Controversy," *Educational Leadership* 47, no 4 (December 1989/January 1990): 52–54.
39. Slavin, "Research on Cooperative Learning."
40. Susan Ellis and Susan Whalen, "Keys to Cooperative Learning," *Instructor* 101, no. 6 (February 1992): 34–37.
41. Grace Pung Guthrie and Larry Guthrie, "Streamlining Interagency Collaboration for Youth at Risk," *Educational Leadership* 49 (September 1991): 17–22.
42. Michael Kirst, "Improving Children's Services," *Phi Delta Kappan* 72, no. 8 (1991): 623–627.

WHAT ARE SCHOOLS FOR?

OBJECTIVES

To explore two fundamental, divergent purposes of schools: transmitting culture and reconstructing society

To identify various purposes and expectations assigned to schools

To discuss criticism leveled at schools

To describe the issues identified in A Nation at Risk *and the other reform reports of the 1980s and 1990s*

To establish your own priorities concerning the purposes of schools

To discuss the significance of choice, charter, privatization, and other recent developments that are redefining the nature of America's schools

A*lthough most of us take school for granted, the proper role of this institution continues to evoke heated debate. Is a school's role to prepare students to adjust to society, or to equip them to change society? Not only do people hold widely divergent views regarding both the goals and the effectiveness of America's schools, these views seem to vary depending on the times.*

In this chapter you will have the opportunity to examine some of the major purposes assigned to schools and some of the major criticisms that have been leveled at them. The chapter will also ask you to consider reform reports that highlight different purposes for schools. Finally, you will be asked to develop your own answers to the question, What are schools for?

A Meeting Here Tonight

Sam Newman has been principal of Monroe High School for just under 5 years. Becoming principal seemed a natural step to take after teaching and coaching for 8 years. There was a big salary boost, and of course it made his family proud to move up a notch on the social status scale. Besides, after 8 years, several thousand students, one state championship, and two runner-up teams, Sam felt that it was time to get out of teaching and coaching and try something new.

But now Sam Newman is having second thoughts. Being principal has not been all he envisioned it to be. He planned to increase school spirit, and that seemed to please the school board enough to give him the principalship over two more-senior candidates. He organized rallies, handed out buttons and pennants proclaiming, "Monroe Is Tops." He even commissioned the music teacher to write a new school pep song. But all that seems long ago.

Sam now spends his time rushing from one emergency to another. Between emergencies, he fills out forms and attends meetings. He spends two nights a week trying to complete federal, state, and school paperwork, and a third night attending meetings. During the day there is an endless parade of students in trouble, teachers with complaints, outraged parents, and, of course, more meetings. Between budgets to balance and supplies to order, Sam rarely has time to think about ways of increasing school spirit or improving education at Monroe. Maybe he ought to commission the music teacher to write a pep song for him.

And now, to top it all off, statewide results show that Monroe students have fallen almost a year behind the norm in math and reading. He must have received a hundred calls from angry parents complaining about higher taxes and inefficient schools. So a meeting has been called to explore solutions to the problem of declining test scores. "They'll be coming out of the woodwork on this one," Sam thought, as he prepared to make his way to the auditorium.

On his way to the meeting Sam turned right, detouring to the bathroom. As he stared into the mirror to comb his thin, graying hair, he noted sadly the almost complete disappearance of his belt buckle beneath his drooping belly. He once prided himself on staying in shape. Now his shape is mostly round.

He allowed himself a brief reminiscence of that naive "I can do anything" time when he first became principal, that time when his belt buckle was still in view. He thought of all the changes he had planned, the increased morale he had sought. But being a principal is not the same as being a coach, and a school is very different from a team. Each passing year has taught him how precious little he knows about schools. Curriculum, philosophy, teaching effectiveness, and psychology are mostly unknown to him. His training was in administration, and that is what he does. He schedules. He budgets. He writes plans. He calms parents. He disciplines students. But all the while, he realizes that he has little time to shape and direct the school. He is not really leading the school—he does not even know where to lead it; he is simply trying very hard to keep it afloat. Although he knows more about flowcharts than about philosophy, a line from his college philosophy course sticks in his mind. The line was Santayana's, and it seems to have a lot of meaning for him and for Monroe High School now: "Fanaticism consists of redoubling one's efforts after having forgotten one's aim."

A look at his watch brought an abrupt end to philosophical speculation. He was already 5 minutes late. He hurried out of the bathroom and down the hallway to the meeting.

• • •

Today's large, comprehensive high schools reflect the diversity and the conflicting interests of the larger society

George Elbright unconsciously tugged at his tie as he mounted the long stairway to Monroe High School. He glanced up at the motto, chiseled in stone for generations to enjoy, "Knowledge Is Power." He thought back to the first time he had read those words, almost 40 years ago, as an underweight, 15-year-old freshman. Fear raced through his heart then, so great that 40 years later the memory still makes him perspire and pull at his tie. Funny how schools do that to you.

For George Elbright, Monroe High conjures up memories of hard work, homework assignments that were graded, midterms so tough that kids sometimes broke down and cried, unable to go on. And finals! The whole year's work riding on one exam. Tests were rough then, but kids learned. Not like today. Not at all.

And that is why George is back at Monroe High. For years he has watched schools disintegrate, and he has complained bitterly about the lack of discipline, the growing permissiveness, the new teaching methods that sound as if the teachers do not have to teach at all, and those courses! Sex education, driver education, drug education, environmental education—everything but education education. No wonder the kids can't read or write. No wonder George, Jr., is doing so poorly. No wonder George Elbright, Sr., is about to attend his first parent-teacher meeting.

George reached into his pocket and pulled out his wrinkled, handwritten list. Slowly he went over each point, making certain that he would neither stumble nor forget any of his suggestions. He had to be clear and forceful. These teachers today have so many answers that you must be totally prepared in order to deal with them. One more time, he slowly rehearsed his list:

1. Teachers must reassume their responsibility. Homework, tests, and drills should be the main activities of the classroom. Free-for-all discussion,

with the teacher acting as a referee instead of a teacher, has to end. Children have to learn that learning is serious business.

2. Students have to learn the importance of discipline and respect. No more kids running the school. Students should learn to dress properly and to speak to adults with respect. Sloppy dress and poor manners lead to lazy attitudes and poor work.

3. The notion that all students must be promoted—no matter what—has to end. Kids who do not pass tests should be left back until they do pass them. We already have far too many high school graduates who can't even read.

4. I am tired of trying to decipher "progress reports" about my child's "social adjustment" and "satisfactory efforts." I want to see report cards with grades and without educational jargon.

5. A school is supposed to teach fundamental skills. Kids should read and write well; forget about sex education, human relations, driver education, and the other frills. No more cafeteria-style electives. It is time that schools get back to the basics.

6. And it is high time that teachers stop bad-mouthing their country. Kids should be instilled with patriotism and love of country. It is time once again to raise Old Glory to the top of the flagpole!

George allowed a smile to cross his lips as he tucked the list safely back into his pocket. Perhaps it will work; perhaps he can get the school back on the right track again. The newspapers are filled with reports that seem to support his point of view. Why, he even read a report that said schools are so weak they jeopardize the security of the nation. At any rate, he has to try for George, Jr.'s sake. All the family's hopes are pinned on him. George, Jr., would be the first Elbright to make it to college. This is no time for the school to let him down. Not with college at stake. Not now.

• • •

Shirley Weiss sat alone in her classroom, sipping lukewarm coffee from a thermos cup. The evening meeting gives her a chance to stay after school and catch up on her paperwork. She finished grading 15 minutes ago but was determined to wait until the last minute before going down to the auditorium for the meeting. Although anxious to make her position known, she is not anxious to get into one-to-one encounters with angry parents. So she waited.

She is amazed at public reaction to the declining test scores. It is, of course, unfortunate that students at Monroe are not doing as well as they should, but given the teacher cuts and the large size of today's classes, it really isn't all that surprising. And to get so worked up over test scores! Incredible.

Everyone seems to be missing the point entirely. Teenagers today simply aren't contemporary versions of the kids who attended Monroe High 10 or 20 years ago. Drugs, violence, alienation, racism, sexism, teen pregnancy—the world is so much more complex. Kids have to find out who they are and where they are going. In comparison with these critical goals, learning about Jackson's fight with the National Bank in 1830 seems to pale into insignificance.

That is why Shirley Weiss restructured her American history course into a contemporary social problems course. If she could only get the kids to understand themselves and their world, the rest would follow. But they have to want to learn and to grow, and that's what her course is all about.

And the students do well in her course. They are genuinely interested. They study and they learn. As a matter of fact, if those test makers ever left their air-conditioned, swanky offices and rejoined the real world, they would revise their tests. A new test would parallel her course, and her kids would probably score in the top percentiles. The problem is not really with the school or the kids at all! It is with the test makers and the parents who blindly believe test scores!

Shirley was good and angry as she pushed back her chair and made her way down to the auditorium.

• • •

Phil Lambert began to fidget as he waited for the meeting to begin. His three-piece suit and the 25-year-old wooden seat were less than perfect fits.

He has not been back to Monroe since his youngest daughter graduated, almost 10 years ago. And he is not overjoyed at being here now. But declining test scores represented a serious problem, not just for Phil but for the entire town.

Phil Lambert is not only the owner of Lambert's, the biggest department store in town; he is also chairman of the chamber of commerce. Every week he is involved with enticing professionals, new industry, and developers to relocate in Monroe. Sooner or later, these discussions always turn to the quality of the school system. In a sense, the success of the schools is a barometer of the town's future growth and development. And now the barometer is falling: stormy days ahead. Declining test scores could cost the town plenty.

But Phil is particularly upset because he has warned people about this problem for years. High school kids are getting into more and more trouble. He has recently been to court three times to deal with teenage shoplifters. And when kids today apply for work, it is so sad it is almost funny! Wearing blue jeans and fouling up the application form, they just come off as irresponsible and stupid. For years Phil has been asking rhetorically, "Didn't you learn *any-thing* in school?" Now his question is no longer rhetorical.

The schools simply have to get down to business, literally, and begin preparing kids for the real world. Our whole nation is in economic trouble because of bad schools. We cannot even compete with the Japanese in international markets. More courses should be offered, stressing not only the basics but also how to get a job and about the importance of the work ethic. Students have to understand that school is not a place where they can come late, dress sloppily, and goof off. Once they understand how serious the real world is, how important getting a job is, they will get serious about their schoolwork. That is why the school has to become business-oriented—in values, in practices, and in courses.

Lambert depressed the button on his digital watch and made a mental note that the meeting was starting 16 minutes late. If he ran the store the way they run the schools, he'd have been bankrupt years ago.

• • •

The late start of the meeting gave Mary Jackson a chance to relax and unwind. She had rushed from her job to make the meeting and was beginning to feel the consequences of her long day.

As she gauged the audience, she realized that once again the "haves" out-numbered the "have-nots." The middle-class, white, well-dressed parents don't look half as tired as Mary Jackson feels. But they sure do seem worried. For the first time, they are getting a small taste of the problem Mary has been fighting for years. Lower achievement scores are shaking them up.

But they could never know the problem as well as Mary does. Compared to the scores of black kids, their kids are doing just fine. Even with the drop in scores for white kids, they are still scoring almost 2 years ahead of the black students. What is their gripe?

Mary has two children enrolled in Monroe High. Both are working hard, yet they cannot seem to catch up to the white students. Mary is concerned with the racism in the school. The teachers seem to mean well, but they just do not understand the realities of the black experience. Why, there's not even one minority faculty member! And tracking is a problem, too. Somehow it seems that white students end up in the honors track. As a result, black kids are not learning much.

To make matters worse, the scores of the girls at Monroe, black and white, are falling behind the boys'. And this is not uncommon, for the report on the test results distributed to all the parents said that girls' scores nationally seem to decrease in high school. The report does not explain why, but Mary has a pretty good hunch. The teachers expect less from girls than from boys. The cards are stacked against them.

So there sat Mary, black and female, caught in the middle with two children, both falling further and further behind the other students at Monroe.

She has tried to make the school aware of the special problems faced by minority students and females. Mary is president of an unofficial group known as the Minority Parents Association, and she has also started an informal discussion group to deal with the matter of sexism. Everyone at Monroe seems sympathetic, from Mr. Newman on down. But nothing has changed, and that makes her feel tired and discouraged—but not tired and discouraged enough to give up.

Mary looked around at the almost completely filled auditorium. The mainly white, middle-class parents overwhelm the few black faces in the audience. But Mary would speak for those would could not come and for those who have given up all hope of changing things. Mary would speak for all those who are being short-changed in the school. The school is failing those who need it the most. Monroe High should be their stepping-stone up, not an obstacle to their advancement. If schools do not improve the status of the minorities, the females, the poor, what would? Mary would tell them. The last few frustrating years have worn her patience thin.

● ● ●

Sam Newman twisted the microphone stand to within a few inches of his mouth and prepared to open the meeting. He looked out at the packed auditorium and began to assess the crowd.

There is Pat Viola, the art teacher. What is she doing here? Art is never assessed on those tests.

Oh, oh! There is Mrs. Jackson, the unofficial spokesperson for black parents. She's not going to pull any punches about those test scores. The black students are 2 years behind the white students on achievement tests.

And Dr. Sweig, the humanities professor from the university, is here. He's probably going to make his pitch about requiring all students to study the classics. He must have given that "cultural literacy for all" speech a dozen times.

Good schools depend on strong community support

Mrs. Benoit, president of the school board, looks pretty unhappy. As long as I can find a solution that pleases everyone and doesn't increase the budget, she'll be satisfied. She needs a magician, not a principal, to run this meeting.

There's Alice Marden, president of the student government. She probably has a long list of demands about making the school more humane and giving the students more rights. That's always good for 15 minutes.

Phil Lambert is here and Shirley Weiss. Isn't that the Elbright kid's father? Wonder what's on their minds?

Sam Newman began to perspire. He felt certain that he knew how the Christians must have felt as they entered the Colosseum to face the lions. He leaned forward and announced, "Okay, let's begin."

Newman's Dilemma

Sam Newman has a dilemma on his hands. Parents and teachers pulling him—and trying to pull the school—in different directions. If it is any comfort to Sam—and it probably is not—he is confronting an old question: What is the purpose of a school?

Having spent much of your life as a student, you may find this question too basic, even obvious. Answers come quickly to mind. We go to school to learn things, to earn good grades, to win a better job, to become a better person—or to please our parents (or even ourselves). But these divergent reasons only represent the view from a student's side of the desk. There are other perspectives, broader views, and more fundamental definitions of the purposes of schools.

While we might have fun brainstorming all the possible reasons for schools, it may be more useful to focus on two fundamental, and somewhat antithetical, purposes of schools.

Purpose 1: To Transmit Society's Knowledge and Values (Passing the Cultural Baton)

Society builds schools for a reason, and society has a vital interest in what schools do and how they do it. Schools reflect and promote society's values. Consider all the options. There is a world of knowledge out there, more than any school can possibly hope to teach. So one of the first tasks confronting the school is to *select* what to teach. This selection creates a cultural message. Each country chooses the curriculum to match and advance its own view of history, its own values, its self-interests, and its own culture. In the United States, we learn about U.S. history, often in elementary, middle, and high school, but we learn little about the history, geography, and culture of other countries or of America's cultural diversity. Even individual states and communities require schools to teach their own state or local history, to advance the dominant "culture" of Illinois or of New York City. But the bases of the selection concern more than merely geographic boundaries. By selecting what to teach—and what to omit—schools are making clear decisions as to what is valued, what is worth preserving and passing on.

Literature is a good example of this selection process. American children read mainly works by U.S. and British writers, while they are rarely asked to read Asian, Latin American, or African authors. This is not because literary genius is confined to the British and U.S. populations; it is because of a selection process, a decision by those keepers of the culture and creators of the curriculum that certain authors are to be taught and talked about and emulated, and others omitted. The same decisions are made concerning which music should be played, which art viewed, which dances performed, which world events studied, which historical figures are worth learning about, and which are of lesser stature. And as each nation makes these cultural value decisions, it is the role of the school to transmit these decisions to the next generation. Schools represent society's attempt to live forever, an academic fountain of youth creating each new generation in the image of the current generation.

As society transmits its culture, it also transmits a view of the world. Being American means valuing certain things and judging countries and cultures from that set of values. Democratic countries that practice religious tolerance and respect individual rights are generally viewed more positively by Americans than are societies characterized by opposing norms, standards, and actions— that is, characteristics that do not fit our "American values." Chinese tanks rolling into Tiananmen Square to repress student demonstrations conflicted with our cultural and political standards, and most Americans were repulsed. Repression of religious, racial, or ethnic minorities usually engenders similar negative feelings. As our national sensitivity to sexism deepens, repression of women in other nations may bring similar disdain. By transmitting culture, schools breathe the breath of cultural eternity into a new generation, and mold its view of the world.

But this process is limiting as well. Schools are teaching students to view the world from the reverse end of a telescope: a constricted, miniaturized view that does not allow much deviation or perspective. From this restricted view, cultural transmission may contribute to feelings of cultural superiority, a belief that "we are the best," that we are "number one!" Such implicitly nationalistic views may decrease tolerance and respect for other cultures and peoples. Historically, such views have led to conflicts and wars between nations and peoples. So while some believe that transmitting cultural values is a purpose of most schools, others, because they find certain cultures and current practices less than ideal, believe that schools need to go beyond simply transmitting values. These people believe that cultural values should be adjusted and improved, and that schools are the perfect place for such midcourse corrections of society.

Purpose 2: Reconstructing Society (Schools as Tools for Change)

If society were perfect, transmitting the culture from one generation to the next would be all that is required of schools. But our world, our nation, and our communities are far from ideal. Poverty, hunger, injustice, pollution, overpopulation, racism, sexism, nuclear dangers, and terrorism are a few societal problems on a depressingly long list of such problems. To *reconstructionists,* schools are instruments of change, a way that society can address and correct these economic and social ills. There is a saying, "If it ain't broke, don't fix it." To reconstructionists, society is broken, it needs to be fixed, and the school is a perfect tool for needed repairs.

Reconstructionists represent a wide spectrum of beliefs and activities. At one end are those who believe that addressing critical social issues, such as poverty and racism, should be part of the school curriculum. They believe that students should be made aware of the ills of society, study these critical, if controversial, areas, and equip themselves to actively confront these issues as they become adults.[1] Other reconstructionists are more action-oriented and believe that schools and students shouldn't wait until the students reach adulthood. They call for a *social action* curriculum in which students actively involve themselves in eliminating social ills. For example, if a poor neighborhood lacks a day care facility for young children of working parents, the students could establish such a center. Students could petition government officials or private

Is the business of schools just academic learning, or might the goals include fostering an awareness of the benefits of community service, such as volunteering to tutor others?

corporations for funds, or work to build equipment for the center, or even serve as teaching assistants.

This idea of students contributing to society is not unique. The Carnegie Foundation for the Advancement of Teaching recommends that every student be required to earn a "service credit," which might include volunteer work with the poor or elderly or homeless. The idea behind a service credit goes beyond that of merely reducing social ills: It includes the goals of providing students with a connection to the larger community and of encouraging students to develop a sense of their personal responsibility for improving the social condition.[2] During the 1980s and 1990s, several states and communities supported the concept of social reconstructionism as described by the Carnegie Foundation, and incorporated service learning activities and credits in their curricula.

While social democratic reconstructionists are reform-minded, economic reconstructionists hold a darker, more radical view of society's ills, and advocate more drastic, even revolutionary, action. They believe that schools generally serve evil purposes by oppressing people, and by teaching the poorer classes to accept their lowly stations in life, to be subservient to authority, to unquestioningly follow the rules while laboring for the economic benefit of the rich. To economic reconstructionists, schools are tools of oppression, not institutions of learning.

Perhaps the most noted of these critics is Paulo Freire, author of *The Pedagogy of the Oppressed,* a book about his efforts to educate and liberate poor, illiterate peasants of Brazil.[3] In his book, Freire describes how he taught these peasants to read in order to identify problems that were keeping them poor and powerless. From this new awareness, peasants began to analyze their problems—such as how the lack of sanitation caused illness—and what they could do to solve specific problems and liberate themselves from their oppressive conditions. Freire highlighted the distinction between schools and education. Schools can either educate and liberate, or miseducate and oppress. But true education liberates. Through education, the peasants learned to read, to act collectively, to improve their living conditions, to reconstruct their lives.

While preserving the status quo and promoting social change represent two fundamental directions available to schools, they are not the only possible expectations. When you think about it, the public holds our schools to a bewildering array of tasks and expectations.

John Goodlad, in his massive study *A Place Called School,* examined a wide range of documents that have tried to define the purposes of schooling over 300 years of history. He and his colleague found four broad goals:

1. *Academic,* including a broad array of knowledge and intellectual skills
2. *Vocational,* aimed at readiness for the world of work and economic responsibilities
3. *Social and civic,* including skills and behavior for participating in a complex democratic society
4. *Personal,* including the development of individual talent and self-expression[4]

Goodlad included these four goal areas, which are illustrated in Figure 5.1, in questionnaires distributed to parents, and he asked them to rate their importance. Generally parents gave "very important" ratings to all four. Ninety percent of elementary, junior high, and high school parents ranked intellectual

FIGURE 5-1
Goals of Schools

Vocational → ← Academic

Personal → ← Social, civic

(academic) goals as very important. The same percentage of elementary school parents rated personal goals as very important, while the perceived importance of this area dropped slightly, to 80 percent, for secondary school parents. Vocational goals were rated only slightly lower by secondary school parents. Seventy-five percent of elementary school parents rated social goals as very important; this dropped to approximately 65 percent at the secondary school level. When Goodlad asked students and teachers to rate the four goal areas, they also rated all as "very important." When pushed to select one of these four as having top priority, approximately half the teachers and parents selected the intellectual area. But for the other half, the first choice was distributed rather evenly among the other three areas. And students spread their preferences fairly evenly among all four categories, with high school students giving a slight edge to vocational goals. When it comes to selecting the purpose of schools, both those who are its clients and those who provide its services resist interpreting the purpose of schools narrowly. What do Americans want from their schools? Evidently they want it all! As early as 1953, Arthur Bestor wrote: "The idea that the school must undertake to meet every need that some other agency is failing to meet, regardless of the suitability of the schoolroom to the task, is a preposterous delusion that in the end can wreck the educational system."[5]

In the 1980s, Ernest Boyer conducted a major study of secondary education and concluded:

> Since the English classical school was founded over 150 years ago, high schools have accumulated purposes like barnacles on a weathered ship. As school population expanded from a tiny urban minority to almost all youth, a coherent purpose was hard to find. The nation piled social policy upon educational policy and all of them on top of the delusion that a single institution can do it all.[6]

Where Do You Stand?

In 399 B.C., the Greek teacher-philosopher Socrates disagreed with his fellow Athenians concerning the purpose of education. He believed that free and open inquiry is a uniquely useful educational technique. But many of his fellow Greeks found his questions disturbing, for his queries sometimes challenged the accepted conventions of the times. Socrates refused to refocus his "school" to avoid controversy, so he was charged with "corrupting" the youth. His steadfast refusal to conform to community pressure regarding the direction of his teaching eventually led to a public trial and his execution by poisoning.

Sam Newman may not have had Socrates in mind when he opened his meeting at the beginning of this chapter, but he realized that his community held strong and diverse opinions about the role and purposes of schools, and he felt the pressure of the conflicting beliefs. The ideological conflict has been dramatized here through the views of Shirley Weiss, Phil Lambert, and others representing a microcosm of America's differing notions about a school's primary and legitimate purposes.

Identifying school goals seems to be everyone's business—parents, teachers, all levels of government, and various professional groups. Over the years, dozens of lists have been published in different reform reports, each enumerating goals for schools. What could be simpler? The problem arises when schools cannot fulfill all of these goals, either because there are too many goals or because the purposes conflict with one another. Then schools must establish priorities and decide which goals to pursue. The two primary, and sometimes conflicting, purposes of schools—to preserve the culture and to reconstruct society—are often broken down into more distinct and immediate goals. It is these smaller pieces that often dominate discussion. Should schools focus on preparing students for college? Should they try to inhibit drug use, or lessen the threat of AIDS? Perhaps schools ought to focus on the economy and train students to be a more productive and efficient workforce, one that can successfully compete in the world marketplace.

Over the years, you too have developed your own ideas about the purpose of schools. You may feel strongly about some of the issues, less firm about others, and really not clear at all on still other possibilities. To help you clarify your thoughts—and raise options you may have not yet explored—we offer the following list of school goals. These goals come from a variety of sources and are sometimes contradictory. But they have been advocated singly and in combination by different groups at different times and have been adopted by different schools. In each case, you register your own judgment on the values and worth of each goal. When you have completed your responses, we shall discuss the significance of these goals, and you can see how your responses fit into the bigger picture.

Circle the number that best reflects how important you think each school goal is.

1 Very unimportant
2 Unimportant
3 Moderately important
4 Important
5 Very important

	Very Unimportant				Very Important
1. To prepare competent workers to compete successfully in a technical world economy	1	2	3	4	5
2. To transmit the nation's cultural heritage, preserving past accomplishments and insights	1	2	3	4	5
3. To encourage students to question current practices and institutions; to promote social change	1	2	3	4	5

	Very Unimportant				**Very Important**
4. To develop healthy citizens aware of nutrition, exercise, and good health habits	1	2	3	4	5
5. To lead the world in creating a peaceful global society, including an understanding of other cultures and languages	1	2	3	4	5
6. To provide a challenging education for America's brightest students	1	2	3	4	5
7. To develop strong self-concept and self-esteem in students	1	2	3	4	5
8. To nurture creative students in developing art, music, and writing; to encourage creative cultural achievement	1	2	3	4	5
9. To educate students in avoiding social pitfalls: unwanted pregnancy, AIDS, drugs, alcoholism	1	2	3	4	5
10. To unite citizens from diverse backgrounds (national origin, race, ethnicity) as a single nation with a unified culture	1	2	3	4	5
11. To provide support to families through after-school child care, nutritional supplements, medical treatment, etc.	1	2	3	4	5
12. To encourage loyal students committed to the United States; to instill patriotism	1	2	3	4	5
13. To teach students our nation's work ethic: punctuality, responsibility, cooperation, self-control, neatness, etc.	1	2	3	4	5
14. To develop academic skills in reading, writing, mathematics, and science	1	2	3	4	5
15. To provide a dynamic vehicle for social and economic mobility, a way for the poor to reach their full potential	1	2	3	4	5
16. To prepare educated citizens who can undertake actions that spark change	1	2	3	4	5
17. To ensure the cultural richness and diversity of the United States	1	2	3	4	5
18. To help eliminate racism, sexism, anti-Semitism, and all forms of discrimination from society	1	2	3	4	5
19. To prepare as many students as possible for college and/or well-paid careers	1	2	3	4	5
20. To provide child care for the nation's children and to free parents to work and/or pursue their interests and activities	1	2	3	4	5

Assessing Your Choices

After reviewing your responses, choose the three goals you consider most important. Your choices reflect your values, just as throughout history different school goals have reflected the nation's ever-changing priorities. In the 1990s, improving school performance—both academically and in terms of international economic competition—was very high on the national agenda. Students are expected to be academically competent and well prepared for the world of work. Statements reflecting this view are clear in items 1, 13, and 14. How did you rate these? Do you agree with this current educational emphasis?

In other periods of American history, different goals have become important. The civil rights and student freedom goals (items 3, 17, and 18) were hallmarks of the 1960s and 1970s. While high marks here do not automatically make you a flower child, a commitment to individual rights and individual differences is captured in these three items.

Some goals rise and fall with the historical tide. For instance, item 17, ensuring cultural diversity, is once again important in schools as new waves of immigrants from Asia, Latin America, the Caribbean, and Eastern Europe join the many ethnic and racial groups already in the United States. If you scored high on this goal, you reflected a sensitivity to our nation's cultural diversity.

While diversity is often valued, so is the need to bind different cultures into a single nation. If you scored high on items 2 and 10, then you value the role schools serve in preparing Americans to adhere to a common set of principles and values. There have been times in our history when this has been a crucial role of schools—during the early forging of the nation, around the turn of the century as large numbers of immigrants arrived, and even today as Latin American, Asian, and other immigrants learn to adjust to the United States. This function of schools has sometimes been termed *"Americanization."*

One goal that has cast a long shadow over U.S. schools during most of the twentieth century, item 12 represents a commitment to national defense. During more than four decades of the Cold War, the focus of education was on national defense, on preparing soldiers to fight, engineers and scientists to build better weapons, and citizens to patriotically support the war effort. If you rated this high, you are responding to this education-defense connection of the past. Or are you ahead of your time, already predicting a potential enemy for the twenty-first century?

How did you rate items 15 and 19? Seeing schools as a step up, a route to social and economic advancement is part of the Horatio Alger folklore of the past. Many Americans have gone from poor to wealthy, from unknown to famous, because of their intellect and talent, developed in public schools and in college. However, critics charge that many students who enter school in poverty leave the same way. A high score here suggests your idealism is untarnished.

The goal of developing healthy citizens (item 4) was made popular by the ancient Greeks, who believed a sound mind and a sound body were necessarily linked. Our current interests in healthful foods, lifestyles, and exercise indicate the endurance of this goal.

Item 20 addresses the fact that the schools give parents free time to pursue work and other interests beyond child care. Few people see schools as babysitters, but without this service, most parents would be overwhelmed. And consider the impact the advent of millions of adolescents would have on the job market. Unemployment would skyrocket and wages would tumble. By minding the children, schools provide parents with time and keep our workforce down to a manageable size.

Teachers and the public do not always agree on these goals. For example, one of the most popular goals among teachers is item 7, developing strong student self-esteem. Teachers believe that if this is accomplished, students will succeed in their studies and beyond. Some education goals have never enjoyed great popularity. Goals that emphasize the needs of gifted students (item 6) or the development of creative and artistic talents (item 8) have rarely won popular support. However, many people do respond to what they see as urgent social needs (item 9). Today teenage pregnancy and AIDS are two such concerns. A few years ago the focus was on drug education and prevention. Before that, driver education was a pressing issue. How did your ratings compare to those of teachers and the general public? Do you find yourself influenced by current trends? Perhaps your ratings are more unique than popular, and you assigned a high priority to the education of gifted and talented students. Why do you think their needs fail to win significant public support?

Seeing the United States as a member of a community of nations (item 5) may be a more popular goal in the years ahead than it has been in the past. The same could be said for item 11, viewing the school as a center for an array of social services in addition to education. If you thought this goal to be important, you are in step with the most recent wave of reform recommendations. If you rated citizenship education (item 16) high, you are in step with schools throughout history. This goal has always garnered widespread support.

What did your ratings teach you about your values and how you view schools? Were your goals popular during particular periods of our history? Or are you more future-oriented? In a later chapter, you will have the opportunity to gain insight into your philosophy of education. You might want to compare your goal choices here with your philosophical preferences in Chapter 13. You may also want to consider whether you lean more toward a view of schools as transmitters of culture, or as change agents for restructuring society. How did you rate the following selected items?

Purpose of Schools			
Transmitting Culture		**Reconstructing Society**	
Focused Item	**Your Rating**	**Focused Item**	**Your Rating**
1	_____	3	_____
2	_____	5	_____
10	_____	9	_____
12	_____	15	_____
13	_____	16	_____
19	_____	18	_____
	Total _____		**Total** _____

Does your total score suggest that you favor one view of the purpose of schools over another? Are you more likely to be a preserver of the culture, or a reformer committed to change? If no clear philosophical leaning is apparent, read on. Actually, read on either way.

You may be wondering about the items not included on these two lists. These items often do not clearly fit into one or the other camp, because they are phrased in a very general way. For example, "developing a strong self-concept and self-esteem" needs further clarification. Is the strong self-concept needed in order to enable students to break out of fixed roles, to consider new options, and to move ahead (reconstructionist view), or in order to assure that they accept and take pride in the status quo (transmitting-culture view)?

Some would even question the appropriateness of some of these items. Are schools really intended to tackle areas such as self-esteem and child care, or are these responsibilities being mistakenly imposed on the school by a society desperate for solutions? That desperation became apparent in the early 1980s when the first in an avalanche of reports was published, indicting the nation's schools and calling for educational reform.

Education Reform

Our Nation is at risk. Our once unchallenged prominence in commerce, industry, science, and technological innovation is being overtaken by competitors throughout the world. This report is concerned with only one of the many causes and dimensions of the problem, but it is the one that undergirds American prosperity, security, and civility. We report to the American people that while we can take justifiable pride in what our schools and colleges have historically accomplished and contributed to the United States and the well-being of its people, the educational foundations of our society are presently being eroded by a rising tide of mediocrity that threatens our very future as a Nation and a people. What was unimaginable a generation ago has begun to occur—others are matching and surpassing our educational attainments.

If an unfriendly foreign power had attempted to impose on America the mediocre educational performance that exists today, we might well have viewed it as an act of war. As it stands, we have allowed this to happen to ourselves. We have even squandered the gains in student achievement made in the wake of the *Sputnik* challenge. Moreover, we have dismantled essential support systems which helped make those gains possible. We have, in effect, been committing an act of unthinking, unilateral educational disarmament.[7]

So began the report of the National Commission on Excellence in Education, *A Nation at Risk: The Imperative for Educational Reform,* released in 1983. The report cited declining test scores, the weak performance of U.S. students in comparison with those of other industrialized nations, and the number of functionally illiterate adults. *A Nation at Risk* condemned the "cafeteria-style curriculum." The report called for a more thorough grounding in the "five new basics" of English, mathematics, science, social science, and computer science. It called for greater academic rigor, higher expectations for students, better-qualified and better-paid teachers. It denounced:

- Watered-down curricula with too many electives
- Illiteracy
- Banal textbooks
- Poor teacher preparation and teacher pay
- Declining graduation standards
- The dropout rate
- Incompetent graduates

This report galvanized Americans, touched a vital nerve, and moved education to center stage. Remember, in 1983 the Cold War with the Soviet Union was still in full swing, and an economic war with Japan had opened up on yet another front. Both our economic well-being and military defense depended upon educated citizens, and the schools were not doing a very good job. With the battle cry sounded, a wave of reports followed (see Appendix 4 for a summary of the salient reform reports). Governors, state legislators, and foundations were mobilized. Within the next two years:

- Nearly 300 state panels were formed.
- More than 40 states increased course requirements for graduation.
- Thirty-three states instituted testing for student promotion or graduation.
- More than 700 state statutes were passed stipulating what should be taught, when it should be taught, how it should be taught, and who should do the teaching.
- Almost half the states passed legislation to increase qualification standards and pay for teachers.
- A majority of states increased the length of the school day and/or school year.
- Most states passed laws that required teachers and students to demonstrate computer literacy.[8]

But while state legislatures passed laws, many critics remained skeptical that such changes would truly improve education. They pointed out that these were top-down approaches, dictates from above and far removed from the real world of the classroom. Teachers felt dumped on (*teacher bashing* was the phrase used to protest this), controlled, and regulated by new rules and requirements. Other critics worried that these new regulations might do more harm than good. Increasing student graduation requirements without providing for special programs could hurt racial and ethnic minorities, non-English speakers, girls, special education students, and other groups not testing well. Different groups struggled to claim their place on the new list of educational priorities. To be left out of the goals for education reform could be costly indeed.[9]

The reform reports—and there were many—came in three waves (see Figure 5.2).

The first wave of reports seemed to view schools and education as a weapon. A stronger defense and a more competitive economy depended on a more educated population. Corporations could no longer afford to teach basic reading and math skills to employees, and the military needed more technically skilled personnel. The nation's well-being depended on its schools.

While there is some truth in this claim, there is some exaggeration as well. Other factors besides education have affected our economy. Lack of reinvestment in capital equipment and inefficient production costs, for example, also place us at an economic disadvantage. But Americans look to their schools to solve problems (both a blessing and a curse for those in the education profession), and schools have not been without fault. The first reform wave was a political battle cry for change.

A second wave of reform reports and books soon followed. These reports did not focus on political and economic issues but concerned themselves with the need to restructure education. These new publications were more likely to be written by educators rather than by politicians. Theodore Sizer, John Goodlad, and Ernest Boyer, all nationally recognized educational leaders, were part of this second wave. Based on more thorough research, these publications stressed the need to change practices at the school level, a bottom-up change.

FIGURE 5.2
Waves of Reform: 1982–Present

Wave I (1982–1985): "Raise the Standards"	Raise educational quality by requiring more courses and more testing of student and teacher performance. States were to assume the leadership in improving existing practices.
Wave II (1986–1991): "Restructure the School"	Again it was state governors who promoted Wave II reforms, which focused on school improvement and accountability. Teachers were to be empowered, given more control over their schools. Some of the educational problems confronting minority groups and some other students facing educational barriers were also addressed.
Wave III (1988–present): "Comprehensive Services"	In this, the most ambitious wave, reformers call for reformulating our notion of schools. Schools should be seen as more than educational facilities. They should also provide health care, social services, and transportation. In short, the whole array of services needed to bring the child into successful adulthood should be offered at the school: one-stop shopping for educational, social, medical, and other services.

Source: Adapted from Joseph Murphy, "The Educational Reform Movement of the 1980s: A Comprehensive Analysis," in Joseph Murphy (ed.), *The Educational Reform Movement of the 1980s* (Berkeley: McCutchan, 1990).

A byproduct of recent calls for educational reform has been an explosion of student (and teacher) testing to ensure that revised school goals are being met.

Gerald Grant, in his "schoolography" of Hamilton High, fits into this second wave. He calls for schools to shape their own destinies and for teachers to be given more power to reshape their schools. The second wave of reformers often criticized burgeoning central offices and cumbersome educational bureaucracies. They noted that rules, regulations, and directives have been showered upon schools and teachers. And, critics claimed, this loss of autonomy resulted in oppressive school climates, bland teaching, and poor academic performance. The second wave emphasized more thoughtful—but no less rigorous—change. It focused on reducing bureaucracy; creating a more professionally trained, treated, and salaried core of teachers; implementing local decision making; and strengthening the role of the school principal. Some authors refer to this as *empowering* teachers, principals, and even students. This second wave has led to many of the current attempts to restructure school organizations, including the use of choice plans, voucher systems, and charter schools, which we will explore in the next section.

The third wave, still underway in the 1990s, is the most radical and comprehensive. It looks beyond schools and focuses on the comprehensive needs of children. Nutrition, health care, transportation, and a host of other kinds of social and medical services are needed to ensure an effective education, according to these critics. In this third reform wave, schools are to become one-stop shopping centers for all of these services. Rather than referring to *school* policy and *school* boards, we will need to develop broader perspectives and more inclusive terminology, such as *children's* policy and *children's* boards. The school, according to third-wave reformers, will become a revitalized institution, the center in a network of social service agencies. Teachers may find themselves in ongoing discussions with social workers, state agency representatives, medical experts—all working together to bring children safely into successful and effective adulthood.

Presidents Reagan, Bush, and Clinton all promoted plans to reform and improve the nation's schools. President Bush worked with the nation's governors to develop six national education goals which were promoted under the "America 2000" plan. President Clinton's "Goals 2000" program encourages states to develop and implement their own educational standards and seeks attainment of national education goals by the year 2000. In addition to the original six referenced in America 2000, Goals 2000 includes 2 objectives for teacher development and parental involvement.

National Education Goals of Goals 2000

- All children in the United States will start school ready to learn.
- The high school graduation rate will increase to at least 90 percent.
- U.S. students will leave grades 4, 8, and 12 having demonstrated competency in a range of challenging subject matter that includes English, mathematics, science, history, and geography; and every school in the United States will ensure that all students learn to use their minds well, so that they may be prepared for responsible citizenship, further learning, and productive employment in our modern economy.
- U.S. students will be first in the world in science and mathematics achievement.
- Every adult American will be literate and will possess the knowledge and skills necessary to compete in a global economy and exercise the rights and responsibilities of citizenship.

- Every U.S. school will be free of drugs, unauthorized firearms, alcohol, and violence and will offer a disciplined environment conducive to learning.
- The nation's teaching force will have access to programs for the continued improvement of their professional skills and will be given the opportunity to acquire the knowledge and instructional skills needed for the next century.
- Every school will foster partnerships that will increase parental involvement and participation in promoting social, emotional, and academic growth of children.[10]

While few disagree with the importance of these goals, critics question how realistic they are. Is it realistic to believe that by the year 2000 we can increase the mathematics and science scores of U.S. students to *number one* in the world? Will *every* school eliminate drugs and violence by the year 2000? Can we achieve *100* percent adult literacy in less than a decade? Or are these not really goals at all; rather are they motivational devices?

Just as questions about the practicality and financing of Goals 2000 were being raised, a new, Republican-dominated Congress arrived in Washington with its own goals—goals that included decreasing the federal presence, increasing state responsibilities, and lowering the federal budget. Goals 2000, like most nonmilitary federal initiatives, came into conflict with the new, conservative agenda, and was put on a back burner. Whether the federal government will eventually lead a national movement to reform the nation's schools, or whether the states will be left with that task, or whether the reform itself will flounder and fade rests on the will of the people as expressed in future elections.

For a growing number of states and communities, the reform effort is already a case of too little, too late. Even teachers have been discouraged by the slow pace of reform. Five years after *A Nation at Risk* was published, a report released by the Carnegie Foundation revealed that 70 percent of over 13,000 teachers surveyed said that the national reform effort deserved a grade of C or less. About 20 percent of the teachers gave the reform movement a D or an F grade.[11] It is no wonder that, by the mid-1990s, communities across the United States were experimenting with their own ideas, creating dynamic new school structures, experimenting with new ways to organize and manage schools, and challenging the very concept of what it means to be a public school.

Beyond the Public School

In 1981, James Coleman released the results from his study showing that private schools seem to do a better job of educating students than public schools do. Students who attend these independent, sometimes religiously affiliated, private schools are not only better-behaved, they also score higher on tests. Coleman noted that private schools enforced more rigorous academic standards, were more intellectual, and gave teachers and administrators more autonomy. Private schools seemed to work; public schools were not working. A possible solution was apparent: Introduce private school practices to the public schools.

The idea of reshaping public schools by introducing private school concepts is not new. In the 1950s, economist Milton Friedman suggested that schools would be more effective if they functioned as a free market. Friedman believed that schools were not working well, even back then, because there

Authors' Corner: Reforming Education—Will It Work?

David: It's about time that national leaders took education seriously. These reform efforts are long overdue. I'm excited about all these changes.

Myra: It's good to see you so animated about education—but don't get overheated. These reforms are destined to fail.

David: How can you say that? Both Democratic and Republican administrations are supporting school reform. We finally made the national agenda. Look to the horizon, Myra. There are big changes coming from the White House and from Congress.

Myra: You got that right. Politics.

David: What do you mean?

Myra: Goals 2000, America 2000, what's next—Pan America 2000? Americation 2000? School, Business, Progress 2050? National slogans have a placebo effect—they make us feel like we are doing something, and eventually we forget that nothing ever happened.

David: Wait a second, there you go again! Look at teacher certification requirements. One college after another has eliminated undergraduate teacher education and required that tomorrow's teachers have a bachelor's degree in an academic area and a master's degree in teacher preparation. What we have now is rampant professionalism.

Myra: What we have is runaway confusion. Look at all the colleges that are keeping their undergraduate education programs. Some states are actually going in the opposite direction and letting people teach with almost no professional preparation. What do you tell tomorrow's teachers? Get a master's—or get no degree at all—and we'll hire you. That's not growing professionalism—that's schizophrenia.

David: But what about the National Board for Professional Teaching Standards? For the first time, we will be able to recognize professionalism—those talented, experienced teachers. It's like medicine—board-certified professionals.

Myra: If the board devises a way to identify really competent professionals—and I'm not sold on that yet—how will these professionals be rewarded? More responsibility? More money? Will they be placed in positions to influence other teachers and enhance teaching? I doubt it. I can hear these faculty meetings now—"Listen to me, I'm board-certified! Please, somebody, listen to me! Anybody!"

David: You are depressing me. You're also forgetting about the new tougher standards for students. States are now testing to make certain that graduation means something. No more 4 years of high school and out. Now students need to show that they've learned something.

Myra: The reformers just don't get it. More testing is

was no competition, no incentive for them to do their best. Parents sent their children to the neighborhood school, the school paid its educators, and a monopoly was created. Because they could afford private school tuition, wealthy parents could bail out if the public school was performing poorly, but poor parents were trapped. According to Friedman, the use of educational vouchers could level the playing field. Vouchers would be given to parents. Parents could "shop" for a school, choose the best one, and give the voucher to the school. The school would then turn the voucher over to the local or state government, and the government would pay the school a fixed sum for each voucher. The more vouchers, the more money a school would get. In this plan, good schools would thrive, while poor schools would not attract "customers" and would go out of business. Some voucher plans would give parents the choice of selecting either a public or private school, while other plans would limit the choice to only public schools. For decades critics have advanced the idea of creating a more competitive school system.

During the reform efforts of the 1980s—and because of tumbling test scores, increased violence, and seemingly unresponsive public school bureaucracy—ideas like the voucher system became more appealing. In 1988, Minnesota instituted "open enrollment," which, similar to the voucher system,

not the answer. That's the same old top-down approach: teach, memorize, test. Some reform! What ever happened to imagination? To American ingenuity? We are increasing the bureaucratic trappings of schools, rather than focusing on education.

David: How would you reform national education? Doesn't that mean making schools work better? Are you quibbling about words?

Myra: I don't know what it means, but I doubt that one answer will do the trick. It's a national challenge, but a local solution. We need faith in local educators, not new names, new tests, new hurdles! We need a different approach.

David: Now I'm really confused.

Myra: I think we need to get the best people into schools as principals and teachers and then wipe the slate clean. No 50-minute periods. No avalanche of rules being issued from faraway places—or even not so far away. Create cooperative work environments and let the educators develop solutions. I don't have the answers, but I have a starting point:

- *Qualified professionals,* paid well in dollars and afforded popular support.
- *Local solutions* rather than national standards.
- *Teachers, not politicians, at the center of change*—their creativity nurtured through cooperation.
- *Opportunities to try new approaches,* even if they don't work. Give us the right to fail and to learn from our mistakes.
- *Time for teachers and principals to plan programs,* to talk to each other, learn, grow, and get rewarded. Maybe even pay teams of teachers rather than paying individual teachers, and foster creative cooperation rather than teacher isolation.

David: Ambitious plans—but you don't know the outcome. Will test scores go up? Will our students do as well as others on international math and science tests? You lack measures for success, national standards, and markers of progress.

Myra: I have faith in teachers. Give them the tools, and let them do the job. And by the way, look at the bright side, no more silly names like "Education 3000" to memorize. We need to put our faith in people, not slogans.

Source: Adapted from David L. Clark and Terry A. Astuto, "Redirecting Reform: Challenges to Popular Assumptions About Teachers and Students," *Phi Delta Kappan* 75, no. 7 (March 1994): 512–520.

encouraged parents to choose the best schools they could find, regardless of location. The closest school no longer had a monopoly on neighborhood children. Arkansas, Iowa, Nebraska, and other states soon followed Minnesota's lead, and began introducing open enrollment legislation. Supportive politicians and educators echoed Friedman's original idea: Competition will strengthen schools. However, not everyone was sold on the idea of a "free market system." Critics warned that the hardest-to-educate students would be left behind in underfunded public schools. Others believed that forcing schools to compete for limited resources was not the answer; they argued that all schools would improve only with greater funding. Advocates of open enrollment countered that dollars for public schools were being wasted on inefficient schools and bloated bureaucracies. For some, neither vouchers nor open enrollment would give results fast enough. They demanded yet another innovation: *charter schools.*

In 1991, Minnesota was also the first state to enact charter school legislation. California followed in 1992, and by 1993 almost 100 charter schools had opened their doors. The charter school concept is simple. Rather than waiting for a voucher or open enrollment, a group—almost any group—petitions to establish its own school. The group could be parents, teachers, a university,

Today, 19 states, including New Jersey, have a law allowing public funding for charter schools, which operate outside normal public school channels to satisfy specific educational goals of the founding group.

even a private company. Each state has different rules as to who can create such a school, and how many charter schools can exist. In some states, only public schools may become charter schools, while in other states a charter school may be established by almost any group. In some states, local school boards are empowered to approve charter schools. In other states, only the state government may grant such a charter. Typical reasons for establishing a charter school might include the desire to improve academic performance or attendance, to explore a new organizational approach or teaching strategy, or to extend the hours of the school day or the length of the school year. While charter schools must follow some of the same rules established for other publicly funded schools (for example, health and safety regulations, agreement not to discriminate), charter schools are exempt from many state and local laws and regulations. The charter (or contract) represents legal permission for the school to break with the past, to try new ways to educate, and to do so with tax dollars. In St. Paul, Minnesota, for example, the City Academy is a year-round charter school serving 40 at-risk students. Metro Deaf is a charter school serving deaf students, while the Teamsters Union and the Minnesota Business Partnership sponsor a vocational and technical school, called "Skills for Tomorrow," that uses internship placements to educate students interested in becoming skilled workers. The Bennett Valley Charter School in California focuses on home-based learning to educate students. While the range of charter school activities is broad, controls are also in place. If the school fails—and accountability for charter schools is typically stronger than it is for other tax-supported schools—then the local or state government retains the right to close the school. Some states have done just that.

But the establishment of charter schools was not the only route to radical reform. A number of school districts—especially urban districts like Hartford, Connecticut, and Baltimore, Maryland—contracted with newly formed companies to take over the management of already existing public schools. Companies such as Educational Alternatives, Inc., (EAI) of Minneapolis and the Edison Project of Knoxville, Tennessee, were created not only to educate students better than the public school system could, but to make a profit doing it. Not that the entrance of private companies onto the public educational scene is completely new. For years, school districts have contracted with private businesses to provide school lunches or bus transportation. But to provide education itself, to be responsible for academic performance, now *that* was new for public schools. Sometimes private companies carefully designed the most effective strategies for entering the education market; other times, educational innovation emerged from chance encounters. For example, in 1990, Benno Schmidt, the president of Yale University, was attending a party in the Hamptons, a posh section of Long Island. At that party, Schmidt met Chris Whittle, an entrepreneur who was involved with various education-related projects. Apparently, they hit it off. Whittle offered Schmidt a high salary, reported to be at about $1 million a year, to leave Yale and assume leadership of the *Edison Project*. The Edison Project was a company formed to implement Whittle's idea for designing a research-based, well-planned private school that would serve as a model for other schools. Once the school was up and running, Whittle wanted to franchise the model nationally. But the costs were enormous, and the franchise idea was not easy to implement. As states began to create charter schools, Whittle saw another, easier way to disseminate his schools.[12]

The Edison Project called for lengthening the school day by 1 or 2 hours, while increasing the school year from 180 days to 210 days. Curricular changes included more school time being spent on math and science, the use of learning contracts to increase student accountability, ethical instruction, and an increased emphasis on reading Great Books. Each student would eventually be linked to the school by a home computer. The computer would give students a virtual library in their homes, and offer both parents and students a constant communications link to teachers. By 1995, the Edison Project had signed contracts with schools in Kansas, Colorado, Texas, Michigan, Ohio, Florida, Hawaii, and Massachusetts. Even though public schools were buying into the Edison concept, questions about the financial stability of the Whittle educational empire persisted.

Other companies were less ambitious in redesigning schools and creating entirely new school programs, but felt that they could nevertheless do a better job than current public school administrators do. In 1994, Hartford, Connecticut, made national news by hiring EAI to manage all of its schools. EAI's primary focus was on cost-effectiveness, which it accomplished by performing regular school operations more economically. The costs of maintenance, supplies, security, transportation, and food contracts—even the salaries paid to teaching consultants—were scaled back, producing a lower school budget overall.

School officials appreciated the cost-cutting efforts of companies such as EAI. They also applauded the improved appearance of schools after private companies invested some money to clean up and dress up the deteriorating inner-city school buildings. The notion was that a more efficient private company—such as EAI—could save the system money, provide schools with more computers, and provide teachers with additional training. The promise of improved academic performance through more efficient school management was just over the horizon. Yet by 1995, questions were being raised about EAI's ability to deliver on its promises as Baltimore and Hartford school districts terminated their contracts with EAI.

Parents' Report Card on Choice

In 1993, 20 percent of children attended schools their families selected (11 percent chose a public school option, 9 percent a private school option). The majority of students, 80 percent, continued to attend the school "assigned" to them. Here are some interesting characteristics of the 20 percent of parents who chose their children's school:

Race Differences

- Black students were more likely than white students to attend a school their parents chose.

Major Reason for Selection of School

- The most common reason for selecting a school was related to ensuring a better academic environment.

Why Do Parents Choose a Private School?

- The second reason, after academics, for choosing a private school concerned moral or religious factors.

Why Do Parents Select a Public School?

- For those parents selecting a public school, the second reason, after academics, was convenience.

Satisfaction Rates

- Over 80 percent of parents who selected their child's public school were positive about their choice.
- Over 90 percent of the parents who selected a private school for their child indicated that they were happy with their selection.

Source: M. C. Rubenstein, R. Hamar, and N. E. Adelman, *Minnesota's Open Enrollment Option* (Washington, DC: Policy Studies Associates, 1992); M. F. Williams, K. S. Hanscher, and A. Huner, *Parents and School Choice: A Household Survey* (Washington, DC: U.S. Department of Education, OERI, 1983).

But the business community has not been timid about investing in public education. The Edison Project, for example, invested at least $40 million in just the start-up phase, and John Walton, son of Walmart founder Sam Walton, invested heavily in EAI, two strong signs indicating the size of the potential profits to be made in the privatization of public schools.[13] Even Walt Disney has entered the school business. In a project called "Celebration," located near Disney World in Florida, the Disney company has joined forces with the Osceola County school district and Stetson University to build and operate a state-of-the-art school. The school will be part of a new residential community "inspired by the main streets of small-town America and reminiscent of Norman Rockwell images."[14] While the community will be visually evocative of an earlier period, the school will also be designed to bring the future closer to today. Disney donated $11 million for the school itself and another $9 million for the creation of an adjacent teaching academy, a place where teachers can be trained in the new techniques and strategies that will be used at the Celebration school. The school district has promised an additional sum of over $15 million to build this "school of tomorrow."

Vouchers, open enrollments, charter schools, privatization, and even the Disney foray into public schools are more than striking examples of public dissatisfaction with the current performance of public schools; they represent the emergence of a growing free market system in the nation's schools. A 1989 Gallup poll found that "the public favors by a two to one margin allowing students and parents to choose which public schools in their communities students will attend."[15] Other studies have shown that as many as 88 percent of African Americans favor choice plans, and that the highest support, 95 percent, comes from families earning less than $15,000 a year.[16] The majority of Americans believe that competition and choice can radically reshape U.S. schools, that a free market economy can redefine public education. Others, including many teachers, hold serious reservations about this approach. Both the National Education Association (NEA) and the American Federation of Teachers (AFT) have criticized many private sector initiatives. NEA president Keith Geiger warned about the incompatibility of "the merchants of greed" with education, and the AFT was openly critical of EAI's Baltimore program, which reduced the wages of paraprofessionals from $12.50 to $7.25 an hour.[17] Some educators warn that the nation's neediest students are the very ones least likely to receive attention and resources in a free market system. Whatever the final resolution, it is likely that public education will undergo fundamental restructuring in the years ahead.

SUMMARY

1. Since their inception, public schools have tried to be all things to all people. Parents, teachers, and students alike expect schools to meet academic, vocational, social, civic, and personal goals. The particulars of these goals are debated constantly, often resulting in bitter disputes. Perhaps nowhere else in our country do personal and societal values conflict so much as when communities examine their schools.

2. People have a myriad of goals and expectations for schools. These include: protecting the national economy and defense; unifying a multicultural society; preparing students for the world of work; improving academic competence; encouraging tolerance for diversity; and providing social and economic mobility, among others.

3. Two fundamental, often-opposing, purposes of schools are to *transmit* society's knowledge and values, passing on the cultural baton, and to *reconstruct* society, empowering students to engineer social change as adults—and, sometimes, as students.

4. The 1983 report *A Nation at Risk* triggered a renewed interest in the quality of public schooling. In response to declining test scores and poor student achievement, measured by worldwide standards, the report called for many back-to-basics measures. A deluge of reports and recommendations ensued, mostly supporting tighter regulation of schools. These reports—the "first wave"—emphasized using schools as tools to transmit rather than reconstruct the culture.

5. A second wave of reports, by Sizer, Goodlad, Boyer, and others, focused on strategies to strengthen the profession and restructure education. These reports and books spring from lengthy observations and research, and focus on empowering educators at the school level, a bottom-up change.

6. The third wave of reform reports viewed the school as a comprehensive institution providing social, medical, and other services to children. Education would be linked to a broader array of student needs, and the child would be the focus of reform.

7. Goals 2000 was President Clinton's plan to enhance the quality of instruction and the performance of U.S. students on a national scale. Congressional budget-cutting, the ambitiousness of the goals identified, and differences among the states jeopardized the long-term effectiveness of this program.

8. Some critics believe that the avalanche of national reports and reform efforts will never be effective, that true reform can only occur at the local, school-district level. Such thinking has fueled a new approach, represented by innovations such as charter schools and the privatization of public schools. Some educators and parents question these innovations as well, and doubt that they will, in the long run, change schools for the better.

DISCUSSION QUESTIONS AND ACTIVITIES

1. Discuss your list of school goals that you recorded with your classmates. Which goals seem to be most important to your classmates? To your instructor? Which do you consider most important? Give reasons for your priorities.
2. Do you believe schools should transmit society's knowledge and values, or do you think schools should prepare students to change society? Find someone of the opposing opinion and hold an informal debate.
3. Summarize the past decade of education reform. What do you think the next reform report will be like?
4. If you were charged with writing a national report on education reform, what would you advocate?
5. Support the statement "More testing is good for American education." Now refute it.
6. Do you agree with the concerns expressed in *A Nation at Risk?*
7. Goals 2000 has won both ardent support and harsh criticism. Identify three arguments supporting and three arguments opposing Goals 2000.
8. Do you agree that every school reflects a value system? What value system did your elementary school reflect? Your secondary school? Your college or university?
9. Imagine you are a school board member and your district is debating whether to move to an open enrollment or to a voucher system. Defend your opinion in a brief memo.
10. If you were to design a charter school, what would it look like? What students would you recruit? What would you look for in your teaching faculty? Would you have a unique physical plan for your building?

NOTES

1. James Shaver and William Strong, *Facing Value Decisions: Rationale Building for Teachers* (Belmont, CA: Wadsworth, 1976).
2. Ernest L. Boyer, *High School: A Report on Secondary Education in America,* The Carnegie Foundation for the Advancement of Teaching (New York: Harper & Row, 1983), pp. 209–210.
3. Paulo Freire, *The Pedagogy of the Oppressed* (New York: Herder & Herder, 1970).
4. John Goodlad, *A Place Called School* (New York: McGraw-Hill, 1984), pp. 35–39.
5. Arthur Eugene Bestor, *Educational Wastelands: The Retreat from Learning in our Public Schools* (Urbana: University of Illinois Press, 1953), p. 75.
6. Boyer, *High School,* p. 5.
7. National Commission on Excellence in Education, *A Nation at Risk: The Imperative for Educational Reform* (Washington, DC: U.S. Government Printing Office, 1983), p. 1.
8. David Hill, "Fixing the System from the Top Down," *Teacher Magazine,* September–October 1989, pp. 50–55.
9. Donald C. Ohlrich, "Education Reforms: Mistakes, Misconceptions, Miscues," *Phi Delta Kappan* 170, no. 7 (March 1989): 512–517.

10. *America 2000: An Education Strategy* (Washington, DC: U.S. Department of Education, 1991); see also Julie Miller, "Clinton, in Attacking Bush's Policies, Pledges 'Real Education Reform' Plan," *Education Week,* May 17, 1992, p. 17; Richard W. Riley, "Reflections on Goals 2000," *Teachers College Record,* 96, no. 3 (Spring 1995): 380–388.

11. Henry J. Perkinson, *The Imperfect Panacea: American Faith in Education* (New York: McGraw-Hill, 1995), p. 191.

12. Joel Spring, *American Education* (New York: McGraw-Hill, 1996), pp. 184–185.

13. Mark Walsh, "Question[s?] About Finances Put Edison Project at Crossroad," *Education Week* 13, no. 40 (August 3, 1994): 18–19; Walter Farrell, Jr., James Johnson, Cloyzelle Jones, and Marty Sapp, "Will Privatizing Schools Really Help Inner-City Students of Color?," *Educational Leadership* 52, no. 1 (September 1994): 72–75.

14. Mark Walsh, "Disney Holds Up School as Model for Next Century," *Education Week* XIII, no. 39 (June 22, 1994): 1, 16.

15. Quoted in Perkinson, *The Imperfect Panacea,* p. 198.

16. Pedro Noguerar, "More Democracy Not Less: Confronting the Challenge of Privatization in Public Education," *Journal of Negro Education* 623, no. 2 (1994): 238.

17. Spring, *American Education,* pp. 185–186.

6

LIFE IN SCHOOLS

The phrase the medium is the message *applies to all forms of mass communication, including schools. By participating in the "medium" of schools—that is, in their environment and basic structure—you inevitably receive subtle messages about the ways teachers are expected to teach and students are expected to learn. These come through loud and clear as you travel from English to math to chemistry every 50 minutes, or as you respond to questions from teachers but seldom ask any of your own. Listening to an hour-long psychology lecture results in mental notes about teaching, as well as written notes about psychology. Being tracked into an advanced class or a remedial section tells you much about schools—and about yourself as a learner. From the moment you first entered school, you have been immersed in an informal and subtle network of interactions that forms a big part of your school's culture.*

This chapter will take you beyond academics to the lesser-known three Rs (rules, rituals, and routine). It also analyzes the subtle dynamics of classroom communication and the role of peer groups, especially within adolescent society. It asks you to assess some of the political realities of schools, such as tracking, and to consider what impact these may have on students. Finally, the chapter summarizes the five factors associated with effective schools and offers examples of each of these factors.

Rules, Rituals, and Routine

"Come Right up and Get Your New Books": A Teacher's Perspective

Dick Thompson looked at the pile of new poetry anthologies stacked on his desk and sighed wearily. Getting new texts distributed and starting a new unit always seemed like such a chaotic ordeal, particularly with seventh graders. But worrying over possible mishaps wouldn't get this new poetry unit launched. Besides, it looked as though the students were getting restless, so he had better get things started.

"Okay, class, quiet down. As you can see, the poetry books we've been waiting for have finally arrived. All right, you can cut out the groans. Give the books a fair trial before you sentence them. I'd like the first person in each row to come up, count out enough books for his or her row, and hand them out."

Students sitting in the first seat of their row charged to the front and made a mad grab for the books. In the ensuing melee, one stack of books went crashing to the floor.

"Hey, kids, take it easy and stop the squabbling. There are plenty of books to go around. Since this procedure obviously isn't working, we'll just have to slow down and do things one row at a time. Bob, you hand out the books for row 1 first, then Sally will come up and get the books for row 2. It will take a little longer this way, but I think things will go more smoothly. When you get your texts, write your name and room number in the stamped box inside the cover."

Since the dispensing of books now seemed to be progressing in an orderly fashion, Mr. Thompson turned his attention to the several hands that he saw waving in the air.

"Yes, Barbara?"

"I can't fill in my name because my pencil just broke. Can I sharpen it?"

"Go ahead. Jim?"

What is the hidden curriculum in teacher-dominated classrooms where teachers actively talk and move about while students passively sit and listen?

"My pencil's broken too. Can I sharpen mine?"

"Yes, but wait until Barbara sits down. Let me remind you that you're supposed to come to class prepared. Now there will be no more at the pencil sharpener today. Bill?"

"Can I use the lav pass?"

"Is this absolutely necessary? All right then (responding to Bill's urgent nod). Now I think we've had enough distraction for one morning. The period's half over and we still haven't gotten into today's lesson. After you get your book and fill in the appropriate information, turn to the poem on page 3. It's called 'Stopping by Woods on a Snowy Evening,' and it's by Robert Frost, one of America's most famous poets. Yes, Donna?"

"I didn't get a book."

"Alan, didn't you hand out books to your row? Oh, I see. We're one short. Okay, Donna, go down to the office and tell Mrs. Goldberg that we need one more of the new poetry anthologies. Now, as I was about to say, I'd like you to think about the questions that I've written on the board: How does the speaker in this poem feel as he looks at the snow filling up the deserted woods? Why does he wish to stop, and what makes him realize that he must go on? The speaker says, 'I have miles to go before I sleep.' He may be talking about more than going to bed for the night. What else may 'sleep' mean in this poem? Yes, Bill, do you have a comment on the poem already?"

"My glasses are being fixed and I can't read the board."

"All right. Take the seat by my desk. You'll see the board from there. April! Maxine! This is not a time for your private gabfest. This is a silent reading activity—and I do mean silent. Okay, class, I think most of you have had enough time to read the poem. Who has an answer for the first question? Tom?"

"Well, I think the guy in this poem really likes nature. He's all alone, and it's private, with no people around to interrupt him, and he thinks the woods and the snow are really beautiful. It's sort of spellbinding."

"Tom, that's an excellent response. You've captured the mood of this poem. Now for the second question. Maxine?"

"I think he wants to stop because. . . ."

Maxine's answer was cut short by the abrasive ring of the fourth-period bell.

"Class, sit down. I know the bell has rung, but it isn't signaling a fire. You'll have time to make your next class. Since we didn't get as far into our discussion as I had hoped, I want to give you an assignment. For homework, I'd like you to answer the remaining questions. Alice?"

"Is this to hand in?"

"Yes. Sue?"

"Should this be done in pen or pencil?"

"I don't care, as long as it's legible. Besides, it's the quality of your answers I'm concerned about—not the nature of your writing instrument. Any other questions? Okay, you'd better get to your next-period class."

As the last student left, Dick Thompson slumped over his desk and wearily ran his fingers through his hair. As he looked down, he spotted the missing poetry anthology under his desk, a victim of the charge of the book brigade. He thought he had counted out enough texts from the supply room. As a matter of fact, the whole lesson was a victim of the book brigade. He had been so busy getting the books dispensed and fielding all the interruptions that he had forgotten to give his brief explanation on the differences between prose and poetry. He had even forgotten to give his motivating speech on how interesting the new poetry unit was going to be. Well, no time for a postmortem now. Stampedelike noises outside the door meant the fourth-period class was about to burst in.

"Come Right up and Get Your New Books": A Student's Perspective

From her vantage point in the fourth seat, fifth row, Maxine eyed the stack of new books on the teacher's desk. She knew they were poetry books because she had flipped through one as she wandered into the room. She didn't care that it wasn't "in" to like poetry; she liked it anyway. At least it was better than the grammar unit they'd just been through. All those sentences to diagram—picking out nouns and pronouns—what a drag that was.

Maxine settled into her seat, began the long wait for her book, and thought about the situation: "Mr. Thompson seems like he's in some kind of daze, just staring at the new books like he's hypnotized or something. Wonder what's bugging him. At last the first kids in each row are heading up to get the books. Oh, brother, they're getting into a brawl over handing out the stupid books. What a bunch of phonies; they must think they're funny or something. Now it'll be one row at a time and will take forever. I suppose I can start my math homework or write some letters."

Maxine got several of her math problems solved by the time her poetry anthology arrived, along with instructions to read the poem on page 3. She skimmed through the poem and decided she liked it. She understood how Robert Frost felt watching the snowy woods and wanting to get away from all the hassles. It sure would be nice to read this poem quietly somewhere without listening to kids going on about pencil sharpeners and lav passes and seat changes. All these interruptions made it hard to concentrate.

As she turned around to share her observation about hassles with April Marston, Mr. Thompson's sharp reprimand interrupted her. She fumed to herself: "Private gabfest. Hmpf. Half the class is talking, and old Eagle Eyes Thompson has to pick on me. And they're all talking about the football game Saturday. At least I was talking about the poem. Oh, well, I'd better answer one of those questions on the board and show him that I really am paying attention."

Maxine waved her hand wildly, but Tom got called for question 1. Maxine shot her hand in the air again for a chance at question 2. When Mr. Thompson called on her, she drew a deep breath and began her response. Once again she was interrupted in midsentence, this time by the fourth-period bell. Disgruntled, she stuffed her poetry book under her arm and fell into step beside April Marston.

"I really knew the answer to that question," she muttered under her breath. "Now we have to write all the answers out. What a drag. Well, next period is science and we're supposed to be giving reports. Maybe we'll have a chance to finish the English homework there."

Delay and Social Distraction

You have just read two capsular replays of a seventh-grade English lesson, one from the vantage point of the teacher, the other from the vantage point of a student. Although the time and the place are identical, the different roles Mr.

Thompson and Maxine play cause them to have very different experiences in this class. In what ways is the same class experienced differently by teacher and student?

One difference you may have noted is that Mr. Thompson was continually leapfrogging from one minor crisis to the next, while Maxine was sitting and waiting. In his perceptive book *Life in Classrooms,* Philip W. Jackson describes how time is spent in elementary school.[1] He suggests that whereas teachers are typically very busy, students are often caught in patterns of delay that force them to do nothing. Jackson goes on to note that a great deal of teachers' time is spent in noninstructional busywork such as keeping time and dispensing supplies. For example, in the slice of classroom life that you just read, Mr. Thompson spent a substantial part of the class time distributing new texts. Indeed, most teachers spend a good deal of time giving out things: paper, pencils, art materials, science materials, exam booklets, erasers, gold stars, special privileges—the list goes on and on. Teachers also select those who will take roll, collect milk money, or take messages to the office. The classroom scene described also shows Mr. Thompson greatly involved in timekeeping activities. Within the limits set by school buzzers and bells, he determines when the texts will be distributed, when and for how long the reading activity will take place, and when the class discussion will begin.

What do students do while teachers are busy organizing, structuring, talking, questioning, handing out, collecting, timekeeping, and crisis hopping? According to Jackson's analysis, they do little more than sit and wait.[2] They wait for the materials to be handed out, for the assignment to be given, for the questions to be asked, for the teacher to call on them, for the teacher to react to their response, for the slower class members to catch up so that the activity can change. They wait in lines to get drinks of water, to get pencils sharpened, to get to the playground, to get to the bathroom, to be dismissed from class. If students are to succeed in school, they must be able to cope with continual delay as a standard operating procedure.

A corollary of this waiting game is denial of desire. Common examples of denied requests include lav passes, a drink of water, use of the pencil sharpener, and being called upon to answer a question. One desire that is rarely granted is that of talking to classmates. Like the character from Greek mythology, Tantalus, who was continually tempted with food and water but was not allowed to eat or drink, students are surrounded by peers and friends but are restrained from communicating with them. In other words, students in the classroom are in the very frustrating position of having to ignore social temptation, of acting as though they are isolated despite the crowd surrounding them. Furthermore, while trying to concentrate on work and ignore social temptations, students are beset by frequent interruptions—the public address system blaring a message in the middle of an exam, the end-of-class bell interrupting a lively discussion, a teacher's reprimand or a student's question derailing a train of thought during silent reading.

Consider how Maxine in Mr. Thompson's English class had to cope with delay, denial of desire, social distraction, and interruptions. She waited for the delivery of her new text. She waited to be called on by the teacher. Her attempt to concentrate on reading the poem was disturbed by frequent interruptions. Her brief communication with a classmate was interrupted by a reprimand. Her head was filled with ideas and questions. In short, there was a lot she would like to have said, but there was almost no opportunity to say it.

The Teacher as Timekeeper

Educators concerned about school improvement have called attention to the inefficient use of time in school, claiming that we lose between one-quarter and one-half of the time available for learning through attendance problems, noninstructional activities such as class changes and assemblies, administrative and organizational activities, and disruptions caused by student misbehavior.[3] Educational researcher Herbert Walberg is even more pessimistic, claiming that while school comprises 13 percent of the waking life of the child's first 18 years, children spend only 3 to 6 percent of their time actively engaged in learning.[4]

In a major study of schools, John Goodlad found a fair degree of consistency in how time is allocated to different activities as children go through the grades. In the early elementary years 2.27 percent of time is allocated to social activities, 5.52 percent to behavior management, 18.99 percent to routines, and 73.22 percent to instruction. By the senior high level, 2.20 percent of time is spent on social activities, 1.29 percent on behavior management, 20.39 percent on routines, and 76.12 percent on instruction.

Although there was relative consistency in time distribution at the different levels of schooling, one of the most astonishing things Goodlad found was the enormous variation in the efficiency with which different schools use time, ranging from a low of 18.5 hours per week allocated to subject-matter learning in one school to a high of 27.5 hours in another. Goodlad was also surprised at the limited amount of time spent on the academic staples such as reading and writing. He found that only 6 percent of time in elementary school is spent on reading. This drops to a minuscule 2 percent at the high school level. In contrast, the amount of time students spend listening to teacher lectures and explanations increases from approximately 18 percent in elementary school to more than 25 percent in high school.[5]

Part of the hidden curriculum of schools is the "culture of waiting" that accompanies the many transition periods throughout the day.

In the Beginning Teacher Evaluation Study, sponsored by the National Institute of Education, researchers also analyzed how time is spent in schools. They found that about 58 percent of the school day is allocated to academic subject matter; 23 percent to music, art, and other nonacademic subjects; and approximately 19 percent of time to noninstructional activities. This study also found a great range in how different teachers allocate time to subject-matter learning.[6]

As you can see, many researchers have spent a lot of their own time analyzing time in schools. Why? Because, as one teacher says, "Time is the currency of teaching. We barter with time. Every day we make small concessions, small trade-offs, but, in the end, we know it's going to defeat us. After all, how many times are we actually able to cover World War I in our history courses before the year is out? We always laugh a little about that, but the truth is the sense of the clock ticking is one of the most oppressive features of teaching."[7]

There is a limited amount of time set aside for the school day. When this valuable resource is spent reprimanding misbehavior, it is lost for learning. Research shows that when more time is allocated to subject-matter learning, student achievement increases. In plain and simple terms, when teachers spend more time teaching reading, students become better readers. Teachers who are skilled at basic classroom management routines have more time available to do what is most fundamental—teach. Looked at from this perspective, Mr. Thompson's class was not only frustrating, it also deprived students of a precious and limited resource—the time to learn.

One of the functions that keeps Mr. Thompson and most other teachers busiest is what Philip Jackson terms *gatekeeping*. As gatekeepers, teachers must determine who will talk, when, and for how long, as well as the basic direction of the communication. In short, teachers stay busy directing both the verbal and nonverbal flow of classroom communication. Since this function is so critical to the teacher's role, we shall look at it a little more closely.

Classroom Interaction

Jackson reports that teachers are typically involved in more than 1,000 verbal exchanges with their students every day.[8] That is a lot of talking, enough to give even the strongest vocal chords a severe case of laryngitis. Count the number of verbal exchanges Mr. Thompson had with his students during our abbreviated classroom scene and you will get some idea of how much and how often teachers talk.

Researcher Ned Flanders developed an instrument called *Flanders Interaction Analysis* (see Figure 1 in Appendix 1) with which he was able to categorize student and teacher verbal behavior. The instrument tells a great deal about the nature and quality of classroom verbal interaction.

As a result of applying his interaction analysis instrument in classroom settings involving 147 teachers, Flanders came up with "the rule of two-thirds." He found that someone is talking during two-thirds of the classroom time. For approximately two-thirds of that time, the person doing the talking is the teacher. Two-thirds of teacher talk is what Flanders calls "direct" talk and includes lecturing and giving directions. Flanders suggests that this two-thirds pattern has unfortunate consequences in that students are forced into a passive role that eventually results in negative attitudes, lower achievement, and a general dependency on the teacher.[9]

Arno Bellack, another researcher, uses a game analogy to describe classroom language patterns. He determined that the language game is composed of the following cycles:

1. Structuring (or setting up the dialogue)
2. Soliciting (or questioning)
3. Responding (answering the questions)
4. Reacting (commenting on the accuracy and quality of the response)

Bellack found that teachers are responsible for most of the moves in the language game—they structure, solicit, and react. In contrast, student participation in this game of language is typically confined to responding to teachers' questions. Bellack found that teachers initiate about 85 percent of these verbal cycles and that they speak approximately three times as many lines of dialogue as do students.[10] In short, as teachers structure the game and control the moves, students are relegated to the passive role of responding to questions.

John Goodlad said that a snapshot of classrooms taken at random would in all likelihood show teachers talking and questioning and students listening and responding. Further, observations in 1,000 classrooms showed that teachers interact less and less with students as they go through the grades. The elementary classroom is more interactive than the high school one; the high school classroom is more interactive than the college. Most students play a more passive role in classroom interaction at the end of the schooling process than at its beginning. Ironically, interviews with students show that they are happiest when they are actively involved in their learning.[11]

An enormous amount of research has focused on the questioning aspect of Bellack's cycles of classroom language. Clearly, questions have been and still are the basis of much classroom talk. Teachers ask a tremendous number of them. An early study showed that teachers of young children asked between three and six questions per minute.[12] More recent studies revealed that elementary school teachers average 348 questions a day. Further, research shows that most of these questions require that students use only rote memory in formulating their responses.[13] Few questions ask students to be creative or to use more complex levels of thought.

Although teachers ask a tremendous number of questions, they exhibit very little patience in waiting for student response. After teachers ask a question, they typically wait only 1 second, and if an answer is not forthcoming within that second, they usually rephrase the question or call on another student. When questions are asked at this "bombing rate," students have hardly any time to think or to construct well-developed and fluent responses. In fact, if teachers are taught to wait 3 to 5 seconds after asking a question, there will be significant positive changes in the quality of student responses. Students will give longer, more complex, and more appropriate answers, and they will exhibit more confidence in their comments.[14]

Ironically, while a major goal of education is to increase students' curiosity and quest for knowledge, it is the teachers, not the students, who do the questioning. Although students do raise questions about the mechanics of

The classroom language game, where teachers talk and students listen, may encourage passivity and boredom.

The Patterns of the Classroom

After observing in more than 1,000 classrooms, John Goodlad and his team of researchers found that the following patterns characterize most classrooms:

- Much of what happens in class is geared toward maintaining order among 20 to 30 students restrained in a relatively small space.
- Although the classroom is a group setting, each student typically works alone.
- The teacher is the key figure in setting the tone and determining the activities.
- Most of the time, the teacher is in front of the classroom teaching a whole group of students.
- There is little praise or corrective feedback; classes are emotionally neutral or flat places.

- Students are involved in a limited range of activities—listening to lectures, writing answers to questions, and taking exams.
- A significant number of students are confused by teacher explanations and feel that they do not get enough guidance on how to improve.
- There is a decline in the attractiveness of the learning environment and the quality of instruction as students progress through the grades.

Goodlad concluded that "the emotional tone of the classroom is neither harsh and punitive nor warm and joyful; it might be described most accurately as flat."

Source: John Goodlad, *A Place Called School* (New York: McGraw-Hill, 1984).

classroom operation (Can I sharpen my pencil? When is the assignment due?), they rarely ask anything about the academic content under discussion. In fact, the typical student asks approximately one question per month.[15] In short, this language game does not train students to be active, inquiring, self-reliant learners. Rather, it teaches them how to be quiet and passive, to think fast (and perhaps superficially), to rely on memory, and to be dependent on the teacher.

Tracking

As students participate in both the formal and the hidden or unofficial curricula of school life, they are continually being evaluated by teachers and administrators. These evaluations eventually show up on the report cards and progress reports that are sent home at regular intervals. They frequently get translated into a **tracking** system that assigns some students to honors classes and others to remedial sections, that places some students in college preparatory programs and others in vocational courses. In short, one very crucial, political function of schools is that of screening and sorting students. Sociologist Talcott Parsons analyzed school as a social system and concluded that the college selection process begins in elementary school and is virtually sealed by the time students finish junior high.[16] Parsons' analysis has significant implications, for he is suggesting that future roles in adult life are determined by student achievement in elementary school. The **labeling** system and training process that determine who will one day wear a stethoscope, who will carry an all-leather executive briefcase, and who will clear the garbage from city streets begin at an early age.

Several researchers consider students' social class a critical factor in this selection system. In 1929, Robert and Helen Lynd, in their extensive study of Middletown, concluded that schools are essentially middle-class institutions that discriminate against lower-class students.[17] Approximately 15 years later,

W. Lloyd Warner and his associates at the University of Chicago conducted a series of studies in New England, the Deep South, and the Midwest and came up with a conclusion similar to the Lynds':

> One group (the lower class) is almost immediately brushed off into a bin labeled "nonreaders, first grade repeaters," or "opportunity class," where they stay for eight or ten years and are then released through a chute to the outside world to become hewers of wood and drawers of water.[18]

In his classic analysis of class and school achievement, August Hollingshead discovered that approximately two-thirds of the students from the two upper social classes but fewer than 15 percent of those from the lower classes were in the college preparatory program.[19] In more recent research on midwestern communities, Robert Havinghurst and associates reported that nearly 90 percent of school dropouts were from lower-class families.[20] In short, it is the upper- and middle-class students who generally get tracked and sorted into academic courses and eventually end up in prestigious occupations, whereas the lower-class students generally end up in the vocational courses and in dropout statistics.

Sometimes tracking seems to be based on race or ethnicity. For example, urban children of color may exhibit behavior that conflicts with school culture and middle-class norms. These students often value cooperation and group teamwork rather than the individual and competitive modes of learning that characterize most school activity. They may also devote time and attention to "stage setting" before beginning a task. Rather than beginning to work immediately, they create an appropriate mood—checking pencils, rearranging posture, and the like. To a teacher unfamiliar with this learning style, such behavior looks like incompetence or avoidance of work. To the student these stage-setting behaviors are necessary before work can begin.[21] Misunderstanding cultural cues, the teacher may inappropriately track these students into lower-ability classes.

Several studies document differences in how students in the high-ability and low-ability tracks are treated. In one ethnographic study, Ray Rist observed a kindergarten class in an all-black ghetto school. By the eighth day of class the kindergarten teacher, apparently using criteria such as physical appearance, socioeconomic status, and language usage, had separated her students into groups of "fast learners" and "slow learners." She spent more time with the "fast learners" and gave them more instruction and encouragement. The "slow learners" got more than their fair share of control and ridicule. The children soon began to mirror the teacher's behavior. As the "fast learners" belittled the "slow learners," these low-status children began to exhibit attitudes of self-degradation and hostility toward one another. This teacher's expectations, formed during 8 days at the beginning of school, shaped the academic and social treatment of children in her classroom for the entire year and perhaps for years to come. Records of the grouping that had taken place during the first week in kindergarten were passed on to teachers in the upper grades, providing the basis for further differential treatment.[22]

Recently there has been a great deal of debate over the morality and consequences of using schools as a sorting system. Many people claim that education is still a key avenue to class mobility and equality of opportunity. "True," they argue, "the school does sort and track students, but this occurs on the basis of individual ability rather than of race, religion, ethnic background, or sex. IQ testing, grouping, and tracking are necessary if we are to educate students according to their ability and future potential."

Others counter with "No sorting system is consistent with the democratic ideal of equality of opportunity. Worse yet," they argue, "the tracking system is not completely based on individual ability; rather, it is badly biased in the direction of white Anglo-Saxon Protestant culture. We must face the reality that lower-class and minority children come to school unprepared to exhibit those academic and social qualities that form the basis of the tracking system. And the school, whose job it is to educate all our children, does little to adapt itself to this situation. The built-in middle-class bias in instructional and counseling procedures, curricular materials, and testing must be overcome before schools are permitted to officially channel students into second-rate courses that prepare them for fourth-rate jobs. In our increasingly credentialed society, this channeling is equivalent to 'a great training robbery,' and the students who are robbed are the minorities and the poor, many of whom have great native ability." As Henry Giroux and Anthony Penna say, "There is little room in social education for tracking and social sorting, hierarchical social relationships, the correspondence between evaluation and power, and the fragmented and isolated dynamics of the classroom encounter, all of which characterize the hidden curriculum."[23]

In fact, the research on **ability grouping** questions the effectiveness and the wisdom of this strategy. It shows that tracking is detrimental to low-ability students. In low-ability groups there are more classroom management problems, and students tend to talk about social rather than academic matters. Teachers hold lower expectations for and make fewer demands of students in low-ability groups. The students receive less constructive feedback. Although small differences in ability do exist initially between children in upper and lower groups, these differences become greater as the year progresses. Over the course of a year, a child in the highest group may move ahead five times as quickly as a child in the lowest group. By the fourth grade, an achievement spread of a full four grades separates children at the top and the bottom of the class. These differences grow even greater as children go through school. Ability grouping seems to increase the achievement range rather than reduce it.[24]

By high school, ability grouping has frequently turned into inflexible tracks. Recent studies of schooling have called for a softening or elimination of this rigid division and implementation of a common core curriculum uniting all students. However, attempts to "detrack" schools are marked by controversy. Many advocates of tracking and ability grouping say these structures are beneficial to high-ability and especially to gifted students. At this point, research is not clear or conclusive as to the effect of ability grouping on very bright students. Tracking is likely to remain an area of controversy in the decade ahead.[25]

Whether discussing school tracking on the basis of race, sex, or class, it is clearly a difficult issue. How do you feel about using schools as a selection system? No matter what your opinion, it is important that you understand the political implications of tracking and that you view the issue in terms of the schools' popularly ascribed missions—to help all students realize their full potential and function effectively within society.

The Power of Peer Groups

When I first walked into the school everyone looked so big to me. Later my teacher showed me around the classroom and I met my classmates. I sure was happy to find children that were my age and were the same size as me. Two boys walked over to me and said, "Hey, you! What's your name?" I just stood there and didn't even know what to say until I finally said, "Ah . . . ah . . . Wood . . . no, Wade. Michael Wade!" Then everyone stood silent and just stared at me with their bally eyes as if I were crazy.

Then I met the principal and I couldn't see anything but his feet. I looked up to see his face and I tell you the truth I almost sprained my neck trying to look at his face. I was so nervous I shook from head to toe. When I had to tell him my name I thought I would faint.

I could never remember my bus number so every day when school was out I couldn't find my school bus. I kept thinking that my bus number was 12,000 or 120,000,000 but it was only 12. When one of the patrols would ask me my bus number I just said, "ah . . . ah . . . ah!" The kind old principal would ask me, "Do you know your bus number?" and I would tell him, "I . . . ah . . . I forgot it." Then the kind old principal got in touch with my bus number as quick as that! Boy, if it hadn't been for that kind old principal I would probably have missed my bus and never gotten home.[26]

This is how Michael, a fourth-grader, remembers his first day at school, a time and place of frightening unfamiliarity where adults were the source of all support and peer groups were as yet unformed.

Educational researcher Raphaela Best wanted to capture a portrait of life in school as a group of elementary schoolchildren experienced it. During a multiyear study, she played the role of participant observer, working with children during class time, playing with them at recess, eating lunch with them in the cafeteria, talking with them, observing them, taking notes. She found that children "organized their own intense, seething little world with its own frontiers, its own struggles, its own winners and losers. It was a world invisible to outsiders, not apparent to the casual observer,"[27] where the peer group became increasingly important in children's lives—eventually competing with and even eclipsing parental influence. Through her study we can enter this invisible world to give you greater insight into the social system of the elementary school and the power of the peer group to affect individual development.

In the first grade, when so much about school seems gigantic and fearful, children look to adults for safety. "What am I supposed to do in the classroom?" "Where do I get lunch?" "How do I find the bus to ride home from school?" Both boys and girls look to the teachers and to the principal for answers and for emotional support. In her study Best found that children would run to their first-grade teacher not only for this practical information, but also for hugs, for praise, and for general warmth and affection. They would climb onto the teacher's lap and rest, secure and comforted.

Their relationship to the teacher was far more important than their interactions with one another. For example, when Anne and Matthew were fighting over how to put a puzzle together, the teacher encircled them in her arms and asked, "Can't we find another way to play?" The children nodded affirmatively. "Good! You're so good and I'm so happy with the way you've been playing, but you know that accidents can happen and someone might have to stay out of school. We wouldn't want that to happen, now would we?"[28] Both children solemnly shook their heads and indicated that they would comply with the teacher's request.

By the second grade, boys began to break away from teacher dependence and place more importance on the peer group. Though loosely structured, this group was largely sex-segregated, with its own leadership hierarchy. In the first grade, boys and girls had sat side by side in the lunchroom, but by the second grade the boys claimed one end of a luncheon table for themselves. To ensure privacy from the female world, the group's meeting place became the boys' bathroom, where the boys talked about kids at school and decided what to play at recess.

By the third grade the boys were openly challenging teacher authority. They banded together to organize formally an all-male club, complete with pecking order, assignments, secrets, and antiestablishment pranks such as stuffing the locks with paper so that the teachers could not get into the building in the morning. Also by the third grade the boys' territorial rights had increased, and they staked out an entire all-male lunchroom table for themselves. The playground also became increasingly sex-segregated, as blacktop and grassy areas were reserved for boys' ball games, and the girls were relegated to the fringe areas where they played hopscotch and jump rope.

Excluded from this all-male society were not only the girls, but also some boys who were considered sissies. For these rejected boys, the consequences of being left out of the dominant male society were painful and severe. As they progressed through their elementary school years, Best found that these excluded male students exhibited an increasing number of social, emotional, and academic problems. Afraid of being teased by the male club, they avoided playing with the girls even though they might have been very happy doing so. Belonging nowhere, they banded together loosely, not out of liking but out of need.

The girls spent the first few years of school helping the teacher, not switching their allegiance to the peer group until the fourth grade. Then, instead of joining a club, they formed best-friend relationships in which pairs of girls pledged devotion to one another. Sometimes fights would break out when two girls would argue over having a third as best friend. In the upper elementary grades the girls also began to fantasize about the "cute" boys in their class and about what being married and having a family would be like. Being a good student and having a pleasing personality were seen as important, but by the upper elementary grades beauty had become the key to social status.

The wall blocking boys and girls from interacting is stronger than barriers to racial integration; there is more cross-race than cross-sex communication during the elementary school years. When Best asked students why there was not more friendship between boys and girls, they reacted with embarrassment. "Everyone would make fun of you," said one girl. Another commented:

If you say you like someone, other kids spread it all over the school and that's embarrassing. . . . If you even sit beside a boy in class, other kids say you like him. And they come to you in the bathroom and tease you about liking the boy. Once some of the girls put J. S. and B. B. on the bathroom walls. That was embarrassing.[29]

Students who experience social rejection by their school peers may also experience adjustment problems as adults.

How children relate to one another is crucial, spilling over into every nuance of school life. For you, as the teacher, a negative peer group dynamic can mean a problem-filled year. For children, the power of the peer group is even more devastating.

"If you hate Graham, sign here." The petition was making the rounds in one fourth-grade classroom not long ago. Fortunately, the teacher intercepted the paper just before it reached Graham's desk. This time, at least, Graham was spared.[30]

In one sense, Graham is not alone. Many children share his predicament. When students respond to *sociograms,* questionnaires designed to measure children's friendship patterns, 10 percent of students emerge as not being anybody's friend. About half of these are just ignored. The other half become the victims of active peer group rejection and hostility.

Most friendless children are aware of their problem and report feeling lonely and unsuccessful in relating to others. Children without friends are more likely to experience adjustment problems in later life. Rejection by the child's peer group is a sensitive indicator of future problems, ranging from juvenile delinquency to mental breakdown. In fact, elementary school sociometric measures predict social adjustment better than most other personality and educational tests do.[31]

As a teacher in charge of an elementary classroom you will need to be aware of both blatant and subtle peer group dynamics. Through this insight, you can structure your classroom to minimize negative and hurtful interaction and maximize the positive power of peer group relations. For instance, you may want to invest time in eliminating social cliques, and race- and gender-based segregation. You can be an "intentional" teacher when assigning students to seats or to group work. Your actions and attention can do much to promote better cooperation among all students, regardless of race, class, or gender. Your perceptiveness and skill in influencing the social side of school can mean a world of difference in the self-esteem of your students as they approach an adolescent society where pressure for popularity becomes increasingly extreme.

High School's Adolescent Society

Rock singer Frank Zappa said, "High school isn't a time and a place. It's a state of mind."

Sociologist James Coleman says that high school is "the closest thing to a real social system that exists in our society, the closest thing to a closed social system."

Sociologist Edgar Friedenberg points out that high school is so insular that it even has its own special mechanism for telling time—not by the clock but by periods, as in "I'll meet you for lunch after fourth period."

Author Kurt Vonnegut says that "high school is closer to the core of the American experience than anything else I can think of."

In his inaugural speech before Congress, President Gerald Ford confided: "I'm here to confess that in my first campaign for president—at my senior class at South High School—I headed the Progressive party ticket and I lost. Maybe that's why I became a Republican."[32]

More than 40 years later, Gerald Ford still remembered high school. No matter where we go or who we become, we can never entirely run away from high school. It is an experience indelibly imprinted on our mind.

More than 13 million students arrive at 20,000 public high schools every day. These schools run the gamut from decaying buildings beset by vandalism and drugs to orderly, congenial places with educators who hold positive expectations and high standards for their students. They vary in size from 50 to 5,000 students, who typically spend days divided into six or seven 50-minute periods.

In his book *Is There Life After High School?*, Ralph Keyes stirs up the pot of high school memories and draws a very lively picture of what life was like during that time and in that place and state of mind. In researching his book he asked many people, both the famous and the obscure, about their high school experience. He was amazed at the vividness and detail with which their memories came pouring out—particularly about the status system, that pattern of social reward and recognition that can be so intensely painful or exhilarating. High school was remembered as a caste system of "innies" and "outies," a minutely detailed social register where one's popularity or lack of it was continually analyzed and contemplated. Using sociological language, James Coleman documents this status phenomenon in *The Adolescent Society* when he states that a high school "has little material reward to dispense, so that its system of reward is reflected almost directly in the distribution of status. Those who are popular hold the highest status."[33]

In a major study conducted almost a quarter of a century after Coleman wrote *The Adolescent Society*, John Goodlad reached a similar conclusion. Junior and senior high school students are preoccupied not with academics but rather with athletics, popularity, and physical appearance. Only 14 percent of junior high and 7 percent of senior high students said "smart students were the most popular." Thirty-seven percent of junior high students said the "good-looking" students were the most popular, and 23 percent said "athletes." In senior high, 74 percent of students said that the most popular kids were "good-looking" and "athletes."[34]

When junior and senior high school students were asked to identify the one best thing about their school, they usually said, "my friends." "Sports activities" ranked second. "Nothing" ranked higher than "classes I'm taking" and "teachers." In some secondary schools, peer group interests bubble so close to the surface that they actually push attention to academic subjects aside and almost take over the classroom. When asked to describe her school, one high school junior said:

> The classes are okay, I guess. Most of the time I find them pretty boring, but then I suppose that's the way school classes are supposed to be. What I like most about the place is the chance to be with my friends. It's nice to be a part of a group. I don't mean one of the clubs or groups the school runs. They're for the grinds. But an informal group of your own friends is great.[35]

These informal groups are rigidly homogeneous, as becomes apparent in the seating arrangements of the secondary school cafeteria. A student in one high school described the cafeteria's social geography like this: "Behind you are the jocks; over on the side of the room are the greasers, and in front of you are the preppies—white preppies, black preppies, Chinese preppies, preppies of all kinds. The preppies are the in group this year; jocks of course are always in and greasers are always out."[36] In some cases, entire sections of the school are staked out by special groups. In a suburban high school near Chicago, the vice principal easily identified the school's different cliques: The "scums" were the group of students who party all the time and are rebelling against their parents. Next to the cafeteria was "Jock Hall," where the male athletes and their popular girlfriends could be found. Close to the library was the book foyer, where the bright kids got together.[37]

Perhaps high school students flock to others most like themselves because making their way in the adolescent society is so difficult. David Owen is an author who wanted to find out what life in high school was like in the 1980s. Although he had attended high school from 1969 to 1973, he returned undercover, almost a decade later. Pretending to be a student who had just moved into the area, he enrolled in what he calls a typical American high school, approximately 2 hours out of New York City. During his experience he was struck by the power of the peer group and how socially ill at ease most adolescents are. He likened adolescents to adults who are visiting a foreign country and a strange culture. Experimenting with new behavior, they are terrified of being noticed doing something stupid.

> Relationships among teenagers are founded on awkwardness more than most of them realize. When a typical high school student looks around at his classmates, he sees little but coolness and confidence, people who fit in better than he does. That was certainly the way I thought of my old high school classmates much of the time; no matter how well adjusted I happened to feel at any particular moment, other people seemed to be doing better. At Bingham, though, I saw another picture. Everyone seemed so shy. The kids hadn't learned the nearly unconscious social habits that

Peer groups appear to be homogeneous and more than anything else tend to define the quality of students' school life.

adults use constantly to ease their way through the world. When kids bumped into each other in the halls, they almost never uttered the little automatic apologies—"Oops," "Sorry"—that adults use all the time. They just kept plowing right ahead, pretending they hadn't noticed. One day, when I was hurrying to my history class, I realized I was on a direct collision course with a girl coming the other way. Each of us made a little sidestep, but in the same direction. Just before we bumped, an expression of absolute horror spread across the girl's face. She looked as though she were staring down the barrel of a gun. The bubble of coolness had been burst. She probably brooded about it for the rest of the day. . . . Being an adolescent is a fulltime job, an all-out war against the appearance of awkwardness. No one is more attentive to nuance than a seventeen-year-old. . . . When a kid in my class came to school one day in a funny-looking pair of shoes that one of his friends eventually laughed at, I could see by his face that he was thinking, "Well, that does it, there goes the rest of my life."[38]

The memory of high school rejection is powerful even for the famous. Mia Farrow recalls the high school dance where every girl was on the dance floor except her. Charles Schulz has not forgotten the day the yearbook staff rejected his cartoon, and Eva Marie Saint recalls the time she did not get a part in the class play. No matter where we were in the high school system, few of us have egos so strong or skins so tough that we fail to get a psychological lift when we learn that Ali McGraw never had a date during high school, that Gregory Peck was regarded as least likely to succeed, that John Denver was called "four-eyes," or that Henry Kissinger is recalled as a little fatso with whom nobody would eat lunch.[39]

The Antiachievement Dilemma

Many students avoid academic excellence because they fear their peers will label them nerds. According to B. Bradford Brown and Laurence Steinberg, who sampled 8,000 high school students in California and Wisconsin, this fear is warranted. Unlike athletes, who are offered adulation, high academic achievers often get resentment instead of respect.[a] To avoid the "nerd" label and the social rejection that comes with it, students learn that they should do well, but not *too* well. This brain-nerd connection causes students to put the brakes on academic achievement, cut corners, and only do what is necessary to get by.

The antiachievement climate is even stronger for African-American students. Signithia Fordham and John Ogbu report the results of a fascinating ethnographic study in a Washington, DC, high school, where the student population was 99 percent black.[b] They found that students actively discourage each other from working to achieve because attaining academic success is seen as "acting white." "Acting white" includes speaking standard English, listening to white music and radio stations, being on time, studying in the library, working hard to get good grades, and getting good grades. Students who do well in school are called "brainiacs," a term synonymous with *jerk*.

Those students who manage to achieve academic success and still avoid the "brainiac" label develop ingenious coping strategies. Some students camouflage high achievement by "acting crazy," as class clowns or comedians. Others choose friends who will protect them in exchange for help with homework. Female achievers are more likely to hide out, keeping a low profile, so their peers will not know they are smart.

What can teachers do to break the brainiac-jerk association? How can the power of peer pressure be unleashed for success instead of mediocrity or failure? What do you think?

[a]B. Bradford Brown and Laurence Steinberg, "Academic Achievement and Social Acceptance," *The Education Digest* 55 (March 1990): 57–60. Condensed from *National Center on Effective Secondary Schools Newsletter* 4 (Fall 1989): 2–4.

[b]Signithia Fordham and John Ogbu, "Black Students' School Success: Coping with the Burden of 'Acting White,'" *Urban Review* 18, no. 3 (1986): 176–205.

For those who remember jockeying unsuccessfully for a place among the inner circle of the high school social register, it may be comforting to learn that the tables do turn. There is no study that shows any correlation between high status in high school and later achievement as an adult. Those who are voted queen of the prom or most likely to succeed do not appear to do any better or any worse in adult life than those whose beauty or yearbook description is less illustrious.

It is not that our basic personality changes after high school. Rather it is that the context changes. What works in that very insular adolescent environment is not necessarily what works in the outside world. One researcher speculates that it is those on the "second tier," those that group just below the top, who are most likely to succeed after high school. He says, "I think the rest of our lives are spent making up for what we did or did not do in high school."[40]

Most students know the feeling of being judged and found wanting by high school peers, and some spend the rest of their lives trying to compensate or get even. In fact, it is this need to repudiate their high school experience that has motivated more than one superstar to drive their way to the top. Mel Brooks sums it up well:

> Thank God for the athletes and their rejection. Without them there would have been no emotional need and . . . I'd be a cracker jack salesman in the garment district.[41]

One of the most astonishing things about high school is how alive the experience was and how vivid and intense the memories are. Dustin Hoffman still remembers himself as an undersized high school student with braces and acne. He lifted weights and dreamed of being popular. When finally he achieved movie stardom he said, "Why couldn't this have happened to me when I was sixteen and needed it?"

For some students, the impact of rejection does not lead to such positive outcomes. These students struggle to break through clique walls that are invisible but impervious. Without the support of friends and peers, they remain on the periphery of high school, where feelings of loneliness can become overwhelming. "I've never really been part of any group. I suppose I don't have anything to offer. It gets awfully lonely sometimes, but after a while you get to like being alone."[42]

The Affective Side of School Reform

According to a Carnegie Foundation survey, by the late 1980s elementary, middle, and senior high school teachers were sounding an alarm bell about the affective side of school, the unmet psychological, emotional, and social needs of the nation's children. Ninety percent of teachers said lack of support from parents was a major concern; 89 percent were concerned about neglected or abused children; 88 percent were worried about the apathy of their students; 87 percent were troubled by children's disruptive behavior; 83 percent pointed to absenteeism as an issue in their schools; almost 70 percent said that undernourishment and poor health were problems for children.[43] When given the opportunity to make open comments to the survey, teachers' anecdotes corroborated the shocking percentages cited above. A kindergarten teacher from an urban school system said:

> The difficult part of teaching is not the academics. The difficult part is dealing with the great numbers of kids who come from emotionally, physically, socially, and financially stressed homes. Nearly all of my kindergarten kids come from single parent families. Most of the moms really care for their kids but are young, uneducated, and financially strained. Children who have had no breakfast, or who are fearful of what their mom's boyfriend will do to them—or their moms—are not very good listeners or cooperative partners with their teachers or their peers. We are raising a generation of emotionally stunted and troubled youth who will in turn raise a generation of the same. What is the future of this country when we have so many needy youngsters?[44]

Those who teach in urban settings warn us that the future of poor and minority children is at risk. But all is not well in suburbia either. Consider this comment from a teacher in suburban New Jersey: "In the large, efficient suburb where I teach the pressure is on kids from kindergarten to high school to get good grades, bring up the test scores, and be the best on the test."[45] Another teacher says that there is such pressure to get high test scores that students are rushed from one workbook to another. There is no time for anything not directly related to cognitive achievement. "We feel guilty," she says, "doing an art lesson or having a wonderful discussion."[46]

In another study of students from 10 very different communities, Frances Ianni describes the affluent lifestyle in the suburb of Sheffield (name fictitious), a place where families keep well-manicured lawns and push their children to succeed. Students are groomed to be good at everything—excellent athletes, adept at social skills, top academic achievers. "People in Sheffield will tell you," Ianni says, "that the two things you never ask at a cocktail party are a family's income and the Scholastic Assessment Test scores of their children."[47] English teacher Patrick Welsh tells of teenagers who take the SATs four and five times, pushed on by their parents' promises of new cars if they score well.

> I've had kids in class with their fingernails bitten to the quick and looking miserable, feeling they have to get As, and their parents going to the point of rewriting their papers for them. Every fall T.C. is gripped by "Ivy League Fever." Sweatshirts marked "Harvard" or "Princeton" start appearing. . . . I got so fed up, that one day in class I horrified everybody by saying I have yet to see anybody wearing an Ivy League sweatshirt get into an Ivy League school. The sweatshirts went back to the drawer after that.[48]

Pushed beyond their abilities and alienated from family, friends, and community, some teenagers develop a "delusion of uniqueness," a sense that "no one knows how I feel, no one else faces these problems, no one cares about me." When children are cut off from what Urie Bronfenbrenner calls "the four worlds of childhood"—family, friends, school, and work—the situation can become serious and even life-threatening.[49] Sara Lawrence Lightfoot describes the following incident that took place in an elite school in a wealthy suburb in the Midwest:

> A student with a history of depression . . . had been seeing a local psychiatrist for several years. For the last few months, however, she had discontinued her psychotherapy and seemed to be showing steady improvement. Since September, her life had been invigorated by her work on *Godspell*—a student production that consumed her energies and provided her with an instant group of friends. After *Godspell,* her spirits and enthusiasm declined noticeably. In her distress, she reached out to a teacher who had given her special tutorial support in the past, and the school machinery was set in motion. A meeting was scheduled for the following day to review her case. That night, after a visit to her psychiatrist, she killed herself.

> The day after, the school buzzed with rumors as students passed on the gruesome news· —their faces showing fear and intrigue. . . . But I heard only one teacher speak of it openly and explicitly in class—the drama teacher who had produced *Godspell.* Her words brought tears and looks of terror in the eyes of her students.

> "We've lost a student today who was with us yesterday. We've got to decide where our priorities are. How important are your gold chains, your pretty clothes, your cars? . . . Where were we when she needed us? Foolish old woman that I am, I ask you this because I respect you. . . . While you still feel, damn it, feel . . . reach out to each other."[50]

Sometimes adults from either the school or the community do reach out to make a startling difference in the lives of children at risk. Researcher Frances Ianni describes Victor, an inner-city child with an unemployed mother and a father who had left home. Victor seldom went to school. Involved in petty theft at an early age, he was first arrested at age 11. By age 13 he was smoking three or four joints of marijuana daily and drinking several cans of beer each night. When, at 14, Victor was arrested for stealing a purse, the court-appointed lawyer took an interest in him.

> At first she really let me have it, telling me I was a real scumbag who made her ashamed of being Hispanic, and I told her I didn't ask for or need any help from her or any other social worker. She really got mad then and said how she could understand how a lot of Spanish kids got into trouble—but that someone smart like me should be using what he had to make other people look up to us rather than feeling for their wallets when one of us walked by.[51]

With the help of his lawyer, Victor was put on probation and into a program for at-risk teens. He says that she changed his life. Now Victor has won a scholarship to a Catholic university where he plans to study law.

Ianni says that several teens she interviewed pointed to a chance encounter, a single individual who changed—or saved—their lives. But the future of the nation's youth is too important to leave to chance. Ianni urges every community to set up a network of mutually reinforcing messages for students, especially adolescents. She calls this network a "youth charter." "Communities," she says, "can create youth charters that encourage youngsters to move from dependence to independence, from the ethnocentrism of early adolescence to the social competence of young adulthood." She urges the community to move from benign neglect or outrage at the young to an organized system of positive involvement and guidance.[52] Many other child advocates are calling for a coordinated system of social services to replace the existing maze of bureaucratic agencies.[53]

Alfie Kohn is one educator who claims that the social and affective side of school must become an explicit part of the formal curriculum. "It is possible to integrate prosocial lessons into the regular curriculum . . . . Indeed to study literature or history by grappling with moral or social dilemmas is to invite a deeper engagement with these subjects." According to Kohn, schools such as the California-based Child Development Project, a long-term effort in prosocial education, can teach children to take responsibility and care for one another.[54]

While most reform reports emphasize increased academic achievement, only a few have recognized the social and emotional needs of children. The Carnegie Council on Adolescent Development report, *Turning Points: Preparing American Youth for the 21st Century,* warned that one in four adolescents—approximately 1 million youth—are in serious jeopardy. Their basic human needs—caring relationships with adults, guidance in facing sometimes overwhelming biological and psychological changes, the security of belonging to constructive peer groups, and the perception of future opportunity—go unmet at this critical stage of life. Millions of these young adolescents will never reach their full potential.[55]

Pointing to a society dangerous to adolescent health—one of drug abuse, poor school performance, alienation, and sexual promiscuity—the report warned that while 25 percent of teens may be extremely vulnerable to the consequences of high-risk behavior, another million are at moderate risk, and half the nation's youth are at low risk of engaging in seriously damaging behavior. The task force called for comprehensive middle-school reform to help protect these youngsters.

> Middle-grade schools—junior high, intermediate or middle schools—are potentially society's most powerful force to recapture millions of youth adrift. Yet all too often they exacerbate the problems youth face. A volatile mismatch exists between the organization and curriculum of middle-grade schools and the intellectual, emotional, and interpersonal needs of young adolescents.[56]

Describing the trauma students face when they shift from a neighborhood elementary school, where they spent most of the school day with one or two teachers who knew them well, to a larger, colder institution where they move through six or seven different classes daily, the report made the following recommendations:

- Divide large schools into smaller "communities" for learning.
- Create a core curriculum.
- Eliminate tracking.
- Emphasize cooperative learning.
- Develop stronger partnerships between schools and communities.
- Assign teams of teachers and students, with an adult adviser for each student.
- Emphasize the link between education and good health.
- Strengthen teacher preparation for dealing with the adolescent age group.

Imagine life in a school that implements these recommendations. You would see a smaller middle school or high school, one emphasizing community activities and moving away from an atmosphere that produces "large-school alienation." Health issues would become more central, linking diet and exercise more directly to education, enhancing the longevity and quality of students' lives well into adulthood. But to create such a caring and healthful school, teacher education itself would need to be changed. As you examine your own teacher education program, can you identify ways that these recommendations are being promoted? How does your teacher education program prepare you to develop school-community partnerships, promote cooperative learning, or respond more effectively to the needs of adolescents? Clearly, significant changes in many teacher education programs across the nation will need to be made if the recommendations of this Carnegie report are to be implemented.

What Makes a School Effective?

While the Carnegie Council's *Turning Points* recommendations are designed to create more sensitive and humane school climates, other studies have offered suggestions for creating more academically demanding schools. Although the major focus of this chapter is on the social and interpersonal side of schools, it is important that academic life not be forgotten. For example, consider the following situation:

Two schools are located in the same neighborhood. They are approximately the same size, and the student populations they serve are similar in all characteristics including socioeconomic level, racial and gender composition, IQ scores upon school entry, and parental education and occupation. However, in one school students have high dropout rates and low scores on national achievement tests. In the other school students score at least at national average on achievement tests, and they are more likely to stay in school. Why should such differences emerge?

Puzzled by situations such as this, researchers attempted to determine what factors have made some schools more effective in encouraging student achievement. As early as 1971, G. Weber studied four schools that seemed successful in teaching reading.[57] Through research such as his, the more effective schools were identified as those in which the achievement of students, especially poor and minority students, was at a uniformly successful level of mastery. One of the best-known studies, conducted by Ronald Edmonds and his colleagues, concluded that in an effective school students of working-class background score as high as middle-class students on tests of basic skills.[58] Other groups around the country, from the Connecticut School Effectiveness Project to the Alaska Effective Schooling program, have conducted research to figure out what makes good schools work. In study after study researchers have found a common set of characteristics that has resulted in a "five-factor theory" of effective schools.[59] Researchers say that effective schools are able, by means of the five characteristics, to reduce the harmful effects of poor socioeconomic background. The values and norms embedded in these five school characteristics create a culture of achievement. Following is a discussion of these five factors and how they contribute to strong school performance.

Factor 1: Strong Leadership

In her book *The Good High School,* Sara Lawrence Lightfoot drew social science portraits of six effective schools.[60] Two, George Washington Carver High School in Atlanta and John F. Kennedy High School in the Bronx, were inner-city schools. Highland Park High School near Chicago and Brookline High School in Brookline, Massachusetts, were upper middle-class and suburban. St. Paul's High School in Concord, New Hampshire, and Milton Academy near Boston were elite preparatory schools. Despite the tremendous difference in the styles and textures of these six schools, ranging from the pastoral setting of St. Paul's to inner-city Atlanta, they all were characterized by strong, inspired leaders, such as Robert Mastruzzi, principal of John F. Kennedy.

When Robert Mastruzzi came to Kennedy, the building was not yet completed. Walls were being built around him as he sat in his unfinished office and contemplated the challenge of not only his first principalship but also the opening of a new school. During his years as principal of John F. Kennedy, his leadership style was collaborative, actively seeking faculty participation. Not only did he want his staff to participate in decision making, but he gave them the opportunity to try new things—and even the right to fail. For example, one teacher made an error about the precautions necessary for holding a rock concert (800 adolescents had shown up, many high or inebriated). Mastruzzi realized that the teacher had learned a great deal from the experience, and he let her try again. The second concert was a great success. "He sees failure as an opportunity for change," the teacher said. Still other teachers described him with hyperbole or superlatives such as "He is the lifeblood of this organism," or "the greatest human being I have ever known."[61]

Mastruzzi seems to embody the characteristics of effective leaders in good schools. Researchers say that students make significant achievement gains in schools where principals:

- Articulate a clear school mission
- Are a visible presence in classrooms and hallways
- Hold high expectations for teachers and students
- Spend a major portion of the day working with teachers to improve instruction
- Are actively involved in diagnosing instructional problems
- Create a positive school climate[62]

Successful principals provide instructional leadership. They spend more of their time working with students and less of their time in the office. They observe what is going on in the classrooms, hold high expectations for teacher performance and student achievement, and provide necessary resources, including their own skills and knowledge. They are active and involved. As a result they create schools that make a positive difference in the lives of students.

Factor 2: A Clear School Mission

When researchers study the working lives of principals, they typically find them in a state of perpetual motion.

A positive, energizing school atmosphere characterized by accepting relationships between students and faculty usually begins in the principal's office.

Generally I am working on four things at a time, but I know my priorities. I may have two students in my office to reinstate. I get a call, telling me there is a fight on the third floor. I sent the students out of my office and lock the door. As I move upstairs, a teacher confronts me, holding a student by the collar, upset about his behavior. I must ignore her to get up to the fight. By the time I reach the third floor, that teacher informs me the situation is under control. All this effort, and what have I accomplished?[63]

A day in the life of a principal can be spent putting out fires and trying to keep small incidents from becoming major crises. But the research is clear; in effective schools good principals somehow find time to develop a vision of what that school should be and to share that vision with all members of the educational community.

Researchers who interviewed successful principals—as well as those who are less effective—found distinct differences in how the two groups responded. Successful principals could articulate a specific school mission, and they stressed innovation and improvement. In contrast, less effective principals were vague about their goals and focused on maintaining the status quo. They made comments such as "We have a good school and a good faculty, and I want to keep it that way."[64]

It is essential that the principal share his or her vision with the teachers so that they too understand the school's goals and work together to achieve them. Research stresses the importance of the school staff's functioning as a team, but when teachers are polled, more than 75 percent say that they have either no contact or infrequent contact with one another during the school day. And 94 percent of teachers say that they would do their jobs better if they were less isolated from their colleagues. In less effective schools, teachers lack a common understanding of the school's mission and function as individuals charting their own separate courses. In her description of the transformation of Pyne Poynt Middle School, then-NEA leader Mary Hatwood Futrell tells what can happen when school administration and faculty work together toward common goals:

> Not long ago, Pyne Poynt Middle School in Camden, New Jersey, fit "the blackboard jungle" stereotype to a T. Teachers regularly confiscated weapons. Parents feared visiting Pyne Poynt after dark. Student achievement was low. Staff morale was lower.
>
> Today Pyne Poynt is a deeply proud school, with abundant reason for pride: Attendance is up, truancy is down. Discipline has returned. Reading and math scores have soared. Parents now volunteer to help with school projects.
>
> What happened? How to explain this metamorphosis? Maureen Reedy, who has taught at Pyne Poynt for 17 years, answers with a single word: communication. In 1979, Reedy explains, the entire school staff recognized that in their efforts to turn Pyne Poynt around, they were neglecting their most valuable resource: each other. The school staff—teachers and administrators together—then began revamping established schedules and procedures to ensure the regular exchange of ideas and insights.

"We became a team," says Pyne Poynt principal Vernon Dover, "and Pyne Poynt became a different place."[65]

The need for the principal to share his or her vision extends not only to teachers but to parents as well. Studies show that mothers typically spend less than half an hour a day talking with or reading to their children; for fathers, the amount of time is less than 15 minutes. The time parents invest in their children differs as much as five-fold from family to family. When parents do spend time with their children—talking with them about school and other aspects of their lives, discussing books, news, and television programs—this curriculum of the home can raise student achievement considerably.[66]

Partnerships between parents and schools have had an outstanding record in improving student achievement.[67] Children who participate in programs to improve the home-learning environment do better than children who do not participate in these programs. In schools where teachers work cooperatively and parents join this team, children are more likely to achieve academic success.

Factor 3: Preventing School Violence: A Safe and Orderly Climate

Theodore Sizer visited more than 80 schools in 15 states, studied what he saw, and reached some conclusions. One thing he discovered is that when a school is allowed to deteriorate physically, the human spirit within the school also declines:

> Most middle- and upper-income Americans would be both shocked by and afraid of some of the places where the young citizens of the poor are now at school. They would be indignant about the Byzantine politics that entangle most understaffed and underfinanced maintenance operations. I have seen a sad poster on the walls of many tattered schools, one that is a poor substitute for the simple courtesies of decently maintained places for learning. It says, simply: I *am* somebody because God don't make no junk.[68]

The conditions of learning demand a safe and orderly climate. In *The Good High School,* Sara Lawrence Lightfoot selected George Washington Carver High School as one of her six effective schools. But Carver was not always a good school. The transformation of that inner-city school from a state of vandalized disrepair and neglect to a safe and orderly place of learning was the result of enormous effort and strong will.

Superintendent Alonzo Crim was ready to close George Washington Carver High, a school on the other side of the tracks in the poorest area of Atlanta. When the community protested, Crim gave Norris Hogans, the ambitious principal of a nearby elementary school, the opportunity and challenge of saving it. A physically imposing and powerful presence, former football player Hogans was shocked when he saw the state of decay into which the school had fallen:

> Roaches were running around like cats. . . . There was dirt and filth everywhere. . . . The band instruments were all broken up. . . . Athletic trophies were falling out of the broken glass cabinets. . . . I can't believe no one stood up and screamed about it.[69]

Hogans believed that chaos and permissiveness are anathema to the education of poor black children. His goal was to turn the school around and create safety and order out of a dangerous environment. To achieve this he literally patrolled the school with a walkie-talkie, barking commands. Bathroom walls were cleaned, graffiti wiped away, broken equipment repaired. Dress codes and behavior codes were established and enforced. Author Lightfoot says that while some teachers and students felt stifled under his tight-ship, authoritarian style, this approach—along with every ounce of Hogans' energy and drive—was needed in order to create a good school.

For more than two decades opinion polls have shown that the public considers lack of discipline among the most serious problems facing schools.[70] The National Institute of Education's Safe School study found that only 1 in every 58 school crimes was reported to the police.[71] The National Parent-Teacher Association reported that the annual cost of vandalism, probably in excess of $600 million, is greater than the nation's total budget for textbooks.

School violence has a direct and tangible impact on teachers and students. When beginning teachers quit, the reason they give most often is that they couldn't cope with discipline problems. When teachers have been the victim of student attack, they are more likely to hold negative feelings toward all students. When there are high rates of violence, students learn fear and the vulnerability of the educational establishment.

In effective schools, where a safe and orderly climate is maintained, discipline is not a major issue. Students are less willing to participate in violent

Good schools have safe environments.

activity if they achieve academic success and enjoy positive relationships with their teachers. Studying 500 schools with good discipline, researchers found eight factors responsible for school safety:

1. Staff members were taught to work together on school problems.
2. There was shared authority for decision making.
3. Students felt a sense of ownership in the school.
4. Rules and procedures were developed to encourage self-discipline.
5. Curriculum was carefully designed to interest and challenge students.
6. School staff helped students deal with personal problems.
7. There was strong school-home cooperation.
8. The school's physical and organizational structure was firmly in place to support these factors.[72]

One of the most important characteristics of a safe school is a clearly articulated and enforced discipline policy that stresses good conduct as well as respect for teachers and academic work. According to *What Works,* a Department of Education publication that assembles research-based effective school practices, successful schools have discipline policies in which misbehavior is clearly defined so that students know what conduct is and is not acceptable. It is helpful to have schoolwide participation in creating this policy. A readable handbook should be developed to inform students and parents about the policy, and the discipline policy should be enforced in a consistent and fair manner.[73]

When schools develop safe and orderly climates, they serve as oases for children in a world that is often confusing and sometimes dangerous. For example, Sara Lawrence Lightfoot tells of the long distances that urban students travel to reach John F. Kennedy High School in the Bronx. One girl, who did not have money to buy a winter coat or glasses to see the board, rode the subway 1 hour and 40 minutes each way to get to school. She never missed a day, because for her school was a refuge—a place of hope where she could learn in safety.[74]

Factor 4: Monitoring Student Progress

The supervisor was puzzled. The students at Edgewood Elementary School were achieving well beyond grade level. But the students at Backwood Elementary were faltering. The schools served similar student populations, and the faculty and administration at both schools seemed to have similar professional credentials. Why was one school more effective than the other in encouraging student achievement and progress? Perhaps a visit to the schools would clear up the mystery.

The first visit was to Edgewood. As the supervisor walked through the hallways and classrooms, she noted the attractive displays of student work mounted on bulletin boards and walls. Also posted were charts clearly documenting class and school progress toward meeting academic goals. Interviews with individual students showed that they had a clear sense of how they were doing in their studies; they kept charts in their notebooks on which they recorded their progress. When the supervisor interviewed teachers, she found them very knowledgeable about the individual strengths and weaknesses of their students. During those interviews, teachers referred to student folders that contained thorough records of student scores on standardized tests as well as samples of classwork, homework, and performance on weekly tests.

The supervisor's visit to Backwood Elementary revealed some striking differences. Bulletin boards and walls were attractive, but there were few student papers posted and no charting of progress toward academic goals. Interviews with students showed that they had only a vague idea of how they were doing or of ways to improve their academic performance. Some students expressed surprise and even anger at recent report card grades. As one student said, "I couldn't believe I got so many C's and D's. I was shocked because I thought I was doing just fine." Teachers also seemed vague about individual student progress. When asked for more information, one teacher sent the supervisor to the guidance office, saying, "I think he keeps some records like the California Achievement Tests. Maybe he can give you what you're looking for."

Following the visit, the supervisor wrote her report: "A very likely reason for the difference in effectiveness is that one school carefully monitors student progress and communicates this information to students and parents. The other school does not."

Effective schools carefully monitor and assess student progress in order to determine whether changes in programs, curricula, and teaching methods are needed. They typically use a variety of assessments:[75]

- **Norm-referenced standardized tests,** such as the Metropolitan Achievement Test (MAT) and the Scholastic Assessment Test (SAT), are used to compare individual students to others in a nationwide norm group. Such tests are given at specified times during each school year.
- **Objective-referenced tests** are used to measure whether a student has mastered some designated body of knowledge rather than how he or she compares to other students in a norm group. These tests measure what students have actually learned. A school district or state may give objective-referenced tests to students at certain points in order to ascertain what instruction is needed and whether students are ready to move on to new tasks.
- Teacher-made tests are also objective-referenced and can be given far more frequently than those assessments administered by the district or the state. Researchers suggest that teacher-made tests should be given fairly often, at least every 2 weeks, because they provide the constant feedback needed to make appropriate modifications in curriculum and instruction.
- Record keeping is another important method of monitoring student progress. Students should keep records of course objectives and their progress toward meeting these objectives in their own folders or notebooks. Wall charts and other observable record-keeping systems are helpful, as are systematic procedures for reporting student progress to parents.
- Homework is one monitoring device that has been the subject of great controversy over the years. In the late 1800s, when educators thought of the mind as a muscle that could be improved through exercise, strenuous homework was considered a mechanism for improving and disciplining the mind. At various points since then (1900–1910, 1930–1940, and 1970–1980), homework has come under attack, usually because of a perceived relationship to student stress and depression. Since publication of

A Nation at Risk, the 1983 report decrying the quality of American education, homework has once again been on the rise.

Although early studies of homework were inconclusive, new research
shows that it does influence student achievement, particularly when accompanied by teacher feedback. Researcher Herbert Walberg and colleagues say that
when homework is assigned without teacher feedback, it raises scores of the
typical student from the 50th to the 60th percentile. When it is graded and
commented on, achievement is increased from the 50th to the 79th percentile.
Walberg and colleagues claim that the correlation between graded homework
and student achievement is among the highest discovered in educational
research.[76] It is an essential step in promoting progress and providing student
feedback.

Factor 5: High Expectations

The teachers were excited. A group of their students had received extraordinary scores on a test that predicted intellectual achievement during the coming year. And just as the teachers had expected, these same children attained
outstanding academic gains that year. And now for the rest of the story.

In reality, the teachers had been duped. The identified students had not
made particularly outstanding scores on the test; rather, they had been selected
at random. However, 8 months later these randomly selected children did show
significantly greater gains in total IQ than another group of children, the control group.

In their highly influential 1969 publication, *Pygmalion in the Classroom,*
researchers Robert Rosenthal and Lenore Jacobson discuss this experiment and
the power of teacher expectations in shaping student achievement. The message of their research: Students will learn as much—or as little—as teachers
expect.[77]

Rosenthal and Jacobson's study sparked a plethora of research on teacher
expectations, some of which replicated their findings, some of which did not.
Although methodological criticisms of the original study abound, those who
report on effective schools say that there is now extensive evidence showing
that high teacher expectations do, in fact, produce high student achievement
and low expectations produce low achievement.[78]

Too often teacher expectations have a negative impact. An inaccurate judgment about a student can be made because of error, unconscious prejudice,
or stereotype. For example, good-looking, well-dressed students are frequently
thought to be smarter than their less attractive peers. Often male students are
thought to be brighter than female students, particularly in math and science,
and minority students are thought to be less intelligent. Sometimes a poor performance on a single standardized test (perhaps due to illness or an "off" day)
can cause teachers to hold an inaccurate assessment of a student's ability for
months and even years. Even a casual comment in the teachers' lounge can
sometimes shape the expectations of other teachers.

Whatever the cause, when teachers have low expectations for certain students, their treatment of these students differs in subtle ways. Typically, they
offer them:

- Fewer opportunities to respond
- Less praise
- Less challenging work
- Fewer nonverbal signs (eye contact, smiles, positive regard)

In most cases, teachers are not even aware of these differences in student treatment. However, when such differential expectations and teacher behaviors do occur, they almost inevitably affect student performance and set in motion a self-fulfilling prophecy.

Another critical way of communicating low expectations is through ability grouping. Although the research on ability grouping is not entirely conclusive, as noted earlier, several studies show that, unless handled with skill and sensitivity, it can have a detrimental impact on lower-track students. Consider the following scenario:

Ms. Pollack dreaded her last-period English class. It was a rambunctious group of eighth graders composed mostly of low achievers who seemed to think school was just a big joke. Often half the period would be over before they would settle down to work. Ms. Pollack decided it was time for a talk.

"Why don't you take your schoolwork and yourselves more seriously?" she confronted them. "You just spend all your time goofing off. My other classes don't act like this."

The charge was met with derision. "Don't try to con us. We're the dumb group, didn't you know that? We're too stupid to learn anything, so why bother?"

This class articulated with shocking clarity how sensitive students are to ability groupings and the accompanying expectations of school and faculty. The scenario also shows how lowered expectations can cause poor achievement not only in a single student but in a whole class or even an entire school.

In effective schools this process is reversed. Teachers hold high expectations that students can learn, and they translate these expectations into teaching behavior. They set objectives, work toward the mastery of those objectives, spend more time on direct instruction, and actively monitor student progress. They are convinced that students can succeed.

Finally, in effective schools teachers hold high expectations for themselves. They believe that they can deliver quality instruction. In *The Good High School,* Sara Lawrence Lightfoot found that this sense of teacher efficacy and power was prevalent at Brookline High, a school near Boston where suburban and urban values met and often clashed. As Lightfoot listened in halls, classes, and the teachers' room, she heard faculty discussion about pedagogy, curriculum ideas, and the problems of individual students. "Star" teachers were respected as models to be emulated: the constitutional history teacher who used innovative role plays and simulation games; the English teacher whose course "The Art of the Essay" encouraged students to respond to one another's work and to write with discipline and honesty. Always striving for excellence, these teachers felt that no matter how well a class went, next time it could be better.

A Note of Caution on Effective Schools Research

Although the research on what makes effective schools has had a major national impact, its findings must be interpreted with caution and applied carefully to individual situations. There are some limitations to this research.[79]

First, there is disagreement over exactly what effective schools are. Researchers who conduct the studies also use varying definitions, ranging from "schools with high academic achievement" to "schools that foster personal growth, creativity, and positive self-concept." The prescriptions of this research are as vague as the term *effective schools.* Although the five factors we have described are helpful, they do not really provide a specific, step-by-step blueprint for developing successful schools.

Another problem is that most of the research has been conducted in the lower grades of elementary schools. Although some researchers suggest applicability to secondary and even higher education, caution must be used in carrying the effective-schools findings to higher levels of education. The generalizability of the research is also limited, since several of the studies were conducted in inner-city schools and tied closely to achievement of lower-order skills in math and science. If one wanted to develop a school that nurtures creativity rather than basic skills, another set of characteristics might be more appropriate. Charles Tesconi has investigated high school effectiveness by focusing on such factors as teacher involvement in school life, the professional climate of the school, and the way that new teachers are introduced to school norms and procedures. According to Tesconi, a high school's policies go a long way in determining its effectiveness.

Although methodological criticisms of effective schools research are numerous, educators have taken the findings and tried to implement them in school improvement projects across the country.[80] As a result of this research, as well as of the reform reports of the 1980s and 1990s, most states have implemented school improvement projects, including additional requirements for high school graduation, and "no pass, no play" rules, where participation in extracurricular activities depends on maintaining academic standards.

The challenge facing teachers and school administrators in the years ahead may well be the thoughtful integration of the research on effective schools and effective teaching with the research on the social and psychological needs of children. How can schools be made more humane and more academic? How can those swirling social forces that so often engulf adolescents be managed and directed so that they enhance not only the students' psychological well-being, but academic success as well?

SUMMARY

1. Typically, teachers keep busy in class, while students spend their time sitting still and waiting. Most children respond by daydreaming or by training themselves to deny their desire to be active.

2. Research studies underscore the importance of the language of the classroom. Teacher talk dominates classroom life. Flanders, Bellack, Goodlad, and others have found that teachers lecture a great deal, and also ask questions, while students are reduced to passive listening, active only when responding to the teacher. This reality is strikingly different from the picture of the curious, inquiring, self-reliant learner that we envision.

3. John Goodlad and others have documented startlingly inefficient use of time in schools. When teachers spend more time teaching, students learn more.

4. Being tracked into slower classes has a negative impact on students' self-esteem and achievement. Also, tracking discriminates against poor and minority students, who are more likely to be labeled as slow learners.

5. Some educators criticize the competition and individualism that permeates school culture. An alternative, cooperative learning, stresses heterogeneous grouping in classes, with students working toward common goals. Some studies show cooperative learning to yield high student achievement and self-esteem, as well as greater tolerance of students from different backgrounds.

6. Beginning in elementary school, peer pressure wields great power in children's lives. Young children's peer groups are rigidly segregated by sex, with boys tending to form hierarchic societies and girls usually forming pairs of best friends. Those left out may develop adjustment problems and emotional difficulties.

7. Educational reform efforts have begun to focus on adolescents' social and personal needs. And schools have begun to take on an increasing number of roles traditionally filled by parents, from sex education to drug and pregnancy counseling. Reports warn of the fragile condition of troubled adolescents, exhorting schools to do more to help the nation's youth.

8. Researchers have set forth a "five-factor theory" of effective schools. These factors can be summed up as (1) strong administrative leadership, (2) clear school goals shared by faculty and administration, (3) a safe and orderly school climate, (4) frequent monitoring and assessment of student progress, and (5) high expectations for student performance.

9. Effective principals articulate a clear school mission, are visible in classrooms and hallways, hold high expectations for teachers as well as for students, spend most of each day working with teachers to improve instruction, become actively involved in diagnosing instructional problems, and create a positive school climate.

10. In effective schools, the principal shares his or her own mission concept with the teachers so that they can work together to achieve the school's goals. These visions should also be shared with parents to aid in student achievement.

11. Where there is a safe and orderly school climate, student behavior is more appropriate and achievement is enhanced. Key to safe schools is a clearly articulated and enforced discipline policy that informs the students and parents about what conduct is and is not permitted.

12. An effective school carefully monitors and assesses student progress in order to determine whether changes in curriculum, teaching methods, or both are necessary. Methods of assessment include norm-referenced standardized tests such as the Scholastic Assessment Test (SAT), objective-referenced tests to measure what the students have already learned, and teacher-made tests. Methods other than testing used to monitor progress include record keeping and homework assignments with teacher feedback.

13. Research has indicated that high teacher expectations produce high student achievement. In addition, in effective schools the teachers hold high expectations not only for their students but also for themselves.

14. Some limitations on research findings on effective schools include the following: (1) There is no one, universally accepted definition of an effective school; (2) research has focused on elementary schools, and thus findings may need to be qualified in their application to secondary and higher education.

15. There are various observation and interview strategies that will aid you in assessing the effectiveness of schools. These strategies are located in the Observation Manual (see Appendix 1). It is important to get information from more than one source so that the most comprehensive and accurate interpretations can be made about school effectiveness.

DISCUSSION QUESTIONS AND ACTIVITIES

1. Observe in a local elementary school. What are the rules and regulations that students must follow? Do they seem reasonable or arbitrary? Do students seem to spend a large amount of time waiting? Observe one student over a 40-minute period and determine what portion of those 40 minutes she or he spends just waiting.

2. Select an elementary or secondary school class and analyze the interaction. How many questions does the teacher ask? How many of these are fact questions and how many involve more complex thought and creativity? How many times does the teacher praise students? Criticize them? Compare your findings with those of your classmates.

3. Visit several classrooms and calculate what percentage of the time is spent on noninstructional activity—administrative duties, reprimanding students, and the like. Share what you find with your classmates.

4. Do you think that the tracking system is a valid method for recognizing meritorious performance? Or do you think it is a mechanism for perpetuating inequality of opportunity based on social class, race, or sex? Develop an argument to support your position and then debate someone in your class who holds an opposing point of view.

5. Spend a day or more in an elementary school classroom. Try to describe the peer groups and cliques. Are the cliques sex-segregated? Who are the most popular students? Who are the isolated ones? Compare your perceptions with those of the classroom teacher.

6. We have noted the vividness and detail with which many people recall their high school years. Try to answer the following:

- Who was voted most likely to succeed in your high school class? (Do you know what he or she is doing today?)
- What was your happiest moment in high school? Your worst?
- Name five people who were part of the in crowd in your class. What were the "innies" in your high school like?

• Is there any academic experience in high school that you remember vividly? If so, what was it?

7. Dig out your senior-class high school yearbook. Read it carefully. How many pictures of you are there in it? What were you doing? What do you wish you had been pictured doing? What does it say under your senior class picture? What do you wish it said? Would you be proud or embarrassed to show this yearbook to your college friends and classmates? How would you feel if you attended your high school reunion and your former classmates said, "Why _____ [insert your name], you haven't changed a bit!"

8. Write a research paper on adolescent alienation. As a result of your research, make some recommendations on how secondary schools could get students to become more involved in academic and extracurricular activities.

9. Read the entire 1989 report *Turning Points: Preparing American Youth for the 21st Century*. Compare this to the 1983 report *A Nation at Risk*.

10. Based on the five characteristics of effective schools, would you consider your elementary and secondary schools effective? If not, why? Share your responses with your classmates.

11. Try out the observation and interview strategies included in the Observation Manual to help you identify effective schools. Develop additional guidelines and activities for finding good schools, and share these with your classmates.

NOTES

1. Philip W. Jackson, *Life in Classrooms* (New York: Holt, Rinehart & Winston, 1968).
2. Ibid.
3. Manuel Justiz, "It's Time to Make Every Minute Count," *Phi Delta Kappan* 65, no. 7 (March 1984): 483–485.
4. Herbert Walberg, "Families as Partners in Educational Productivity," *Phi Delta Kappan* 65, no. 6 (February 1984): 397–400.
5. John Goodlad, *A Place Called School* (New York: McGraw-Hill, 1984).
6. C. Fisher, N. Filby, E. Marliave, L. Cohen, M. Dishaw, J. Moore, and D. Berliner, *Teacher Behaviors, Academic Learning Time, and Student Achievement,* Final Report of Phase III-B, Beginning Teacher Evaluation Study (San Francisco, CA: Far West Laboratory for Educational Research and Development, 1978).
7. Quoted in Ernest L. Boyer, *High School* (New York: Harper & Row, 1983).
8. Jackson, *Life in Classrooms.*
9. Ned Flanders, "Intent, Action, and Feedback: A Preparation for Teaching," *Journal of Teacher Education* 14, no. 3 (September 1963): 251–260.
10. Arno Bellack, *The Language of the Classroom* (New York: Teachers College Press, 1965).
11. Goodlad, *A Place Called School.*
12. Romiett Stevens, "The Question as a Measure of Classroom Practice," in *Teachers College Contributions to Education* (New York: Teachers College Press, 1912).
13. Myra Sadker and David Sadker, "Questioning Skills," in James Cooper (ed.), *Classroom Teaching Skills* (Lexington, MA: D. C. Heath, 1986).
14. Mary Budd Rowe, "Wait Time: Slowing Down May Be a Way of Speeding Up!" *Journal of Teacher Education* 37 (1986): 43–50.
15. W. D. Floyd, *An Analysis of the Oral Questioning Activity in Selected Colorado Primary Classrooms.* Unpublished doctoral dissertation, Colorado State College, 1960.

16. Talcott Parsons, "The School as a Social System: Some of Its Functions in Society," in Robert Havinghurst, Bernice Neugarten, and Jacqueline Falk (eds.), *Society and Education* (Boston: Allyn & Bacon, 1967).

17. Robert Lynd and Helen Lynd, *Middletown: A Study in American Culture* (New York: Harcourt Brace Jovanovich, 1929).

18. W. Lloyd Warner, Robert Havinghurst, and Martin Loeb, *Who Shall Be Educated?* (New York: Harper & Row, 1944).

19. August Hollingshead, *Elmtown's Youth* (New York: Wiley, 1949).

20. Robert Havinghurst et al., *Growing Up in River City* (New York: Wiley, 1962).

21. Shirl Gilbert and Geneva Gay, "Improving the Success in School of Poor Black Children," *Phi Delta Kappan* 67, no. 2 (October 1985): 133–138.

22. Ray Rist, "Student Social Class and Teacher Expectations. The Self-Fulfilling Prophecy of Ghetto Education," *Harvard Education Review* 40, no. 3 (1970): 411–451.

23. Henry Giroux and Anthony Penna, "Social Education in the Classroom: The Dynamics of the Hidden Curriculum," in Henry Giroux and David Purpel (eds.), *The Hidden Curriculum and Moral Education: Deception or Discovery?* (Berkeley, CA: McCutchan, 1983), p. 118.

24. Jeannie Oakes and Martin Lipton, "Detracking Schools: Early Lessons from the Field," *Phi Delta Kappan* 73, no. 6 (February 1992): 448–454.

25. Susan Allan, "Ability Grouping Research Reviews: What Do They Say About Grouping and the Gifted?" *Educational Leadership* 48, no. 6 (March 1991): 60–65; Adam Gamoran, "Alternative Use of Ability Grouping in Secondary Schools: Can We Bring High-Quality Instruction to Low-Ability Classes?" *American Journal of Education* 102 (1993): 1–22; Robert E. Slavin, "Achievement Effects of Ability Grouping in Secondary Schools: A Best-Evidence Synthesis," *Review of Educational Research* 60 (1990): 471–499.

26. Quoted in Raphaela Best, *We've All Got Scars* (Bloomington: Indiana University Press, 1983), p. 9.

27. Best, *We've All Got Scars*.

28. Ibid., p. 10.

29. Ibid., p. 162.

30. Steven Sher, "Some Kids Are Nobody's Best Friend," *Today's Education,* February–March, 1982.

31. "Unpopular Children," *The Harvard Education Letter,* Harvard Graduate School of Education in association with Harvard University Press, January–February 1989, pp. 1–3. See also Lisa Wolcott, "Relationships: The Fourth 'R,'" *Teacher* (April 1991): 26–27.

32. Zappa, Coleman, Friedenberg, Vonnegut, and Ford are quoted in Ralph Keyes, *Is There Life After High School?* (Boston: Little, Brown, 1976).

33. James Coleman, *The Adolescent Society* (New York: Free Press, 1961).

34. Goodlad, *A Place Called School.*

35. Quoted in Boyer, *High School,* p. 202.

36. Ibid., p. 206.

37. Sara Lawrence Lightfoot, *The Good High School* (New York: Basic Books, 1983).

38. David Owen, *High School* (New York: Viking Press, 1981).

39. Keyes, *Is There Life After High School?*

40. Lloyd Temme, quoted in Keyes, *Is There Life After High School?*

41. Mel Brooks and Dustin Hoffman are quoted in Keyes, *Is There Life After High School?*

42. Quoted in Boyer, *High School.*

43. Ernest L. Boyer, "What Teachers Say About Children in America," *Educational Leadership* 46, no. 8 (May 1989): 73–75.

44. Quoted in Boyer, "What Teachers Say About Children in America," p. 73.

45. Ibid.

46. Ibid., p. 74.

47. Frances Ianni, "Providing a Structure for Adolescent Development," *Phi Delta Kappan* 70, no. 9 (May 1989): 677.

48. Patrick Welsh, *Tales Out of School* (New York: Viking, 1986), pp. 41–42.

49. Urie Bronfenbrenner, "Alienation and the Four Worlds of Childhood," *Phi Delta Kappan* 67, no. 6 (February 1986): 430–435.

50. Lightfoot, *The Good High School.*

51. Quoted in Ianni, "Providing a Structure for Adolescent Development," p. 679.

52. Ianni, "Providing a Structure for Adolescent Development, p. 680.

53. Grace Pung Guthrie and Larry Guthrie, "Streamlining Interagency Collaboration for Youth At Risk," *Educational Leadership* 49, no. 1 (September 1991): 17–22.

54. Alfie Kohn, "Caring Kids: The Role of Schools," *Phi Delta Kappan* 72, no. 7 (March 1991): 496–506.

55. Carnegie Council on Adolescent Development, *Turning Points: Preparing American Youth for the 21st Century,* excerpted in "The American Adolescent: Facing a Vortex of New Risks," *Education Week* 8, no. 39 (June 21, 1989): 22.

56. Ibid.

57. G. Weber, *Inner-City Children Can Be Taught to Read: Four Successful Schools* (Washington, DC: D.C. Council for Basic Books, 1971).

58. Ronald Edmonds, "Some Schools Work and More Can," *Social Policy* 9 (1979): 28–32.

59. Barbara Taylor and Daniel Levine, "Effective Schools Projects and School-Based Management," *Phi Delta Kappan* 72, no. 5 (January 1991): 394–397. See also Herman Meyers, "Roots, Trees, and the Forest: An Effective Schools Development Sequence." Paper delivered at the American Educational Research Association, San Francisco, April 1992.

60. Lightfoot, *The Good High School.*

61. Ibid., p. 67.

62. David Clark, Linda Lotto, and Mary McCarthy, "Factors Associated with Success in Urban Elementary Schools," *Phi Delta Kappan* 61, no. 7 (March 1980): 467–470. See also David Gordon, "The Symbolic Dimension of Administration for Effective Schools." Paper delivered at the American Educational Research Association, San Francisco, April 1992.

63. Quoted in Boyer, *High School,* p. 221.

64. William Rutherford, "School Principals as Effective Leaders," *Phi Delta Kappan* 67, no. 1 (September 1985): 31–34. See also R. McClure, "Stages and Phases of School-Based Renewal Efforts." Paper presented at the annual meeting of the American Educational Research Association, New Orleans, 1988.

65. Mary Hatwood Futrell, "An Educator's Opinion, Reform Demands Restructured Schools," *The Washington Post,* April 6, 1986, p. c5.

66. United States Department of Education, *What Works* (Washington, DC: U.S. Department of Education, 1986).

67. Joyce Epstein, "Paths to Partnership," *Phi Delta Kappan* 72, no. 5 (January 1991): 344–349.

68. Theodore Sizer, *Horace's Compromise: The Dilemma of the American High School* (Boston: Houghton Mifflin, 1984).

69. Quoted in Lightfoot, *The Good High School,* p. 43.

70. Stanley M. Elam, Lowell C. Rose, and Alec M. Gallup, "The 24th Annual Gallup Poll of the Public's Attitudes toward the Public Schools," *Phi Delta Kappan* 74, no. 1 (September 1992); Stanley M. Elam, Lowell C. Rose, and Alec M. Gallup, "The 26th Annual Gallup Poll of the Public's Attitudes toward the Public Schools," *Phi Delta Kappan* 74, no. 1 (September 1994).

71. Keith Baker, "Recent Evidence of a School Discipline Problem," *Phi Delta Kappan* 66, no. 7 (March 1985): 482–487.

72. William Wayson, "The Politics of Violence in Schools: Double Speak and Disruptions in Public Confidence," *Phi Delta Kappan* 67, no. 2 (October 1985): 127–132.

73. U.S. Department of Education, *What Works.*

74. Lightfoot, *The Good High School.*

75. Wilbur Brookover, Laurence Beamer, Helen Efthim, Douglas Hathaway, Lawrence Lezotte, Stephen Miller, Joseph Passalacqua, and Louis Tornatzky, *Creating Effective Schools* (Holmes Beach, FL: Learning Publications, 1982).

76. Herbert Walberg, Rosanne Paschal, and Thomas Weinstein, "Homework's Powerful Effects on Learning," *Educational Leadership* 42 (1985): 76–79.

77. Robert Rosenthal and Lenore Jacobson, *Pygmalion in the Classroom* (New York: Holt, Rinehart & Winston, 1968).

78. Patrick Proctor, "Teacher Expectations: A Model for School Improvement," *Elementary School Journal* (March 1984): 469–481.

79. Larry Cuban, "Effective Schools: A Friendly but Cautionary Note," *Phi Delta Kappan* 64, no. 10 (June 1983): 695–696.

80. Daniel Levine, "Creating Effective Schools: Findings and Implications from Research and Practice," *Phi Delta Kappan* 72, no. 5 (January 1991): 389–393.

7

WHAT STUDENTS ARE TAUGHT IN SCHOOL

OBJECTIVES

To consider the place of the extracurriculum in school life

To assess the impact of the hidden curriculum

To become aware of contemporary curriculum trends and innovations

To differentiate between the formal and the hidden curriculum

To analyze historical trends and issues in curriculum development

What did you learn in school today? This is a time-honored question asked by parents, and many jokes have been made about the responses children give. What children learn varies depending on whether they are more alert to the formal curriculum made up of objectives and textbook assignments or to the hidden curriculum that emerges from the social procedural organization of the school. What children learn in school also shifts with the changing societal values of different times.

This chapter will provide a brief profile of what is taught in today's elementary and secondary schools. Through a series of time capsules, you will gain historical perspective on the issues and controversies that have marked curriculum development from the Puritans' two Rs (reading and religion) to the current controversy over national curriculum standards. The chapter will also examine the educational pendulum and analyze how the curriculum swings back and forth to reflect the interests of progressive and traditional educators.

What Is a Curriculum?

As soon as she opened the door, Mary Jean knew she would like the teachers' room. There was the good smell of fresh coffee, and although it was early, groups of teachers were already clustered about the room talking about their work and their lives.

As Mary Jean filled her cup and reluctantly turned away from the donuts, she scanned the room. There they were, Mr. Battersea and Mrs. Schwartz, sitting at a round table in the corner.

"I hope I'm not late," Mary Jean apologized as she slipped into the remaining seat at the table. "Is it after eight?"

"Oh no, you're right on time," said Mr. Battersea. "We've been here for a while. We get here early to plan for the day. As soon as you start teaching, those college days of sleeping late are over. So enjoy it while you can."

"He's so lively in the morning," Mrs. Schwartz grimaced. "Personally, I hate the morning. Maybe after I finish this cup of coffee I'll be more coherent." Then she gave Mary Jean a broad wink. "Just kidding. I gripe about the mornings as a matter of principle. I've gotten used to the early hours—well, almost used to them. You said that you needed to conduct an interview for your Introduction to Education class. How can we help you?"

Mary Jean pulled out the sheet her professor had distributed in class. "It says here I'm supposed to ask two teachers at the school where I'm observing to give me their definition of *curriculum*. So I guess that's the big question. What's a curriculum?"

"Kind of a big, broad topic, isn't it?" Mr. Battersea looked puzzled.

"I know. Our professor said you might feel that it was a very general question. But that was the idea. We are all supposed to get different reactions from the teachers in class and then compare them."

"I like that idea," said Mrs. Schwartz, looking a little more lively as she drained the coffee cup. "In fact, I'd like to be a fly on the wall and listen in on your class discussion. I'll try to answer your question. A curriculum. . . . Hmm. . . . What is a curriculum? Well. . . . Obviously it's what kids learn in school. It's the goals and objectives our country sets for the different grade levels, and they certainly set an awful lot of them. We discuss those goals and objectives as a faculty here at Thomas Jefferson. Sometimes we add new objectives of our own, and we'll often decide, based on the needs of our own students, which to emphasize and what are our priorities."

Carol Schwartz glanced at Mary Jean, who was scribbling furiously. "Got all that, dear? Then, a curriculum is also the textbooks that are selected. Students are working with texts of one kind or another throughout the day. So what a text emphasizes becomes an important part of the curriculum. What we teachers do in class—our own interests and specialties—that becomes the curriculum too. For example, I love to travel. Every summer I go to a different country, and then all during the year I take some time to talk with the children about that place. Sometimes I'll bring in food or show them postcards and slides. I guess that becomes the curriculum too. A curriculum is simply what students learn from their teachers and textbooks in their classrooms."

"Carol, I think you've made some great points for Mary Jean, but for me the curriculum is more than what is taught in classrooms. It's everything kids learn in school. For example, we have a drama group that's putting on a rock version of Shakespeare's *A Midsummer Night's Dream.*" Mary Jean stopped writing and stared at Mr. Battersea. "Oh, I know it sounds weird," he grinned, "but the kids are doing a great job, and the drama teacher is very creative. Kids who are participating in that play are learning a tremendous amount—music, theater, Shakespeare. Other students participate in band, in chorus, in sports. There's a computer club. We even have a Special Friends Club, where the students work with the kids who have disabilities—take them bowling, play with them during lunch, teach them. . . . Children learn a lot through these experiences. I think extracurricular activities are an important part of what students learn in school."

"You're right, Jim. I was thinking about the formal academic curriculum. And what children learn in school is broader than that. I also remember one of my education professors talking about a hidden curriculum. I wasn't quite sure what he meant at the time, but over the years I've been teaching, I've grown more and more aware of just how powerful this hidden curriculum is."

"I'm with you there. I couldn't agree with you more." Jim Battersea leaned forward. "What Carol and I are talking about, Mary Jean, is all that subtle, incidental learning that occurs as children interact with each other, with the teacher, with all the different sides and angles of this thing we call school. For example, those kids in the drama club are learning so much more than Shakespeare. How does it feel to be on stage in front of 500 people? Are they nervous? How do they handle stage fright? What do they do if they forget their lines? Can they improvise? Do they help each other and cooperate, or do they compete? And think what a tremendous amount students learn about themselves and human nature when they work with kids with disabilities in the Special Friends Club. This hidden curriculum is an undercurrent of the formal class structure, too. What do kids learn when they're playing a game in class and no one chooses them for the team? What messages do they take away if a teacher treats them unfairly or explodes in anger? Or, think of all a youngster will learn from that teacher who sits down to talk with him or her about hobbies, goals, problems."

"I know just what you're talking about." Mary Jean put down her pencil. "Like right now. I've learned a lot more than formal definitions of the curriculum. I know what the teachers' room is like early in the morning. I know how early you get here, and that you take time out of your busy schedules to talk with someone who wants to be a teacher. I've learned about curriculum and about teaching as well."

• • •

In 1962 the highly regarded educator Hilda Taba said, "Learning in school differs from learning in life in that it is formally organized. It is the special function of the school to so arrange the experiences of children and youth that desirable learning takes place. If the curriculum is to be a plan for learning, its content and learning experiences need to be organized so that they serve the educational objectives."[1] Today most educators regard the formal **curriculum** as the organization of intended outcomes for which the school says it is responsible.

In *A Place Called School,* one of the most important and influential studies of school life, John Goodlad refers to an explicit and an implicit curriculum.[2] The *explicit curriculum* is reflected in curriculum guides, courses offered, syllabi describing courses, tests given, materials used, and teachers' statements of what they want students to learn. The *implicit,* or *hidden, curriculum* emerges incidentally from the interaction between the students and the physical, social, and interpersonal environment of the school. The **extracurricu-**

lum includes student activities such as sports, clubs, governance, newspaper, and the like. Before we look at the formal, or explicit, curriculum of elementary and secondary schools, perhaps we should examine the powerful, less formal, extracurriculum.

Extracurriculum or Cocurriculum

"The Battle of Waterloo was won on the playing fields of Eton," said the Duke of Wellington, perhaps becoming the first to highlight the importance of extracurricular activities. Today the justification for the extracurriculum is similar to that provided in Wellington's time. Through sports, academic and social clubs, band, chorus, orchestra, and plays, crucial skills and values are developed. Students who participate in athletics learn leadership, teamwork, persistence, diligence, and fair play. Through involvement in plays and concerts, creativity and talent are nurtured. Academic clubs—science, languages, computers, debate—enhance not only academic learning but social skills as well. Advocates see these activities as so important that they refer to them not as the *extracurriculum* but as the *cocurriculum.*

Students also see these experiences as worthwhile, at least if their patterns of involvement are any measure. In the mid-1980s, 80 percent of students nationwide were participating in some form of extracurricular activity. Students from small schools were more likely to get involved; and the smarter the student, the higher the rate of participation.

Sports attract the most students, with 55 percent of high school boys and 30 percent of high school girls participating. While the percentage of girls participating in sports grew dramatically after passage of Title IX in 1972, a law prohibiting gender discrimination in educational programs receiving federal aid, this increase has slowed down in the past few years. If the current trend continues, it will take high schools until the year 2033 to achieve gender parity in their sports programs.[3] Areas such as music, drama, and debate comprise the second-most-popular extracurricular activities, with 28 percent of students

Although opinions vary over the long-term value of extracurricular activities, no one can deny that the experiences they produce are far more memorable than academic learning experiences.

participating. Academic clubs are the third-most-popular activity, with one-quarter of all students taking part in one by their senior year. While the overall rate of student participation in academic clubs has not changed since the early 1970s, gender imbalance is less an issue than underrepresentation of low socioeconomic students.[4] Today's academic clubs are called Odyssey of the Mind and Future Bowl and promote cross-curricular interests and creative problem-solving skills.

Advocates proclaim the value of the extracurriculum to life both within and far beyond the high school years. Allyce Holland and Thomas Andre found that:

- Extracurricular activities encourage student self-esteem and civic participation.
- The extracurriculum, especially athletics, improves race relations.
- Participating students have higher SAT scores and grades.
- Involvement in the extracurriculum is related to high career aspirations, especially for boys from poor backgrounds.[5]

Recently, the benefits of sports participation specifically for girls have received special attention. Organizations such as the Women's Sports Foundation have publicized studies showing that, overall, girls who participate in sports are less likely to get involved in drugs, less likely to get pregnant, and more likely to graduate from high school than are those who do not play sports.[6] Moreover, they are 30 percent less likely to get breast cancer by age 40.[7]

Not all research reports agree about the positive effects of extracurricular involvement. More skeptical than others about any real benefit to students, researcher B. Bradford Brown concludes that the best we can say "is that the effects of extracurricular participation on secondary school students' personal development and academic achievement are probably positive, but very modest, and are definitely different among students with different social or intellectual backgrounds."[8]

While all must be involved in the formal, academic curriculum, participation in the extracurriculum is voluntary and results from a variety of personal and social factors. If you think back to your own high school days, you may remember both high- and low-profile students: the extracurricular superstar so involved in everything from the student council to the yearbook that she walked around with a little black calendar in her backpack to keep activities straight; the nominal participants, involved in a few activities (this is where most students fall); and the nonparticipants, those who are alienated or feel excluded from the extracurricular side of school.

Think about your own involvement in the extracurriculum. Were you a high-profile student? Nominal? Alienated or uninvolved? What did you learn from the extracurricular side of school? Did you gain important skills and knowledge, or did you think the extracurriculum was a frill, diverting important resources and attention from formal academic coursework? If you were active in extracurricular activities, what were your motives?

High-profile students have a complex network of reasons for participating. For some, there is genuine interest and enjoyment. Others see the extracurriculum as a path to social success. One study found that only 16 percent of students surveyed said getting good grades increases status among peers. However, 56 percent of students said that extracurricular activities can lead to popularity.[9] Other calculating students base their choice of activities not on their own interests but rather with an eye to the interests of admissions officers who select the chosen few for the nation's most prestigious colleges and universities.

When controversies arise over the extracurriculum, they are usually over its uneasy relationship with the academic side of school. For example, the current emphasis on a rigorous academic curriculum has spilled over in the form of policies that bar students who have failed a course from extracurricular participation. In Texas and other states, "no pass, no play" rules deny students in poor academic standing the right to participate in varsity sports.

Such policies raise puzzling questions and issues. Should poor performance in the formal curriculum be used as a reason to deny participation in the extracurriculum? If the extracurriculum is a vital part of the learning offered in school, can students be denied access? According to data from the longitudinal study *High School and Beyond,* African-American and Latino males are most likely to be affected by these policies, since one-third fail to maintain a 2.0 grade point average.[10] Since the top academic students, more likely to be wealthy and white, already dominate the extracurriculum, will no pass, no play regulations make this curriculum even more exclusive, driving deeper divisions between the haves and have-nots and further segregating racial and ethnic groups?

An ongoing concern is that to many the extracurriculum means only one thing—varsity sports. On any autumn Saturday in thousands of small towns across the United States, entire communities, accompanied by bands, parades, and pep rallies, cheer the hometown football teams with a level of adulation that can only be dreamt of by academic stars. Media publicity and multibillion-dollar markets too often emphasize the profit motive above and beyond academic concerns. All the hoopla can lead hopeful high school athletes down a treacherous road. While more than 5 million students across the nation play interscholastic varsity sports, 49 out of 50 will never make a college team. For every 100 college athletes, only one will play professional sports. Many critics worry that the tail is wagging the dog in a system where athletics get the resources, the hope, and the attention, while academics slide into the shadows.

The Hidden Curriculum

While the relationship between the formal curriculum and the extracurriculum is occasionally controversial, they have one thing in common: Both have goals and methods that are explicit and intentional. Those who study schools have uncovered a third curriculum. Incidental and unintentional, not found in the official school catalog, it is powerful nonetheless. Researchers call this the *hidden curriculum.*

Jules Henry is an anthropologist who has analyzed the hidden curriculum of the elementary school and studied the values and behavior it teaches. He concludes that students are capable of learning many things at one time and that the school teaches far more than academic content. For example, Henry describes a fourth-grade classroom where a spelling bee was taking place. Team members were chosen by two team captains. When a student spelled a word correctly on the board, a hit was scored. When three spelling errors were made, the team was out. Students cheered or groaned, depending on the outcome for their team.

According to Henry, these students were learning about more than spelling. They were learning about winning and losing, competition, and the feelings that accompany success and failure. If they were chosen early for a team, they learned about group support and recognition. If they were chosen late, they learned about embarrassment and rejection. Some of the more thoughtful students also learned about the absurdity of a spelling lesson being taught as a baseball game.[11]

Here is another example. The formal academic curriculum stresses the importance of preparing students to become active citizens in a democracy. Courses in government, civics, and history are offered to meet this goal. In the extracurriculum, elections to student government schoolwide and to offices in individual classes and clubs supposedly promote democratic participation. But the subtle and powerful message of the hidden curriculum may lead to some very different learning, learning entirely opposite to that which is intended.

Elections, as they are run in most schools, may teach students that "selecting the best person for the job" is really little more than judging a popularity contest. Or that the candidate with the best posters, rather than the best platform, is most likely to win. Or that it does not matter if the winner has intelligent positions on issues, or the snazziest posters, or the most friends, because nothing changes anyway. Perhaps the fact that a large segment of the electorate fails to vote in national elections is a testament to the power of the hidden curriculum.

The Formal Curriculum

There are striking similarities in the courses of study put forth by each of the 50 states. National curriculum standards, already developed for math, science, social studies, geography, history, the performing arts, and other subject areas, will continue to make state curricula increasingly similar in the coming years. The sections below offer a synopsis of what is taught in the formal curriculum in today's schools. They also summarize current tension points and trends that may shape what is taught in the schools of tomorrow.

Language Arts and English

Topics

Language arts programs emphasize multiple goals, including effective oral and written communication, comprehension and listening skills, problem solving, and language and literature appreciation. In elementary school, the language arts curriculum addresses the essentials of how to use language—reading, grammar, spelling, handwriting, composition, capitalization, punctuation, and dictionary use. At the secondary level, language arts instruction (or simply, English class) usually shifts the focus, with an increasing emphasis on literature. Senior high school students usually read classics by authors such as Shakespeare, Poe, Whitman, and Austen.

Tension Points and Trends

Today approximately one in six adults in the United States is functionally illiterate, a shocking statistic that results in the loss of an estimated $6 billion annually in related unemployment compensation and welfare costs.[12] Adult illiteracy underscores the continuing debate over how to best teach reading skills. Basal readers, which have traditionally dominated reading instruction, emphasize discrete components of reading, such as phonics, in which students learn to read by sounding out letters in order to form words. *Whole language*—a newer movement that focuses on the construction of meaning, early and extensive writing, and having students read relevant literature instead of the classics—treats reading as an integrated behavior. Many teachers seek, and sometimes struggle, to incorporate principles of both phonics and whole language into their language arts instruction.[13]

Improving generally poor reading performance is not the only language arts challenge: Poor writing performance also remains a concern. The 1992 "snapshot of student writing" study collected the best writing samples of 2,200 fourth and eighth graders. Analysis showed that most students do not write at any length and do not write analytical or research papers, and that only 1 percent revise their work.[14]

Another trend worth noting is that, during the past century, the list of authors taught in English classes has become increasingly American. In 1907, 9 of the 40 most frequently assigned authors were American; by 1990, 29 of the 40 were American.[15] In recent years, many English teachers have strived to include literature by women and minorities in their syllabi, a trend that some fear is jeopardized by current efforts to instill a core curriculum of "classic" literature, traditional selections more familiar to many adults.

Mathematics

Topics

The curriculum and evaluation standards issued by the National Council of Teachers of Mathematics (NCTM) in 1989 have been virtually unanimously accepted by teachers nationwide. These standards emphasize problem solving, reasoning, technology, communication, and real-life application of mathematical concepts.

Mathematics instruction in elementary school focuses on basic skills and concepts: addition, subtraction, multiplication, division, fractions, decimals,

A major focus of current curriculum reform is how to reverse girls' progressive decline in mathematics test scores.

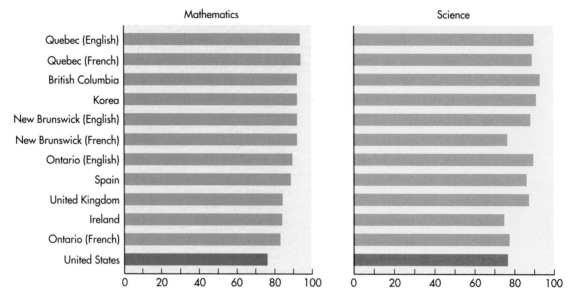

Source: National Center for Education Statistics, *An International Assessment of Educational Progress, A World of Differences* (Washington, DC: U.S. Department of Education, 1989).

FIGURE 7.1
Percentage of 13-Year-Olds with a Score of 400 or Higher on an International Mathematics and Science Test, by Selected Countries and Provinces, 1988

percentages, and the rudiments of geometry. In secondary school, algebra, geometry, trigonometry, calculus, and computer programming are taught.

Tension Points and Trends

According to the National Assessment of Educational Progress (NAEP), average mathematics performance improved between 1973 and 1990 for students at ages 9 and 13 while achievement remained stagnant for 17-year-olds.[16] International assessments suggest that Americans do not compare favorably with students from other countries in mathematics skills (see Figure 7.1). Also, there is a gender gap in mathematics achievement, with boys outperforming girls by high school graduation. Since mathematics is the "critical filter" for a wide array of professional and technological careers, the comparatively poorer performance by women and minorities is an issue of current and future concern.

In 1992 the NCTM published *A Core Curriculum: Making Mathematics Count for Everyone.* The document suggested innovative directions for the teaching of mathematics, including the transition from ability grouping and tracking to a core mathematics curriculum for all students. While algebra was previously taught only to eighth-grade students in the high-ability group, it is now increasingly likely to be taught to all students. Also emphasized in the report is the need for students to see real-world applications of math; the report emphasizes the use of computer and calculator graphics to investigate these connections.[17]

Social Studies

Topics

As the study of the relationship between people and their ideas and actions, social studies curricula draw upon the disciplines of history, government, geography, economics, sociology, anthropology, and psychology. However, in most programs, especially those at the secondary level, history is paramount.

The early elementary school social studies program emphasizes self, family, and community. Upper elementary school students begin the study of history, geography, and civics. At the high school level the focus is on U.S. history and government, but a wide array of electives, such as economics, sociology, law, world history, anthropology, and current events, is also offered. The curricular emphasis in most high schools is still predominantly domestic. Today, about half of all U.S. high school graduates have never studied world history; most of the other half have studied it for a year or less.[18]

Tension Points and Trends

At all levels of instruction there is insufficient attention to international topics, and today's students are shockingly ignorant of the history, politics, and geography of other nations. One out of three students cannot locate France on a map, and one out of five cannot locate the United States.[19] While the performance of U.S. students is disappointing in general, the even poorer performance of minority students and, to a lesser extent, of female students, is of special concern (see Figure 7.2).

The increasingly interdependent world economy has prompted a renewed drive to promote international understanding through social studies instruction.

FIGURE 7.2
Average U.S. History and Civics Proficiency by Grade, Sex, and Race, or Ethnicity, 1988

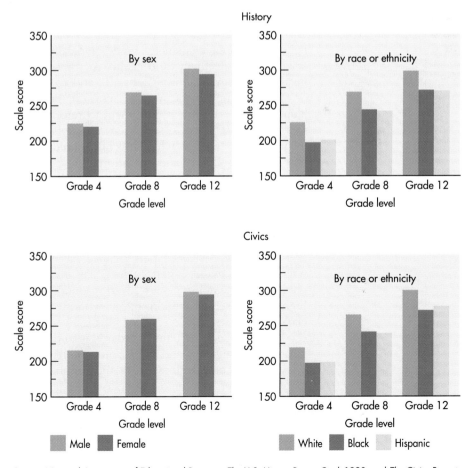

Source: National Assessment of Educational Progress, *The U.S. History Report Card,* 1990, and *The Civics Report Card* (Princeton, NJ: Educational Testing Service, 1990).

For example, in 1989, the National Governors' Association issued a report called *America in Transition,* which asserted that the United States is not well-prepared for international trade and called for increased business support for international education in schools.[20]

Civics, a social studies area under particular scrutiny at this time, is seen as a potential course through which to acquaint a diverse student population with the democratic tradition. The 1990 NAEP showed that better civics education is sorely needed. More than 40 percent of high school seniors were not aware that the Declaration of Independence affirms the right to life, liberty, and the pursuit of happiness. Half of all twelfth graders do not know that the amendments to the Constitution guarantee religious freedom and other basic rights.[21] Along with all its other tension points, history has become the battleground for curriculum wars between multiculturalists and advocates of a core curriculum (see Chapter 8). While the curriculum battle still rages, history teaching has changed dramatically over the past generation, moving away from a narrow emphasis on political and economic landmarks and toward a broader perspective of social life and daily human struggles.[22]

Science

Topics

In the early elementary grades science instruction emphasizes the child's orientation to the natural world—plants, animals, seasons, heat, sound, color, and light. The upper elementary grades typically study weather and climate, the solar system, electricity, and health. At the secondary level, science curriculum includes biology, chemistry, physics, and earth and space sciences.

In 1985, the American Association for the Advancement of Science (AAAS) launched Project 2061, a movement to reform science, mathematics, and technology. In 1993, AAAS released *Benchmarks for Science Literacy,* which includes statements of what students should know and be able to do by the end of grades 2, 5, 8, and 12. Reforming science curricula will continue in the years ahead.

Tension Points and Trends

In international comparisons with students from other countries, U.S. students generally rank low in science achievement. According to the 1990 NAEP, fourth- and eighth-grade science performance has stagnated over the past 20 years, while twelfth graders' performance has dropped. Only 9 percent of twelfth graders can demonstrate advanced scientific procedures. Fully 41 percent of high school seniors report never working on homework for their science classes.[23]

The science curriculum standards issued by the AAAS emphasize learning through investigation and higher-order thinking instead of rote memorization. They also recommend reducing the number of concepts that are currently taught in order to promote deeper understanding of key scientific principles. As with mathematics standards, the science standards are intended to promote heterogeneous grouping by defining basic levels of core knowledge for all students, regardless of background, ability level, or future aspirations. A challenge to the successful implementation of these new standards will be the need for resources and equipment to conduct appropriate experimentation.[24]

Foreign Languages

Topics

Before World War II, most foreign language instruction stressed reading and writing. The 1950s saw the introduction of an audiolingual approach designed to develop competence in listening and speaking. As a result the number of language laboratories increased from a handful to 8,000 by the mid-1960s. However, the audiolingual approach met with mixed success, so the use of language labs subsequently declined.[25]

Today the language taught most often is Spanish, followed by French and German. The junior high school language curriculum focuses on grammar, vocabulary development, pronunciation, and simple conversation. In senior high school the curriculum focus switches to conversational fluency, with more emphasis on cultural awareness.

Tension Points and Trends

In a world where 2,700 languages are spoken, only 15 percent of its people are native English speakers. The language with the most speakers is Chinese, and Hindustani comes in second. Within this context, the United States is the most monolingual of all the developed countries.

In 1915, 36 percent of all high school students studied a foreign language. By 1980, this percentage had been slashed by more than half, and only 5 percent of high school students continued their study of a foreign language more than two years. Recently, however, many colleges have reestablished foreign language requirements and enrollments in foreign language courses are climbing once again. Further, educators are calling for earlier emphasis on the study of foreign language—by the fourth grade and even before—and for blocks of time longer than 40 or 50 minutes a day for the study of language.[26]

The Arts

Topics

Visual arts and music are emphasized in elementary school, where regular classroom teachers do most of the instruction. Children color, paint, and use clay. In music, children learn sight reading and sing traditional childhood favorites, patriotic songs, and music from other lands. In secondary school the arts curriculum typically expands to include graphic arts, design, crafts, drama, dance, cinema, photography, ceramics, sculpture, orchestra, band, chorus, and more specialized music courses. Goals of the arts program include developing the ability to create art forms, understanding art as a cultural phenomenon, and developing greater aesthetic appreciation and perception.

Tension Points and Trends

Many educators consider the arts to be shamefully neglected—the last to come and the first to go when the budget ax falls. One study found that elementary schools commit only 4 percent of their school week to art instruction. Only 25 percent of that time is provided by trained art teachers. Further, some critics charge that there is too much emphasis on students' acquiring technical and performance skills rather than gaining greater appreciation of aesthetics and human creativity. In 1994, a panel of 38 artists, educators, and business

Periodic curriculum reform efforts are nearly always motivated by competitive national goals such as defense and economics. Should these goals always dominate the noncompetitive, humanistic concerns of the arts?

representatives approved new, voluntary standards for arts curriculum that call for more ambitious and sequential instruction. The standards specify that, by high school graduation, students should have a basic level of competency in each of the four arts disciplines—dance, music, theater, and visual arts.[27]

Physical Education

Topics

Education by and through human movement, physical education focuses on fitness, skill and knowledge development, and social and psychological development including leadership, teamwork, and cooperation. During the 1960s physical education emphasized competitive skills development, an approach that often led to frustration and embarrassment for those who did not excel. During the past few decades, there has been a shift in focus to fitness and lifelong activity such as tennis, golf, and swimming.

Elementary programs are often structured around games that develop skill in movement. Programs vary from little more than teacher-monitored recess to well-organized sports programs. Course offerings in secondary school typically include aerobic conditioning, archery, badminton, basketball, bowling, dance, football, gymnastics, hockey, pool, tennis, track, tumbling, wrestling, and yoga. Today physical education program goals include enhancing fitness by increasing aerobic capacity, strength, and flexibility and helping students to participate in appropriate individual and group activities. Research shows that the involvement of students in physical education provides lifelong health dividends.

Tension Points and Trends

National assessments continue to show that American children are less physically fit than is desirable. According to the President's Council on Physical Fitness and Sports, American children are in bad shape: Forty percent of boys cannot do more than one pull-up; 55 percent of girls cannot do any.[28] According to a study by the Department of Health and Human Services, 40 percent of U.S. children between the ages of 5 and 8 exhibit obesity, hypertension, or high cholesterol.[29] The trends toward decreased childhood fitness and increased body fat are attributed primarily to high-fat diets and a lack of physical activity.

Health Education

Topics

Health education is incorporated into the curriculum at both the elementary and secondary levels, but topics are not typically addressed in great detail until upper elementary school or later. Areas of instruction include disease prevention and control, mental and emotional health, consumer health, family life, sexuality, nutrition, and substance abuse.

Tension Points and Trends

Health education is often embroiled in controversy, especially in the areas of sex education and AIDS prevention. (See Chapter 15 for a discussion of health issues.)

Vocational and Career Education

Topics

Career education occurs informally in elementary school, with individual lessons on different occupations. At the secondary level, the vocational education curriculum is clearly targeted to specific types of work, and course titles such as "cosmetology," "auto body repair," "vocational printing," and "meal management" abound in high school catalogs. During the 1960s and 1970s vocational education experienced enormous growth, peaking in 1984. Since then enrollment in vocational education has been declining.[30]

Despite the common belief that vocational education constitutes a discrete academic track for low-ability students who plan to work full-time after high school, a recent survey revealed that vocational education plays a much broader role in the high school curriculum. More than 97 percent of high school students take at least one vocational education course before graduation. In fact, the average high school student takes more credits of vocational education (4.2 credits) than of English (4.0 credits). Nearly half of all vocational education classes are taken by students who plan to attend a 4-year or community college after high school.[31]

Tension Points and Trends

Some critics decry vocational education as it is now taught. Pointing to statistics showing that students who graduate from vocational programs do not have an advantage in the job market, they charge that vocational education is caught between inadequacy and irrelevance. Lacking modern equipment and well-trained staff, the programs cannot prepare students for high-tech fields. And the skills needed for low-paying jobs, such as work in fast-food restaurants, are better learned on the job than in school. Other opponents charge that a vocational curriculum tracks students into worthless nonacademic courses and should be abolished.

In 1990, Congress passed the Carl D. Perkins Vocational and Applied Technology Act, signaling the start of a new era of reform for vocational education. This legislation calls for a shift from the traditional job-skills orientation of vocational education to a broader integration with academic instruction. Proponents of this approach argue that higher-order thinking skills should be emphasized in all vocational courses in order to adequately prepare students for today's job market. The Perkins Act also channels federal funds to school districts with the highest proportions of poor students, promotes nonsexist career choices, assists displaced homemakers as they reenter the job market, and offers support for post–high school vocational training programs. But by 1995, congressional budget cuts had jeopardized the future of the Perkins Act.

How the Curriculum Developed: A Historical Perspective

Curricula serve a dual function. On the one hand, they preserve and transmit to students the culture and traditions of the past. On the other hand, they anticipate the knowledge, skills, and abilities that today's students will need in order to function effectively in tomorrow's society. Sometimes these two roles—preserving and anticipating—come into conflict, and then some difficult curricular decisions must be made. When this clash occurs, it is important that the curriculum not be viewed as sacred and immutable, but as living and evolv-

Dear Ms. Kirincich,

The Mouse and the motorcycle was a great idia it mostly teaches us how to spell bedder. It was fun. Kelly

Love
your student,
Gioia.

ing, flexible enough to meet the emerging needs of a continually developing society.

Many of today's adults have witnessed a variety of curriculum changes in their lifetime. For example, males who went to junior high school in the 1950s and 1960s took a required course called "industrial arts," which was for boys only. Females who went to junior high school during this time took a required course called "home economics," which was only for girls. Today some women can whip up a mean souffle but are bewildered when confronted with even minor home repairs. Some men can fathom the intricacies of a house wiring system but work on one level when it comes to cooking—burned. There is nothing genetic about the ability to hammer a nail or measure a cup of flour: It was the junior high school curriculum of a few decades ago that stereotyped people in this manner.

Today this artificial split between industrial arts and home economics is disappearing as a result of the women's movement, federal law, and economic necessity. Girls now enroll in industrial arts, and boys now take home economics in related courses. In many schools these old course titles have been replaced by newer ones such as "life survival skills." In such courses, girls and boys together learn to use both needles and wrenches, to change flat tires and to cook dinner. In short, they learn whatever skills are necessary in order to function effectively in a society where once-traditional roles for women and men are no longer traditional.

Although most of you left high school just a few years ago, the curriculum you knew has changed even in that short span of time. The curriculum is continually evolving in response to new needs and new perspectives, and your earlier experiences as students are now a part of history. To see the way curricula change with time, let us look at the curricula of some earlier time periods. Our brief journey in time will reflect the process of change and adaptation that has matched curriculum development to social change in this country. Because Chapter 9, The History of American Education, will offer you a look at U.S. schooling from colonial times through the progressive era, this chapter will offer only brief reviews of those periods. However, we will take a closer look at how curricula developed from the 1950s through the 1980s, the time period that sets the context for what and how you will teach. Imagine what it might have been like to have been a student in schools past. To borrow the words of a famous news commentator, "You are there."

Time Capsule 1: The Two Rs in the Seventeenth Century

In the seventeenth century, religion underlay all human activity. Reading the Scriptures provided the route to salvation, and the "two R" curriculum, a blend of reading and religion, prevailed. As a white elementary student in those times, you would acquire the rudiments of reading and religion from the **hornbook,** parchment attached to a paddle-shaped board and covered with a piece of transparent horn. If you were a white student toward the end of the century, you would be treated to a fear-inspiring dose of Puritan morality from America's first basal reader, *The New England Primer*. After elementary school you would put away your hornbook if you were female. Secondary schooling was not offered to girls, while African-Americans and Native Americans were routinely denied any formal education. If you were male and financially well off, you might go to the **Latin grammar school.** There you would learn Latin,

Greek, and more Latin. If you grew weary of conjugating Latin verbs and translating Greek, you could always get a change of pace by reading the Bible and other religious texts.

Time Capsule 2: Curricula in the Eighteenth Century

New immigrants came to America, there was an upsurge in trade and commerce, and the boundaries of the frontier stretched westward. These were optimistic times, with great faith in the progress and potential of humanity, dreams of fortunes to be made, and a growing commitment to life in the present instead of salvation after death. This shift from the spiritual to the secular began to free the curriculum from the tight bonds of religion. As a white elementary student, you would still work on *The New England Primer.* Studies focused on reading, religion, and morality, although writing and arithmetic were beginning to get more attention.

For secondary students there were some new alternatives to the Latin grammar school. You could, if you wished, attend the **English grammar school** to learn vocational skills such as surveying, bookkeeping, accounting, or navigating. Or, by the middle of the century, thanks to the efforts of Benjamin Franklin, you would have a third option—the **academy.** These academies were a merger of the Latin and the English schools, and they housed two different courses of study. You could choose either the traditional Latin curriculum or the English course of study, which included English grammar, some history, and foreign languages. And the academy broke with tradition in another way, for its doors were open to women as well as men.

Time Capsule 3: A Secularized Curriculum for More Students in the Nineteenth Century

The forces of nationalism, democratization, and industrial development spread across the land. As a result, universal literacy, vocational competence, and preparation for citizenship became curricular aims.

As an elementary school student, you would have traded in your *New England Primer* for McGuffey's readers. The course of study expanded to include writing, arithmetic, spelling, geography, and good behavior.

As a secondary student, you would probably be enrolled in the academy, which by the middle of the century had become the dominant form of secondary school in America. You could choose either the Latin curriculum, which continued to focus on Latin, Greek, and arithmetic, or the expanding English curriculum, which included English grammar, public speaking, geography, history, and sometimes science, geometry, algebra, and a modern language (a long way from the two Rs of the 1600s).

Time Capsule 4: Progressive Education in the First Half of the Twentieth Century

Migration changed a once agrarian nation into one that was primarily urban. New and diverse waves of immigrants (Irish, Polish, German, Jewish, Italian, Slovak, Greek, and Finnish) continued to pour ashore, and the schools were

Immigrant children such as these were expected to be "Americanized" by the schools of the late nineteenth and early twentieth century.

expected to Americanize them into a homogeneous and productive workforce. New educational philosophies also migrated from Europe, and these culminated in the progressive movement, with John Dewey as its chief spokesperson.

As an elementary student, you would now have time for creative expression in the form of drawing, painting, music, dance, and craftwork. Moreover, the rigid distinctions that separated content fields were breaking down. Rather than studying history, geography, and civics, you would face an integrated course called *social studies*. And *language arts* was a broad rubric that encompassed reading, writing, speaking, and listening.

As a secondary student, you would attend the **junior high school,** which grew in popularity during the 1920s. Here you might participate in a core curriculum that stressed the integration of different subject areas, studying topics from "conservation in the development of American civilization" to "how I can use my spare time." During this period, high school changed from a college-oriented institution organized to meet the needs of the elite to a secondary school for most white Americans. By 1918 vocational courses such as typing, stenography, bookkeeping, domestic science, and industrial arts joined the curriculum.

Time Capsule 5: *Sputnik* in Space and Structure in Knowledge

After World War II, the vocational and service-oriented courses of progressivism became known as *life-adjustment education*. As a student you might have enrolled in courses such as "developing an effective personality" or something called "common learning," in which you would have studied your own social and personal problems. By the 1950s the life-adjustment curriculum was ridiculed as anti-intellectual and undemocratic, and progressive education was under attack from many sides.

In 1957 the iciest of Cold War fears seemed to be realized with the launching of the Russian *Sputnik*, the first artificial satellite. The schools were made the scapegoat for the country's failure in the race for space. *Life* magazine urged an end to the "carnival" in the schools; Congress passed the National

Defense Education Act (NDEA) and appropriated nearly a billion dollars for programs in science, math, modern languages, and guidance. Academicians and the lay public both decried the schools' lack of intellectual rigor.

As a student during this time, you and your classmates would have enrolled in a foreign language and rigorous math and science courses. Prestigious academicians became involved in curriculum development, particularly in math and science. One of these scholars was Jerome Bruner, a Harvard psychologist, who served as secretary of a conference of scholars, scientists, and educators at Woods Hole, Massachusetts, and his report on this conference, *The Process of Education* (1960), had a major impact on curriculum. Translated into 20 languages and read by educators worldwide, this report put forward the premise that "any subject can be taught effectively in some intellectually honest form to any child at any stage of development."[32] Bruner conceptualized a discipline not as a collection of facts but rather in terms of its structure—the principles and methods of inquiry most central to its study. Bruner believed that if students could learn these methods of inquiry, they could then study a field at different levels of sophistication. He envisioned the curriculum as a spiral in which students would return to the principles at the heart of the discipline and study them in progressively more complex and advanced forms. In terms of teacher training, Bruner advocated the *discovery method,* in which teachers would assist students in uncovering meanings for themselves.

Bruner's emphasis on the structure of the discipline intrigued scholars and curriculum developers. The new curriculum developers, often prestigious academicians from colleges and universities, sought to structure or to sequence each body of knowledge so that students could grasp and build upon basic principles and relationships rather than memorize seemingly unrelated pieces of information. The result of this curriculum revolution was an array of discipline-oriented curricula, particularly in science and math.

Time Capsule 6: Social Concern and Relevance

During the late 1960s and the early 1970s, Cold War competition seemed irrelevant, as racial strife and the war in Vietnam tore at the very fabric of our society. As a student of the times, you might have thought that the discipline-oriented curricula of the past decade were out of touch with the needs of disadvantaged children and alienated youth, the movement for civil rights, and the devastation of war overseas.

Once again school curricula became the object of critical scrutiny, and once again they were found lacking—this time by a group of critics who have been variously labeled the "radical," "compassionate," or **"romantic" critics.** Whatever their label, these critics were concerned about the irrelevance of curricula that emphasized academics at the expense of social reality.

New courses and topics burgeoned, spinning the curriculum into new areas. You would probably have found yourself studying an array of issues from multicultural curricula to your own attitudes and values. Many of these developments continue to influence the school curriculum today.

Women's Studies and Multiethnic Curricula

During the 1970s curriculum developers began to design lessons, units, even entire programs, around the needs and contributions of women. These programs generally focused on patterns of sex bias, and they sought to compensate for the omissions of history and literature books, where women and their contributions have often been systematically ignored. Another development in educational institutions at all levels was the drive to sensitize students to the various **ethnic groups** that comprise American society. As a result, ethnic studies programs were developed, particularly in the social studies, language arts, and humanities.

Individualized Education Programs for Children with Disabilities

Public Law 94-142, the 1975 Education for All Handicapped Children Act, specified the components of the **individualized education program (IEP)** for each child who is eligible for special education: (1) assessment of the child's present achievement levels, (2) identification of goals and of the services needed to achieve those goals, and (3) systematic progress checks to see if the goals are being met or if they need to be revised. The IEP statement also indicates the extent of the child's participation in regular school programs. This act, renamed the Individuals with Disabilities Education Act (1990), remains highly influential today.

Social Issues: Death, War and Peace, the Environment

During the 1970s, some educators, psychologists, and parents began asserting that death is a universal concern and that children have a need and a right to learn about it:

> There is a need for guidance and knowledge about dying, grief, and bereavement, but accent needs to be given to the death education of children and youth, for that has been relatively ignored. Ideally, death education should be that process whereby each person is helped to develop from childhood through maturity and to senescence with an acceptance of death as a fact of life.[33]

Educators also began to note the pervasive impact of violence and war and to call for a peace curriculum through which students could analyze the conditions of peace, the causes of war, and the mechanisms for the nonviolent resolution of conflict. Courses in **peace studies** were first instituted in the 1960s, and by 1974, 29 colleges and universities offered either a certificate or an academic major in peace studies. In some cases, elements from these courses filtered down to secondary and elementary schools.

During this time many educators and citizens became concerned that students should receive more appropriate information about pollution, overpopulation, and the waste of our natural environment. As a result of such concern, new programs in ecology and **environmental education** emerged. These programs reflected the urgent need to preserve our planet's intricate environmental balance, and they continue to influence curricular materials today.

The Open Classroom

In 1967 in Great Britain the Plowden Committee, a Parliamentary commission, encouraged all English primary schools to adopt a child-centered approach to education called the **open classroom.** This open classroom approach enjoyed great popularity in this country during the 1970s. Based on the work of the Swiss child psychologist Jean Piaget, the open classroom was decentralized and divided into flexible areas called **interest,** or **learning, centers.** The children were encouraged to explore the classroom and select the activities they wished to pursue in the various learning centers. The room and the different centers were rich in learning resources and materials of all kinds to stimulate the children's interest and involvement in learning. The teacher typically worked with individual students and small groups, and trust in the child was the paramount characteristic of the teacher-student relationship.

A visitor to such a classroom in the 1970s might have seen students discussing their beliefs and commitments on topics ranging from war to changing sex roles; learning about the culture and heritage of different ethnic groups; studying topics such as sexuality, peace, drug or consumer education; and moving freely from one interest center to another within the classroom. However, even as these innovations were occurring, newspaper editorials and articles in professional journals reflected a disenchantment with some or all of these new curriculum trends. The comments went something like this: "National tests show that our students are having trouble with reading, writing, and math. In view of this, what business do schools have dabbling in all these curricular frills? It's time to get back to the basics."

Time Capsule 7: Back to Basics and a Core Curriculum

There was no unifying manifesto for those who advocated **"back to basics."** The meaning of this movement varied from one individual and school to another. In the early 1980s a composite of what many back-to-basics advocates wanted schools to do went something like this:

1. Devote most of the elementary school day to reading, writing, and arithmetic.
2. Place heavy secondary school emphasis on English, science, math, and history.
3. Give teachers more disciplinary latitude, including the authority to use corporal punishment.
4. Use instructional procedures that stress drill, homework, and frequent testing.
5. Adopt textbooks that reflect patriotism and reject those that challenge traditional values.
6. Eliminate electives, frills, innovations, and such "social services" as guidance, sex education, humanistic education, and peace education programs.
7. Test, test, and test. Tie student promotion from grade to grade and graduation from high school to demonstrated proficiency on specific examinations. Issue traditional report cards frequently to communicate and monitor student progress.[34]

The conservative *National Review* summed it up this way: "Clay modeling, weaving, doll construction, flute practice, volleyball, sex education, laments about racism, and other weighty matters should take place on private time." The public defined *back to basics* more succinctly as attention to the traditional subject areas of reading, writing, and arithmetic.[35]

The issue of declining test scores gave the movement its major impetus. Between 1952 and 1982, student scores dropped 50 points on the verbal part of the SAT and almost 30 points on the mathematics part. The National Assessment of Educational Progress indicated that 17-year-olds knew less about the natural sciences, were less skillful in using reference works, wrote less coherent essays, and made less accurate inferences in reading in the academic year 1973–1974 than in the academic year 1969–1970. Parents and citizens were concerned about academic decline. In 1977 the College Board appointed a blue-ribbon panel to study the problem. They identified a number of issues, including absenteeism, grade inflation, a lack of homework, and a profusion of watered-down electives.

Many researchers focused with alarm on this burgeoning number of electives as a cause for achievement decline. Philip Cusick found a mushrooming curriculum at the high schools he studied. For example, one high school had 31 separate courses in English; another had 27. There was a proliferation of easy electives, such as "girl talk," "what's happening?," "personal relations," and "trouble shooter." Also, activities that used to be extracurricular—yearbook, student council, newspaper, band, glee club—were often given academic credit.[36] Sara Lawrence Lightfoot, in her study *The Good High School,* also found a bewildering array of electives. One of the schools she visited had a 188-page catalog with more than 500 course descriptions. Career courses alone took up 23 pages.[37]

Even though proliferation of electives may reflect academic richness, there is no doubt that students began to avoid the more rigorous courses. A U.S. Department of Education study showed that between 1964 and 1980 students flocked from academic study to "personal service and social development" courses. In the 1960s, 12 percent of high school students were enrolled in the "general" program, which is more open-ended than the academic program and has more opportunity for electives. By the 1970s, enrollment in the general program had skyrocketed to 42 percent.

When faced with the question of whether to tilt in the direction of student choice or of a curricular core, most reform reports opted for the latter. For example, the National Commission on Excellence report, *A Nation at Risk,* called for new basics—4 years of English, 3 years of mathematics, 3 years of science, 3 years of social studies, and one-half year of computer science. .

In his book *High School,* Ernest Boyer also called for a **core curriculum,** with the proportion of required courses changed from one-half to two-thirds of the total number of units necessary to graduate. He said that this core should include literature, history, math, science, foreign languages, the arts, civics, non-Western studies, technology, the meaning of work, and health. He advocated the abolition of the three traditional high school tracks (academic, general, and vocational), calling instead for the integration of all students into one track with a pattern of electives radiating from the center of a common core of learning. Boyer also advocated a new unit for a service requirement, which would involve students in volunteer work in their communities.[38]

Influential in the reform movement, John Goodlad's *A Place Called School* also recommended a core, but it stated that a common set of topics should not form the basis of the core. Rather, the core should comprise "a common set of concepts, principles, skills and ways of knowing."[39] Theodore Sizer's *Horace's Compromise* fueled the movement to reform public schools, and it too emphasized the process of knowing. Arguing that less is more, Sizer believed that only certain essentials such as literacy, numeric ability, and civic understanding should be mandated.[40]

The reform report that placed the most stringent emphasis on core requirements was developed by philosopher and educator Mortimer Adler, in his controversial "The Paideia Proposal." This program advocated a required course of study that was the same for every child through the first 12 years of schooling. The only choice was the selection of which second language to study. Adler thought that electives only allow students "to voluntarily downgrade their own education."[41]

With an expanded perspective on the implications of a core curriculum, E. D. Hirsch, Jr., brought the issue into the national spotlight with his best-selling *Cultural Literacy*. The ability to understand what one reads is dependent on a shared, taken-for-granted context of information, a network of names, places, dates, and ideas—what Hirsch calls **cultural literacy.** According to Hirsch, the core components of this background knowledge can be identified. He has even extracted these components as terms and compiled them as a several-hundred-item list of what literate Americans know.[42]

Hirsch believes that this network of background information, key to standard literate culture, remains stable over time and can be taught directly to students. He worries that in recent years schools have abandoned their responsibility to teach this standard, literate culture. He warns, "When the schools of the nation cease to transmit effectively the literate language and culture, the unity and effectiveness of the nation will necessarily decline."[43]

Time Capsule 8: New Directions for the Curriculum

While academic excellence and the core curriculum remain important issues, a new vocabulary and different perspectives are shaping curricula. Many educators are urging a widening of the core, an expansion to include more minorities and women. Others advocate a culturally specialized curriculum, such as Afrocentric education, to meet the unique needs of different ethnic and racial groups (see Chapter 8). This struggle to make the core more inclusive—or to change it—is complex, volatile, and not likely to be resolved easily. The volatility of this conflict became apparent in the hotly contested debate over what should be included in national history standards (an issue also explored in the next chapter).

Another trend is toward a more integrated curriculum. Some reformers are frustrated by the dissected nature of the curriculum, its "egg carton" division of content into separated and disconnected academic disciplines. These divisions, they say, make it difficult for students to perceive and understand the intellectual links between content areas. How, they ask, can you teach the Renaissance, for example, without connecting history, literature, music, and art? To slice knowledge into somewhat arbitrary and separated segments denies students a rich, textured, and coherent understanding of the past and present world.

There are many entrenched barriers to curricular integration, including class schedules, the physical structure of school buildings, and teachers themselves. A truly integrated curriculum makes enormous demands on the knowledge base of teachers, especially at the secondary level. Suppose, for example, you are a high school English teacher and your class is about to read *The Red*

The integrated curriculum uses activities that are innately interesting to create a variety of learnings. Here, students performing in this play might incorporate literature and history lessons, artistic expression, and social learnings among others.

Badge of Courage, Stephen Crane's novel set during the Civil War. You have a B.A. in literature, with several credits toward your master's, and you have spent years developing and honing your academic specialty. However, your general knowledge is not as strong. You haven't had a history, math, or science course in years. How, you wonder, can you connect this novel to the history, music, and art of the Civil War? How can you possibly integrate scientific developments of the time—and work in some math as well?

"You would integrate one step at a time," say curricular reformers, "and you wouldn't have to do it alone." There are many different models for helping students to connect their learning. Working more closely with teachers from other departments and grade levels is an important way to begin. In the case above, for example, you could find out when the history teacher plans to teach the Civil War, and coordinate your lessons on the novel with his or her schedule. Teachers from other disciplines could be included in planning, so they could relate lessons, or segments of lessons, to this curricular theme.

From these initial steps the development of a connected curriculum can become a far more complex and sophisticated effort. As one advocate says, the connected curriculum would:

> shun education which shortchanges insight, . . . which takes knowing a lot as a substitute for understanding, which tolerates the chocolate box model of learning—because learning like that will go stale the week after the test. It would emphasize connection—making performances within and across subject matter knowledge, performances that both build and show understanding. It would help to bring insight home to the classroom.[44]

As you have read how the curriculum has changed during the past decades, you may have felt a sense of *déjà vu,* with each innovation echoing past developments. There seems to be an ongoing struggle between educators who hold differing visions of what a school is for. This debate between progressives and traditionalists has yielded a history of curricular fads swinging with the motion of a pendulum. While other professions demonstrate steady, long-term progress, researcher Robert Slavin says that "education resembles such fields as fashion and design, in which change mirrors shifts in taste and social climate and is not usually thought of as true progress."[45] Many educators yearn for a more stable time when the radical curricular swing will be fine-tuned, so that innovation will depend more on research about what works than on the politics of who is in power. Only then can a reasonable and thoughtful compromise accommodate the legitimate concerns of different groups and best meet the needs of our students.

SUMMARY

1. There are various forms of curricula in schools. One, the explicit, or formal, curriculum, includes the courses offered, syllabi description of courses, tests given, materials used, and teachers' statements of what they want students to learn. Another, the implicit, or hidden, curriculum, emerges incidentally from the interaction between the students and the physical, social, and interpersonal environment of the school. A third, the extracurriculum, or cocurriculum, includes student activities such as sports, clubs, student government, school newspapers, and the like.

2. Extracurriculars have become fixed in the culture of American schooling, with 80 percent of all students participating in activities such as athletics, musical groups, and academic clubs. Proponents of the extracurriculum argue that it encourages student self-esteem and civic participation, improves race relations, and raises children's aspirations as well as their SAT scores. Many remain skeptical, however, seeing extracurricular activities as having very little, if any, effect on achievement and personal development.

3. Controversies over the extracurriculum usually arise from conflict with the academic side of school. Some states have instituted "no pass, no play" rules, excluding low-achieving students from participating in varsity sports. Since these rules tend to affect minority students disproportionately, many people see these rules as making the extracurriculum exclusive and discriminatory. Others criticize the degree to which schools pour resources and attention into athletics, when that support could be going toward academics.

4. In addition to planned lessons, schools teach a hidden curriculum, subtle messages that students receive from teachers' and other students' behaviors.

5. School subjects are taught in the formal curriculum, which is currently undergoing scrutiny and revision. National standards have already been developed for math, science, geography, and other subject areas. The scope of these changes, as well as tension points, are reviewed in this chapter.

6. Curricula have two functions. One function is to *preserve* and transmit to students the culture and traditions of the past. The other is to *anticipate* the knowledge, skills, and abilities that today's students will need in order to function effectively in tomorrow's society. Sometimes these two functions of preserving and anticipating may clash.

7. The seventeenth century witnessed the "two R" curriculum, with a heavy emphasis on reading and religion. The only secondary schooling available was the Latin grammar school, which was open only to white male students who could afford the cost.

8. The eighteenth-century curriculum shifted toward the secular. The English grammar school and the academy became options for secondary schooling. Girls were allowed to attend the academy.

9. As a result of nationalism, democratization, and industrial development, the curriculum in the nineteenth century moved toward universal literacy, vocational competence, and preparation for citizenship. Elementary school studies included writing, arithmetic, spelling, geography, and good behavior. The academy was the dominant form of nineteenth-century secondary schooling until the last quarter of the century, when the academy gave way to tax-supported public high schools.

10. In the first half of the twentieth century, the curriculum was influenced by John Dewey and the progressive movement. Creative expression, social skills, and a more integrated study of subject areas were stressed. The junior high emerged during the 1920s. The mission of high schools was to meet the needs of all the students, not only the college-bound. By 1918 vocational coursework had become an important part of the curriculum.

11. In 1957 the Russians launched *Sputnik,* and weak American schools were viewed as the reason for the country's defeat in the race for space. As a result the curriculum became discipline-oriented, particularly in math and science.

12. The curriculum in the late 1960s and the 1970s focused on social issues, with particular emphasis on the needs and contributions of women and minorities. Public Law 94-142, the Education for All Handicapped Children Act (later renamed the Individuals with Disabilities Education Act), required developing an individualized education program for each special needs child. Other issues emphasized in the curriculum were peace studies, ecology, and secular presentation of topics relating to death.

13. Popular in the 1970s, open classrooms were divided into flexible areas called interest or learning centers. Children were encouraged to explore the classroom and choose activities that they wished to pursue.

14. The curriculum of the 1980s was marked by the back-to-basics movement. Triggered by the problem of declining test scores, this movement stressed achievement in the traditional subject-matter areas. Today there is an ongoing debate over emphasizing a curricular core versus presenting the student with a variety of electives. Most reform reports urge a return to a core curriculum. There is also currrent movements toward an integrated or connected curriculum, and toward national standards as a way of unifying and improving schools. This controversial approach is described in the next chapter.

DISCUSSION QUESTIONS AND ACTIVITIES

1. To some students, it is the hidden curriculum and the extracurriculum that are central to their high school experience. Define the roles of these unofficial curricula experiences in your own high school education. If you were placed in charge of a high school today, how would you change these hidden and extracurricular experiences? Why?

2. Discuss your reactions to the current curriculum with your classmates. Were there any topics you studied that you now see as irrelevant? What subjects should be taught differently? Are there any subjects that are not included in the curriculum but that should be there?

3. If you were given the job of developing a core curriculum for elementary school, what would it look like? What would you include in a core curriculum for secondary school? For postsecondary education?

4. Do you think the proliferation of electives during the 1970s was a positive or a negative development? Did it reflect intellectual wealth or an abandonment of standards?

5. Consider past and present curricular developments and think about the changes in contemporary society. Then, with the help of your instructor and classmates, formulate what the school curriculum may be like in the year 2025.

NOTES

1. Hilda Taba, *Curriculum Development: Theory and Practice* (New York: Harcourt Brace Jovanovich, 1962).

2. John Goodlad, *A Place Called School* (New York: McGraw-Hill, 1984).

3. Feminist Majority Foundation, *Empowering Women in Sports,* 1995.

4. National Center for Education Statistics, *Trends Among High School Seniors, 1972–1992* (Washington, DC: U.S. Department of Education, 1995).

5. Allyce Holland and Thomas Andre, "Participation in Extracurricular Activities in Secondary School: What Is Known, What Needs to Be Known," *Review of Educational Research* 57, no. 4 (Winter 1987): 437–466.

6. Women's Sports Foundation. Based on information in *Women's Sports Facts,* 1989, updated July 1995.

7. J. Raloff, "Exercising Reduces Breast Cancer Risk," *Science News* 149, no. 14 (October 1, 1994): 215.

8. B. Bradford Brown, "The Vital Agenda for Research on Extracurricular Influences: A Reply to Holland and Andre," *Review of Educational Research* 58, no. 1 (Spring 1988): 107–111.

9. National Association of Secondary School Principals, *The Mood of American Youth* (Reston, VA: National Association of Secondary School Principals, 1984).

10. Data from *High School and Beyond* reported in "Extracurricular Activity Participants Outperform Other Students," *OERI Bulletin* (September 1986): 2.

11. Stephen Hamilton, "Synthesis of Research on the Social Side of Schooling," *Educational Leadership* 40, no. 5 (February 1983): 65–72.

12. Martha L. Brown, "Fighting Illiteracy: Let's Not Slight School Literacy," *Network News and Views* 8, no. 10 (October 1989): 61. Reprinted from *Chicago Tribune,* August 22, 1989.

13. Carla Haymesfeld, "Filling the Hole in Whole Language," *Educational Leadership* 46, no. 6 (March 1989): 65–68.

14. Mary Jordan, "Snapshot of Student Writing Finds Care Absent," *The Washington Post,* April 17, 1992, p. A-3.

15. Sandra Stotsky, "Whose Literature? American's!" *Educational Leadership* 49, no. 4 (December 1991/January 1992): 53–56.

16. Eugene Owen (compiler), *Trends in Academic Progress* (Washington, DC: National Center for Educational Statistics, 1991).

17. Peter West, "'Common Core' High-School Math Curriculum Offered," *Education Week,* April 8, 1992, p. 8.

18. John Fonte and Andre Ryerson (eds.), *Education for America's Role in World Affairs* (Lanham, MD: University Press of America, 1994), p. 44.

19. Diane Ravitch and Chester Finn, Jr., *What Do Our 17-Year-Olds Know?* (New York: Harper & Row, 1987).

20. Fonte and Ryerson (eds.), *Education for America's Role,* p. 44.

21. Ernest L. Boyer, "Civic Education for Responsible Citizens," *Educational Leadership* 48, no. 3 (November 1990): 5–7.

22. Philip Cohen, "Challenging History: The Past Remains a Battleground for Schools," *Association for Supervision and Curriculum Development Curriculum Update* (Winter, 1995): 2.

23. Annette Licitra, "Kids Start Strong in Science But Few Show Advanced Skills," *Education Daily,* March 26, 1992, p. 1; see also Owen (compiler), *Trends in Academic Progress.*

24. Hugh McIntosh, "What Should Students Know? How Should Teachers Teach?" *National Research Council NewsReport* 43, no. 1 (Winter 1993): 2–6; Project 2061 (American Association for the Advancement of Sciences), *Benchmarks for Science Literacy* (New York: Oxford University Press, 1993).

25. Gerald Hayn, "High School Language Instruction in the 1970s," *Hispania* 56 (March 1973): 94–99.

26. Sara Melendy, "A Nation of Monolinguals, A Multilingual World," *NEA Today* (January 1989): 70–74.

27. Debra Viadero, "38-Member Panel Adopts 81 Standards for the Arts," *Education Week* 23, no. 20 (February 9, 1994): 5.

28. William Bennett, *American Education: Making It Work* (Washington, DC: U.S. Department of Education, 1988).

29. Scott O. Roberts, "Fit Kids," *American Health* 11 (September 1992): 70–73.

30. Kenneth Gray, "Vocation Education in High School: A Modern Phoenix?" *Phi Delta Kappan* 72, no. 6 (February 1991): 437–445.

31. John G. Wirt, "A New Federal Law on Vocational Education: Will Reform Follow?" *Phi Delta Kappan* 72, no. 6 (February 1991): 425–433.

32. Jerome Bruner, *The Process of Education* (Cambridge, MA: Harvard University Press, 1960).

33. Donald Irish, in Betty Green and Donald Irish (eds.), *Death Education: Preparation for Living* (Cambridge, MA: Schenkman, 1971).

34. Ben Brodinsky, "Back to the Basics: The Movement and Its Meaning," *Phi Delta Kappan* 58, no. 7 (March 1977): 522–527.

35. George Gallup, "Gallup Poll of the Public's Attitudes Toward the Public Schools," *Phi Delta Kappan* 64, no. 1 (September 1982): 39.

36. Philip Cusick, *The Egalitarian Ideal and the American High School* (New York: Longman, 1983).

37. Sara Lawrence Lightfoot, *The Good High School* (New York: Basic Books, 1983).

38. Ernest L. Boyer, *High School: A Report on Secondary Education in America,* The Carnegie Foundation for the Advancement of Teaching (New York: Harper & Row, 1983).

39. Goodlad, *A Place Called School,* p. 298.

40. Theodore Sizer, *Horace's Compromise: The Dilemma of the American High School* (Boston: Houghton Mifflin, 1984), p. 89.

41. Mortimer Adler, "The Paideia Proposal," *The Rotarian,* September 1982.

42. E. D. Hirsch, Jr., *Cultural Literacy* (Boston: Houghton Mifflin, 1987).

43. E. D. Hirsch, Jr., "Cultural Literacy: Let's Get Specific," *NEA Today,* January 1988, p. 18.

44. D. N. Perkins, "Educating for Insight," *Educational Leadership* 49, no. 2 (October 1991): 4–18.

45. Robert Slavin, "PET and the Pendulum: Faddism in Education and How to Stop It," *Phi Delta Kappan* 70, no. 6 (June 1989): 752.

CONTROVERSY OVER WHO CONTROLS THE CURRICULUM

OBJECTIVES

To describe the various social forces that influence school curricula

To consider the advantages and disadvantages of a national curriculum

To analyze current controversies over curricula

To evaluate the role of the teacher as a developer of the curriculum

To debate the strengths and weaknesses of the "saber-tooth" curriculum and its relationship to today's schools

"We shape our buildings and afterwards our buildings shape us," said Winston Churchill. Had the noted statesman been a noted educator, he might have rephrased this epigram, substituting curriculum *for* buildings; *for what children learn in school today will affect the kinds of adults they become and the kind of society they will eventually create. In fact, it is the power of curriculum to shape students and, ultimately, society that takes curriculum development out of the realms of philosophy and education and into the political arena.*

In this chapter you will be asked to analyze the various groups and social forces that influence what students are taught in today's schools. After considering the role of the teacher as instructional decision maker, you will be asked to debate the strengths and weaknesses of the "saber-tooth" curriculum and to consider what knowledge is most worthy for inclusion in the curriculum of today's schools.

Censorship and Curriculum

Consider the following scenario: You have started your first job teaching English at an excellent high school, and you are thoroughly enjoying the experience. A college course in children's literature has given you extensive knowledge of contemporary adolescent fiction, and you have managed to establish a classroom library that is relevant to the concerns of your students and is of good literary quality as well. As a result, your students have been reading more than ever before and have been involved in exciting discussions about the books.

However, your sense of well-being and accomplishment is shattered by an early-morning stop at your mailbox, where you pick up an official-looking memo from the principal. You read:

Dear Ms./Mr. _____
(fill in your name)

Last night I had a long conference with Ms. Robinson, who is very upset with some of the books her daughter is reading in your class. She takes particular exception to *The Outsiders,* which she claims is a glorification of gang warfare and violence, and to *Forever* because she does not want her daughter exposed to any kind of knowledge about premarital sex.

Ms. Robinson has called for a special meeting of the school board to discuss what she terms "this serious crisis of providing inappropriate materials for impressionable adolescents." I have asked her to come to my office at the close of school today. The meeting will take place at 3:30 P.M. I'd like you to be there, too—and bring the books.

Gail Nirok
Principal

Would you be ready to meet with Ms. Robinson and Ms. Nirok, or do you feel that censorship conflicts, like traffic accidents, happen only to others?

The point is that nearly everyone—teachers, parents, the general public, and various special interest groups—wants some say as to what is and is not in the school curriculum. No matter what a particular textbook or course of study is like, someone is likely to consider it too conservative or too liberal, too traditional or too avant-garde, too racist, sexist, anti-Semitic, violent, un-Christian, or pornographic. There is, in fact, no such thing as a totally safe, acceptable, uncontroversial book or curriculum. For example, each of the following has been subjected to censorship at one time or another:[1]

- Mary Rodgers's *Freaky Friday:* "Makes fun of parents and parental responsibility."
- George Eliot's *Silas Marner:* "You can't prove what that dirty old man is doing with that child between chapters."
- Plato's *Republic:* "This book is un-Christian."
- Jules Verne's *Around the World in Eighty Days:* "Very unfavorable to Mormons."
- William Shakespeare's *Macbeth:* "Too violent for children."
- Fyodor Dostoyevsky's *Crime and Punishment:* "Serves as a poor model for young people."
- Herman Melville's *Moby Dick:* "Contains homosexuality."
- Anne Frank's *Diary of a Young Girl:* "Obscene and blasphemous."

In a multicultural society, to what extent should vocal community groups concerned about a particular issue (sex, religion, abortion, politics) be allowed to influence the school curriculum?

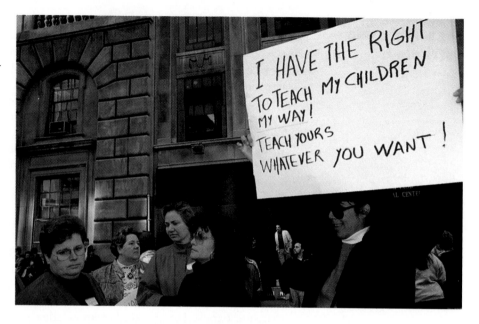

- E. B. White's *Charlotte's Web:* "Morbid picture of death."
- Robert Louis Stevenson's *Treasure Island:* "You know what men are like and what they do when they've been away from women that long."
- J. R. R. Tolkien's *The Hobbit:* "Subversive elements."
- Roald Dahl's *Charlie and the Chocolate Factory:* "Racist."
- William Steig's *Sylvester and the Magic Pebble:* "Anti-police" (one of the police officers is drawn as a pig).
- *Webster's Dictionary:* "Contains sexually explicit definitions."

According to People for the American Way, during the 1994-1995 school year there were 458 incidents of attempted censorship in 49 states.[2] Topping the list of the most frequently challenged books between 1982 and 1995 were:[3]

- John Steinbeck's *Of Mice and Men*
- J. D. Salinger's *The Catcher in the Rye*
- Robert Cormier's *The Chocolate War*
- Mark Twain's *The Adventures of Huckleberry Finn*
- Maya Angelou's *I Know Why the Caged Bird Sings*
- Roald Dahl's *The Witches*
- Alvin Schwartz's *Scary Stories to Tell in the Dark*
- Alvin Schwartz's *More Scary Stories to Tell in the Dark*
- Anonymous *Go Ask Alice*
- Katherine Paterson's *Bridge to Terabithia*

In one-half of the cases, the attempts at censorship were successful: The materials were either removed from the curriculum or school or placed on restricted-access shelves in libraries.[4]

The heart of the case against censorship is the First Amendment, which guarantees freedom of speech and of the press. Those who oppose censorship say that our purpose as educators is not to indoctrinate children but to expose them to a variety of views and perspectives. The case for censorship is made by those who believe adults have the right and the obligation to protect children from harmful influences, including what they read in school. From the classroom to the courtroom, each side has made a compelling case for its own point of view, and the controversy is symbolic of how politicized the curriculum debate has become. What knowledge is of most worth? Who decides? How is it transmitted? Who gets access to it? What information is left out? These questions are fundamentally political. Those who determine what should be known and who should know it have powerful influence over how a society thinks and behaves. This chapter will sort through the controversy to examine the different groups that want to control the curriculum and the many aspects of the issues.

Who (and What) Shapes the Curriculum

Parent and Community Groups

The scenario at the beginning of this chapter illustrates the power of parents to control classrooms, curricula, and instructional materials. Some citizens have pressured schools to provide courses as varied as drug education, sex education, ethnic studies, and studies of changing sex roles. In more conservative communities, religious fundamentalists have objected to the influence of secular humanism. Still others, who feel that job preparation is a key purpose of schools, want heavy emphasis on career and vocational education. Others want all these courses abolished so that schools can focus on a core curriculum.

Students

Students are sometimes skeptical about the wisdom and honesty of people in high places; schools, being the institution they are most familiar with, have received a large share of their criticism and censure. During the 1960s and 1970s, student protests covered all phases of the school curriculum. Demanding relevance, students tried to infuse more practical application into the academic curriculum and to liberalize the rules and rituals that constituted the hidden curriculum. Although students have not been particularly influential in curriculum development recently, as times change so may their interest and involvement in deciding what they are being taught.

Administrators

Sometimes administrators play an important role at the building or central-office level. The emphasis on the principal not only as a manager but also as an instructional leader has, in some cases, generated greater administrator involvement in curriculum development. For example, an elementary school principal may attend an in-service course on critical thinking skills and then urge all teachers in his or her building to include this topic in what they teach in their classrooms. Sometimes central-office personnel, such as social studies coordinators, play a major role in curriculum change in a system or district. Although they may involve teachers, community members, and students in curriculum planning, they usually retain the right to make final decisions.

The Federal Government

The federal government influences curriculum by periodically sponsoring school-related legislation tied to some long-term national goal. For example, the National Defense Education Act (NDEA) of 1958 encouraged schools to emphasize math, science, and foreign languages in order to train future scientists for the space race with the former Soviet Union. The Elementary and Secondary Education Act (ESEA) of 1965 influenced the curriculum in various ways, perhaps most notably in the development of special programs for children from low-income families. Many educators think that Goals 2000 could eventually result in a national curriculum.

Federal school legislation normally provides funds with which to finance the new program or policy. Consequently, such legislation usually contains provisions for supervising schools to see that they spend the money for the intended purpose. Often educators at the local level interpret such federal supervision as "if we [the federal government] are going to pay for it, then it belongs to us," and this leads to resentment and charges of federal control of education.

The State Government

The states influence school curricula through both legislative acts and administrative policies as well as through curriculum guides implemented by a department of public instruction or a state board of education. As states have assumed a stronger leadership role in education in recent years, their interest in curriculum matters has sharpened.

States often have requirements as to what should be included in the curriculum. For example, if a state mandates that every student take a course in computer literacy, this will obviously affect every school in the state. Many states also have requirements concerning what cannot be taught in the public schools. For example, there are many prohibitions today pertaining to the teaching of communism. In 1925, Tennessee had a law that prohibited teaching about human evolution in any way that was inconsistent with Biblical interpretation. In a famous case popularized as the "monkey trial," John Scopes, a young high school biology teacher, challenged this law, claiming that there was scientific merit in Darwin's theory of the origin of species. The nation's attention was riveted on the oratorical clash between Clarence Darrow, the famous trial lawyer representing Scopes, and William Jennings Bryan, "the silver-tongued orator" who was the prosecuting attorney. Scopes was found guilty of breaking Tennessee's law and was given a $100 fine. Today, as in the 1920s, individual teachers may encounter state laws that limit the topics they can teach or the points of view they are allowed to express.

Some states either prescribe the texts that schools can use or approve a limited listing of texts from which local school personnel must select. For example, a state may appoint a commission to determine what content and points of view a text must include in order to be *adopted* for use in that state. Among other things, a commission may insist that adopted texts contain an accurate portrayal of females, males, and minority group members. Clearly, such state adoption committees can have a significant impact on what you teach in your classroom.

Local Government

Local school boards, composed of locally elected or appointed citizens, make a variety of curriculum decisions that teachers and administrators are required to implement. The boards' requirements may run the gamut from courses in sex education to instruction in Latin. Some educators and citizens feel that local school boards should have a strong voice in curriculum decision making because they are in touch with the needs of the local community and have a clear sense of the abilities and interests of the students. Others feel that school board members lack the training and the broad perspective needed to maintain a flexible curriculum that is in touch with the national pulse. Although school boards are supposed to be representative of all groups within the community, in reality their membership is usually upper middle class and male. Consequently, their decisions often tend to be conservative in nature and protective of the status quo.

Colleges and Universities

Institutions of higher learning influence curricula through their entrance requirements, which spell out courses students must have taken in order to gain admittance. Many secondary schools base their academic curricula on these college and university requirements. As Bartlett Giamatti noted when he was president of Yale University:

> The high schools in this country are always at the mercy of the colleges. The colleges change their requirements and their admissions criteria and the high schools . . . are constantly trying to catch up with what the colleges are thinking. When the colleges don't seem to know what they think over a period of time, it's no wonder that this oscillation takes place all the way through the system.[5]

During the 1970s, half the nation's colleges set no specific course requirements and 75 percent did not consider the kinds of courses a student had taken in their admissions decisions. This had a drastic impact on enrollments and curriculum offerings in high school foreign languages and advanced math and science courses. During the 1980s and 1990s colleges tightened standards again, and enrollments have been increasing in these courses.

National Test Results

The results of national testing, such as the National Assessment of Educational Progress (NAEP), can influence what is taught in the schools. If students in a school fall short of national norms in certain areas, there will usually be attempts to strengthen the curriculum in these weak spots. In schools where there is student and community interest in admission to selective colleges, the Scholastic Assessment Test (SAT) may have a great deal of influence on what is taught in school. Because an increasing number of states are requiring new teachers to take tests in the Praxis series, these tests may become a major force in shaping the curricula in schools of education. If Benjamin Bloom's *Taxonomy of Educational Objectives* (see pages 52 to 53) is included in the Praxis tests, schools of education across the nation will stress the six levels of the taxonomy in their courses.

National tests can have a positive influence in holding the school curriculum to high standards. Their influence is less beneficial when teachers allow the tests to dictate their teaching styles and curricula.

Education Commissions and Committees

From time to time in the history of U.S. education, various committees, usually on a national level, have been called to study some aspect of education. Their reports often draw national attention and subsequently influence elementary and secondary curricula. For example, in 1968 the president's National Commission on Civil Disorders had widespread impact with its recommendation for the expansion of vocational education to meet the needs of alienated youth. The 1983 report by the National Commission on Excellence in Education called for new basics, with increased emphasis on academic subjects. The 1989 education summit of the governors convened by then President George Bush called for establishing clear national performance goals, and President Clinton continued this emphasis.

Professional Organizations

Many professional organizations, such as the National Education Association (NEA), the American Federation of Teachers (AFT), and the Association for Supervision and Curriculum Development (ASCD), publish journals and hold conferences that emphasize a variety of curriculum needs and developments. One year an organization may stress the need for attention to ecology or peace studies. The next year a conference theme may stress "back to basics." The topics highlighted by professional associations may filter down to the local level and influence what is taught in the schools. (Figure 8.1 summarizes all the groups that shape the curricula.)

Creating Curricular Standards: An Awkward Attempt to Create a National Curriculum

As you might expect, the collision of these various interest groups has created curricula that are not particularly characterized by logic or planning. In fact, frustrated education reformers have often cited the haphazard, disorganized manner in which schools create their curriculum as an obstacle to improving education and have targeted this process for change. In the early 1990s, the Bush administration began funding a project that harnessed the efforts of experts in mathematics, history, English, physical education and other fields in a project aimed at giving some order and direction to the nation's curriculum development. The National Education Standards and Improvement Council was formed to oversee the project. Working with organizations such as the National Council for Geographic Education, the National Council of Teachers of Mathematics, and the National Academy of Sciences, educators and content area experts worked to develop specific subject-matter guidelines detailing precisely what students across the United States should know at each grade level. The

FIGURE 8.1
Groups Shaping the Curriculum

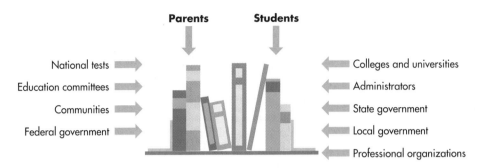

Parents   Students

National tests ➡
Education committees ➡
Communities ➡
Federal government ➡

⬅ Colleges and universities
⬅ Administrators
⬅ State government
⬅ Local government
⬅ Professional organizations

guidelines would serve as a national yardstick, enabling one school district to compare its performance with others.

More to the point, the institution of national guidelines and standards was intended to improve school performance. With higher, uniform national curricular goals in place, educators in local school districts would need to develop more rigorous programs, and all students would need to work harder. The end result of this effort would be "world-class" students as U.S. students moved from the bottom, or near-bottom, ranks in international tests to the top. The popular Republican plan was also a popular Democratic plan, and President Clinton continued this effort with the Goals 2000 plan. But soon things began to unravel, especially in history.

> "Plan to Teach U.S. History Is Said to Slight White Males"
> (*New York Times* headline)
> "History Hijacked"
> (Charles Krauthammer, *Washington Post*)
> "The History Thieves"
> (*Wall Street Journal* headline)

The publication of the proposed history standards prompted a storm of criticism. The critics were led by Lynne Cheney, a former official in the Bush administration, who argued that, in the new curriculum, white men were being slighted, business leaders maligned, historical heroes omitted. Lynne Cheney characterized the new history standards as "a warped view of American history."[6] Her criticism was seen as particularly harsh, pointed, and ironic—in part because when she headed the National Endowment for the Humanities years earlier, she had initiated the history standards project that she later found so abhorrent.

No such outburst accompanied the publication of the national standards for mathematics 5 years earlier. Forty-one states quickly adopted the mathematics standards, and math textbooks were modified accordingly. For mathematics, a national curriculum took shape.[7] Why was the process of adopting standards easy for math and difficult for history? The basic reason is that mathematics raises few values questions, while other disciplines, such as history, live and breathe values. Here are just some of the values questions raised by history standards:

• Should traditional heroes, sometimes called "DWM" (*dead white males*)—such as Washington, Jefferson, and other revered Americans—be the focus of the curriculum, or should the experiences and contributions of women and minorities, usually overlooked, be researched and included?

- Should history continue to emphasize European roots, or should Afrocentric issues be included? What about the views of other groups? For instance, should a penetrating view of European settlement of the Americas as seen through the eyes of Native Americans be taught to schoolchildren?
- Should U.S. history tell only a story of victors and triumphs, or should it also relate varied views of social and economic issues?

The new history standards did not please those with more traditional Eurocentric values, both because of what the standards omitted—for example, familiar names like Daniel Webster, Paul Revere, the Wright brothers—and for whom and what they included. Myra Colby Bradwell, for example, was included. Who was she? She was the first woman who took her bid to be admitted to the Illinois bar all the way to the Supreme Court. The Civil War received a different perspective as well, going beyond a chronology of battles to include an account of Northern riots by poor laborers who were being drafted for the deadliest war in American history while rich men simply paid $300 and avoided the draft. Whichever route the creators of the new history standards pursue, it is clear that some groups will be offended and protest.[8]

So touchy is the issue of a national curricular movement that—like "Newspeak"—even the words used to designate it carry hidden meaning. If this effort had been termed a *standard, federal curriculum,* rather than *national standards,* it would have encountered even greater opposition. *Federal* suggests enforcement, a "strong arm" approach. But *national* indicates that everyone will be included—a far less offensive concept. *Standards* for a curriculum suggests that there may be multiple routes for meeting each standard, that schools can choose from different materials and a variety of approaches in order to accomplish these goals. But *standard curriculum* suggests inflexibility, a lock-step program that all must follow. Political criticisms—reinforced by federal budget cuts—have put the future of the national standards movement in doubt, despite the attempts at more sensitive, less offensive wording.

The Textbook Shapes the Curriculum

While national standards in all subjects remain a distant prospect, the textbook continues to dictate the curriculum in most of today's classrooms. Students spend from 70 to 95 percent of classroom time using textbooks, and teachers base more than 70 percent of instructional decisions on them. Given this heavy reliance on texts, there is no doubt that they have a major daily influence on what is taught in schools. In fact, they are so pervasive and so frequently used that they constitute a curriculum of their own.

Before 1850 textbooks were made up of whatever educational materials children had in their homes. Students would bring these books to school, and class instruction would be based on them. Picture yourself trying to teach a class with the wide array of random materials children have in their homes. Although it might work as a supplementary technique, this approach would make it impossible to conduct most kinds of group instruction. In fact, despairing teachers appealed for common texts so that all students could use the same materials. Local legislators responded by requiring schools to select appropriate books, and then parents were required to buy them. When families moved,

National Curriculum Balance Sheet 1
Performance

The Good News
With Higher Standards, We Become More Economically Competitive. . .

If we are going to compete effectively with economic powerhouses such as Japan and Western Europe, our workers must be well-educated, able to acquire new information and technical skills in a rapidly changing economic world. The skill and talents of our workforce will be our real advantage—or our Achilles heel. See what is happening without these standards. Today, too many high school graduates must be retrained or brought to a level of basic literacy by the companies that hire them. This sort of educational inefficiency has lowered our standard of living. With national standards, we can once again mobilize the nation's resources and successfully meet the economic challenges from abroad.

The Bad News
Performance: For Many Students and Schools, National Standards Are a Step Down

Any set of national standards must be viewed as a compromise, standards that can be met by the weakest as well as the strongest school districts. It is likely that the strongest schools will already be operating above and beyond such compromised standards. National standards would do nothing for them. And simply establishing higher standards to be met would become little more than an exercise in frustration for the poorer schools. If these struggling schools are to successfully reach these higher goals, they will need resources, not merely reminders of how weak they have become. A set of national standards would provide neither incentive to the nation's best schools, nor the funding needed by the weakest.

National Curriculum Balance Sheet 2
Unity

The Good News
A National Curriculum Will Bind the Nation. . .

If we are to survive as a united nation, we need a unifying experience. Schools provide that cohesive thread. As children we all learn the same stirring stories of national leaders, the development of our social institutions, and our common heritage. This shared destiny and history ties our mainly immigrant nation together. So does a shared literary experience, as all students read and discuss the same great books, and understand how our ideas and experiences have formed our culture. Without such a curriculum, we can become dangerously pluralistic and suffer the risk of becoming not one nation, but several. There are already examples of countries that have lost this common thread, and whose cultures have disintegrated.

The Bad News
The Effort to Create a National Curriculum Will Divide the Nation

While it is comforting to believe, as Hirsch and Bloom do, that cultural literacy can be defined, that we can all decide on what stirring stories to tell and which national leaders to study, we simply cannot agree on a single list of what is important, what is worth knowing. In fact, while learning popular facts and dates may be wonderful preparation for being a contestant on *Jeopardy,* or winning at "Trivial Pursuit," it does not create a common, national culture. Too many groups have been left out. What is important to one group may be unimportant to another. In fact, the effort to create such a national curriculum only highlights the obvious fact that there is no such consensus. The holy quest to find a national curriculum will divide our people: The proposed history standards started that process and created a dangerous and divisive controversy.

National Curriculum Balance Sheet 3
Local Control

The Good News
Local Parochialism Will Be Eliminated. . .

Instituting national standards will decrease the power of local school boards, which have often opted to restrict the range of views offered to their students. Today many of our children are being shaped and indoctrinated by a liberal or a conservative community, by a particular religious viewpoint, or by a single racial or ethnic climate. Implementation of national standards can stop this parochialism by broadening their horizons, teaching them other points of view, and, ultimately, ending the narrow-mindedness of so many communities.

The Bad News
Central Control of Our Lives Will Grow

The authors of the Constitution had it right—freedom and individual liberties are best protected without a "big brother" telling us what to believe, what is important. Every time there is an election, values change, new messages are sent. There is no central, federal wisdom. Local communities and individuals hold the wisdom that made this nation great. All we need is faith in the common sense of Americans.

National Curriculum Balance Sheet 4
Testing

The Good News
Everyone Is Not Above Average. . .

Garrison Keillor, in his *Lake Wobegon* radio show, always describes the students in his town as "above average." Sometimes it seems that all of the nation's students are "above average," until you compare them to students from other countries—then it is obvious that they are well below average. Too many standardized achievement tests do not do the job needed. And because too many different tests are in use, no sense can be made of their scores. Even the SATs and ACTs are only taken by a select group. National standards would mean national assessments, honest numbers showing us how our schools are doing. They are long overdue.

The Bad News
Everyone Is Not the Same

Testing, testing, testing—it creates as many problems as it solves. Subjects not included on national tests will quickly be eliminated from the curriculum, because only "tested subjects" will affect a school's status or a student's future. Paper-and-pencil tests will dominate, but not all knowledge lends itself to paper-and-pencil exams. Moreover, some students "freeze" on such tests. In fact, the more unique the student's talent, from art to creative thinking, the less likely we will test for it. How many unique talents will be lost? National tests will reduce our schools and our students to the lowest common denominator.[9]

they often had to buy new books. Concerned about the costly burden this lack of consistency placed on families, legislators mandated commonly used textbooks across larger geographic areas.

Today the process of how textbooks are developed and adopted has come under intense criticism. One of its chief critics, Harriet Tyson Bernstein, says:

Imagine a public policy system that is perfectly designed to produce textbooks that confuse, mislead, and profoundly bore students, while at the same time making all the adults in the process look good, not only in their own eyes, but in the eyes of others. Although there are some good textbooks on the market, publishers and editors are virtually compelled by public policies and practices to create textbooks that confuse students with nonsequitors, that mislead them with misinformation, and that profoundly bore them with pointedly arid writing.

None of the adults in this very complex system intends this outcome. To the contrary, each of them wants to produce good effects, and each public policy regulation or conventional practice was intended to make some improvement or prevent some abuse. But the cumulative effects of well-intentioned and seemingly reasonable state and local regulations are textbooks that squander the intellectual capital of our youth.[10]

Here's how the system works and why Bernstein and other opponents are so angry. In 1900, when our current textbook system was designed, 22 states enacted laws that put in place a centralized adoption system. Today 21 states, located mainly in the South and the West, are **state adoption** states. These states are indicated in Figure 8.2.

Under a state adoption system, local school districts typically select their texts from an official, state-approved list. As you can well imagine, a publisher's dream fulfilled would be to capture the market in a populous state adoption state that offers its school districts a short list of approved books to select from.

Those in favor of statewide adoption claim that this process results in the selection of higher-quality texts. It creates a common, statewide curriculum, which unites educators on similar issues and makes school life easier for students who move to different schools within the state. It saves time and work for educators at the local level, and it results in less expensive books because of the large numbers of books purchased.

FIGURE 8.2
State Adoption States

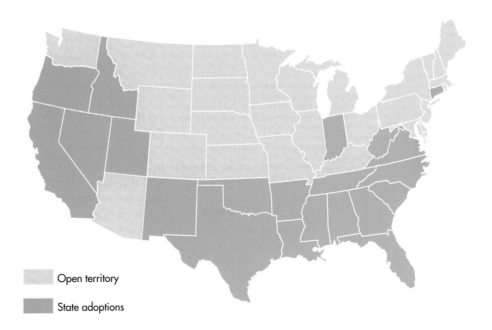

Open territory

State adoptions

There is also criticism of statewide adoptions, much of it attacking the "Texas and California effect." When these populous states buy textbooks for all the students in all their schools, the result is enormous income for the publishing companies. Critics charge that the huge revenues involved give these populous states unfair influence over textbook development. Another problem is that there is wide variation in the care and expertise with which different states handle the textbook adoption procedure. For example, some states try out and evaluate texts in the classroom for an extensive period of time, even as long as a year, while others use a very brief pilot testing that lasts only one or two weeks. In some states, publishers make special presentations to adoption committees. In other states, all personal contact between the publishing companies and the adoption committee is forbidden.

Criticism has also been leveled at the adoption process at the district and school levels. For example, most teachers and administrators have never received any training in how to evaluate curriculum materials for classroom use. Without effective training, these educators could easily be influenced by the cosmetic effect of the text—the cover, the graphics, the headings, the design. Further complicating this aspect of the issue are the severe time constraints that hamper careful decision making. Given the need to review a large number of books in a brief period of time, harried committee members sometimes merely flip through a book to determine its merit. Publishers are well aware of this "flip phenomenon" and make sure that their books have "eye appeal." While visual attractiveness can have a positive effect on learning, it is no substitute for well-chosen, well-written content.

Frequently adoption committees are given criteria sheets to assist them in determining textbook quality. There is variation in how good these criteria are. Some lists are too brief and general; some, in a well-intentioned attempt to be comprehensive, become too cumbersome to be used efficiently.[11]

Another area that has drawn criticism is the widespread use of **readability formulas.** Readability formulas use quantitative measures to determine the difficulty of the text. Typically the readability level is determined by sampling several passages from the text and applying the formula to a number of aspects, most often word difficulty and sentence length.

Initially the use of readability formulas seemed a promising development. What could be more reasonable than determining the reading level of a book to make sure it was appropriate for children in the designated grade? But as these formulas have become more pervasive, so have problems associated with their use. For example, to determine the readability level of a text, you would determine the overall readability level of several passages sampled throughout the book. The problem is that readability levels vary widely from passage to passage within a single text. It is possible to find eleventh-, eighth-, seventh-, and fourth-grade passages in a single book designated as fifth-grade level. To complicate the problem further, the different readability formulas are not always reliable. For one text, the Spache readability formula indicated a 3.1 grade level, the Dale-Chall 4.2, the Gunning 4.0, and the Fry put the text at the seventh-grade (7.0) level.[12]

Since some states will buy texts only if they have a specified readability level, publishers are under pressure to develop books that advertise appropriate readability levels. Often authors will avoid difficult words and long sentences so that, for example, *esophagus* becomes *food tube* and *protoplasm* becomes *stuff*. The result, according to former secretary of education Terrell Bell and other critics, is the "dumbing down" of the textbook. Ironically, authors who write for the readability formula may make books harder, not easier, to read. When authors try to simplify vocabulary, they may replace precise and clear terminology with vague, ambiguous words. When authors shorten sentences, they often leave out the connective issue—*and, but, therefore*—words that clarify the relationships between events and ideas. Again, this shortening of sentences to meet the readability formulas' requirements can have the unanticipated result of making comprehension more difficult.

Writing to the readability level not only hurts comprehension but "squeezes the juice out of some very fine tales."[13] Here, for example, is one such distorted basal reader version of "The Tortoise and the Hare":

> Rabbit said, "I can run. I can run fast." "You can't run fast," Turtle said. "Look Rabbit. See the park. You and I will run. We'll run to the park."
>
> Rabbit said, "I want to stop. I'll stop here. I can run, but Turtle can't. I can get to the park fast." Turtle said, "I can't run fast. But I will not stop. Rabbit can't see me. I'll get to the park."[14]

In this textbook version, the characterization is gone. So is the moral. So is the meaning.

Another problem is that many textbooks skim over a content area, simply in order to cover it, rather than providing the student with sufficient information for genuinely understanding it. Critics charge that books try to include too many subjects and gloss over them to such a degree that students do not really understand what is going on. Students are as frustrated by this "mentioning phenomenon" as the adult critics. They say:

> Sometimes they just mention a person's name and then don't talk about them anymore in the whole book.
>
> They should talk more about each topic. For the War of 1812 there should be more information about the fighters and the treaties. What did the Treaty of Ghent contain? Who wrote it?[15]

Part of the problem is the knowledge explosion. But another reason behind the mentioning phenomenon can once again be traced to the adoption process. In their quest for higher scores on standardized tests, many states have called for aligning the curriculum in textbooks with what is assessed on standardized tests. Adoption committees have delineated in minute detail all the names, dates, and places they want included. In many districts, textbooks are required to cover all the topics in a course syllabus; consequently publishers, who must try to appeal to many districts and a variety of course syllabi, frequently trade off reasonable explanations and clarifying examples in favor of mentioning lots of names, places, and dates. When authors try to include everything, any sense of coherence is lost. The context essential for comprehension is deleted. So are vignettes that would give more flavor to the narrative. Sometimes even important adjectives are dropped. Talented children's literature authors often refuse to write for school texts for fear their work will be mangled.

Researchers have also found that basal readers and other texts, in attempting to be inoffensive to potential purchasers, include only a limited range of story types, often devoid of interpersonal and internal conflict.[16] In their efforts to satisfy local and regional groups, some companies even publish alternative versions of the same book. For example, in some texts Thanksgiving is truly a "movable feast": If you grew up in Massachusetts, your social studies book may have told you that the first Thanksgiving took place in Plymouth; if you went to school in Virginia, you may have learned that this great celebration occurred in Jamestown.

Another problem is that texts, especially in social studies, still largely chronicle the events of white men. Although women and minorities are included more frequently than in the past, they still suffer from unrealistic portrayal, and American society as a whole is presented in an idealized manner. As one disgruntled critic concludes: "Adoption states, special interest groups, and readability formulas have all contributed to produce textbooks designed by a committee, written by a committee, and selected by a committee to please all and offend none."[17] Despite these efforts to please all and offend none, textbooks often seem to please none and offend all.

Textbook Controversy: The Portrayal of Women and Minorities

A great many people become passionate about what textbooks should teach children. The 1970s, the decade of relevance in the curriculum, was characterized by confrontations over social issues—fundamentalists and scientists battling over whether to include Darwinism or creationism, feminists protesting portrayals of apron-clad women relegated to the kitchen, minorities objecting to the lack of multiracial and multiethnic texts. Fierce battles raged between the more liberal groups and the more conservative community members who were wary of curriculum change. Textbook companies and professional associations, such as the American Psychological Association, issued guidelines for nonracist and nonsexist textbooks, and, as a result, textbooks became more fair in their representation of women and minority group members. Concerned that textbooks may revert to unrepresentative portrayals of women and minorities, educators who advocate multicultural texts often monitor textbooks. Following is a description of six forms of bias, which you can use to monitor and evaluate instructional materials.[18] Although these are commonly used to identify bias against women or racial and ethnic groups, they can help you assess the portrayal of any minority group, such as the elderly, those with disabilities, or gays and lesbians.

Six Forms of Bias in Instructional Materials

Invisibility

Perhaps the most fundamental form of bias in instructional materials is the complete or relative exclusion of a particular group or groups from representation or consideration in text narrative and/or illustrations. Research suggests, for example, that textbooks published prior to the 1960s largely omitted any consideration of African Americans within contemporary society and, indeed, rendered them relatively invisible in accounts of or references to the United States after Reconstruction. Latinos, Asian Americans, and Native Americans were largely absent from most textbooks as well. Many studies indicate that women, who constitute more than 51 percent of the U.S. population, represented approximately 30 percent of the persons or characters referred to throughout the textbooks in most subject areas. All of these are examples of the existence of bias through exclusion or invisibility.

Stereotyping

Stereotyping may occur in reference to any of a number of variables: physical appearance, intellectual attributes, personality characteristics, career roles, domestic roles, social placement. Some of the stereotypes most frequently seen in textbooks include the portrayal of:

Teachers serving on text-book adoption committees apply specific criteria to determine text suitability for their curriculum.

- African Americans primarily as ignorant servants and manual workers
- Asian Americans primarily as laundry workers or cooks
- Mexican Americans primarily as peons or migrant workers
- Native Americans as either "blood-thirsty savages" or "noble sons and daughters of the earth"
- Women as passive, dependent persons defined in terms of their home and family roles
- Men in a wide variety of occupational roles (and only occasionally as husbands and fathers) and as strong, assertive persons defined primarily in terms of their work outside the home

Imbalance and Selectivity

Textbooks may perpetuate bias by presenting only one interpretation of an issue, situation, or group of people. These imbalanced accounts restrict student knowledge of complex issues by denying the varied perspectives that may apply to a particular situation. Through selective presentation of information, instructional materials may distort reality and ignore differing points of view. Examples of these distortions include the following:

- The origins of European settlers in the New World are emphasized, while the origins and heritage of African Americans are frequently omitted.
- The history of the relations between Native Americans and the federal government is frequently described in terms of treaties and "protection," rather than with reference to broken treaties and progressive government appropriation of Native-American lands.
- Textbooks refer to the fact that "women were given the vote" but omit the physical abuse and sacrifices suffered by the leaders of the suffrage movement.

Unreality

Many researchers have noted the tendency of instructional materials to ignore facts that are unpleasant or that indicate negative positions or actions by individual leaders, states, or the nation as a whole. Instructional materials often ignore the existence of prejudice, racism, discrimination, exploitation, oppression, sexism, and intergroup conflict. When controversial topics are glossed over, this unrealistic coverage denies children the information they need to recognize, understand, and perhaps some day conquer the problems that plague society. Examples of unreality may be found in materials that present:

- Minorities and women as having economic equality with white males, when reality suggests that the economic gap remains substantial

- Women's congressional representation as approaching parity with the representation of men—as the result of recent election gains—when in reality women are profoundly underrepresented

Fragmentation and Isolation

Bias through fragmentation and isolation takes two primary forms. First, content regarding minority groups and women may be physically or visually fragmented or isolated and delivered only in separate chapters (for example, "Black Americans and the Winning of the West," "Bootleggers, Suffragettes, and Other Diversions"), or even in boxes at the side of the page (for example, "Ten Distinguished Black Americans," "Ten Women Achievers in Science"). Second, racial and ethnic minority group members and women may be depicted as interacting only with persons like themselves, never in contact with the majority culture. Fragmentation and isolation imply that the history, experiences, and situations of minorities and women are somehow unrelated to those of the dominant culture, and they ignore the dynamic relationships of these groups to the development of our current society.

Linguistic Bias

Language is a powerful conveyor of bias in instructional materials, both in blatant and subtle forms. For example:

- Native Americans are frequently referred to as "roaming," "wandering," or "roving" across the land. These terms might be used to apply to buffalo or wolves; they suggest a merely physical relationship to the land, rather than a social or purposeful relation. Such language implicitly justifies the seizure of Native lands by "more goal-directed" white Americans who "traveled" or "settled" their way westward.
- Immigrant groups are often referred to as "hordes" or "swarms." These terms serve to dehumanize and to reduce the recognition of diversity and variation within any group of people.
- Such words as *forefathers, brotherhood,* and *mankind* serve to deny the contributions and existence of the 51 percent of the U.S. population that is female.

Textbook Controversy: Religion and Secular Humanism

Some parents and educators argue that publishers have not gone far enough in producing nonsexist, multicultural books, but others are outspoken with criticism of a different kind. The publishers, they claim, have gone much too far. In the 1970s it was liberals who challenged the curriculum, but censorship attacks in the 1980s and 1990s were more likely to come from conservative groups.

> Pressures from the politically organized religious Right have made it risky for publishers to discuss evolution. If evolution is discussed at all, it is often confined to a chapter in the book. Students are conducted on a forced march through the phyla, and given no understanding of the overarching theory (evolution) that gives taxonomy life and meaning. Touchy subjects like dinosaurs, the fossil record, genetics, natural selection, or even the sci-

entific meanings of the words "theory" and "belief" are treated skimpily or vaguely in order to avoid the ire of the Bible fundamentalists.[19]

National attention has been riveted on court cases dealing with **secular humanism,** religion in texts, and what children should and should not be allowed to read in school.

A 1986 case in eastern Tennessee made headlines when a group of fundamentalist Christian families objected to secular humanism in a series of Holt, Rinehart & Winston readers and supported this charge with items they found objectionable, including an illustration in a first-grade reader showing a kitchen scene with a girl reading while a boy cooks (he is making toast). The plaintiffs argued that "the religion of John Dewey is planted in the first graders [*sic*] mind that there are no God-given roles for different sexes."[20] The plaintiffs also objected to *The Diary of Anne Frank,* which was cited as being antireligion in its acceptance of diversity in religious belief and practice. Consider the following passage:

Anne: *(Softly)* I wish you had a religion, Peter.
Peter: No, thanks! Not me.
Anne: Oh, I don't mean you have to be Orthodox . . . or believe in heaven and hell and purgatory and things . . . I just mean some religion . . . it doesn't matter what. Just to believe in something! When I think of all that's out there . . . the trees . . . the flowers . . . and seagulls . . . when I think of the dearness of you, Peter . . . and the goodness of the people we know . . . Mr. Kraler, Miep, Dirk, the vegetable man, all risking their lives for us everyday. . . . When I think of these good things, I'm not afraid anymore.[21]

Other categories called "offensive" included "futuristic supernaturalism, one-world government, situation ethics or values clarification, humanistic moral absolutes, pacifism, rebellion against parents or self-authority, role reversal, role elimination, animals are equal to humans, the skeptic's view of religion contrasting belief in the supernatural with science, false views of death and related themes, magic, other religions, evolution, godless supernaturalism . . . and specific humanistic themes."[22]

In his ruling, Judge Thomas Hull found that the plaintiffs held sincere religious convictions that were violated by the total context of the textbooks and that they should be entitled to protection under the Free Exercise clause of the First Amendment. The judge said that the plaintiff students had been deprived of a free public education and of free exercise of religion because the Hawkins County Public Schools had insisted that the children use the Holt, Rinehart & Winston series. Therefore he granted the plaintiffs' request that the children from the conservative Christian families be allowed to "opt out" of class during the reading period and go to the study hall or the library; their actual reading instruction would be provided at home.

The Tennessee case raised practical as well as philosophical issues. For the teachers, procedural questions surfaced immediately: When does the reading class begin and end? What if topics taught in reading class surface in discussion later in the day? Should the plaintiff children get up again and go to the library? How will these disruptions affect teaching?

The case also highlighted questions of a more philosophical and legal nature: "Does reading material have to be so limited that it never offends any groups' religious beliefs? Must a public school system accommodate 'belief'—whatever the size of the group of believers? Or is the purpose of a public school to expose students to a variety of beliefs, to conflicting ideas, to the thoughts of humankind as reflected in literature, in society, in the arts, in politics?"[23]

An explosive textbook-suitability case in Mobile, Alabama, went even further in attacking secular humanism. With its roots in classical Greek literature, *humanism* is defined in the dictionary as a belief that people can live ethically without recourse to the supernatural. In the Mobile case, Judge W. Brevard Hand banned more than 40 social studies, history, and home economics texts because they advanced the secular humanism "religion." In his 1986 ruling, Judge Hand said, "The most important belief of this religion is its denial of the transcendent or supernatural: There is no God, no creator, no divinity." This ruling was the first federal court decision to support the fundamentalist Christian claim that secular humanism is a religion taught in the public schools.

The decisions in both the Tennessee case and the Alabama case were reversed on appeal, with the courts ruling that the textbooks promoted neither secularism nor any religious views. But a new censorship controversy was brewing. Consider the following case. During the spring of 1988, an assignment from Robert Marzano's *Tactics for Thinking* unleashed a storm of controversy in southern Indiana. Protestors charged that the following exercise could induce a self-hypnotic trance:

> Have students focus their attention on some stimulus (e.g., a spot on the wall). Explain to them that you want them to focus all of their energy for about a minute and ask them to be aware of what it is like when they are really trying to attend to something.[24]

Many community members were persuaded that the book was brainwashing children into believing in a one-world government and religion. In Battle Ground, Washington, a group of citizens claimed that *Tactics for Thinking* was teaching the occult. In at least a dozen other states there were protests against the New Age movement and global education.

It is hard to define the New Age movement with any clarity. Some critics see it as an outgrowth of secular humanism, and book banners charge New Age and secular humanism with similar outrages—global education, the occult, values clarification, Eastern mysticism, and a belief in a one-world government and religion. Since his experience with textbook censorship, Marzano has studied the writings of a movement known as *Christian reconstructionism*. He says this group is not synonymous with *Christian fundamentalism* but rather is a grass-roots movement aimed at restoring Christianity to the public schools. Marzano says the group is growing at a geometric rate and is responsible for the increasing number of censorship attacks on books used in public schools.[25]

Many are puzzled and concerned about these cases. They find charges against secular humanism and the New Age movement to be ludicrous and bizarre. But those who have been involved directly in book-banning cases do not dismiss them lightly. Even when based on unfounded charges, censorship attacks can tie a school system into knots of controversy and pose a genuine threat to academic freedom.

While most people are perplexed by the notion of secular humanism and "New Ageism" as school-promoted religions, they are becoming aware of an

Scenes like this one involving overt religious prayer have been banned from the school curriculum. Should the study of religion as a vital social force also be banned or watered down because it is politically dangerous?

important intellectual problem: texts' omission of the role of religion in history and culture. Three studies of public school textbooks, funded by the Department of Education, Americans United for the Separation of Church and State, and People for the American Way, have agreed that textbooks minimize the importance of religion in American life. Although 96 percent of Americans believe in God or a universal spirit and 58 percent go to a place of worship at least once a month, history texts do not reflect the impact of religion.[26] For example, analysis of 40 social studies texts for grades 1 to 4 found that the majority of these books made no reference to any kind of religious activity. In one sixth-grade book, "Thank God" was changed to read "thank goodness" in an Isaac Bashevis Singer story. One history book told about the life of Joan of Arc without ever noting her religious beliefs, and other books described Thanksgiving without referring to the religious beliefs of the Puritans. In one book the Pilgrims were defined as "people who make long trips," and in another fundamentalists were described as rural people "who follow the values or traditions of an earlier period." The importance of religion in inspiring social movements such as the labor movement, prohibition, abolition, civil rights, and protests against the Vietnam War is rarely noted.

There is an important difference between teaching *about* religion and actually promoting it, but the omission of religion is actually part of a larger textbook phenomenon: the failure to discuss adequately many issues that are intellectually complex and socially controversial. Not only is the treatment of religion inadequate, but also many other potentially controversial topics—such as slavery, evolution, the Holocaust, and even sexual references in plays by Shakespeare—are given short shrift. Columnist Ellen Goodman pushes publisher fear of controversy in texts to an inevitable conclusion:

If textbook publishers keep retreating to a shrinking patch of safe ground, they will end up editing chunks out of "The Three Little Pigs." The strength of our system, what's worth telling the young, is not that Americans deny their differences or always resolve them, but that we have managed, until now, to live with them.[27]

Ellen Goodman was closer to the truth than she may have realized. Thomas McDaniel, dean of Converse College, reports that in 1992 in South Carolina, Marzano's *Tactics For Thinking* and secular humanism were still under attack. In one county, "St. George and the Dragon," "Puss in Boots," and *Sylvester and the Magic Pebble* were dropped from the reading curriculum. Parents objected because they were about magic.[28]

Textbook Controversy: Cultural Literacy or Cultural Imperialism?

Both George Orwell and Aldous Huxley were pessimists about the future, but the two authors were, as Neil Postman points out, concerned about it in different ways, "What Orwell feared were those who would ban books," Postman writes. "What Huxley feared was that there would be no one who wanted to read one."[29]

Concern for the cultural literacy of the young continues to spark debate over elective diversity versus a common curricular core. Novelist and teacher John Barth summarizes the problem as seen from the perspective of one who laments the loss of a core curriculum:

In the same way you can't take for granted that a high school senior or a freshman in college really understands that the Vietnam War came after World War II, you can't take for granted that any one book is common knowledge even among a group of liberal arts or writing majors at a pretty good university.[30]

With both E. D. Hirsch, Jr.'s *Cultural Literacy* and Allan Bloom's *The Closing of the American Mind* on the nation's bestseller list, 1987 was a banner year for debate about the curriculum. *The Closing of the American Mind* sounded the trumpet of alarm for a curriculum canon at risk. Bloom, professor of social thought at the University of Chicago, took aim at the university curriculum as one without a vision of what an educated individual should know. He claimed that his university students were ignorant of music, literature, and art. He says:

Imagine such a young person walking through the Louvre or the Uffizi, and you can immediately grasp the condition of his soul. In his innocence of the stories of Biblical and Greek or Roman antiquity, Raphael, Leonardo, Michelangelo, Rembrandt and all the others can say nothing to him. All he sees are colors and forms—modern art. In short, like almost everything else in his spiritual life, the paintings and statues are abstract. No matter what much of modern wisdom asserts, these artists counted on immediate recognition of their subjects and, what is more, on their having a powerful meaning for their viewers. The works were the fulfillment of these meanings, giving them a sensuous reality and hence completing them. Without those meanings and without there being something essential to the viewer as a moral, political and religious being, the works lose their essence. It is not merely the tradition that is lost when the voice of civilization elaborated over millennia has been stilled in this way. It is being itself that vanishes beyond the dissolving horizon.31

To renew the voice of civilization, Bloom recommended a Great Books curriculum through which students read texts generally recognized as classic and requisite to a liberal education.

In *Cultural Literacy* E. D. Hirsch, Jr., not only called for a national canon of learning, he translated this call into an actual list of "What Literate Americans Know." Pointing to test results showing that one-third of our students do not know when the Civil War was fought and only half can identify Don Quixote, Byron, Keats, and Wordsworth, Hirsch claimed that schools have failed in their obligation to transmit the network of information that is our national culture. Without this common culture, Hirsch warns, our nation's well-being is at risk. He says we need to transmit the history and literature of our country if we are to instill a sense of national values and unity. Both Bloom and Hirsch would be comfortable with the idea of a national curriculum.

Cultural literacy for every child in the land, according to Hirsch, is the only way to make the Jeffersonian ideal of democracy a reality. Since children, especially those from impoverished homes, will not become culturally literate by osmosis, Hirsch advocates teaching them directly through a list of names, dates, places, events, and quotes that every literate American should know. From "Achilles" to "Homer," from "Uriah Heep" to "John Bull," from *"je ne sais quoi"* to "Pike's Peak," from "phylum" to "ukelele.", from "Uncle Tom" to "Emile Zola."[32] In 1991, Hirsch published the first two volumes of the core knowledge series, *What Your First Grader Needs to Know* and *What Your Second Grader Needs to Know,* mass-marketed to parents and schools through bookstores and supermarkets. All this is part of Hirsch's plan to identify what students should know so that this network of background information can be transmitted in schools.[33]

As the wave of articles and books rolled on advocating a common culture taught to all schoolchildren, a growing number of educators began to take exception. They raised the questions at the heart of curriculum development. What knowledge is of most worth? Who decides? How is it transmitted? Who gets access to it? What information is left out? Which are the books that should be included on a list of great books that everyone is supposed to read? What are the names that all American schoolchildren should know? Which names are left out? Who gets to choose? E. D. Hirsch? A blue-ribbon committee of Very Smart People? Will the Great Books of literature and history reflect only the European tradition? What about Africa? Asia? E. D. Hirsch, Jr.'s list comprises mainly white males. What will happen to all the exciting new information about the contributions women and minorities have made to our culture? If we return to the Great Books or if the Hirsch list is followed, the nation's schoolchildren may become literate in the culture of a white male club—Eurocentric, exclusionary, myopic, limited.

As a result of these concerns, a resurgence of interest in a multicultural curriculum has been sparked. Multiculturalists call, often passionately, for a more inclusive telling of the American story, one that has room for the poor as well as the powerful. The curriculum, they say, must weave the contributions of minorities and of women as well as of white males into the textbook tapestry of the American experience. Multicultural advocates say that minority and female students will achieve more, like learning better, and have higher self-esteem if they see themselves in the pages of their textbooks. New immigrants should learn about their homelands and the experiences of their people. African-American children must understand their connection to their homeland, and they are entitled to the pride that comes from learning about the enormous cultural and historical contributions they have made to the United States. As James Banks, a pioneer in the development of multicultural education, says:

> People of color, women, and other marginalized groups are demanding that their voices, visions, and perspectives be included in the curriculum. They ask that the debt Western civilization owes to Africa, Asia, and indigenous America be acknowledged.... However, these groups must acknowledge that they do not want to eliminate Aristotle and Shakespeare, or Western civilization, from the school curriculum. To reject the West would be to reject important aspects of their own cultural heritages, experiences, and identities.34

To many educators, parents, and students this approach sounds wise and rational. But those who worry about the vanishing curricular core, one they

What balance should schools seek between teaching a common core curriculum that binds all Americans together and a curriculum that celebrates the many cultures that have been brought to the United States?

see as necessary to shape a common identity for the nation, raise practical questions. "Education," they say, "is a zero sum game." When something new goes into the curriculum, something that used to be there must come out. There is just not enough time to cover everything. Any history teacher who has struggled to reach the Civil War by December knows this only too well.

The heated curriculum wars reach a boiling point around the topic of Afrocentric education. *Afrocentrists* see African-American children as dislocated—first by their ancestors' removal from Africa and today by a school that devalues their history and culture. Their ideas have led to innovations such as the African-American immersion schools.

> A is for Armstrong, B is for Banneker, C is for Carver. For children at Victor Berger Elementary School, African-American culture is the foundation of all instruction.
>
> The first graders are learning to count from 1 to 10 in Swahili as well as English. They know that the colors of the African-American flag are red, black, and green just as surely as they know the American flag is red, white, and blue. And at art time, the children identify the pipe cleaner spiders they are making not as the itsy-bitsy spider in the well-known song but as the clever Anansi of African folk tales.[35]

Critics claim that this kind of curriculum has no place in a public school, where common American values and culture should be taught. They worry about the disuniting of American school and society. Who learns the Afrocentric curriculum? African-American children only? Or all children? Should there be a curriculum that is centered on Latin America? Should this be further divided into separate strands for children from Mexico, Cuba, Puerto Rico, Nicaragua, El Salvador? If students spend all this time learning about Africa (or another country, depending upon their land of origin), will they lose out on knowledge essential to functioning effectively in the American mainstream? As noted historian Arthur Schlesinger wonders:

> What good will it do young black Americans to take African names, wear African costumes, and replicate African rituals, to learn by music and mantras, rhythm and rapping?... Will such training help them understand democracy better? Help them fit better into American life?... The best way to keep a people down is to deny them the means of improvement or achievement and cut them off from the opportunities of the national life.[36]

Advocates of a core curriculum claim that it will empower the poor and the disadvantaged. Opponents say it will rob them of the chance to see their experiences reflected in history and literature. What some call "cultural literacy" others see as cultural imperialism. "Whose knowledge is of most worth?" is the question of the day. It will continue to drive the debate about what culture should be in the curriculum.

A View from the Teachers' Room

In the midst of new trends and tension points is the classroom teacher, a force in his or her own right in determining what and how children are taught in school. Let us listen in on some different perspectives in the teachers' room.

Jo: Were you at yesterday's faculty meeting? The sales representatives from the publishing company showed their new textbook series.

Flo: No, I had an emergency dentist appointment—a root canal. Talk about pain! What was the textbook series like?

Jo: Fabulous. It must've cost them a fortune—glitzy cover, beautiful artwork. And talk about your supplementary materials! They have everything. The objectives are all spelled out so that we know exactly what we have to do. There's a step-by-step teacher's guide saying exactly how to teach each objective. There are discussion questions to ask after each reading assignment, and a student workbook with activities for the kids to do after we've finished the reading. They even have huge banks of test questions for weekly tests and unit exams.

Flo: What's so great about that?

Jo: What's so great about it? You know how hard we work! The paperwork alone is endless. Anything that saves me time, I appreciate. And these books look like a great time saver. They've thought of everything.

Flo: Jo, you and I have been through so many TGIF afternoons—you know I appreciate the need to save time. But some of these new comprehensive textbook systems make me nervous.

Jo: What do you mean?

Flo: I'm not so sure the people in those faraway offices who write those fancy textbooks know what's best for our kids. What makes them so smart that they can determine what we should tell our students? Children they've never even met! What kind of expertise do they have to tell us how to teach? When was the last time those textbook writers were in a classroom, anyway? I'm not so sure that I want to turn over that much of my professional control over what I teach and how.

Although many groups attempt to influence the school curriculum, in the final analysis it is the classroom teacher who must plan the day-to-day instruction that matches the specific learning needs of his or her students.

The Culture of the Curriculum

No educational issue has sparked more controversy than the debate over the curriculum. Should all children study a core curriculum? If so, should it emphasize this nation's Eurocentric roots? Should there be a multicultural curriculum? For all children? Or should a particular curriculum be developed to match each group in this country's diverse population? The following quotes represent different voices and views on the issue. As you read these, try to formulate your perspective. And if you're puzzled that there is so much interest and debate over the culture of the curriculum, it may be instructive to remember the party slogan from George Orwell's 1984: *"Who controls the past controls the future; who controls the present controls the past."*

When my colleagues and I insist on diversifying the curriculum, what we are trying to do . . . is to include more of the other elements that have been systematically excluded from entering into this great pot. . . . Society is already fissured by race, class, and gender. Unlike what [columnist] George Will says, a multicultural curriculum doesn't contribute to the fissures; it's meant to address the fissures, to redefine what our common culture is.

What other country has the potential to house so many ethnic identities and produce a new blend? We are talking about the weave of a new kind of tapestry. The bland monochrome that is part of official American ideology, which we can no longer afford, no longer fits with the facts of the world.[a]

If the public schools abandon their historic mission as the common schools of the nation, if they instead foster racial and ethnic separatism, they will forfeit their claim to public support. If the public schools relinquish their responsibility for teaching children an awareness of their American identity, then they will lose their privileged status as public schools. Such a trend would inevitably encourage a flight from public education

by those who are repelled by relentless ethnic struggles for control of the curriculum.[b]

African-American children who have never heard the spirituals; never heard the names of African ethnic groups; never read Paul Laurence Dunbar, Langston Hughes, and Phillis Wheatley nor the stories of High John de Conqueror, Anansi, and the signifying monkey, are severely injured in the most fragile part of their psyches. Lacking reinforcement in their own historical experiences, they become psychologically crippled, hobbling along in the margins of the European experiences of most of the curriculum.[c]

Our schools and colleges have a responsibility to teach history for its own sake—as part of the intellectual equipment of civilized persons—and not to degrade history by allowing its contents to be dictated by pressure groups whether political, economic, religious, or ethnic. . . . The question America confronts as a pluralistic society is how to vindicate cherished cultures and traditions without breaking the bonds of cohesion—common ideals, common political institutions, common language, common culture, common fate—that hold the republic together.[d]

Celebrating Diversity
because we are so different,
we have so much to share.[e]

[a]Henry Louis Gates, quoted in David Holmstrom, "A Vision of a New Racial Tapestry," *Christian Science Monitor,* April 10, 1992, p. 11.
[b]Diane Ravitch, "A Culture in Common," *Educational Leadership* 49, no. 4 (December 1991/January 1992): 8–11.
[c]Molefi Kete Asante, "Afrocentric Curriculum," *Educational Leadership* 49, no. 4 (December 1991/January 1992): 28–31.
[d]Arthur Schlesinger, *The Disuniting of America* (New York: Norton, 1992).
[e]Hall poster, found in Chesterbrook Elementary School, Fairfax County, VA, 1989.

Jo: I hadn't thought of it that way.
Flo: The other day I was talking with Mary, the new teacher who works across the hall from me. She just graduated from college a few years ago, and she has some terrific ideas. She's using an individualized reading program, and she's really got the kids going. Instead of the basal reading selections, she's got the class reading everything from Judy Blume

to Tolkien. And they are learning to love reading. On all counts, it looks like a tremendous success. But instead of being happy, she's worried—afraid she's harming her students' reading development, because she's not following the basal reader.

Jo: You're kidding!

Flo: I wish I were.

Jo: So you're saying that some teachers trust the textbooks more than they trust their own professional training and expertise.

Flo: I think we walk a fine line between being technicians and professionals. While it's good to have texts that save us time, I want to make the decisions about how and when the textbook is used. The way I figure it, that's an important part of my professional role as a teacher.

The Teacher as Curriculum Developer

Sometimes it seems that everyone controls the curriculum except the teacher, but nothing could be further from the truth. Many schools have textbook selection committees, comprised primarily of teachers, that determine what texts the school will purchase. More important, it is the classroom teacher who has the power to interpret and adapt whatever official text or curriculum guide has been assigned. As a teacher, you can stress certain points in a text and give scant attention to others; you can supplement or replace official texts with your own teacher-made materials; you can even introduce lessons on units that are completely unrelated to the assigned text.

It is important to remember that textbook authors and curriculum specialists work with a broad audience in mind. They have no way of knowing about the specific needs, interests, and abilities of the students in your class. Knowing this is your responsibility, just as it is up to you to see that textbooks and curriculum guides are adapted to fit these needs, interests, and abilities. This freedom to modify and transform the official curriculum has led many to conclude that the real curriculum is whatever teachers actually choose to do in their classrooms.

Despite this current freedom and influence, some critics warn that new trends in textbook production are a potential threat to the teacher's professional role in curriculum development. During the *Sputnik*-inspired curriculum revisions of the 1960s, there was an attempt to infuse more rigor into the math and science curricula. Many of the curriculum developers, taking something of an elitist attitude toward teachers, tried to "foolproof" the curriculum, specifying almost everything the teacher was supposed to say and do. This signaled a new trend: less on-site, local curriculum development by teachers and more purchasing of commercial systems, complete with teaching activities, student activities, diagnostic tests, achievement tests, and the like. Today's emphasis on the comprehensive textbook and highly sophisticated instructional design echoes this trend.

Obviously, there are positive elements in this trend toward comprehensive, commercially developed textbook systems. They can save overburdened teachers (especially new teachers) a great deal of time, which the teachers can then devote to individualized instruction as well as a variety of classroom management duties. The potential danger is that teachers may become mere technicians, executing someone else's instructional goals and ideas. What will happen to local control?

The Career of a Master Builder

In this salute to teaching, Robert Cole describes how his talented first-grade teacher left the classroom to become "the master architect of the city schools' curriculum." Do you think Betty Fisher had the opportunity to use her curriculum development skills as a classroom teacher? How could classroom teachers become empowered as "architects of the curriculum"?

Betty Fisher, my first-grade teacher, retires this month. She was my favorite teacher of all, and I think I was her favorite student. It doesn't matter, of course, whether I was or not. I thought I was; that's the gift she gave me. A third of a century later, I don't remember what Miss Fisher taught me, but I remember her teaching. I remember her, teaching.

I remember them all, really—the good, the bad, and the hapless. Miss Tarbutton (truly), who flooded my first-grade life with books. Miss Fritz, who had taught my father Latin and who taught me terror (and Caesar, too). Mr. Morrison, the martinet, who reprimanded students who dared to learn more than he had assigned. Louise Leonard, whom I still mention in nearly every speech I give. The incomparable A. J. McGowan, hounded from his job by cowards and knaves. Harold Garriott, who never lost faith in me (or, if he did, never showed it). I remember them all. But Betty Fisher . . .

In 1955, not long after my third-grade year, Miss Fisher stopped teaching. (Was it something I said?) She took the job of language arts supervisor, a position she held for five years before becoming elementary supervisor for the district. Ten years after that, she was named elementary curriculum coordinator

and, four years later, director of elementary curriculum—the post she held until her retirement. She must have been good at her job (which doesn't surprise me). The Springfield newspaper called her "the master architect of the city schools' curriculum" and said that she was "well known throughout the state" for her skill in preparing curriculum documents. School district officials said she "left a legacy . . . which perhaps will never be duplicated by any educator."

But like so many other wonderful teachers, she left the classroom. And today, just as 30 years ago, we need all the Betty Fishers we can get in our classrooms. . . .

Teachers, good teachers—choosing them, training them properly, initiating them, evaluating their worth and paying them commensurately, and creating various innovative and challenging career paths for them—are the issue of the day. Good teachers are assets we must work to cultivate and to keep. They're worth remembering.

Just as Miss Fisher remembered me. Long after our brief time together, when I returned to Springfield to give a speech, there she was in the front row, and I was reminded yet again of what it is to be a teacher. The best teachers, architects of the human soul, stay with us always. Their influence never lessens. They never stop, never go away. And we shouldn't let them.

Source: Robert Cole, the Editors' Page, *Phi Delta Kappan* 67, no. 6 (February 1986): 410. Reprinted by permission of author and publisher.

What impact will this have on teachers' involvement in curriculum development? How will it affect teacher autonomy and creativity?[37] When teachers stop developing their own curricula, they give up control over their expertise, time, and activities. "Hence the tendency of the curriculum to become totally standardized and systematized, totally focused on competencies measured by tests and largely dependent on predesigned commercial materials, may have consequences exactly the opposite of what we intend. Instead of professional teachers who care about what they do and why they do it, we may have only alienated executors of someone else's plans."[38]

If teachers cease to practice **curriculum development,** other problems will soon emerge. As the view of teachers as technicians rather than as professional decision makers gradually spreads, they will become increasingly expendable during budgeting season. After all, anyone can administer "fool-proof" materials, can't they? Eventually the "technician" teacher will even lose the ability to adapt these norm-referenced materials to the diagnosed needs, abilities, and interests of his or her own, local students. A depersonalized curriculum developed in the faraway offices of commercial publishers will rule our classrooms. George Orwell's vision of a centrally planned and administered society will be a giant step closer.

"Knowledge is power," the saying goes, and in the final analysis the degree of power and talent you exert as an architect of the curriculum will depend on your own knowledge and skills. If you are supposed to teach a unit on the Civil War but you know little about it yourself, it will be all you can do to implement commercially prepared materials. If you are to teach a unit on poetry but always avoided literature classes in college, you will be at the mercy of whatever the publishers or the test makers tell you to do and say. If your knowledge of science is limited to that terrible memory of when you tried to dissect a frog, you may gratefully follow to the last dot on the i whatever instructions are in the teacher's manual (and pray for the science specialist to come in and do it for you). Knowledge and skill are the result of a strong liberal arts program combined with courses in pedagogy. This background will give you the power to put into action one of the most creative functions of teaching: shaping what your students learn in school.

The Saber-Tooth Curriculum

When you develop curricula, it is important always to question whether your instructional objectives and learning activities will provide students with skills for effective functioning in today's world—and tomorrow's. Here is what curriculum development scholar Michael Apple considers essential:

> The curriculum must simultaneously be both conservative and critical. It must preserve the ideals that have guided discourse in the U.S. for centuries: a faith in the American people, a commitment to expanding equality, and a commitment to diversity and liberty. Yet it must also empower individuals to question the ethics of their institutions and to criticize them when they fail to meet these ideals.[39]

Unless we carefully consider what a school is for and what kind of curriculum can meet those goals, we might end up with a "saber-tooth curriculum." Since many of you may never have read this classic satire on Paleolithic curriculum written by Abner Peddiwell, known in real life as Harold Benjamin, we will summarize the story of *The Saber-Tooth Curriculum* for you here. As you learn about this clever parody, you will become aware of the flaws of a saber-tooth curriculum. Are there any positive aspects of this kind of curriculum?

• • •

New-Fist was a brilliant educator and thinker of prehistoric times. He watched the children of his tribe playing with bones, sticks, and brightly colored pebbles, and he speculated on what these youngsters might learn that would help the tribe derive more food, shelter, clothing, security, and, in short, a better life.

Eventually, he determined that in order to obtain food and shelter, the people of his tribe must learn to fish with their bare hands and to club and skin little woolly horses; and in order to live in safety, they must learn to drive away the saber-tooth tigers with fire. So New-Fist developed the first curriculum. It consisted of three basic subjects: (1) "Fish-Grabbing-with-the-Bare-Hands," (2) "Woolly-Horse-Clubbing," and (3) "Saber-Tooth-Tiger-Scaring-with-Fire."

New-Fist taught the children these subjects, and they enjoyed these purposeful activities more than playing with colored pebbles. The years went by, and by the time New-Fist was called by the Great Mystery to the Land of the Setting Sun, all the tribe's children had been systematically schooled in these three skills; the tribe was prosperous and secure.

All would have been well and the story might have ended here had it not been for an unforeseen change—the beginning of the New Ice Age, which sent a great glacier sliding down upon the tribe. The glacier so muddied the waters of the creeks that it was impossible for people to catch fish with their bare hands. Also, the melted water of the glacier made the ground marshy, and the little woolly horses left for higher and dryer land. They were replaced by shy and speedy antelopes with such a scent for danger that no one could get close enough to club them. And finally, as if these disruptions were not enough, the increasing dampness of the air caused the saber-tooth tigers to contract pneumonia and die. The tigers, however, were replaced by an even greater danger: ferocious glacial bears, who showed no fear of fire. Prosperity and security became distant memories for the suffering tribe.

Fortunately, a new breed of brilliant educators emerged. One tribesman, his stomach rumbling with hunger, grew frustrated with fruitless fish-grabbing in cloudy waters. He fashioned a crude net and in one hour caught more fish than the whole tribe could have caught had they fish-grabbed for an entire day. Another tribesman fashioned a snare with which he could trap the swift antelope, and a third dug a pit that captured and secured the ferocious bears.

As a result of these new inventions, the tribe again became happy and prosperous. Some radicals even began to criticize the school's curriculum and urged that net-making, snare-setting, and pit-digging were indispensable to modern life and should be taught in the schools. But the wise old men who controlled the schools objected:

> With all the intricate details of fish-grabbing, horse-clubbing, and tiger-scaring—the standard cultural subjects—the school curriculum is too crowded now. We can't add these fads and frills of net-making, antelope-snaring, and—of all things—bear-killing. Why, at the very thought, the body of the great New-Fist, founder of our paleolithic educational system, would turn over in its burial cairn. What we need to do is to give our young people a more thorough grounding in the fundamentals. . . . The essence of true education is timelessness. It is something that endures through changing conditions like a solid rock standing squarely and firmly in the middle of a raging torrent. You must know that there are some eternal verities, and the saber-tooth curriculum is one of them.[40]

• • •

The Saber-Tooth Curriculum was written in 1939, but it has meaning today. Clearly educators need to avoid a curriculum out of touch with the reality of today's students and thoughtlessly programmed for obsolescence. No educator worth his or her salt wants to be caught waving unnecessary firebrands at tigers long extinct. Today's debate over curricula for different ethnic groups versus a common, Eurocentric core is related to issues raised in *The Saber-Tooth Curriculum*. Is Latin a "saber-tooth" subject? What about the ancient history of the Romans and Greeks? Should these topics make way for subjects more relevant, useful, or culturally inclusive? If we omit these, do we lose an important part of the nation's cultural heritage? Is there room for everything? If not, how do we establish priorities? Perhaps it all comes back to questions fundamental to the development of the curriculum: What knowledge is of most worth? What is included in the curriculum? What is left out? What is education for? And who decides?

SUMMARY

1. The curriculum can be influenced by many different groups and data. These include students, parents, administrators, the federal government, the state government, the local government, colleges and universities, national test results, education commissions and committees, and professional organizations.

2. The effort to establish national curricular standards has moved forward for subjects such as mathematics, but has encountered a vocal opposition in more value-laden disciplines such as history, where no national consensus exists as to what should be included. While some Americans believe that institution of national standards will enhance the level of learning and national unity, critics argue that funding for additional resources rather than national standards are needed in order to improve America's schools.

3. While the debate on national standards continues, both presidents Bush and Clinton have proposed national objectives designed to improve the performance of America's schoolchildren. President Clinton's plan was named "Goals 2000."

4. Twenty-one states, mainly located in the South and the West, are state adoption states. Typically, in this centralized adoption system, local school districts select their texts from an official, state-approved list.

5. Those who are in favor of the state adoption system believe that this process leads to the selection of higher-quality texts and creates a common statewide curriculum. Those who criticize the state adoption system claim that large, populous states have unfair influence over textbook development.

6. Under pressure to publish books that will have appropriate readability levels, publishers and authors "dumb down" the textbook or substitute simplified, shorter words or phrases for more complex ones. This may result in books in which sophisticated ideas are simplified into meaningless ideas. Critics of textbooks cite the "mentioning phenomenon" as another problem. Critics claim that the books try to include too many subjects and gloss over them to such a degree that students fail to gain sufficient depth or context.

7. Six types of bias may characterize textbooks. These are invisibility, stereotyping, imbalance and selectivity, unreality, fragmentation and isolation, and linguistic bias.

8. Controversies over religion and secular humanism have characterized textbook adoption in recent years. In some communities, these controversies have led to book banning and censorship.

9. Debate continues over the impact of a core curriculum. Proponents of a core curriculum feel that it will benefit the disadvantaged and transmit the culture essential for well-educated citizens. Multiculturalists feel it will deny women and minorities the opportunity to see their experiences reflected in history and literature.

10. Although most classroom teachers cannot choose their own textbooks, they have the power to interpret the materials and emphasize or skim over content. While detailed guides and workbooks may save time and effort, they rob the teaching role of autonomy and professionalism.

11. When developing curricula, it is important to keep in mind the satire of *The Saber-Tooth Curriculum*. A curriculum must include objectives and activities that will teach students how to preserve the past, function effectively in the present, and become prepared for the future.

DISCUSSION QUESTIONS AND ACTIVITIES

1. This chapter has presented an overview of the various groups and forces that influence what children are taught in schools. In your opinion, which of these groups and forces have the most influence on curricula? Why?

2. What subjects would spark the greatest debate and controversy to creating a single, national curriculum? Are there strategies to help reach a consensus on these issues? How might a national history curriculum written today differ from one written a century from now? A century ago? Why?

3. Do you believe that children's educational materials should be censored? Are there any benefits to censorship? Any dangers? What kinds of materials would you refuse to let elementary school students read? Secondary students? Postsecondary students?

4. Are you in favor of a comprehensive textbook system, or do you think this inhibits teachers from pursuing one of the important professional aspects of their work?

5. Collect textbooks from your local elementary and secondary schools and analyze them according to the following criteria:

- Do they include instructional objectives? Do these require students to use both recall of factual information as well as more analytical and creative thinking skills?
- Were readability formulas used in the preparation of the textbook? If so, did this appear to have a negative or positive impact on the quality of the writing?
- Are females and minority group members included in the textbook narrative and illustrations? Are individuals with disabilities included?
- When these individuals are included, are they portrayed in a fair or a stereotyped manner?

6. Is American society best characterized as a melting pot? A salad? A stew? Stir-fry in a sauce? Why? Is there another metaphor that better captures the nature of American society?

7. Do we have a saber-tooth curriculum today? Through satire, Abner Peddiwell made a persuasive case against the saber-tooth curriculum. Can you write a satire in its defense?

8. Consider the courses and textbooks used on your campus in history and literature courses. Do you think a traditional or a multicultural perspective is reflected?

NOTES

1. Myra Sadker and David Sadker, *Now upon a Time: A Contemporary View of Children's Literature* (New York: Harper & Row, 1977).
2. *Attacks on the Freedom to Learn,* People for the American Way, 1994–1995 report.
3. Ibid.
4. Ibid.
5. Paul Barry, "Interview: A Talk with A. Bartlett Giamatti," *College Review Board* (Spring 1982): 48.
6. John Elson, "History, The Sequel," *Time* 144 (November 7, 1994): 53; see also Von Wiener, "History Lesson," *The New Republic,* January 2, 1995: 9–11.
7. Joel Spring, *American Education* (New York: McGraw-Hill, 1996), pp. 237–241.
8. Lyn Nell Hancock with Nina Archer Biddle, "Red, White—and Blue," *Newsweek* 1224 (November 7, 1994): 54.
9. Jack Nelson, Kenneth Carlson, and Stuart Palonsky, *Critical Issues in Education,* (New York: McGraw-Hill, 1996), pp. 241–261.
10. Harriet Tyson Bernstein, *A Conspiracy of Good Intentions: America's Textbook Fiasco* (Washington, DC: The Council for Basic Education, 1988), p. 2.
11. Rodger Farr and Michael Tulley, "Do Adoption Committees Perpetuate Mediocre Textbooks?" *Phi Delta Kappan* 66, no. 7 (March 1985): 467–471.
12. Bonnie Ambruster, Jean Osborn, and Alice Davison, "Readability Formulas May Be Dangerous to Your Textbooks," *Educational Leadership* 42, no. 7 (April 1985): 18–20.
13. Susan Ohanian, "Ruffles and Flourishes," *Atlantic Monthly,* September 1987: 20–22.
14. Quoted in Bernstein, *A Conspiracy of Good Intentions,* p. 19.
15. Quoted in David Elliott, Kathleen Carter Nagel, and Arthur Woodward, "Do Textbooks Belong in Elementary School Studies?" *Educational Leadership* 42, no. 7 (April 1985): 22–25.
16. Jean Osborn, Beau Fly Jones, and Marcy Stein, "The Case for Improving Textbooks," *Educational Leadership* 42, no. 7 (April 1985): 9–16; see also Michael Apple, "Regulating the Text: The Social Historical Roots of State Control." Paper delivered at the American Educational Research Association, San Francisco, April 1992.
17. Connie Muther, "What Every Textbook Evaluator Should Know," *Educational Leadership* 42, no. 7 (April 1985): 48.
18. The forms of bias were developed by Myra Sadker and David Sadker for Title IX equity workshops.
19. Bernstein, *A Conspiracy of Good Intentions,* pp. 35–36.
20. Quoted in Edward B. Jenkinson, "The Significance of the Decision in 'Scopes II,' " *Phi Delta Kappan* 68, no. 6 (February 1987): 446.
21. Frances Goodrich and Albert Hackett, *The Diary of Anne Frank.* In *Great Waves Breaking* (New York: Holt, Rinehart & Winston, 1983), p. 387.
22. Transcript of proceedings in *Mozert,* July 14, 1986, p. 24, as quoted in Jenkinson, *Scopes II.*
23. Jenkinson, *Scopes II.*
24. Robert Marzano and David Arredondo, *Tactics for Thinking—Teacher's Manual* (Alexandria, VA: Association for Supervision and Curriculum Development, 1986), p. 11; quoted in Edward Jenkinson, "The New Age of Schoolbook Protest," *Phi Delta Kappan* 10, no. 1 (September 1988): 66.
25. Debra Viadero, "Christian Movement Seen Trying to Influence Schools," *Education Week* 11, no. 30 (April 15, 1992): 8.
26. Anthony Podesta, "For Full Discussion of Religion in the Schools," *The Wall Street Journal,* November 12, 1986, p. 32.
27. Ellen Goodman, "Denying Diversity," *The Washington Post,* November 11, 1986, p. A21.

28. Thomas McDaniel, "On Trial: The Right to Think," *Educational Leadership* 49, no. 4 (December 1991/January 1992): 85.
29. Quoted in Lynne Cheney, *Humanities in America: A Report to the President, Congress and the American People* (Washington, DC: National Endowment for the Humanities, 1988), p. 17.
30. Quoted in William Bennett, *American Education: Making It Work* (Washington, DC: U.S. Department of Education, 1988).
31. Allan Bloom, *The Closing of the American Mind* (New York: Simon and Schuster, 1987), p. 63.
32. E. D. Hirsch, Jr., *Cultural Literacy* (Boston: Houghton Mifflin, 1987).
33. E. D. Hirsch, Jr., *What Your First Grader Needs to Know,* and *What Your Second Grader Needs to Know* (New York: Doubleday, 1991).
34. James Banks, "Multicultural Education: For Freedom's Sake," *Educational Leadership* 49, no. 4 (December 1991/January 1992): 32–36.
35. Marge Scherer, "School Snapshot: Focus on African-American Culture," *Educational Leadership* 49, no. 4 (December 1991/January 1992): 17–21.
36. Arthur Schlesinger, *The Disuniting of America* (New York: Norton, 1992).
37. Eliot Eisner, "Should America Have a National Curriculum?" *Educational Leadership* 49, no. 4 (October 1991): 76–81.
38. Michael Apple, "Curriculum in the Year 2000: Tensions and Possibilities," *Phi Delta Kappan* 64, no. 5 (January 1983): 323.
39. Apple, "Curriculum in the Year 2000."
40. Abner Peddiwell (Harold Benjamin), *The Saber-Tooth Curriculum* (New York: McGraw-Hill, 1939).

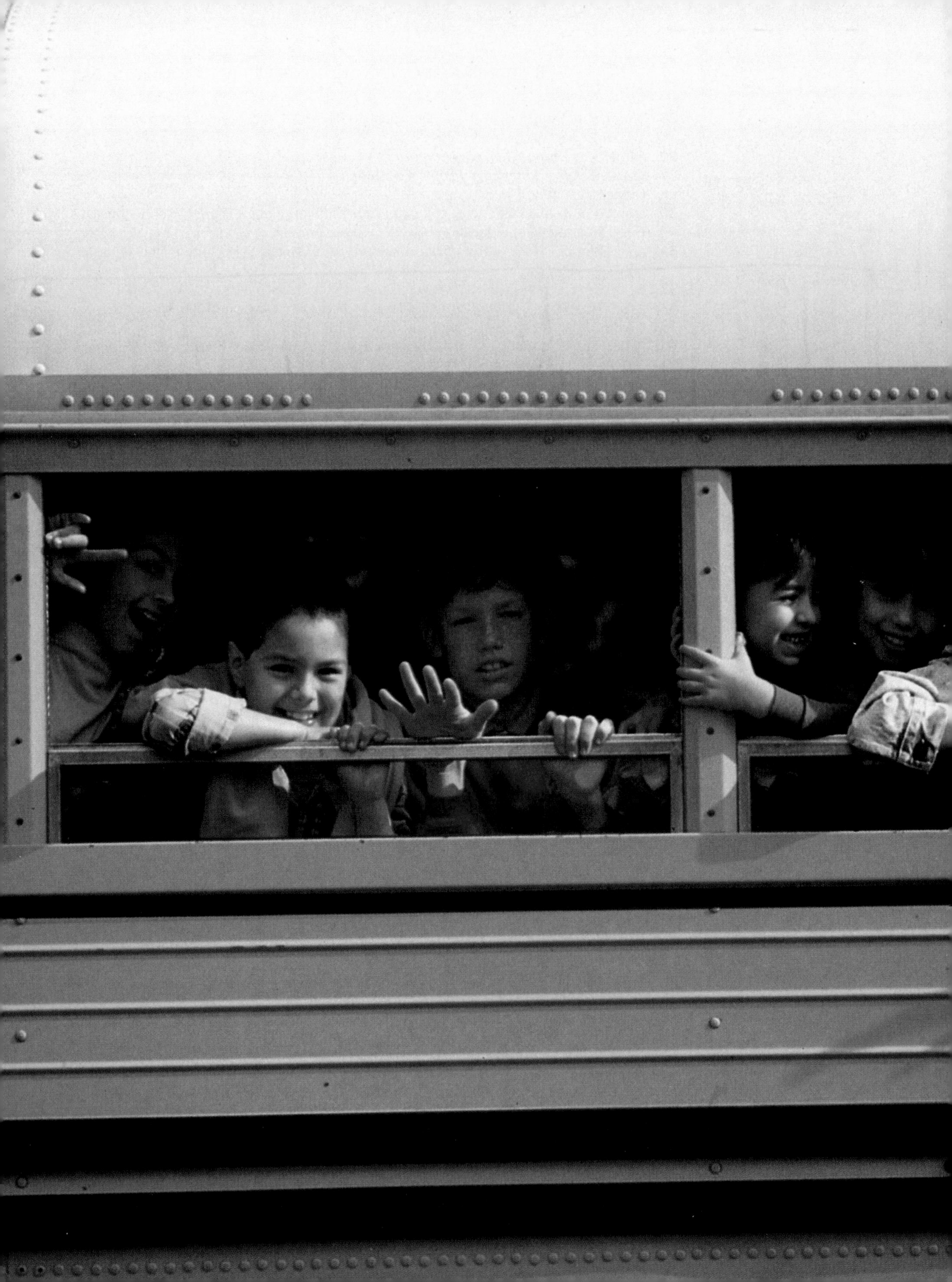

THE HISTORY OF AMERICAN EDUCATION

OBJECTIVES

To describe the major historical events in the development of American education

To analyze the role of local, state, and federal governments in the creation of America's schools

To trace the development of elementary and secondary schools

To explore the educational barriers and breakthroughs experienced by girls, women, and minorities

To identify the significant contributions of individuals in shaping today's educational practices

Your classroom is a living tribute to past achievements and events. As a teacher, you are the latest link in a long line of individuals who have shaped America's schools. Understanding the history of America's schools will not actually provide practical classroom strategies, but it will offer you a sense of perspective—a place in your new profession. Knowledge of the events and forces that have brought us to this place in time will provide insight into the culture and milieu of teaching and an appreciation of the struggle, sacrifices, and achievements of those who came before.

This chapter will trace American education from colonial times to the present. Education during the colonial period was intended to further religious goals and was offered primarily to white males. Although the experience of females is less well-known, it is also described in this chapter.

For minority groups, a very different story unfolds. For these groups, education was far more difficult, if not impossible, to attain. In Chapter 14, "The Struggle for Equal Educational Opportunity," we give their stories the focus and space they deserve. In this chapter, the efforts of Benjamin Franklin, Horace Mann, Emma Hart Willard, and others are described as they fought to free America from historical biases. To a great extent, the story of American education is a story of increasing access, of opening the schoolhouse door to more and more of our citizens.

As education became more widely available, individuals, groups, and governments influenced the direction of public schools. Should the schools' purpose be college preparation and academic training, or should they prepare children for vocations? Can schools neutralize social problems? Should schools educate all children?

The complex network of expectations surrounding today's schools is the product of a society that has been evolving for over three centuries. In the colonial era, however, the goals were simple: to teach the Scriptures and to develop a religious community. This review begins by looking into Christopher Lamb's classroom in New England more than three centuries ago.

Back to the Future

The frigid, wintry wind knifed through Christopher Lamb's coat, chilling him to the bone as he walked in the predawn darkness. The single bucket of firewood that he lugged, intended to keep his seventeenth-century New England schoolroom warm all day, would clearly not do the job. Once the fire was started, Christopher focused on his other teaching tasks: carrying in a bucket of water for the class, sweeping the floor, and mending the ever-so-fragile pen points for the students. More than an hour after Christopher's predawn activities began, Margaret, the first student, arrived. As other students trickled in, they were directed to either the boys' bench or the girls' bench, where, in turn, they read their Testament aloud. Those who read the Scriptures without error took their place at the table and wrote on their slates.

Christopher was amazed at how poorly some students read, tripping over every other word, whereas others read quite fluently. The last student to finish, Benjamin, slowly rose from the bench, cringing. Christopher called out, "Lazy pupil," and a chorus of children's voices chimed in: "Lazy pupil. Lazy pupil. Lazy pupil." Benjamin, if not totally inured to the taunts, was no longer crushed by them either. He slowly made his way to the end of the student line.

After the recitation and writing lessons were completed, all the children were lined up and examined, to make certain that they had washed and combed. A psalm was sung and Mr. Lamb exhorted the students to walk in God's footsteps. For 10 minutes, the class and teacher knelt in prayer. Each student then recited the day's biblical lesson. Those who had memorized their lessons received an "O," written on their hand in crayon, a mark of excellence. Those who failed to recite their lessons correctly after three attempts once again were called lazy pupil by the entire class, and this time their names were written down. If by the end of the day the lesson was finally learned, the name was erased from the list and all the children called out "Diligent!" to the student.

Christopher Lamb was an apprentice teacher for 5 years before he accepted this position. He rejected the rod approach used so frequently by his master teacher. Using the children to provide rewards and punishments was far more effective than welts and bruises, the products of a quickly moving teacher's rod. Yes, Christopher was somewhat unorthodox, perhaps even a bit revolutionary, but the challenges of contemporary seventeenth-century society demanded forward-thinking educators like Christopher Lamb.

Colonial New England Education: God's Classrooms

Although there are striking differences (as well as discomforting similarities) between Christopher Lamb's colonial classroom and today's schools, certainly one of the crucial differences is the role of religion in education. The religious fervor that drove the Puritans to America was the same force that drove the Puritans to provide for the education of their young. In Christopher Lamb's classes, the purpose of education was to save souls, to teach children to read the holy word, to beat the Devil. Reading the Bible would protect children from Satan. Education provided a path to heaven, and reading, writing, and moral development all revolved around the Bible. Although the Puritans made New England the cradle of American education, they did not wait for the construction of school buildings to begin the educational process.

Before Christopher Lamb had a classroom, before there were formal schools, the Puritans provided for the education of their youth. Early colonial education, both in New England and in other colonies, took place in the home, in the church, and through apprenticeship programs. It was at home that most children learned to read. The family was the major educational resource for youngsters. Values, manners, social graces, and even vocational skills were taught by parents and grandparents. Home instruction eventually became more specialized, as some women began to devote their time to teaching children in the community reading, writing, and computation. This resulted in the creation of **dame schools,** schools held in the homes of women interested in teaching. A "dame," or well-respected woman with an interest in teaching, was a forerunner of today's teacher.

Paralleling home instruction and dame schools was an apprenticeship program. Children, sometimes as young as 7 years of age, were sent to live with masters who taught them a trade. Apprenticeship programs involved not only learning skilled crafts but also managing farms and shops. Many colonies required that masters teach reading and writing as well as vocational skills. The master would serve *in loco parentis*—that is, in place of the child's parent. The church also provided education to the Puritans. This collection of diverse educational opportunities reflected disparate teaching standards. The competencies of masters guiding apprentices varied greatly, as did the talents

Recitation lesson in a colonial classroom.

of family members, dames, ministers, and others fulfilling the teaching role. Clearly, more formal structure was needed.

Twenty-two years after arriving in the New World, the Puritans living in the Commonwealth of Massachusetts passed a law requiring that periodic checks be made on parents and masters of apprentices to ensure that children were being taught properly. Five years later, in 1647, Massachusetts took even more rigorous measures to ensure the education of its children. The Massachusetts Law of 1647, which is more commonly known to us as the **"Old Deluder Satan Law"**—the Puritans' attempt to thwart Satan's trickery with Scripture-reading citizens—required that:

- Every town of 50 households must appoint and pay a teacher of reading and writing.
- Every town of 100 households must provide a (Latin) grammar school to prepare youths for the university, under a penalty of £5 for failure to do so.[1]

By 1680 the Massachusetts laws had spread throughout most of New England. The settlement patterns of the Puritans, living in towns and communities rather than scattered throughout the countryside, made the establishment of schools a practical reality. After learning to read and write, most girls returned home to learn the art of housekeeping. Boys who were able to continue their education went on to a **Latin grammar school.** In 1635, only 15 years after arriving in America's wilderness, the Puritans had established their first Latin grammar school in Boston. The Boston Latin Grammar School was similar to the classical schools of Europe and was the origin of today's high schools.

The Latin grammar schools were not unlike "prep" schools for boys. Tuition was charged to teach boys between the ages of 7 and 14 the classics of the Greek and Roman civilizations. Students were expected to read, recite, and discuss (in Latin, of course) the works of Cicero, Ovid, and Erasmus. In Greek, they read the works of Socrates and Homer. (This was a real back-to-basics curriculum!) Those who graduated from the Latin grammar schools were expected to go on to college and become the ministers and leaders of the colonies. By the eighteenth century, the grammar school had modified its practices and incorporated mathematics, science, and modern languages. However, the new curriculum offerings did not alter the lengthy school day. Classes started at 7:00 A.M., recessed at 11:00 A.M., and picked up from 1:00 P.M. until 5:00 P.M.

Within a year of the founding of the Boston Latin Grammar School, Harvard College was established to prepare ministers. Founded in 1636, Harvard was the first college in America, the jewel in the Puritans' religious and educational crown.[2]

But this new system was far from inclusive. Blacks, in America since 1619, and Native Americans, who preceded the Europeans, were offered few educational opportunities—typically by religious groups, such as the Quakers.[3] The growing institution of slavery, coupled with racism, not only denied formal schooling to many Native Americans and blacks, it eventually led to laws prohibiting their education. (See Chapter 14, "The Struggle for Equal Educational Opportunity," for a more complete review of these issues.) Nor did girls fare much better. After they had learned the rudiments of reading and writing, girls focused on housework. Apprenticeships for females frequently included not skills and vocations outside the home, but the tasks that fell to the mother and

Today's communities often retain the name "School Street" indicating where early school buildings, like this one, were first constructed.

*School Street
North Side
1645–1748*

wife. Those attractive samplers that we see in antique stores symbolize the stunted education provided to women. They learned various stitches. They mastered and sewed the alphabet. They memorized and sewed religious sayings. As much as we value these young women's samplers today, at the time they marked the terminal degree—the academic finish line for girls, the diploma of a second-rate education, a depressing denial of equal educational rights that we describe later in this chapter.

Wealth played a critical role in determining educational opportunity. The least desirable types of apprenticeships were left to the poor. Few other educational options existed: Some civic-minded communities made education available, but only to families who would publicly admit their poverty by signing a "Pauper's Oath." Broadcasting one's poverty was no less offensive in colonial times than it is today, and many chose to have their children remain illiterate rather than sign such a public admission. The result was that most poor children remained outside the educational system.

Geography also played a role. The northern colonies were settled by Puritans who lived in towns and communities relatively close to one another. Their religious fervor and geographic proximity made the creation of community schools dedicated to teaching the Bible a predictable development.

In the middle and southern colonies, educational opportunity differed markedly from that in New England.[4] The range of European religious and ethnic groups (Dutch, Swedes, Puritans, Catholics, Mennonites) in the middle colonies created, if not a melting pot, a tolerance for diversity (except for Native Americans and African Americans). Various religious groups established schools, and apprenticeships continued to train youngsters for a variety of careers, including teaching. The economic needs of the middle colonies also affected schools. The development of commerce and mercantile demands promoted the formation of private schools devoted to job training. By the 1700s, private teachers and night schools were functioning in Philadelphia and New York, teaching accounting, navigation, French, and Spanish.

The rural, sparsely populated southern colonies developed a cultural and educational system that was responsive to plantation society. The wealthy plantation owners brought tutors into their homes to teach their children not only basic academic skills but also social graces appropriate to their station in life. Plantation owners' children learned the proper way to entertain guests and treat slaves, using such texts as *The Complete Gentleman*. Wealthy young men seeking higher education were sent to Europe. Girls made do with just an introduction to academics in addition to their social responsibilities. Poor white children made do with rudimentary home instruction in reading, writing, and computation. Black children made do with no instruction, and as time went by, with laws prohibiting their education entirely.[5]

Education has come a long way from colonial days and from Christopher Lamb's class—or has it? Consider the following:

1. The colonial experience established many of today's educational norms:

   • Local control of schools was established.
   • Compulsory education was legislated.
   • Tax-supported schools were created.
   • State standards for teaching and schools were developed.

2. The colonial experience highlighted many of the persistent tension points that continue to challenge our schools today:

   • What is the proper role of religion in the classroom?
   • How can we respond fairly in order to equalize the disparate quality of education available in different communities?
   • How can the barriers of racism, sexism, religious intolerance, and classism be eliminated so that all children receive equal educational opportunity?
   • How can we identify and ensure appropriate competencies for the teaching profession?

More than three centuries ago Christopher Lamb trudged to school carrying his firewood. The contributions and sacrifices of the thousands of Christopher Lambs who preceded us forged the traditions and identified the challenges that persist in our schools today. Figure 9.1 lists the first 15 colleges and universities in the United States in order of their establishment.

FIGURE 9.1
The Development of Colonial Higher Education

Many of today's colleges and universities began as small, religiously sponsored institutions founded to train the clergy. The first 15 institutions of higher education established in the colonies were all affiliated with a religious denomination.

Year	Institution	Year	Institution
1636	Harvard University	**1766**	Queen's College (Rutgers University)
1693	College of William and Mary	**1769**	Dartmouth University
1701	Yale University	**1782**	Washington College
1746	Princeton University	**1782**	Washington and Lee University
1754	King's College (Columbia University)	**1783**	Hampton-Sidney College
1755	University of Pennsylvania	**1783**	Transylvania College
1765	Brown University	**1783**	Dickinson College
		1784	St. John's College

A New Nation Shapes Education

As the eighteenth century unfolded, the ideas that led to the American Revolution also revolutionized our schools. European beliefs and practices, which had pervaded America's schools, were gradually abandoned as the new national character was formed. None of these beliefs had been more firmly adhered to than the integration of the state and religion.

In sixteenth- and seventeenth-century England, the Church of England was created not only as a religious entity, but also to replace the Catholic church for political reasons. Individuals affiliated with other religions were viewed as disloyal, not only to the Church but to England. Religious dissenters, such as the Puritans, were viewed as potentially subversive. Their desire to reform the Church of England led to both religious and political conflict, and they looked to the New World as an escape from persecution. However, they came to America *not* to establish religious freedom, as our history books sometimes suggest, but to establish their own church as supreme, both religiously and politically. The Puritans were neither tolerant of other religions nor interested in separating religion and politics. Nonconformers, such as Roger Williams (who went on to establish Rhode Island), were vigorously persecuted. The purpose of Massachusetts was to establish the "true" religion of the Puritans, to create a "new Israel" in America. Schools were simply an extension of the religious state, designed to teach the young whatever they had to know in order to read and understand the Bible and to do honorable battle with Satan.

During the 1700s, education was seen as meeting broader, nonsectarian goals. Leaders like Thomas Jefferson wanted to go beyond educating a small elite class or providing only religious instruction. He maintained that education should be more widely available to white children from all economic and social classes. Public citizens began to question the usefulness of rudimentary skills taught in a school year of just 3 or 4 months. They also questioned the value of mastering Greek and Latin classics in the Latin grammar schools when so many practical skills were in short supply in the New World.

In 1749 Benjamin Franklin wrote *Proposals Relating to the Youth of Pennsylvania,* suggesting a new kind of secondary school to replace the Latin grammar school—the **academy.** Two years later, the Franklin Academy was established, free of religious influence and offering a variety of practical subjects including mathematics, astronomy, athletics, navigation, dramatics, and bookkeeping. Students at the Franklin Academy were able to choose some of their courses, thus setting the precedent for elective courses and programs at the secondary level. By the late 1700s it was the Franklin Academy and not the Boston Latin Grammar School that was considered the most important secondary school in America.[6]

The innovative Franklin Academy accepted both girls and boys who could afford the tuition, and the practical curriculum became an attractive innovation. Franklin's academy sparked the establishment of 6,000 academies in the century that followed. Several of those academies survive today, including Phillips Academy at Andover, Massachusetts (1778), and Phillips Exeter Academy in Exeter, New Hampshire (1783). The original Franklin Academy eventually became the University of Pennsylvania.

Jefferson's commitment to educating all white Americans, rich and poor, at government expense, and Franklin's commitment to a practical program of nonsectarian study offering elective courses, severed American educational thought

In addition to serving two terms as president, Thomas Jefferson was the colonial era's most eloquent spokesman for education and was the founder of the University of Virginia.

From the Hornbook to the Terminal

A rich variety of textbooks, media, library books, and computer software provides today's teachers with curricular resources unimaginable just a few years ago. As a teacher, you will undoubtedly come across references to some of the limited, but influential, curriculum materials of the past. Here is a brief profile of the best-known instructional materials from yesterday's schools.

Hornbook

The most common teaching device in colonial schools, the hornbook consisted of the alphabet sheet covered by a thin, transparent sheet made from a cow's horn. The alphabet and the horn covering were tacked to a paddle-shaped piece of wood and often hung by a leather strap around the student's neck. Originating in medieval Europe, the hornbook provided colonial children with their introduction to the alphabet and reading.

New England Primer

The first real textbook, the *New England Primer* was a tiny 2½- by 4½-inch book containing 50 to 100 pages of alphabet, words, and small verses accompanied by woodcut illustrations. First published in 1690, it was virtually the only reading text used in colonial schools until about 1800. The *Primer* reflected the religious orientation of colonial schools. A typical verse was:

> In Adam's Fall
> We sinned all.

> Thy Life to mend,
> This Book attend
> The idle fool
> Is whipt at School.

American Spelling Book

The task undertaken by Noah Webster was to define and nourish the new American culture. His *American Spelling Book* replaced the *New England Primer* as the most common elementary textbook. The book contained the alphabet, syllables, consonants, rules for speaking, reading, short stories, and moral advice. The bulk of the book was taken up by lists of words. Royalty income from the sale of millions of copies of this book supported Webster in his other efforts to standardize the American language, including his best-known work, which is still used today, the *American Dictionary*.

McGuffey's Readers

William Holmes McGuffey was a minister, professor, and college president who believed that clean living, hard work, and literacy were the virtues to instill in children. He wrote a series of readers that emphasized the work ethic, patriotism, heroism, and morality. It is estimated that well over 100 million copies of McGuffey's readers educated several generations of Americans between 1836 and 1920. McGuffey's readers are noteworthy because they were geared for different grade levels and paved the way for graded elementary schools.

from its European roots. Although many years would pass before these ideas became widely established practices, the pattern for change, for innovation, for a truly American approach to education was taking shape.

After the American Revolution, the new nation demonstrated a unique approach to education with the passage of the Land Ordinance Act of 1785 and the Northwest Ordinance of 1787. These acts, which dealt with the disposition of the newly settled territories bounded by the Ohio and Mississippi rivers and the Great Lakes, required that each township reserve a section of land for educational purposes. The ordinances contained a much-quoted sentence underscoring the new nation's faith in education: "Religion, morality, and knowledge being necessary to good government and the happiness of mankind, schools and the means of education shall forever be encouraged."

Despite the strong faith that Americans placed in education, the United States Constitution was written without reference to it. Some historians believe that since the individual colonies had established different educational practices, the framers of the Constitution did not want to devise new requirements that might create dissension. Others think that education was omitted from the Constitution because Americans wanted to ensure that schools would not be controlled by a central authority, as they had been in Europe. Some historians suggest that the framers of the Constitution, in their haste, bartering, and bickering, simply forgot about education (what a depressing thought!). Whatever the reason, the responsibility for education was not assigned to the new federal government, and the Tenth Amendment dictated that areas not assigned to the federal government would be the responsibility of each state. Consequently, each state created its own system for instructing students, preparing teachers, and funding education.

The Constitution also radically altered education through the First Amendment, which separated church and state. U.S. education would become secular, and no single religion would become state endorsed and prevail over other religions. These two constitutional provisions created a unique educational system, secular and decentralized. This new system has left us with a legacy of conflict as we struggle to define the educational roles of the state and federal governments and the limits of religious activities appropriate for U.S. classrooms. Chapter 11 describes the conflict and confusion over how to interpret and implement the Constitution in today's schools.

The Common School Movement

During the early decades of the nineteenth century, education was often viewed as a luxury item. However, even parents who could afford such a luxury had limited choices. The town schools still existed in Massachusetts, and some charity schools served the poor and orphans. Dame schools varied in quality. In some areas religious schools of one denomination or the other prevailed, while in rural areas and the South few schools existed at all. The United States was a patchwork quilt of schools tied together by the reality that money was needed to attain a decent education.

During the early decades of the nineteenth century, the common people—immigrants, small farmers, and urban laborers—demanded greater participation in the democracy. With the election of Andrew Jackson in 1828, their voices were heard in the government. However, they sought access to the schoolhouse as well. No longer should ignorance lock their children into poverty when education could provide them with a means to move up in society.

Horace Mann became the nation's leading proponent for the establishment of what we know today as the public **elementary school,** a school open to all, an education not dependent on family wealth. Horace Mann is considered by historians to be the outstanding proponent of the school for the common person (the **common school** movement), and he is often referred to as "the father of the public school." Educated as a lawyer at Brown University, Mann served in the state legislature and became an outspoken advocate for state-supported quality education. He helped in the creation of the Massachusetts State Board of Education and in 1837 became secretary of the board, a position that today would be similar to a state superintendent of schools. Mann saw the need for public education in both practical and idealistic terms. In practical terms, both business and industry would benefit from educated workers, and we would develop a more productive economy. In idealistic terms, public schools should help us identify and nurture the talents in all our children—the poor as well as the rich.[7]

The idea of public education is so commonplace today that it seems difficult to imagine another system. But Horace Mann, along with allies such as Henry Barnard of Connecticut, fought a long and difficult battle to win acceptance of public elementary schools. The opposition was powerful. First there were the business interests, predicting disaster if their labor pool of children was taken away. Then there were the concerned taxpayers, protesting the additional tax monies needed to support public education. There was also the competition. Private schools and religious groups sponsoring their own schools protested the establishment of free schools. Americans wondered what would become of a nation where everyone received an elementary education. Would this not produce overeducated citizens, questioning authority and promoting self-interest? The opposition to public elementary schools was often fierce, but Horace Mann and his allies prevailed.

As he fought for public schools for all, Mann also waged a battle for quality schools. He worked for more stringent teacher-licensing procedures to establish a core of competent teachers. He continually attempted to build new and expanded schools to teach more and more students. Mann emphasized practical subjects useful to children and to adult society, rather than mastery of Greek and Latin. He also promoted newer teaching methods to improve the quality of classroom instruction. Horace Mann saw education as a great investment, for individuals and for the country, and he worked for many years to make free public education a reality.

Contributing to the school reforms of the nineteenth century were the poor physical conditions that characterized most U.S. schools.

By the time of the Civil War, this radical notion of the public elementary school was widespread and widely accepted. Educational historian Lawrence Cremin summarizes the advance of the common school movement in his book *The Transformation of the School:*

> A majority of the states had established public school systems, and a good half of the nation's children were already getting some formal education. Elementary schools were becoming widely available; in some states, like Massachusetts, New York, and Pennsylvania, the notion of free public education was slowly expanding to include secondary schools; and in a few, like Michigan and Wisconsin, the public school system was already capped by a state university. There were, of course, significant variations from state to state and from region to region. New England, long a pioneer in public education, also had an established tradition of private education, and private schools continued to flourish there. The Midwest, on the other hand, sent a far greater proportion of its school children to public institutions. The southern states, with the exception of North Carolina, tended to lag behind, and did not generally establish popular schooling until after the Civil War.[8]

The Secondary School Movement

With Mann's success in promoting public elementary schools, more and more citizens were given a basic education. By 1880 almost 10 million Americans were enrolled in elementary schools, and at the upper levels of schooling, both private and public universities were established. But the gap between the elementary schools and the universities remained wide.

Massachusetts, site of the first tax-supported elementary schools and the first college in America, was the site of the first free **secondary school.** Established in Boston in 1821, the English Classical School enrolled 176 students (all boys); shortly thereafter, 76 students dropped out. The notion of a public high school was slow to take root. The name of the school was changed to The English High School, to emphasize the more practical nature of the curriculum.

As secondary schools spread, they generally took the form of private, tuition-charging academies. Citizens did not view the secondary schools as we do today, as a free and natural extension of elementary education.[9] In 1855, 263,000 secondary students were enrolled in 6,000 tuition-charging private academies. These academies were the link between elementary and college education. The curricula of these academies varied widely, some focusing on college preparation and others providing a general curriculum for students who would not continue their studies. In academies founded for females or in coeducational academies, "normal" courses were often popular. The normal course prepared these academy graduates for teaching careers in the common schools. A few academies provided military programs of study.

One of the chief stumbling blocks to the creation of free high schools was public resistance to paying additional school taxes. This was the same argument that Mann had had to contend with a half a century earlier in promoting the public elementary school. But in a series of court cases, especially the Kalamazoo, Michigan, case in 1874, the courts ruled that taxes could be used to support secondary schools. In the Michigan case, citizens already had access to free elementary schools and a state-supported university. The courts saw a lack of rationality in not providing a bridge between the two. As a result of these legal and political efforts, the U.S. high school could legally be supported by tax funds.

During the last half of the nineteenth century, significant changes spurred the development of the public high school. The nation moved from agrarian to industrial, from rural to urban, and people viewed the elementary school as inadequate to meet the needs of a more sophisticated and industrialized society. More parents viewed the high school as an important stepping-stone to better jobs. With the gradual decrease in demand for teenage workers, high school attendance grew. Half a century earlier, the public elementary school reflected the growing dreams and aspirations of Americans and their changing economy. Now the public high school was the benchmark of these changes.

The high school developed in a uniquely American way. As a school for white students from various social classes, ethnic and religious backgrounds, and both sexes, the American secondary school was a radical departure from the rigid tracking system of Europe. The secondary schools of Europe segregated academic students from those who would not go beyond a secondary education. Relatively early in a student's career, the limits of secondary education were set, with class status and wealth often primary factors. In the United States, although the high school also served the dual purposes of vocational and college preparation, there was no rigid tracking system, no early decision determining a young child's destiny. The high school became a continuation of elementary education, a universal right to further schooling, a stepping-stone to public higher education, and an affirmation of democracy.

During the twentieth century, attendance at the secondary level grew significantly, and the demands on the high school increased. Organizational changes included the creation of **junior high schools** in 1910 and, more recently, the creation of **middle schools,** which typically consist of grades 6, 7, and 8. The development of elementary and secondary schools is described in Figure 9.2.

Almost from their inception, America's high schools have been viewed as means of enculturating immigrant students into the mainstream of American life.

FIGURE 9.2
The Development of American Schools

Elementary Schools

Dame schools (1600s)
These private schools taught by women in their homes offered child care for working parents willing to pay a fee. The "dames" who taught here received meager wages, and the quality of instruction varied greatly.

Local schools (1600s–1800s)
First started in towns and later expanded to include larger districts, these schools were open to those who could afford to pay. Found generally in New England, these schools taught basic skills and religion.

Itinerant schools (1700s) and tutors (1600s–1900s)
Rural America could not support schools and full-time teachers. As a result, in sparsely populated New England, itinerant teachers carried schooling from village to village; they lived in people's homes and provided instruction. In the South, private tutors taught the rich. Traveling teachers and tutors, usually working for a fee and room and board, brought varying levels of education to small towns and wealthy populations.

Private schools (1700s–1800s)
Private schools, often located in the middle colonies, offered a variety of special studies. These schools constituted a true free market, as parents paid for the kind of private school they desired. As you might imagine, both the curricula and the quality of these schools varied greatly.

Common schools (1830–present)
The common school was a radical departure from earlier ones in several ways. First, it was free. Parents did not have to pay tuition or fees. Second, it was open to all social classes. Previously, schools usually taught either middle-class or upper-class children. Horace Mann's common school was intended to bring democracy to the classroom. By the mid-nineteenth century, kindergarten was added. In the last few decades many common schools, now called *elementary schools*, have also added Head Start and other prekindergarten programs.

Secondary Schools

Latin grammar schools (1600s–1700s)
These schools prepared wealthy men for college and emphasized a classical curriculum, including Latin and some Greek. From European roots, the curriculum in these schools reflected the belief that the pinnacle of civilization was reached in the Roman Empire.

English grammar schools (1700s)
These private schools moved away from the classical Latin tradition to more practical studies. These schools were viewed not as preparation for college but as preparation for business careers and as a means of instilling social graces. Some of these schools set a precedent by admitting girls, thus paving the way for the widespread acceptance of females in other schools.

Academies (1700s–1800s)
The academies were a combination of the Latin and English grammar schools. These schools taught English, not Latin. Practical courses were taught, but history and the classics were also included. Some academies emphasized college preparation, while others prepared students to enter business and vocations.

High schools (1800s–present)
These secondary schools differed from their predecessors in that they were free; they were governed not by private boards but by the public. The high school can be viewed as an extension of the common school movement to the secondary level. High schools were open to all social classes and provided both precollege and career education.

Junior high schools (1909–present) and middle schools (1950s–present)
Junior high schools (grades 7–9) and middle schools (grades 6–8) were designed to meet the needs of preadolescents and to prepare them for the high school experience.

The Forgotten Majority: Educating America's Girls

Day after day, the young girl in Hatfield, Massachusetts, hurried to finish her spinning, sewing, and knitting, familiar chores for girls in colonial America. Once her tasks were completed, she would rush off to the place she enjoyed the most: school. But not to attend, for girls were considered mentally and morally inferior to boys and were not allowed in school. Instead, she peered through the window, spellbound. She listened as boys recited their lessons. Her education ended at the schoolhouse door.

For almost two centuries girls were barred from America's schools. In fact, the education of America's girls was so limited that fewer than a third of the women in colonial America could even sign their names. For centuries women fought to open the schoolhouse door. It was not until the 1970s and 1980s that they were admitted to the male Ivy League colleges. In the 1990s, tax-supported colleges, like the Citadel and the Virginia Military Institute, continued to wage a legal battle to deny women admission. And subtle forms of gender bias persist today. Despite this long history of gender discrimination, most Americans seem remarkably unaware of the female struggle for equal educational opportunities. It has been a slow, mostly silent, and painful struggle.

In some areas of colonial America, a few schools experimented with limited education for females, but not always for altruistic reasons. Some schools and teachers agreed to educate girls in the wee hours of the morning, or late in the afternoon, at times that would not interfere with prime-time learning—the time reserved for boys. Often this was done for financial reasons. Girls and their families were charged hefty sums for their off-hours education. During the 1800s, when high schools were opened to educate boys beyond the rudimentary skills, growing pressure from parents of girls eventually forced high schools to admit females as well. Once girls were admitted, new questions arose. What should girls be taught? Since their futures were to be strikingly different from boys' (they were expected to raise families and stay at home), preparing them for vocations or college seemed dangerously inappropriate. A second question concerned how girls should be taught, in separate or in coed classes, which back then were called "mixed classes." Most schools began educating girls separately, offering them a less challenging curriculum. But soon the higher cost of gender-segregated schools and classes convinced taxpayers to put girls in the same schools, and sometimes in the same classes, as boys. It was simply too expensive to maintain separate facilities. But not everyone thought this to be a good development.

For those families financially able to educate their daughters beyond elementary school, and disenchanted with coeducation, female seminaries became a popular option. Some of these seminaries were destined to become well known for their quality and impact on women, and still exist today. In New York, Emma Hart Willard struggled to establish the Troy Female Seminary, while in Massachusetts, Mary Lyon created Mount Holyoke, a seminary that would one day become a noted women's college. Religious observance was an important part of seminary life in institutions like Mount Holyoke. Prayers were recited early in the morning and late at night, and girls were housed in the same building as the instructors so that they could be supervised around the clock. Self-denial and strict discipline were considered important elements of molding devout wives and Christian mothers. By the 1850s, with help from Quakers like Harriet Beecher Stowe, Myrtilla Miner established the Miner Normal School for Colored Girls in the nation's capital, providing new educational opportunities for African-American women. While these seminaries sometimes offered superior educations, they were also trapped in a paradox they could never fully resolve: They were educating girls for a world not ready to accept educated women. Seminaries sometimes went to extraordinary lengths to reconcile this conflict. Emma Willard's Troy Female Seminary was devoted to "professionalizing motherhood" (and who could not support motherhood?). But en route to reshaping motherhood, seminaries reshaped teaching.

Over 80 percent of the graduates of Troy Female Seminary and Mount Holyoke became teachers. Since school was seen as an extension of the home and another arena for raising children, seminary graduates were allowed to become teachers—at least until they decided to marry. Once married, a woman's teaching career came to an end. Seminary leaders such as Emma Hart Willard and Catherine Beecher wrote textbooks on how to teach and on how to teach more humanely than was the practice at the time. In their books they denounced corporal punishment and promoted more cooperative educational practices. At the superior seminaries, coursework compared favorably with the first 2 years of college education provided men. At the less advanced ones, little was taught beyond home crafts and skills. But for the teaching profession, seminaries became the source of new professionals and new ideas. In fact, Horace Mann was a strong proponent of female seminaries, which supplied him with the teachers he needed so desperately to staff his common schools. Female teachers were particularly attractive to school districts—not just because

Historically, low teacher salaries can be traced back to the late nineteenth century, when communities found that they could hire capable women teachers for approximately 60 percent of what men teachers were paid.

of their teaching effectiveness, but also because they were typically paid one-third to one-half of the salary paid to male teachers.

In what was considered a radical move back in 1833, Oberlin became the first college to admit both men and women to the same institution. In 1862, Oberlin achieved another first, graduating the first African-American woman, Mary Jane Patterson. But by today's standards, not all of Oberlin's activities would be viewed so positively. Like other colleges that would later accept female students, Oberlin created a model of the "Ladies' Course," a sub-college-level program that segregated and supervised the women, a curriculum that offered them limited options and prepared them for few careers. Moreover, female students at Oberlin were expected to wash men's clothing, clean their rooms, listen to male orations, serve the men's meals, and themselves remain generally silent: Even at Oberlin, women were kept in subservient roles.

By the end of the Civil War, a number of colleges and universities, especially tax-supported ones, began accepting female students. However, the reasons for admitting women were, again, less than altruistic. This time dollars and the promise of large endowments opened some college doors to women. Colleges and universities were desperate for dollars. During the Civil War, an enormous number of men were killed on both sides of the conflict. Institutions of higher learning experienced a serious student shortage, and women became the source of much-needed tuition dollars.

Female funding did not buy even on-campus equality. Women often faced separate courses and continual hostility, from both other students and professors: At state universities, male students would stamp their feet in protest when a woman entered a classroom. On other campuses, women were confronted as they walked to class. By the late 1800s, Harvard became a national leader in protesting the arrival of women. Harvard professor Edward Clarke found more than political reasons for opposing women at Harvard; he suggested there were medical reasons as well. According to Clarke, women needed to avoid colleges for their own well-being.

In *Sex in Education* (1873), Dr. Clarke, a member of Harvard's medical faculty, explained his thesis. As girls matured into women, the development of their reproductive organs was central. Women attending high school and college were at risk because the blood destined for the development and health of their ovaries would be redirected to their brains. The stress of study was no laughing matter. Too much education would leave women with "monstrous brains and puny bodies . . . flowing thought and constipated bowels." Clarke recommended that the health risk could be reduced by providing females with a less demanding education, easier courses, no competition, and "rest" periods so that their reproductive organs could develop. He maintained that allowing girls to attend places such as Harvard would pose a serious health threat to the women themselves, with sterility and hysteria potential outcomes. Had health warnings been invented back then, Clarke would probably have advocated one that said: "WARNING: The Surgeon General has determined that higher education poses a serious health risk to women."

Clarke's concerns were widely circulated as his book saw amazing sales. Even successful women like M. Carey Thomas, future president of Bryn Mawr and one of the first women to earn a Ph.D. in the United States, wrote in her diary about the profound fears she experienced as she was studying: "I remember often praying about it, and begging God that if it were true that because

I was a girl, I could not successfully master Greek and go to college, and understand things, to kill me for it."[10] In 1895, the faculty of the University of Virginia concluded that "women were often physically unsexed by the strains of study." Parents, fearing for the health of their daughters, would often place them in less demanding programs reserved for females, or keep them out of advanced education entirely. Even today, the echoes of Clarke's warnings resonate, as some people still see well-educated women as less attractive, or view advanced education as "too stressful" for females, or believe that education is more important for males than for females.

Despite Clarke's writings, by the 1890s even Harvard was educating women, but with strong restrictions in place in order to "protect" the male students. Females were not allowed to attend Harvard itself, but were segregated in "the Annex" (later to become Radcliffe). Professors would walk a few blocks from Harvard Yard to the Annex, where female students lived and learned in boardinghouses, and repeat their lectures for the women. In addition to their regular Harvard salaries, these professors would collect money from the women for these lectures, an early form of "double dipping." Women attending the Annex, the invisible women's college at Harvard, were allowed to use the university's great library, but only within carefully proscribed limits. Women were not allowed to set foot in the library themselves, for fear that they would "distract" the men. They had to send messengers to the library in order to retrieve books. But even the messengers' activities were proscribed. They could only check out books after the library closed each evening, and the books needed to be returned before the library opened the next morning. "Burning the midnight oil" was not an empty phrase at the Annex.

In the twentieth century, women won greater access to educational programs at all levels, although well into the 1970s gender-segregated programs were the rule. "Commercial courses" prepared girls to become secretaries, while "vocational programs" channeled them into cosmetology and other low-paying occupations. Although females attended the same schools as males, they often received a less valuable education. After World War II, for example, it was not unusual for a university to require a married woman to submit a letter from her husband granting her permission to enroll in courses before she would be admitted. By the 1970s, with the passage of Title IX of the Education Amendments of 1972, females saw significant progress toward gaining access to educational programs, but not equality. Today, women encounter a second generation of barriers, subtle and insidious barriers that continue to short-circuit their educations and careers.

In *Backlash,* Susan Faludi documents the negative impact on women resulting from the conservative political gains of the 1980s and 1990s. Most of the educational programs designed to assist girls and women have been eliminated. In certain areas, such as engineering, physics, chemistry, and computer science, few women can be found. In other areas, such as nursing, teaching, library science, and social work, few men can be found. A "glass wall" still keeps women from the most lucrative careers and keeps men from entering traditionally "female" areas. The gender gap in test scores persists, with girls beginning school by scoring ahead of boys on the vast majority of standardized achievement tests, only to fall behind in high school and college. In fact, females are the only group to begin school with a testing advantage and to leave school with a testing disadvantage. Even in areas where tremendous progress has been made, like medicine and law, a second generation of bias persists. In both professions, women find themselves channeled into the least prestigious, least profitable areas. During the early years after graduating from medical schools, for example, the average male physician earns $153,600. The average female physician earns $92,800, just 60 percent of the male salary. Similar income gaps persist in other fields, and gender bias in schools continues to be documented in curricular materials, staffing patterns, and teaching behaviors. Given the powerful and painful history of gender bias in U.S. schools, it is surprising that so many Americans are unaware of the past efforts to achieve gender equity, or of the subtle (and not so subtle) barriers that still exist.[11]

School Reform Efforts

In 1890 the United States was a vibrant nation undergoing a profound transformation. Vast new industries were taking shape; giant corporations were formed; labor was restive; massive numbers of immigrants were arriving; population was on the upsurge; and traditional patterns of life were changing. How should education generally, and the new high schools specifically, respond to these changes?

In 1892 the National Education Association (NEA) established the **Committee of Ten** to develop a national policy for high schools.[12] Chaired by Charles Eliot, president of Harvard University, the committee was composed, for the most part, of college presidents and professors who wanted to bring consistency and order to the high school curriculum. This committee of college professors viewed high schools in terms of preparing intellectually gifted students for college. The Committee of Ten did not envision today's high school, one that serves all our youth. Nonetheless, many of the committee's recommendations have been influential in the development of secondary education. The committee published its reports in 1893 and recommended that:

- A series of traditional and classical courses should be taught sequentially.
- There should be few electives offered.
- Each course lasting for 1 year and meeting four or five times weekly should be awarded a **Carnegie unit.** Carnegie units would be used in evaluating student progress.
- Students performing exceptionally well could begin college early.

A generation later, in 1918, the NEA once again convened a group to evaluate the high school. Unlike the Committee of Ten, this new committee consisted of representatives from the newly emerging profession of education. Education professors, high school principals, the U.S. commissioner of education, and other educators focused concern not on the elite moving on to college, but on the majority of students for whom high school would be the final level of education. This committee asked the question: What can high school do to improve the daily lives of citizens in an industrial democracy? The position paper of this committee, entitled ***Cardinal Principles of Secondary Education,*** identified seven goals for high school. These were (1) health, (2) worthy home membership, (3) command of fundamental academic skills, (4) vocation, (5) citizenship, (6) worthy use of leisure time, and (7) ethical character. The high school was seen as a socializing agency to improve all aspects of a citizen's life.

Since the *Cardinal Principles* were published in 1918, not a decade has passed without a committee or commission reporting on the ills and reforms needed to improve U.S. schools. During the 1930s, the Progressive Education Association (PEA) provided suggestions to promote social adjustment as well as individual growth. Similar findings reported in the 1940s and 1950s noticeably influenced the evolution of our high schools. More electives were added to the high school curriculum. Guidance counselors were added to the staff. Vocational programs were expanded. The result was the formation of a new, comprehensive institution.

In recent years, the series of national reports on education has come full cycle, echoing the original call for intellectual rigor first voiced by the Committee of Ten in 1893. The federal government's National Commission on Educational Excellence issued a report calling for a more rigorous educational program. In its report, *A Nation at Risk: The Imperative for Educational Reform,* the commission declared that the inadequate level of U.S. education had put the nation at risk and in danger of losing ground to other nations in commerce, industry, science, and technology. The report indicated that mediocrity, not excellence, characterized U.S. schools, and it called for fewer electives and a greater emphasis on academic subjects.

Reports on the status of education and their recommendations for school reform have become a U.S. tradition. These reports have underscored a built-in schizophrenia in public education, a conflict between intellectual excellence and basic education for the masses, between college preparation and vocational training, between student-centered education and subject specialization. Some of the reports have called for more focus on the student, on programs to enhance the student's entrance into society and the workplace. Others have cited the need for more emphasis on academic and intellectual concerns, on programs to enhance the student's preparation for college. This dichotomy has been and continues to be an integral feature of American education, both troubling and invigorating. Yet regardless of the particular reforms advocated, all the reports, from the 1890s to the 1990s, share a common theme: a faith in education. The reports have differed on solutions but concur on the central role of the school in maintaining a vibrant democracy.

John Dewey and Progressive Education

John Dewey was quite possibly the most influential educator of the twentieth century—and probably the most controversial one as well. Some saw him as a savior of U.S. schools; others accused him of nearly destroying them. But rather than become engrossed in the heated controversy surrounding Dewey, let us look at the roots of *progressivism,* the movement with which he is closely associated. The same forces that created the public high school also helped to shape progressivism.

Progressive education included several components. First, it broadened the school program to include health concerns, family and community life issues, and a concern for vocational education. Second, progressivism applied new research in psychology and the social sciences to classroom practices. Third, progressivism emphasized a more democratic educational approach, accepting the interests and needs of an increasingly diverse student body. As early as 1875, Francis Parker, superintendent of schools in Quincy, Massachusetts, introduced the concepts of progressivism in his schools. By 1896 John

Dewey, the most noted proponent of progressivism, established his famous **laboratory school** at the University of Chicago. But it was not until the 1920s and 1930s that the progressive education movement became more widely known.

During the 1920s and 1930s, the Dalton and Walden schools in New York, the Beaver Country Day School in Massachusetts, the Oak Lane Country Day School in Pennsylvania, as well as laboratory schools at Columbia and Ohio State universities, began to challenge traditional practices. The progressive education approach soon spread to suburban and city public school systems across the country. Different school systems adapted or modified progressive education, but certain basic features remained constant.

The focus of the program was to build on child-centered interests and needs rather than traditional academic subjects presented by the teacher. For example, as a result of classroom discussions, a teacher might become aware of the fact that many of the students had learned to sail during the summer. Learning this, the teacher might initiate discussions of sailing. These discussions might encourage a group of students to design a model boat; a second group might be encouraged to investigate the techniques used by early sailors, including the Egyptians, the Phoenicians, and Europeans. This progression of events should eventually lead to a geography lesson.

This model of education assumed that students learn best when they study what they are most interested in. Passively listening to the teacher, according to the progressive movement, is not the most effective learning strategy. The role of the teacher is to identify student needs and interests and provide an educational environment that builds upon them.

Although not involved in all the progressive education programs, in many minds John Dewey is the personification of progressive education as well as

Progressive educators like John Dewey believed that participation in democratic decision making, whether in or out of school, develops rational problem-solving abilities and social skills and, consequently, is educational.

its most notable advocate. (See the "Education Hall of Fame" on pages 293–303 for a description of Dewey and his achievements.) In no small part, this is due to the tens of thousands of pages that Dewey wrote during his long life. (Dewey was born on the eve of the Civil War in 1859 and died during the Korean War in the early 1950s.) Toward the end of Dewey's life, both he and progressive education came under strong attack.

The criticism of Dewey and progressive education originated with far-right political groups, for it was the era of Senator Joseph McCarthy and his extremist campaign against communists. While McCarthy's hunt for communists was primarily directed at the government and the military, educators were not immune from attack. Some saw progressive education as a communistic, atheistic, and un-American force that had all but destroyed the nation's schools. Others maintained that students had been allowed to run wild, to accept any values, and to turn away from American traditions. Because students were allowed to explore and question, many critics were able to cite examples of how traditional values were not being taught. Although these critics were generally ignorant of Dewey's ideas and progressive practices, a second group was more responsible in its approach.

This second wave of criticism came not from the radical right but from individuals who felt that the school curriculum was not academically sound. Hyman Rickover, a famous admiral and developer of the nuclear submarine, and Arthur Bestor, a liberal arts professor, were among the foremost critics decrying the ills of progressive education. They called for an end to "student-centered" and "life-adjustment" subjects and a return to a more rigorous study of traditional courses. While the arguments raged, the launching of *Sputnik* by the Soviet Union in 1957 redirected America's attention. Now the United States would be involved in a race with the Soviets, a race to educate scientists and engineers, a race toward the first moon landing. Although many still argue vociferously over the benefits and shortcomings of progressive education, the issue has faded from the forefront of current educational dialogue.

Before leaving progressive education, however, it will be beneficial to examine one of the most famous studies of the progressive movement. The PEA, formed in 1919, initiated a study during the 1930s that compared almost 3,000 graduates of progressive and of traditional schools as they made their way through college. The study, called the **Eight-Year Study,** was intended to determine which educational approach was more effective. The results indicated that graduates from progressive schools:

1. Earned a slightly higher grade point average
2. Earned higher grades in all fields except foreign languages
3. Tended to specialize in the same fields as more traditional students
4. Received slightly more academic honors
5. Were judged to be more objective and precise thinkers
6. Were judged to possess higher intellectual curiosity and greater drive

The Modern Era (1945–Present)

As World War II drew to a close, the United States found itself the most powerful nation on earth, responsible for reconstructing a war-ravaged world economy and defending the West in the Cold War. For almost half a century, the United States would grapple with this new role at home and abroad.

In education, the federal government exerted more vigorous leadership, reflecting new economic and military world responsibilities. For example, toward the end of World War II and again during the Vietnam War, the government passed the **G.I. Bill of Rights,** which provided an income to veterans interested in continuing their education. In this way the government rewarded those who fought in these wars; consequently, schools and colleges throughout the nation saw a significant increase in student enrollment. Moreover, many of these veterans became teachers, so the G.I. bill had an impact on both public and private elementary and secondary schools.

But even before World War II, the impact of the Great Depression forced the federal government to become more directly involved in local education. During the 1930s, the federal government built schools, provided food to schoolchildren, instituted part-time work programs for high school and college students, and even established educational programs for individuals involved in the Civilian Conservation Corps, devoted to preserving the nation's natural resources. With unemployment, hunger, and desperation rampant, the states welcomed federal efforts to alleviate these problems. More and more Americans were coming to realize that some educational challenges were beyond the resources of the individual states, and the federal government's involvement became increasingly accepted and welcome.

The federal government built on these efforts and increased its influence in schools during the 1940s and 1950s; in fact, the United States viewed its schools as an important aspect of national defense, particularly after the Soviets launched *Sputnik.* Consequently, Congress passed the **National Defense Education Act (NDEA)** in 1958 to enhance "the security of the nation" and to develop "the mental resources and technical skills of its young men and women." The NDEA supported the improvement of instruction and curriculum development in a number of subjects; funded teacher training programs; provided loans and scholarships for college students, encouraging many of them to enter fields deemed important to the national defense (such as teaching); and in the 1960s expanded these efforts beyond math and science to improve the teaching of geography, English, history, and reading.

The 1960s was also a time when America took inventory at home. In *Brown v. Board of Education of Topeka* (1954), the U.S. Supreme Court had ruled that segregating children in schools "from others of similar age and qualifications solely because of their race generates a feeling of inferiority as to their status in the community that may affect their hearts and minds in a way unlikely to ever be undone." The federal government struggled to desegregate schools in the 1950s and early 1960s, and the passage of the 1964 **Civil Rights Act** marked a significant step forward in these efforts. Schools that continued to practice discrimination would be prohibited from receiving federal funds. Special programs were established to assist low-income and minority students. The **Elementary and Secondary Education Act (ESEA)** of 1965 provided compensatory funding to assist disadvantaged students. The 1960s and 1970s witnessed the federal government's attempt to reduce and eliminate the discriminatory educational practices that existed in many states.[13]

One of the most significant pieces of legislation developed during the 1970s responded to discrimination directed at students with disabilities. For many years, the education of a physically or mentally disabled child was viewed as the responsibility of the family. Private educational opportunity or very limited public education was frequently all that was available. These ignored students

The supreme court decision in *Brown v. Board of Education* followed by the 1964 Civil Rights Act made it possible for students of all races, cultures, and disabling conditions to receive a desegregated education.

became more visible with the creation in 1967 of the Bureau of Education for the Handicapped (BEH), a federal agency that sponsored training for special education teachers to work with children handicapped by mental retardation, speech problems, emotional disorders, deafness, blindness, and other disabilities. But it was the 1975 passage of **Public Law 94-142,** the Education for All Handicapped Children Act, later renamed **Individuals with Disabilities Education Act (IDEA),** which radically altered the earlier policy, by establishing public responsibility for educating physically and mentally challenged children.

The federal involvement in this area was a response to the wide differences among states in providing education for the country's 8 million children with disabilities, as well as a moral commitment to ensure educational opportunities for all Americans. The act required that all disabled learners between 3 and 21 years of age be provided with a free public education. Schools were encouraged to create the "least-restrictive environment," ensuring that children with disabilities are educated with nondisabled children to the greatest extent possible, not segregated into separate schools or classrooms. This has become widely known as **mainstreaming.**[14]

The 1960s and 1970s were a time of great ferment in schools. "Romantic" critics wrote best-selling books about educational joys and tragedies. Neill's *Summerhill* (1960), Ashton-Warner's *Teacher* (1963), Holt's *How Children Fail* (1964), and Kozol's *Death at an Early Age* (1967) created national excitement about the problems and promise of schools. Student protests against the war in Vietnam and racism at home affected life in classrooms. Students became involved in governance and curricular decisions; they demanded more electives and more personal and individualized education experiences. (See Chapter 7 for a more complete description of these curricular developments.)

But as protests at Kent State, Ohio, and Jackson State, Mississippi, resulted in student deaths, and as new waves of immigrants from Asia and Latin America crowded classrooms with urgent educational and social needs, some believed things were getting out of hand. Adding to this social unrest were clear academic danger signs. Between 1963 and 1980 Scholastic Assessment Test (then known as the Scholastic Apptitude Test) scores fell nearly 100 points.[15] These events set the stage for the decisions of the Reagan and Bush administrations.

The conservative movement of the 1980s and 1990s seriously challenged the federal government's growing role in education. Federal support for education began to decrease in the 1980s, as many **categorical grants** (funds designated to help specific groups or promote specific purposes) were replaced by **block grants** (funds given to states without specific programs or students in mind). Through the 1990s, conservative politicians fought to eliminate the U.S. Department of Education and to shift responsibility for educational programs to the state level. Believing that the federal government is often wasteful and too distant from local school realities, critics argued that the states themselves are better able to determine local priorities and more efficiently administer educational programs. Many critics disagree. If this line of reasoning is carried further, they argue, local towns and cities—and not the state governments—should make the critical decisions, since they are closer still to understanding local educational challenges. Other critics assert that state governments are neither wiser nor more efficient than the federal government, and that involvement of the federal government is needed in order to ensure that all students are treated equally, regardless of which state is educating them. States can differ dramatically in the quality of their educational programs. Clearly, the debate over central versus local control will continue in the years ahead.

Although the laws and events of recent times provide an important framework for understanding education today, they offer a somewhat distant, even sterile perspective. To experience the human dimension in recent history, we turn our attention to a single school to see the day-to-day influences these laws and events had on the lives of children and teachers.

The World We Created at Hamilton High: A Schoolography

In 1988, Gerald Grant published a fascinating book describing life at Hamilton High School (real school, fictitious name) from the 1950s to the 1980s. Like a biography that helps us understand the forces shaping and directing individual lives, *The World We Created at Hamilton High* may be thought of as "schoolography," offering powerful insights into the forces that have shaped today's schools. The events at Hamilton probably mirror many of the developments in the life of the school that you attended, or the one in which you will be teaching. The biography of Hamilton High offers a microcosm of the roots and reasons behind the current demand for educational reform.[16]

A Super School (If You're on the Right Side of the Tracks), 1953–1965

In 1953, Hamilton High opened its doors to students growing up in one of the new suburban developments, a prototype of those that were sprouting up all across postwar America. Carefully coiffed girls in sweaters and skirts and neatly dressed boys with crewcuts and baggy khakis relished their new school with its tennis courts, modern design, and strong academic offerings. The social life of the Northern, all-white, middle-class school was driven by fraternities and sororities that prohibited or limited membership of Catholics and Jews. The principal, a former coach, did not provide instructional leadership but certainly did run a tight ship. The purpose of the school was college preparation, and an evaluation of Hamilton written in 1960 reported that a "strong, almost pathological resistance to taking non–college preparation courses exists in this school community." While letters in the school paper debated whether school spirit was dwindling and what would happen if girls were allowed to wear miniskirts, the school board was approving a desegregation plan that would bring the "southern problem" to Hamilton and open a second, more volatile chapter of the school's history.

Social Unrest Comes to School, 1966–1971

Northern desegregation was as difficult as Southern desegregation, with white teachers unprepared to teach black students and both black and white students discovering racism. SAT scores fell, racial incidents and conflicts rose, and white families began leaving the neighborhood. The number of African-American students in the school system jumped from 15 to 33 percent. As racial confrontations grew, Hamilton was forced to close several times because of bomb threats and the cloud of threatened violence. Fear gripped the school, teachers became physically ill trying to survive the tension, and several principals, unable to control or eliminate the problems, came and went during this period. By the fall of 1971, more than 70 percent of the teachers who had taught at Hamilton in 1966 had left the school.

The Students' Turn, 1972–1979

The old world of fraternities, sororities, and a social structure that was discriminatingly clear disintegrated in the race riots of the 1960s and split the faculty: Some were sympathetic to the curricular change and protest goals of the students; others opposed such changes. The administration used uneven standards of discipline, with white children penalized less harshly than black. There was a lack of trust between the old and the young, parents and the school, and even between students and administration at all levels as protests over the Vietnam War and the draft grew more intense. As America's social fabric unraveled, the Supreme Court handed down several influential decisions awarding greater liberties to students, including grievance procedures and due process rights. Many teachers and administrators were unclear about what constituted legal or illegal discipline. As a result, they found it legally smarter not to discipline students. An abyss was created, with power unclear and the rules in limbo.

From this maelstrom, student leaders (with some faculty supporters) emerged, and student demands began to reshape the world at Hamilton. While teachers and administration tolerated minor and major student infractions of the rules (for fear of being drowned in litigation), students suffered no such inhibitions. They flexed their legal muscles by bringing suits against parents, guardians, and teachers. In class, students felt free to play their radios—that is, when they attended; most students reported that they regularly skipped classes. Drinking and gambling became a part of the school parking-lot landscape, and the students even published an underground newspaper that kept them up-to-date on their legal rights as well as strategies for cutting classes without being caught. Not that the classes themselves were difficult or demanding. In fact, course requirements were reduced significantly. Electives were the choice of the day. Some students were revitalized by the new curriculum, but others took "gut" courses and graduated from Hamilton without much to show for their high school years.

In 1978, a new principal came to the high school, a veteran educator considered tough enough to handle the problems. A uniform discipline code for blacks and whites was established, administrators were taught to back up teachers in their discipline efforts, and the avalanche of easy courses was replaced by a more demanding curriculum. Student suspensions soared. That year 30 seniors who had cut too many classes were prohibited from participating in graduation. Ever so slowly, adult authority was reestablished and Hamilton's experiment in rule by students came to an end.

New Students, Old School, 1980–1985

Racial desegregation and student protests radically changed Hamilton during the 1970s; the enrollment of disabled students sparked the school's second transformation. Although a new federal law (PL 94-142) required that special education students be mainstreamed and taught in regular classes, teachers were unprepared to respond to their needs, and a number of Hamilton's students were hostile to the new arrivals. Disabled students were mainstreamed—and taunted. Mentally retarded, emotionally disturbed, and physically disabled students both caused and experienced frustration when placed in regular classrooms.

During these years, immigrants from Southeast Asia were introduced to Hamilton through the English as a second language (ESL) program. Tension between the newly arrived Vietnamese and Cambodian students and African Americans at Hamilton led to fights. While Hamilton searched for peace and consensus with its new student populations, some students escaped from reality through drug use. By 1984 a third of Hamilton's students were experimenting with drugs, typically marijuana. However, an increase in adult authority had checked the escalation of black-white tensions and increased academic demands. The decline in national test scores at Hamilton had stabilized, and "white flight" had ceased. The school was settling down. But Hamilton was not a particularly inspiring or dynamic institution. The academic star of the 1950s had become an academic has-been of the 1980s. Many people were disappointed in their school.

The disappointment at Hamilton High has been felt in other communities. In 1983, *A Nation at Risk* was published, and initiated a national evaluation of schools. Analysis and questioning of education goals and school quality continued throughout the 1980s and 1990s. How effective is our educational system? Is it accomplishing its goals? (These and other questions were considered in Chapter 5, "What Are Schools For?") Before turning your attention to the Education Hall of Fame, you might find it useful to review the education milestones presented in Figure 9.3.

FIGURE 9.3
Education Milestones

Seventeenth Century
Informal family education, apprenticeships, dame schools, tutors

1635	Boston Latin Grammar School	**1647**	Old Deluder Satan Law
1636	Harvard College	**1687–**	*New England Primer*
		1890	published

Eighteenth Century
Development of a national interest in education, state responsibility for education, growth in secondary education

1740	South Carolina denies education to blacks	**1783**	Noah Webster's *American Spelling Book*
1751	Opening of the Franklin Academy in Philadelphia	**1785, 1787**	Land Ordinance Act, Northwest Ordinance

Nineteenth Century
Increasing role of public secondary schools, increased but segregated education for women and minorities, attention to the field of education and teacher preparation

1821	Emma Willard's Troy Female Seminary opens, first endowed secondary school for girls	**1839**	First public normal school in Lexington, Massachusetts
1821	First public high school opens in Boston	**1855**	First kindergarten (German language) in U.S.
1823	First (private) normal school opens in Vermont	**1862**	Morrill Land Grant College Act
1827	Massachusetts requires public high schools	**1874**	*Kalamazoo* case (legalizes taxes for high schools)
1837	Horace Mann becomes secretary of board of education in Massachusetts	**1896**	*Plessy v. Ferguson* Supreme Court decision supporting racially separate but equal schools

Twentieth Century
Increasing federal support for educational rights of poor, females, minorities, and disabled; increased federal funding of specific (categorical) education programs

1909	First junior high school in Berkeley, California	**1958**	National Defense Education Act funds science, math, and foreign language programs
1919	Progressive education programs	**1964– 1965**	Job Corps and Head Start funded
1932	New Deal education programs	**1972**	Title IX prohibits sex discrimination in schools
1944	G.I. Bill of Rights	**1975**	Public Law 94-142, Education for All Handicapped Children Act, passed
1954	*Brown v. Board of Education of Topeka* Supreme Court decision outlawing racial segregation in schools		
1957	*Sputnik* leads to increased federal education funds	**1979**	Cabinet-level Department of Education established

Source: Compiled from Edward King, *Salient Dates in American Education, 1635–1964* (New York: Harper & Row, 1966); National Center for Education Statistics, U.S. Department of Education, *Digest of Education Statistics 1994.*

The Education Hall of Fame[17]

A "hall of fame" recognizes individuals for significant contributions to a field. Football, baseball, and basketball all have halls of fame to recognize outstanding athletes. We think education is no less important and merits its own forum for recognition. Although we lack the funds to build a physical structure to honor educators, we can share with you our nominations for this honor.

Obviously, not all influential educators have been included in these brief profiles, but we believe that the process of recognizing significant educational contributions is an important one to begin. Although other individuals could be included, the individuals presented here have significantly affected U.S. education. Indirectly or directly, they have influenced your life as a student and will influence your career as a teacher. We nominate them for membership in the Education Hall of Fame.

For his pioneering work in identifying developmental stages of learning and his support of universal education—

Comenius, born Jan Komensky (1592–1670)   A teacher and administrator in Poland and the Netherlands, Comenius's educational ideas were revolutionary for his day. Abandoning the notion that children were inherently bad and needed corporal punishment to encourage learning, Comenius attempted to identify the developmental stages of learners and to match instruction to these stages. He approached learning in a logical way and emphasized teaching general principles before details, using concrete examples before abstract ideas, sequencing ideas in a logical progression, and including practical applications of what is taught. He believed that education should be built upon the natural laws of human development and that caring teachers should gently guide children's learning. Comenius supported universal education, and his ideas were later developed by Rousseau, by Pestalozzi, and, nearly 400 years later, by the progressive education movement in the United States.

For his work in distinguishing schooling from education and for his concern with the stages of development—

Jean-Jacques Rousseau (1712–1778)   The French philosopher Rousseau viewed humans as fundamentally good in their free and natural state, but corrupted as a result of societal institutions such as schools. Like Comenius, he saw children as developing through stages and believed that the child's interests and needs should be the focus of a curriculum. In *Emile,* a novel written in 1762, Rousseau described his educational philosophy by telling the story of young Emile's education, from infancy to adulthood. Emile's education was to take place on a country estate, under the guidance of a tutor and away from the corrupt influences of society. The early learnings would come through Emile's senses and not through books or the words of the teacher. The senses, which Rousseau referred to as the *first teachers,* are more efficient and desirable than learning in the schoolroom. Nature, geography, and the natural sciences were acquired through careful observation of the environment. Only after Emile reached age 15 would he be introduced to the corrupt influences of society to learn about government, economics, business, and the arts. Rousseau emphasized the senses over formalized teaching found in books and classrooms, nature over society, and the natural instincts of the learner over the adult-developed curriculum of school. Rousseau's visionary education for Emile can be contrasted with the sexist education he prescribed for Sophie, the book's female character. Sophie's education amounted to little more than obedience school, because Rousseau expected women to be totally subservient to men. This terribly restricted view of the role of women is an indication that even members of the Hall of Fame have their limitations.

Rousseau was a pioneer of the contemporary deschooling movement as he separated the institution of the school from the process of learning. His work led to the child study movement and served as a catalyst for progressive education. Rousseau's romantic view of education influenced many later reformers, including Pestalozzi.

For his recognition of the special needs of the disadvantaged and his work in curricular development—

Johann Heinrich Pestalozzi (1746–1827) The Swiss educator Pestalozzi read, agreed with, and built upon Rousseau's ideas. Rather than abandoning the monotonous and ill-conceived practices of schools, Pestalozzi attempted to reform them. He established an educational institute at Burgdorf to educate children as well as to train teachers in more effective instructional strategies. He identified two levels of effective teaching. At the first level, teachers were taught to alleviate the special problems of poor students. Psychological, emotional, and physical needs should be remediated by caring teachers. In fact, the school environment should resemble a secure and loving home, contributing to the emotional health of the child.

At the second level, teachers should focus on teaching students to learn through the senses, beginning with concrete items and moving to more abstract ideas, starting with the learner's most immediate surroundings and gradually moving to more complex and abstract topics.

Pestalozzi's ideas are seen today in programs focused on the special needs of the disadvantaged student. His curricular ideas emerge in today's expanding-horizons social studies curriculum, where children learn first about their family, then their community, their state, and eventually the national and world community. Pestalozzi's ideas influenced Horace Mann and other U.S. educators committed to developing more effective school practices.

For establishing the kindergarten as an integral part of a child's education—

Friedrich Froebel (1782–1852) Froebel frequently reflected on his own childhood. Froebel's mother died when he was only 9 months old. In his recollections, he developed a deep sense of the importance of early childhood and of the critical role played by teachers of the young. Although he worked as a forester, chemist's assistant, and museum curator, he eventually found his true vocation as an educator. He attended Pestalozzi's institute and extended Pestalozzi's ideas. He also saw nature as a prime source for learning and believed that schools should provide a warm and supportive environment for children.

In 1837 Froebel founded the first **kindergarten** ("child's garden") to "cultivate" the child's development and socialization. Games provided cooperative activities for socialization and physical development, and materials used (sand, clay, and so on) were designed to stimulate the child's imagination. Like Pestalozzi, Froebel believed in the importance of establishing an emotionally secure environment for children. Going beyond Pestalozzi, Froebel saw the teacher as a moral and cultural model for children, a model worthy of emulation. (How different from the earlier view of the teacher as disciplinarian!)

In the nineteenth century, as German immigrants came to the United States, they brought with them the idea of kindergarten education. The wife of the noted German-American Carl Schurz established a German-language kindergarten in Wisconsin in 1855. The first English-language kindergarten and training school for kindergarten teachers was begun in Boston in 1860 by Elizabeth Peabody.

For his contributions to moral development in education and for his creation of a structured methodology of instruction—

Johann Herbart (1776–1841)   The German philosopher Herbart believed that the primary goal of education is moral education, the development of good people. He believed that through education individuals can be taught such values as action based on personal conviction, concern for the social welfare of others, and the positive and negative consequences associated with one's behavior. Herbart believed that the development of cognitive powers and knowledge would lead naturally to moral and ethical behavior, the fundamental goal of education.

Herbart also believed in a coordinated and logical development of all areas of the curriculum. He was concerned with relating history to geography and both of these to literature—in short, in clearly presenting to students the relationships among different subjects. Herbart's careful and organized approach to the curriculum led to the development of a structured teaching methodology, including the development of student readiness, relating new material to previously learned information, the use of examples, and student application of the information learned.

Herbart's concern for moral education paved the way for contemporary educators to explore the relationship between values and knowledge, between a well-educated scientist or artist and a moral, ethical adult. His structured approach to curriculum encouraged careful lesson planning—that is, the development of a prearranged order of presenting information. Teachers who spend time classifying what they will be teaching and writing lesson plans are involved in the kinds of activities suggested by Herbart.

For opening the door of higher education to women and for promoting professional teacher preparation—

Emma Hart Willard (1787–1870)   The sixteenth of 17 children on a farm in Connecticut, Willard was fortunate enough to be born of well-educated and progressive parents who nurtured new ideas. At a time when it was believed that women could not learn complex subjects, Willard committed her life to opening higher education to women. In her own education, she pursued as rigorous an academic program as was permitted women at the time. She mastered geometry on her own by the age of 12. At 17, she began her career in teaching. In 1814, she opened the Middlebury Female Seminary. In reality, the seminary offered a college-level program, but the term *college* was avoided and *seminary* was used so as not to offend the public. Although she herself was denied the right to attend classes at nearby Middlebury College, she learned college-level material on her own and incorporated this curriculum into the subjects she taught her female students at the seminary.

She put forth her views on opening higher education to women in a pamphlet entitled *An Address to the Public; Particularly to the Members of the Legislature of New-York, Proposing a Plan for Improving Female Education* (1819).

The pamphlet, written and funded by Willard, won favorable responses from Thomas Jefferson, John Adams, and James Monroe, but not the money she sought from the New York State Legislature to open an institution of higher learning for women. Eventually, with local support, she opened the Troy Female Seminary, establishing a rigorous course of study for women, more rigorous than the curriculum found in many men's colleges. Moreover, the seminary was devoted to preparing professional teachers, thus providing a teacher education program years before the first normal (teacher training) school was founded. To disseminate her ideas and curriculum, Willard wrote a number of textbooks, especially in geography, history, and astronomy. In 1837 she formed the Willard Association for the Mutual Improvement of Female Teachers, the first organization to focus public attention on the need for well-prepared and trained teachers.

Emma Hart Willard was a pioneer in the struggle for women's intellectual and legal rights. She wrote and lectured in support of the property rights of married women and other financial reforms, and she dedicated her life to promoting the intellectual and educational freedom of women. Her efforts also promoted the recognition of teaching as a profession and the creation of teacher education programs. In the years that followed, colleges, graduate schools, and the professions were to open their doors to women. It was Emma Hart Willard's commitment to providing educational opportunities for women that has shaped the last two centuries of progress, not only for women, but for all Americans.

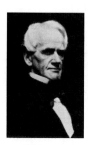

For establishing free public schools, expanding the opportunities of poor as well as wealthy Americans, and for his visions of the central role of education in improving the quality of American life—

Horace Mann (1796–1859)   Perhaps the most critical factor in shaping the life of Horace Mann was not what he was given, but what he was denied. Although he proved to be an able and gifted student, he was not afforded very much in the way of formal schooling. Forced to learn on his own, he acquired an education and was eventually admitted to Brown University. Before him was a career in law as well as a career in politics, but neither influenced his life as much as his struggle to gain an education. He worked to ensure that others would not be denied educational opportunities. That struggle directed his life and altered the history of U.S. education.

As an educator and a member of the Massachusetts House of Representatives, he worked to improve the quality of education. Corporal punishment, floggings, and unsafe and unsanitary school buildings were all denounced by Mann in speeches, letters, and his lobbying efforts before the state legislature and the U.S. Congress. He worked to lengthen the school term, to increase teacher salaries, and, by establishing the first public normal school in 1839, to prepare better teachers. He established school libraries and encouraged the writing of textbooks that included practical social problems. Mann's efforts also resulted in the establishment of the Massachusetts Board of Education, and he became the board's first secretary of education, a position equivalent to a state superintendent of schools.

Of the numerous challenges Mann confronted, he was probably most violently denounced for his efforts to remove religious instruction from schools.

Of the many achievements attributed to Mann, he is probably best remembered for his leadership in the common school movement, the movement to establish free, publicly supported schools for all Americans. He viewed ignorance as bondage and education as a passport to a promising future. Through education the disadvantaged could lift themselves out of poverty, blacks could achieve freedom, and children with disabilities could learn to be productive members of society. Mann's credo was that social mobility and the improvement of society could be attained through a free education for all. Nor was Mann's fervor confined to establishing quality public education. As a member of Congress, he denounced slavery, child labor, worker exploitation, hazards in the workplace, and the dangers of slum life. Later, as president of Antioch College, he provoked further controversy by admitting women and minority members as students. In the 1850s this was not only a radical move; for many it suggested the imminent collapse of higher education. Mann did more than verbalize the importance of freedom and education; his life and actions were a commitment to these principles. The fruits of Mann's efforts are found in our public school system; the education of minorities, the poor, and women; and efforts to provide well-trained teachers working in well-equipped classrooms.

For her integrity and bravery in bringing education to African-American girls—

Prudence Crandall (1803–1889) Born of Quaker parents, Prudence Crandall received her education at a school in Providence, Rhode Island, founded by an active abolitionist, Moses Brown. Her upbringing within Quaker circles where discussions of abolition were common may have inspired her interest in racial equality, an interest that would lead her to acts of personal courage as she strove to promote education among people of all colors.

After graduating from the Brown Seminary around 1830, Crandall taught briefly in Plainfield, Connecticut, before founding her own school for girls in the neighboring town of Canterbury. However, her decision to admit a black girl, Sarah Harris, daughter of a neighboring farmer, caused outrage. While African Americans in Connecticut were free, a large segment of the white population within Canterbury supported the efforts of the American Colonization Society to deport all freed blacks to Africa, believing them to be inherently inferior. Many were adamant that anything but the most basic education for African Americans would lead to discontent and might encourage interracial marriage. Townspeople also voiced fears that Crandall's school would lead to devaluation of local property by attracting a large number of blacks to the area. Prudence Crandall was pressured by the local population to expel Sarah Harris. However, she was determined to defy their wishes. When the wife of a prominent local clergyman suggested that if Harris remained, the school "could not be sustained," Crandall replied, "Then it might sink then, for I should not turn her out."

When other parents withdrew their children, Crandall advertised for pupils in *The Liberator*, the newspaper of abolitionist William Lloyd Garrison. A month later, the school reopened with a student body comprising 15 black girls. However, the townspeople made life difficult for Crandall and her students. Supplies were hard to obtain, and Crandall and her pupils faced verbal harassment, as well as being pelted with chicken heads, manure, and other objects. Nonetheless, they persisted.

In 1833, only one month after Prudence Crandall had opened her doors to African-American girls, the Connecticut legislature passed the notorious "Black Law." This law forbade the founding of schools for the education of African Americans from other states without the permission of local authorities. Crandall was arrested and tried. At her trial her counsel advised the jury, "You may find that she has violated an act of the State Legislature, but if you also find her protected by higher power, it will be your duty to acquit." Her conviction was later overturned on appeal, but vandalism and arson continued. When a gang stormed the building with clubs and iron bars, smashing windows and rendering the downstairs area uninhabitable, the school finally was forced to close.

Prudence Crandall's interest in education, racial equality, and women's rights continued throughout her life. Several of her students continued her work, including her first African-American student, Sarah Harris, who taught black pupils in Louisiana for many years.

For her work in identifying the educational potential of young children and crafting an environment in which the young could learn—

Maria Montessori (1870–1952)   Montessori was no follower of tradition or past practices, in her private life or in her professional activities. Rather than follow the traditional path of Italian women, she broke new ground. Shattering sex-role stereotypes, she attended a technical school and then a medical school, becoming the first female physician in Italy. Her work brought her in contact with children regarded as mentally handicapped and brain-damaged, but her educational activities with these children indicated that they were far more capable than many believed. By 1908 Montessori had established a children's school called the *Casa dei Bambini,* designed to provide an education for disadvantaged children from the slums of Rome.

Montessori's view of children differed from the views held by her contemporaries. Her observations led her to conclude that children have an inner need to work at tasks that interest them. Given the right materials and tasks, children need not be rewarded and punished by the teacher. In fact, she believed that children prefer work to play and are capable of sustained periods of concentration. Young children need a carefully prepared environment in order to learn.

Montessori's curriculum reflected this specially prepared environment. Children learned practical skills, including setting a table, washing dishes, buttoning clothing, and basic manners. They also learned formal skills such as reading, writing, and arithmetic. Special materials included movable sandpaper letters to teach the alphabet and colored rods to teach counting. Children developed motor skills as well as intellectual skills in a carefully developed sequence. The Montessori teacher worked with each student individually, rather than with the class as a whole, to accomplish these goals.

The impact of Montessori's methods continues to this day. Throughout the United States early childhood education programs use Montessori-like materials. A number of early childhood institutions are called *Montessori schools* and adhere to the approach she developed almost a century ago. Although originally intended for disadvantaged students, Montessori's concept of carefully preparing an environment and program to teach the very young is used today with children from all social classes.

For his work in developing progressive education, for incorporating democratic practices in the educational process—

John Dewey (1859–1952)   John Dewey's long life began before the Civil War and ended during the Korean War. During his 93 years, he became quite possibly the most influential educator of the twentieth century. Dewey was a professor at both the University of Chicago and Columbia .University, as well as a prolific writer whose ideas and approach to education created innovations and provoked controversies that continue to this day.

Dewey's educational philosophy has been referred to as *progressivism, pragmatism,* and *experimentalism.* Dewey believed that the purpose of education is to assist the growth of individuals, to help children understand and control their environment. Knowledge is not an inert body of facts to be committed to memory; rather it consists of experiences that should be used to help solve present problems. Dewey believed that the school should be organized around the needs and interests of the child. The learner's interests serve as a springboard to understanding and mastering contemporary issues. For example, a school store might be used to teach mathematics. Students involved in the store operation would learn mathematics by working with money and making change. Dewey was committed to child-centered education, to learning by doing, and to the importance of experience. Classrooms became laboratories in which students could experiment with life and learn to work together.

Dewey's philosophy was founded on a commitment to democratic education. The student should be free to explore and test all ideas and values. Basic American beliefs and institutions should be investigated and restructured when necessary. There are no sacred cows. Education consists of change and of reconstructing experiences. Children, like adults, should learn how to structure their lives and develop self-discipline. Autocratic governments and authoritarian schools are both disservices to democracy. All students, regardless of background, should participate in shaping their education as children, so that they can continue the process and shape their world as adults.

The disciples of Dewey's philosophy became a powerful force in education. It was they who founded the Progressive Education Association which influenced education well into the 1950s. Today, Dewey's writings and ideas continue to motivate and intrigue educators, and there still exist educational monuments to Dewey, both in a variety of school practices and in professional organizations such as the John Dewey Society. Dewey's philosophy helped to open schools to change and innovation and to integrate education with the world outside the school.

For her contributions in moving a people from intellectual slavery to education—

Mary McLeod Bethune (1875–1955)   The first child of her family not born in slavery, Bethune rose from being a field hand picking cotton to become an unofficial presidential adviser. The last of 17 children born to South Carolina sharecroppers, she was committed to the critical need of providing education to the newly freed African Americans. Whenever a respite in her fieldwork occurred, she put it to use studying, and when a Colorado seamstress offered to pay the cost of educating one black girl at Scotia Seminary in Concord, New Hampshire, she was selected. Bethune's plans to become an African missionary changed as she became more deeply involved in the need to educate newly liberated American blacks.

With $1.50, five students, and a rented cottage near the Daytona Beach city dump in Florida, Bethune began a school that eventually became Bethune-Cookman College. She became a national leader, founding a number of black civic and welfare organizations, serving as a member of the Hoover Commission on Child Welfare, and acting as an adviser to President Franklin D. Roosevelt.

Mary McLeod Bethune demonstrated commitment and effort in establishing a black college against overwhelming odds and by rising from poverty to become a national voice for African Americans. Her inclusion in the Hall of Fame is not only a tribute to her considerable achievements; it is also symbolic of the achievements of the many African-American educators too often omitted from the pages of our history.

For his creation of a theory of cognitive development—

Jean Piaget (1896–1980)   As a student at the University of Paris, the Swiss psychologist Piaget met and began working for Alfred Binet, who developed the first intelligence test (a version of which we know today as the Stanford-Binet IQ test). Binet was involved in standardizing children's answers to various questions on this new test, and he enlisted Jean Piaget to assist. Piaget not only followed Binet's instructions, he went beyond them. He not only recorded children's answers, he also probed students for the reasons behind their answers. From the children's responses, Piaget observed that children at different age levels see the world in different ways. From these initial observations, he conceptualized his theory of cognitive or mental development, which has influenced the way educators have viewed children ever since.

Piaget's theory outlines four stages of cognitive development. From infancy to 2 years of age, the child functions at the *sensorimotor stage*. At this initial level, infants explore and learn about their environment through their senses—eyes, hands, and even mouths. From 2 to 7 years of age, children enter the *preoperational stage* and begin to organize and understand their environment through language and concepts. At the third stage, *concrete operations*, occurring between the ages of 7 and 11, children learn to develop and use more sophisticated concepts and mental operations. Children at this stage can understand numbers and some processes and relationships. The final stage, *formal operations*, begins between 11 and 15 and continues through adulthood. This stage represents the highest level of mental development, the level of adult abstract thinking.

Piaget's theory suggests that teachers should recognize the abilities and limits at each stage and provide appropriate learning activities. Children should be encouraged to develop the skills and mental operations relevant to their mental stage and should be prepared to grow toward the next stage. Teachers, from early childhood through secondary school, need to develop appropriate educational environments and work with students individually according to their own level of readiness.

Piaget revealed the interactive nature of the learning process, the importance of relating the learner's needs to educational activities. His work also led to increased attention to early childhood education and the critical learning that occurs during these early years.

For his contributions in establishing a technology of teaching—

Burrhus Frederick (B. F.) Skinner (1904–1990) When poet Robert Frost received a copy of the young B. F. Skinner's work, he encouraged the author to continue writing. But Skinner's years of serious writing in New York's Greenwich Village were unproductive. As Skinner explained, "I discovered the unhappy fact that I had nothing to say, and went to graduate study in psychology, hoping to remedy that short-coming."

Skinner received his doctorate from Harvard, where he eventually returned to teach. He found himself attracted to the work of John B. Watson, and Skinner's ideas became quite controversial. One critic described him as "the man you love to hate."

Skinner's notoriety stemmed from his belief that organisms, including humans, are totally the products of their environment; engineer the environment and you can engineer human behavior. Skinner's view of human behavior (called *behaviorism*) irked individuals who see it as a way of controlling people and enslaving the human spirit. Skinner's response was that he did not create these principles but simply discovered them and that a constructive environment can "push human achievement to its limits."

Skinner's early work included the training of animals. During World War II, in a secret project, Skinner trained or conditioned pigeons to pilot missiles and torpedos. The pigeons were so highly trained that they were capable of guiding a missile right down the smokestack of an enemy ship.

Skinner believed that children could be conditioned to acquire desirable skills and behaviors. By breaking down learning into small, simple steps and rewarding children after the completion of each step, learning mastery is achieved. By combining many of these steps, complex behaviors can be learned efficiently. To advance his ideas he developed the "teaching machine," a device that used these principles of step-by-step instruction requiring and rewarding student responses. This approach laid the foundation for the later development of behavior modification and computer-assisted instruction.

Skinner's inventiveness and productivity resulted in both creative inventions and numerous books. The "Skinner box" enabled researchers to observe, analyze, and condition pigeons and other animals to master tasks, while teaching machines translated these learning principles to human education. Skinner's books, including *Walden Two, The Technology of Teaching,* and *Beyond Freedom and Dignity,* spread his ideas on the importance of environment and behaviorism to educators, psychologists, and the general public. He provided guiding principles about the technology of learning, principles that can be used to unleash or to shackle human potential.

For her creative approaches placing children at the center of the curriculum—

Sylvia Ashton-Warner (1908–1984) Sylvia Ashton-Warner began her school career in her mother's New Zealand classroom, where rote memorization constituted the main avenue for learning. The teaching strategies that Ashton-Warner later devised, with their emphasis on child-centered learning and creativity in the classroom, stand in opposition to this early experience.

Ashton-Warner was a flamboyant and eccentric personality, and throughout her life she considered herself to be an artist rather than a teacher. She focused on painting, music, and writing. Her fascination with creativity was apparent in the remote New Zealand classrooms where she encouraged self-expression among the native Maori children. As a teacher she infuriated authorities with her absenteeism and unpredictability, and in official ratings she was never estimated as above average in her abilities. However, during the peak years of her teaching career, between 1950 and 1952, she developed innovative teaching techniques that were to influence teachers around the world and especially in the United States.

Realizing that certain words were especially significant to individual pupils because of their life experiences, Ashton-Warner developed her "key vocabulary" system for teaching reading to young children. Words drawn from children's conversations were written on cards. Using these words children learned to read. Ashton-Warner asserted that the key to making this approach effective lay in choosing words that had personal meaning to the individual child: "Pleasant words won't do. Respectable words won't do. They must be words organically tied up, organically born from the dynamic life itself. They must be words that are already part of the child's being."

Bringing meaning to children was at the center of Ashton-Warner's philosophy. This belief provided the foundation of several reading approaches and teaching strategies used throughout the United States. Her work brought meaning to reading for millions of children. In her best-selling book, *Teacher,* she provided many future teachers with important and useful insights. Her emphasis on key vocabulary, individualized reading, and meaningful learning is evident in classrooms today in America and abroad.

For his work in identifying the crippling effects of racism on all American children and in formulating community action to overcome the educational, psychological, and economic impacts of racism—

Kenneth Clark (1914–   ) Born in the Panama Canal Zone, Clark was influenced by a forceful mother who relocated the family to New York City when Clark was 5 years of age in order to provide better educational opportunities for her children. Working as a seamstress in a New York sweatshop, she helped to organize the International Ladies' Garment Workers Union. Clark attributes to his mother the lessons he learned concerning the importance of "people doing things together to help themselves."

Clark attended schools in Harlem, where he witnessed an integrated community become all black and felt the growing impact of racism. He attended Howard University and received his doctorate from Columbia University, but his concern with the educational plight of African Americans generally and the Harlem community in particular was always central in his professional efforts.

Clark participated in the landmark study of racial segregation undertaken by Gunnar Myrdal, which resulted in the publication of *An American Dilemma* in 1944. In his own work, he investigated the impact of segregated schools in New York City, concluding that black students received an education inferior to that of whites. To counter this problem, he established several community self-help projects to assist children with psychological and educational problems. One of those programs, called HARYOU (Harlem Youth Opportunities Unlimited), was designed to prevent school dropouts, delinquency, and unemployment. His efforts also served as a catalyst for government action, with both New York City and the federal government providing funds to enhance educational opportunities for minority students.

Kenneth Clark was the first African American appointed to a faculty position at the City College of New York. In books such as *Prejudice and Your Child,* he analyzed the impact of racism on both whites and blacks. The Supreme Court, in its 1954 *Brown* decision, cited Clark's work as psychological evidence for the need to desegregate U.S. schools. His psychological studies and community efforts represented pioneering achievements in desegregating U.S. schools and enhancing U.S. education. As Clark was to note decades ago: "A racist system inevitably destroys and damages human beings; it brutalizes and dehumanizes blacks and whites alike."

For his contribution in establishing an American school of cognitive psychology and for his insights in shaping school curriculum—

Jerome Bruner (1915–   ) As a graduate student in psychology at Harvard, Jerome Bruner found himself deeply involved in the study of animal perceptions and learning. Psychology was then a new field, and U.S. psychologists, heavily influenced by the behaviorist tradition, turned a deaf ear to studying anything as "unscientific" as human thinking and learning. But Bruner's involvement in World War II altered the direction of his efforts and helped to initiate an American school of cognitive psychology, a movement to study human behavior.

During the war Bruner worked in General Eisenhower's headquarters studying psychological warfare. His doctoral dissertation concerned Nazi propaganda techniques. After the war he published works showing how human needs affect perception. For example, poor children are more likely to overestimate the value of coins than are richer children. Adult values and needs affect the way they see the world as well, and realities that do not conform to these needs and beliefs are mentally altered. Bruner showed that human behavior can be observed, analyzed, and understood in an objective way. By 1960 he had helped to found Harvard University's Center for Cognitive Studies. Bruner helped legitimize the systematic, objective, and scientific study of human learning and thinking.

Bruner's thoughtful and practical approach to issues was applied to the study of the school curriculum. He was a leader of the Woods Hole conference, a conference of scientists, educators, and scholars interested in reforming education. (The conference followed the Soviet success in launching *Sputnik*.) His report on the conference was published in *The Process of Education* (1960), hailed as a practical and readable analysis of curriculum needs. In his book Bruner argued that schools should not focus on facts but should attempt to teach the "structure," the general nature of a subject. He also stressed the need for developing intuition and insights as a legitimate problem-solving technique. Finally, in his best-known quotation from *The Process of Education,* Bruner stated: "Any subject can be taught effectively in some intellectually honest form to any child at any stage of development." Bruner has cogently argued for more problem solving and direct involvement in the process of education for all learners, from young children to adults. *The Process of Education* has been translated into 22 languages and is studied by teachers around the world.

SUMMARY

1. In early colonial days, most education took place in the home, in the church, and through apprentice programs, with instruction dominated by religious teachings. While today's public school system hardly resembles its colonial roots, many of our current challenges date back three centuries, especially inequities in educational opportunities for women, minorities, and the poor.

2. In 1647 in Massachusetts, the "Old Deluder Satan Law" was passed, requiring that every town of 50 households appoint and pay a teacher of reading and writing, and every town of 100 households provide a Latin grammar school. This law offered a model for other towns and communities and made the establishment of schools a practical reality.

3. Colonial Latin grammar schools prepared white boys for a university education. In the 1700s academies were established; they were more secular and practical in their curriculum and also open to girls.

4. The Constitution has helped to determine the shape of modern education in two ways. First, the separation of church and state secularized public schooling. Second, by omitting any mention of national education policies, the Constitution called upon the states to set up their own policies, practices, and means of funding schools.

5. During the nineteenth century, the public began to feel that schools should serve the poor as well as the wealthy. As leader of the common school movement, Horace Mann is sometimes called the father of the public school. By the time of the Civil War, the concept of the elementary public school was widely accepted.

6. Public high schools caught on much more slowly than elementary schools. But, as the country moved from agrarian to industrial and from rural to urban, resistance to high schools gave way. Eventually high schools came to represent democratic ideals of equal opportunity; later they attempted to serve as a panacea for societal problems.

7. From the Committee of Ten in 1892 to the 1983 publication of *A Nation at Risk,* efforts to reform American education have come in and out of the public spotlight. While reform movements have disagreed about countless aspects of schooling, one idea remains key: Schools should have a central role in maintaining a vibrant democracy.

8. Over the course of its development the nation's educational system has been supported by a rich variety of instructional materials including the colonial hornbook; the nation's first real textbook, *The New England Primer;* Noah Webster's *American Spelling Book,* which replaced *The New England Primer* as the most widely used elementary textbook; and McGuffey's readers, emphasizing hard work, patriotism, and morality. McGuffey's readers sold more than 100 million copies between 1836 and 1920.

9. Decades of struggle were needed before girls and women gained access to the nation's schools and colleges. Once admitted, they were often segregated into gender-restricted programs and careers. Even today, subtle bias and traditional sexist patterns and behavior continue to shortchange the education and career potential of females.

10. Progressivism, with John Dewey as its most notable advocate, had a significant impact on education in the twentieth century. Its emphasis on learning by doing and shaping curricula around children's interests has influenced many educators to this day. Dewey and others have come under frequent attack, however, first by conservative extremists of the 1950s, who saw progressivism as communistic and contrary to American values. Later, in the wake of the Soviet *Sputnik* launching, progressivism was blamed for causing U.S. students to lag behind in important subjects. While progressivism has ceased to be the organized educational movement it once was, many of its ideas continue to be debated and reexamined.

11. While the Constitution leaves most of the responsibility for schooling to the states, the federal government has played an increasing role in education over the last century. National programs have included the G.I. Bill of Rights, the National Defense Education Act, and extensive legislation designed to fight segregation and other forms of discrimination in the schools. During the 1980s and 1990s, more conservative forces have called for decreased federal influence in education. But an increasing concern about the quality of U.S. education has resulted in ongoing federal participation in and support for the nation's schools.

DISCUSSION QUESTIONS AND ACTIVITIES

1. the colonial period a number of factors influenced the kind of education you might receive. Describe how the following factors influenced educational opportunities:

   - Geography
   - Wealth
   - Race/ethnicity
   - Sex

2. Identify current educational practices that are similar to or had their roots in the colonial period. What colonial educational practices are no longer with us?
3. Contrast the Latin grammar school with the Franklin Academy.
4. "The United States was founded on a commitment to the importance of education, yet failed to develop a national strategy for shaping education." Support both parts of this statement.
5. Identify the arguments that Horace Mann needed to overcome in order to establish state-supported elementary schools.
6. In what ways are U.S. secondary schools different from European high schools?
7. "New England, more than any other region, was the birthplace of educational innovation." Support this statement using examples from elementary, secondary, and postsecondary education.
8. Compare the report of the Committee of Ten (1893) with the reports on the status of education issued during the 1980s.
9. "Curricular materials used in schools reflect the changing nature of American education and the maturity of the new nation." Support this quote

with examples from the *New England Primer,* the *American Spelling Book,* and McGuffey's readers.

10. Visit a school and see how many examples of sexism are apparent. Are boys and girls separated? Check the bulletin boards and other displays and determine the proportion of females represented. Examine the textbooks to assess the portrayal of females.

11. Read Sadker and Sadker's *Failing at Fairness: How Our Schools Cheat Girls* (New York: Touchstone Press, 1995). Discuss the more subtle forms of bias in education reported in the book.

12. Progressive education has sparked adamant critics and fervent supporters. Offer several arguments supporting the tenets of progressivism as well as arguments against this movement.

13. If you were asked to design a role for the federal government in education, how would your plan differ from the role provided in the United States Constitution?

14. Can you relate any of the stages of Grant's Hamilton High to your own high school? How would you describe the most recent chapter in the life of your high school, from 1986 to the present?

15. What characteristics do members of the Education Hall of Fame share? Whom would you add to the roster of this Hall of Fame?

NOTES

1. Sheldon Cohen, *A History of Colonial Education, 1607–1776* (New York: Wiley, 1974).

2. Nathaniel Shurtlett, ed., *Records of the Governor and Company of the Massachusetts Bay in New England, II* (Boston: Order of the Legislature, 1853); see also H. Warren Button and Eugene F. Provenzo, Jr., *History of Education and Culture in America* (Englewood Cliffs, NJ: Prentice-Hall, 1983).

3. James Hendricks, "Be Still and Know! Quaker Silence and Dissenting Educational Ideals, 1740–1812," *Journal of the Midwest History of Education Society,* Annual Proceedings, 1975; R. Freeman Butts and Lawrence A. Cremin, *A History of Education in American Culture* (New York: Holt, 1953).

4. Lawrence A. Cremin, *American Education: The Colonial Experience, 1607–1783* (New York: Harper & Row, 1970); see also Button and Provenzo, *History of Education and Culture.*

5. James C. Klotter, "The Black South and White Appalachia," *Journal of American History,* March 1980: 832–849.

6. John H. Best, *Benjamin Franklin on Education* (New York: Teachers College Press, 1962).

7. Jonathon Messerli, *Horace Mann: A Biography* (New York: Alfred A. Knopf, 1972).

8. Lawrence Cremin, *The Transformation of the School: Progressivism in American Education, 1876–1957* (New York: Alfred A. Knopf, 1961).

9. Edward A. Krug, *The Shaping of the American High School, 1880–1920, I* (New York: Harper & Row, 1964); see also John D. Pulliam, *History of Education in America,* 4th ed. (Columbus, OH: Merrill, 1987); Joel Spring, *The American School, 1642–1985* (New York: Longman, 1986).

10. M. Carey Thomas, "Present Tendencies in Women's Education," *Education Review* 25 (1908): 64–85. Quoted in David Tyack and Elisabeth Hansot, *Learning Together: A History of Coeducation in American Schools.* (New Haven: Yale University Press, 1990), p. 68.

11. Adapted from "Through the Back Door: The History of Women's Education" and "Higher Education: Colder by Degrees," Myra and David Sadker, *Failing at Fairness: How Our Schools Cheat Girls* (New York: Touchstone Press, 1995).

12. National Education Association, *Report of the Committee on Secondary School Studies* (Washington, DC: U.S. Government Printing Office, 1893).

13. John Ogbu, *Minority Education and Caste, The American System in Cross-Cultural Perspective* (New York: Academic Press, 1978); see also Earle H. West (ed.), *The Black American and Education* (Columbus, OH: Merrill, 1972); Eric Lincoln and Milton Meltzer, *A Pictorial History of the Negro in America,* 3d ed. (New York: Crown, 1968); *Historical Statistics of the United States, Colonial Times to 1970, Vol. 1* (Washington, DC: U.S. Government Printing Office, 1975); Franklin Frazier, *The Negro in the United States,* rev. ed. (New York: Macmillan, 1957).

14. Wayne Sailor and Doug Guess, *Severely Handicapped Students* (Boston: Houghton Mifflin, 1983).

15. *Condition of Education, 1990. Vol. 1, Elementary and Secondary* (Washington, DC: National Center for Education Statistics, 1990).

16. Gerald Grant, *The World We Created at Hamilton High* (Cambridge, MA: Harvard University Press, 1988).

17. Special thanks to Kate Volker for developing the Crandall and Ashton-Warner biographies.

10

SCHOOL GOVERNANCE

OBJECTIVES

To describe the governance structure of schools

To describe the role, responsibilities, and conflicts associated with school superintendents

To review the nature and function of local school boards

To discuss the tension points in current school governance

To differentiate between hidden and formal school governance

To discuss recent trends affecting school organization, including partnerships, consolidation, the increasing role of state governance, and school-based management

To analyze the role of the federal government in education

You probably know very little about the governance of U.S. schools, but your effectiveness as a teacher can be greatly enhanced if you are able to identify and to work with those who hold official and unofficial power in the schools. Unless you become familiar with the fundamentals of school governance, you may find yourself victimized by a system you do not understand. Conversely, your knowledge of the world of educational decision making can be a powerful ally in establishing a successful teaching career.

This chapter provides insights concerning the roles of school boards, superintendents, and others who are officially charged with governing our public schools. You will also learn about the unofficial power and influence wielded by school secretaries, parents, and the business community. In the past few years, several new and exciting trends have emerged that are influencing school organizations. To find out what you know, think you know, or do not have the foggiest idea about regarding school governance, take the school governance quiz at the beginning of the chapter. Good luck!

School Governance Quiz

The following quiz (all scores are confidential) should help you focus on some issues discussed in this chapter. The answers are found immediately following the quiz. The remainder of the chapter is organized around a discussion of these questions.

1. Most school board members are (*choose only one*):
   a. Conservative, male, and middle or upper class
   b. Liberal, middle-class homemakers, about half of whom have been or are teachers
   c. Middle of the road politically, about evenly divided between men and women, and representing all socioeconomic classes
   d. So diverse politically, economically, and socially that it is impossible to make any general characterizations
   e. The Supreme Court abolished school boards in the landmark 1975 *Ginzburg v. Des Moines* case.

2. The chief state school officer is called:
   a. Superintendent
   b. Commissioner
   c. Secretary
   d. All of the above are true.
   e. None of the above is true.

3. School boards and chief state school officers are:
   a. Elected by the people
   b. Elected by the people's representatives
   c. Appointed by the governor
   d. Appointed by officials other than the governor
   e. All of the above are true.
   f. None of the above is true.

4. During the past decade, control and influence over education have increased at the:
   a. Federal level
   b. State level
   c. Local level

5. The influence of the business community in U.S. schools can best be characterized as:
   a. Virtually nonexistent
   b. Felt only in vocational and commercial programs
   c. Extensive and growing
   d. A recent phenomenon

6. Your job security as a classroom teacher is considerably influenced by the (*you may choose more than one*):
   a. Principal
   b. State school superintendent
   c. U.S. secretary of education
   d. School secretary
   e. Parents
   f. National Labor Relations Board

7. If you asked for a raise, your greatest support would probably come from (*choose only one*):
   a. Parents
   b. City council (or finance committee)
   c. U.S. Department of Education

    d. Governor

    e. Tax-payers union

    f. State parole board

8. The major responsibilities of school district superintendents include all of the following, *except:*

    a. Manage personnel

    b. Plan and administer budgets

    c. Effectively communicate with the public

    d. Win local elections

    e. Provide instructional and curricular leadership

9. School superintendents can be characterized as:

    a. Mediating frequent conflicts

    b. Civil service–type administrators

    c. Female and minority, between the ages of 45 and 60

    d. Generally powerless figureheads

10. The number of school districts in the nation is:

    a. Increasing

    b. Decreasing

    c. Remaining constant

11. The share of public education paid for by the federal government is:

    a. More than 90 percent

    b. About 50 percent

    c. Less than 50 percent

    d. Less than 10 percent

    e. 0

12. One current and expanding organizational trend is the:

    a. Formation of educational partnerships

    b. Elimination of the superintendent position

    c. Increasing number of school districts

    d. Creation of "super" school boards, responsible for numerous school systems

    e. Replacement of the school principal with an educational manager

13. In most schools, teachers are expected to:

    a. Design the policies guiding their schools

    b. Collaborate with principals and district officials to create policies to suit their schools

    c. Comply with policy decisions made by principals and by district and state officials

    d. Comply with policy decisions that seem appropriate and change those that do not

Here are the answers—score yourself.

    0 to 1 wrong: The John Dewey Award

    2 to 3 wrong: Candidate for tenure

    4 to 5 wrong: Read chapter carefully

    6 or more wrong: Take detailed notes on this chapter; find a friend to quiz you.

9. a

1. a   3. e   5. c   7. a   10. b   12. a

2. d   4. b   6. a,d,e   8. d   11. d   13. c

The following sections review and discuss the quiz you have just taken, beginning with the first three questions.

The Legal Control of Schools

1. *Most school board members are* . . . conservative, male, and middle or upper class.
2. *The chief state school officer is called* . . . superintendent, commissioner, or secretary.
3. *School boards and chief state school officers are* . . . elected by the people, elected by the people's representatives, appointed by the governor, or appointed by officials other than the governor.

As the responses to the above questions indicate, there is great diversity in the legal governance of our schools. In some states, school boards and chief state school officials are elected; in others, they are appointed. Not only does the title of the chief state school officer change from state to state, but so do the responsibilities of the job. Although some say that "variety is the spice of life," you are probably thinking, "How will I ever sort out this strange system?"

The best way to unravel the complexity of our system of educational governance is to understand how it developed. Historically, local control can be traced to colonial times, when our country had local community governments but no national government. The first educational legislation was enacted almost 150 years before the U.S. Constitution was written. As noted in the previous chapter, this legislation was enacted in the Massachusetts Bay Colony in 1647 in order to meet a clear and present danger from the "evil menace." (You may recall that Massachusetts was already busy stamping out witches. In this early legislation, Massachusetts armed its citizens to battle with the Devil himself.) The weapons: reading and writing. The means: Every town of 50 families or more was required to provide instruction in reading and writing, since "one chief point of that old deluder, Satan, is to keep men from knowledge of the Scriptures." The effectiveness of the Old Deluder Satan Law is a matter of record.

By the time the Constitution was written, the control of schools by local communities was well established. The Constitution did not assign education to the national government but recognized and reaffirmed the state's responsibilities in this area under the Tenth Amendment: "The powers not delegated to the United States by the Constitution, nor prohibited by it to the States, are reserved to the states, respectively, or to the people."

Today the United States is unusual in this respect. Whereas most nations have a national ministry of education that determines what and how children are taught in all parts of those nations, in the United States the legal responsibility for public education resides within each of the 50 states and the District of Columbia. Since few governors or state legislators possess special competence in the area of education, state governments have not earned a reputation for effective, decisive, or progressive educational leadership. In fact, state governments have delegated much of their authority to state boards of education, superintendents, and departments of education.

Probably the best way for you to learn how the different state educational agencies and offices actually function is through a specific example. Although this example is not representative of all states (no single example could be), it will provide you with an insight into the mechanics of state governance and how state actions can affect you.

State-level policy making usually begins when someone suggests a new educational need or goal, such as the need to improve student writing skills, or the need for a more equitable system for financing schools, or the need to limit the number of students in each class. In this example, let us assume that the new policy concerns state teacher certification standards and that it specifically requires all candidates for certification to have completed at least three courses involving techniques for teaching exceptional children (students with learning, emotional, or physical disabilities).

Perhaps your next question is, "Who thinks up those policies?" Policy suggestions originate from all kinds of sources: professional educators, school board members, state legislators, superintendents, court decisions, special interest groups, and the general public. Whatever their source, suggestions cannot become official policy until the state board of education has voted their approval. In short, the role of the state school board is to consider recommendations for educational policy and to vote for or against their implementation.

The implementation of this policy is the responsibility of the chief state school officer and the state department of education. The chief state school officer is given different titles in different states (superintendent, director, commissioner, or secretary of education) and is usually the executive head of the state department of education. Together, the superintendent and the state department enforce state laws, evaluate teachers and schools, plan for future educational developments, and provide training and information to educators throughout the state. In our example, the superintendent would be responsi-

FIGURE 10.1
Structure of a Typical State School System

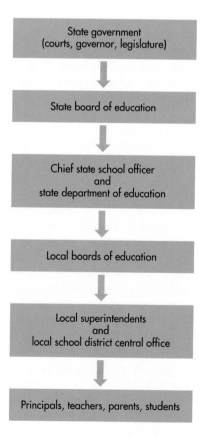

ble for informing all school systems in the state of the new certification requirement. If you applied for a teaching license in the state, someone in the state department of education would review your transcript to make certain that you had successfully completed at least three special education courses. If this and other requirements were met, you would be issued your teaching certificate.

But what about a job? States issue teaching certificates, but the actual hiring and firing of teachers is done by the local education districts. Altogether, there are more than 15,000 school districts across the country, and they are the most visible agency of educational governance—the ones you read about most often in your local newspaper. These districts are actually agencies of state rather than local governments, but they exercise control over such local matters as recruitment of school staff, curriculum formulation, and budgets—including teacher salaries and school building programs.

Most of these local districts elect their board members, although a few appoint them. Each local board then hires a local superintendent to provide educational leadership within the community. So, in any given state, educational governance involves not only a state superintendent and a state school board of education, but also hundreds of local superintendents and local school boards. In many instances, local superintendents and school boards influence education more than do their counterparts at the state level. In reality, each state is unique in the way it delegates and administers its educational program. Figure 10.1 shows an example of a state school system's structure.

Listed below are the main agents of school governance.

Boards of Education

Constituted at the state and local levels, these agencies are responsible for formulating educational policy. The members are sometimes appointed, but at the local level they are more frequently elected. In order to implement their policies, a chief state school officer (often called a *superintendent*) is selected.

Chief School Officer

Called *superintendent, commissioner, secretary of education,* or *director of instruction,* this executive officer is responsible for managing, regulating, and planning school policies and activities. The school superintendent is responsible for implementing the policies of the board of education. The superintendent is sometimes elected but more frequently appointed, usually by the board of education. There is a superintendent at the state level as well as a superintendent in each local school district.

State Department of Education

This agency performs the administrative tasks needed to implement state policy. This includes certifying teachers, testing student progress, providing information and training to teachers, distributing state and federal funds, seeing that local school systems comply with state laws, and conducting educational

FIGURE 10.2
Who Controls What? Levels of Educational Power

State Governments

- Levy taxes
- License teachers and other educators
- Set standards for school attendance, safety, etc.
- Outline minimum curricular and graduation standards (sometimes including specific textbooks to be used and competency tests for student graduation and teacher certification)
- Regulate the nature and size of local school districts

Local Governments

- Implement state regulations and policies
- Create and implement local policies and practices for effective school administration
- Hire school personnel
- Provide needed funds and build appropriate facilities
- Fix salaries and working conditions
- Translate community needs into education practice
- Initiate additional curriculum, licensing, or other requirements beyond state requirements
- Create current and long-range plans for the school district

research and development. The state superintendent usually oversees the operation of state department of education activities.

School Districts

All states except Hawaii have delegated much of the responsibility for local school operations to local school districts. (Hawaii treats the entire state as a single school district.) These school districts vary in size from those with only a few students to those with more than a million. Most have their own school boards and superintendents and are responsible for school construction, taxing, budgeting, hiring school personnel, making curriculum decisions, and formulating local school policy. Although these districts operate at the local level, their authority derives from the state, and they must operate within the rules and regulations specified by the state. Figure 10.2 summarizes the relationships between state and local control of schools.

State Government

4. *During the past decade, control and influence over education have increased at the . . .* state level.

If you interpreted the Constitution quite literally and had no knowledge of the way education developed in the United States, you would be quite surprised to find the federal government and local communities involved in education at all. The Constitution clearly assigns responsibility for education to the states. Yet we have seen how the states assign much of their responsibility to local communities, and how the federal government makes its influence felt. Beginning in the 1980s a variety of factors reversed these trends and moved more of the control of education back to the state level.

State governments have been squeezed into action by both the retreat of federal influence and by public demands that exceeded the capabilities of local districts. A series of reports emanating from both government and private foundations detailed and decried the sorry state of American education, and both the media and the public began calling for reform. Whereas the federal government traditionally responded to such calls for national reform by providing funding to correct the problem, as a result of conservative election victories in the 1980s and 1990s, federal leadership in these issues has all but disappeared. Consequently the states were pushed into action. By the mid-1980s, approximately 30 high-level state commissions were studying the quality of education. A number of reforms ensued:

- Tougher high school graduation requirements were legislated in a majority of states.
- More than a score of states revised curriculum standards and textbook requirements.
- A number of states increased the length of the school day and/or the school year (for example, North Carolina increased its school year from 180 to 200 days).
- States increased teacher certification standards. Some states began testing not only new teachers, but all teachers, and acted to terminate experienced teachers who did not pass these competency exams.
- Many states also provided additional funding to assist in raising educational standards.[1]

These changes represent examples of some of the seven areas of power and control available to state governments committed to altering education. State governments can:

1. Set accreditation standards and procedures for teachers and other school personnel
2. Establish how revenues will be raised
3. Establish how revenues will be spent
4. Develop and select curriculum materials
5. Determine school organization (for example, size of school districts or composition of school boards)
6. Set accreditation standards for professional programs
7. Evaluate school programs and student progress (including standards)[2]

While the states undergo these major changes, the impact is being felt at the local level. In towns, counties, and cities across the United States, local school boards find themselves under a new barrage of criticism.

School Boards Under Fire

School boards have long been a sacred U.S. institution. They represent the public's interest in shaping the policies and practices of their local schools. Forged in the hamlets of colonial New England, for centuries they have been a symbol of U.S. small-town democracy. School board meetings represent the

Superintendents (mostly white males) along with members of state and local boards of education comprise the official governance system of schools.

essence of Americana—the kind painted by Norman Rockwell and made into a Frank Capra movie starring Jimmy Stewart as the beleaguered, but triumphant, school board president. Therefore, it was a great shock to many when in 1992 America's school boards came under scrutiny. (See Figure 10.3 for statistics on school boards.)

One of the most intensive studies of school boards in recent times was conducted by the Twentieth Century Fund and the Danforth Foundation. They recommended a total overhaul of the system. Their report, added to other criticisms of the U.S. education system, has led to serious reevaluation of the role of school boards. Here are some of the major criticisms:[3]

- School boards have become *immersed in administrative details,* at the expense of more important and appropriate policy issues. One study of West Virginia school boards showed that only 3 percent of all decisions made concerned policy.
- School boards are *not representing local communities,* but only special interest groups. Elections to the school board receive little public support. In one recent New York City school board election, only 7 percent of the voters participated.
- The *politics of local school board elections* have a negative impact on attracting and retaining superintendents and lead to conflict with state education agencies.
- The composition of the boards is *not representative,* with minorities, women, the poor, and the young unrepresented or underrepresented.
- School boards are often *barriers to change.* Suburban boards serve as buffers to keep out minority groups, women, and the poor. This becomes an obstacle to reducing persistent educational problems.
- School boards have been in the *backseat when it comes to educational change and reform.* As a matter of fact, many school boards do not sup-

port current educational reform proposals. Only 16 percent of board members favor vouchers, and a minority supports the choice option. Although not everyone approves of vouchers, especially for private schools, public school choice is an idea with a great deal of appeal. School boards, on the other hand, are slow to change.

- The education of children goes beyond school issues to include health, social, and nutritional concerns. School boards are *too limited in scope* to respond to all the contemporary concerns of children.
- If schools continue to be *financed less from local funds* and more from state funds, local boards could become less influential.
- Many of the new reforms call for *new governance organizations,* site-based management, or choice programs that relegate the school board to a less important, perhaps even unnecessary, role.

While these criticisms suggest a dismal future for the more than 15,000 school boards, preparing their obituary may be premature. Supporters point out that boards may be more representative of Americans than foundations, state governments, and special task forces that issue reform recommendations. School boards, they say, have endured a long time and may be around long after many of the reform recommendations are forgotten.

But clearly, school board practices need to be improved. Board membership should be more representative of the communities they serve, including women, minorities, and other groups. Board responsibilities may need to be expanded to include nutrition, preschool programs, health care, welfare benefits, and other issues influencing the well-being of children outside of school. Perhaps school boards will need a name change, such as Children's Education and Development Boards, to better reflect their broader responsibilities. Some educators suggest that we need to rethink how we select our current boards, depending less on elections and more on appointments of nonpolitical

---

FIGURE 10.3

Everything You Always Wanted to Know About School Boards But Never Thought to Ask

- The first school board was established in 1721 in Boston.
- In the United States, there are over 15,000 school boards in charge of 42 million students in 84,000 schools.
- Three-quarters of the school districts are small, with fewer than 2,500 students in each.
- Just 1 percent of the school districts in urban areas enroll more than 25 percent of all students in the United States.
- Eighty-five percent of local school boards are elected.
- School board members are typically white (93.5 percent), male (61 percent), financially secure (more than half earning above $50,000, and more than a quarter earning over $80,000), and middle-aged (75 percent being above 41 years of age).
- School boards hire superintendents who look much like themselves (97 percent of the superintendents are white, 96 percent are male, 95 percent are married).

Source: Data compiled from C. Emily Feistritzer, "A Profile of School Board Presidents." In Patricia First and Herbert Walberg (eds.): *School Boards: Changing Local Control* (Berkeley: McCutchan, 1992); Jesse L. Freeman, Kenneth E. Underwood, and Jim C. Fortune, "What Boards Value," *American School Board Journal* 178 (January 1991): 32–37.

educators. Too often school board membership is seen as a political stepping-stone to higher office, or as a way of paying back political debts, instead of as an educational responsibility.

Finally, the relationship between school boards and superintendents needs to be improved. If you look at the official organization of a school district, the school board formulates policy and hires the superintendent to administer the schools. The superintendent, as an employee of the board, manages the day-to-day school district activities. So much for the official version. The unofficial version is quite different. Superintendents in many districts actually control their school boards. The increasing complexity of educational practice, law, and research makes the superintendent the expert and the school board members the amateurs. As a result, the superintendent often prepares the agenda for the school board members, and many important educational issues are never discussed. Most school board members do not have a research staff, and they rely on the superintendent for advice. In fact, board members rarely get paid. Clearly, reform and change are needed if school boards are to regain their leadership in formulating policy and monitoring school district performance.[4]

The Business of America Is Business

5. *The influence of the business community in U.S. schools can best be characterized as* . . . extensive and growing.

The involvement of the business community in the nation's schools is not new. Early in the century most school board members were business and professional men, and many public school activities were modeled on business practices. In fact, for many Americans a major—if not *the* major—purpose of schools was to prepare students to enter the business world. With the dramatic economic challenges of today, business involvement in education has become even more extensive. But how does the business community influence schools? And is this influence positive or negative?

President Calvin Coolidge once remarked that "The business of America is business," an observation that can be paraphrased as "The business of America's schools is to promote the values of business." Through both the overt and the hidden curricula, most of today's schools systematically espouse the business creed. Children are taught to work hard and to compete with one another. They are taught the importance of punctuality, neatness, and a sense of duty and loyalty to the school, of following rules and directives, of the sanctity of private property, and of the advantages of conformity. Studies have indicated that students believe that hard work should be considered an important factor in deciding academic grades—totally distinct from any consideration of the quality of that work.[5]

Students also learn to view success in comparative and competitive terms rather than according to personal standards. Receiving a mark of 85 on an examination is considered "good" if other students scored lower and "bad" if the average grade was 95. How much or how well something is learned takes on meaning only when compared with the achievements of others and has led to the earth-shattering cry that reverberates through school corridors across the country: "Whad-ja-get?"

Competition and other business-oriented values have become so familiar and pervasive in our schools that we have become inured to them. When you consider them carefully, you begin to realize that many of these practices have little or no educational merit. Schools have adopted them, in part, to prepare students to accept and adhere to the business ethic.

Of course, there are those who applaud this. They say that competition, punctuality, and the rest are not just business values; they are the basic values on which U.S. society was built, and consequently, students must learn these values if they are to cope with the real world beyond the classroom walls. These advocates recognize and encourage the role of business in the schools' hidden government and believe that the impact of the business community on schools is right on the money.

So intertwined have business values and school practices become that educators have adopted the business vocabulary. An education leader is called a *superintendent,* the same title originally given to a factory supervisor. A school building, like a factory, is called a *plant.* Terms such as *quality control, accountability, management design,* and *cost overruns* have also been expropriated from business and applied to the educational process. Therefore, it is understandable that so many school superintendents have become more management- than education-oriented, more involved in cost-effectiveness formulas than in educational innovation, and more in touch with management design than with education research.

In addition to all this, the National Association of Manufacturers (NAM), the public relations organ of the business community, runs a very active campaign to promote the values of the business community in the schools. As a teacher you are likely to receive "free" teaching materials from the NAM or from individual business firms: materials ranging from useful records, films, and software to heavily probusiness propaganda. In more than one case, these materials have promoted a specific company's products, and, cumulatively, the

Competition and other business-oriented values have become so familiar and pervasive in our schools that we have become inured to them.

cost of their production has been estimated as greater than the cost of school textbooks.[6]

For some educators, business involvement in education might already be too intrusive, but trends indicate that it is still on the increase. In 1986, Dennis Doyle, of the American Enterprise Institute, stated: "The most far-reaching initiative in education to emerge in recent years is the growing corporate interest in public schools."[7] This is still true today. This interest stems from deep-rooted problems in the economy. A 1995 survey by *Business Week* of 408 senior executives at large corporations revealed that improving the education system ranked second only to balancing the federal budget as the issue "most important to American business."[8] Thus the business community, confronted with increased competition from abroad, is looking for solutions to help meet these new challenges. Of particular importance is the need for a competitive labor pool. Consider the following trends:

- Although the education level of the U.S. workforce is generally increasing—one in four U.S. workers is a college graduate—the lack of basic skills among entry-level workers has prompted corporations to teach reading, writing, and computing to their employees or to form partnerships with local school systems that then do so.
- The growth of information technologies and the demise of assembly-line production demands new skills of tomorrow's workers.
- International competition will increase as other countries achieve higher levels of technical and scientific competence. Although the United States has the world's largest technically educated workforce, other countries are realizing the importance of technical education for economic growth and are making tremendous strides in this area.[9]

Given these trends, it is not surprising that the business community has experienced a renewed interest and involvement in education. The U.S. worker's effectiveness is seen as being determined years before an employment application is filled out, in the elementary, secondary, and college classrooms of the nation. For survival and success, business needs effective schools. Theodore Schultz, in his Nobel Prize–winning research, reported that capital investment in education yielded economic profits to business, to the nation, and to the individual.[10]

Those who applaud business involvement in schools have many examples to choose from because business involvement has not only been increasing, it has taken a variety of forms. For example, umbrella organizations have served to coordinate joint business and education sponsorship of job programs for youth. Businesses have invested their expertise and materials in school management, accounting, and career awareness programs. The following examples illustrate the rich variety of business involvement in schools.

Boston. The Bank of Boston established a $1.5 million endowment that distributed $15,000 grants to schools to increase basic skills, computer literacy, critical thinking, and multicultural education. The John Hancock Insurance Company likewise established a $1 million endowment to improve basic skills and intramural programs in Boston's middle schools.

Arkansas. A group of Arkansas businesses established Project IMPAC (Instructional Microcomputer Project for Arkansas Classrooms). The project donated computers, software, and teacher-training services to improve basic skills.

Chicago. AMOCO, working with the Chicago Public Schools and the University of Chicago, funded the School Mathematics Project, designed to restructure the elementary math program. Elementary teachers were trained to teach algebra and geometry to students earlier than usual, and computers and calculators were introduced in elementary classrooms.

Coca-Cola and RJR Nabisco. These two corporations are leaders among a growing number of companies funding national education efforts. By the early 1990s, these corporations had allocated $80 million for public schools.

For-Profit Education Companies. The Edison Project, Educational Alternatives Incorporated, and Channel One represent a new generation of business involvement in schools. These companies view education as a profit center. Some companies contract to provide specific services, ranging from school transportation and maintenance to televised instruction. Other companies actually compete with public schools by forming their own schools, for-profit enterprises that they believe can do a better job of educating children.[11]

In addition to the distribution of microcomputers to schools, numerous business organizations have provided regional or national incentives. Among these companies is Dr. Pepper, which awarded college scholarships to Tennessee and Pennsylvania students going into teaching. Pizza Hut distributed millions of pizzas to students in all 50 states to promote reading. Burger King provided seminars for educators concerned with student attitudes, federal involvement in education, and the quality of students. This corporate involvement represents just the tip of the iceberg, as national and local businesses become more and more involved in schools.

Even as the trend of ever greater corporate involvement in education continues, many business leaders have become frustrated in recent years by the slow pace of school reform. Accustomed to fast results and rapid return on investment, some corporations have scaled back their education-related efforts. Meanwhile, leading corporate groups such as the Business Roundtable and the National Alliance of Business remain committed to advancing their programs for education reform.[12]

Over the next few years, the relationship between business and education will undergo a series of stresses. Will the business community maintain and increase its financial support of schools? Is the business community's assessment of the educational needs of its future labor force accurate? Will this movement increase to include more small and medium-size companies? And perhaps most important, will education maintain its independence and integrity, or will it become even more influenced and shaped by business mores and goals?

Covert Power in Schools

6. *Your job security as a classroom teacher is considerably influenced by the . . .* principal, parents, and perhaps the school secretary.

The principal is usually the individual most responsible for the school personnel decisions, including hiring and firing. But do not overlook parents, who can make their displeasure felt and sometimes significantly influence person-nel actions. The school secretary, depending on the particular school, can also exert extraordinary influence. These three—principal, parents, and perhaps the school secretary—can be quite influential in your success as teacher.

> 7. *If you asked for a raise, your greatest support would probably come from*
>   . . . parents.

Although all of the groups cited might oppose salary and benefit increases, the best support has traditionally come from parents.

There are no absolute answers to questions 6 and 7, but the choices given are representative of the situation in most schools, and they help to distinguish between official and unofficial control in the schools. Most students think only in terms of school officials (principals, superintendents, school boards, and so on) when pondering the question: Who's in charge of schools? Although prin-cipals and superintendents are legally responsible for the operation of schools, it would be a mistake to believe that these officials hold a monopoly on edu-cational decision making. In reality, many other individuals and groups both inside and outside the educational establishment influence the policies and practices of our schools. In fact, in many school districts, vocal individuals and community groups exert as much power as, or even more power than, school boards and superintendents. These unofficial, but highly involved, persons and groups constitute the **hidden government** of schools.

The concept of hidden government is not unique to schools. In fact, most of our institutions have developed their own unique forms of hidden govern-ment. For example, army generals frequently ask for and follow the advice of lowly sergeants rather than staff officers because they realize that sergeants rep-resent a source of grass-roots power, knowledge, and experience. As a result, sergeants often outrank some officers in terms of the real decision-making power that constitutes the army's hidden government.

Another example of hidden government is provided by the White House. There, presidential decision making was and is often influenced more by old colleagues back home than by the president's official advisers, the cabinet members. Likewise, congressional representatives are besieged and influenced by a horde of lobbyists who pressure and cajole them to pass legislation favor-able to their special interests. In fact, lobbyists represent a powerful element of our country's hidden government.

How does hidden government operate in schools? Here are some examples:

Example 1 A first-year teacher in a New England junior high school was totally committed to his teaching career. He would spend long hours after school preparing lessons and working with students. As admirable as all this appeared, the school secretary, Ms. H., advised the teacher not to work with female students after school hours, because "You may get your fingers burned." The teacher smiled, ignored the secretary's advice, and continued providing students with afterschool help.

Within a week, the principal called the teacher in for a conference and suggested that the teacher provide extra help to students only if male and female students were both present. The teacher objected to the advice and objected to the secretary's complaining to the principal. The principal listened

As dispenser of supplies and information and gate-keeper to the principal, the school secretary holds a pivotal role in the covert power system of the school.

and carefully explained, "You're new here, and I can understand your concern. But what you have to learn is that Ms. H. is more than a secretary. She knows this school better than I do. Follow her advice and you'll do just fine."

• • •

Example 2 A young teacher in an elementary school in the Midwest was called into the principal's office for a conference. The principal evaluated her teaching as above average but suggested that she maintain greater discipline. Her classroom was simply too noisy, and the students' chairs were too often left in disarray. The conference was over in 10 minutes.

The teacher did not really understand the principal's remarks. She did not agree that her classroom was too noisy; and the chairs were always arranged in a neat circle. Moreover, the principal had only visited her class for 5 minutes, and during that time the students had said hardly a word.

The next day in the teacher's lounge, it all became clear when she discussed the conference with another teacher. The teacher nodded, smiled, and explained:

"Mr. Richards."

"The custodian?"

"Yup. He slowly sweeps the halls and listens for noisy classrooms. Then he tells the principal. He also hates it when the chairs are in a circle, since it makes sweeping harder. Nice straight rows are much easier. Don't worry about it; just make sure your classroom is quiet when he's in the halls and have your students put the chairs in neat, straight rows at the end of the day. That's the ticket for getting a really good evaluation!"

Although both these examples are true, they are also somewhat extreme. While most custodians and secretaries do not run schools, they often have an inside track to the principal.

• • •

Example 3 An elementary school teacher in a rural Southern community was put in charge of the class play. Rehearsals were under way, costumes were being sewn, and the sets were being built when the teacher received a note to stop by the principal's office at 3:00 P.M.

The principal had received a call from a parent who was quite disappointed at the small part her daughter had received in the play. The teacher said that she could understand the parent's disappointment, but the parts had been assigned on the basis of auditions. Nevertheless, the principal wanted the teacher to consider giving the child a larger part. "After all," he explained, "her mother is quite influential in the PTA and other community groups, and her father is one of the town's most successful businessmen. It's silly for you to alienate them. Give her a bigger part. Life will be easier for both of us, and we may be able to get her parents' support for the next school bond issue. That would mean a raise for all of us."

> *Lesson 1:* You can't always tell which people hold the real power by their official position.
>
> *Lesson 2:* Do not assume that school secretaries merely type and file. The school secretary frequently works more closely with the principal than anyone else and is often the eyes and ears of the principal. In some cases, the secretary is actually in charge of the day-to-day operations of the school.
>
> *Lesson 3:* School custodians are often a source of information for principals and of supplies for teachers. They make very helpful allies and powerful adversaries.
>
> *Lesson 4:* Parents can be very influential in school decisions by applying pressure on principals, school boards, and community groups. When you choose to make a stand in the face of parental pressure, try to choose a significant rather than a trivial issue and be able to substantiate your facts. Do not abandon your beliefs or actions for fear of parental disapproval, but do not forget the role and influence that parents can play in the hidden government of schools.

Professional organizations constitute another element in the hidden government of schools. In Chapter 2 we discussed the growing power of national teacher organizations such as the National Education Association (NEA) and the American Federation of Teachers (AFT). In many communities, especially those in and around large urban areas, teacher organizations exercise considerable power, influencing curricula and school policies as well as teachers' salaries and benefits.

The School Superintendent

8. *The major responsibilities of school district superintendents include all of the following, except* . . . win local elections.
9. *School superintendents can be characterized as* . . . mediating frequent conflicts.

The first superintendents were hired to relieve school boards of their growing administrative obligations. The year was 1837, and these new superintendents worked in Buffalo and Louisville.[13] As the nineteenth century progressed, more communities followed this example. Superintendents were expected to supervise and hire teachers, examine students, and buy supplies. These tasks had become too burdensome for the school boards themselves, and so the school superintendency was created. Superintendents kept school records, developed examinations, chose textbooks, and trained teachers.

Over the century, the superintendent's role changed from the board's administrative employee to its most knowledgeable educational expert—from helper to chief executive officer. Today the superintendent is the most powerful education officer in the school district. The superintendent recruits, hires, demotes, and fires personnel. The superintendent is responsible for budgets, buildings, new programs, daily operations, long-term goals, and short-term results. When things are going well, the superintendent enjoys great popularity. But when things are going poorly, or school board members are not pleased, or local community groups are angry, or teacher organizations turn militant, or . . . you get the picture. The superintendent does *not* run in elections, but if the public and the board are not pleased, the superintendent can be—and frequently is—fired. The superintendent lives and works in a fishbowl, trying to please different groups while managing the school district. It is a very insecure existence of sidestepping controversies, pleasing school board members, responding to critics, juggling many different roles and goals, and managing conflict. As one superintendent reported, "It's always a balancing act because there are so many pressure groups. . . . Now I have so many different constituencies out there with so many different interests that my problem is to try to keep them appeased."[14] Historically, this conflict has led to the frequent terminating of superintendents, especially during difficult times.

Superintendent turnover was particularly high during the 1920s as progressive school reformers, determined to increase school efficiency, worked for small school boards appointed from the ranks of business and the professions. With the increase in appointed boards of education and an emphasis on the business ethic, superintendents received professional training and attempted to insulate themselves from political bickering. It did not work. From the beginning until today, superintendents have remained immersed in political conflict. During the 1960s and 1970s, civil rights, community participation, accountability, enrollment declines, and economic recession were controversial issues that precipitated high superintendent turnover, especially in large urban school districts. Even in the more conservative era of the 1980s and 1990s, the superintendency has not been viewed as a secure, long-term position. In 1992, for example, 25 of 47 major urban school districts were looking for new superintendents.

One need not look hard for the reasons for this turnover. Successful superintendents must win and maintain public support and financing for their schools. This involves forming political coalitions to back their programs and to ward off attacks from those more concerned with rising taxes than with the school budget. In an era when the majority of citizens in many communities do not have children in schools, this becomes a real test of political acumen.

In addition to the role of politician, the superintendent must also be a manager. School systems can range from quite small, one-school affairs to complex organizations serving hundreds of thousands of students. Developing budgets, overseeing facilities, establishing rules and policies, responding to problems, even ensuring that transportation needs are met—all are part of the superintendent's managerial responsibilities. If not attended to, they can result in the departure of a superintendent. For instance, a superintendent in a large metropolitan school district was terminated when the textbooks used in a number of schools were not delivered until Thanksgiving. In another case, a rural school superintendent was sent job hunting because the community did not agree with the selection of snow days, the canceling of school because of weather conditions. Although supported by a professional staff, the school superintendent is ultimately responsible for the district's management.

Finally, the school superintendent is expected to be an instructional leader who is responsible for evaluating student progress, training teachers and administrators, and instructing school board members and the community about the educational needs and goals of the system. The competency examinations of teachers and students that emerged in the 1980s underscored once again the instructional accountability of the superintendent. This accountability is seen in school districts such as Minneapolis, Philadelphia, and Los Angeles, which have adopted performance-based contracts that link superintendent compensation directly to student performance.[15]

The school superintendent needs to be a masterful politician, an effective manager, and a sound instructional leader. He or she must combine all these roles effectively in responding to the needs of different community groups—a challenging task that has made the stay of many school superintendents short-lived.

Consolidation of School Districts

10. *The number of school districts in the nation is . . .* decreasing.

For the past century, there has been a decrease in the number of school districts and an increase in their average size. This organizational shift to fewer, larger districts, which is called **consolidation,** is not a new phenomenon. In the early part of this century, the growth of industry and the advent of the automobile (and the intrepid school bus) increased consolidation. (See Figure 10.4.) Clearly, the one-room schoolhouse and small school districts lacked the resources to provide diversified programs and specialized courses for an increasingly sophisticated society.

Although small was clearly inadequate, the ideal size for a school district is not at all clear. Some studies have suggested that 10,000 to 12,000 students is the ideal size, whereas other studies' estimates have gone as high as 50,000 and even 100,000 students as most desirable.[16] The ideal size has yet to be determined, but most school districts still have fewer than 2,000 students, and many have only a few hundred. The process of consolidation will likely continue into the future as these smaller school districts are combined and consolidated into larger ones in order to offer students a richer curriculum.

Although most school districts will remain small, the majority of students are enrolled in the larger urban and suburban school districts. This has created another problem: When is big too big? Large urban and suburban schools may provide richer course offerings than small rural schools do, but not without a price. Roger Barker and Paul Gump[17] indicate that students in smaller schools have more opportunities to participate in school activities. Alienation and apathy often afflict large schools, and a student lost in the crowd may not be reap-

FIGURE 10.4
Consolidation in Action

The following numbers show the dramatic reduction in the number of school districts as smaller ones consolidate. Still, 75 percent of the remaining districts are fairly small, servicing fewer than 2,500 students each.

School Year	Number of Public School Districts
1929–1930	119,001
1939–1940	117,108
1949–1950	83,718
1959–1960	40,520
1970–1971	17,995
1980–1981	15,912
1989–1990	15,367

Source: Digest of Education Statistics 1991, U.S. Department of Education, National Center for Education Statistics.

ing great benefits from plentiful curriculum offerings. Moreover, a study sponsored by the National Institute of Education investigated consolidation and found some serious concerns, suggesting that some **decentralization** of school districts into smaller and more responsive units might be beneficial. One of these concerns was the price tag, since increased transportation and administration costs often make consolidation an expensive proposition. Further, there is little evidence that student achievement increases as a result of consolidation. Consolidation is a fact of life in U.S. education, but its benefits are still in doubt.[18]

The Federal Government

11. *The share of public education paid for by the federal government is . . .* less than 10 percent.

Although the federal government's financial contribution to our nation's educational system is surprisingly small, the government nevertheless has exerted tremendous influence on our schools as a result of federal laws and court actions. In fact, in 1979 President Jimmy Carter established the **Department of Education,** raising federal involvement in education to cabinet status. This department, which withstood an attempt by President Ronald Reagan to abolish it, is charged with initiating research, disseminating information, and administering federal grants.

Since the Constitution assigns educational responsibility primarily to the states, the federal government has been a reluctant financial partner in this arena. On the other hand, since the quality and direction of public education clearly affect national interests, the federal government has necessarily become a junior partner in educational finance.

Historically, most federal aid has been through **categorical grants**—that is, directed at specific educational needs such as library construction, the acquisition of new audiovisual equipment, the training of teachers and administrators, providing lunches for poor children, supporting educational research, and providing loans to college students. By targeting funds into these specific areas or categories, federal aid has had a limited but highly visible impact on schools. For example, the federal government has spent billions of dollars a year on educating the disadvantaged, a group that has benefited significantly under categorical grants.

As you might suspect, the federal government has attached rules and regulations to its financial aid. These rules stipulate not only how the funds are to be used but also what kinds of federal reports must be filed and what federally sponsored legislation (for example, fair and nonbiased hiring practices) must be adhered to in order to qualify for the funds. More than one school system has refused federal aid rather than comply with these rules. Although the regulations and their attendant paperwork are sometimes demanding, most school districts seek and accept federal aid.

The obligations, rules, and even competition associated with seeking federal dollars were greatly reduced in the 1980s and 1990s, with the election of more conservative politicians. The Reagan administration passed the Education Consolidation and Improvement Act (ECIA), which was designed to reduce the rules, regulations, competition, and many of the categorical programs traditionally associated with federal financial support. States were awarded **block grants,** lump sums of money, and given great latitude in how to spend this money. As a result, there were educational winners and losers in the quest for federal dollars.

> *Winners.* Under the block grant system, more funds went to purchase instructional materials, including microcomputers. Rural communities that often lacked the resources even to apply—much less compete— for federal dollars received federal support, and the paperwork for all districts was reduced.
>
> *Losers.* Desegregation efforts were reduced by two-thirds under the block grant approach. Minority, disadvantaged, and urban students received less support. Long-range programs were less likely to be supported, and accountability for how the funds were spent was greatly weakened.[19]

Some educators thought that local control and decision making on how to spend federal dollars was a change for the better. Others expressed concern over the lost aid to special populations, including disadvantaged students. Although the Reagan administration also proposed to reduce the overall amount of money spent on education, Congress refused to go along with this reduction. Congress also refused to eliminate the cabinet-level status of the Department of Education as proposed by the administration. By the time the Clinton administration took office, the role of the federal government in education was still being debated.

Trends in School Governance

12. *One current and expanding organizational trend is the* . . . formation of educational partnerships.
13. *In most schools, teachers are expected to* . . . comply with policy decisions made by principals and by district and state officials.

The past decade has witnessed the involvement of new players in the field of school governance. An informal community self-help response, generally called *educational partnerships,* arose. Parents, community organizations, and, as previously discussed, the business sector contributed significant resources to local school systems. As these partnerships gained publicity, renewed interest in teacher professionalism and empowerment also came to the forefront of national attention. As a result, innovative experiments involving teachers in school governance began to spring up across the country. The following section will discuss these new trends. Since we have already talked about business participation, partnerships involving family and community groups will be highlighted here.

Educational Partnerships: Family

Education does not start and stop at the schoolhouse door. Although educators can exert enormous influence on children, children spend 87 percent of their time outside of school, mostly under the influence of their parents. According to public opinion polls, many parents want to become more actively involved in their children's education. But a 1992 survey suggested, for the most part, that parents are earning less than a C grade: Thirty percent of the high school students who participated in the study agreed that their parents were rarely, if ever, involved in their school work.[20] And 44 percent said their parents were only "somewhat" involved. Yet parents are critically important.

According to numerous research studies, factors such as class size, dollars spent per student, or private versus public schools contribute less to a student's academic success than do such home- and school-related factors as student motivation and ability and the amount and quality of instruction.[21] Other factors less directly related to student performance include the degree of academic stimulation in the home, the psychological climate of the classroom, the academic orientation of the peer group, and the amount of time spent viewing low-quality television. There is great disparity in how families deal with these factors and how much time they invest in their children.[22]

Homework provides a concrete illustration of how families differ in their time investment in children. Children who diligently complete their homework achieve higher scores than those who do not (not too surprising). In fact,

When parents work with the school to make sure homework is completed, student achievement increases.

whether a student regularly completes homework has three times as much impact on school performance as the socioeconomic background of the student's family does. One surprise finding reported by James Coleman in his study of high schools was that the average high school student spends 4 hours a week on homework and 30 hours a week on television. Thus, despite the importance of homework on school performance, few families invest the time and attention needed to ensure that homework is done. Similarly, too many teachers also take the course of least resistance and either do not assign or do not correct homework activities. By pulling families more closely into the education of their children, schools hope to build important and effective family-school ties.

Some states have done just that. By 1990, 20 states had enacted parent involvement legislation.[23] Examples of state and city efforts include:

Arizona. Teachers organized a basic skills program to assist parents working with children. Published in English, Spanish, and Navajo by the state department of education, the program provides parents with a step-by-step guide to assist children in accomplishing school activities and objectives.

California. California launched a major campaign to incorporate parents into the learning process. The slogan "Parents are teachers, too" was printed on 12 million shopping bags in 500 stores, and numerous television stations also carried the message. A brochure was printed suggesting several ways that parents could work with their children, including talking with children about current events and school activities, encouraging and discussing reading, monitoring television, supervising homework, taking trips to museums and other cultural attractions, and showing affection for their children and interest in their schoolwork.

Illinois. In an attempt to revitalize some schools crippled by bureaucracy, low morale, and poor academic performance, the Illinois legislature enacted a state law empowering parents. For example, each of Chicago's 570 schools was given its own school council consisting of the principal, two teachers, two community representatives, and six parents. In one legislative move, authority and power were transferred from a distant district office to each local school and its community. Kentucky has passed similar legislation. Time will tell whether these dramatic moves prove successful.

Missouri. The state provided $165 per family to fund an ambitious program called Parents as First Teachers. The program included seminars for parents on language development of children, home visits by teachers, parental instruction on activities to promote hand-eye coordination, and testing of children's vision, hearing, speech, and motor development. Missouri saw this funding as an investment in the future and a preventive measure to avoid the high cost of remedial programs for these children in later years.

A growing number of jurisdictions are integrating parents into the education process. Fairfax, Virginia, Albuquerque, New Mexico, New York City, Houston, Texas, and Wichita, Kansas, are several of the metropolitan areas that provide homework assistance to parents through Dial-a-Teacher programs. These efforts are impressive, but much still remains to be done.[24]

Dorothy Rich, in *The Forgotten Factor in School Success—The Family,* provides a series of suggestions to enhance the home-school partnership. She asks, "Does your school:

- Link parent involvement directly to the learning of their own children?
- Provide ways for families to reinforce academic skills at home?
- Link the school's work to the community and distribute home-learning activities at workplaces, gas stations, and grocery stores?
- Provide for parent involvement at all levels of schooling?
- Support and assign educational responsibilities to the family?
- Provide families with practical information they need in order to help educate their children?
- Respond to family diversity and differing needs of employed mothers and single-parent families?
- Encourage an active role for fathers?
- Provide teachers with training and information to help them work well with families?
- Provide for family involvement at all levels?
- Use school facilities for community needs, including the care of children before and after school?
- Find ways to coordinate teacher-school schedules to work with schedules of today's families?
- Emphasize early prevention of learning problems?"[25]

Educational Partnerships: Community Groups

Beyond the immediate family, schools have also developed partnerships with a variety of community groups. In Pittsburgh, the American Jewish Committee and the Urban League raised funds for schools. In Houston, architects taught students insights into the history and structure of the city's buildings. In Juneau, Alaska, the university provided teachers in the isolated Northern Arctic School District with workshops via television. In St. Louis, lawyers held mock court in schools to teach students about the real workings of the legal system. School districts across the country assessed the variety and wealth of educational resources available in their community and established a great array of educational partnerships.

Obviously, wealthier and larger districts have the potential for greater variety and sophistication in community partnerships. Regardless of size, however, all schools have educational resources available in their community or in neighboring communities. Most of these resources can be grouped into nine major categories:

1. Professional associations (architects, doctors, lawyers, and engineers)
2. Environmental and conservation organizations
3. Museums, galleries, and other cultural attractions
4. Social and civic groups (League of Women Voters, Rotary and Lions clubs, fraternities and sororities)
5. Colleges and universities
6. Ethnic and cultural groups
7. Health agencies and hospitals

8. Senior citizens

9. Artists, musicians, and craftspeople

As schools reach out to family, community, and business sectors, they are enhancing their chances of improving the quality and effectiveness of education. Only time will tell whether these partnerships, often initiated on an informal basis, become an institutionalized part of the school system. Partnerships with the home, the community, or the business world demand good communication and cooperation as well as close supervision to avoid the possibility of undue business or community pressure on school practices. Partnerships may turn out to be an educational fad or a new fact of life, a cornucopia of resources or a loss of school independence. What do you think?

Teacher Employment and School-Based Management

While parents, community groups, and the business sector carve out new roles in school participation, teachers traditionally have been omitted from meaningful involvement in school governance. Imagine that you are the senior faculty member at Someplace High School. Having taught there for 30 years, you know the school like the back of your hand. You are regarded as an excellent teacher, an expert at judging the needs of your students. Should you participate in making decisions affecting the management of your school?

Despite their professional expertise, most teachers have almost no role in making important decisions that will affect the quality of life in their schools. A survey of 8,000 teachers disclosed that only 30 percent of those responding said they made key decisions concerning textbooks and instructional materials. About half made none of the decisions affecting their in-service training. More than 60 percent never had the opportunity to observe their colleagues in action in the classroom. Less than one-quarter said they had a voice in choosing the subjects and grade levels they teach.[26] A 1989 poll showed teachers to be highly dissatisfied with the amount of control they had over the educational process.[27] Teachers were most frustrated by their lack of involvement in setting academic standards and establishing the school schedule. While teachers may request improvements or suggest changes, rarely do they have a significant voice in decisions made outside their own classrooms.

To get a sense of how little say teachers have once they leave their own classrooms, let's join the first faculty meeting of the fall at Someplace High. The principal, Mr. Will E. Tell, is discussing the new teacher assessment forms with the faculty.

Mr. Tell: If you all look in your folders, you'll see the criteria on which you will be assessed when I observe in your classrooms. Look these forms over carefully, and let me know if you have any questions. I'll be scheduling my school observation visits with you shortly.

Another issue I wanted to raise with you concerns our need to develop better relations with the community. As you can see, I've passed around a sign-up sheet for a committee to improve parent-teacher relations. Many of you have said that there has been low turnout for parent conferences. I thought that a committee would be in order. I know that a number of you haven't signed up for any committees yet, and it won't take that much time. What I have in mind is a car wash or a bake sale or some other fundraising activity to bring the community together. Ms. Johnson, you have a question?

Ms. Johnson: Yes, Mr. Tell. I thought that we were going to talk about getting new textbooks for the history department. The ones we've got now are too awful to use.

Mr. Tell: You're absolutely right, Louise, and I'm glad you raised the topic. That was going to be our first order of business, but I'm happy to report that the district office called yesterday and has promised us new textbooks by the second semester. They tell me that the new books are excellent.

I'll be getting out my first newsletter to the faculty in a few weeks, and I'll be announcing the in-service training sessions for the fall semester. I heard some interesting speakers at the national convention I attended, and I think I'm going to be able to get some of them to come to our district.

Before we end the meeting, I want to introduce our new faculty member. I hired Ms. Wetherby over the summer, an she'll join the teachers in our English department. I know you'll all do everything you can to make sure that Ms. Wetherby feels welcome.

Now, if there are no further topics for discussion, let's all get back to our classrooms. Tomorrow the kids arrive. It's time for a new year.

When the faculty of Someplace High head back to their classrooms, they can ignore a lot of Mr. Tell's decisions. Rather than confronting school officials in an open showdown, they can, for example, ignore awful textbooks and choose to teach from mimeographed handouts and carefully developed notes.

But from listening in on this faculty meeting, you can tell that many of the most crucial decisions have been made before the teachers arrive for work. Whether they teach advanced placement literature classes or remedial English

Teachers, who know more than anyone in the educational chain about the needs and interests of individual students, have until recently been virtually excluded from school management and policy-making.

is a decision usually made by the principal. Teachers do not participate in setting graduation requirements, in scheduling classes, in hiring new teachers, or in developing criteria by which their teaching will be evaluated.

While many of the school reforms of the mid-1980s demanded increased regulation of teachers, objection to top-down decision making by principals and school district authorities prompted a broad movement to give teachers a greater role in school governance.[28] This role is still so experimental that educators have not even settled on a term to describe it. You may hear phrases such as *participatory management, shared leadership, teacher empowerment,* and *faculty-led renewal*. During the last decade, two of the most widely adopted reforms were the related actions of moving decision-making authority to individual schools (known as **site-based** or **school-based management**) and dispersing the authority more broadly within schools (known as **collaborative decision making**). Large urban school systems such as those in Chicago, Miami, Los Angeles, San Diego, and Rochester, New York, led the trend of adopting school-based management. At least four states—Colorado, Kentucky, North Carolina, and Texas—made some form of collaborative decision making mandatory at every school.[29]

Today, all over the country, different visions and versions of **school-based management** and teacher empowerment are influencing how schools are governed. When anything is new, problems need to be worked out and questions need to be answered. This innovation is no exception. Will there be confusion in who is supposed to make what decisions? What will happen if there are clashes between teachers and principals? Could teacher collegiality be shattered by fights over how the school should run? Might teacher energy be diverted from what is most important—classroom instruction and attention to students? Will managing schools become less efficient and more expensive?

Despite all the unknowns, there is growing commitment to the concept of the principal as a leader of leaders in school-based decision making. The future promises to be exciting for those teachers who wish to extend their influence beyond the classroom and make a difference in the policy and practice of how their schools are governed.

While there is a general consensus that teacher morale and parent involvement have increased at schools that have made these changes, the impact on student achievement has been more difficult to discern. In order to be truly effective, most experts suggest that school-based management must be part of a broader strategy for improving education. One parent involved in school governance summarized the situation this way: "Site-based management is an innovation, yet it is trying to fit into an administration and a school board that were made 92 years ago. It doesn't fit together . . . we need to look at a new system."[30]

SUMMARY

1. According to the U.S. Constitution, education is the responsibility of each of the individual states.

2. At the state level, the legislature, state board of education, state superintendent, and state department of education provide the policy and administration of schools. The state also delegates some of its power to local school boards and superintendents who administer individual school districts.

3. The board of education at both the state and local levels is responsible for formulating educational policy. The chief state school officer, often called the *superintendent,* is responsible for implementing the policies of the board of education.

4. The state department of education's tasks are administrative and include certifying teachers and distributing state and federal funds.

5. On the local level, the responsibility of school operations rests with the local school districts, which generally have their own school boards and superintendents. Although they are required to operate within the rules and regulations of the state, the local school districts are responsible for school construction, hiring school personnel, and formulating school policy.

6. The business community has had a significant impact on schools. Certain business-oriented values, such as competitiveness and punctuality, have been adopted by schools. Moreover, many businesses are becoming directly involved in schools, donating products, dollars, and volunteers to work with students.

7. Parents, school secretaries, and custodians can be influential in a teacher's success. They are part of the hidden government of schools.

8. Consolidation has decreased the number of school districts while increasing the average size of schools. Those who oppose consolidation claim that it leads to higher costs for transportation and administration but does not increase student achievement. Supporters of consolidation believe that it increases educational opportunities and efficiency by absorbing small school districts with limited educational resources and electives into larger districts.

9. Although educational responsibility rests with the states, the federal government still plays an important part in educational finance and in improving educational practices and raising standards.

10. Recently educational partnerships involving parents, community groups, and the business sector have had a significant impact on local school systems.

11. Traditionally teachers have not had a significant role in school governance. However, the recent trends of school-based management, site-based management, and collaborative decision making may provide teachers with a more influential position in school governance.

DISCUSSION QUESTIONS AND ACTIVITIES

1. Have you had any personal experience in an organization that had both a formal and a hidden government? Explain how these governments operated.
2. Identify both the advantages and the disadvantages of the unusual U.S. form of local control over schools.
3. Based on your own experiences in school, can you recall examples of how business values were taught to you? Do you feel that this is a positive or a negative aspect of public education? Why?
4. If you had the power to reorganize the governance structure of public education, what changes would you make?
5. Someone once said, "What is good for General Motors is good for the country." If we were to paraphrase this statement to apply to U.S. schools, would you agree or disagree? Why?

6. Have you ever had first-hand experience with the power of the hidden or the legal government of schools? Describe these experiences.

7. Support or refute the following statement: "The least critical expertise needed by school superintendents is knowledge about teaching, learning, and children."

8. Describe the advantages and disadvantages of:

  • Increasing state influence on education
  • Decreasing federal influence on education

9. If you were responsible for creating school partnerships, what businesses, community groups, or other organizations would you seek out to contribute to the education process? Why?

10. Why has the twentieth century been marked by school consolidation? What problems does consolidation bring?

11. Identify at least five powers that states have to influence education.

12. Find a school that has implemented site-based or collaborative decision making. Interview a teacher to find out what the effects have been for teachers.

NOTES

1. Michael W. Kirst, "The Changing Balance in State and Local Power to Control Education," *Phi Delta Kappan* 66, no. 3 (November 1984): 189–191.

2. Douglas Mitchell and Dennis Encarnation, "Alternative State Policy Mechanisms for Influencing School Performance," *Educational Researcher,* May 1984, pp. 4–11.

3. Chester Finn, "Reinventing Local Control," in Patricia First and Herbert Walberg (eds.), *School Boards: Changing Local Control* (Berkeley: McCutchan, 1992); Emily Feistritzer, "A Profile of School Board Presidents," in *School Boards: Changing Local Control;* Neal Pierce, "School Boards Get Failing Grades, in Both the Cities and the Suburbs," *The Philadelphia Inquirer,* April 27, 1992, p. 11; Mary Jordan, "School Boards Need Overhaul, Educators Say," *The Washington Post,* April 5, 1992, p. A-51.

4. Thomas Shannon, "Local Control and 'Organizations,'" *School Boards: Changing Local Control;* Jacqueline Danzberger and Michael Usdan, "Strengthening a Grass-Roots American Institution: The School Board," in First and Walberg (eds.), *School Boards: Changing Local Control;* Arthur Blumberg and Phyllis Blumberg, *The School Superintendent: Living with Conflict* (New York: Teachers College Press, 1985).

5. David Sadker, *A Factor Analytic Study of Student Perceptions of the Elementary School Environment.* Unpublished doctoral dissertation, University of Massachusetts, 1971.

6. William O. Stanley, *Education and Social Integration* (New York: Columbia University Press, 1953).

7. Quoted in "Building Better Business Alliances," *Instructor,* Winter 1986 (special issue), p. 21.

8. Mark Walsh, "Businesses' Enthusiasm for Reform Seen Flagging," *Education Week,* June 14, 1995, p. 11.

9. Joseph F. Coates, Jennifer Jarratt, and John B. Mahaffie, "Future Work," *The Futurist* 25, no. 3 (May/June 1991): 9–19.

10. Quoted in Herbert J. Walberg, "Families as Partners in Educational Productivity," *Phi Delta Kappan* 65, no. 6 (February 1984): 397.

11. "Building Better Business Alliances"; Brian Dumaine, "Making Education Work," *Fortune,* Spring 1990 (special issue), pp. 12–22.

12. Walsh, "Businesses' Enthusiasm for Reform Seen Flagging."

13. Charles Russo, "The Legal Status of School Boards in the Intergovernmental System," in First and Walberg (eds.), *School Boards: Changing Local Control.*

14. Arthur Blumberg and Phyllis Blumberg, *The School Superintendent: Living with Conflict* (New York: Teachers College Press, 1985), p. 67.

15. Joanna Richardson, "Contracts Put Superintendents to Performance Test," *Education Week,* September 14, 1994, pp. 1, 12.

16. William H. Roe and Thelbert L. Drake, *The Principalship,* 2d ed. (New York: Macmillan, 1980); J. Lloyd Trump, *A School for Everyone* (Reston, VA: National Association of Secondary School Principals, 1977); Howard A. Dawson, *Satisfactory Local School Units,* Field Study No. 7 (Nashville, TN: George Peabody College for Teachers, 1934); Paul R. Mort and Francis G. Cronell, *American Schools in Transition* (New York: Teachers College Press, 1941); Paul R. Mort, William S. Vincent, and Clarence Newell, *The Growing Edge: An Instrument for Measuring the Adaptability of School Systems,* 2 vols. (New York: Teachers College Press, 1955); Mario D. Fantini, Marilyn Gittell, and Richard Magat, *Community Control and the Urban School* (New York: Praeger, 1970); A. Harry Passow, *Toward Creating a Model Urban School System* (New York: Teachers College Press, 1967); *Summary of Research on Size of Schools and School Districts* (Arlington, VA: Education Research Service, 1974).

17. Roger G. Barker and Paul V. Gump, *Big School, Small School* (Stanford, CA: Stanford University Press, 1964).

18. Jonathan P. Sher and Rachel B. Tompkins, *Economy, Efficiency and Equality: The Myths of Rural School and District Consolidation* (Washington, DC: National Institute of Education, U.S. Department of Health, Education and Welfare, 1976).

19. Anne C. Lewis, "Washington Report: House Democrats Criticize (in Unison) the Education Block Grant: Republicans Sing a Different Tune," *Phi Delta Kappan* 65, no. 6 (February 1984): 379–380.

20. Mary Jordan, "Pupils Give Their Parents 'D' for School Involvement," *The Washington Post,* May 12, 1992, p. A-3.

21. Herbert J. Walberg, "Families as Partners in Educational Productivity," *Phi Delta Kappan* 65, no. 6 (February 1984): 397–400.

22. Russel Hill and Frank Staffor, "The Allocation of Time to Preschool Children and Educational Opportunity," *Journal of Human Resources,* Spring 1974, pp. 323–341.

23. Frank E. Nardine and Robert D. Morris, "Parent Involvement in the States," *Phi Delta Kappan* 72, no. 5 (January 1991): 365.

24. Meg Sommerfeld, "National Commitment to Parent Role in School Sought," *Education Week,* April 15, 1992, p. 1. See also Don Davies, "Schools Reaching Out: Family, School, and Community Partnerships for Student Success," *Phi Delta Kappan* 72, no. 5 (January 1991).

25. Quoted in *Instructor and Teacher,* Winter 1986 (special issue), p. 16.

26. "Here's What You Care About Most," *Instructor,* May 1986, p. 31.

27. Ann Bradley, "Teachers Tell Pollster Lack of Support from Parents Impedes School Reform," *Education Week* 8, no. 31 (June 14, 1989): 6.

28. Terry Stimson and Richard Appelbaum, "Empowering Teachers: Do Principals Have the Power?" *Phi Delta Kappan* 70, no. 4 (December 1988): 313–316. See also Sarah Caldwell and Fred Wood, "School-Based Improvement—Are We Ready?" *Educational Leadership* 46, no. 2 (October 1988): 50–53. See also John Lane and Edgar Epps (eds.), *Restructuring the Schools: Problems and Prospects* (Berkeley, CA: McCutchan, 1992).

29. Ann Bradley and Lynn Olson, "The Balance of Power: Shifting the Lines of Authority in an Effort to Improve Schools," *Education Week,* February 24, 1993, p. 10.

30. Ibid.

SCHOOL LAW

OBJECTIVES

To describe the legal rights and responsibilities of teachers

To describe the legal rights and responsibilities of students

To apply court decisions and federal laws to specific case studies

To identify prudent steps teachers can take to decrease their risk of being sued

To describe court cases and major federal laws affecting educational programs and practices

To review crucial court decisions concerning the civil rights of teachers and students

A single teacher in one community is fired for living with her boyfriend. In a neighboring town, another teacher is fired because of union activity. Across the country, a teacher is suing a school board for a large sum of money, claiming that she has been slandered. And in a large urban system, a student is seeking a court action to allow him to publish a controversial student paper. Lawyers and judges are more and more becoming a part of school life.

In this chapter you will have the opportunity to respond to actual legal situations that have affected teachers and students. In the process you will learn about the laws and court decisions that affect your life in the classroom. You will also have the opportunity to review some of the major federal laws that have shaped and directed many school programs.

Classroom Law: New Frontiers for Teachers

You have probably heard it before: The United States is a litigious society. "Take them to court," "I'll sue," and "Have your lawyer call my lawyer" are phrases that have worked their way into the American lexicon. And action follows the words. People sue companies. Companies sue people. Governments sue companies. Companies and people sue governments. Parents sue teachers. We tend to seek redress for all kinds of problems in the courts, from divorce to physical injury, from protecting our beliefs to complying (or not complying) with laws.

The story is told that when the federal government ordered new antipollution standards in automobiles, U.S. and Japanese companies responded quite differently. Japanese automobile manufacturers increased the number of engineers working to solve the problem and design cars to meet the new antipollution standards. American corporations, on the other hand, increased the size of their legal budgets in order to fight the new standards. Both strategies met with some success. The Japanese developed and sold cars that met the new standards, while the American companies won delays in implementing those standards.

Despite the growing importance and influence of school-related law, many educators are still unaware of their basic legal rights and responsibilities. This can be a costly professional blind spot.[1]

What rights do you have in the classroom? To some, this complex question can be reduced to a single formula. Consider the following conversation between a college professor and a former associate superintendent of public instruction for California:

Superintendent: Teaching is a privilege, not a right. If one wants this privilege, he or she has to give up some rights.
Professor: Just what constitutional rights do people have to give up in order to enter teaching?
Superintendent: Any right their community wants them to give up.[2]

Although such simplistic attitudes still exist, recent years have seen extraordinary changes in the legal rights of both teachers and students. Once the victims of arbitrary school rules and regulations, today's teachers and students can institute legal action if they believe that their constitutional rights are being threatened. In an ever-increasing number of cases, the courts are finding school administrators guilty of violating the rights of both teachers and students.

As a classroom teacher, what can you legally say and do? Can you legally copy material for classroom use? What disciplinary methods are acceptable? How does your role as teacher limit your personal activities? Your lifestyle? Your freedom of speech? Before you step into a classroom, you should be aware of the laws that shape what you can and cannot do as a teacher.

It is impossible to review here all the court rulings and federal laws pertaining to teacher and student rights, but it is important for you to be aware of both your own legal rights and responsibilities as a teacher and those of your students. You will have an ongoing responsibility to keep abreast of changes in school laws, since what the courts consider legal today may be found illegal tomorrow, and vice versa.

While teachers would like to know definitively what is legal and what is not, courts often set forth standards with vague terms. Requirements that people act with "reasonable care" or "appropriately under the circumstances" may be susceptible to differing interpretations when applied to different sets of facts. Teachers should be sensitive to the courts' difficulties in framing clear, precise legal standards, given that very often they are called upon to balance legitimate concerns that can be raised on both sides of an issue.

What Is Your Rights Quotient?: Teachers' Rights

The following quiz focuses on several vignettes, each based on a court case or a federal regulation.[3] The quiz will test your legal knowledge regarding a number of common teaching situations.

The quiz is divided into two parts: teachers' rights and students' rights. In each case, an issue is identified, a situation is described, and you are asked to react to the situation by selecting an appropriate legal response. After your selection, the correct response and relevant court decisions or laws are described. Keep track of your successes and misses; a scoring system at the conclusion of the quiz will help you determine your RQ (rights quotient). Good luck!

Issue

Civil rights in applying for a teaching position

Situation 1

You are completing your student teaching and are beginning to interview with several local school districts for a teaching position. A representative from a district you would love to work for has come to campus to interview teacher candidates. Mr. Thomas seems quite impressed with your credentials, and the interview is going very well. Mr. Thomas explains that the system invests considerable training and resources in new teachers and wants to make certain that they will be committed to and remain with the school system. Mr. Thomas asks if you plan to get married soon, and if so, will you be starting a family right away?

_____ You answer the question, realizing that the district is entitled to know about your long-range plans.

_____ You do not answer the question.

Federal and State Laws, Court Decisions Not too long ago, school districts regularly gave hiring and promotion consideration to marital status and parenthood. For women, these were critical factors in being offered a job. Now a variety of federal and state laws and court decisions make such inquiries illegal. Generally, interview questions must be related to the job requirements. Questions about race, creed, marital status, sex, religion, age, national origin, physical or other disabilities, and even a request for photographs along with an application are generally illegal. **Title IX of the Education Amendments (1972)** and **Title VII of the Civil Rights Act (1964)** are two federal laws that prohibit many of these practices. In the situation described above, the questions are inappropriate and illegal, and you need not answer them. You may wish to notify the school district or even the Office for Civil Rights in order to stop the school district from asking such discriminatory questions in the future.[4]

Issue

Sexual harassment

Situation 2

After surviving the sex discriminatory interview, you are offered a teaching position and decide to take it. After all, you like the community and the children, and with any luck you will never run into Mr. Thomas (the interviewer) again. You are very excited as you prepare for your first day. You are up an hour early, you rehearse your opening remarks, and you feel hopeful and optimistic as you enter the school. Then it's your worst nightmare. You meet the new principal, Mr. Thomas, recently transferred from the personnel office. You spend the next year dodging his lewd comments, his unwanted touches, and his incessant propositions. At the end of the year, you find yourself in counseling and worried about your job. You decide that:

_____ Your initial instincts were right. You should never have taken this job. Quit before things get worse.

_____ Enough is enough. Sue the district for damages.

Court Decision   Anita Hill's charges against Supreme Court nominee Clarence Thomas awakened millions of Americans to the issue of sexual harassment, and the principal's behavior, both verbal and physical, is clearly an example of this problem. In 1992, the Supreme Court ruled that victims of sexual harassment are also victims of sex discrimination and can recover monetary damages. Keeping a record of the principal's behavior and having witnesses will strengthen your case; but you certainly can sue, and if you are successful, you may be awarded significant monetary damages.[5]

Issue

Personal lifestyle

Situation 3

A teacher in your community is creative and effective in the classroom and well-liked by students and colleagues, but her life outside the classroom is not appreciated by school officials. She is unmarried and living with her boyfriend, and school officials believe that she is behaving as a poor role model for her students. The school system publicly announced that because she is cohabiting, her behavior is having a negative influence on her elementary-age students. The school board suspends the teacher.

_____ The teacher is the victim of an illegal action and should sue to be reinstated.

_____ The school board is within its rights in dismissing the teacher and removing a bad role model from the classroom.

Court Decision   This case is typical of various issues, all related to the degree of personal freedom an individual abandons when assuming the position of a teacher and becoming a role model for students. Although decisions by the courts have varied, the following general standard should be kept in mind: Does the teacher's behavior significantly disrupt the educational process or erode the credibility of the teacher with students, colleagues, or the community? If the school district can demonstrate that the teacher has disrupted education or lost credibility, then the teacher may be fired.

In the case presented here, the teacher sued the school district (*Thompson v. Southwest School District*). The court indicated that until the school district took action to suspend the teacher on grounds of immorality, the public was generally unaware of the teacher's cohabitation with her boyfriend. The court decided that it was unfair of the board of education to make the issue public in order to gain community support for its position. Furthermore, the court ruled that the teacher's behavior had not interfered with her effectiveness in the classroom. With neither a loss of credibility nor a significant disruption of the educational process, the board lost its case and the teacher kept her job.

Issues concerning the personal lifestyles of teachers have emerged in a series of court cases ranging from drinking problems to smoking marijuana, from church attendance (actually, a lack of church attendance) to personal appearance. Sometimes court decisions have differed from state to state. Driving while intoxicated or smoking marijuana was found to be grounds for dismissal in one state but not in another, depending on whether the behavior resulted in "substantial disruption" of the educational process. On the other hand, attempting to dismiss a teacher because she did not attend church was not upheld by the court. In fact, the teacher in this case actually won financial damages against the school district.

What about your personal appearance? What can a school district legally require in terms of personal grooming and dress code for teachers? Courts have not been consistent in their decisions, although if the dress requirements are reasonable and related to legitimate educational concerns, the courts may uphold the legality of dress codes for teachers.[6]

Issue	**Situation 4**
Teachers' academic freedom	As a social studies teacher you are concerned about your students' apparent insensitivity to racism in the United States. You have found a very effective simulation game that evokes strong student feelings on racial issues, but the school board is concerned by this activity and has asked you to stop using the game. The board expressed its concern over your discussion of controversial issues. Committed to your beliefs, you persist; at the end of the year you find that your teaching contract is not renewed.

_____   Since you think your academic freedom has been violated, you decide to sue to get your job back.

_____   You realize that the school board is well within its rights to determine curriculum, that you were warned and now you must pay the price for your indiscretion.

Court Decision   The right to **academic freedom** (that is, to teach without coercion, censorship, or other restrictive interference) is not absolute, and the courts will balance the teacher's right to academic freedom with the school system's interests in its students' learning appropriate subject matter in an environment conducive to learning. Courts look at such factors as whether the teacher's learning activities or materials are inappropriate, irrelevant to the subjects to be covered under the syllabus, obscene, or substantially disruptive of

Academic freedom protects a teacher's right to teach about sensitive issues such as AIDS or other sex education topics as long as the topic is relevant to the course, is not treated in an obscene manner, and is not disruptive of school discipline.

school discipline. In the case of the simulation game involving racial issues, the activity appears to be appropriate, relevant, and neither obscene nor disruptive. If you sued on the grounds of academic freedom, you would probably get your job back.[7]

Issue

Legal liability (negligence)

Situation 5

You are assigned to cafeteria duty (lucky break). Things are pretty quiet, and you take the opportunity to call up a guest speaker and confirm a visit to your class. While you are gone from the cafeteria, a student slips on some spilt milk and breaks his arm. His parents hold you liable for their son's injury and sue you for damages.

_____ You will probably win, since you did not cause the fall and were on educational business when the accident occurred.

_____ The student's parents will win, since you left your assigned post.

_____ The student who spilt the milk is solely responsible for the accident.

_____ No one will win, because the courts long ago ruled that there is no use crying over spilt milk.

Court Decision In recent years, litigation against teachers has increased dramatically. The public concern over the quality of education, the bureaucratic and impersonal nature of many school systems, and the generally litigious nature of our society have all contributed to this rising tide of lawsuits. Negligence suits against teachers are no longer uncommon. In the cafeteria example, you would be in considerable jeopardy in a legal action. A teacher who is not present at his or her assigned duty might very well be charged with negligence, unless the absence is "reasonable." The courts are very strict about what is "reasonable" (leaving your post to put out a fire is reasonable, but going to the telephone to make a call is unlikely to be viewed as reasonable). It is good practice to stay in your classroom or assigned area of responsibility unless there is a real emergency.

Teacher liability is an area of considerable concern to many teachers. Courts generally use two standards in determining negligence: (1) whether a reasonable person with similar training would act in the same way; and (2) whether or not the teacher could have foreseen the possibility of an injury. Here are some common terms and typical situations related to teacher liability:

Misfeasance. This is failure to conduct in an appropriate manner an act that might otherwise have been lawfully performed; for example, unintentionally using too much force in breaking up a fight is **misfeasance.**

Nonfeasance. This applies to failure to perform an act that one has a duty to perform; for example, the cafeteria situation described above is **nonfeasance,** since the teacher did not supervise an assigned area of responsibility.

Malfeasance. This refers to an act that cannot be done lawfully regardless of how it is performed; for example, starting a fistfight or bringing marijuana to school is **malfeasance.**

Educational malpractice. Although liability litigation usually involves physical injury to students because of what a teacher did or failed to do, a new line of litigation, called **educational malpractice,** is concerned with "academic damage." Some students and parents have sued school districts for failing to provide an adequate education. Many courts have rejected these cases, pointing out that many factors affect learning and that failure to learn cannot be blamed solely on the school system.

Issue	**Situation 6**
Teachers' freedom of speech	As a teacher in a small school district in Illinois, you are quite upset with the way the school board and the superintendent are spending school funds. You are particularly upset with all the money being spent on high school athletics, since these expenditures have cut into your proposed salary raise. To protest the expenditures, you write a lengthy letter to the local newspaper criticizing the superintendent and the school board. After the letter is published, you find that the figures you cited in the letter were inaccurate.
	The following week, you are called into the superintendent's office and fired for breaking several school rules. Among them are your failure to communicate your complaints to your superiors and the harm you have done to the school system by spreading false and malicious statements. In addition, the superintendent points out that your acceptance of a teaching position obligated you to refrain from publicizing critical statements about the school. The superintendent says that although no one can stop you from making public statements, the school system certainly does not "have to pay you for the privilege." You decide to:

_____ Go to court to win your position back.

_____ Chalk it up to experience, look for a new position, and make certain that you do not publish false statements and break school rules in the future.

Court Decision This situation is based on a suit instigated by a teacher named Marvin Pickering. After balancing the teacher's interests, as a citizen, in commenting upon issues of public concern against the school's interests in efficiently providing public services, the Supreme Court ruled in favor of the teacher. It found that the disciplined operation of the school system was not seriously damaged by Pickering's letter and that the misstatements in the letter were not made knowingly or recklessly. Moreover, there was no special need for confidentiality on the issue of school budgets. Hence, concluded the Court, prohibiting Pickering from making his statements was an infringement of his First Amendment right to freedom of speech. You, too, would probably win in court if you issued public statements on matters of public concern unless your statements were intentionally or recklessly inaccurate, disclosed confidential material, or hampered either school discipline or your performance of duties.[8]

Issue	**Situation 7**
Copying published material	You read a fascinating two-page article in a national magazine, and since the article concerns an issue your class is discussing, you duplicate the article and distribute it to your students. This is the only article you have distributed in class, and you do not bother to ask either the author or the magazine for permission to reprint it. You have:

_____ Violated the copyright law, and you are liable to legal action.

_____ Not violated any copyright law.

Federal Law Until recently, teachers could reproduce articles, poems, book excerpts, or whatever they pleased with virtually no fear of legal repercussions. But in January 1978, PL 94-553 was passed, and teachers' right to freely reproduce and distribute published works was greatly curtailed. Under this law, in order to use a published work in class, teachers must write to the publisher or author of the work and obtain written permission. This sometimes requires the payment of a permission fee, something that teachers on a limited budget are usually unwilling to do. Under certain circumstances, however, teachers may still reproduce published material without written permission or payment. This is called **fair use**, a legal principle that allows the limited use of copyrighted materials. To use copyrighted materials, teachers must observe three criteria in selecting the material: brevity, spontaneity, and cumulative effect. As we review these criteria, you can apply them to the example outlined in the vignette to determine if in this case you stayed within the limits of the new copyright law.

1. _Brevity_ means that a work can be reproduced if it is not overly long. Poems or excerpts from poems must be no longer than 250 words. Articles, stories, or essays of less than 2,500 words may be reproduced in complete form. Excerpts of any prose work (such as a book or an

article) may be reproduced only up to 1,000 words or 10 percent of the work, whichever is less; such excerpts must be a minimum of 500 words. Only one illustration (photo, drawing, diagram) may be reproduced from the same book or journal. The brevity criterion limits the length of the material that a teacher can reproduce and distribute from a single work. If you were the teacher in this example and you reproduced only a two-page article, you would not have violated the criterion of brevity.

2. The second criterion, *spontaneity,* allows a teacher to reproduce material if there is not enough time to secure written permission. If a teacher has an inspiration to use a published work and there is simply not enough time to write for and receive written permission, then the teacher may reproduce and distribute the work. The teacher in our vignette has met this criterion and, consequently, is acting within the law. If the teacher wishes to distribute the same article to a class during the next semester or the next year, written permission would be required, since ample time exists to request such permission.

3. The final criterion, *cumulative effect,* limits the number of published works that may be used in a course. The total number of works reproduced without permission for class distribution must not exceed nine instances per class per semester. Within this limit, only one complete piece or two excerpts from the same author may be reproduced, and only three pieces from the same book or magazine. Cumulative effect limits the number of articles, poems, excerpts, and so on, that can be reproduced even if the criteria of spontaneity and brevity are met. From the description in the vignette, the teacher has not reproduced other works and therefore has met this criterion also.

Under the fair use principle, single copies of printed material may be copied for your personal use. So if you want a single copy for planning a lesson, that is not a problem. Whenever multiple copies are made for classroom use, each copy must include a notice of copyright.

Three new areas should also be considered: videotapes, computer software and data, and mixed media. Without a license or permission, educational institutions may not keep copyrighted videotapes (for example, from a television show) for more than 45 days. The tape should not be shown more than once to students during this period, and then it must be erased. The growing use of computers prompted amendment of the Federal Copyright Act in 1990 to prohibit the copying of software for commercial gain. Teachers should observe all copyright restrictions when using software. For other materials, including mixed-media products that combine text, graphics, and film images, it is always advisable to check with your local school district officials to determine school policy and procedures.[9]

Issue
Labor rights

Situation 8
Salary negotiations have been going badly in your school district, and at a mass meeting teachers finally vote to strike. You honor the strike and stay home, refusing to teach until an adequate salary increase is provided. During the first week of the strike, you receive a letter from the school board stating that you will be suspended for 15 days without pay at the end of the school year owing to your participation in the strike. You decide:

_____ To fight this illegal, unjust, and costly suspension.

_____ To accept the suspension as a legal action of the school board.

Court Decision In a number of cases, courts have recognized the right of teachers to organize, to join professional organizations such as the NEA and the AFT, and to bargain collectively for improved working conditions. You cannot legally be penalized for these activities. On the other hand, courts have also upheld legislation that prohibits teachers from striking because they provide a vital public service, so unless you are working in one of the few states that allow teacher strikes (for example, Hawaii, Pennsylvania), you are breaking the law by honoring the strike. The school board is within its rights to suspend and penalize you for striking.

Although about half of the states have laws that prohibit strikes, many communities choose not to prosecute striking teachers. If they do prosecute, the teachers may be penalized. Conversely, even though membership in teacher organizations and the right to collective bargaining have been upheld by the courts, some communities and school boards are adamantly opposed to such organizations and refuse to hire or to renew contracts of teachers who are active in them. Such bias is clearly illegal; nevertheless, it is very difficult to prove in court, and consequently, it is very difficult to stop.

In summary, law and reality do not always coincide. Legally speaking, teachers may belong to teacher organizations but are prohibited from striking by state law. In reality, however, striking teachers are rarely prosecuted or penalized, although many others suffer from discriminatory school board actions because of their active involvement in teacher organizations. Finally, if you should choose to strike, do so with the realization that such activity makes you liable to legal sanctions.[10]

Although most states have laws prohibiting teachers from striking, most communities choose not to penalize striking teachers, since it has become commonplace in the past two decades.

What Is Your Rights Quotient?: Students' Rights

Issue
Student records

Situation 9
You are a high school teacher who has decided to stay after school in order to finish working on some student personnel folders. As you are working, Phyllis, a 16-year-old student of yours, walks in and asks to see her folder. Since you have several sensitive comments recorded in the folder, you refuse. Within the hour, the student's parents call and ask if they can see the folder. At this point you:

_____   Explain that the information is confidential and sensitive and cannot be shared with nonprofessional personnel.

_____   Explain that the parents can see the folder and describe the procedure for doing so.

Federal Law   The *Family Rights and Privacy Act,* commonly referred to as the *Buckley amendment* (1974), allows parents and guardians access to their children's educational records. The amendment also requires that school districts inform parents of this right and establish a procedure for providing educational records on request. Moreover, written parental permission is needed before these records can be shared with anyone other than professionals connected with either the school the student attends or another school in which the student seeks to enroll, health or safety officials, or persons reviewing the student's financial aid applications. If the student has reached 18 years of age, he or she must be allowed to see the folder and is responsible for granting permission for others to review the folder. ·

Under this law you should have chosen the second option, for it is the parents' right to see this information.[11]

Issue
Distribution of scholarships

Situation 10
As a secondary teacher, you are concerned with the manner in which scholarships and other financial awards are distributed at graduation. You notice that nearly all the awards are going to boys. You mention this to the principal, who explains to you that most of the scholarships are given to boys because the burden of supporting a family falls more on men than women. The principal says that although this is not exactly equitable, it is realistic. You decide that:

_____   It is an unfortunate but realistic policy.

_____   It is unfair, unreasonable, and unrealistic given our society's divorce rate. You file a complaint with the Office for Civil Rights.

Federal Law   Using sex as a criterion by which to grant awards, scholarships, or financial aid is one of the many areas of sex discrimination prohibited under Title IX. Objective criteria fairly applied without regard to sex should be the appropriate policy in awarding these funds. If it turns out that the most qualified students in a given year are predominantly or entirely of one sex, that is acceptable as long as the procedures and criteria were fairly applied. But sex itself should not be a criterion; this example is a violation of Title IX and should be reported.[12]

Issue
Suspension and discipline

Situation 11
You are teaching a difficult class, and one particular student is the primary source of trouble. After a string of disorderly episodes on this student's part, the textbooks for the entire class mysteriously disappear. You have put up with more than enough, and you send the student to the principal's office to be suspended. The principal backs you up, and the student is told not to return to school for a week. This action is:

____ Legal and appropriate (and probably long overdue!).

____ Illegal.

Court Decision Although troublesome and disorderly students can be disciplined, suspension from school represents a serious penalty, one that should not be taken lightly. In such cases, the Supreme Court has ruled (*Goss v. Lopez*) that teachers and administrators are required to follow certain procedures in order to guarantee the student's **due process** rights. In this case, the student must be informed of the rule that has been broken and of the evidence. The student is also entitled to tell his or her own side of the story in self-defense. For suspensions in excess of 10 days, the school must initiate more formal procedures. School officials can be held personally liable for damages if they violate a student's clearly established constitutional rights (*Wood v. Strickland*).

If you look back at this vignette, you will notice that you do not know for sure that this student is responsible for the missing textbooks. Nor is the student given the opportunity for self-defense. If you selected "illegal," you chose the correct response.

While looking at discipline, let us look at the legality of **corporal punishment.** In *Ingraham v. Wright* (1977), the Supreme Court ruled that physical punishment may be authorized by states. The Court ruled that the corporal punishment should be "reasonable and not excessive," and such factors as the seriousness of the student offense, the age and physical condition of the student, and the force and attitude of the person administering the punishment should be considered. Although the courts have legalized corporal punishment, many states and school districts do not believe in it and have prohibited the physical punishment of students; other districts and states provide very specific guidelines for its practice. You should be familiar with the procedures and norms in your district before you ever use this disciplinary strategy.[13]

Issue
Freedom of speech

Situation 12
During your homeroom period you notice that several of your more politically active students are wearing green arm bands. You call them to your desk and ask them about it. They explain that they are protesting censorship on the Internet. You tell them that you share their concern but that wearing the arm bands is specifically forbidden by school rules. You explain that you will let it go this time,

since they are not disturbing the class routine, but that if they wear any more arm bands they will be suspended.

Sure enough, the next day the same students arrive at school still wearing the arm bands, and you send them to the principal's office. The students tell the principal that although they understand the rule against arm bands, they refuse to obey it. The principal, explaining that school rules are made to be followed, suspends them. The principal's action is:

_____ Legally justified, since the students were given every opportunity to understand and obey the school rule.

_____ Illegal, since students have the right to wear arm bands if they so desire.

Court Decision In December 1965, three students in Des Moines, Iowa, demonstrated their opposition to the Vietnam War by wearing black arm bands to school. The principal informed them that they were breaking a school rule and asked that they remove the arm bands. They refused and were suspended.

The students' parents sued the school system, and the case finally reached the Supreme Court. In the landmark *Tinker* case, the Court ruled that the students were entitled to wear the arm bands as long as the students did not

Courts have upheld student's freedom of speech in a number of cases, so long as the protests were not disruptive of other students' right to learn and were not obscene.

substantially disrupt the operation of the school or deny other students the opportunity to learn. Since there was no disruption, the Court ruled that the school system could not prohibit students from wearing the arm bands or engaging in other forms of free speech. The school system in the vignette acted illegally; it could not prevent students from wearing arm bands.[14]

The issue of allegedly "obscene" speech has been more recently considered by the Supreme Court. In a 1986 decision (*Bethel School District v. Fraser*), the Court evaluated the First Amendment rights of a high school senior, Matthew Fraser. Fraser presented a speech at a school assembly that contained numerous sexual innuendos, though no explicit, profane language. After Fraser was suspended for his speech and told that he was no longer eligible to speak at his class's graduation, his father sued the school district. The Court upheld the suspension on the grounds that the language in the speech was indecent and offensive and that minors should not be exposed to such language.[15]

Issue	Situation 13
School prayer	A student in your class objects to the daily prayer recitation. You are sensitive to the student's feelings, and you make certain that the prayer is nondenominational. Moreover, you tell the student that he may stand or sit silently without reciting the prayer. If the student likes, he may even leave the room while the prayer is being recited. As a teacher, you have:

_____ Broken the law.

_____ Demonstrated sensitivity to individual needs and not violated the law.

Court Decision You were sensitive but not sensitive enough, because you violated the law. The Court has ruled that schools must be completely neutral with regard to religion and may neither encourage nor discourage prayer. Schools should not allot time for any kind of religious observance, nor even for a moment of silence. As a result of leaving the room, the student might be subjected to embarrassment, ostracism, or some other form of social stigma. The Court has ruled that the separation of church and state prevents religious activities of any kind in public schools.[16]

Issue	Situation 14
Search and seizure	The drug problem in your school is spreading, and it is clear that strong action is needed. School authorities order a search of all student lockers, which lasts for several hours. Trained police dogs are brought in, and each classroom is searched for drugs. The dogs sniff suspiciously at several students, who are taken to the locker rooms and strip-searched.

_____ School authorities are well within their rights to conduct these searches.

_____ Searching the lockers is legal, but strip-searching is inappropriate and illegal.

_____ No searches are called for, and all of these activities represent illegal and unconstitutional violations of student rights.

Court Decision Courts have ruled that school authorities have fewer restrictions than do the police in search-and-seizure activities. Courts have indicated that school property (such as lockers, or cars parked in the school lot) are actually the responsibility of the school. Moreover, the school has a parentlike responsibility (termed *in loco parentis*) to protect children and to respond to reasonable concerns about their health and safety.

In the situation described above, the search of lockers is legal. However, using police dogs to sniff students (rather than things) is allowable only if the dogs are reliable and the student is a reasonable suspect. The strip-search is illegal.

The second choice is the correct response. Although school personnel have great latitude in conducting school search and seizures, educators should be familiar with proper legal procedures and should have thought carefully about related ethical issues.[17]

Student locker searches for contraband items are permissible since schools have parentlike responsibility for the safety of their students.

Issue
Freedom of the press

Situation 15
The *Argus* is the official student newspaper, written by students as part of a journalism course, but it has run afoul of school administrators. First the student newspaper printed a story critical of the school administration. In the next edition, the paper included a supplement on contraception and abortion. With their patience worn thin, school administrators closed the publication for the remainder of the school year.

_____ Closing the student newspaper is a legal action.

_____ Closing the student newspaper is an illegal action.

Court Decision In 1988, a relatively conservative Supreme Court appointed largely by President Reagan ruled in the *Hazelwood* case that student newspapers may be censored under certain circumstances. The Court held that student newspapers written as part of a school journalism course should be viewed as part of the official school curriculum. School administrators, according to the Court, can readily censor such a paper. Since the case presented in the above hypothetical situation indicated that the publication was part of a journalism course, closing the school newspaper would be legal.

If, on the other hand, the newspaper was financed by the students and not associated with an official school course, the students would enjoy a greater degree of freedom. By the way, additional grounds for censoring a school newspaper include obscenity, psychological harm, and disruption of school activities.[18]

Issue
AIDS-infected students

Situation 16
As you enter school one morning, you are met by a group of angry parents. They have found out that Randy, one of your students, is HIV positive and hence can transmit the AIDS-related virus to others. There is no cure for AIDS, and there is no compromise in the voices of the parents

confronting you. Either Randy goes or they will keep their children at home. You listen sympathetically, but find your mind wandering to your own contact with Randy. You worry that you, too, may be at risk. In this case you decide:

_____   It's better to be safe than sorry, so you ask Randy to stay home. There is no cure for AIDS, and no reason to put every child's life in jeopardy.

_____   It's probably okay for Randy to attend school, so you check with your principal and try to calm the parents down.

Court Decision   Once confined predominantly to gay men and drug users, AIDS and its root, the HIV virus, are finding their way into the general population. In a case very similar to the one described above, Randy, a hemophiliac, and his brothers were denied access to De Soto County Schools in Florida when they tested positive for the HIV virus. The court determined that the boys' loss of their education was more harmful than the remote chance of other students' contracting AIDS. In fact, in this 1987 case, Randy's parents actually won an out-of-court settlement in excess of $1 million for the pain the school system inflicted on the family. In another case, the court determined that AIDS-infected students are protected under *PL 94-142, Individuals with Disabilities Education Act*. Clearly, medical guidelines direct the court. If some AIDS children present more of a public risk (for example, because of biting behavior, open sores, engaging in fights, and so on), more restrictive school environments may be required. To date, however, AIDS-infected students and teachers are not viewed as a significant risk to the health of the rest of the population and cannot be denied their educational rights.[19]

Issue
Sexual harassment

Situation 17
One of your favorite students appears particularly upset. You are concerned, so you go over to Pat and put your arm around him. Pat stiffens his shoulder and pushes you away. He is obviously distressed about something. The next day you offer to take Pat to a local diner after school, to cheer him up with a hot fudge sundae. He refuses to go but thanks you for the gesture. A few weeks later, the principal calls you into her office to explain that you have been charged with sexual harassment.

_____   You feel bewildered and betrayed that your gestures of kindness have been misconstrued. You decide to fight the suit, believing that you have been victimized.

_____   You decide to apologize, realizing that you have overstepped the boundaries of propriety.

Court Decision   In *Franklin v. Gwinnett* (1992), the Supreme Court extended the reach of Title IX, allowing students to sue a school district for monetary damages in cases of sexual harassment. The Gwinnett County case involved a Georgia high school in which a student was sexually harassed and abused by the teacher, a case much more serious than the pat on the back and offer of a hot fudge sundae described in the vignette. In Georgia, the teacher's behavior was extreme and the school district's response inadequate. The school district was instructed to pay damages to the student—establishing a precedent.[20]

Sexual harassment complaints being filed against teachers have been increasing. Teachers need to realize that sexual harassment laws protect individuals not only from extreme actions, as in the Georgia case, but from offensive words and inappropriate touching. The mild scenario of comforting words, touching, and an offer of ice cream that was described above can indeed lead to problems. While the teacher's intention might have been pure and caring, the student's perception might have been quite different. The threat of the legal broadside that can result from this gap between teacher intentions and student perceptions has sent a chill through many school faculties. Teachers now openly express their fears about the dangers of reaching out to students, and some teachers are vowing never to touch a student or be alone in a room with a student, no matter how honorable the intention. Many teachers lament the current situation, recalling earlier times when a teacher's caring, kindness, and closeness would affect students in a positive way.

Prudent teacher actions can go a long way in avoiding difficult situations or student accusations about misbehavior. (See the next section about precautions teachers can take to avoid potential litigation.) However, it is important to remember that while your actions, and the actions of most teachers, may be honorable, incidents of sexual harassment in schools are evidently quite numerous. A 1993 survey sponsored by the American Association of University Women (AAUW) found that over 70 percent of boys and over 80 percent of girls experienced some form of sexual harassment in school. For boys, harassment usually took the form of comments challenging their sexuality. While most boys suffered from some form of harassment, gay boys were particularly vulnerable. Female students indicated a more long-term impact, reporting that they were less likely to want to speak in class or to continue their schooling as a result of being harassed.

The AAUW survey surprised many Americans, who did not realize the extent of the problem. One out of 4 girls, and 1 out of 10 boys reported being harassed by a school employee, ranging from administrators to custodians. Yet 93 percent of the students who said that they were victimized by a school employee also said that they never reported the incident to school officials. As students become increasingly aware of their rights, sexual harassment complaints will more likely be reported in the future, and teachers will be encouraged to adopt more cautious and more prudent behaviors.[21]

Scoring

To determine your RQ, the following scoring guide may be useful:

15 to 17 correct: Legal Eagle
13 to 14 correct: Excellent
11 to 12 correct: Pretty good
9 to 10 correct: Fair
8 or fewer: In need of remedial legal training

This brief review of the legal realities that surround today's classroom is not meant to be definitive. These situations are merely intended to highlight the rapid growth and changing nature of school law and the importance of this law to teachers.

However, this sample of teacher and student rights underscores the legal side of the classroom. Ignorance of the law, to paraphrase a popular saying, is no defense. More positively, knowledge of fundamental legal principles allows you to practice "preventive law"—that is, to avoid or resolve potential legal conflicts so that you can attend to your major responsibility: teaching.

Charged with Child Abuse

- In a case that received a great deal of media coverage, a Connecticut middle school teacher was accused of inappropriate sexual contact with a student. The teacher faced legal charges and was placed on an 18-month probation by the school district.
- A group of Illinois elementary students came forward to claim that a substitute teacher had molested them. While an investigation was being carried out, the teacher was suspended.
- In Texas, a sixth-grade student crawled through electrical wiring, shaking a table full of equipment, and refused to follow the teacher's directions. The teacher pulled the student from under the table by grabbing and tugging the student's leg. The teacher was accused of assault and removed from the classroom.

Although still a relatively infrequent occurrence, charges of teacher abuse have increased in the past decade—as has litigation. While allegations of abuse can occur at any grade level and against any teacher, the middle and junior high school years see the largest number of such complaints, and male teachers are more likely to be targeted than female teachers. What do the three cases above have in common? In each instance, the teacher was found innocent. The charges of sexual abuse brought forward in Connecticut and Illinois were groundless, each motivated by totally unrelated student grievances. In fact, the Illinois case, in which a number of students accused the teacher of molestation, was a well-orchestrated act of revenge. A 9-year-old girl, concerned about the repercussions of her classroom misbehavior, offered nine of her classmates $1 each if they would claim that the teacher molested them. The third case, in Texas, in which the teacher pulled the student (who was enmeshed in electrical wires beneath the computer table) from this dangerous position, also featured an innocent teacher who was eventually reinstated by the school board. But while none of these teachers were guilty, they endured public abuse and, in some cases, a trial in the media for their alleged offenses. Teachers are not immune from lawsuits. While there is no foolproof way to protect yourself from groundless charges, you can take actions to better your chances of weathering such legal storms.[22]

- When meeting with students individually, keep classroom and office doors open. When possible, schedule such appointments for times when other adults or students are present.
- Separate your personal and professional lives. Don't inundate students with personal stories, or invite students to your home, or involve yourself with sensitive and personal issues—yours or the students'.

How Private Is Your Personal Life?

Courts are constantly asked to draw the line between a teacher's personal freedom and the community's right to establish teacher behavior standards. Historically, the scales have tilted toward the community, and teachers were fired for wearing lipstick, joining a different church, or getting married. Today's courts make more deliberate efforts to balance personal liberty and community standards. Although each case must be judged on its own merits, some trends do emerge.

The courts have ruled that the community has the right to fire a teacher for:

- Making public homosexual advances to nonstudents
- Incorporating sexual issues into lessons and ignoring the approved syllabus
- Inciting violent protest among students
- Engaging in sex with students
- Encouraging students to attend certain religious meetings
- Allowing students to drink alcohol
- Drinking excessively
- Using profanity and abusive language toward students
- Having a sex-change operation
- Stealing school property (even if it is returned later)
- Not living within their school district if that is listed as a condition of employment

On the other hand, courts have ruled that teachers should not be fired for:

- Smoking marijuana
- Private homosexual behavior
- Obesity (unless it inhibits teaching performance)
- Adultery
- Using vulgar language outside of school

Why are teachers dismissed in some cases and not in others? Often the standard courts use is whether the behavior under question reduces teacher effectiveness. Public behavior, or behavior that becomes public, may compromise a teacher's effectiveness. In such cases, the courts find terminating the teacher reasonable and legal. If the behavior remains private, if the teacher shows discretion, the teacher's "right to privacy" often prevails.

What lies ahead? Courts continue to draw the line between the private and public lives of teachers. Courts have disagreed on whether the following three situations constitute grounds for dismissal of a teacher. If you were the judge, how would you rule on:

- Unwed cohabitation?
- Unwed parenthood?
- Conviction for shoplifting?

Source: These examples have been adapted from Louis Fischer, David Schimmel, and Cynthia Kelly, *Teachers and the Law* (New York: Longman, 1991).

- Avoid telling jokes that some may find offensive or off-color. You should preview videotapes and other materials for profane, sexual, or otherwise potentially offensive language or images.
- Physical force often invites litigation. Involve other adults—security personnel, if possible—whenever physical restraint of a child is required.
- If a child is injured in class, seek immediate medical assistance. Write up precisely what occurred, and identify witnesses.
- Many attorneys believe that the best advice they can offer teachers is simply not to touch students under any circumstances.
- If you are charged with some violation, do not contact the accuser. Do not give interviews or respond to questions without having an attorney present (both the NEA and the AFT can provide guidance in this area). Writing down the specifics of the case can also be extremely helpful.
- Finally, remember that *not* acting can also target you for legal action. For example, failure to report suspected child abuse places you in legal jeopardy. If you suspect that a child has been the victim of abuse—at home or anywhere else—you are required to report your suspicions to the child

protective services, and often to your school district as well. Even if your suspicions are proved wrong, you are protected from potential lawsuits as long as your report has been made in good faith.

Worrying about how best to protect yourself from litigation is no fun. After all, many of us preparing to become teachers have a desire to reach out to students, to touch their lives and to make a positive difference in their futures. Yet lawyers advise us to use discretion in such cases and to draw clear boundaries. How and where to draw these boundaries is up to you.

Federal Acts Shaping Education

The federal government impacts schools not only through federal regulations and court decisions, as described previously, but also by passing legislation to promote specific educational programs and practices. If we were to resort to "pop" psychology, we might describe the federal government's education laws as a carrot-and-stick view of its place in schools. It uses carrots to entice and reward the creation of certain educational activities and a stick to punish or prohibit other practices. Its attempts to direct certain educational activities from behind the scenes have met with uneven success. In most instances, the federal government has maintained a low profile while quietly collaborating with the states to implement educational policies. Let us look at this carrot-and-stick approach as it is reflected in federal laws.

Even before the Constitution was ratified, under the old Articles of Confederation, the central government developed the notion of indirectly aiding education. Passed in 1785 and 1787, the Land Ordinance Act and the Northwest Ordinance provided a system for local funding of schools. Almost 100 years later, in 1862, the Morrill Land Grant College Act promoted the establishment of **land-grant colleges.** Although these were indirect means of influencing education, this action established three fundamental precedents of federal legal involvement in education:

1. The federal government can and will influence schooling.
2. The federal government, whenever possible, will work cooperatively with the states in educational matters.
3. The role of the federal government will be to provide a carrot—that is, a financial incentive—to encourage certain education activities.

This cooperative and indirect federal involvement in education eventually assumed another characteristic, *targeting funds*. The Smith-Hughes Act (1917) provided federal assistance to encourage specific curricular activities, including agriculture, industrial arts, and home economics. In 1958, targeted support reappeared with the passage of the National Defense Education Act (NDEA), which provided federal dollars to stimulate math, science, and foreign languages, a national response to the Soviet challenge represented by the launching of *Sputnik*. In 1965, with the passage of the Elementary and Secondary Education Act, special needs students were targeted. Low-income and educationally disadvantaged children were now provided with additional educational resources. The targeting of special populations continued with the passage of the 1975 Education for All Handicapped Children Act, now called *Individuals with Disabilities Education Act (PL 94-142),* which required states to ensure effective educational opportunities for children with disabilities.

This evolutionary development from the 1700s to today ensures that no educational issue is immune from federal influence. Although the conservative administration of the 1980s attempted to severely curtail the educational role of the federal government, that indirect yet influential role continues.

The following is a partial list of federal legislation indicating the long history of federal involvement, as well as the categorical or specific focus of federal interest in education.

1. *Land Ordinance Act* and *Northwest Ordinance* (1785 and 1787). These two ordinances provided for the establishment of public education in the territory between the Appalachian Mountains and the Mississippi River. In these new territories, 1 square mile out of every 36 was reserved for support of public education, and new states formed from these territories were encouraged to establish "schools and the means for education."

2. *Morrill Land Grant College Acts* (1862 and 1890). These acts established 69 institutions of higher education in the various states, some of which are among today's great state universities. These acts were also called simply the *Land-Grant College Acts,* since public land was donated to establish these colleges.

3. *Smith-Hughes Act* (1917). This act provided funds for teacher training and program development in vocational education at the high school level.

4. *Servicemen's Readjustment Act* (G.I. Bill of Rights, 1944). This act paid veterans' tuition and living expenses for a specific number of months, depending on the length of their military service.

5. *National Defense Education Act* (1958). In response to the Soviet launching of *Sputnik,* the NDEA provided substantial funds for a variety of educational activities, including student loans, the education of school counselors, and the strengthening of instructional programs in science, mathematics, and foreign languages.

6. *Elementary and Secondary Education Act* (1965). In this omnibus piece of education legislation, the federal government attempted to remedy educational inequities between states and communities. This law provided for financial assistance to school districts with low-income families, provided for funding to improve libraries and for instructional materials, promoted educational innovations and research, and provided for funds to improve the quality and services of state departments of education. In the 1970s this legislation was expanded to include funding for bilingual education, drug education, and school lunch and breakfast programs, as well as for the education of Native Americans.

7. *Project Head Start* (1964–1965). This act provides medical, social, nutritional, and educational services for children 3 to 6 years of age who come from low-income families.

8. *Bilingual Education Act* (1968). In response to the needs of the significant number of non-English-speaking students, Congress authorized funds to provide relevant instruction to these students. The primary focus was on Spanish-speaking students from Mexican, Puerto Rican, and Cuban backgrounds, almost 70 percent of whom were failing to graduate from high school. Although many other languages besides

Spanish are included in this act, a relatively small percentage of non-English-speaking students participate in these programs due to funding shortfalls.

9. *Title IX of the Education Amendments* (1972). This regulation prohibits discrimination on the basis of sex "under any education program or activity receiving federal funds." The regulation is quite comprehensive and protects the rights of both males and females from preschool through graduate school. Title IX prohibits sexual discrimination in sports, financial aid, employment, counseling, school regulations and policies, admissions, and other areas. Although Title IX has the potential for promoting sex equity, its enforcement has been lax, and many schools are currently in violation of one or more aspects of the regulation.

10. *Individuals with Disabilities Education Act* (1975). This act provides financial assistance to local school districts to provide free and appropriate education for the nation's 8 million children with disabilities who are between 3 and 21 years of age.

LEGAL LANDMARKS
Teachers' and Students' Rights

What rights do students and teachers have when they enter school? What rights do school authorities have? The judicial system has frequently been called upon to resolve these conflicting viewpoints. The following brief summaries highlight the critical cases that have defined the boundaries of civil rights and liberties in American schools. You may not agree with all the decisions, and the current, more conservative Supreme Court may modify some of these rulings. But for now, they are the law of the land.

Students' Rights
Freedom of Speech (Symbolic)

Tinker v. Des Moines Independent Community School District, 393 U.S. 503 (1969)

Facts: During the Vietnam War, three public school students attended classes wearing black arm bands as a form of protest against the war. The school authorities suspended the students until they agreed to return to school without the arm bands. The students brought suit, alleging that wearing the black arm bands is a form of speech protected under the First Amendment. The school authorities argued that the wearing of the arm bands could lead to a substantial and material disruption within the school and, thus, should be prohibited.

Holding: The Supreme Court ruled in favor of the students. Unless there is substantial disruption in the school caused by the wearing of the arm bands, the school board cannot deprive the students of their First Amendment right to freedom of speech. Students do not shed their constitutional rights at the school door.

(Box continues on next page.)

West Virginia State Board of Education v. Barnette, 319 U.S. 624 (1943)

Facts: A compulsory flag-salute statute in the public school regulations required all students and teachers to salute the U.S. flag every day. Two Jehovah's Witness students refused to salute the flag because doing so would be contrary to their religious beliefs. Consequently, they were not permitted to attend the public schools. The students sued, alleging that the compulsory flag salute was unconstitutional.

Holding: Students may not be compelled to pledge allegiance to the flag in public schools. Their right not to salute the flag is protected by the First Amendment. In so deciding, the Supreme Court overruled its own decision in *Minersville v. Gobitis* three years earlier. Today, compulsory flag salutes are unconstitutional.

Freedom of Speech (Verbal)

Bethel School District v. Fraser, 478 U.S. (1986)

Facts: A high school senior delivered a controversial speech during a school assembly; its purpose was to nominate fellow classmates for school office. The speech contained sexual innuendos but not profane language. The school authorities refused to allow the student to speak at graduation and suspended him for his "offensive" speech. The student's father sued the school authorities for depriving his son of his First Amendment right to freedom of speech.

Holding: The Supreme Court held in favor of the school authorities. To reach its holding, the Court balanced the student's freedom to advocate controversial ideas with the school's interests in setting the boundaries of socially appropriate behavior. The Court found that the First Amendment is not so broad as to prevent school authorities from disciplining students for speech that is lewd and offensive. The Court relied on previous case law recognizing society's interest in protecting minors from being exposed to offensive and vulgar speech.

Freedom of Press

Hazelwood School District v. Kuhlmeir, 108 S.Ct. 562 (1988)

Facts: Written by students as part of a journalism class, the high school newspaper, *Spectrum,* was sponsored and funded by the school. Two articles, one discussing the effect of divorce on teenage children, the other concerning teenage pregnancy, were deleted by the principal, who felt that they were inappropriate. The students who wrote these articles brought suit, alleging that the principal had violated their First Amendment right to freedom of speech (via the press).

Holding: The students lost their battle against the principal. The Supreme Court held that since *Spectrum* was school sponsored and funded and was part of the school's journalism class, the school principal had the right to control its content. Similar to the balancing test applied in *Bethel School District v. Fraser,* the school authorities' right to control the content of school curriculum took priority over the students' First Amendment rights.

Compare *Hazelwood* with *Burch v. Barker,* 861 F.2d 1149 (9th Cir. 1988), in which the Ninth Circuit Court of Appeals (a federal appellate court) held that school authorities may not censor student newspapers produced at the students' own expense and off school property. The court found that schools may not censor such newspapers because they are not part of any school's curriculum.

Freedom of Access to the Printed Word

Board of Education, Island Trees Union Free School District No. 26 v. Pico, 457 U.S. 853 (1982)

Facts: A school board decided to remove nine books from the school library because the members of the board felt the books were objectionable and improper for students. Students brought suit contending that the board's action had violated their First Amendment rights.

Holding: School boards lack the authority to remove books from a school library based solely on their feelings that the material contains bad or unpopular viewpoints. The Supreme Court ruled that school boards may not suppress ideas by removing books from the school library.

Freedom to Due Process

Goss v. Lopez, 419 U.S. 565 (1975)

Facts: Several high school students were disciplined by being suspended from school for 10 days. The students were not notified of the reason for suspension, nor were they given the opportunity for a hearing to explain their side. The principal's action was based on a state law that allowed such suspensions. The students brought suit, challenging the constitutionality of this state law.

Holding: The Supreme Court held that this law was unconstitutional. Before a principal can suspend a student, he or she must present the student with the charges. If the student denies the charges, the principal must provide detailed evidence. In addition, the principal must give the student a hearing, or an opportunity to present a defense against the charges. (These presuspension procedures do not apply in cases where the student poses a threat to people, property, or the academic program in the school.) The procedures mandated as a result of this decision can be compared to the "Miranda rights" mandated in criminal cases.

The *Goss* decision set forth the due process requirements for students suspended for up to 10 days. Schools may be required to establish even greater due process procedures than those mandated in *Goss* before suspending students for more than 10 days.

Ingraham v. Wright, 430 U.S. 651 (1977)

Facts: Two students were punished by being hit with a flat wooden paddle. The paddling caused one student to lose full use of his arm for a week and the other student to seek medical attention and remain absent from school for over a week. Although a Florida statute allowed corporal punishment, the students sued. They alleged that the paddling constituted cruel and unusual

(Box continues on next page.)

punishment, which is prohibited by the Eighth Amendment, and that they were deprived of their right to liberty guaranteed under the due process clause of the Fourteenth Amendment.

Holding: The students lost their battle against the school authorities. The Court held that corporal punishment, such as the paddling involved in this case, does not necessarily deprive the student of his or her right to due process under the Fourteenth Amendment. In addition, the Court explained that paddling does not fall under the definition of cruel and unusual punishment prohibited by the Eighth Amendment. The Court held that corporal punishment, subject to specific restrictions, is legal within the schools.

Teachers' Rights
Freedom of Association

Shelton v. Tucker, 364 U.S. 479 (1960)

Facts: A statute required all teachers in public schools to list all of the organizations they had belonged to or contributed to during the preceding 5 years. This requirement was mandatory as a condition of employment. Teachers brought suit, alleging that this statute was unconstitutional in that it interfered with their right of freedom of association.

Holding: The Court held in favor of the teachers. It said that teachers could *not* be required, as a condition of employment, to list all of the organizations they had belonged to or contributed to during the previous 5 years. The state has a right to request information relevant to its teachers' fitness and competence. However, this right is limited and does not include investigating membership in associations. The First Amendment, in particular the right to freedom of association, protects the teachers from overboard statutes such as the one in this case.

Keyishian v. Board of Regents, 385 U.S. 589 (1967)

Facts: Under New York State law, individuals were not allowed to teach in the New York school system if they were members of the Communist Party or members of any other party listed as subversive. These were referred to as *loyalty laws*. Many New York State teachers refused to declare openly whether or not they were members of these types of organizations. Consequently, they were fired from their positions as teachers. These teachers brought suit, alleging that the New York loyalty laws were unconstitutional.

Holding: The Court struck down the New York loyalty laws as unconstitutional. The teachers' right to freedom of association was protected by this decision. Political association alone could not constitute an adequate ground for denying employment.

Freedom of Speech

Pickering v. Board of Education, 391 U.S. 563 (1968)

Facts: A teacher wrote and sent to the newspaper a letter that criticized the school board. The letter included language criticizing the board's allocation of school funds between educational and athletic programs and the board's methods of informing taxpayers about the need for additional revenue. Most of the statements made in the letter were truthful; however, some were false. The false statements were not knowingly or recklessly made, but rather the result of incomplete research by the teacher. The teacher was fired by the school board for writing this letter and sending it to the newspaper. The teacher sued the school board, alleging that this dismissal was unconstitutional.

Holding: The teacher was successful in his suit against the school board. To reach its holding, the Supreme Court balanced the teacher's (and society's) First Amendment interests in discussing publicly issues of societal concern against the school's interests in providing educational services efficiently. The Court determined that the teacher's letter neither seriously damaged the disciplined operation of the school, nor disclosed confidential information, nor contained any misstatements that were made knowingly or recklessly. Under the First Amendment, a teacher has the same rights as all other citizens to comment on issues of legitimate public concern, such as a school board's decisions in allocating funds.

Separation of Church and State

Engel v. Vitale, 370 U.S. 421 (1962)

Facts: A local school board instructed that a prayer composed by the New York Board of Regents be recited aloud every day by each class. The prayer was nondenominational and voluntary. Students who did not want to recite the prayer were permitted to remain silent or leave the classroom while the prayer was said. Parents of the students sued, alleging that the state and the school district violated the **establishment clause** of the First Amendment by ordering the recitation of the prayer (that is, state involvement in support for religion).

Holding: Official, organized prayer in school is not permitted. The Supreme Court held that the New York statute authorizing the prayer in school violated the First Amendment, particularly the establishment clause.

Wallace v. Jaffree, 472 U.S. 38 (1985)

Facts: Alabama enacted a law that authorized a 1-minute period of silence in all public schools for meditation or voluntary prayer. A parent of a student in the public schools sued, alleging that this law violated the establishment clause of the First Amendment.

Holding: The Supreme Court held that the Alabama law violated the establishment clause. To determine whether the Alabama law was constitutional, the Court applied the tripart test established in 1971 in *Lemon v. Kurtzman,* 403 U.S. 602 (1971), for interpreting the First Amendment's establishment clause. Under *Lemon,* to avoid violating the establishment clause, a statute or government policy must: (1) have a secular purpose, (2) have a primarily secular effect, and (3) avoid excessive government entanglement with religion. In *Wallace,* the statute was found to have a religious rather than a secular purpose and was thus ruled unconstitutional, even though prayer was not required during the moment of silence.

(Box continues on next page.)

McCollum v. Board of Education, 333 U.S. 203 (1948)

Facts: An Illinois school district allowed privately employed religious teachers to hold weekly religious classes on public premises. Those students who chose not to attend these classes in religious instruction pursued their secular studies in other classrooms in the building. A local taxpayer brought suit, alleging that this program violated the establishment clause and was unconstitutional.

Holding: The Court ruled that a program allowing religious instruction inside public schools during the school day is unconstitutional because it violates the establishment clause.

Stone v. Graham, 449 U.S. 39 (1980)

Facts: A Kentucky statute required the posting of a copy of the Ten Commandments, purchased with private contributions, on the wall of each public classroom in the state. On the bottom of each of these posters, there was a statement in fine print explaining that the Ten Commandments are secular and are fundamental to the legal code of Western civilization and the common law of the United States.

Holding: Despite the fact that the copies of the Ten Commandments were purchased with private funds and had a notation describing them as secular, the statute requiring that they be posted in every public school classroom was declared unconstitutional. Under the three-part *Lemon* test, the Court concluded that the statute requiring posting of the Ten Commandments failed under part 1 of the test in that it lacked a secular purpose. Merely stating that the Ten Commandments are secular does not make them so.

Note: The section on legal landmarks was written by Nancy Gorenberg.

SUMMARY

1. As a teacher, it is important to be aware of your own legal rights and responsibilities as well as those of your students.

2. When applying for a teaching position in your local county, you should be aware of your rights. Under Title IX of the Education Amendments and Title VII of the Civil Rights Act, you do not have to answer questions an interviewer may ask that are unrelated to the job requirements, and you are also protected from words and behaviors that can be considered sexual harassment.

3. The general standard, resulting from court decisions, is that if a teacher's behavior or personal life does not disrupt or interfere with teaching effectiveness, he or she cannot be suspended or fired because of it.

4. Generally, courts hold that the teacher's right to academic freedom is not absolute and each case depends on its own unique facts.

5. When determining whether a teacher has been negligent in a situation, courts will judge whether a reasonable person with similar training would act in the same way and whether or not the teacher could have foreseen the possibility of injury. A teacher may be liable for misfeasance, nonfeasance, or malfeasance.

6. As stated by the Supreme Court in *Pickering v. Board of Education,* teachers are protected under the First Amendment to exercise freedom of speech and to publicly express themselves, unless their statements are malicious, intentionally inaccurate, disclose confidential material, or hamper teaching performance.

7. Teachers must be sure to comply with Public Law 94-553 when distributing copies of other people's works in the classroom, observing the three criteria of brevity, spontaneity, and cumulative effect.

8. Under the Buckley amendment (the Family Rights and Privacy Act), parents and guardians have the right to see their child's educational records. Upon reaching 18 years of age, the student is allowed to see the record, and he or she becomes responsible for providing permission for others to see it.

9. Under Title IX, students may not be discriminated against based on gender for awards, scholarships, or financial aid.

10. Students have constitutionally protected rights to due process before they can be disciplined or suspended from school. Although corporal punishment is rarely used, courts have upheld the school's authority to administer it as long as it is reasonable and not excessive.

11. In *Tinker v. Des Moines Independent Community School District,* students were successful in protecting their First Amendment right to freedom of speech. As long as students do not disrupt the operation of the school or deny other students the opportunity to learn, they have the right to freedom of speech within the schools.

12. Schools must be neutral with regard to religion. Thus school prayer is not permitted under the doctrine of separation of church and state.

13. Students, like teachers, have the right to freedom of the press. However, student publications can be censored if they are an integral part of the school curriculum, such as part of a course, or if they are obscene, psychologically damaging, or disruptive.

14. Teachers today are potential targets of litigation. Sexual harassment and child abuse charges can short-circuit the careers of even innocent teachers. Taking appropriate precautions to avoid even the appearance of impropriety is advised.

15. The federal government has had a significant impact on education. Important acts such as the Bilingual Education Act of 1968 and Title IX of the Education Amendments of 1972 have been created to help ensure both quality and equity in the provision of education.

DISCUSSION QUESTIONS AND ACTIVITIES

1. Assume that the federal government decides to increase its financial support of education from 6 percent to 30 percent. How will this affect:

- The operation of schools?
- The quality of education for different populations and different regions of the country?
- Federal influence on school practices?
- Educational financing policies?

2. Assume that the federal government decides to eliminate all financial support of education. How would that affect the areas listed in question 1?

3. If you were to suggest a federal law to improve education, what would that law be?

4. How have minority groups and females benefited from federal involvement in schools?

5. What are the relative advantages and disadvantages of (a) block grants and (b) categorical grants?

6. What are some supporting and opposing arguments for the following: "Teaching is not a job; it is a special responsibility. Working with impressionable minds, teachers must be held accountable for all their behaviors that influence children, both in the classroom and outside the classroom."

7. Distinguish between malfeasance, misfeasance, and nonfeasance. Give an example of each.

8. What are the legal factors you should keep in mind if you are about to discipline a student?

9. Define and evaluate the concept of "educational malpractice."

10. What kinds of questions is an employer prohibited from asking during an interview?

11. Outline the limits of academic freedom.

12. "The *Tinker* decision sent a strong message that students do not abandon their constitutional rights at the schoolhouse door." Do you agree or disagree with this statement? Support your position with specific examples.

13. The role of religion and prayer in schools has always been controversial. Offer some examples of how a school system should neither *encourage* nor *discourage* religious observance.

14. In each of the following cases, indicate if there are grounds for dismissing a teacher:

- Being homosexual
- Publicly criticizing the school system
- Hitting a student
- Photocopying material without permission
- Striking
- Carrying the HIV virus
- Reaching the age of 70
- Sexually harassing a student

15. Construct an argument to support the principle that students and their property should not be searched without the students' consent.

16. "The Buckley amendment increased the access to, but decreased the value of, student records." Explain.

NOTES

1. Julius Menacker and Ernest Pascarella, "How Aware Are Educators of Supreme Court Decisions That Affect Them?" *Phi Delta Kappan* 64, no. 6 (February 1983): 424–426.

2. Louis Fischer and David Schimmel, *The Civil Rights of Teachers* (New York: Harper & Row, 1973).

3. The legal situations and interpretations included in this text are adapted from a variety of sources, including Myra Sadker and David Sadker, *Sex Equity Handbook for Schools* (New York: Longman, 1982); Fischer and Schimmel, *The Civil Rights of*

Teachers; and *Your Legal Rights and Responsibilities: A Guide for Public School Students* (Washington, DC: U.S. Department of Health, Education and Welfare, n.d.).

4. Sadker and Sadker, *Sex Equity Handbook for Schools.*

5. Richard Carelli, "Top Court Says Sexually Harassed Students May Sue Schools," Associated Press, February 26, 1992; Greg Henderson, "Court Says Compensatory Damages Available Under Title IX," UPI, February 26, 1992.

6. *Thompson v. Southwest School District,* 483 F. Supp. 1170 (W.D.M.W. 1980). See also *Board of Trustees v. Stubblefield,* 94 Cal. Rptr. 318, 321 [1971]; *Morrison v. State Board of Education,* 461 P. 2d 375 [1969]; *Pettit v. State Board of Education,* 513 P. 2d 889 [Cal. 1973]; *Blodgett v. Board of Trustees, Tamalpais Union High School District,* 97 Cal. Rptr. 406 (1970); Fernand Dutile, *Sex, Schools and the Law* (Springfield, OH: Charles Thomas, 1986).

7. *Kingsville Independent School District v. Cooper,* 611 F. 2d 1109 (5th Cir. 1980); *Parducci v. Rutland,* 316 F. Supp. 352 (M.D. Ala. 1979); *Brubaker v. Board of Education, School District 149, Cook County, Illinois,* 502 F. 2d 973 (7th Cir. 1974). See also Martha McCarthy and Nelda Cambron, *Public School Law: Teachers' and Students' Rights* (Boston: Allyn & Bacon, 1981).

8. *Pickering v. Board of Education of Township High School District 205, Will County,* 391 U.S. 563 (1968); *Givhan v. Western Line Consolidated School District,* 439 U.S. 410 (1979). See also Robert Monks and Ernest Proulx, *Legal Basis for Teachers* (Bloomington: Phi Delta Kappa Educational Foundation, 1986).

9. Miriam R. Krasno, "Copyright and You," *Update,* Winter 1983; Thomas J. Flygare, "Photocopying and Videotaping for Educational Purposes: The Doctrine of Fair Use," *Phi Delta Kappan* 65, no. 8 (April 1984).

10. Leroy Peterson, Richard A. Rossmiller, and Marlin M. Volz, *The Law and Public School Operation,* 2d ed. (New York: Harper & Row, 1978), pp. 132–134. See also Michael La Morte, *School Law: Cases and Concepts* (Englewood Cliffs, NJ: Prentice-Hall, 1987).

11. E. Gordon Gee and David J. Sperry, *Education Law and the Public Schools: A Compendium* (Boston: Allyn & Bacon, 1978). See also Louis Fischer, David Schimmel, and Cynthia Kelly, *Teachers and the Law* (New York: Longman, 1991).

12. Sadker and Sadker, *Sex Equity Handbook for Schools.* See also Fernand Dutile, *Sex, Schools and the Law* (Springfield, OH: Charles Thomas, 1986).

13. *Goss v. Lopez,* 419 U.S. 565 (1975); *Wood v. Strickland,* 420 U.S. 308 (1975); *Ingraham v. Wright,* 430 U.S. 651 (1977).

14. *Tinker v. Des Moines Independent Community School District,* 393 U.S. 503 (1969).

15. *Bethel School District No. 403 v. Fraser,* 478 U.S. 675 (1986).

16. *Engel v. Vitale,* 370 U.S. 421 (1962); *School District of Abington Township v. Schempp* and *Murray v. Curlett,* 373 U.S. 203 (1963).

17. *Bellnier v. Lund,* 438 F. Supp. 47 (N.Y. 1977); *Doe v. Renfrou,* 635 F.2d 582 (7th Cir. 1980), *cert. denied,* 101 S.Ct. 3015 (1981).

18. *Hazelwood School District v. Kuhlmeier,* 108 S.Ct. 562 (1988); *Shanley v. Northeast Independent School District,* 462 F.2d 960 (5th Cir. 1972); *Gambino v. Fairfax County School Board,* 564 F.2d 157 (4th Cir. 1977).

19. Fischer, Schimmel, and Kelly, *Teachers and the Law.*

20. Joel Spring, *American Education* (New York: McGraw-Hill, 1996), p. 276.

21. Millicent Lawson, "False Accusations Turn Dream into Nightmare in Chicago," *Education Week,* August 2, 1994, p. 16; Louis Harris and Associates Poll, *Hostile Hallways* (Washington, DC: American Association of University Women, 1993).

22. Mike Rose, "Legal Minefields," *American Teacher* 79, no. 4 (December 1994/January 1995): 12–13.

FINANCING AMERICA'S SCHOOLS

*D*uring the 1980s, educational attention in the United States focused on reform. How could we improve our schools? What new methods, tests, or school organizations would raise student achievement scores? The decade of the 1990s has focused more on the cost of education reform. From coast to coast, school districts and states faced monumental financial challenges. Where would they find dollars to support not only reform but ongoing educational needs? And how would they spend these dollars fairly in poor as well as wealthy districts? Finding the funds and distributing them equitably was near the top of the 1990s educational agenda.

This chapter is designed to give you an understanding of how state and local governments work together in raising and distributing over 90 percent of the funds supporting the nation's schools. Also included are reviews of public resistance to paying for the cost of education and the impact of that resistance on your life in the classroom.

The courts have also entered the picture through their efforts (1) to ensure that students attending schools in poor districts receive as effective an education as students who attend schools in wealthy districts and (2) to *decide whether public funds can be used to support private education. The recent controversy surrounding educational vouchers and school choice programs will also be explored. Finally, the chapter will discuss possible future trends in educational finance.*

State Funding for Schools: A View from the Governor's Office

In an annual poll of perceived problems facing public schools, "lack of discipline" was cited as the top concern in the early 1980s and "use of drugs" ranked highest from the mid-1980s through the early 1990s. But by 1992, a third issue surpassed these ongoing concerns: "Lack of financial support" was cited most frequently as the major issue facing public schools. Consider the following—a fictitious scenario but one that presents a very real dilemma: The lights burned late in the governor's office as she tried again and again to fit the pieces together. There was no denying that the schools needed more money. From computers to vocational education to teacher salaries, significant increases in school funding could no longer be delayed. But where would these funds be found?

She turned to her administrative assistant, Harriet Schukel. They had been together for almost 20 years. In that time they had overcome numerous obstacles. Certainly school finance could be mastered.

"Harriet," the governor said, "where will we find those dollars for the schools?"

"Probably the simplest way would be to hike the sales tax. Even a 1 percent hike would raise millions of dollars."

Sales Tax

The governor thought that increasing the sales tax was not an unattractive option. The business community would simply add an extra 1 percent charge to all sales, and the state would receive the money. The state would not have to create any special fundraising system or hire additional employees. Consumers would pay a few extra pennies for small purchases or a few extra dollars for large purchases, and the money would go from the sale directly to the state treasury. There was a lot of appeal for the governor in this not too painful system. After all, more than 40 states had a sales tax, usually between 2 percent and 8 percent, and these funds accounted for 30 percent of the typical state's income.[1] Increasing the state's sales tax would be a reasonable, proven, and widely used system for increasing state revenues for education.

The governor's train of thought was broken by Harriet's voice. As she focused on her aide's comments, she realized that there were problems.

"Governor," Harriet continued, "we need to nurture business in this state. The sales tax could kill your economic revitalization program."

The governor turned her attention to the problems posed by increasing the sales tax.

The current sales tax was already fairly high, and increasing it by just 1 percent would add to the cost of almost everything sold in the state (food and medical items were exempted). With higher costs, the business community might lose sales to neighboring states, thus stifling the state's economic growth. Moreover, poor families living a marginal economic existence would be particularly

The governor, working with the state legislature, is responsible for providing direction and financing for the state's schools.

hurt by a higher sales tax, and the governor's margin of victory in the last election had come from these poorer families.

There was also the gamble with the national economy to which the various states were inevitably linked. If the national economy continued to be healthy, then state sales and sales taxes would almost certainly grow. But what if the predictions of a national recession proved to be accurate? A higher sales tax on fewer sales would not raise more funds at all. In fact, a bad recession would reduce revenues despite the higher sales tax. Perhaps an additional sales tax was not as attractive as it had first appeared. The governor turned to her aide.

"What are our other options?"

"The best is the personal income tax. It's probably the fairest."

Personal Income Tax

Increasing the state's personal income tax was well worth considering. All but nine states use a personal income tax to raise funds totaling more than 25 percent of state revenues.[2] Again, the governor was attracted to the simplicity of this plan. Like the federal income tax, the personal income tax was collected through payroll deductions, even before a worker received his or her paycheck. Increasing the state income tax would simply increase the size of the deductions, and more money would be available for education. And Harriet was right: This approach would also be relatively fair. The tax was based on a taxpayer's ability to pay. Individuals with a high income paid a higher amount, and those less able to pay, although taxed at the same percentage, were taxed on their lower income and paid fewer dollars in tax. One of the governor's concerns was to ensure that whatever new funds were raised were raised equitably, and she appreciated the equity built into the income tax. In fact, the state income tax rules already recognized the special circumstances of some of the state's taxpayers and made provisions for dependents, the disabled, and those with high medical bills and other special needs.

As usual, however, Harriet was quick to point out the problems: "Naturally, there is a downside to increasing the state income tax. Some of our wealthy citizens are not paying their fair share now; their accountants always manage to find tax loopholes. In fact, a good many manage to evade both the federal and state income tax completely. And like the sales tax, if the economy sours and people's income drops, the increased income tax might result in no additional income."

After discussing the pros and cons of a tax increase, the governor decided to explore other options as well.

"Harriet, let's look beyond the traditional, tried-and-true systems used by most states. Are there any other revenue sources that we can tap—anything new?"

"Well, governor, we could institute a state lottery. That's popular all across the country. Here's someone who would support a lottery."

State Lottery

Harriet gave the governor a copy of the day's newspaper containing the following headline: "Unemployed Worker Wins Million Dollar Lottery." The story described the good fortune of a Maryland man who bought a $1 lottery ticket and became an instant millionaire. Perhaps a state lottery would do the trick. Many states had already established lotteries, an activity some called a form of legalized gambling. Individuals bought a lottery ticket, usually for a dollar, and chose a series of numbers (or allowed a computer to select a series of numbers). If those numbers were selected, the lucky ticket holder could win an amount ranging from a few dollars to millions. Although some groups opposed lotteries as immoral gambling, there was a growing acceptance of this approach as a relatively painless and voluntary method of raising funds for education. After the winners collected their millions in prize money, there would still be enormous profits remaining, profits which could be spent on education and other state needs.

Roughly two-thirds of the states now have lotteries, and nearly half of those claim to dedicate at least a portion of the revenues to education. In reality, however, most states use lottery revenues to fund, not supplement, parts of an established education budget.[3] Even if the lottery were structured to enhance educational resources, other social needs within the state would likely compete for the funding as well. The governor concluded that a lottery would be unlikely to provide significant additional long-range funding.

The governor was running out of options and began to review a potpourri of other tax sources.

Other Taxes

Rather than increase the sales tax or the personal income tax, or institute a lottery, the governor considered a series of small, targeted taxes in several different areas. Raising the state tax on tobacco, gasoline, and liquor (generally called *excise taxes*) might work. The excise tax on gasoline alone accounted for approximately 9 percent of all state revenues (but these funds usually went for highway construction, not education). A tax on tobacco and alcohol (sometimes called a "sin" tax) could be implemented. At least one state relied almost exclusively on the sin tax to support education. But its schools were critically underfinanced. A tax on the state's mineral wealth (*severance tax*) would help raise some funds. So would an increase in the motor vehicle license fee (*car registration*). Increasing estate or gift taxes was yet another possibility. But increasing many of these taxes would affect some citizens a lot more than others, and might adversely affect business. Excise tax, sin tax, severance tax—the list seemed endless.

The governor glanced at her watch: Two-thirty in the morning. She began to question Harriet, but Harriet had closed her eyes 5 minutes earlier. The governor reviewed her four options, the fundraising strategies used in most states:

1. Sales tax
2. Personal income tax
3. State lottery
4. Tax package (excise, severance, sin tax, and so on)

The governor decided to postpone her decision one more day, to sleep on this problem until her morning cabinet meeting and then to solicit the advice of her staff.

If you were on her staff, which options would you recommend? Could you devise an entirely new scheme to raise funds for the state's underfinanced schools?

Wealthy versus Poor States

As John F. Kennedy once remarked, "Life is unfair." Although Kennedy was talking about the draft, his observation applies to education as well. The most important educational decision we make may not be where to go to college but rather where to be born. In short, our most critical educational decision is out of our hands. Some communities and states take pride in their excellent schools, while others lament the low quality of their educational efforts. In a sense, the struggle to improve U.S. education is a struggle to reduce the inequity of geography. In this chapter, we shall discuss the importance of both state and local communities in funding and shaping education. But, since we began in the governor's office, let's continue with differences among the states.

State wealth shapes education. A state with a relatively wealthy citizenry can spend quite a bit on education and still have money for other things. Because its citizens have relatively high incomes, a wealthy state can tax these large incomes at a lower rate and still receive a great deal of income.

Conversely, a state in which more people have lower incomes has a much tougher road to travel. Poorer states may impose higher tax rates and still end up with fewer dollars for education. For example, in a wealthy state where the average income is $25,000, a 3 percent education tax would provide $750 per income to spend on schools. But in a poor state where the average income is only $11,000, the same 3 percent tax would provide only $330 per income for schools—$420 less per income than the rich state obtained. Even if the poorer state doubled the tax rate to 6 percent, only $660 (still $90 less per

FIGURE 12.1
**Per Pupil Expenditures
in Public Schools,
1991–1992**

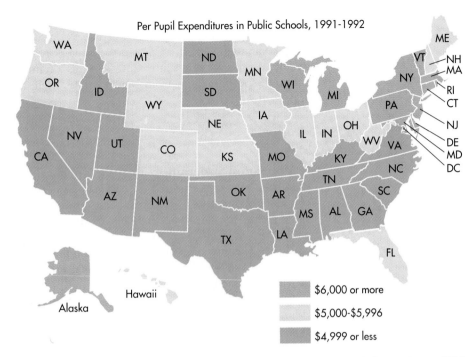

Per Pupil Expenditures in Public Schools, 1991-1992

$6,000 or more

$5,000–$5,996

$4,999 or less

Source: U.S. Department of Education, National Center for Education Statistics, *Digest of Education Statistics* 1994.

income) would be brought in. And many poorer states are unable or unwilling to increase their taxes substantially.

While wealth affects a state's ability to pay for education, how it chooses to raise funds is also important. A state that has a wide array of taxes is in a better, more stable position than a state that relies heavily on just one or two funding sources. If these few sources of funds run into hard times, the state's education program suffers. For example, Delaware, New Hampshire, Oregon, and Montana have no sales tax, while other states do not tax individual incomes or corporations. These states become more vulnerable to economic downturns than do states relying on numerous and varied funding sources.

As we will see later in this chapter, a great deal of attention—and court action—has been given to equalizing economic differences *within* a state. Since education is a state rather than a federal responsibility, the courts have had little to say about educational differences *between* the states. Yet these differences are real (see Figure 12.1). Students cannot choose where to be born or, typically, where to attend school, but as a teacher you can choose where to work. As you decide, you may find yourself thinking about the wealth and stability of the taxing system in various states.

**State Programs
to Fund Local
School Districts**

In the past decade, a number of states have initiated efforts to improve **school financing.** Like the governor in the previous scenario, state officials must devise and implement strategies to raise funds for schools. As difficult as that task may be, it is only part of the challenge. Once the funds are secured, decisions need to be made as to how best to distribute state funds to local school districts. During the first half of this century, states used a rather simplistic formula that awarded funds to local districts based on how many students were enrolled, or teachers employed, or classrooms in operation (a "flat grant" to local communities). Later, state policymakers realized that local needs differed widely, as did local wealth. New systems of financial aid were created, and although specifics differ from state to state, there are similarities in the general approaches used.

Foundation Programs

A **foundation program** establishes a minimal level, or "foundation," to be spent by each school district on each student. The state requires that each local community establish a certain tax rate and spend a certain amount for each student. Just as states vary in their ability to pay for education, local communities vary as well. The foundation program ensures that, regardless of the wealth or poverty of an individual community, the state will provide the necessary funds to see that at least a minimal level of educational services will be provided to each student in the state.

The foundation-level program is the most popular state approach in providing state aid, and more than 20 states currently use some variation of this model. The plan not only guarantees a minimum level of educational services (measured in per-student expenditures, or teacher-student ratio, or minimum teacher salaries) but also includes the idea of taxpayer equity. Each jurisdiction is required to tax at some minimal rate (the state will not fund a local education budget entirely). Clearly, in a wealthy district a tax of 2 percent would raise more funds than the same 2 percent tax in a poor district. The foundation plan requires that the same minimum tax be levied in all districts throughout the state, with the state providing the difference to ensure that minimum monies are provided for education.

Although the foundation program promises equity to both taxpayers and children, the promise is not fully kept. The foundation for minimum educational expenditures established by the states is frequently far below actual expenditures. For instance, a state might establish a foundation level of $1,500 per student. But if the average expenditure per pupil is actually $3,000, no equalization would occur, since the foundation is so low. In addition, the foundation level usually does not respond to the higher educational costs required for some students, including vocational and special education students. Coupled with other problems, the popular foundation program of distributing aid has been abandoned by some states.

Guaranteed Tax Base

Some states distribute aid by matching local tax revenues, not on a dollar-for-dollar basis, but at a fluctuating rate. Under this guaranteed tax base plan, the state adds to the tax dollars raised at the local level, the poorer communities receiving state funds at a higher rate than the wealthy ones. Local districts use these state funds in their regular educational budgets. Since more funds are provided to poorer districts, the impact of the guaranteed tax base approach is to raise the educational budgets of school systems, especially poorer ones. Because poorer districts receive a greater percentage of their tax rate in matching state funds, they are able to work with an education budget that is fairly

Bonds Build Schools

Did you ever enter a school that was in such disrepair the memory lingered long after you left? You know what those schools look like: floors worn out, walls defaced and pockmarked, poor lighting, broken lockers, and bathroom graffiti that would keep a psychologist busy for years. Some of the desks and fixtures in such schools are actually sold (for a very nice price, mind you) as antiques. These schools should have been torn down years ago, but the money to renovate or, better yet, replace them simply was not there. A new school might cost $10, $15, or even $20 million, quite a burden for local and state taxes. The money to support this one-time major building project usually comes from the sale of bonds. For many communities, **school bonds** build schools.

Here is how it works: Rather than attempt to raise $20 million in 1 year, a very difficult task, communities sell bonds. This gives them 15 or 20 years to pay off the construction costs, because the bonds mature or come due in that time. Each year the community pays off interest to the bond holders and puts some additional money away to pay back the bond when it is due.

If you bought a school construction bond, you would do very well economically. Your interest would be tax-free (government bonds are not taxed). So you would end up with more money than you would get from interest on a savings bank account, because savings interest is taxed. After 15 or 20 years you get all your original money back.

equal to that of a typical or average school district. Unlike the foundation plan, this approach does not specify a maximum level of state spending. The guaranteed tax base enables local communities to use state funds as if they were their own.

Foundation–Tax Rate Combination

Other states combine these two programs by providing a guaranteed tax base on top of a foundation program. By combining these two approaches, states ensure both a minimum educational spending level and a minimum tax level. Local districts are provided with autonomy in deciding how to spend their funds, and poorer school districts continue to receive more state assistance than wealthier ones.

In addition to these basic funding plans, it is worth noting the changing role of states in financing education. While states contributed less than 17 percent of the total cost in 1919,[4] today their average contribution generally exceeds that of local governments (see Figures 12.2 and 12.3). This increase in state support has been driven by the more costly needs of special student populations and by demands for more equitable funding among local communities.

Local Funding and the Property Tax

The sources of state revenues—from sales taxes to income taxes—have already been discussed, but we have not yet identified the sources of local education funding. Traditionally, local communities have provided most of the money for education, and although the state share of education has been growing, local communities still provide nearly half the cost of education. A discussion about local funding of education is in fact a discussion about property tax.

More than 90 percent of local revenues provided for education are derived from property taxes. Individuals who own property (usually real estate such as homes and businesses, but also personal property such as automobiles) are

FIGURE 12.2
Sources of Revenue for Public Elementary and Secondary Schools, 1970–1971 to 1991–1992

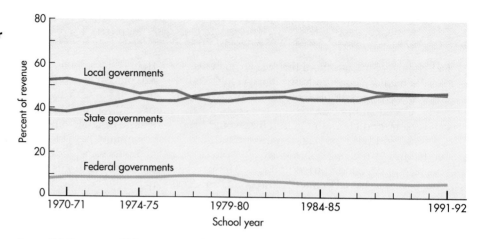

Source: U.S. Department of Education, National Center for Education Statistics, *Statistics of State School Systems; Revenues and Expenditures for Public Elementary and Secondary Education;* and Common Core of Data surveys.

FIGURE 12.3
Sources of Educational Funds for a Typical School District

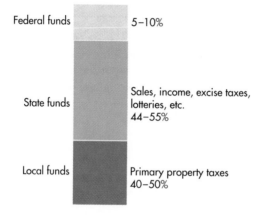

taxed each year. Taxing a certain percentage of the estimated value of a home, for example, typically provides from several hundred to several thousand dollars a year to the local community, with most of these funds going to education. Dating from colonial times, property tax is based on an agrarian economy in which the measure of one's wealth is equated directly with real estate.

This is no longer the case. Although many people still own real estate, it is no longer the single measure of wealth. Yet local communities continue to rely on property taxes to raise revenues. Inequities, confrontations, and protests have been the result. Consider the following grievances raised at Anytown's annual meeting:

Joe Adams: I've lived in this town for 40 years. I paid off my mortgage a decade ago and I haven't had a child in the schools for almost 20 years. I'm tired of paying over $2,000 a year to schools I don't use. And my retirement check isn't getting any bigger!

Claire Vitalis: The property tax is killing the downtown. Businesses are folding. If they invest money and improve their buildings, their property taxes go sky high and they will go bankrupt. This tax is killing any chance for economic revitalization.

Harry Hopkins: The Mega Company has decided to locate its new plant elsewhere. They said that the property tax rates were too high. That's not going to help our unemployment problem.

Thelma Ridgely: I'm concerned about the assessment of my house. The house right across the street is the exact same model. It's assessed by the county at $185,000. My house is assessed at $235,000. Why is my house valued at $50,000 more than the exact same house across the street? I'm paying more property taxes because some bureaucrat thinks my house is worth more than my neighbor's.

Sam Mallory: Why are we home owners bearing this burden? There must be other ways of raising money without sticking it to us.

Diane Carmody: Every 2 or 3 years my property tax is reassessed and I pay more taxes. But we are not educating more students. And test scores aren't going up. Why are taxes going up?

The property tax approach has many problems. It is an inequitable system that treats the citizens of a community differently, sometimes without apparent rhyme or reason. Home owners without children may pay much higher taxes than families with many children who rent their residence. Renovation and rehabilitation of homes and businesses are discouraged because of the prospect of much higher taxes. In some communities, it is even difficult to collect property taxes. Certainly one of the worst characteristics of the property tax is visibility. Unlike the state sales tax, lotteries, or other tax schemes, the property tax does not quietly nibble at people's income. It is a major and very visible tax and, as such, a major target.

Meetings, such as the fictional Anytown get-together, helped to fuel the taxpayer revolt of the late 1970s. Prompted by passage of Proposition 13 in California, more than 20 other states have imposed similar limits on property taxes and spending. These limits caused early school closings, a deterioration

Steadily increasing property taxes have led to taxpayer revolts in states like California, Texas, and Massachusetts where voters passed propositions limiting such taxes.

of school buildings, shortage of supplies, and teacher layoffs and continue to place significant constraints on school funding levels.

As we have discussed, most states require a minimum property tax for local communities to qualify for state aid. Most local communities find it necessary to tax beyond this minimum rate to raise enough funds for schools and other local services. The tax revolt has made voter approval of these higher local taxes far less likely. However, recent polls suggest that a new popular sentiment is on the rise. More taxpayers are voicing their support for better schools through higher taxes. These two currents are colliding in local communities across the nation.

A Tale of Two Cities

Just as the state economies vary in their ability to finance education, economic differences also exist within states, for all states have relatively wealthy and relatively poor communities. Helpful as state aid is, local discrepancies persist. In wealthy school districts, per-pupil expenditures may be two to four times greater than in poor districts. Because the amount of wealth in a community may affect the quality of education, the issue has attracted the interest of state and federal courts.

In 1968, in a poor Latino section of San Antonio called Edgewood, a 48-year-old sheetmetal worker named Demetrio Rodriquez looked with despair at the school his children attended. Not only did Edgewood Elementary School lack adequate books and air conditioning, the top two floors were condemned and almost half the teachers were not certified.[5] Yet 10 minutes away in affluent Alamo Heights, children learned in comfortable surroundings with ample materials. In Alamo Heights, all children were taught by certified teachers. The educational cards were stacked against Rodriquez and his neighbors because the methods of financing schools are stacked against poorer communities.

It was not that Edgewood residents were not taxed heavily. In fact, they paid one of the highest tax rates on their property of any Texas community. The problem was that the property itself was not worth much; so paying a high rate on poor property did not provide much money for education. Edgewood raised only $37 per student; Alamo Heights raised $412 per student.

And herein lies the tale of two cities: the challenge of how to fund U.S. schools fairly. Property taxes in wealthy communities produce wealthy schools. Taxes on poor property produce schools like Edgewood Elementary School. So Rodriquez went to court.

On March 21, 1973, the Supreme Court, in a hotly contested 5-to-4 decision, ruled against Rodriquez, claiming that education was not a "fundamental right" under the U.S. Constitution. So the inequities continued. By the mid-1980s, when Edgewood had neither typewriters nor a playground, affluent Alamo Heights had modern computers and a swimming pool. These two schools mirrored the continuing inequity throughout Texas where, in the 1980s, the 100 wealthiest districts were averaging $7,233 per student, while the 100 poorest were averaging $2,978. In fact, from poorest to richest, the range was $2,112 to $19,333 per student. The educational spending gap was an economic chasm.

In the *Rodriquez* case, the U.S. Supreme Court decided that although the local property tax might violate state constitutions, it did not violate the U.S. Constitution. The vote was close (5 to 4), and the Supreme Court may eventually reverse itself—a reversal that would impact even more state governments. One thing is certain: A number of justices made it clear that educational funding through the property tax is a seriously flawed system. Justice

Potter Stewart stated that "the method of financing public schools . . . can be fairly described as chaotic and unjust." Justice Thurgood Marshall, dissenting from the majority opinion, charged that the decision "is a retreat from our historic commitment to equality of educational opportunity." For better or worse, the Court ruled that educational reform would have to occur—if it was to occur at all—at the state level.

While the Supreme Court did not find this economic chasm a violation of the Constitution, on October 2, 1989, in *Edgewood v. Kirby,* the Texas supreme court justices agreed unanimously that such differences violated the Texas constitution.

Because of the vast differences in the property values of different communities, school taxes based on property values have resulted in widely differing school funding between communities. To equalize local school expenditures across communities, many states are now assuming primary responsibility for school funding.

The differences between Alamo Heights and Edgewood are representative of differences throughout the nation. In fact, these differences had been brought to the attention of the state courts in California several years earlier. In California, the two communities were poor Baldwin Park and wealthy Beverly Hills (even before it became the subject of a popular television series). Almost 30 years ago, Beverly Hills was spending $1,232 per student, and Baldwin Park only $577. Once again the reason for these differences was to be found in the value of property. Beverly Hills is where the rich and famous buy big and expensive homes, and designer fashion shops line the streets of Rodeo Drive. All this meant Beverly Hills had well-funded schools, and Baldwin Park did not.

In August 1971, the California supreme court, in a 6-to-1 decision, found that heavy reliance on the local property tax "makes the quality of a child's education a function of the wealth of his parents and neighbors." The court went on to state: "Districts with small tax bases simply cannot levy taxes at a rate sufficient to produce the revenue that more affluent districts produce with a minimum effort." This landmark decision was known as *Serrano v. Priest*.

The *Serrano* decision in California, the *Edgewood* decision in Texas, and similar decisions in other state courts have put the responsibility on the states to equalize local educational expenditures. No easy task. While Americans are philosophically for educational equality, in practical terms many become upset when they see their tax dollars spent outside their local communities. The economic recession of the late 1980s also made equity a difficult challenge. For example, by the late 1980s, California had equalized per-pupil expenditures in 96 percent of its school districts.[6] But because of the limits placed on raising funds under Proposition 13, California dropped dramatically in per-pupil expenditures compared to other states—from near the top to near the bottom. In addition, the state has taken responsibility for 60 percent of school funding, a greater financial burden than many other states have assumed, but an acceptance of economic responsibility that other states may soon need to emulate. Equalizing local expenditures may require ever-increasing state involvement, especially since the federal government's support is at best unreliable and meager.

Inequalities: Savage and Other

Few things in life seem as bland, colorless, and uninspiring as finances, tax rates, and school budgets. It is easy to forget that behind these numbers are people whose lives are shaped, and sometimes destroyed, by the impact of educational funding.

Jonathan Kozol is not one to forget. In his best-selling book, *Savage Inequalities* (1991), Kozol describes the impact of funding differences through his eyewitness accounts of life in poor schools from East St. Louis to the Bronx.[7] The differences between the haves and have-nots are enormous. For example, the science labs in East St. Louis schools are 40 years out of date. The physics lab has six work areas, each with its own hole where pipes had once carried water. The average temperature in the lab is 100 degrees, because the school's heating system tends to roast that side of the building—while simultaneously freezing the other half of the school. At Morris High School in the South Bronx, the blackboards are so badly cracked that students are told not to use them for fear they will cut themselves. Plaster and paint chips fall from the ceiling with such regularity that students shower after school to wash the paint out of their hair. In the band room, chairs are positioned to avoid falling acoustical tiles. When it rains, water cascades down a staircase located just under a hole in the ceiling.

Kozol writes of schools in poor neighborhoods that have no computers and would gladly settle for used typewriters. Schools report a chronic lack of textbooks. Some students go for part, most, or all of the year without a book. Others attend classes so overcrowded that students get desks only when enough other students are absent.

The teachers who tough it out in these schools often demonstrate a commitment too often overlooked. One teacher in East St. Louis gave up law school to teach in the toughest situation he could find. After 30 years, his salary is only $38,000, $10,000 to $20,000 less than he would be earning in the suburbs. Another committed teacher sees her dilapidated school as a destructive force, an inanimate object that actively keeps kids from learning.

The heart of these savage inequalities, according to Kozol, is the economic gap between poor and rich communities in the United States. For example, all the property in Camden, New Jersey—all of the property wealth in the entire community—is valued at $250 million. That is less than the value of one casino in Atlantic City. When those levels of economic disparities live side by side in the United States, children go without textbooks—and worse.

Kozol documents not only how little these schools receive but how much they need. Students attend these schools for months with untreated toothaches. On Fridays, they fill their pockets with chicken nuggets from the school cafeteria to carry them through the hungry weekend. And for most, the conclusion of school is not a formal graduation, a commencement, a beginning, but a withering away, a quiet departure. Of the 1,400 students who make it to Wilson High School in Camden (some drop out before they ever reach Wilson), only 600 stay for graduation, and only 60 take the Scholastic Assessment Tests (SATs). According to Kozol, in New York City, only one in four African-American students and only one in five Latino students graduate from high school. The nation's failure to fairly fund its schools goes beyond court cases and tax rates; it represents an ongoing human tragedy.

By the mid-1990s, more than 40 states were facing legal challenges to their school finance systems.[8] These legal cases have led to "Robin Hood laws"—so named because courts have been redistributing wealth *a la* the hero of Sherwood Forest, by taking from the rich and giving to the poor. New Jersey is a case in point. In Camden, New Jersey, the poor district that attracted so much of Kozol's interest, court action has led to an $80-million increase in state aid. These funds were taken from more affluent districts, like Cherry Hill. With these redistributed state funds, Camden has established afterschool homework centers, provided free tutoring, purchased computers, updated science labs, created parent education and teacher training programs, purchased new textbooks, and begun to develop a new curriculum.[9] Yet Cherry Hill and other wealthy school districts were still able to spend thousands of dollars more on each student's education than could Camden. Robin Hood was creating change, but not equality. While some critics believe that Robin Hood laws go too far, others believe that they do not go far enough.

A growing number of state courts have taken up this challenge and now consider not only *financial input,* but *educational outcome* as well. Believing that financial reform in itself is not enough to ensure equal educational opportunities, these courts have adopted a more active role in order to promote educational changes. State courts in Massachusetts, Montana, Texas, and Kentucky have gone beyond the economics of schooling, to schooling itself. In Kentucky, for example, the court ruled that the state's "entire system of common schools was infirm." Concerned with the differences in funding in the richest versus the poorest districts, the court invalidated the method for funding schools; concerned with differences in test scores between rich and poor districts, the court threw out the state's education laws and regulations. The court defined an "efficient" educational system as one that provides students with oral and written communications skills; knowledge of economics, history, and social systems; and sufficient preparation for academic and career success. As a result, the state legislature enacted the Kentucky Education Reform Act in 1990, funding this court-inspired reform by increasing state income taxes. Kentucky schools underwent radical changes: Rewards were tied to school performance; preschool programs for marginal students were initiated; statewide performance tests were developed, as was a new curriculum; and of course, great disparities in per-pupil expenditures were eliminated. Like the Kentucky court, in the years ahead other state courts may pursue fundamental changes not only in school finances, but in school practices as well.[10]

In times of economic retrenchment and budget balancing, funding educational reform poses a serious challenge. Recruiting talented teachers, promoting them along the career ladder, increasing teacher salaries, purchasing computers, redesigning curricula, reducing class size—these reforms cost money, and require the goodwill and financial support of the American people. But not everyone agrees with the wisdom of spending more money on schools. Some critics argue that dollars do not make that much difference, and that the quality of education is not directly related to the size of the school budget. They point out that although per-pupil expenditures have risen more than 25 percent (adjusted for inflation) over the past decade, student achievement has not seen a corresponding improvement. Critics argue that schools are simply inefficient, and that almost one-half of the school budget gets lost on overhead and never makes it into the classroom. These critics believe that schools need to adopt better business practices by using staff and facilities more efficiently.[11]

The shift to more of a business, or free market, mentality in the world of education, popular in the 1990s, contributed to the creation of "choice" plans. (See Chapter 5, "What's a School For?") These plans were designed to increase competition by giving parents the opportunity to choose from among a variety of schools, a system that was intended to weed out costly and ineffective schools while promoting successful ones. Competition, long a central aspect of the U.S. business community, had now made its way to public schools.

LEGAL LANDMARKS
Educational Finance

- *Serrano v. Priest* (California, 1971). Dependence on the property tax to fund education is unconstitutional in California because it "invidiously discriminates against the poor." Similar rulings have been made by courts in other states.
- *San Antonio Independent School District v. Rodriquez* (U.S. Supreme Court, 1973). By a 5-to-4 vote, the Supreme Court ruled that the property tax did

not violate the U.S. Constitution but might violate state constitutions. The close vote moved the issue to the state level but did not rule out possible future decisions from the highest court as membership changed.

- *Serrano II* (California, 1976). Reaffirming the unconstitutionality of the property tax under the California constitution, the state court noted "a distinct relationship between cost and the quality of educational opportunities afforded."
- *Levittown v. Nyquist* (New York, 1982). In a setback for the school finance reform movement, the New York State Court of Appeals declared that the property tax approach had a "rational basis" and that any attempt to enforce a uniform property tax would undermine local control of schools.
- *Rose and Blandford v. Council for Better Education et al.* (Kentucky, 1989). In perhaps the most dramatic state ruling, the Kentucky supreme court declared the entire system of public education to be the cause of inequities. As a result, the legislature has radically reshaped education. A new finance system is only a part of this restructuring effort. Local school policies are now carried out by councils of parents, teachers, and administrators rather than school boards. Teacher certification is open to college graduates who do not hold education degrees. More preschool opportunities for the disadvantaged have been mandated. Schools institute "ungraded" primary classes and develop greater governing autonomy. For Kentucky, equitable education went well beyond equitable financing to include the restructuring of education.
- *Edgewood v. Kirby* (Texas, 1989). Taking the lead from the 1973 *Rodriquez* decision, the Texas supreme court declared that heavy reliance on property taxes led to major inequities in tax rates and per-pupil expenditures and violated the Texas state constitution. This decision led to a 1991 state law that redistributed wealth from wealthier districts to poorer ones in their geographic area.
- *Abbott v. Burke* (New Jersey, 1990). The state court ordered that the funding of the 30 poorest school districts be raised to the average level of the state's 108 richest school districts. More state funds would go to these poorer districts, and fewer state monies would be given to wealthier districts. However, a number of middle-income and wealthy districts objected, and this has delayed implementation.

Source: Adapted from Thomas Toch, "Separate But Not Equal," *Agenda* 1 (Spring 1991): 15–17

School Financing Balance Sheet 1
Equitable Financing Laws: The Robin Hood Approach[12]

We need to redistribute educational funds equitably because . . .

As Kozol and others have poignantly documented, children born in poorer districts are denied an effective, even an adequate, education only because of the accident of geography. Their schools have fewer facilities and fewer programs, their teachers are less well-paid, and their graduation rates are quite low. In many urban areas, dilapidated schools are even dangerous, and quality education is all but impossible.

Forced redistribution of educational funds is a terrible mistake because . . .

While it may sound harsh, everyone is not equal. In our system, those who work hard and are talented are rewarded, while the less capable and less ambitious do less well. That reality motivates people, and it makes our system work so well. Government intrusion disrupts this process and, by equalizing funding, deprives people of motivation. Good schools reward hardworking parents and motivate

In these schools the scarcity of textbooks, lack of computers, rats "sharing" the classrooms, health code violations, and the threat of violence are constant reminders of America's broken promise to the poor. When the lack of dollars denies educational opportunity, the United States is weakened. We as a people are supposed to be committed to equality and fairness, yet paying twice as much to educate the children of the rich, while barely providing minimum education to the poor, makes a mockery of U.S. justice. The poor are being horribly short-changed. Education is a basic right for all.

It is cost-effective, in the long run, to have all our schools and all our students be successful. When schools in poor areas do not do an effective job, society pays the bill. Teenage pregnancy, juvenile delinquency, and crime haunt students—and the rest of society. Underfunded schools lead to underemployed or unemployed adults. The decision is ours: We can pay for more effective, more successful schools today, or get ready to spend far more on welfare, unemployment, and prisons tomorrow.

America is based on the notion of one person, one vote. The idea that everyone enjoys equal political power regardless of race, gender, wealth, or geography, is fundamental to our democracy. Education is as important, as central, as voting. Each child is entitled to equal educational opportunity. When students in one part of the state are given two, or even three, times more dollars for their education, that contradicts the idea of equal education for all. Educational dollars, like political votes, are fundamental to the survival of our democracy and must be shared equally.

The federal and state governments do not spend enough money on education in general, and poorer students suffer most. The United States ranks eleventh out of the top 14 industrialized nations in the percentage of gross national product spent on elementary and secondary schools. While wealthier communities can and do make up the gap out of their personal wealth, poorer school districts do not have these resources. Ironically, it is the poorer students—whose educational needs are the greatest—who are most likely to suffer because of the relatively low level of public dollars spent on education.

their children. If less productive parents were simply "given" good schools, what would motivate them to do better? In fact, if we were to take money from successful parents and simply give it to less successful ones, we would negatively impact our most effective citizens. We would "demotivate" them. Our system of rewards is not always perfect, but it is better than the others available. The demise of the Soviet Union, the great equalizer and demotivator, is a classic example that the forced-equality approach is destined to fail.

The idea that the size of a school budget determines the quality of a school's education is not only simplistic . . . it is inaccurate. Big school budgets create carpeted classes, well-paid teachers, and expansive parking lots so that students can park their expensive cars—all very nice accessories, but not really related to education quality. Wealthy schools can afford to spend money on luxuries, but that does not result in better education. In the end, students motivated to learn will succeed. There are too many examples of rich students doing poorly and poor students doing well for us to buy this "bigger budget, better school" argument.

The reality is that education is a state function, not a national democratic right. It is true that states can make some efforts to equalize spending among schools within the state (if they so choose), but what about differences between the states? Some states spend much more on education than do others, and there is no way of equalizing differences among the states. So attempts to equalize expenditures *within* a state, even if totally effective, would not change the funding differences in the United States. It is a futile effort.

Attempts to equalize education through funding are destined to fail. Many poorer districts are simply inefficient, even corrupt. There are too many examples of urban educators who use funds unwisely, if not illegally. Throwing dollars down rat holes is not a good idea. Moreover, states trying to equalize educational efforts will discover that the weaker districts will never reach the level of the stronger ones. Should the best districts be given less money or told to lower their student achievement scores? There will always be differences, and throwing dollars at weaker schools will not eliminate these gaps.

The Controversy over Choice

For almost three decades an explosive, some say revolutionary, idea lurked in the background of the U.S. Department of Education. Under the Reagan and Bush administrations, it moved to center stage. The approach is to restructure U.S. schools into a more competitive organization, one in which different schools actually vie with one another for students. Families would not be forced to channel their children into the neighborhood school; rather, they would "shop" for a school the same way they might shop for other goods and services. The idea is called *choice*.

The choice concept would not make much sense if parents were forced to choose from schools that are pretty much alike, as is the case today. The power behind choice is the power of the open market. Schools would have to compete for students. No students, no school. Schools would have to develop strong or unique programs in order to attract students and parents. Schools failing to compete successfully would simply go out of business. The monopoly that the school has on the local neighborhood would be broken.

The theory is that a program of choice will create more effective schools. Many, however, are less swayed by the idea of choice. They fear a loss of standards, a profit motive crowding out educational goals, even the intrusion of religious values and other biases into the public schools. Most choice programs include only the public schools, although some people have proposed expanding the plan to include private, even religious, schools as well.

The financial impact of a choice plan that includes private schools could be quite damaging to the nation's public schools. Critics point out that, in such a plan, schools might also choose not to accept certain students. This would result in the most difficult students being left behind in the public schools. Others suggest that wealthy parents, already sending their children to private schools, would now receive extra money from the state to support their decision—a state subsidy to those who need it least.

Those for and against the idea of creating a competitive school market are often fervent about their positions. This would be, after all, a very fundamental change in public education. To get a better sense of what the furor is all about, let's eavesdrop on a community deeply embroiled in this controversy. Welcome to the Cabin Cove Town Meeting.

For centuries, this small New England city has prided itself on its annual experiment in democracy: the town meeting. But as the citizens of Cabin Cove approached the high school, it was clear that this would be no typical community get-together. Demonstrators crowded around the front door as the police strained to keep the entrance clear. Their placards shouted their emotions: "Choice, Not Chance"; "End the Education Monopoly"; "Special Schools for Special Kids"; "Parents Have Rights Too!"

The noise actually seemed to increase inside the school auditorium, where nearly 4,000 Cabin Cove residents filled every seat, overflowing into the aisles. The efforts of the overambitious school furnace contributed to the crowd's fervor as Mayor DeCarlo, flanked by the school board and the superintendent, called the meeting to order.

I appreciate this turnout tonight. It demonstrates our pride in three centuries of quality education here in Cabin Cove and our community's commitment to ensuring that quality education will continue in the future for our children and their children.

It is important that we remain calm and reasoned tonight, and I will maintain strict order. The decision before us is clear—to maintain the current neighborhood school tradition, or to develop distinctly different schools throughout the city, with citywide open enrollment. Each citizen who requested the right to speak will be given 2 minutes at the microphone. Please keep your speeches brief. First on the list is Ann Sinclair, who is here tonight representing the governor.

Smartly dressed in a navy wool suit, Ann Sinclair surveyed the audience. This was one of her first public speeches as the governor's representative, and she was nervous. She adjusted the microphone to suit her 5'3" height and began.

Thank you, Mayor DeCarlo, Governor Jensen asked me to speak to you tonight and to share with you her strong support for the development of the choice plan in Cabin Cove. In 1986, the National Governors' Association threw its support behind the development of a choice plan for America's public schools. Governor Jensen supports choice. She believes that parents and educators should be given the freedom to create educational

Some experts fear that school-choice programs are more apt to produce competitive and sometimes misleading school advertising programs than genuine school improvement efforts. School-choice fairs might extend from colleges all the way down to elementary schools.

diversity. Schools should not be produced with a cookie cutter, all looking the same. We should create special schools for special interests and talents and learning styles. Cabin Cove parents should be able to choose from schools that develop musical talents or intellectual gifts or special vocational interests or whatever areas Cabin Cove chooses. The governor believes that the citizens of Cabin Cove, like the rest of the citizens of the state, should develop original schools, not educational clones. We deserve no less. Thank you.

Dressed informally in jeans and a cardigan sweater, Nick Lane, the president of the local teachers' association, was visibly agitated as Ann Sinclair concluded her remarks. Respected by both teachers and parents, he was well known as an advocate of teachers' rights. As the next speaker to address the group, he virtually bolted to the microphone.

That all sounds wonderful, but I've taught in Cabin Cove for 18 years, and I'm really concerned about the seduction of words. *Choice* sounds better than *no choice*. It's as American as apple pie. But let's not get confused. A choice program can destroy our schools.

The neighborhood school is our democratic laboratory. Learning how to live with students of different talents and abilities is an important lesson in a democratic society. We don't need more segregation in our schools—we need more harmony. Building an educational "gulag" of specialized schools is divisive. Choice might sound good, but it's basically undemocratic. Neighborhood schools are real melting pots and should be preserved.

And another thing. Advocates of choice say good schools will be "rewarded" with more students. Yet who's to say bigger is necessarily better? I can just picture it now: a good school ruined because it attracts too many students for its own good.

One more comment before I sit down. What happens to the teachers in a choice plan? Teachers deserve more than insecurity. Each summer we will have to wait to find out which schools have gained enrollment and which have lost pupils; which teachers will be working and which will be unemployed. Are teachers to be asked to abandon their security? Or should they be "flexible" and change their philosophies according to the type of school that has teacher positions available? What kind of teachers will this system produce? Phonies? Unemployed? This system will kill the heart of our schools—our teachers.

As Nick took his seat, a number of teachers and some parents broke into applause.

As chair of the education department at Cabin Cove College, Professor Humphrey, the next speaker, was active and well known in the community. He also had a reputation for independence and because of that enjoyed significant respect. His position on choice, however, was not known, so the crowd waited with anticipation as he took the microphone.

I understand Nick's concerns. If the Cabin Cove choice program is to work, certain safeguards need to be set in place. But I believe that we must move ahead on the choice program because it offers great promise.

To give it a fair test, I suggest that we make certain that our teachers are guaranteed not only jobs but free training when appropriate. They too must be allowed to choose in this plan. They should be trained for special schools and guaranteed jobs.

I'm also worried about "hucksterism." When schools exist only if they are attractive to parents and children, I'm afraid that some schools might stoop to some pretty shady practices. For example, a school might get carried away with self-promotion, resulting in false or misleading advertising. Or a school might try to appeal to a select group of families by establishing discriminatory recruitment and admissions policies that exclude certain classes or races or the like. Basically, we need to establish a regulatory body to ensure that schools under the choice plan do not engage in unfair or discriminatory practices. Without such a regulatory body, a choice plan could cause far more damage than good.

A woman in her sixties moved slowly to the microphone. Doris Parlen had been one of the most active parents in her community, having served as president of the Parents' Associations for her children's elementary, middle, and high schools. The mother of seven children, all of them educated in the Oak Knoll area of Cabin Cove Public School District, she had become one of the city's unofficial community spokespersons.

I'm against this choice plan 100 percent. My seven children have all attended Oak Knoll Elementary School. I'm pleased with the school and with the education they received. What would choice do? They learned their basic skills: reading, writing, mathematics, social studies, science, art, and music. What choice should they have—not learn their basics? Should we have schools that teach elementary children only art or film making or science? There should be no choice concerning whether elementary schoolchildren should learn the basics. Teaching the basics is the only job of elementary schools.

High school is different. Some students need to prepare for college, while others need to prepare for a career. But our high schools are rich in choices and tracks. Students with different interests and abilities make choices every day. Moreover, if they change their minds they can switch programs without switching schools. It's actually easier to choose in today's high schools than under a choice plan. And I agree with Nick Lane's comments—not only because my children did well in his class but because the comprehensive high school is more democratic. All races and types of students mix freely in the hallways, in special school activities, and in some courses. Choice would segregate these kids. How will they learn to live and work together?

I know that choice sounds good, but we have choice right now where we should, and no choice in elementary schools, where it doesn't make any sense. Mr. Mayor, this is a bad idea, and it could hurt all the work we've already put into our schools.

As the mayor looked at the crowd, he saw a number of heads nodding in agreement with Ms. Parlen. For the first time, he was worried that the Cabin

Cove choice plan might not pass. Next on the list was Father Ghiradelli, whom the mayor knew to be a strong supporter of the plan. But the good father might create more problems. The mayor wiped his brow with a handkerchief and called the priest to the microphone.

My name is Father Ghiradelli, and I'm the principal of the Sacred Heart High School. While I can't speak for the archdiocese, I can tell you that the parochial schools in Cabin Cove not only support this choice plan but would like to see it expanded. All our parents at Sacred Heart are veterans of choice—they chose to send their children to our school to ensure that they receive not only an academic education but a Catholic one as well. And they are paying tuition, above their taxes, to ensure that. We believe that all citizens of Cabin Cove should have the opportunity to send their children to any private or parochial school they choose, but without tuition charges. Cabin Cove should include private and parochial schools in its plan and pay the tuition for either.

A murmur emerged from the crowd. Clearly, many objected to this, and the priest anticipated their objections.

I know what you're thinking: Why support a Catholic school with general taxes? I'll tell you why—because we've been supporting public schools with our taxes and schools. I'm only asking you to consider fair play.

At Sacred Heart, we educate more than 800 children. Their parents pay taxes but don't send their children to the public schools. Cabin Cove uses our tax dollars to educate other children. We receive no benefits for our tax dollars. Then our parents must pay again for education at Sacred Heart. Our parents are paying twice for their children's education. Moreover, you don't have to hire teachers or buy books or build schools for the children of our parents. This just isn't fair!

And look at what you're getting! Our students receive a wonderful education. As many of you know, students in our school have significantly higher SAT scores than do students from the public schools. We often serve as a beacon for the public schools, experimenting with new curricula or new teaching techniques, many of which they eventually adopt. That's one of the many advantages that private schools offer Cabin Cove: We provide an important alternative, a real choice to public schools. Real choice means allowing parents to choose from parochial schools or military academies or Montessori schools or elite schools or ghetto schools that focus on the classics. Private schools have always competed in the real marketplace. If we do not offer a better product, we must close our doors. We started this effort called *choice;* please, don't exclude us now. God bless you.

The crowd was visibly disturbed as the priest left the podium. Although almost 25 percent of the students in Cabin Cove attended private schools, most parents were against using public tax dollars to pay for private school tuition. The mayor quieted the audience as the next speaker, Hazel Adams, approached the microphone.

As an attorney and president of the local chapter of the Educational Rights and Liberties Committee, let me express my profound concern with and objection to this bizarre plan. Let's be rational, what will this plan accomplish? It's quite simple: Each family will choose schools that reflect its own values. But not only values, biases as well. Those who believe in a literal translation of the Bible will pick fundamentalist schools. Should we pay for that with public monies? Perhaps poor families will help to create schools that emphasize strong discipline and control and stress basic academic skills. Those kinds of schools reflect blue-collar values and will provide poorer families with their preferred choice, but it will also prepare their kids for dead-end jobs. These blue-collar schools will teach lower-class kids how to follow orders but will not teach them managerial or professional skills. Is that the kind of education we seek under this choice plan? This plan will not educate our students, it will simply reinforce the biases and limitations of class and family backgrounds. And I suspect that this choice plan will increase racially segregated schools, since minority students are more frequently found among the poorer classes. We had choice programs before, in the 1960s. We called it *segregation.*

Mayor DeCarlo had been in politics for most of his 57 years. He prided himself in his "sixth sense," his ability to read an audience. He knew that he was losing this one. But perhaps there was hope. David Rodriguez, a resident of a nearby county, was introducing himself at the microphone.

I have been invited here to tell you about the experiences we have had in Pelham County. We began our choice program almost 2 years ago, and we are very pleased. Our teachers, parents, and students all worked together to plan our schools. We never thought it could be so exciting. Everybody really got into it; for the first time, we feel in control of our schools. We developed a bilingual school, a maritime school, a performing arts school, and an academically gifted school. Teachers are excited about planning new programs and teaching children who are interested in these areas. Parents feel as though they have a real part in their schools. And students are enjoying school; they're not bored.

We're happy with our choice plan, but we still have some fine-tuning to do. Segregation still exists, but, of course, it existed before. We don't know how the achievement tests and SAT scores will come out. And not everyone is happy. Some teachers want transfers. Some schools are too crowded, while others are underenrolled. Some parents and neighborhoods feel left out, because the schools they wanted to create were not included in the plan. People are also concerned about the cost and time involved in transportation. But all that is to be expected. After all, this is all new. But it works better than before. We are really proud of our choice plan. Thank you.

The mayor sensed movement. Rodriguez had influenced a lot of opinions, but had he changed enough minds? DeCarlo just wasn't sure anymore. You never know how these town meetings will go or how the final vote will turn out. Was Cabin Cove wedded to three centuries of neighborhood schools, or was it willing to move toward a citywide choice program? Mayor DeCarlo no longer knew. He searched his speakers' list, found his place, and announced the next speaker.

School Financing Balance Sheet 2
The School Choice Plan

Pro	Con
Free to choose from different schools (guided by their parents), children will no longer be forced to attend their neighborhood school. Education will finally be democratic.	The neighborhood school is a community of neighbors learning to work together. This is the real meaning of democracy.
Choice will lead to competition. As schools compete, they will develop their unique strengths to attract students to their programs. Without students, they will be forced to close. Only good schools will survive and prosper.	Transplanting businesslike competition into the education arena would be a disaster. False advertising, "special" promotions, a feel-good education—all the hucksterism of the marketplace will mislead students and their parents.
The choice program will overcome the racism and classism of the neighborhood school and promote integrated schools open to all.	The choice program would deteriorate to the prejudice of private academies of the past, where race, religion, even disability factors will be used to keep certain students from attending.
Teachers will enjoy the opportunity to leave the bureaucracy of the current system. Lifetime professionals, they will be free to create and manage their own schools.	Teachers will lose their tenure and work at the whim of the community. No professional should be forced to work from year to year without basic job security.
For the first time, poor families will be given authority to choose a school that works instead of attending neighborhood schools they know don't work. Finally, poor Americans will be given some control over their educational futures.	Poor families will be the most victimized under a choice plan. Without education or experience, poor families are more susceptible to false advertising and misleading claims.
The choice system will increase national test scores. Schools will compete with each other academically, raising student achievement scores overall. In addition, unique and different types of schools will be more successful with different kinds of students.	The choice system will lower the nation's already low scores. All these different schools will teach and emphasize different topics. Without a central, accepted curricular core, fewer students will be prepared for national, standardized tests.

Private Schools and Public Funding

While the citizens in Cabin Cove debate the choice plan, many Americans, like Father Ghiradelli, believe that private schools should be included in the options presented to parents. Currently, most choice plans only include public schools. But parents and educators involved in private schools believe that they are not receiving a fair deal under the current system. Take a minute and put yourselves in their shoes.

Imagine that you are a parent who wants to send your child to Persimmon Tree Country Day School. The school has a wonderful reputation, but the tuition is $7,000 per year. You understand, regrettably, that it is your responsibility to pay the tuition, but you are frustrated because you must also support the public schools. You pay your property taxes, state income and sales taxes, and all of your other obligations, and yet, because you are not sending

Parents whose children attend expensive private schools generally support voucher proposals that include private as well as public schools, since they are paying both public school taxes and private school tuition.

your child to the public schools, you are not benefiting from the services you are paying for. In fact, by not sending your child to the public schools you are saving the government the cost of educating your child. Yet you are paying twice, which does not seem fair.

For many parents, private school educators, politicians, and religious leaders, the lack of government support for private schools is a frustrating and painful fact of life, one they would dearly love to change. Nor is this a small minority. Private schools represent a significant proportion of U.S. education. There are more than 26,000 private schools in the United States, employing 13 percent of all teachers and educating nearly 5 million elementary and secondary students.[13]

Approximately three out of every four of these private schools are religiously affiliated, and one-third of the private school students attend Catholic schools. Parents who send their children to private schools often are seeking an educational environment that is not available in public schools. Most frequently this is religious, but sometimes it is one that strives for a greater level of individualization and institutional responsiveness. Private school teachers usually earn less than public school teachers but choose private school teaching because of personal convictions and working conditions that include fewer discipline problems, less absenteeism, more supportive parents, and a strong emphasis on academic achievement.

Those opposed to public support of private schools may or may not sympathize with this problem of nongovernment support, but they believe firmly in the First Amendment to the U.S. Constitution: "Congress shall make no law respecting an establishment of religion or prohibiting the free exercise thereof."

Using public funds to support religious education (remember, most private schools are religiously affiliated) has generated not only strong public opposition but successful legal challenges as well. However, two financial plans that would help support private schools continue to garner a large number of supporters: educational vouchers and tuition tax credits. But there is some debate about their impact, as one educational writer notes:

> Are the supermarkets available to different economic groups anything like so divergent in quality as the schools? Vouchers would improve the quality of schooling available to the rich hardly at all; to the middle class, moderately; to the lower-income class, enormously. Surely the benefit to the poor more than compensates for the fact that some rich or middle-income parents would avoid paying twice for schooling their children. . . .

> But, what makes the voucher approach unique is that parents will be able to send their children to schools that will reinforce in the most restrictive fashion the political, ideological, and religious views of the family. That is, school will be treated as a strict extension of the home, with very little opportunity for students to experience the diversity of backgrounds and viewpoints that contributes to the democratic process.[14]

Although educational vouchers and tuition tax credits first emerged as issues decades ago, these finance plans regained popularity in the 1980s and 1990s. Both plans are ways to financially assist private schools and, according to their proponents, increase diversity, freedom of choice, and the quality of U.S. schools.

Probably the best-known technique for implementing a choice plan is **educational vouchers.** In fact, some people use these terms interchangeably, although the choice plan is actually a broader concept. Here is how a voucher would work. Imagine once again that you are a parent who wants to send your child to the Persimmon Tree Country Day School, the school with the $7,000 a year tuition. You, along with other parents in your community, are awarded a voucher (or coupon). The voucher might represent the average annual cost of educating a child, and you are allowed to use the voucher at any school of your choice, public or private. You are pleased to learn that your child has been accepted at Persimmon Tree Country Day School, and you gladly turn your voucher over to the school's finance office. It in turn sends the voucher to the appropriate government agency and receives a check equivalent to the cost of educating a child in the local schools (typically about $5,000). In some plans, the school needs to make do with the voucher (in our case, worth $5,000) and cannot charge its regular $7,000 tuition. In other variations of this plan, the parent must come up with the difference between the value of the voucher ($5,000) and the cost of tuition ($7,000). Under the voucher plan, the cost of sending your child to a private school could be as little as nothing or as much as $2,000. The voucher plan literally returns your tax dollars to you and in effect tells you: "Here is your money—you choose your school." In many plans, the voucher might be worth considerably less than the average cost of educating a child, and parents are expected to pay a far greater share of the tuition.

The **tuition tax credit** program is not as beneficial to you as the educational voucher system, but it does help defray some costs. Under this plan all or part of your tuition is reported as a tax credit; that is, it is subtracted from the amount you owe as income tax. In a typical proposal, your income taxes might be reduced by $500. Although you would still have to pay Persimmon

Jonathan Kozol: "I have some problems with the idea of choice, and I want to tell you why . . ."

Jonathan Kozol, author of the best-selling Savage Inequalities, *spoke at the University of Tennessee–Knoxville about the terrible disparities among public schools in this country. At the end of his speech, members of the audience were invited to ask questions. Here, reprinted with permission, is Jonathan Kozol's response to the question:* **What are your views on the proposed voucher system for public schools?**

The first time I ever heard vouchers proposed in the U.S. was by Milton Friedman, an economist respected among scholars for some of his pure economics work but better known to some people as the former economics advisor to Augusto Pinochet: the fascist dictator of Chile.

The first time I heard of schools of choice, it was after the Brown decision in the 1950s, when schools in many Southern states set up schools of choice—that was the word. They called them Freedom of Choice Schools as a ploy to avoid desegregation. That's the history.

What have I actually seen? Well, first of all, the idea behind choice (within the district), basically, is that if you let people choose, everybody will get the school they want. Everybody will have an equally free choice; everybody will have equal access. And, those I hear defend choice say it will not increase class or racial segregation. In fact, in virtually every case that I have seen, none of these conditions is met. People very seldom have equal choices, and even when they theoretically have equal choices, they rarely have equal access.

People can't choose things they've never heard of, for example. And lots of the poorest folks in our inner cities are functionally illiterate. I've written a book about that, as some of you know. In many of our inner cities, as many as 30 percent of our adults cannot read well enough to understand the booklets put out by school systems delineating their choices. That's one point.

Even if they can understand and even if the school system is sophisticated enough to print these

things in five different languages for all the different ethnic groups in cities like New York or Chicago, there's a larger point that those who hear about new schools, good schools, first are almost always the well connected. They're almost always the people whose friends are in the school system, the people like myself who went to college with the principal or the superintendent or some of the people who run the system. Word of mouth always favors the children of the most wealthy or best educated.

And so, what often happens is that while everybody theoretically has the right to choose any school, the affluent, the savvy, the children of the academics, the children of the lawyers, the children of the doctors, the children of the school superintendent tend to end up in the same three little boutique elementary schools. And I call them boutique schools because they're always charming, and the press loves them, and they always have enough racial integration so it looks okay for the newspaper or the TV camera. But, in fact, they are separated by both race and class, and more and more by class.

What happens is that the poorest of the poor often do not get into these schools or get in in very small numbers. Large numbers of the kids who nobody wants end up concentrated in the schools that no one chooses except by default.

That's my profound reservation. I've been at it a long, long time. I've seen that happen. I'd add that there are some exceptions, as in an enlightened program in East Harlem. But there are unusual aspects of this program that are seldom found in choice plans elsewhere.

When you have choice *across* school districts, it gets even trickier. In Massachusetts, we now have a statewide plan called Massachusetts 2000. . . . What's happened? Eight hundred kids transferred to other districts within two months after the plan's initiation. Who were those kids? Ninety-three percent of them were white and middle class. Not one child

Tree Country Day School the full $7,000 tuition, as well as pay all your property and state taxes, you would receive some recognition of this expense in reduced federal taxes.

Like the voucher system, open enrollments and charter schools (discussed earlier in the text) are based on increasing educational options for parents. Fundamental to all these approaches is the notion of breaking up what is seen

transferred from a rich district to a poor district, which does tell us something about the value of money doesn't it?

Let me give you a simple case study. Two adjacent districts in Massachusetts: One is a small industrial town of 80- to 100,000 people, called Brockton, an old mill town. Half the people in Brockton are nonwhite, half are very poor—the same half largely. And the others are working class. There are few middle-class people in the town. About 1,000 kids in the school system are bilingual, that is, they are definitely not proficient in English. Of the kids who transferred from Brockton, only 5 percent were low-income and only one of these children was a bilingual student.

Brockton, last year, which already was in dire straits because of the recession, lost $850,000 to the neighboring, white affluent suburb of Avon, Massachusetts. $850,000! That's happening in every paired situation (where there are neighboring rich and poor schools) across our state. So what has choice done in Massachusetts? It has unleashed the flight of rich and middle class from poor; of white from black, Hispanic, and Asian. . . .

What happens when you take choice to the ultimate, and let people take public money and go to a private school? It sounds wonderful, just like choice. It sounds so reasonable. Why shouldn't people have the right to do that? Secretary of Education Lamar Alexander says rich people already have the right to go to private school; why shouldn't we give poor children this right? Listening to his words, one might almost think he had undergone a conversion and was ready to give the poor black kids of Washington, D.C. a $15,000 voucher so they could go to Andover. But no, despite the disarming simplicity and the subtlety of his formula, that's not what he intends at all. The choice plan he points to involves about $1,000 in vouchers. . . .

Class distinctions will remain unaltered. They will remain the same. I'm very much against voucher plans. . . .

Now the dark, terrifying prospect of vouchers or a choice agenda, of a so-called market basis for our public schools, is that rather than encourage a sense of common loyalties among people, choice will particularize loyalties. It will fragmentize ambition, so that the individual parent will be forced to claw and scramble for the good of her kid and her kid only, at whatever cost to everybody else. There will no longer be a sense of "What I choose for my child, I choose for everybody." There's a wonderful quote from John Dewey. He said "What the best and wisest parent wants for his own child, that must the community want for all its children. Any other ideal for our schools is narrow and unlovely. Acted upon, it destroys our democracy."

Just a tiny postscript: A lot of the people who are for vouchers don't know that much about vouchers. They're not right-wing or bigots or anything like that. They might be people who say, "Well, nothing else works. Why don't we try them?" That's a common mood in this country.

The best known voucher advocate, John Chubb, of the Brookings Institution, in Washington, says something—I'm paraphrasing him—like this: "Democratic governance of schools is what's wrong with schools. We need a voucher plan in order to break the bonds of democratic education, because it hasn't worked." That's what he says.

When I hear that, I think to myself, "Wait a minute. We've never tried democratic education." We haven't yet given equal, wonderful, innovative, humane schools—at the level of our finest schools—to all our children. I do not agree to "break the bonds" of democratic education. I think we should try it first, see how it might work.

Source: Reprinted with permission of *Educational Leadership* 50, no. 3 (November 1992): 90–92.

as an educational monopoly that is stifling the schools. Through competition and choice, advocates of these programs want to reshape the educational landscape and dramatically change public schools. But even some public school critics express reservations when private schools become the beneficiaries of tax dollars. They fear that providing tax dollars to private schools may start an exodus of the best and brightest students, who would abandon public education for now-affordable private education. With weaker and more difficult students to educate, and fewer parents with children enrolled in public schools, public education would be in great jeopardy.

The furor surrounding public aid to private schools has not abated, and most public funds requested by private schools have been disallowed by the Supreme Court as a violation of the First Amendment's prohibition of state support of religious activities. However, some minimal public aid does find its way to private schools, especially nonreligious private schools.[15] The Supreme Court has allowed state funds to be used to provide therapeutic services (speech classes, remedial reading), diagnostic services, and the administration of standardized tests. The Court has rejected the use of public funds for teacher salary supplements, instructional materials, and even for the costs of field trips. The criterion used in these cases is avoiding "excessive entanglement" (that is, government involvement in promoting religious beliefs, and so on), but the history of Court decisions that determine what constitutes "excessive entanglement" has not been consistent. It is conceivable that a more conservative Supreme Court might allow public funds to be used even more extensively in the future. However, the fate and legality of major public financing such as tuition tax credits and educational vouchers has yet to be determined.

Looking to the Future

The 1980s brought controversy and conflict to school finance—taxpayers' revolts, shifting governmental responsibility, and public clamor for less expensive but more effective schools. The 1990s witnessed new challenges to school finance (see Figure 12.4). Here are some trends and issues likely to surface in the years ahead.

Accountability

The fact that many school districts have increased educational expenses without parallel improvements in school performance has created a great deal of public frustration. The public desires evidence that their tax dollars contribute to academic progress and are being used efficiently. The popular colloquial-

FIGURE 12.4

Current Expenditure per Student in Average Daily Attendance in Public Elementary and Secondary Schools, 1970–1971 to 1993–1994

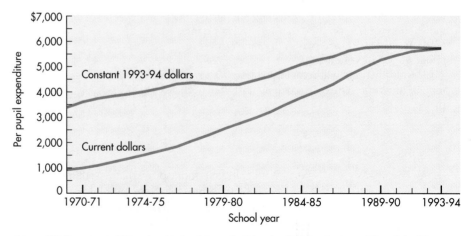

Source: U.S. Department of Education, National Center for Education Statistics, *Statistics of State School Systems; Revenues and Expenditures for Public Elementary and Secondary Education;* and Common Core of Data surveys.

ism for this phenomenon is "getting the biggest bang out of the educational buck." The formal term is **accountability.**

The desire for accountability will lead to a continuation of testing. Students will be tested, and so will educators. Graduation will be based less on time spent in school and more on proven performance. Teaching tenure also may be more difficult to obtain. Educational overhead, including the number of administrators and supervisors, may be reduced in order to put a lid on expenses. Schools will be required to identify specific goals, such as minimal achievement levels on standardized test scores, and will then be held responsible for reaching these goals. As states increase their support of schools, it is reasonable to anticipate that they will develop new standards of performance for their schools. In fact, organizational changes, new staff structures, merit pay, teacher dismissals, and alternative learning programs are all potential outcomes of this accountability movement.

Economic Challenges

The substantial federal debt and the vulnerability of the economy to potential problems (including foreign competition) suggest that the budget crisis will continue. A weakened national economy ripples down to state and local economies, and schools are always among the primary victims of economic hard times. Given the cyclical nature of the economy, the enormous federal debt, and the trade imbalance, it is reasonable to anticipate cycles of school budget cuts.

State and Federal Support of Education

The recent shift toward more state and less local support of education will probably level off in the years ahead. State revenues have their limits. Local communities once again will be put to the test in raising educational revenues, and property taxes may increase again. At the national level, many view education more and more as a national issue. To compete economically with Japan and other nations, and to reduce the cost of illiteracy and poverty at home, it is reasonable to expect that the federal government will initiate new programs and increase its funding of education. Reasonable, but by no means guaranteed. Budget balancing at the federal level, differences among states in their support for education, and local economic conditions make the future funding of public education unpredictable (see Figure 12.5). Various reform efforts, from charter schools to privatization, create additional uncertainties about the funding and management of the nation's schools.

Robin Hood Responses

As state courts continue their efforts to redistribute education dollars and to funnel additional state resources to poorer districts, parents in wealthier districts increasingly find such actions distasteful. Some of these parents have turned to private schools, while others have become supporters of voucher plans or charter schools. But parents choosing to keep their children in the public schools are developing creative strategies to insure that the educational

FIGURE 12.5
Federal On-Budget Support for Education, by Category

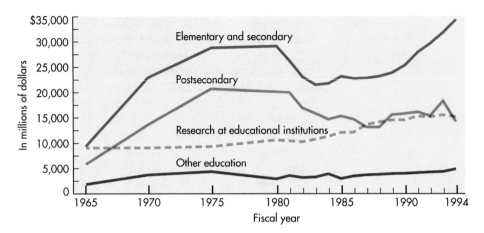

Source: U.S. Office of Management and Budget, *Budget of the U.S. Government,* fiscal years 1967 to 1995; National Science Foundation, *Federal Funds for Research and Development,* fiscal years 1967 to 1994; and unpublished data.

wealth and success of their schools are not endangered. One such strategy has prompted the formation of *educational foundations.*

About 2,000 public high schools, or 13 percent of the high schools in the United States, have created foundations. Funded by private donations, these foundations provide schools with additional revenues for a wide variety of projects, including acquiring advanced science equipment, computers, special devices for disabled students, and providing college scholarships. While the funds raised from such foundations amount to only a fraction of official school budgets, these foundations have a significant educational impact, because the dollars are spent directly on educational improvements and are not used for ongoing expenses like maintenance and salaries. Wealthy communities like La Jolla, California, Edgemont, New York, and Bellaire, Texas, have devoted time and dollars to creating foundations that support public schools with private resources. Supporters of such foundations believe that wealthy parents and their children "will flee to private school if they don't perceive the public education to be excellent."[16]

School Buildings

The physical condition and location of school buildings will continue to be an economic problem in the years ahead. As some neighborhoods lose their young families and school-age populations, school buildings will be forced to close. In the same school district, however, new neighborhoods of young families with school-age children will create a need for new schools. The result will be the costly enterprise of simultaneously closing and building schools, a reflection of housing costs, population shifts, and other factors.

The structural condition of many of the nation's schools is yet another financial problem looming in the future. Many schools are in a critical state of disrepair. Plumbing, heating, electrical wiring, roofing, masonry, and so on, are deteriorating at a rapid rate. The deteriorating school **infrastructure** is the result of deferred or inferior repairs, cost-cutting building programs, vandalism, and plain old age. Many school buildings currently in use are 50 to 100 years old. Asbestos, a carcinogenic building material, was used in constructing many of these schools, and removing this material is a costly endeavor. Lead in paint represents yet another health risk, highlighting the need for the physical reconditioning of U.S. schools. Widespread health, safety, and environmental violations need to be corrected. The cost of repairing and rebuilding the nation's schools has been estimated at more than $112 billion.[17]

SUMMARY

1. Funding for education presents serious problems year after year for state and local officials. Each of the most common strategies to fund schools—property tax, sales tax, personal income tax, state lottery, and others—has drawbacks. Funding is especially difficult for poorer communities and states, where even high taxes do not provide enough money for the schools. In the past decade, some states have experimented with new funding methods, such as foundation programs, a guaranteed tax base for all districts, and a combination of programs to help poorer communities fund schools; but none has proved very successful.

2. States provide approximately half of the cost of education, with local communities providing most of the rest. Local communities generally fund their schools through a property tax, which many people consider outdated and unfair. Since some areas are wealthier than others, some school districts generate more than enough money while others must struggle to keep schools open.

3. Local funding disparities have led to a series of state court decisions mandating new state formulas for funding schools. These decisions have been called "Robin Hood laws," since they require that funding-level differences between wealthy and poor districts be reduced or eliminated. Some courts are even mandating changes based on differences in educational outcomes.

4. In the 1980s and 1990s, the issue of choice in schooling moved to center stage. Similar to competitive organizations, schools under a choice plan must compete to attract students, each school advertising its strong attributes and special programs. Some argue forcefully that such a system pushes schools to become more effective, but others respond just as forcefully that choice is divisive and harmful, benefiting some students at the expense of others.

5. Educational vouchers, tuition tax credits, and parental options to choose any school for their children are three strategies for implementing choice plans. Many feel that choice plans should include private schools, three-quarters of which have religious affiliations. So far, funding for private schools has been blocked on the grounds that public funds should not support religious education.

6. An educational voucher may be valued at a thousand dollars, or at several thousand dollars, or at the average annual cost of sending a child to public school. Under this choice plan, parents would have the option of using their voucher at any school they wish. Some voucher plans include private schools, while others apply only to public schools. If private schools are included, the voucher might not cover all expenses. In one form of the voucher plan, parents sending children to expensive private schools would have to pay the difference; in another form of the plan, the schools would have to make do with the voucher.

7. Tuition tax credits would not be worth as much money as vouchers, but they would help defray the costs of education. Under this plan, parents paying private school tuition would receive financial help by having their taxes reduced.

8. Choice plans that allow parents to select any school for their children became popular in the 1980s and 1990s. Minnesota, for example, allows students to attend any school, not just neighborhood schools.

9. The 1990s saw a number of new challenges to school finance, including accountability for funding, budget crunches resulting from lack of adequate funds, a leveling off of state support for education, deteriorating school buildings and materials, and a search for the funds to support educational reform.

DISCUSSION QUESTIONS AND ACTIVITIES

1. Why has state support for local school systems grown?
2. Briefly describe the major sources of state and local funds for schools.
3. What are the major programs for state distribution of education funds?
4. Create a plan for (a) raising funds for education and (b) distributing funds equitably to all school districts within a state.
5. How can the differences in state wealth be dealt with to ensure that all students, regardless of the state they live in, benefit from equal educational expenditures?
6. If you were a state judge, would you focus more on financial resources (input) or educational output?
7. Do you believe that educational expenditures and educational quality are directly related? Support your position.
8. If educational vouchers were applied only to public schools, what would be the result?
9. Contrast the *Serrano* and *Rodriquez* court decisions.
10. If you were a superintendent of schools, what steps would you take to avoid taxpayer opposition to increasing school funding levels?
11. What are some of the costs associated with educational reform?
12. Why does a high property tax not always result in a well-funded school program?
13. Describe the pros and cons of a choice plan.

NOTES

1. Thomas Toch, "Separate But Not Equal," *Agenda* 1 (Spring 1991): 15–17.
2. Peter Keating, "How to Keep Your State and Local Taxes Down," *Money* 24, no. 1 (January 1995): 86–92.
3. Bill Norris, "Losing Ticket in Lotteries," *The Times Educational Supplement* 4003 (March 19, 1993): 17.
4. U.S. Department of Education, *Disparities in Public School District Spending 1989–90* (Washington, DC: U.S. Department of Education, February 1995), p. 56.
5. Barry Siegel, "Parents Get a Lesson in Equality," *Los Angeles Times* (Washington edition), April 13, 1992, pp. A1, A18–A19.
6. Ted Wilson, "Equal and Adequate Funding for Urban Schools," *Equity Coalition for Race, Gender, and National Origin* 2, no. 2 (Summer 1991).
7. Jonathan Kozol, *Savage Inequalities: Children in American Schools* (New York: Crown, 1991).
8. L. Harp, "Momentum for Challenges to Finance Systems Still Seen Strong," *Education Week*, September 27, 1993, pp. 1, 26.
9. Indira A. R. Lakshmanan, "New Jersey Schools Offer Omen for Massachusetts," *Boston Sunday Globe*, June 20, 1993, p. 1.

10. W. E. Thro, "The Third Wave: The Impact of the Montana, Kentucky and Texas Decisions on the Future of Public School Finance Reform Litigation," *Journal of Law and Education* 119, no. 2 (Spring 1990): 219–250; Robert F. McNergney and Joanne M. Herbert, *Foundations of Education: The Challenge of Professional Practice* (Boston: Allyn & Bacon, 1995), pp. 475–478; Chris Pipho, "Stateline: The Scent of the Future," *Phi Delta Kappan* 76 (September 1994): 10–11.

11. Larry Hedges, Richard Laine, and Rob Greenwald, "Does Money Matter? A Meta-Analysis of Studies of the Effects of Differential School Inputs on Students' Outcomes" *Educational Researcher,* April 1994, pp. 5–14; Michael J. Mandel with Richard A. Melcher, Dori Jones Yang, and Mike McNamee, "Will Schools Ever Get Better?"; *Business Week,* April 17, 1995, pp. 64–68.

12. Jack L. Nelson, Kenneth Carlson, and Stuart B. Palonsky, *Critical Issues in Education: A Dialectic Approach* (New York: McGraw-Hill, 1996), pp. 108–131.

13. U.S. Department of Education, *Schools and Staffing Survey 1993–94* (Washington, DC: National Center for Education Statistics, 1995).

14. Julie Miller, "Private School Groups Postpone Quest for Vouchers," *Education Week,* April 15, 1992, p. 15.

15. "State Supreme Court Upholds Milwaukee Choice Program," *Education Daily,* March 9, 1992, p. 3.

16. Jay Mathews, "More Public Schools Using Private Dollars," *The Washington Post,* August 28, 1995, pp. A-1, A-8.

17. Anne Lewis, "Washington Seen: Buildings in Disrepair," *Education Digest* 60, no. 8 (April 1995): p. 71.

PHILOSOPHY OF EDUCATION

Daniel Spiro, Lynette Long, and Elizabeth Ihle

OBJECTIVES

To describe the contributions to philosophy of Socrates, Plato, and Aristotle

To define philosophical terminology, including metaphysics, epistemology, ethics, political philosophy, aesthetics, and logic

To describe alternative positions that may be taken on certain key issues of philosophy

To describe key educational philosophies, including essentialism, perennialism, progressivism, existentialism, and behaviorism

To identify key educators associated with each philosophy

To develop your own philosophy of education

Philosophy is the love of wisdom. For thousands of years, philosophers have been wrestling with many of the same questions: What is most real—the physical world or the realm of mind and spirit? What is the basis of human knowledge? What is the nature of the just society? These and other philosophical questions influence education. Educators must take stances on such questions before they can determine what and how students should be taught.

Since educators do not agree on the answers to these questions, different philosophies of education have emerged. Although there are similarities, there are also profound differences in the way leading educators define the purpose of education, the role of the teacher, the nature of curriculum and evaluation, and the method of instruction.

This chapter will introduce you to the philosophy of three ancient Greeks: Socrates, Plato, and Aristotle. It will then examine some of the key questions of philosophy that are important to teachers. In addition, the chapter will discuss five major educational philosophies and describe examples of each in practice. Biographical sketches of some important philosophers are included. The chapter encourages you to attempt to resolve the ultimate questions of philosophy and challenges you to create a consistent position on education and schools.

What Is Your Philosophy of Education?

Each of us has a philosophy of education, a set of fundamental beliefs regarding how we think schools should be run. What is your philosophy of education? To find out, read each of the following statements about the nature of education. Decide whether you agree or disagree with each statement. Use the following numbers to express your response:

5 Agree strongly

4 Agree

3 Neutral

2 Disagree

1 Disagree strongly

_____ 1. The curriculum of the schools should be subject-centered. In particular, student learning should be centered around basic subjects such as reading, writing, history, math, and science.

_____ 2. The curriculum of the schools should focus on the great thinkers of the past.

_____ 3. Many students learn best by engaging in real-world activities rather than reading.

_____ 4. The students should be permitted to determine their own curriculum.

_____ 5. Material is taught effectively when it is broken down into small parts.

_____ 6. The curriculum of a school should be determined by information that is essential for all students to know.

_____ 7. Schools, above all, should develop students' abilities to think deeply, analytically, and creatively; this is more important than developing their social skills or providing them with a useful body of knowledge about our ever-changing world.

_____ 8. Schools should prepare students for analyzing and solving the types of problems they will face outside the classroom.

_____ 9. Reality is determined by each individual's perceptions. There is no objective and universal reality.

_____ 10. People are shaped much more by their environment than by their genetic dispositions or the exercise of their free will.

_____ 11. Students should not be promoted from one grade to the next until they have read and mastered certain key material.

_____ 12. An effective education is not aimed at the immediate needs of the students or society.

_____ 13. The curriculum of a school should be built around the personal experiences and needs of the students.

_____ 14. Students who do not want to study much should not be required to do so.

_____ 15. Programmed learning is an effective method of teaching information.

_____ 16. Academic rigor is an essential component of education.

_____ 17. All students, regardless of ability, should study more or less the same curriculum.

_____ 18. Art classes should focus primarily on individual expression and creativity.

_____ 19. Effective learning is unstructured and informal.

_____ 20. Students learn best through reinforcement.

_____ 21. Effective schools assign a substantial amount of homework.

_____ 22. Education should focus on the discussion of timeless questions such as "What is beauty?" or "What is truth?"

_____ 23. Since students learn effectively through social interaction, schools should plan for substantial social interaction in their curricula.

_____ 24. The purpose of school is to help students understand themselves and find the meaning of their existence.

_____ 25. Frequent objective testing is the best way to determine what students know.

_____ 26. The United States must become more competitive economically with countries such as Japan, and schools have an affirmative obligation to bolster their academic requirements in order to facilitate such competition.

_____ 27. Students must be taught to appreciate learning primarily for its own sake rather than because it will help them in their careers.

_____ 28. Schools must place more emphasis on teaching about the concerns of minorities and women.

_____ 29. Each person has free will to develop as he or she sees fit.

_____ 30. Reward students well for learning and they will remember and be able to apply what they learned, even if they were not led to understand why the information is worth knowing.

_____ 31. U.S. schools should attempt to instill traditional American values in students.

_____ 32. Teacher-guided discovery of profound truths is a key method of teaching students.

_____ 33. Students should be active participants in the learning process.

_____ 34. There are no external standards of beauty. Beauty is what an individual decides it to be.

_____ 35. We can place a lot of faith in our schools' and teachers' ability to determine which student behaviors are acceptable and which are not.

_____ 36. Schools must provide students with a firm grasp of basic facts regarding the books, people, and events that have shaped the nation's heritage.

_____ 37. Philosophy is ultimately as practical a subject to study as is computer science.

_____ 38. Teachers must stress for students the relevance of what they are learning to their lives outside, as well as inside, the classroom.

_____ 39. It is more important for a student to develop a positive self-concept than to learn specific subject matter.

_____ 40. Learning is more effective when students are given frequent tests to determine what they have learned.

Now that you have responded to all 40 items, write the number of your response to each statement in the spaces below. Add the numbers in each column to determine your attitudes toward key educational philosophies.

A Essentialism	B Perennialism	C Progressivism	D Existentialism	E Behaviorism
1. _____	2. _____	3. _____	4. _____	5. _____
6. _____	7. _____	8. _____	9. _____	10. _____
11. _____	12. _____	13. _____	14. _____	15. _____
16. _____	17. _____	18. _____	19. _____	20. _____
21. _____	22. _____	23. _____	24. _____	25. _____
26. _____	27. _____	28. _____	29. _____	30. _____
31. _____	32. _____	33. _____	34. _____	35. _____
36. _____	37. _____	38. _____	39. _____	40. _____

The scores in columns A through E, respectively, represent how much you agree or disagree with the beliefs of five major educational philosophies: essentialism, perennialism, progressivism, existentialism, and behaviorism. The higher your score, the more you agree with philosophers who represent that viewpoint. The highest possible score in any one area is 40, and the lowest possible score is 8. Scores in the mid to high 30s indicate strong agreement, and scores below 20 indicate disagreement with the tenets of a particular philosophy. Compare your five scores. What is your highest? What is your lowest? Now you have done some initial examination of what you believe about education, and you have even given yourself a philosophical label. But what do these philosophical labels or terms mean? In this chapter you will learn about all five of these educational philosophies as well as the beliefs that underlie them. After you finish reading the chapter, you may want to take another look at the above quiz to gain a better understanding of what you believe at this point in your education.

What Is Philosophy?

The root for the word _philosophy_ is made up of two Greek words: _philo,_ meaning "love," and _sophos,_ meaning "wisdom." As lovers or seekers of wisdom, students of philosophy grapple with the issues of most fundamental significance to humankind. In so doing, they attempt to uncover profound truths: the meanings that underlie the facts of their world.

Their search may have begun when they were children; they may have wondered, for example, about the existence of God or immortality, or whether it is fair for some people to be so rich while others are so poor. Upon discovering literature, they may have found books that discussed some of their own deepest thoughts and feelings and built upon them. Other books may have presented ideas with which they were previously unfamiliar, but that somehow added to the meaning and richness of their lives. Gradually, a philosophy of life emerges by which they interpret their world and locate themselves in it.

More than resolving dilemmas, philosophy raises questions. And each question leads to another. Yet, in raising questions and providing different approaches to answering them, philosophy makes a tremendous contribution to humankind. Each student of philosophy comes to his or her own opinion about which conclusions to philosophical questions are most acceptable. Depending on which conclusions students reach, their beliefs, feelings, and actions will be affected substantially.

The study of philosophy builds various qualities, including the ability to think deeply and analytically. It uncovers for students interrelationships among different academic subjects in the curriculum and develops in them an appreciation for those great philosophers and other historical figures who courageously devoted their lives to their principles. Above all, it builds a sense of awe and wonder that inevitably accompanies serious thinking about the age-old questions facing humankind.

Philosophy pervades all aspects of education, and this chapter highlights the philosophical issues that are most relevant to teachers. For example, consider the following philosophical questions: Is knowledge best acquired through observing and analyzing nature scientifically? Developing reasoning skills? Or cultivating intuitive and emotional faculties? Depending on how they resolve that philosophical issue, teachers decide which capacities of their students to develop most fully.

The Three Legendary Figures of Classical Philosophy

While a full discussion of the history of philosophy is beyond the scope of this book, we will provide an introduction through the teachings of the great thinkers from ancient Greece, the birthplace of Western philosophy. Three thinkers in particular—Socrates, Plato, and Aristotle—represent the apex of the Greek philosophical tradition. Reflecting upon their examples, many a modern student has come to affirm a Greek saying that may well be called the philosopher's creed: The unexamined life is not worth living.

The city-state of Athens in the fifth century B.C. was not, according to modern standards, a democratic society. Its economy rested fundamentally on slave labor. Women were forbidden to own or inherit property; even wealthy women were forced to spend most of their time secluded from public life. Girls were generally considered unworthy of education.

Nevertheless, relative to other societies of its time, ancient Athens was the pinnacle of participatory democracy. Those adult males fortunate enough to be citizens of Athens served as equals in the legislative assembly, which made the major decisions governing Athenian society. Those citizens, at least, enjoyed the benefits of a society that cultivated both self-expression and interaction among politically empowered individuals. Not surprisingly, science, art, and literature flourished in this environment. So, too, did philosophy.

Perhaps the most inspiring figure to emerge from ancient Athens was, on the surface, anything but the picture of classical Greek beauty. He had, among

Socrates (469-399 B.C.) developed the famous "Socratic method," that involved testing his students' ideas through repeated questioning and disputation.

other undesirable physical features, a snub nose and a sizable belly, and he would habitually walk about town barefoot in shabby old clothes. Far from achieving favor with the ruling class of Athens, he was sentenced to death for impiety, which in his case meant "corrupting" the youth of the city with unorthodox ideas and "neglecting" the gods that Athenians traditionally worshipped. After his death, however, this man was to be hailed as the personification of wisdom and the philosophical life. His name was *Socrates*.

Socrates (469–399 B.C.) did not write down his thoughts. Rather, he walked about Athens engaging people in provocative dialogues about questions of ultimate significance. Disdaining wealth and status as values, Socrates is depicted as an exemplar of human virtue and piety whose goal was to help others find the truths that lie within their own minds. In that regard, he described himself as merely a "midwife."

The **Socratic method** is the term given to Socrates' approach to helping students understand their own deepest thoughts. By repeatedly questioning, disproving, and testing the thoughts of his pupils on such questions as the nature of "love" or "the good," Socrates was confident that he could help his pupils eventually discover invaluable guides to a virtuous life.

Socrates may be best known today for the noble manner in which he died. During his trial for "impiety," Socrates vigorously defended his philosopher's mission. After he was found guilty, the court offered him the option of proposing an appropriate penalty. Socrates first suggested, semiseriously, that he be rewarded rather than punished, and thereafter he proposed that he pay only a relatively small fine. The court then voted to approve the death penalty, a result Socrates presumably foresaw but nevertheless preferred to concessions that would appear to acknowledge his guilt. At peace with his decision to accept death and maintain his virtue, Socrates willingly drank the poisonous hemlock given in execution of his sentence.

We know about Socrates and his teachings through the writings of his disciples, one of whom was *Plato* (427–347 B.C.). The son of a wealthy family, Plato initially entered the field of politics. However, after the death of his

An Example of the Socratic Method in Action

Teacher: Today we will try to understand what we mean by the concepts of right and wrong. What are examples of conduct you consider wrong or immoral?

Student: Lying is wrong.

Teacher: But what if you were living in Germany around 1940 and you were harboring in your house a certain Mr. Cohen who was wanted by the Nazis. If asked by a Nazi if you knew the whereabouts of that Mr. Cohen, wouldn't it be acceptable, even *obligatory,* to lie?

Student: I suppose so.

Teacher: So could you rephrase what you meant when you said that lying is wrong or immoral?

Student: I think what I meant is that it is usually wrong to lie. But it is true that there are times when lying is acceptable, because the overall effects of the lie are good. Look at how much your "Mr. Cohen" was helped; the lie about where he was may have saved his life.

Teacher: So you are saying that it is okay to lie as long as the consequences of the lie are positive. But consider this hypothetical situation: I am a business tycoon who makes millions of dollars selling diamonds to investors. I sell only to very rich people who can afford to lose the money they invest in my diamonds. I tell my customers that my diamonds are worth $10,000 each, but they really are fakes, worth only $2,000 each. Rather than keeping the profits myself, I give all the money to the poor, helping them obtain the food and shelter they need to live.

If you look at the obvious consequences of my business—the rich get slightly poorer, the needy are helped out immensely—you may conclude that my business has a generally positive effect on society. And yet, because the business was based on fraud, I find it immoral. Do you agree?

Student: Yes, I find it immoral. I suppose I was wrong in saying that whenever a lie has generally good results, it is morally acceptable.

In your diamond example, unlike the Nazi example, the lie was directed at innocent people and the harm done to them was significant. I want to change my earlier statement that a lie is acceptable whenever it has generally good results. What I want to say now is that you should never lie to innocent people if that would cause them significant harm . . . .

As is typical of Socrates' dialogue, this one could go on indefinitely, because there is no simple "correct" solution to the issues being discussed—the meaning of right and wrong and, more specifically, the contours of when a lie is morally acceptable. By asking questions, the teacher is trying to get the student to clarify and rethink his or her own ideas, to come eventually to a deep and clear understanding of philosophical concepts such as right and wrong.

teacher, Socrates, he became disillusioned with Athenian democracy and left the city for many years. Later he returned to Athens and founded the Academy, considered by some to be the world's first university. At the Academy, students learned such disciplines as math, astronomy, music, logic, politics, and ethics.

Plato's writing is renowned not only for its depth but for its beauty and clarity. His most famous works were dialogues, conversations between two or more people, that presented and critiqued different philosophical viewpoints in the form of a drama. Socrates is the major character in Plato's dialogues. He questions and challenges others about what they are confident is true, and he often presents his own philosophical positions. Precisely which thoughts attributed by Plato to the character Socrates were truly those of the historical Socrates is something we will probably never learn.

Plato is associated with the doctrine that a realm of eternally existing "ideas" or "forms" underlies the physical world. To Plato, truth, beauty, and justice were not mere abstractions; they are truly existent entities in a world hidden from our senses but accessible to those people governed by reason. In that other world exist not only the forms of truth or beauty, but the universal forms of material objects, such as the "bed," the "tree," or the "artichoke."

Aristotle's doctrine of the Golden Mean, or the notion that virtue lies in a middle ground between two extremes, has influenced countless political and moral philosophers down through the ages.

In Plato's philosophy, the human soul has three parts, intellect (or reason), spirit (or passion), and appetite (or basic animal desires). He believed that these three faculties interact with each other to determine human behavior. Plato urged that the intellect, the highest faculty, be trained to control the other two. Plato also taught that, although the body dies, the human soul is immortal.

Just as Plato was the student of Socrates, *Aristotle* (384–322 B.C.) was the student of Plato. Aristotle entered Plato's Academy at age 18 and stayed there for 20 years until Plato died. In 342 B.C. he went to northern Greece and, for several years, tutored a young boy named Alexander. That boy, now known as Alexander the Great, became king and, through his conquests, helped to disseminate Greek culture. After educating Alexander, Aristotle returned to Athens to set up his own school, the Lyceum, adjacent to Plato's Academy.

Whereas Aristotle's prose is not generally considered to have the beauty of Plato's, the depth and breadth of his ideas were unsurpassed in ancient times. In addition to tackling difficult philosophical questions, Aristotle wrote influential works on biology, physics, astronomy, mathematics, psychology, and literary criticism.

Aristotle placed more importance on the physical world than did Plato. Aristotle's teachings can, in fact, be regarded as a synthesis of Plato's belief in the universal, spiritual forms, and a scientist's belief that each animal, vegetable, and mineral we observe is undeniably real. Aristotle's views about the true nature of reality were extremely influential to those who shaped Christian, Jewish, and Islamic philosophy in the Middle Ages.

Plato's Political Philosophy and the "Parable of the Cave"

Plato's political philosophy was set forth in his most well known dialogue, the *Republic*. In that work, Plato showed himself to be one of the pioneers in envisioning the essential relationship between education and government. A son of a wealthy landowner, Plato's ideal, or "utopian," republic is anything but democratic. He envisioned a society with three classes of people: the common people, the warriors, and the rulers (or philosopher-kings). Only the last group, according to Plato, was entitled to political power.

The most famous passage of the *Republic* is known as the "Parable of the Cave." In that timeless passage, Plato compares the realm of human affairs as we know it to an underground cave. That cave is populated by prisoners who are tied down such

that they can only see straight ahead of them. A light in the cave creates shadows on the cave wall, and the prisoners stare intently at the shadows. Those who see the shadows most clearly and can best explain their movements are praised by their fellow prisoners. They, presumably, are the people who, in a nonideal society, rule over business and government. In an ideal society, on the other hand, the philosopher-kings must be educated to escape from the cave and head up to the outside world, the world of sunlight. That world is the transcendent realm of "forms" or "ideas." While leaving the cave is painful at first, a life spent contemplating the world of forms is truly pleasant. However, concludes Plato, the philosopher-kings must eventually return to the cave (that is, participate in practical politics) for 15 years in order to obtain the experience necessary to rule over society with wisdom.

Aristotle is also renowned for his ethical and political theories. He wrote that the highest good for people is a virtuous life, fully governed by the faculty of reason, with which all other faculties are in harmony. Aristotle envisioned a properly functioning society as one that would give each person the role most appropriate to his or her own abilities and inclinations. Like Plato, Aristotle was convinced that the innate capacities of people vary tremendously.

In his writings, Aristotle promoted the doctrine of the Golden Mean, or the notion that virtue lies in a middle ground between two extremes. Courage, for example, is an Aristotelian virtue, bordered on the one side by cowardice and on the other side by foolhardiness.

Many of the ideas first formulated by the ancient Greeks have long been integrated into Western culture. By now, these ideas may seem obvious, whereas they once were startling and profound. We should never lose sight of how remarkable they were, given the time of human history when they were developed.

Why We Remember Socrates, Plato, and Aristotle

- **Socrates.** His philosophical lifestyle; the Socratic method, in which students are provocatively questioned so that they can rethink what they believe; his noble death
- **Plato.** Discussions of philosophy through eloquent dialogues; theory of "forms" or "ideas" that exist in an eternal, transcendent realm; vision of

utopia, where an elite group of philosopher-kings rules over other members of society
- **Aristotle.** Breadth of his knowledge; synthesis of Plato's belief in the eternal "forms" and a scientist's belief in the "real" world that we can see, touch, or smell; theory of the Golden Mean (everything in moderation)

Basic Philosophical Issues and Concepts

Philosophy has many subdivisions that are of particular significance to educators. These include metaphysics, epistemology, ethics, political philosophy, aesthetics, and logic. Before you can formulate your own educational philosophy, you must first become familiar with key terms, issues, and concepts. These are displayed in Figure 13.1 and are discussed below.

Metaphysics and Epistemology

Metaphysics and epistemology are closely related philosophical disciplines. **Metaphysics** deals with the nature of reality, its origin, and its structure. Metaphysicians ask, What really is the nature of the world in which we live? **Epistemology** examines the nature and origin of human knowledge. Epistemologists are interested in how we use our minds to distinguish valid from illusory paths to true knowledge. It may be easiest to remember the scope of these disciplines by considering that epistemology and metaphysics address, respectively, *How we know* (epistemology) . . . *what we know* (metaphysics) . . . about reality.

Is Reality Composed Solely of Matter?

Though *metaphysics* literally means "beyond physics," one of the most basic metaphysical issues is whether anything exists other than the physical, material realm that we experience with our senses. Many philosophers assert the existence only of the physical. This philosophy, because it affirms fundamentally the existence of matter, is called *materialism*. Other philosophers assert that the realm of physical objects is but an illusion. To support their position, they point out that matter is known only through the mind. These philosophers claim that innermost reality is composed solely of mind (also referred to as *soul* or *spirit*). This philosophy is called *spiritualism* or *idealism*. Still a third group of philosophers asserts that reality is composed of two dissimilar substances: body and mind. That belief is associated with the French philosopher René Descartes and is called *Cartesian dualism*.

By emphasizing in their curriculum the study of nature through scientific observation, modern public schools suggest that the physical world is real and important. Teachers must decide for themselves whether to agree with critics

FIGURE 13.1
Branches of Philosophy

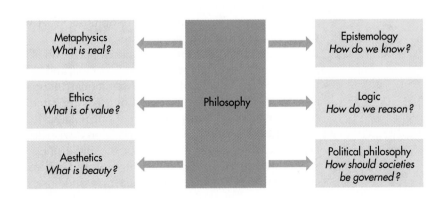

who claim that the modern public schools do not adequately discuss spiritual entities, such as God or the Platonic forms.

Is Reality Characterized by Constant Progress through Time?

Metaphysicians also reflect on the apparent existence of change or flux in nature and address such issues as whether nature is constantly progressing or improving through time. The belief that progress is inevitable is widely held today, particularly by those who champion the political and cultural reforms of recent centuries. Those who do not believe that progress is inevitable may hold a number of alternative views. For example, some philosophers believe that change is cyclical, moving from one point in a cycle through different points, and then back to the initial point, after which the process repeats. The phrase *what comes around goes around* is a statement of this view. Other philosophers hold that change is truly illusory and that a realm of timeless, static forms underlies all reality.

Some teachers believe in the inevitability of progress. They may seek new approaches to teaching and new subjects to be taught, thereby "keeping up with the times." Other teachers are less concerned about, or enamored with, change. Deemphasizing the importance of presenting new ideas and technologies, they may desire that schools teach everlasting, timeless truths, which were discovered by people such as Plato and Aristotle and should be rediscovered by each successive generation.

Is There a God? If So, What Is God's Nature?

The question of God's existence and nature is another key issue of metaphysics. *Theism,* the doctrine that the world was created by an omnibenevolent, omniscient, and omnipotent diety, is familiar to us all. Similarly, most of us are familiar with *atheism,* the doctrine held by materialists. Unlike agnostics, who claim that whether or not God exists is something we cannot know, atheists believe firmly that there is no God.

Less known to people in the Western world are alternatives to these two perspectives on God. One such alternative was set forth by the Dutch philosopher Baruch Spinoza (1632–1677). Spinoza was abhorred by the Jewish and Christian leaders of his day for his unconventional religious views; the orthodox even called him an atheist. Spinoza taught that underlying the world is a single, creative, and aware being: the true God. Contrary to theist beliefs, Spinoza claimed that God did not create the world in accordance with a humanlike will; that is, God did not act based on any desires, such as bestowing grace. Rather, Spinoza contended, God merely expresses himself effortlessly in accordance with his own nature. To Spinoza, what we perceive as evil is merely God unfolding his complex nature.

In recent years, some educators have questioned whether our public schools spend enough time discussing God and religion. They urge that more time be spent talking about the traditional theistic conception of God. They also point out that the Supreme Court has repeatedly indicated that it is appropriate for public schools to teach about religion in a neutral manner. Teachers who address religion in their classes may wish to consider whether, in addition to teaching about the God of the Bible, they should also present discussions about alternative, nontheistic views of God, many of which have achieved considerable popularity in the Eastern world.

What Is the Basis of Our Knowledge?

Before you can decide how best to teach your students, it is important first to reflect on which paths to knowledge are most valid, and which are illusory. This is an underlying issue in both epistemology and education.

One group of philosophers holds that sensory experiences (seeing, hearing, touching, and so on) are the ultimate source of all human knowledge. They deny that we possess inborn awareness or that we can learn about the world solely through the exercise of reason. This philosophy is called **empiricism.** To empiricists, sensation is the ultimate basis of knowledge, but it is not the sole determinant. Empiricists assert that we experience the external world by sensory perception; then, through reflection, we conceptualize ideas that help us interpret that world. For example, when we see the sun rise every day, we can formulate the belief that it will rise again tomorrow.

The empiricist doctrine that knowledge is gained most reliably through scientific experimentation is the most widely held belief in our Western culture. People want to hear the latest research or be shown evidence that something is true. Even children demand of one another, "prove it." Science teachers rely on experimental research to draw conclusions about the physical world.

Rationalists disagree with empiricists about the extent to which knowledge must be grounded on sensory experience. **Rationalism** emphasizes the power of reason—in particular, the principles of logic—to derive true statements about the world. Rationalists point out that the field of mathematics has generated considerable knowledge that is not based on our senses. For example, we can reason that 7 cubed equals 343 without having to count seven times seven times seven objects to verify our conclusion empirically. Not surprisingly, rationalists encourage schools to place a greater emphasis on teaching about mathematics as well as such nonempirical disciplines as philosophy.

Some philosophers oppose both rationalism and empiricism. They believe that our emotions or innermost intuitions are our surest sources of truth. For example, according to the French philosopher Jean-Jacques Rousseau, we all possess in the depth of our being certain feelings and passions. Only when these feelings and passions are first shielded from polluted influences in our culture, and then liberated and allowed to control our conduct, may we possess true understanding and virtue. Rousseau's novel *Emile* set forth his educational philosophy. (For a biography of Jean-Jacques Rousseau, see the Education Hall of Fame in Chapter 9.)

Ethics, Political Philosophy, and Aesthetics

In discussing ethics, political philosophy, and aesthetics, philosophers move from what "is" to what "ought to be." They confront openly and directly the issue of what we should value or hold in esteem.

Ethics, or morality, studies what is "good" or "bad" in human behavior, thoughts, and feelings. It analyzes how individuals ought to treat other people or animals. It inquires into the nature of "the good life," so that people can learn not only how to treat others properly but how properly to treat themselves. To reach judgments about what is good or bad, ethics seeks an understanding of human nature.

Just as an ethicist must understand the principles of psychology, a political philosopher must understand the principles of such fields as political science and economics. **Political philosophy** analyzes how past and present societies are arranged and governed and proposes ways to create better societies in the future. Many treatises in political philosophy, such as Plato's *Republic,* describe ideal, or utopian, societies and suggest how we can create them.

Aesthetics is concerned with the nature of beauty. It asks: What is beauty? How can we evaluate the beauty or lack of beauty in the world? Is beauty solely in the eyes of the beholder? Or do different objects, people, and works of art each possess different amounts of beauty, some being objectively more beautiful than others?

Controversy over whether beauty is solely in the eyes of the beholder is an example of a larger debate that inquires about what is of most value. One school of thought, *absolutism,* claims that values exist independently of any human being. Objective and universal, they exist for all. Whenever a universal value is identified (for example, one of the Ten Commandments), all people must follow it, or they are acting outside the boundaries of a virtuous life. The opposing school of thought is called *relativism.* It argues that values are determined by the interests, perceptions, or desires of each individual. An old Latin saying *De gustibus non est disputandum,* or "Don't argue with someone else's taste," reflects the relativist point of view.

Ethics, political philosophy, and aesthetics underlie much of the official school curriculum and have extensive influence in shaping the hidden curriculum as well. For example, some critics argue that our schools' emphasis on equal educational opportunities, as well as the relative lack of resources targeted specifically to gifted and talented students, indicates an overly democratic bias on the part of our nation's educators. Others, however, argue that by tracking students into various ability groups, schools in fact have created an elitist system of education in which only a small group of children are prepared to compete in the world of business and government. For another example, consider how different aesthetic viewpoints influence the literature, music, and fine arts curricula of schools. A teacher may include or exclude novels, plays, or works of music or art based on his or her aesthetic values.

Logic

Logic is the branch of philosophy that deals with reasoning. It focuses on how to move from a set of assumptions to valid conclusions and examines the rules of inference that enable us to frame our propositions and arguments. While epistemology defines reasoning as one way to gain knowledge, logic defines the rules of reasoning.

Schools teach children to reason both deductively and inductively. When teaching **deductive reasoning,** teachers present their students with a general rule and then help them to identify particular examples and applications of the rule. Inductive reasoning works in the opposite manner. When teaching **inductive reasoning,** teachers help their students to draw tentative generalizations after having observed specific instances of a phenomenon.

A teacher who explains the commutative property of addition (a + b = b + a) and then provides the student with specific examples of this rule (3 + 2 = 2 + 3, or 5 + 1 = 1 + 5) is teaching deductive reasoning. Contrast this with a teacher who begins a lesson by stating a series of addition problems of the form 3 + 2 = 5 and 2 + 3 = 5. After presenting the series of problems, the teacher poses the question "What do you notice about these examples?" If students can draw a tentative generalization about the commutative property of addition, they are reasoning inductively.

One way of remembering the difference between inductive and deductive reasoning is by recalling the Sherlock Holmes mysteries. In those stories, detective Holmes was involved in sifting through a myriad of evidence to reach general conclusions about a crime. When he reached such a conclusion, he was inevitably rewarded by the praise of his assistant, Dr. Watson, who would exclaim "brilliant deduction." But, in fact, Holmes had not made a deduction. He was reasoning inductively. That is, he was reasoning from the particulars to the general.

Philosophies of Education

[I]n modern times there are opposing views about the practice of education. There is no general agreement about what the young should learn either in relation to virtue or in relation to the best life; nor is it clear whether their education ought to be directed more towards the intellect than towards the character of the soul. . . . [A]nd it is not certain whether training should be directed at things useful in life, or at those conducive to virtue, or at nonessentials. . . . And there is no agreement as to what in fact does tend towards virtue. Men do not all prize most highly the same virtue, so naturally they differ also about the proper training for it. (*Aristotle*)[1]

Aristotle wrote that passage more than 2,300 years ago, and today educators are still debating the issues he raised. Different approaches to resolving these and other fundamental issues have given rise to different schools of thought in the philosophy of education. We will examine five such schools of thought: essentialism, progressivism, perennialism, existentialism, and behaviorism. Each has many supporters in U.S. education today. Taken together, these five schools of thought do not exhaust the list of possible educational philosophies you may adopt, but they certainly present strong frameworks from which you can create your own educational philosophy.

Essentialism

1. Gripping and enduring interests frequently grow out of initial learning efforts that are not appealing or attractive.
2. The control, direction, and guidance of the immature by the mature is inherent in the prolonged period of infancy or necessary dependence particular to the human species.
3. While the capacity for self-discipline should be a goal, imposed discipline is a necessary means to this end. Among individuals, as among nations, true freedom is always a conquest, never a gift.
4. Essentialism provides a strong theory of education, its competing school (progressivism) offers a weak theory. If there has been a question in the past as to the kind of educational theory that the few remaining democracies of the world need, there can be no question today. (*William Bagley*)[2]

Profiles in Teaching: William Bagley

William Bagley (1874–1946) popularized the concept of essentialism as an educational philosophy. He served as a professor at the University of Illinois and at Columbia University's Teachers' College. He was also president of the National Council on Education and an editor of two education-related journals.

Bagley believed that the major role of the school is to produce a literate, intelligent electorate that will protect U.S. democracy. Bagley saw the school not as a vehicle for social change but as a stabilizing force in society, where cultural heritage is passed on from one generation to the next. Bagley argued against electives and stressed the value of thinking skills to help students apply their academic knowledge. A major critic of progressivism, he used his forum as editor of the *National Education Association Journal* to voice his concerns.

In California, our educational philosophy can be categorized as "essentialist," or traditional. It holds that many of our students can profit by a traditional academic curriculum, whether or not they are college bound. Thus, we have concentrated our efforts on raising expectations, providing a core curriculum, and increasing the amount of homework. (*Bill Honig*)[3]

Essentialism refers to the traditional, or back-to-basics, approach to education. It is so named because it strives to instill students with the "essentials" of academic knowledge and character development. The term *essentialism* as an educational philosophy was originally popularized in the 1930s by the U.S. educator William Bagley (1874–1946). The philosophy itself, however, had been the dominant approach to education in America from the beginnings of American history. Early in the twentieth century, essentialism was criticized as being too rigid to prepare students adequately for adult life. But with the launching of *Sputnik* in 1957, interest in essentialism revived. Among modern supporters of this position are members of the President's Commission on Excellence in Education. Their 1983 report, *A Nation at Risk,* mirrors essentialist concerns today.

Underlying Philosophical Basis

American essentialism is grounded in a conservative philosophy that accepts the social, political, and economic structure of U.S. society. It contends that schools should not try to radically reshape society. Rather, essentialists argue, U.S.

schools should transmit the traditional moral values and intellectual knowledge that students need in order to become model citizens. Essentialists believe that teachers should instill such traditional American virtues as respect for authority, perseverance, fidelity to duty, consideration for others, and practicality.

Reflecting its conservative philosophy, essentialism tends to accept the philosophical views associated with the traditional, conservative elements of U.S. society. For example, U.S. culture traditionally has placed tremendous emphasis on the central importance of the physical world and of understanding the world through scientific experimentation. As a result, to convey important knowledge about our world, essentialist educators emphasize instruction in natural science rather than in nonscientific disciplines such as philosophy or comparative religion.

The Essentialist Classroom

Essentialists urge that the most essential or basic academic skills and knowledge be taught to all students. Traditional disciplines such as math, natural science, history, foreign language, and literature form the foundation of the essentialist curriculum. Essentialists frown upon vocational, life-adjustment, or other courses with "watered-down" academic content.

Elementary students receive instruction in skills such as writing, reading, measurement, and computing. Even when learning art and music, subjects most often associated with the development of creativity, the students are required to master a body of information and basic techniques, gradually moving from less to more complex skills and detailed knowledge. Only by mastering the required material for their grade level are students promoted to the next higher grade.

Essentialist programs are academically rigorous, for both slow and fast learners. The report *A Nation at Risk* reflects the essentialist emphasis on rigor. It calls for more core requirements, a longer school day, a longer academic year, and more challenging textbooks. Moreover, essentialists maintain that classrooms should be oriented around the teacher, who ideally serves as an intellectual and moral role model for the students. The teachers or administrators decide what is most important for the students to learn and place little emphasis on student interests, particularly when such interests divert time and attention from the academic curriculum. Essentialist teachers focus heavily on achievement test scores as a means of evaluating progress.

In an essentialist classroom, students are taught to be "culturally literate"— that is, to possess a working knowledge about the people, events, ideas, and institutions that have shaped U.S. society. Reflecting the essentialist emphasis on technological literacy, *A Nation at Risk* recommends that all high school students complete at least one semester of computer science. Essentialists hope that when students leave school, they will possess not only basic skills and an extensive body of knowledge, but also disciplined, practical minds, capable of applying schoolhouse lessons in the real world.

Essentialism in Action: The Amidon School

Carl Hansen was superintendent of schools for the District of Columbia when he founded the Amidon Elementary School. Created in 1960, 3 years after the Soviet Union launched *Sputnik,* the Amidon School was an experiment in essentialist, back-to-basics education in an urban public school. Its goal was to provide a rigorous academic program that would prepare students for effective citizenship. The curriculum of the Amidon School was organized into the following traditional subjects: reading, writing, spelling, penmanship, speaking, grammar, math, science, U.S. history, geography, music, art, and health and physical education. Students received organized presentations of the facts and principles considered basic to each of these subjects. They were expected to learn the subject matter presented and to apply their knowledge to concrete situations. Promotion from one grade to the next hinged upon successful student achievement.

Hansen presented the case for essentialist education in *The Amidon Elementary School: A Successful Demonstration in Basic Education*.[4] As an essentialist, Hansen focused on achievement tests as a measure of a school's success. He presented statistics indicating that the Amidon School's test scores for the first group of students were substantially higher than scores of other schools with comparably intelligent students. Hansen concluded from these test results that the instruction provided at Amidon was of superior quality.

The Amidon School did change. In the late 1960s, following community protests that the school was not responsive to the needs of all the children, the Hansen model was replaced with a more child-centered, less rigorous approach.

Progressivism

[W]e may, I think, discover certain common principles amid the variety of progressive schools now existing. To imposition from above is opposed expression and cultivation of individuality; to external discipline is opposed free activity; to learning from texts and teachers, learning through experience; to acquisition of isolated skills and techniques by drill is opposed acquisition of them as means of attaining ends which make direct vital appeal; to preparation for a more or less remote future is opposed making the most of the opportunities of present life; to statistics and materials is opposed acquaintance with a changing world. (*John Dewey*)[5]

Progressivism's respect for individuality, its high regard for science, and its receptivity to change harmonized well with the U.S. environment in which it was created. The person most responsible for the success of progressivism was John Dewey (1859–1952). Dewey entered the field of education as a liberal social reformer with a background in philosophy and psychology. In 1896, while a professor at the University of Chicago, Dewey founded the famous Laboratory School as a testing ground for his educational ideas. Dewey's writings and his work with the Laboratory School set the stage for the progressive education movement, which, beginning in the 1920s, has produced major lasting innovations in American education. (For a biography of John Dewey, see the Education Hall of Fame in Chapter 9.)

The progressivist movement stimulated schools to broaden their curricula, making education more relevant to the needs and interests of students. Its influence waned during the 1950s, particularly after the 1957 launching of *Sputnik* by the Soviet Union prompted schools to emphasize traditional instruction in math, science, foreign languages, and other defense-related subjects. In the late 1960s and 1970s, under the guise of citizenship education and educational relevance, many of Dewey's ideas enjoyed a renewed popularity that decreased again during the education reform movement of the 1980s.

The Roots of Progressivism: John Dewey's Philosophy

Dewey regarded the physical universe as real and fundamental. He also claimed that the one constant truth about the universe is the existence of change. For Dewey, change was not an uncontrollable force; rather, it could be directed by human intelligence. He explained that as we alter our relationship with our environment, we ourselves are made different by the experience.

Dewey not only believed in the existence of change but welcomed it. He regarded the principles of democracy and freedom espoused in the United States as representing tremendous progress over the political ideas of earlier times. Nevertheless, Dewey found much that was wrong with U.S. society, and he had little affection for the traditional U.S. approach to education. He hoped that his school reforms would alter the American social fabric, making it a more democratic nation of free-thinking, intelligent citizens.

Dewey taught that people are social animals who learn well through active interplay with others and that our learning increases when we are engaged in activities that have meaning for us. Book learning, to Dewey, was no substitute for actually doing things. Fundamental to Dewey's epistemology is the notion that knowledge is acquired and expanded as we apply our previous experiences to solving new, meaningful problems. Education, to Dewey, is a reconstruction of experience, an opportunity to apply previous experiences in new ways. Relying heavily on the scientific method, Dewey proposed a five-step method for solving problems: (1) Become aware of the problem; (2) define it; (3) propose various hypotheses to solve it; (4) examine the consequences of each hypothesis in the light of previous experience; and (5) test the most likely solution.

Progressivism in the Schoolhouse

Believing that people learn best from what they consider most relevant to their lives, progressivists center the curriculum around the experiences, interests, and abilities of students. Teachers plan lessons that arouse curiosity and push the students to a higher level of knowledge. In addition to reading textbooks, the students must learn by doing. Often students leave the classroom for field trips during which they interact with nature or society. Teachers also stimulate the students' interests through thought-provoking games. For example, modified forms of the board game Monopoly have been used to illustrate the principles of capitalism and socialism.

In a progressivist school, students are encouraged to interact with one another and to develop social virtues such as cooperation and tolerance for different points of view. Also, teachers feel no compulsion to focus their students' attention on one discrete discipline at a time, and students may be responsible for learning lessons that combine several different subjects.

Progressivists emphasize in their curriculum the study of the natural and social sciences. Teachers expose students to many new scientific, technological, and social developments, reflecting the progressivist notion that progress and change are fundamental. Students are also exposed to a more democratic curriculum that recognizes accomplishments of women and minorities as well as white males. In addition, in the classroom, students solve problems similar to those they will encounter outside of the schoolhouse; they learn to be flexible problem solvers.

Progressivists believe that education should be a perpetually enriching process of ongoing growth, not merely a preparation for adult lives. They also deny the essentialist belief that the study of traditional subject matter is appropriate for all students, regardless of interest and personal experience. By including instruction in industrial arts and home economics, progressivists strive to make schooling both interesting and useful. Ideally, the home, workplace, and schoolhouse blend together to generate a continuous, fulfilling learning experience in life. It is the progressivist dream that the dreary, seemingly irrelevant classroom exercises that so many adults recall from childhood will someday become a thing of the past.

Progressivism in Action: The Laboratory School

Based on the view that educators, like scientists, need a place to test their ideas, Dewey's Laboratory School eventually became the most famous experimental school in the history of U.S. education, a place where thousands observed Dewey's innovations in school design, methods, and curriculum. Although the school remained under Dewey's control for only 8 years and never enrolled more than 140 students (ages 3–13) in a single year, its influence was enormous.

Dewey designed his school with only one classroom but with several facilities for experiential learning: a laboratory, an art room, a woodworking shop, and a kitchen. Children were likely to make their own weights and measures in the laboratory, illustrate their own stories in the art room, build a boat in the shop, and learn chemistry in the kitchen. They were unlikely to learn through isolated exercises or drills, which, according to Dewey, the students consider irrelevant. Since Dewey believed that students learn well from social interaction, the school used many group methods such as cooperative model making, field trips, role playing, and dramatizations. Dewey also maintained that group techniques make the students better citizens, developing, for example, their willingness to share responsibilities.

Children in the Laboratory School were not promoted from one "grade" to another after mastering certain material. Rather, they were grouped according to their individual interests and abilities. For all its child-centered orientation, however, the Laboratory School remained hierarchical in the sense that the students were never given a role comparable to that of the staff in determining the school's educational practices.

Perennialism

The Paideia Program seeks to establish a course of study that is general, not specialized; liberal, not vocational; humanistic, not technical. Only in this way can it fulfill the meaning of the words "paideia" and "humanities," which signify the general learning that should be in the possession of every human being. (*Mortimer Adler*)[6]

The great books of ancient and medieval as well as modern times are a repository of knowledge and wisdom, a tradition of culture which must initiate each generation. (*Mortimer Adler*)[7]

Textbooks have probably done as much to degrade the American intelligence as any single force. (*Robert M. Hutchins*)[8]

Perennial means "everlasting"; for example, a perennial flower is one that comes up year after year. Espousing the notion that some ideas have lasted over centuries and are as relevant today as when they were first conceived, **perennialism** urges that these ideas should be the focus of education. According to perennialists, when students are immersed in the study of those profound and enduring ideas, they will appreciate learning for its own sake and become true intellectuals.

The roots of perennialism lie in the philosophy of Plato and Aristotle, as well as that of St. Thomas Aquinas, the thirteenth-century Italian whose ideas continue to shape the nature of Catholic schools throughout the world. Perennialists are generally divided into two groups: (1) those who espouse the religious approach to education adopted by Aquinas and (2) those who follow the secular approach formulated in the twentieth-century United States by such individuals as Robert Hutchins and Mortimer Adler. We will be concentrating here on this second branch of perennialism. It strives above all to develop our capacity to reason, and regards training in the humanities as particularly essential to the development of our rational powers.

Similarities to Essentialism

While Hutchins and Adler regard perennialism as a badly needed alternative to essentialism, the two philosophies have many similarities. Both aim to rigorously develop all students' intellectual powers, first, and moral qualities, second. Moreover, both advocate classrooms centered around teachers in order to accomplish these goals. The teachers do not allow the students' interests or experiences to substantially dictate what they teach. They apply whatever creative techniques and other tried-and-true methods are believed to be most conducive to disciplining the students' minds.

As with essentialism, perennialism accepts little flexibility in the curriculum. For example, in his *Paideia Program,* published in 1982, Mortimer Adler recommends a single elementary and secondary curriculum for all students, supplemented by years of preschooling in the case of the educationally disadvantaged. He would allow no curricular electives except in the choice of a second language.

The perennialists base their support of a universal curriculum on the view that all human beings possess the same essential nature: We are all rational animals. Perennialists argue that allowing students to take vocational or life-adjustment courses denies them the opportunity to fully develop their rational powers. As Plato might claim, by neglecting the students' reasoning skills, we deprive them of the ability to use their "higher" faculties to control their "lower" ones (passions and appetites).

Differences from Essentialism

Unlike essentialism, perennialism is not rooted in any particular time or place. The distinctively American emphasis on the value of scientific experimentation to acquire knowledge is reflected in essentialism, but not in perennialism. Similarly, while essentialism reflects the traditional U.S. view that the "real" world is the physical world we experience with our senses, perennialism is more

Profiles in Teaching: Robert M. Hutchins

Robert M. Hutchins (1899–1979) was a primary spokesperson for the perennialist movement in U.S. education. In 1929, a year after he was appointed dean of the Yale Law School, he was named president of the University of Chicago. During the 16 years he served as president of that university, Hutchins developed and implemented his philosophy of education. Stressing intellectual attainment and the need for a liberal education, he argued against the vocational emphasis in U.S. education. While at the University of Chicago, he also abolished the course credit system, since he was opposed to granting a degree based on the number of credits a student earned. Instead, his plan for undergraduates measured achievement by comprehensive examination. In addition, Hutchins abolished fraternities, football, and compulsory attendance and introduced the Great Books program into various levels of the University of Chicago curriculum. In the Great Books program, students read works by history's finest minds, including Plato, Newton, Rousseau, and Darwin, but few books by women or non–Western authors.

open to the notion that universal spiritual forms—such as those posited by Plato or by theological philosophers—are equally real.

Perennialists seek to help students discover those ideas most insightful and timeless in understanding the human condition. The study of philosophy is thus a crucial part of the perennialist curriculum. Perennialists regard essentialism, and its view that knowledge stems primarily from the empirical findings of scientists, as undermining the importance of our capacity to reason as individuals—that is, to think deeply, analytically, flexibly, and imaginatively.

Recognizing that enormous strides have been made in our knowledge about the physical universe, perennialists teach about the processes by which scientific truths have been discovered. Perennialists emphasize, though, that students should not be taught information that may soon be obsolete or found to be incorrect because of future scientific and technological findings. They would not be as interested as the essentialists, for example, in teaching students how to use current forms of computer technology.

Like progressivists, perennialists criticize the vast amount of discrete factual information that educators traditionally have required students to absorb. Perennialists urge schools to spend more time teaching about concepts and explaining how these concepts are meaningful to students. Particularly at the high school and university levels, perennialists decry undue reliance on textbooks and lectures to communicate ideas. Perennialists suggest that a greater emphasis be placed on teacher-guided seminars, where students and teachers engage in Socratic dialogues, or mutual-inquiry sessions, wherein students develop an enhanced understanding of history's most timeless concepts. In addition, perennialists recommend that students learn directly from reading and analyzing the Great Books. These are the creative works by history's finest thinkers and writers, which perennialists believe are as profound, beautiful, and meaningful today as when they were written.

Perennialists lament the change in universities over the centuries from places where students (and teachers) pursued truth for its own sake to mere glorified training grounds for the students' careers. University students may learn a few trees, perennialists claim, but many will be quite ignorant about the forests: the timeless philosophical questions.

Perennialism in Action: St. John's College

The best-known example of perennialist education today takes place at a private institution unaffiliated with any religion: St. John's College, founded in 1784 in Annapolis, Maryland. It adopted the Great Books as a core curriculum in 1937 and assigns readings in the fields of literature, philosophy and theology, history and the social sciences, mathematics and natural science, and music. It seeks to promote a truly liberal education that will help develop free and rational people "committed to the pursuit of knowledge in its fundamental unity, intelligently appreciative of their common cultural heritage, and conscious of their social and moral obligation."[9] Students write extensively and attend seminars twice weekly to discuss assigned readings. They also complete a number of laboratory experiences and tutorials in language, mathematics, and music, guided by the faculty, who are called *tutors*. Seniors take oral examinations at the beginning and end of their senior year and write a final essay that must be approved before they are allowed to graduate.

Since the St. John's experience thrives best in a small-group atmosphere, the college established a second campus in 1964 in Santa Fe, New Mexico, to handle additional enrollment. Although grades are given in order to facilitate admission to graduate programs, students receive their grades only upon request and are expected to learn only for learning's sake. St. John's alumni can be found in all fields, but most have gone into law, theology, medicine, education, and philosophy.

Existentialism

Childhood is not adulthood; childhood is playing and no child ever gets enough play. The Summerhill theory is that when a child has played enough he will start to work and face difficulties, and I claim that this theory has been vindicated in our pupils' ability to do a good job even when it involves a lot of unpleasant work. (*A. S. Neill*)[10]

The bestowal of freedom is the bestowal of love. . . . Children do not need teaching as much as they need love and understanding. They need approval and freedom to be naturally good. (*A. S. Neill*)[11]

Man is nothing else but what he makes of himself. Such is the first principle of existentialism. (*Jean-Paul Sartre*)[12]

Existentialism *as a Philosophical Term*

The existentialist movement in education is based on an intellectual attitude that philosophers term **existentialism.** Born in nineteenth-century Europe, existentialism is associated with such diverse thinkers as Søren Kierkegaard (1813–1855), a passionate Christian, and Friedrich Nietzsche (1844–1900), who wrote a book entitled *The Antichrist* and coined the phrase *God is dead*. While the famous existentialists would passionately disagree with one another on many basic philosophical issues, what they shared was a respect for individualism. In particular, they argued that traditional approaches to philosophy do not adequately respect the unique concerns of each individual.

Jean-Paul Sartre's classic formulation of existentialism—that, for humans, "existence precedes essence"—means that there exists no universal, inborn human nature. We are born and exist, and then we ourselves freely determine our essence (that is, our innermost nature). Some philosophers commonly associated with the existentialist tradition never fully adopted the "existence precedes essence" principle. Nevertheless, that principle is fundamental to the educational existentialist movement.

Existentialism as an Educational Philosophy

Just as its namesake sprang from a strong rejection of traditional philosophy, educational existentialism sprang from a strong rejection of the traditional, essentialist approach to education. (Hereafter in this chapter, *existentialism* will refer simply to the movement in education associated with that term.) Existentialism rejects the existence of any source of objective, authoritative truth about metaphysics, epistemology, ethics, and aesthetics. Instead, individuals are responsible for determining for themselves what is true or false, right or wrong, beautiful or ugly. For the existentialist, there exists no universal form of human nature; each of us has the free will to develop as we see fit.

In the existentialist classroom, subject matter takes second place to helping the students understand and appreciate themselves as unique individuals who accept complete responsibility for their thoughts, feelings, and actions. The teacher's role is to help students define their own essence by exposing them to various paths they may take in life and creating an environment in which they may freely choose their own preferred way. Since feeling is not divorced from reason in decision making, the existentialist demands the education of the whole person, not just the mind.

Although many existentialist educators provide some curricular structure, existentialism, more than other educational philosophies, affords students great latitude in their choice of subject matter. In an existentialist curriculum, students are given a wide variety of options from which to choose.

To the extent that the staff, rather than the students, influence the curriculum, the humanities are commonly given tremendous emphasis. They are explored as a means of providing students with vicarious experiences that will help unleash their own creativity and self-expression. For example, rather than emphasizing historical events, existentialists focus upon the actions of historical individuals, each of whom provides possible models for the students' own behavior. In contrast to the humanities, math and the natural sciences may be deemphasized, presumably because their subject matter would be considered "cold," "dry," "objective," and therefore less fruitful for self-awareness. Moreover, vocational education is regarded more as a means of teaching students

Profiles in Teaching: A. S. Neill

A. S. Neill (1883–1973) was a famous existentialist educator and the founder of Summerhill, an English experimental school. Born in Scotland, he was such a poor student that he was the only one of eight children not to go to college. Instead, at age 14, he began work in a factory. Frustrated with that job, he then went to work for his father, who was a schoolmaster. In this way, Neill became a teacher and launched an influential career that would culminate in the establishment of Summerhill, a school based on his belief in freedom and student government. Founded in 1924, Summerhill became the most famous model of existentialist philosophy. It is still in operation.

Neill's attitude toward education stemmed from his own problems as a student and from his observations of the students he met and taught across the Scottish countryside. Many of those students were bored with school and wanted to learn only that information they saw as personally useful. According to Neill, the best treatment for these students was noninterference—allowing them to make decisions for themselves. Summerhill exemplified this philosophy. At Summerhill, the students governed the school and issued all punishments. The students even decided whether or not they wanted to attend class.

Today Summerhill is still in operation; but according to a 1992 *Wall Street Journal* report, freedom has turned to anarchy. Students rarely attend classes, and discipline problems occur frequently.

about themselves and their potential than of earning a livelihood. In teaching art, existentialism encourages individual creativity and imagination more than it does copying and imitating established models.

Existentialist methods focus on the individual. Learning is self-paced, self-directed, and includes a great deal of individual contact with the teacher, who relates to each student openly and honestly. Although elements of existentialism occasionally appear in public schools, this philosophy has found wider acceptance in private schools and in alternative public schools founded in the late 1960s and early 1970s.

Existentialism in Action: The Sudbury Valley School

After A. S. Neill established the Summerhill school in England in the early 1920s, a number of existentialist private schools were founded in the United States. One of those schools, which remains in operation today, is the Sudbury Valley school, established in 1968 in Framingham, Massachusetts.

Sudbury Valley operates on the principle that education should be founded upon children's natural tendencies toward wanting to grow up, to be competent, to model older children and adults, and to fantasize. No fixed curriculum is set forth, and no activity takes place unless a student asks for it. Instead, the school offers a wide variety of educational options, including instruction in standard subjects in both group and tutorial formats; field trips to Boston, New York, and the nearby mountains and seacoast; and the use of facilities that include a laboratory, a woodworking shop, a computer room, a kitchen, a darkroom, an art room, and several music rooms. School governance is democratic, with each student and staff member having one vote. Parents participate, along with students and teachers, in deciding the school's budget, tuition rates, and questions of general policy.

Sudbury Valley is fully accredited. It accepts anyone from 4-year-olds to adults and charges low tuition so as not to exclude anyone. No evaluations or grades are given except upon request. A high school diploma is awarded to those who complete relevant requirements, which mainly include the ability to be a responsible member of the community at large. The majority of Sudbury's graduates have continued on to college.

Behaviorism

Give me a dozen healthy infants, well-formed, and my own specified world to bring them up in and I'll guarantee to take anyone at random and train him to become any type of specialist I might select—doctor, lawyer, artist, merchant-chief, and yes, even beggar-man and thief, regardless of his talents, penchants, tendencies, abilities, vocations, and race of his ancestors. (*John B. Watson*)[13]

While educational existentialism is based on the notion that we possess free will to shape our innermost nature, behaviorism is derived from the belief that free will is an illusion. According to a pure behaviorist, any human being is shaped entirely by his or her external environment. Alter a person's environment, and you will alter his or her thoughts, feelings, and behavior. Provide positive reinforcement whenever students perform a desired behavior, and soon they will learn to perform the behavior on their own.

Behaviorism has its roots in the early 1900s in the work of the Russian experimental psychologist Ivan Pavlov (1848–1936) and the U.S. psychologist John B. Watson (1878–1958). By refining and expanding their studies, Harvard professor B. F. Skinner (1904–1990) was the driving force behind the spread of behaviorism within modern U.S. culture. Skinner developed the now-famous "Skinner box," which he used to train small animals by behavioral techniques. He also invented a World War II guided missile system that employed pecking pigeons to keep a projectile on course, a controversial air crib for keeping babies in a climatically controlled environment, and programmed learning. (For a biography of B. F. Skinner, see the Education Hall of Fame in Chapter 9.)

Underlying Philosophical Basis

Behaviorism asserts that the only reality is the physical world that we discern through careful, scientific observation. People and other animals are seen as complex combinations of matter that act only in response to internally or externally generated physical stimuli. We learn, for instance, to avoid overexposure to heat through the impulses of pain our nerves send to our brain. More complex learning, such as understanding the material in this chapter, is also determined by stimuli, such as the educational support you have received from your professor or parents, or the comfort of the chair in which you sit when you read this chapter.

Human nature, according to behaviorism, is neither good nor bad, but merely the product of one's environment. It is not human nature but defective environments that are responsible for harmful things that people do to themselves and others. To a behaviorist, there is no such thing as free will or the autonomously acting person; such ideas are only myths that may make us feel better but do not correspond to scientific observation.

Skinner recommends that moral standards ought to be derived from the scientific observation of human behavior. We should identify through experimentation those environments that best utilize humankind's potential. In such environments, we would find the moral code that people ought to follow. That scientifically developed code would be much preferable to our present codes, which are derived from the histories and cultures of particular groups.

Regarding aesthetic appreciation, behaviorists consider our sense of beauty environmentally formed. Have you ever wondered why something believed to be beautiful by another culture appears ugly to you? Behaviorism says that the reason lies in the way your environment has shaped your tastes. A good example is the effect of the media on your appreciation of clothing styles. Over a few months or years, the media may convince you to regard as beautiful a style you previously found unattractive.

Behaviorism in the Classroom

Behaviorism urges teachers to use a system of positive reinforcement (pleasant stimuli or "rewards") to encourage the types of behavior that the school desires. According to Skinner, students may be able to learn material even if they do not fully understand why it will have value in their futures. Rather, it is most important that the students be rewarded whenever they demonstrate the desired response and thus begin to associate the accomplishment of learning with the pleasurable feeling of the reward. Gradually they will firmly acquire that knowledge or moral virtue their schools consider important.

To the extent possible, behaviorists advocate positive rather than negative steps (unpleasant stimuli or "punishment"). Punishment is considered to make the undesirable behavior disappear temporarily, while rewards increase desired behavior and make the students feel better about themselves. A **behavior modification** program usually begins by consistently giving the student extrinsic rewards (a smile, candy, and so on) each time he or she performs a desired behavior. As the student continues to behave in the desired manner, the extrinsic rewards are gradually lessened because the targeted behavior has now acquired, through association, the ability to produce its own reward (self-satisfaction). The length of time this process takes depends on the complexity of the learning desired and on the past environment of the learner. The interval could vary from a few minutes to many years.

After a visit to his daughter's fourth-grade arithmetic class, Skinner developed *programmed learning,* a technique often used by behaviorists. By presenting segments of information to be learned, then eliciting responses to that information, and finally providing immediate feedback regarding the correctness of those responses, teachers allow students to set their own learning pace. By carefully sequencing the material so that most responses are accompanied qby positive feedback, the teachers allegedly make the learning process more enjoyable.

Behaviorist philosophy has produced a great deal of controversy. Critics decry the behaviorists' disbelief in the autonomy of the individual. They also question whether any educator is qualified to exert the extent of control over our youth that behaviorists demand. However, many mainstream educators defend the use of behavior management techniques, claiming that such techniques are particularly helpful when working with young learners, as well as disruptive students of all ages.

Behaviorism in Action: Token Economies in Schools

Although many teachers use social reinforcers such as smiles and nods, the behaviorist programs that have received the most attention are those using more tangible reinforcements.

Little Rock, Arkansas A federal grant helped one inner-city school with a history of severe disciplinary problems and corporal punishment implement a positive reinforcement program in which teachers issued tokens for both acceptable behavior and good academic work. During a special period each week, the students could exchange their tokens for tickets to variously priced activities. Students with insufficient tokens spent the time quietly reading or studying. During its first year, the program successfully eliminated corporal punishment but did not completely solve all disciplinary problems. Often, the most disruptive children were unable to earn enough tokens to benefit from the system.[14]

Gilman, Vermont Billed as a "microeconomy" designed to teach students about real-life economics, the "thaler system" (pronounce it like *tailor*) at a small middle school let students earn up to $8 weekly in thalers (tokens) during nonclass hours for working around the school, operating their own business, or working in their system's own bank, court system, recreation office, or redemption center. The system even had a welfare program financed through taxes on the tokens earned by employed students. Thalers could be spent for extra cafeteria food, access to games, special trips, or at one of the student businesses. Twenty-five percent of students' incomes could also be used to buy items through a mail-order catalog. This program differed from the one mentioned above in that its rewards were not given by teachers and the system was totally separate from the school's academic program. Both student and community responses were favorable, and the program eliminated almost all disciplinary problems. Although there is no proof that the thaler system was responsible, students' academic achievement climbed as well.[15]

Five Philosophies Meet

The school board of Bingham County has decided to establish a magnet high school as an alternative to the county's more traditional schools. Funds from next year's budget have already been allocated, but now the school board needs to describe more precisely what this magnet school will be like. In order to help with this decision, a planning team consisting of five teachers from Bingham County has been selected to determine the school's mission and curriculum. Their recommendations will be submitted to the school board for implementation. Listen to the first meeting of the planning team as the five teachers try to come to agreement on what the new magnet school should look like.

Marcus Washington: Back to basics, back to basics! That's all I've heard since *A Nation at Risk* came out. Our schools are becoming a series of courses to pass, a body of knowledge to memorize. We need to offer an alternative. We can't afford to waste time teaching our students *what* to think. We need to teach them *how* to think. Children must learn how to solve problems. I don't mean the math or history problems at the end of a textbook chapter. I'm talking about real problems that students will find meaningful. When I was in eighth grade, my class took a 3-week trip around the United States by train. Most of the semester was spent planning this trip. We worked together, researching the different areas of the country and deciding where we wanted to go. We learned how to read train schedules and maps because we had to. We discovered the importance of being organized and running meetings effectively. If we weren't organized, nothing got done. Math, history, geography, writing . . . all the subjects were involved. The curriculum was totally integrated. We learned by living. The teachers structured our experiences. I still remember that trip and what went into it as a high point in my life. I want all students to have that kind of experience.

Alice Baker: I agree with what you're saying, but you haven't gone far enough. In the school I envision, the focus of education would be on the students themselves. The teachers of this school would have training in counseling. They need to learn how to listen effectively and guide students toward their personal goals. Not every teacher would be suited for this school, because most of the teachers I know wouldn't be comfortable being so nondirective or so open to views they didn't agree with. The youngest or least able child would have a voice equal to the head of the school in governance and decision making. The resources of the school and faculty would be used to help students learn about themselves and find their own interests. Parents and teachers would not dictate what students should learn or how they should learn it. Instead, methods and curriculum would be decided by each student. They must assume primary responsibility for their own learning. It's not enough to tinker with education. We must change the whole structure.

Jackie Pollack: I can't believe what I'm hearing! We can't let students wander around the country hoping they'll learn what's important or sit around looking at the clouds until they feel interested in learning. We can't afford these luxuries. The very health of our nation's economy is being threatened by other industrialized nations like Japan. Their students outscore ours on many standardized tests. Do you think the Japanese are going to sit still while our young people meander around trying to find themselves?

The school we establish must provide all students with factual knowledge and skills to apply that knowledge; this is what they need in a competitive world. I want a school with a solid curriculum and high academic standards; one that's willing to assign a lot more homework and demand a lot more student discipline than do our present schools. Students must be trained in the traditional academic disciplines, such as English, math,

FIGURE 13.2
Five Philosophies of Education

	Underlying Basis: Metaphysics	Underlying Basis: Epistemology	Focus of Curriculum	Sample Classroom Activity	Role of Teacher	Goals for Students	Educational Leaders
Essentialism	The physical world is the basis of reality	We learn through reasoning, primarily empirical reasoning	Core academic curriculum; students learn traditional academic subjects and such modern "basics" as computer science; students are taught to extol traditional American virtues	Teacher instructs entire class by lecturing about "essential" information or supervising the development of particular skills	Model of academic and moral virtue; center of classroom	To become intelligent problem solvers, culturally literate individuals, and model citizens, educated to compete in the modern economic world	William Bagley
Progressivism	The physical world is the basis of reality; the world inevitably progresses over time	We learn best from meaningful life experiences, social interaction, and scientific experimentation	Flexible; integrated study of academic subjects around activities that reflect personal integrity, needs, and experiences of students; embraces concerns of women and minorities	Learning by doing—for example, students plan a field trip through Shenandoah National Park and Monticello, the home of Thomas Jefferson, in order to learn about history, geography, and natural sciences	Guide or director; must be creative in finding integrated learning activities that can be presented as meaningful to the students	To become intelligent problem solvers, to enjoy learning, to live comfortably in the world while also helping to reshape it	John Dewey

Perennialism	The realm of thought, of spirit, may be at least as real and substantial as the physical world; all human beings are by nature rational animals	We learn through reasoning; particularly through creative, deep, and logical analysis	Core, academic curriculum; students at higher levels read and analyze great works of literature; students learn timeless principles of science rather than technological and scientific information that may later become obsolete with new discoveries	Socratic dialogue analyzing a philosophical issue or the meaning of a great work of literature	Scholarly role model; philosophically oriented, he or she helps students seek the truth for themselves	To increase their intellectual powers and to appreciate learning for its own sake	Robert Hutchins; Mortimer Adler
Existentialism	Reality is whatever each individual determines it to be; people shape their innermost nature in accordance with their free will	Each individual determines how he or she learns best; important life decisions are made by engaging the emotional as well as the intellectual faculties	Each student determines the pace and direction of his or her own learning	Students choose their preferred medium—such as poetry, prose, or painting—and depict their own image of what is beautiful and ideal	One who seeks to relate to each student honestly and directly and is skilled at creating a free, open, and stimulating environment	To accept personal responsibility for their own lives; to understand deeply and be at peace with one's own unique individuality	A. S. Neill
Behaviorism	The physical world is the basis of reality; human beings are primarily shaped by their environmental influences; free will does not exist	Learning is a physiological response to stimuli; it is best induced through positive reinforcement for correct behavior	Curriculum is determined by school staff rather than students; students learn organized bits of information and discrete skills	Students engage in programmed learning	Expert in conditioning the students; one who understands how to apply the techniques of behavioral engineering	To act and think in a manner congruent with the school's objectives	B. F. Skinner

history, geography, and science. They must also learn about computer science, since it's so important in the modern economy. We can't let students decide for themselves what is "right" or "wrong"; we must instill in them the traditional values that have made America a great nation. We need a school that will develop leaders to carry on the traditions of democracy. We can't afford to waste tax dollars on anything else.

Robin Johnson: Jackie, you and I agree that schools must rigorously develop the intellectual powers of all students. But we differ tremendously as to why and how a school should strive to accomplish that goal. You want students to learn merely so that they can become model citizens who are successful in a career. I want students to pursue learning for its own sake, for the wisdom it produces. A life spent reading books by history's greatest thinkers is rewarding in ways a nonintellectual person can never understand. The ideas of the great minds are relevant now and always; they help us solve problems that have plagued humankind for centuries. The beauty of Plato or Shakespeare rivals that of nature itself. Once exposed to it, the students will want more and more; they will see education as a wondrous process that is never-ending.

Given the existence of Plato's *Republic* and other marvelous books, I can't possibly understand why your students learn mainly from textbooks. Those textbooks I've seen are dryer than the Sahara. They succeed in breaking down human knowledge into such minute parts that students rarely can tell why the lessons they are learning are meaningful. The school I envision would focus its curriculum on the timeless ideas that underlie all academic disciplines. Students would learn largely from classic works of literature and art. And lessons would often involve philosophical dialogues between the students and the teacher, as pioneered by the greatest educator of them all, Socrates.

Margaret Nava: Human knowledge has come a long way since the time of the ancient Greeks, Robin. Experimental psychologists applying the methods of science have learned a tremendous amount about the causes of human actions and whether what people call *free will* truly exists. The psychologists have found that our nature is not determined primarily by our genes or our "free," conscious choices. Rather, who we are is determined essentially by our environment. As educators, what we need is an environment that's engineered to maximize learning for the students. Tasks should be broken down into small parts, and student learning should be monitored in order to see what objectives the students have mastered and which components they need to relearn. Modern technology can be used to monitor the students and generate new methods of teaching.

Illiterate students are graduating from high school every day. That would never happen in the school I'd design. Besides being carefully monitored, students would also be systematically reinforced for learning as well as for good behavior. In my school, everything would be carefully designed and controlled.

The discussion has just begun in what promises to become a long afternoon meeting, but chances are that none of these teachers will get precisely what he or she wants. Their goals and philosophies are too divergent for group consensus, and this planning team will either break up in frustration or reach a compromise.

If these five teachers manage to hammer out a philosophical blueprint for a new school, it is likely that the mission and curriculum will reflect **eclecticism**—that is, components of each philosophy that are consistent with one another and can be integrated. The key word here is *consistency*. Philosophies that are diametrically opposed to and inconsistent with one another cannot be combined. For example, the existentialist belief that people determine their innermost nature by the exercise of free will cannot be combined consistently with the behaviorist belief that free will is illusory and we are instead determined by the influence of our environment.

Is your philosophy of education most congruent with a particular member of this planning team? Do you agree with the progressivism of Marcus Washington, the existentialism of Alice Baker, the essentialism of Jackie Pollack, the perennialism of Robin Johnson, or the behaviorism of Margaret Nava? (See Figure 13.2 for a summary of the five philosophies.) Or are you beginning to develop a more eclectic approach, identifying components of each philosophy that are compatible and congruent with one another? It is important for you as prospective teachers to reflect and clarify your educational philosophy, because what you believe will tremendously shape how and what you teach.

SUMMARY

1. Behind every school and every teacher is a set of related beliefs—a philosophy of education—that influences what and how students are taught. Philosophies of education are based on the way the schools and teachers resolve the various philosophical questions that have puzzled thinkers since the time of the ancient Greeks.

2. Socrates, Plato, and Aristotle are the three most legendary ancient Greek philosophers. Socrates is hailed today as the personification of wisdom and the philosophical life. He gave rise to what is now called the *Socratic method,* in which the teacher repeatedly questions the students to help them clarify their own deepest thoughts. His death is renowned as a model of courage and sincere devotion to moral principles.

3. Plato, Socrates' pupil, crafted eloquent dialogues that present different philosophical positions on a number of profound questions. He believed that a realm of externally existing "ideas" or "forms" underlies the physical world. He also believed that preferable to a democracy is a society governed by an elite group of philosopher-kings who are schooled in philosophy as well as the world of practical politics.

4. Aristotle, Plato's pupil, was remarkable for the breadth as well as depth of his knowledge. He provided a synthesis of Plato's belief in the universal, spiritual forms and a scientist's belief in the physical world we observe through our senses. He taught that the virtuous life consists of controlling desires by reason and by following the moderate path between extremes.

5. Philosophical questions include: Is reality composed solely of matter? Is it characterized by constant progress through time? Is there a God? If so, what is God's nature? (*Metaphysics*) What is the basis of human knowledge? (*Epistemology*) What is the nature of the good life? (*Ethics*) The just society? (*Political philosophy*) Beauty? (*Aesthetics*) What are the principles behind human reasoning? (*Logic*)

6. This chapter presents five educational philosophies: essentialism, progressivism, perennialism, existentialism, and behaviorism. Essentialism focuses on teaching whatever academic and moral knowledge is needed for children to become productive citizens. Essentialists urge that schools get back to the basics; they believe in a strong core curriculum and high academic standards.

7. Progressivism is based largely on the belief that lessons must seem relevant to the students in order for them to learn. Consequently, the curriculum of a progressivist school is built around the personal experiences, interests, and needs of the students.

8. Perennialism focuses on the universal truths that have withstood the test of time. Perennialists urge that students read the Great Books and develop their understanding of the philosophical concepts that underlie human knowledge.

9. Existentialism is derived from the belief in human free will. Students in existentialist schools are allowed to control their own education. They are encouraged to understand and appreciate their uniqueness and to assume responsibility for their actions.

10. Behaviorism is founded on the views that human beings are primarily the product of their environment and that children can become moral, intelligent people if they are rewarded for proper behavior. Behaviorists break down material into small lessons, test the students after each lesson, and reward the students for proper responses on the tests.

11. While essentialism is currently the most popular of these five educational philosophies, there exist schools based primarily on each of the other four philosophies, as well. Many schools do not ascribe to any one of these philosophies in a pure form; they are considered eclectic in approach.

12. You should continue to develop and reflect on your own philosophy of education; it will shape the kind of teacher you become.

DISCUSSION QUESTIONS AND ACTIVITIES

1. The creators of the various educational philosophies had a tremendous impact on their students. Pick a teacher who had an impact on you and describe that teacher's philosophy of education.

2. Suppose that you are a student who must choose one of five schools to attend. Each reflects one of the five philosophies. Which would you choose and why? Which school would you choose to work in as a teacher? Why?

3. Interview a teacher who has been teaching for several years. Find out what that teacher's philosophy was when he or she started teaching, and what it is today. Is there a difference? If so, try to find out why.

4. If you could meet one of the great philosophers discussed in this chapter, who would it be and what would you ask him?

5. Reread the five statements by the teachers of Bingham County. In what areas do you think these teachers could agree? In what areas are their philosophies inconsistent?

6. Which of the statements by the five teachers of Bingham County do you agree with most? Are there elements of each teacher's philosophy that you agree with and could combine to form your own philosophy of education?

7. How would you describe your own philosophy of education?

NOTES

1. Aristotle, *Politics,* trans. and intro. by T. A. Sinclair (Middlesex, England: Penguin, 1978), at 300.
2. William Bagley, "The Case for Essentialism in Education," *National Education Association Journal* 30, no. 7 (1941): 202–220.
3. Bill Honig, "The Educational Excellence Movement: Now Here Comes the Hard Part," *Phi Delta Kappan* 66, no. 10 (June 1985): 675–681.
4. Carl Hansen, *The Amidon Elementary School: A Successful Demonstration in Basic Education* (Englewood Cliffs, NJ: Prentice-Hall, 1962).
5. John Dewey, *Experience and Education* (New York: Macmillan, 1963).
6. Mortimer Adler, *The Paideia Program* (New York: Macmillan, 1982), p. 3.
7. Mortimer Adler, *Reforming Education* (Boulder, CO: Westview Press, 1977), pp. 84–85.
8. Robert M. Hutchins, *The Higher Learning in America* (New Haven, CT: Yale University Press, 1962), p. 78.
9. *St. John's Program, 1985–1986.*
10. A. S. Neill, *Freedom—Not License* (New York: Hart, 1966).
11. A. S. Neill, *Summerhill: A Radical Approach to Child Rearing* (New York: Hart, 1960).
12. Jean-Paul Sartre, *Existentialism,* trans. by Bernard Frechtman (New York: Philosophical Library, 1947), p. 13.
13. John B. Watson, *Behaviorism* (New York: Norton, 1924), p. 82.
14. Richard Elardo, "Behavior Modification in an Elementary School," *Phi Delta Kappan* 59, no. 5 (January 1978): 334–338.
15. Richard Bumstead, "The Thaler System: A Slice of Life Curriculum," *Phi Delta Kappan* 59, no. 10 (June 1978): 659–664.

THE STRUGGLE FOR EQUAL EDUCATIONAL OPPORTUNITY

OBJECTIVES

To become aware of major developments in the educational history of the following groups: African Americans, Latinos, Native Americans, Asian/Pacific Americans, and women

To analyze key ways that bias and discrimination continue to operate in today's classrooms

To identify contemporary educational developments that serve to reduce discrimination in the educational process

To become sensitive to the enormous diversity that characterizes learners in today's schools

To identify curricular and instructional strategies that teachers can use to help children reach their full potential

To analyze the tension points between equity and excellence in U.S. schools

*H*ave you ever felt what it is like to be an outsider trying to get "in"? Some of you may have lived the outsider experience when the "in" clique in your school, camp, job, or neighborhood seemed to have no place for you. Others of you may have felt the cold slap of rejection because of race, religion, color, sex, language, national origin, social class, or physical or learning disability. Too often, the majority population, the mainstream, has no tolerance for those who are in some way "different." As most of us know from personal experience, when you happen to be the one who is outside—the one who is deprived even briefly of the benefits, the privileges, the status of the inside group—the feeling of being labeled "inadequate" can be very painful.

Ideally, education should be for all children; it should help each child reach her or his full potential. In reality, education has often served to label, track, discard, and exclude students who are in some way different. These children have too often met prejudicial treatment early, right at the schoolhouse door. This chapter will analyze the nature of prejudicial treatment faced by African Americans, Latinos, Asian/Pacific Americans, Native Americans, and women.

It will also review the major developments that have served to pry the school door open and to bring these once excluded learners into the educational mainstream. At times, this process of breaking down the barriers of bias and discrimination has seemed to turn the process of education inside out, as educators have struggled to cope with federal regulations and court decisions. They have also been forced to question their own value systems and the biases that are ingrained in curriculum materials and sometimes in the very nature of the instructional process. Since the racial and ethnic diversity of the nation's student population is increasing dramatically, schools and society will need to respond so that both equity and excellence can become a reality.

Black Americans: The Struggle for a Chance to Learn

Much of the history of African-American education in the United States has been one of denial. The first law denying slaves the opportunity for education was passed in South Carolina in 1740. During the next hundred years, many states passed similar and even stronger compulsory-ignorance laws. For example, an 1823 Mississippi law prohibited six or more Negroes from gathering for educational purposes. In Louisiana, an 1830 law imposed a 1- to 12-month prison sentence on anyone caught teaching a slave to read or write.[1] However, because education has always been integral to African Americans' struggle for equal opportunity, they have risked the penalties of these laws and even the dangers of violence for a chance to learn. They formed clandestine schools throughout most large cities and towns of the South. Suzie King Taylor described what it was like to attend one of those secret schools in Savannah, Georgia:

> We went every day about nine o'clock with our books wrapped in paper to prevent the police or white persons from seeing them. We went in, one at a time, through the gate, into the yard to the L Kitchen which was the schoolroom. . . .

> The neighbors would see us going in sometimes, but they supposed we were there learning trades. . . . After school we left the same way we entered, one by one, when we would go to a square, about a block from the school, and wait for each other.[2]

The Civil War brought an end to policies of compulsory ignorance and an affirmation of black people's belief in the power of education. Education gave former slaves a new sense of pride. Robert Fitzgerald, a black teacher in Amelia County, Virginia, found the freedmen's and freedwomen's response to education overwhelming:

> It [education] made a vast difference in their lives. It would take some of them quite a while to move the awkward distance from saying "Master" to saying "Mister," but it had taken them no time at all to respond with glowing faces to "ladies" and "gentlemen" and "scholar." It gave them a new image of themselves.[3]

Most of the schooling of African Americans immediately following the Civil War was carried out by various philanthropic societies in cooperation with the

The famous Tuskegee Normal School founded by Booker T. Washington became a national symbol for the educational aspirations of African Americans.

Freedmen's Bureau, the federal agency established to provide various services, including the establishment of schools. School staffs were usually a mixture of instructors from the North and newly freed literate blacks.

Many white Southerners responded to the education of blacks with fear and anger. Sometimes there was terrorism against black schools. In North Carolina, for example, African-American teachers were protected by armed guards. In the end, however, politics replaced violence as the principal means of denying blacks equal educational opportunity following the Civil War.

Reconstruction unofficially ended in the South as conservatives began regaining political power. In state after state, laws were passed that explicitly provided for segregated schools. With the 1896 ***Plessy v. Ferguson*** Supreme Court decision, white supremacy and segregation became a legally sanctioned part of the American way of life. In this landmark case, the Court developed the doctrine of **separate but equal** in relation to railroad travel, a doctrine that was immediately used to develop a segregated school system that in many states lasted for more than 50 years.

The **racial discrimination** of "separate but equal" was clearly visible in the different funding patterns for white and black schools. For example, in 1907, Mississippi spent $5.02 for the education of each white child but only $1.10 for each black child. In 1924, the state paid more than $1 million to transport whites long distances to schools. No money was spent for blacks, and for them a daily walk of more than 12 miles was not out of the question. Attending schools without enough books, seats, space, equipment, or facilities taught African-American children the harsh reality of "separate but unequal": In the South, a dual school system based on race was in existence. This was **de jure segregation**—that is, segregation by law or by official action.

In the North, school assignments were based on both race and residence. **De facto** (unofficial) **segregation** occurred as the result of segregated residential patterns, patterns that were often prompted by discriminatory real estate practices. As housing patterns changed, attendance zones often were redrawn to ensure the separation of white and black children in schools. In schools that were not entirely segregated, black children were often placed in special classes or separate academic tracks, were counseled into low-status careers, and were denied access to extracurricular activities. Whatever the obstacle, however, African Americans continued their struggle for access to quality education. As W. E. B. DuBois noted: "Probably never in the world have so many oppressed people tried in every possible way to educate themselves."[4]

In May 1954, following 20 years of steady political gains by blacks as the result of Franklin Roosevelt's New Deal policies and their own participation in World War II, the Supreme Court made one of its most historic decisions ever. In the case of ***Brown v. Board of Education of Topeka*** (Kansas), the Court unanimously ruled that "in the field of public education the doctrine of 'separate but equal' has no place. Separate educational facilities are inherently unequal. . . ." In indicating how quickly desegregation of Southern schools was to take place, the Court used the phrase "with all deliberate speed." In effect, the Court established a vague timetable, one without a deadline of any kind. So yet another generation of black children experienced segregated education. Ten years after *Brown,* almost 91 percent of African-American children in the South still attended all-black schools.

In schools that did achieve some measure of desegregation, there was extensive ability grouping or tracking. The typical pattern was a virtually all-white college preparatory track and a basic or remedial track that was virtually all-black. The educational rationale behind tracking was to provide remedial work so that all students could eventually move to higher tracks. In reality, this rarely occurred. For example, 7 years after tracking began in the District of Columbia, approximately 97 percent of junior high school students remained in the track they had occupied 2 years earlier.

The integration of Southern schools was not without violence, as the following account by a black minister in Alabama indicates. When in 1957 the Reverend Fred L. Shuttlesworth went to enroll his children in the local white school:

> A mob of people armed with chains, brass knuckles, pipes, and knives set upon us. . . . Mrs. Shuttlesworth was stabbed in the hip. Ruby Fredericks, our second daughter, had her foot hurt in a car door by one of the men and I was beaten with a chain and brass knuckles, knocked several times to the ground, had most of the skin scrubbed off my face and ears, and was kicked in my face and side as members of the mob really set out to kill me.[5]

Such experiences were not uncommon, and **desegregation** made only small apparent gains. But a new movement in the form of nonviolent protest emerged among African Americans. Dr. Martin Luther King, Jr., encouraged black high school and college students to focus their efforts on voting rights.

While the South's dual school system was under attack, segregation continued in the North. New migrations of African Americans to the North during the 1950s and 1960s increased the size of already segregated black neighborhoods and, in so doing, intensified de facto segregation. There were also many instances of deliberate segregation through the altering of school district boundaries. Whenever and however segregated schools appeared, the result was a pattern of unequal achievement for black students.

Scenes like this one became commonplace all across America in the years following the landmark *Brown v. Board of Education of Topeka* decision in 1954 and the passage of the Civil Rights Act in 1964.

In 1964, Congress moved boldly to eradicate racial segregation and discrimination in schools by passing the **Civil Rights Act.** This omnibus act included two titles of particular importance to schools. **Title IV** gave the U.S. Commissioner of Education the power to help desegregate and the U.S. Attorney General the power to initiate law suits to force school desegregation. **Title VI** prohibited the distribution of federal funds to schools with racially discriminatory programs of any kind. Together, these two titles produced more desegregation in their first 4 years than the Supreme Court's decision in *Brown* had produced during the preceding 14.

During the late 1960s and the early 1970s, the Court handed down a series of decisions indicating its impatience with the slow pace of desegregation. The time for "all deliberate speed" was drawing to a close. During this period, the Court also began attacking de facto segregation stemming from racially imbalanced neighborhoods. In Charlotte–Mecklenburg County, North Carolina, a U.S. district judge ordered extensive **busing** of pupils to achieve integration. In addition to busing, the courts later supported devices such as racial quotas and school pairing in attempts to eradicate school segregation. In short, the courts became the primary battleground in the African-American communities' fight for equal educational opportunity.

Because initial desegregation activity was directed at Southern schools, by the 1970s they were among the most integrated in the country. The Court then turned its attention to the North and West, where de facto segregation continued.

The conservative Reagan presidency and the tremendous economic growth of the 1980s shifted attention away from the desegregation issue. As liberal justices were replaced by more conservative appointees, the Supreme Court began to turn to the right. This conservative trend has led to rulings that have loosened the federal government's influence on state and local institutions. The conservative nature of the courts has resulted in retreats from civil rights initiatives such as affirmative action.

A Different Kind of Public School

To respond to the needs of special populations, such as minority groups, working students, or students who for one reason or another have never finished high school, school systems have created some unusual options.

These responses show that public education can go beyond traditional approaches when the need is clear.

- *Alternative school.* Alternative schools were created to reach out to students who were not succeeding in more traditional settings. Some alternative schools are quite informal and offer a less structured, more learner-centered climate. A look into one type of alternative school might reveal students working individually, or with the teacher in small groups. Other alternative schools are called "schools without walls," where students spend a significant amount of time learning

in settings ranging from museums to the City Hall. For students who work during the day, alternative schools can be night schools, providing students with a way to earn a high school diploma while they continue to earn a salary. Yet another kind of alternative school is a magnet school, a popular alternative option with a history all its own.

- *Magnet school.* Created in 1976 under an amendment to the Emergency School Aid Act (ESAA), magnet schools were conceived as tools to attain voluntary desegregation. Magnet schools offer a specialized curriculum, whether in mathematics, the arts, foreign language, the sciences, or some other discipline. Students from different neighborhoods, races, and ethnic backgrounds are drawn to the "special school," and they learn in an integrated setting.

The Tools and Impact of Desegregation

During the 1970s mandatory busing was a key desegregation tool, one that created turmoil and upset a lot of parents. Consequently, many school districts began to experiment with other remedies more acceptable to school families. Typically these procedures involved more freedom of choice and greater emphasis on improved instruction. Such remedies included magnet schools, controlled choice plans, and voluntary metropolitan desegregation arrangements.

Magnet schools attempt to attract a desegregated student population by providing unique and outstanding instructional opportunities not available in other neighborhood schools. Sometimes magnet schools use quota systems to attain desegregation goals. In the past, schools that functioned as magnets had rigorous entry requirements and served an elite student clientele. Today's magnet schools place greater emphasis on what students are interested in rather than the scores they achieve on an entrance exam.

Across the country magnet schools are offering an impressive array of specialties, including foreign language, performing arts, technology, math, and science. Preliminary studies of these schools are encouraging. They attract multiracial enrollments, provide outstanding educational opportunities, encourage business and community support, and result in increased achievement across racial and ethnic groups.[6]

While the limited research on magnet schools is positive, it is highly unlikely that alone they will accomplish the nation's desegregation goals. Other strategies are necessary.

Controlled choice plans are a desegregation tool initiated during the 1980s. Parents indicate three or four schools of choice for their children, and

Magnet schools offer students exceptional educational opportunities and attract culturally diverse students.

the school system tries to place the students in their chosen schools. The system must also provide transportation to the schools that families have selected. Enrollments are controlled to meet designated goals of racial and ethnic composition. The controlled choice plan appears to be most effective in small districts where distances between schools are not too far for travel and where minority enrollment does not exceed 40 or 50 percent. Big-city schools are often more than 70 percent minority, and the majority of these enroll very poor students. In such situations, desegregation plans must involve metropolitan arrangements that include both city and suburbs. Metropolitan desegregation has been brought about both through court orders and through voluntary cooperation between suburban and city school districts.

Controversy surrounds school desegregation. Detractors question whether the process is worth all the effort, expense, and conflict. However, it does appear that desegregation, particularly when combined with emphasis on effective instruction, has both cognitive and affective benefits.

Studies show that in desegregated schools the scores of minority students increase while, for the most part, the scores of white students are not affected. When students attend desegregated schools, other aspects of their later lives—college, employment, social situations—also tend to be desegregated. Similarly, segregation appears to be self-perpetuating. African Americans and other minorities who attended segregated schools are more likely to send their children to segregated schools. Both black and white students who go to desegregated schools have more positive attitudes toward future interracial situations. Further, blacks from desegregated schools get higher college grades, have higher graduation rates, appear to have better employment opportunities, and earn more income. In fact, desegregation researchers have concluded: "We have considerable evidence that school desegregation is a necessary step to insure equality of economic opportunity to minorities in U.S. society."[7]

Hypersegregated Big-City Schools

During the early to mid-1900s, there was a shift in the nation's population so significant that it is now considered a migration: the movement of Southern blacks to Northern cities. Today in the Northeast and throughout the nation, African-American and Latino enrollment is concentrated in big-city schools. In these urban centers segregated housing patterns result in segregated schools. These systems are particularly resistant to integration.

One of the reasons for these hypersegregated urban centers is the withdrawal of both majority and minority middle-class families. The 1970s and the 1980s witnessed an exodus of both middle-class white and minority families from schools and neighborhoods with substantial minority representation. When middle-class families left the cities, they took with them the skills and values that had created and maintained local businesses, churches, schools, and recreational facilities, the infrastructure that was the backbone of the city. They also took with them information and role models that should connect inner-city youth with mainstream U.S. culture.[8]

With the withdrawal of the middle class, these role models are no longer available. In addition, big cities have been hurt badly by the loss of manufacturing jobs and the shift to a service and information-processing economy requiring higher levels of skill and education. The result is a socially isolated population, mainly minority, collectively different from earlier times, characterized by hopelessness and despair. "I don't have any goals," said a black male student in a Houston high school. "I live with my grandmother and she tells me to do my school work, but she can't read so she can't help me. Nobody can help me."[9]

Problems and Progress

In 1968, the Kerner commission appointed by President Johnson issued a warning: "Our nation is moving toward two societies, one black, one white—separate and unequal." The commission charged that white society must assume responsibility for the black ghetto. "White institutions created it, white institutions maintain it, and white society condones it."[10] The report's warning is relevant to this day. Consider the following:

- African Americans have the lowest average Scholastic Assessment Test (SAT) scores in both verbal and math among the nation's major racial and ethnic groups.
- The percentage of blacks in special education classes remains unacceptably high, and the percentage of blacks in accelerated and gifted and talented school programs remains unacceptably low.
- Teen-age pregnancies, alcohol and drug abuse, and dropout and school suspension rates among black students remain at high levels.[11]

While these statistics reflect patterns of educational and economic poverty among African-American students, there has also been substantial academic progress. There are some hopeful signs. High school completion rates have increased for African-Americans from 74 percent in 1972 to nearly 84 percent in 1993.[12] This progress must be maintained and built upon, for as noted child psychiatrist James Comer points out:

Past and present policies and practices which made it extremely difficult for black Americans to achieve at the level of their ability are like dropping the baton. And black America is not another team in competition with white America. Black Americans are part of America's team. If America keeps running without the baton, no matter how fast or how far, we're going to lose.[13]

Implications for Schools

Recently, there has been much debate over how to educate African-American schoolchildren, especially what should be taught and how it should be taught. The "Afrocentric" curriculum, one of the ideas resulting from this debate, was designed to offset the traditional, "Eurocentric" curriculum, criticized as alienating to African-American children. It was intended that African-American students would become more involved in a curriculum based on the culture and traditions of their African heritage. Another, more radical, idea is that black male students, who run the greatest risk of falling out of the educational system, should be segregated by both gender and race and taught only by black male teachers who can provide positive role models. Moderates, such as Harvard professor Henry Gates, feel that the solution lies in widening the traditional curriculum to include not only African-American but all cultures.[14] Although it is too soon to tell what the outcome of this debate will be, one thing is certain: It has changed the way that we think about educating African-American children.

While the controversy over what and how to teach black children rages, there are some positive actions that can help facilitate the struggle for equal educational opportunity for African Americans. Teachers, schools, and society can and should:

- Increase access to academically challenging programs for black students
- Create alliances among schools, churches, businesses, and social and civic organizations to provide role models for students
- Increase parental involvement in the education process
- Develop a truly multicultural curriculum that accurately portrays African-American achievement
- Ensure that black students begin their education with the skills necessary for successful learning[15]

Latinos: The Youngest Minority

More than 26 million Latinos live in the United States, up 70 percent since 1980. They constitute 10 percent of the nation's population. Because many Latinos immigrated to the United States to escape economic and political repression, not all of them entered the country legally. Consequently, the actual percentages may be much higher. This ongoing legal and illegal immigration, together with high birth rates for young families in their child-bearing years, have made Latinos the youngest and fastest-growing *school-age* population in the United States.

Hispanics are not a monolithic group but rather are made up of several subgroups who share some characteristics, such as language, but differ in oth-

In terms of absolute numbers, Hispanic students represented the fastest growing minority group during the 1980s.

ers, such as location, age, income, and educational attainment. The three largest Hispanic subgroups are Mexican Americans, Puerto Ricans, and Cuban Americans. There is also significant representation from other Latin-American and Caribbean countries, such as the Dominican Republic, El Salvador, Nicaragua, and Honduras. In contrast to these new immigrants, many from war-torn countries, there is also an "old" population of Spanish descent living in the Southwest with as long a history in this country as those who trace their ancestors to the original New England colonies. This population of Spanish origin numbers about 1 million; they are older, wealthier, and better educated than any of the other Latino subgroups.

Cuban Americans

Following the Castro-led revolution in the 1950s, Cuban immigration to the United States increased significantly. During the 1960s, the Cubans who settled in the United States were primarily well-educated, professional, and middle and upper class. By 1980, 800,000 Cubans—10 percent of the population of Cuba— were living in the United States. For the most part Cubans have settled in Miami and other locations in southern Florida, but there are also sizable populations in New York, Philadelphia, Chicago, Milwaukee, and Indianapolis. Cubans tend to be more prosperous, better educated, and more conservative than most of the other Latino groups.

During the 1980s there was a major exodus of 125,000 immigrants from Cuba to the United States. Attention and concern were focused on the 4,000 "Marielitos," criminals Castro had released from Cuban jails. In this second immigration wave there were many more black Cubans, who have not been accepted as readily into communities in the United States.

Puerto Ricans

Puerto Ricans have encountered more educational and economic hardships than have Cubans. During the nineteenth century many of the Puerto Ricans in the United States were highly respected political exiles striving for the independence of their homeland. Since 1898, when the island was annexed to the United States, Puerto Ricans have emigrated to escape unemployment and poverty. Immigration to the United States peaked during the 1950s, with the majority of Puerto Ricans settling in New York City. By 1974 there were more than a quarter of a million Puerto Rican students in the New York City public schools.

In 1957 *The Puerto Rican Study* addressed problems Puerto Ricans face in speaking English as a second language and in adjusting to life in the United States. Although the report was issued many decades ago, its recommendations, never implemented successfully, are still relevant today. The study called for teaching that relates directly to the experiences and culture of Puerto Rican students; the need for exploration, socialization, and cooperative learning with peers; culturally appropriate toys, games, and learning materials; and the importance of teachers who are warm, sympathetic, and understanding.[16]

New Immigrants from Latin America

Since the 1960s, 34 percent of the nation's new immigrants, legal and illegal, have come from Latin America, mainly Mexico, El Salvador, Guatemala, and Nicaragua. For example, after the Sandinista revolution in the 1980s, 200,000 Nicaraguans fled to the United States. Half a million Salvadorans also came in the 1980s; over half settled in Los Angeles, making it the second-largest Salvadoran city.

Many of the new Latin-American immigrants have survived war, torture, and terrorism in their homelands of El Salvador, Guatemala, and Nicaragua. These children bring both physical and psychological scars into the schools of their new land. Mental health professionals note the symptoms of trauma and stress that too often characterize these children: depression, nightmares, insomnia, and guilt. A man from El Salvador describes "countless situations where children were in the classroom and their teacher was killed." An education advocate from New York City counsels an 8-year-old girl who "saw her father put up against the wall and shot by government troops."[17] Trauma, poverty, and limited ability to speak English present enormous educational obstacles for these new Latino immigrants.

About half of the Mexican and Central American children now in California schools entered the United States illegally, a situation causing political upheaval and more restrictive legislation. Sometimes desperate attempts to cross the border have put children in terrifying circumstances. A 7-year-old Mexican boy tells of his perilous journey:

> I still have nightmares. It was scary. We went separate across. I was caught the first time and sent back to my aunt's house. This time she paid a lot of money to get me across. The coyote put me in a sack in the back of the truck with potatoes and told me to be totally quiet until he came. I

was so hot and couldn't breathe. I cried with no sound. After hours, I think, he came to me. We had gotten across, but where was my mother? She had given me an address, but I didn't know how to get there and was afraid to ask for help.[18]

Because such a large proportion of Latino students come from Mexico, the following section tells their history in more detail.

Mexican Americans

At the end of the United States' war with Mexico (1846–1848), those Mexicans who decided to stay in the new U.S. territories were guaranteed full citizenship. By 1900 approximately 200,000 Mexican Americans were living in the Southwest. Within the context of the dominant Anglo society, most of these Mexican Americans were viewed as a source of cheap labor and were exploited as such.

The schools mirrored this conception. They operated in a manner that ensured that Mexican Americans knew their place and stayed in it. One superintendent in Texas explained why education was actually dangerous for Mexican Americans:

> Most of our Mexicans are of the lower class. They transplant onions, harvest them, etc. The less they know about everything else, the better contented they are. You have doubtless heard that ignorance is bliss; it seems that it is so when one has to transplant onions. . . . If a man has very much sense or education, either, he is not going to stick to this kind of work. So you see it is up to the white population to keep the Mexican on his knees in an onion patch. . . . This does not mix well with education.[19]

The devices that were used to deny educational opportunity to Mexican Americans were similar to those imposed on African Americans. By 1920 a pattern of separate and unequal Mexican-American schools had emerged throughout Texas and California. Not only were the facilities in these schools far inferior to those in white schools, but the school year was only half as long because many of the children worked in the fields during the harvest seasons.

Mexican Americans who were enrolled in Anglo schools frequently suffered abuse and indignities from their classmates. One youngster from Nueces County, Texas, remembers the insults and patterns of exclusion:

> I was the only Mexican in my high school, and well liked by the Americans. I used to go to picnics with them and drink water out of the same cups and pitchers. Then we came to the Alamo in our study of history, and then it was "gringo" and "greaser." They expelled me from the baseball nine and would not sit with me any more and told me to drink water out of my own cup.[20]

Patterns of bias continue as the language and cultural history of Mexican Americans are typically ignored within the school curricula today.

In the late 1960s Cesar Chavez led the fight of migrant Mexican-American laborers to organize themselves into a union and to demand a more responsive education that included culture free IQ tests, instruction in Spanish, smaller classes, and greater cultural representation in the curriculum.

Problems and Progress

The problems that Latinos have historically faced persist to this day, and in some cases have grown worse. Although Latino children are the fastest-growing segment of the school population, they continue to be underrepresented at all grade levels. Consider the following statistics:

- Latinos have the lowest high school completion rate of any ethnic group.
- In 1990, 51 percent of all Latinos over 25 had high school diplomas, compared to 81 percent for non-Latinos.
- Latinos were the only ethnic group to show a decline in graduate school enrollment between 1986 and 1988.[21]

A portion of these grim statistics can be attributed to economic conditions. It is estimated that two out of every five Latino children live in poverty.[22] However, there are many other factors contributing to these statistics. Unequal access to educational resources, lack of positive role models, low expectations of teachers and students, inadequate funding for schools, and differences in language and culture all contribute to the problem.

Implications for Schools

The Latino population is composed of many subgroups whose individual members vary greatly in terms of experience and priorities. Still, it is possible to make some generalizations about traditional Latino values connecting these various groups:

- A strong sense of identity with family, community, and ethnic group translates into achievement patterns that are cooperative rather than competitive. Latino children frequently express a desire to achieve for the sake of family approval and pride rather than for individual gain.
- Latino children often desire close interpersonal relationships with teachers and a curriculum that focuses on human beings and their social interac-

tions. A respect for one's roles and responsibilities in the family and community translates into respect for teachers who are both firm and supportive.

• An acceptance of Catholic ideology that stresses respect for authority may cause strong guilt feelings when the students do not live up to their school obligations. Since guilt can lead to further academic failure, it is important that teachers learn to recognize this guilt-failure cycle and intervene.[23]

It is important that teachers and schools be sensitive to the individual and cultural differences of Latino students and employ teaching strategies and multicultural curricula that are matched to their needs.

Native Americans: A History of Miseducation

In the beginning, God gave to every people a cup of clay, and from this cup they drank their life. They all dipped in the water, but their cups were different. Our cup is broken now. It has passed away. (*Digger Indian Proverb*)

Over the centuries the impact of white people on the forms of tribal life and Native American education has been one of conquest and the attempted and often successful destruction of tradition and culture. The early attempt of whites to provide their own brand of education for Native Americans was carried out by church missionary societies. They operated schools for Native Americans, although the tribes themselves provided most of the funds for their own education. Many Native Americans responded enthusiastically to the white approach to their education—as long as this approach did not attempt to eradicate their cultures. The missionaries, however, often saw their goal as one of "civilizing" and Christianizing the tribes. They ignored or actively suppressed the languages of their pupils and tried to teach exclusively in English.[24]

Despite such adverse conditions, Native Americans achieved some extraordinary educational accomplishments. For example, in 1822 Sequoyah invented a Cherokee syllabary. This permitted the Cherokee language to be written; books were published in Cherokee; Cherokee schools became bilingual; and the Cherokee nation wrote, edited, and published the *Cherokee Phoenix,* a bilingual weekly newspaper. There have been many other Native American achievements in education, accomplishments that rejected white attempts to deny tribal heritages and languages. However, as federal intervention became more organized, the tribes' control over their own education diminished.

After the Civil War, the federal government dominated the education of Native Americans. Education became a tool of conquest, and the reservations saw more and more white superintendents, farm agents, teachers, inspectors, and missionaries who ravaged tribal cultures. For example, the largest of the tribes, the Navajos, despite their years of resistance, were assigned to a reservation. The treaty with the Navajos promised that schools would be built to educate their children. In 1892, almost 20 years after the treaty was signed, only 75 students attended the one and only school on the reservation. This represented less than 0.5 percent of the Navajo population.

Indian boarding schools were established to assimilate young Native Americans into the dominant European-American values: veneration of property, individual competition, European-style domesticity, toil, and European standards of dress and hygiene.

Often, Native American parents refused to send their children to reservation schools. One such case involved a group of Hopi parents, and the white response was harsh. There are several reports of federal troops forcing Hopi children into wagons and carrying them off to faraway boarding schools. The children would often run away and hide, and in one case, 75 Hopi men were arrested and sentenced to 90 days at hard labor until they agreed to send their children to these schools.

For those Hopi children who did attend school, the white approach to education was alien to and in conflict with their cultural heritage. The children were not allowed to speak the Hopi language. They were bewildered and alienated by strict school rules and regulations that were out of touch with the greater freedom of time and space that characterized tribal life. One Hopi student recalled: "Seems like that was the first English we learned. 'Get in line, get in line,' all the time we had to get in line."[25]

In all areas of the country, the story of Native American education has been one of broken promises, discrimination, and cultural repression. For example, treaties with the Sioux included provisions for schools, but often the schools were not built. When they did exist, they were overcrowded, understaffed, and inadequate. Similar patterns of promises not kept, schools not built, and educational needs not met emerged for the tribes of the Northern Plains, Eastern woodlands, and the Pacific Coast. In Alaska a dual school system existed: there was one set of schools for whites and "civilized" children of "mixed blood" and another set of schools for Indian and Inuit students.

By 1920 reservation education was based firmly on the policies and practices of white cultural superiority. It was mandated that instruction take place in English, and textbooks written in native languages were forbidden. In place of their heritage, Native American children were given occupational education. But the jobs for which they were trained were mismatched and incongruent with the patterns of reservation life. The teachers in those schools knew little of the culture of their pupils, and their appointments were based more on political patronage than on instructional skill.

Native Americans often refused to send their children into such unresponsive and destructive environments. Arrest and kidnapping were common practices in forcing Native American children to attend. Rations were often withheld from parents as a means of compelling them to send their children to school.

After 1920 there was an increase in political and legal activity as Native Americans fought for tribal and educational rights. In two particular instances, Native Americans challenged the federal government for violating treaties, including failure to provide adequate education. In both cases, the federal courts were not responsive. It was on the state level that greater gains were made, and in several state court cases Native Americans won the right to attend public schools.

Financial appropriations meant to aid Native American students were frequently misused. The **Johnson O'Malley Act** of 1934 was a federal assistance program designed to provide supplemental funds to school districts with large numbers of Native American children. However, the Johnson O'Malley funds were often diverted from their purpose, merged with general school funds, and used to aid non–Native American children. During the 1970s, research disclosed vast differences in the quality of education provided in schools with heavy Native American enrollments located near reservations and schools that enrolled primarily non–Native American children. "The differences," said the researchers, "are so obvious as to lead to the inescapable conclusion that Indians are not receiving an equal share of anything."[26]

Problems and Progress

The last few decades have witnessed increased activity by Native Americans to win control of the reservations, including the schools. The tribes feel strongly that such control will enable them to maintain their cultural identity as well as to increase the academic achievement of their children. Recently, signs of academic progress are becoming evident. For example, between the years 1987 and 1991, the average American College Testing Program (ACT) Examination score increased at a higher rate for Native Americans than for any other ethnic group.[27]

Unfortunately, problems continue to plague Native American students:

- The mean SAT score for Native Americans in 1990 was 91 points below the national mean score.
- Native American students are overrepresented in special education programs and underrepresented in gifted and talented programs.
- Native American parents have participated only minimally in the formal education of their children.[28]

Implications for Schools

One does not teach an Indian how to become a white person, but how to use his own values to take advantage of vocational and education opportunities in the dominant society. . . . How can he learn to make the best of two cultures. . . . without losing his identity?[29]

These are the views and the question of Annemarie Brewer, an Oglala Sioux who taught at Red Cloud Indian School on the Pine Ridge Indian Reservation. From her own experience, she concluded that the most effective teachers in that school, whether Native American or white, were those who learned about the culture of their students. Many other teachers of Native American students have also learned from first-hand experience how necessary it is to be sensitive to the culture and heritage of the particular tribe. They offer the following suggestions:

• It is a tradition not to ask someone his or her name directly. In order to make a student more comfortable, learn his or her name from a friend.
• Inquire before bringing any animals into the classroom. Some animals are not to be touched or looked upon for various reasons.
• Some of the people believe in reincarnation. All forms of life are to be treated with respect.
• When preparing foods in the classroom, find out the proper way in the culture to prepare and serve them.
• Family ties are very strong and the children call their cousins brothers and sisters; this tie is as strong as true sibling ties in the Anglo culture. Respect this custom and don't tell them they are not brothers and sisters.
• Native American children may be repelled by a classroom environment in which students are forced to compete individually and "pushed" for answers.[30]

Beyond learning tribal culture and traditions, teachers are also encouraged to:

• Develop a multicultural curriculum that includes Native Americans.
• Provide positive role models for Native American students—individuals who are well-educated and retain their sense of cultural identity.
• Increase parental involvement in the educational process. Traditional distrust of the schools must be replaced with positive relationships.
• Use cooperative learning and other noncompetitive techniques.[31]

Asian/Pacific Americans: A Study in Diversity

More than 500,000 Asian/Pacific Islanders immigrate to the United States each year. As the largest and most culturally diverse group to enter our nation legally since the 1970s, Asian/Pacific Americans account for approximately 3 percent of the population. Demographers predict that this figure will increase several fold by the year 2050.

This group has attained a high degree of educational and economic success. Despite outstanding accomplishments, the statistics hide problems that many of the new immigrants from Southeast Asia and the Pacific Islands face. Cultural conflict, patterns of discrimination, and lower educational achievement are all hidden by the title "model minority." This section will describe the differing experiences of the three largest Asian immigrant groups—Chinese, Japanese, and Filipinos—as well as problems faced by refugees from Southeast Asia and the Pacific Islands.[32]

Chinese Americans

When the Chinese first began immigrating to the West Coast in the 1850s, they were considered a curious and exotic people. It was mostly young unmarried men who left China, a country ravaged by famine and political turmoil, to seek their fortune in the "Golden Mountains" across the Pacific and to bring their wealth back to their homeland.

Because the California gold mines were largely depleted by the time they arrived, most Chinese took other jobs. Almost single-handedly they built the Pacific segment of the transcontinental railroad over rugged western terrain. The celebration that signified its completion also signaled a loss of jobs for almost 25,000 Chinese laborers. Many found that the hope of bringing fortunes home to their families in China was an impossible dream.

By 1880, approximately 106,000 Chinese had immigrated to the United States, and by that time a vicious movement—its rallying cry: "The Chinese must go"—had emerged to keep them out of the United States. With the passage of the Immigration Act of 1882, along with a series of similar bills, further Chinese immigration was blocked for decades. Those Chinese already in this country responded to increasing physical violence by moving eastward and consolidating into ghettos called *Chinatowns*. Inhabited largely by male immigrants unable to bring their wives, these ghettos offered a grim and sometimes violent lifestyle, one with widespread prostitution and gambling. However, Chinatowns did provide some sense of solidarity as well as relief from discrimination on the outside.

Despite active prejudice and discrimination, the progress of Chinese Americans of today is outstanding, with both median income and educational attainment above that of white Americans. With a rapidly increasing population, the impact and contributions as well as the special needs of Chinese Americans are likely to receive increasing attention.

Japanese Americans

Only when the Japanese government legalized emigration in 1886 did Japanese come to the United States in significant numbers. In 1870, there were only 50 people of Japanese ancestry here, but by 1920, the number had increased to more than 110,000.

With the immigration of Chinese halted by various exclusion acts, Japanese immigrants filled the need for cheap labor. Like the Chinese, most of the early Japanese immigrants were male and they hoped to return to their homeland with the fortunes they earned in the United States. This remained an unfulfilled dream for most.

Few women were among the early Japanese immigrants. However, the practice of "picture brides," the arrangement of marriages by exchange of photographs, established Japanese families in the United States. Many researchers say that the strong Japanese family structure, perpetuated in the early system of picture brides, is key to the extraordinary success of Japanese Americans today.

Praised for their willingness to work when they first arrived in California, the Japanese began to make other farmers nervous with their great success in

Asian Americans represent the most culturally diverse and most academically successful group of minority children.

agriculture and truck farming. Anti-Japanese feelings became prevalent along the West Coast. Slogans such as "Japs must go" and warnings of a new "yellow peril" were frequent. In 1913 a bill was passed making it difficult for Japanese to lease land. In 1924 anti-Japanese forces won a major victory when Congress passed an immigration bill that halted Japanese immigration to the United States.

After Japan's attack on Pearl Harbor on December 7, 1941, fear and prejudice about the "threat" from Japanese Americans was rampant. Terror of the "yellow peril" spread down the West Coast. On February 19, 1942, President Franklin Roosevelt issued Executive Order No. 9006, which resulted in the West Coast's being declared a "military area" and the establishment of federal concentration camps. Approximately 110,000 Japanese, more than two-thirds of whom were U.S. citizens, were removed from their homes in the "military area" and sent to 10 "relocation" camps in California, Idaho, Utah, Arizona, Wyoming, Colorado, and Arkansas. Located in geographically barren areas, guarded by soldiers and barbed wire, these camps made it very difficult for the Japanese people to keep their traditions and cultural heritage alive. Almost half a century later, the U.S. goverment officially acknowledged this wrong and appropriated a symbolic payment to the victims of this action.

Despite severe discrimination in the past, by all measures the Japanese Americans of today are very successful. With high median family incomes and educational attainment, Japanese Americans are considered model citizens. However, although their current success is unquestionable, their future is uncertain. Their success is at least partially due to traditional values, a heritage some fear may be weakened by increasing assimilation. Others, however, suggest that their values will not be eroded but will expand to enrich the U.S. mainstream.

Filipino Americans

After the 1898 Spanish–American War, the United States acquired the Philippines. Seen as a source of cheap labor, Filipinos were recruited to work in the fields of Hawaii and the U.S. mainland. Thousands left the poverty of their islands to seek their fortune.

But the Filipino experience in the United States has been particularly difficult. Because of the scarcity of women (in 1930 the male-female ratio was 143 to 1) and because of the mobility of their work in farms and as field hands, the Filipinos had difficulty establishing cohesive communities. Like other Asian immigrants, they came with the goal of taking their fortunes back to their homeland; like other Asian immigrants, most found this an impossible dream.

By the 1920s Filipinos were immigrating in greater numbers, and fear of the "yellow peril" became pervasive. Riots, especially in California, where most of the Filipinos had settled, resulted in further violence. Because of their unique legal status (the United States had annexed the Philippines in 1898), Filipinos were not excluded as aliens under the Immigration Act of 1924. However, the Tydings-McDuffie Act of 1934 was a victory for those who wanted the Filipinos excluded from the United States. Promising independence to the Philippines, this act limited immigration to the United States.

In 1965 a new immigration act resulted in a significant increase in Filipino immigration. Between 1970 and 1980 the Filipino population in the United States increased 132 percent. Concentrated in urban areas of the West Coast, Filipinos are the second-largest Asian-American ethnic group in the United States. The newer immigrants come to the United States with professional skills, and they seek jobs commensurate with that training. Although most indexes of educational and occupational success show Filipino Americans doing very well, this must not be allowed to mask problems and difficulties this group continues to confront.

Indochinese Americans

Before 1975 the United States saw only small numbers of immigrants from Indochina, the area in Southeast Asia including Vietnam, Laos, and Kampuchea/Cambodia. Their arrival was related directly to the end of the Vietnam War and resulting communist rule.

In 1973 a formal peace treaty among North Vietnam, South Vietnam, the National Liberation Front, and the United States was signed in Paris. A few months later U.S. troops left Vietnam. Although the South Vietnamese continued to fight for approximately 2 more years, the United States was not ready with a well-thought-out evacuation plan when the Saigon government finally fell. The evacuation was chaotic, reaching a state of panic in the last hours, with North Vietnamese troops on the heels of the fleeing people of South Vietnam. A few Americans, mainly news correspondents and missionaries, were left behind, along with thousands of Vietnamese. Many of these struggled over the next several years to find a way to leave Vietnam.

The refugees came from all strata of society. Some were wealthy, others poverty stricken. Some were widely traveled and sophisticated, others farmers and fishing people who had never before left their small home villages. Most came as part of a family, and almost half were under age 18 at the time of their arrival. To assist with admission and to provide a transition period, refugee camps were established. The camps dispensed food, clothing, medical assistance, and temporary housing, as well as an introduction to U.S. culture and some training in English as a second language.

By December 1975 the last refugee camp had closed and the government had succeeded in its purpose of resettling large numbers of Indochinese across the nation without too high a concentration in any one location. This concept of widespread dispersement was well-intentioned, but it often left the refugees feeling lonely and isolated. In fact, many moved from original areas of settlement to cities where large numbers of Asian Americans were already located.

A second wave of Indochinese refugees followed in the years after 1975. Cambodians and Laotians came because of poverty and starvation in their homelands and because of fear of political reprisals. Many tried to escape in small fishing boats not meant for travel across rough ocean seas. Called *boat people* by the press, almost half of them, according to estimates, died before they reached the shores of the United States.

Despite the hardships and terrible ordeals, by 1985 more than a million Indochinese were living in the United States. These refugees were less affluent and less educated than those who had come earlier. They had health problems, and some had suffered shock and trauma from war or the ordeals experienced in their efforts to escape. Some have prospered, but others, suffering from culture shock and depression over family left behind, have experienced psychological difficulties, generational conflict, and poverty.

Sometimes the children bring memories of terrible tragedy to school. A teacher in San Francisco was playing hangman during a language arts lesson. As the class was laughing and shouting out letters, she was shocked to see one child, a recent immigrant, in tears. The girl spoke so little English she could not explain the problem. Finally another child translated. The game had triggered a traumatic memory. In Cambodia the girl had watched the hanging of her father.[33]

Parents are especially baffled by the new ways of a new land. One father misunderstood his daughter's report card. He knew that A was the best grade and that it went downhill from there. When his daughter brought home a report card with three S's (for satisfactory), he beat her for what he thought was inadequate performance.[34]

Pacific Islanders

The islands in the South Pacific spread across an area that is larger than the continent of North America. The label of *Pacific Islander* is used to describe a large and diverse population that includes peoples from Guam, Samoa, Tonga, and countless other islands. Like many of the immigrants from Southeast Asia, Pacific Islanders often have limited educational or vocational training and have trouble getting jobs. It is estimated that one-quarter of all Samoans living on Hawaii are on welfare.[35] Culturally, many Pacific Island students find the competitive style of education, with its emphasis on the individual, at odds with their traditional style, which emphasizes cooperation and experiential learning. Pacific Islanders often come into conflict with a school system that knows little about their cultures or background.

Problems and Progress

Frequently Asian/Pacific Americans see education as a way to regain status that was lost when they immigrated to the United States; it is also viewed as a means to gain acceptance in U.S. society. These two powerful motivators have driven many to succeed in school, giving rise to the stereotype of the model minority. However, as with many stereotypes, there is a certain element of truth and a good deal of misconception.

1. Fully 40 percent of Asian Americans completed 4 years of college in 1990.
2. Typically, Asian Americans scored approximately 50 points higher than the national average on the math portion of the SAT.
3. Although they are 3 percent of the total population, Asian Americans have a much higher representation at prestigious universities such as Harvard and Stanford.[36]

These successes mask many problems.

1. While approximately 80 percent of Japanese Americans finish high school, only about 60 percent of Vietnamese and Samoan Americans graduate.
2. Currently, fewer than 10 percent of all Pacific Islanders have graduated from college.
3. Today Pacific Island and Southeast Asian Americans are greatly under-represented at colleges and universities.[37]

Implications for the Schools

To teach these groups effectively, particularly those who are recent immigrants, educators must know about the lifestyle changes they have experienced. For many immigrants, family cohesiveness is diminished or lost entirely if parents have been left behind. Traditional family roles may be altered and even turned upside down. In Asian homelands the father's role was typically that of patriarch. In the United States this role may be threatened as wives also become breadwinners. Young children assume new status, since they may become the only English-speaking members of the family, and, therefore, an essential link to the outside world.[38]

Communicating can cause many problems, both verbal and nonverbal.[39] For example, in Vietnam one person rarely touches another's head, perhaps because it is considered sacred, housing the soul. When teachers pat children on the head, they may upset Indochinese students. Cultural differences concerning gender are a major area of confusion. In Southeast Asian cultures it is not unusual for two male friends or two female friends to walk together holding hands. These students are unprepared for the ridicule with which U.S. students often greet these customs because of our more homophobic U.S. culture. One teacher tells of Vietnamese parents who were furious to see their daughter, for whom they had always stressed modest dress and behavior, doing jumps and spins in an abbreviated cheerleading costume.

Differences in the very process of schooling can also create problems. Since Indochinese teachers are accorded great respect, students will often bow before them, refrain from asking questions, and avoid eye contact. In the United States the relationship between student and teacher is far more casual and may be startling to Southeast Asian parents. One junior high school teacher tells of a classic situation of cross-cultural misunderstanding. She requested a conference

Classroom Tips for Non-Sexist, Non-Racist Teaching

Questioning Strategies

- *Calling on students* Do not rely on the "quickest hand in the West," which is usually attached to a male. Relying on the "quickest hand in the West" will skew the pattern of classroom participation. Develop other strategies for student participation besides hand raising—for example, writing each student's name on a card and using the cards to select students. Instead of a few students "carrying" the class, all students will be pulled into the learning process.
- *Wait Time 1* Wait time can be a big help in promoting equity. Giving yourself 3 to 5 seconds before you call on a student allows you more time to think, to choose which students have not been participating and could benefit from your extra attention. Research indicates that females and minorities will particularly benefit from this strategy.
- *Wait Time 2* Give yourself more wait time *after* a student speaks, as well. Research shows that boys get more precise feedback than girls do. Waiting will give you the opportunity to think about the strengths and weaknesses of a student's answers, to be more specific in your reactions, and to provide girls with more specific feedback as well.

Classroom Organization

- *Segregation* Avoid segregated seating patterns or activities. Sometimes teachers segregate: "Let's have a spelling bee—boys against the girls!" Other times students segregate themselves. Gender or race or ethnic groups that are isolated alter the dynamics of the classroom and create barriers to effective communication among students, as well as obstacles to equitable teaching. If necessary, you will need to move students around to create a more integrated class.

- *Mobility* Students sitting in the front row and middle seats receive the majority of the teacher's attention. This is because the closer you get to students, the more likely you are to call on them. If you move around the room you will get different students involved. By the way, students are mobile too. You may want to change their seats on a regular basis to more equally disperse classroom participation.
- *Cooperative Education* Research suggests that when students choose their own cooperative learning groups, inequity also emerges. For instance, in cooperative learning groups, girls tend to assist both other girls and boys, while boys are more likely to help only other boys. Boys get help from everyone in the group, but girls must make do with less support. In addition, some students (usually boys) may dominate the group, while others (usually girls) are quiet. It is a good idea to monitor your groups, in order to intervene and stop these inequitable patterns.
- *Displays* Check your bulletin boards, your displays, your textbooks. Are women and minority groups represented? Should you find other resources to supplement these materials and create a more equitable classroom climate? Do you remember the phrase, "If the walls could speak"? Well, in a sense they do. What messages are the classroom walls and curriculum sending to your students?

And by the way . . . all these strategies are not meant to be secret. You should explain why you are working to include all students in class discussions. Students need to learn how important it is for them to be able to speak publicly both at school and at work. With this knowledge, students could enhance their learning in school and their success after graduation.

with the parents of a student who, she felt, was not participating fully in class. The father came and insisted that the boy apologize to the teacher. When the student offered an American-style apology, he was struck by the father, who ordered him to kneel and bow. When the boy did so, the teacher became upset; as the stunned father watched, she knelt on the floor beside the student, declaring that no one in the United States had to kneel before anyone else.

Another schooling difference between Southeast Asia and the United States involves the parent's role in education. Indochinese parents often view the teacher as the expert and feel it inappropriate to voice their opinion about the education of their children. Consequently they are baffled by and rarely take active roles in organizations such as the PTA.

U.S. teaching strategies may seem odd to children from Southeast Asia. For example, public recognition of any kind is often uncomfortable. Even praise and compliments can be embarrassing and are more effective when given in private. Indochinese students have come from schools where the lecture method was predominant, and they may need special assistance in order to participate in discussions and independent projects.

To help Asian/Pacific Americans achieve equality of educational opportunity, teachers and schools should use teaching strategies that take into account cultural differences and develop curricula including Asian/Pacific Americans.[40]

Women and Education: A History of Sexist Schooling

A woman . . . cannot afford to risk her health in acquiring knowledge of the advanced sciences, mathematics, or philosophy for which she has no use. . . . Too many women have already made themselves permanent invalids by overstrain of study at schools and colleges.[41]

From a contemporary point of view, you may regard such a comment as bizarre and outlandish. However, it is symptomatic of past attitudes toward women, attitudes of bias that have prevented females from gaining access to education at all levels and that have ensured differential and unequal treatment when access was won.

Although a woman gave the first plot of ground for a free school in New England, female children were not allowed to attend the school. In 1687 the town council of Farmington, Connecticut, voted money for a school "where all children shall learn to read and write English." However, the council quickly qualified this statement by explaining that "all children" meant "all males." Today, the bias is far more subtle, but the bias persists.

Classroom Interaction

If asked whether or not they treat male and female students equally, most contemporary teachers would probably respond somewhat indignantly, "Of course I do!" If observed closely, however, a good many differences can usually be detected. For example, many teachers expect boys to be active, aggressive, and independent, good in math and science. Conversely, they expect girls to be quiet, dependent, and cooperative, good in reading and the language arts. Such attitudes are in evidence when teachers consistently ask boys to do tasks that require physical activity or mechanical skills and girls to do those that are more sedentary, such as grading papers. These assignments inform students that different behaviors and skills are appropriate for male and female students.

Research on teacher interaction patterns tells us that teachers talk differently to female and male students. For example, boys are reprimanded more often (one study shows that they receive 8 to 10 times as many control messages as girls do) and are punished more harshly. Not only do teachers

Liberty: American Women Shaping Our Future

An old soothsayer sat down, discouraged. "Women can't go very far—just to a point." With trepidation she picked up her crystal ball, rubbed it, and looked into the future. Her eyes opened wide. "A woman leader!" she cried. "A woman general too! How did this happen? Perhaps," she speculated, "the roots of this miracle are in the past."

Again she looked into the crystal ball, this time toward the past, searching for more brave women. Suddenly the globe radiated with the courage of pioneer women riding covered wagons. Then Molly Pitcher came into view, firing the cannon for her sick husband. Her image faded as a new figure emerged. Harriet Tubman was boldly leading her

people from slavery. Then came Elizabeth Cady Stanton, shaper of the suffrage movement. Elizabeth Blackwell appeared next, first woman doctor in the United States.

"Many intrepid women of the past have shaped our future, but what about today?" the old woman wondered. Again, the answer was in the crystal ball. A silver space shuttle loomed over the darkness and Christa McAuliffe spoke, "I hope kids in the future reach the stars." The old woman smiled. She knew they would.

Source: Jackie Sadker, age 11, 1986 Winner National Women's Hall of Fame Essay Contest, Seneca Falls, New York.

---

punish boys more, they also talk to them more, listen to them more, and give them more active teaching attention. A 3-year study conducted in more than 100 elementary and secondary classrooms in four states and the District of Columbia showed that:

- Teachers interact more frequently with male students.
- White male students were asked questions most frequently.
- Minority females were asked the fewest number of questions.
- One of the reasons boys get to answer more questions and talk more is that they are assertive in grabbing teacher attention. Boys are eight times more likely than girls to call out the answers to questions. However, when boys call out the answers to questions, teachers are likely to accept their responses. When girls call out the answers to questions, teachers often remind them to raise their hands.
- When teachers initiate interaction with a male student, they are likely to keep calling on male students for several more interactions. There is the same tendency to continue questioning female students after an initial interaction with a female, but it is not as strong. One of the reasons for this pattern of same-sex interactions may be the sex-segregated seating arrangements in many classrooms.
- It does not matter if the teacher is male or female, minority or majority; the same patterns of boys being given the opportunity to answer more questions persist.[42]

When teachers learn that in many classrooms boys get more than their fair share of questions, they often express disbelief. "This certainly doesn't apply to me" is a common reaction. "I direct questions to all my students. I interact with them equally."

Of course, not all teachers interact more with boys. But for most teachers, who are immersed in a dizzying number of interactions with students—as many as 1,000 a day—it is impossible to track questioning patterns accurately. Frequently, when the teachers are shown videotapes or codings of questioning patterns in their classrooms they are surprised and shocked at the disparities in interaction.

The overwhelming majority of teachers are fair people who strive for excellence and equity in their teaching. When they become aware of inequities and are provided with appropriate training, they can change their interaction patterns to become more fair and effective for all students.

The Impact of Title IX

As educators have become aware of the impact of **sex bias,** they are beginning to confront and eliminate sexist patterns in curriculum and instruction. Many publishing companies have issued guidelines to help authors and illustrators avoid **sexism** and racism in their work. Further, **Title IX** of the 1972 Education Amendments Act specifically prohibits many forms of **sex discrimination** in education. The opening section of Title IX states:

> No person in the United States shall, on the basis of sex, be excluded from participation in, be denied the benefits of, or be subjected to discrimination under any education program or activity receiving federal financial assistance.

Every public school and most of the nations' colleges and universities are covered under Title IX, which prohibits discrimination in school admissions, in counseling and guidance, in competitive athletics, in student rules and regulations, and in access to programs and courses, including vocational education and physical education. Title IX also applies to sex discrimination in employment practices, including interviewing and recruitment, hiring and promotion, compensation, job assignments, and fringe benefits. The power of Title IX was attenuated for a short time by a 1984 Supreme Court decision, *Grove City College v. Bell*. In this decision, Title IX coverage was limited to specific activities that receive federal financial assistance. If, for example, a math program received federal financial assistance but no other program on campus received such aid, the college would be allowed to discriminate in all programs and activities except those involving mathematics.

However, on March 22, 1988, Congress enacted the Civil Rights Restoration Act over President Reagan's veto. This act overturned the Supreme Court's earlier decision; it restored Title IX coverage to apply to the entire education institution no matter where federal funds are utilized. In a 1992 case, *Franklin v. Gwinnett County Public Schools,* involving sexual harassment, the Supreme Court ruled unanimously that students can sue for monetary damages under Title IX.

Although enforcement of the law has at times been slow, there is still cause for optimism, because the most critical force for creating nonsexist education is the power of teachers. As teachers begin challenging **sex-role stereotyping** for 5-year-old girls who think that only boys can be doctors and for 11-year-old boys who hate poetry and ballet, they will be advancing gender equity and equality of opportunity for all our children.

Before Title IX, only girls took home economics and only boys took shop. During the past decade, the barriers of sexism have steadily eroded.

But some barriers persist. In college, physics, engineering, business and computer science programs continue to be overwhelmingly male. At the same time, home economics, nursing, teaching, and library science courses are populated mainly by women. Universities place greater resources in programs dominated by men, and these programs lead to more prestigious (and profitable) career paths. The battle against sexism is not yet won.

Report Card: The Cost of Sexism in School

Below is a report card you will not find in any elementary or secondary school. Nevertheless, it is an important evaluation. It reflects the loss that both girls and boys suffer because of gender bias in society and in education. Years after the passage of Title IX of the Education Amendments Act of 1972, the law that prohibits sex discrimination in schools receiving federal financial assistance, gender inequities continue to permeate schools.

Academic

Girls

- Girls start out ahead of boys in speaking, reading, and counting. In the early grades, their academic performance is equal to that of boys in math and science. However, as they progress through school, their achievement test scores show significant decline. The scores of boys, on the other hand, continue to rise and eventually reach and surpass those of their female counterparts, particularly in the areas of math and science. Girls are the only group in our society that begins school ahead in standardized evaluations and ends up behind.
- Sex differences in mathematics become apparent at the junior high school level. Male superiority increases especially in problem solving, and is evident even when the number of mathematics courses taken by males and females is the same.
- The National Assessment of Educational Progress (NAEP) has conducted four assessments of reading achievement. Although girls continue to outperform boys at the 9-, 14-, and 17-year-old levels, the achievement gap between the sexes has narrowed: as girls' performance has remained stable, boys continue to make achievement gains.
- Males outperform females on the Scholastic Assessment Test (SAT) and the American College Testing Program Examination (ACT). The largest gap is in the math section of the SAT, followed by the ACT natural science reading, the ACT math usage, and the ACT social studies reading.
- The SAT II tests are required for admission to more selective colleges and universities. On these achievement tests, males outperform females in European history, American history, biology, physics, chemistry, math, and many foreign languages.

- Girls attain only 36 percent of the more than 6,000 National Merit Scholarships awarded each year. These awards are based on the higher Preliminary Scholastic Assessment (PSAT) scores attained by boys.
- On tests for admission to graduate and professional schools, males outperform females on the Graduate Record Exam (GRE), the Medical College Admissions Test (MCAT), and the Graduate Management Admissions Test (GMAT).
- In spite of performance decline on standardized achievement tests, girls frequently receive better grades in school. This may be one of the rewards they get for being more quiet and docile in the classroom. However, their silence may be at the cost of achievement, independence, and self-reliance.
- Girls are more likely to be invisible members of classrooms. They receive fewer academic contacts, less praise and constructive feedback, fewer complex and abstract questions, and less instruction on how to do things for themselves.
- Girls who are gifted are less likely to be identified than are gifted boys. Those girls who *are* identified as gifted are less likely to participate in special or accelerated programs to develop their talent. Girls who suffer from learning disabilities are also less likely to be identified or to participate in special education programs than are learning-disabled boys.

Boys

- Boys are more likely to be scolded and reprimanded in classrooms, even when the observed conduct and behavior of boys and girls does not differ. Also, boys are more likely to be referred to school authorities for disciplinary action than are girls.
- Boys are far more likely to be identified as exhibiting learning disabilities, reading problems, and mental retardation.
- Not only are boys more likely to be identified as having greater learning and reading disabilities, they also receive lower grades, are more likely to be grade repeaters, and are less likely to complete high school.
- The NAEP indicates that males perform significantly below females in writing achievement tests.

(Box continues on next page.)

Psychological and Physical
Girls

- Although women generally achieve better grades than men do, they are less likely to believe they can do college work. Females exhibit lower self-esteem than males do during secondary and post-secondary education.
- Girls have less confidence than boys in their mathematical ability. The sex typing of mathematics as a masculine discipline may also be related to low female confidence and performance.
- Girls have a less positive attitude toward science than do boys. High school girls view science, especially physical science, as a "masculine" subject.
- In athletics, females also suffer from sex bias. For example, although there has been some progress, women's athletic budgets in the nation's colleges are only a modest percentage of men's budgets.
- One in 10 teenage girls becomes pregnant every year. More than 40 percent of all adolescent girls who drop out of school do so because of pregnancy. Teenage pregnancy is related to a constellation of factors, including poverty, low self-esteem, academic failure, and the perception of few life options.

Boys

- Society socializes boys into an active, independent, and aggressive role. But such behavior is incongruent with school norms and rituals that stress quiet behavior and docility. This results in a pattern of role conflict for boys, particularly during the elementary years.
- Hyperactivity is estimated to be nine times more prevalent in boys than in girls. Boys are more likely to be identified as having emotional problems, and statistics indicate a higher suicide rate among males.
- Boys are taught stereotyped behaviors earlier and more harshly than girls. There is a greater probability that such stereotyped behavior will stay with them for life.
- Conforming to the male sex-role stereotype takes a psychological toll. Boys who score high on sex-appropriate behavior tests also score highest on anxiety tests.
- Males are less likely than females to be close friends with one another. When asked, most men identify women as their closest friends.

- Until recently, programs focusing on adolescent sexuality and teen pregnancy were directed almost exclusively at females. Males were ignored, and this permissive "boys will be boys" attitude translated into sexual irresponsibility.
- Family planning experts say that 50 percent of sexually active single males will contract a sexually transmitted disease by the time they are 25. The highest incidence of venereal disease occurs in young men between 15 and 25.
- Males are more likely to succumb to serious disease and be victims of accidents or violence. The average life expectancy of men is approximately eight years shorter than that of women.

Career and Family Relationships
Girls

- Starting at the junior high school level, girls say that mathematics is less important and useful to career goals. The majority of girls still enter college without completing 4 years of high school mathematics. This lack of preparation in math serves as a "critical filter" inhibiting or preventing girls from entering many careers in science, math, and technology.
- Girls from lower socioeconomic backgrounds are less likely to have plans for college than are those from more affluent families. Limited family finances are more likely to limit the college attendance of females.
- Teenagers who become mothers earn only about half the income of females who delay child bearing. When families are headed by young mothers, they are six times as likely to be in poverty.
- In urban areas, 43 percent of young males who drop out of school are likely to return to school. For young females who drop out, the return rate is only 25 percent.
- The preparation and counseling girls receive in school contribute to the economic penalties that they encounter in the workplace. Although over 90 percent of the girls in U.S. classrooms will work in the paid labor force for all or part of their lives, the following statistics reveal the cost of the bias they encounter:
  - More than a third of families headed by women live below the poverty level.
  - A woman with a college degree will typically earn less than a male who is a high school dropout.

- The typical working woman will earn 70 cents for every dollar earned by a male worker.

Boys

- Teachers and counselors continue to advise boys to enter sex-stereotyped careers and limit their potential in occupations such as kindergarten teacher, nurse, or secretary.
- Many boys build career expectations that are higher than their abilities. This results in later compromise, disappointment, and frustration.
- Both at school and at home, boys are taught to hide or suppress their emotions; as adults, they may find it difficult or impossible to show feelings toward their family and friends.
- Boys are actively discouraged from playing with dolls (except those that play sports or wage war). Few schools provide programs that encourage boys to learn about the skills of parenting. Many men, through absence and apathy, become not so much parents as "transparents." In fact, the typical father spends only 12 minutes a day interacting with his children.
- Men and women vary in their beliefs of the important aspects of a father's role. Men emphasize the need for the father to earn a good income and to provide solutions to family problems. Women, on the other hand, stress the need for fathers to assist in caring for children and in responding to the emotional needs of the family. These differing perceptions of fatherhood lead to family strain and anxiety.
- Scientific advances involving the analysis of blood and other body fluids now make possible genetic testing for paternity. Such testing, along with the passage of stricter laws and enforcement procedures for child support, have major implications for the role of males in parenting.

Source: Adapted from Myra Sadker and David Sadker, "Gender and Educational Equity," in James Banks and Cherry McGee Banks (eds.), *Multicultural Education* (Boston: Allyn & Bacon, 1989), pp. 114–117. © Myra Sadker and David Sadker. See also Myra Sadker, David Sadker, and Susan Klein, "The Issue of Gender in Elementary and Secondary Education," in Gerald Grant (ed.), *Review of Research in Education* (Washington, DC: American Educational Research Association, 1991), pp. 269–334.

Tension Point: Are Equity and Excellence Compatible?

An issue frequently debated is whether equity and excellence are philosophically and practically at odds or whether they are compatible with one another. Some who claim that these two goals are a contradiction in terms see education as a pie of a limited number of slices. If one area, such as equity, receives attention, that much less of the pie will remain for other educational needs. As they view it, equity diverts resources from excellence.

Others see these values as working in basic opposition to one another. For example, the push for excellence that has fueled reform reports has resulted in state after state raising its standards for high school graduation. Those concerned about equity worry that this will cause at-risk students to drop out. In this situation, equity and excellence seem to be diametrically opposed.

Those who say that educational equity and excellence must complement rather than contradict each other put their arguments in practical as well as philosophical terms; they say that when education is effective in helping those least successful, the whole system benefits. For example, *Sesame Street* was designed for poor youngsters, but it has benefited middle- and upper-class children as well. Cooperative learning approaches were initially devised to promote racial harmony, but they have also been successful in raising achievement levels for all students. In the case of higher graduation standards mentioned above, an advocate for equity and excellence being mutually supportive might put it this way: "Raising graduation requirements implies increased quality of education; but if higher standards cause students at risk to drop out, this will mean more quality education for some students, but less quality for others. However, if additional assistance and programs supplement and buttress higher standards, then the result might be educational quality and equality for all."

The basic question may be: Can education be excellent if it is not excellent for all? Facing this same issue two centuries ago, Thomas Jefferson said:

> I know of no safe depository of the ultimate powers of the society but the people themselves; and if we think them not enlightened enough to exercise their control with a wholesome discretion, the remedy is not to take it from them, but to inform their discretion.

A democratic society requires educational excellence and educational equity. If quality education is only for some, democracy cannot survive.

LEGAL LANDMARKS
Discrimination in the Schools

During the last century charges of discrimination on the basis of race, gender, ethnicity, and national origin have been lodged against schools. Following is a summary of landmark cases that have brought education to court.

Race

Plessy v. Ferguson, 163 U.S. 537 (1896)

Facts: An 1890 Louisiana law required that railway passenger cars have "separate but equal" accommodations for the white and "colored" races. Plessy, an African-American man, brought suit after being arrested for refusing to vacate a seat in the area for whites, alleging this Louisiana law to be unconstitutional.

Holding: The law was upheld as constitutional. The doctrine of "separate but equal" was established in this case. The decision in *Plessy* was overruled 58 years later in the case of *Brown v. Board of Education*.

The doctrine of "separate but equal" stemming from the *Plessy* decision applied to public education for over half a century. In *Cumming v. Board of Education,* 175 U.S. 528 (1899), black taxpayers unsuccessfully sought an injunction requiring the school board to discontinue the operation of a high school for white children until the board resumed operation of a high school for black children. In *Gong Lum v. Rice,* 275 U.S. 78 (1927), the court permitted state authorities to classify Chinese children with black children and required them to attend a school for blacks, under the doctrine of "separate but equal."

Brown v. Board of Education of Topeka, 347 U.S. 483 (1954)

Facts: This case combined four cases from the states of Kansas, South Carolina, Virginia, and Delaware. In each of these cases, African-American children were seeking permission to be admitted to the public schools in their community on a nonsegregated basis. South Carolina, Virginia, and Kansas denied relief to the children and based their refusal on the "separate but equal" doctrine. Delaware permitted blacks to attend white schools only because the schools that black children attended in that area were substantially inferior.

Holding: The Supreme Court reversed its doctrine of "separate but equal" and concluded that in the field of public education separate educational facilities are inherently unequal. Even if the physical facilities and other tangible factors appear to be equal, race segregation has a negative psychological and educational impact.

Green v. County School Board, 391 U.S. 430 (1968)

Facts: The population of New Kent County in Virginia was approximately 50 percent black. There was no residential segregation, yet the two elementary and high schools in the county were segregated until 1964. In 1965 the school board adopted a "freedom-of-choice" plan in order to continue receiving federal funds under federal guidelines. After three years of the freedom-of-choice program, the schools continued to be segregated. The freedom-of-choice plan was challenged in the courts.

Holding: Under the equal protection of the Fourteenth Amendment and the *Brown* decision, school boards must provide for effective desegregation. A desegregation plan such as the freedom-of-choice plan in *Green* is ineffective, and it is the responsibility of the school board to establish a more desegregated plan.

Swann v. Charlotte–Mecklenburg Board of Education, 402 U.S. 1 (1971)

Facts: This case involved desegregation of the Charlotte, North Carolina, metropolitan area school district. The plan that was implemented by the school board proved to be ineffective. The district court imposed its own plan, one that required extensive busing and was regarded by many as impractical. This plan was challenged as too burdensome.

Holding: If school authorities cannot effectively remedy segregation, the district courts have the power and wide discretion to step in and create a plan to achieve an integrated school system. Specifically, the court may (1) order teachers to be reassigned to achieve faculty desegregation, (2) rearrange plans for construction of schools that would aid in segregation, (3) impose flexible racial quotas in the beginning of the desegregation plan, and (4) rearrange school zones and require reasonable busing in order to achieve integration.

National Origin

Lau v. Nichols, 414 U.S. 563 (1974)

Facts: Many students enrolled in the San Francisco school system spoke Chinese, and the school system did not provide them with any remedial instruction to learn English. The students brought suit alleging that the school board was violating the equal protection of the Fourteenth Amendment and Title VI of the Civil Rights Act of 1964, which prohibits recipients of federal aid from discriminating against students on the basis of race, color, or national origin. Because the Chinese students were not provided with instruction in the English language, they were not able to participate successfully in the rest of the education program.

(Box continues on next page.)

Holding: Under Title VI of the Civil Rights Act of 1964, a school district that is receiving federal aid has an affirmative duty to provide special instruction for non-English-speaking students in order for them to receive an effective education. The *Lau* decision required school districts to attend to the needs of non-English-speaking students.

Sex

Grove City College v. Bell, 465 U.S. 555 (1984)

Facts: Title IX of the 1972 Education Amendments Act prohibits sex discrimination in any education program receiving federal financial assistance. At Grove City College the only federal aid was to students for loans and grants. Since Grove City College received federal aid, the U.S. Department of Education claimed that the entire college should comply with Title IX. Grove City College refused to comply with the regulations, and consequently the U.S. Department of Education sought to revoke any financial assistance to its students. The college and several students sued, seeking to obtain the federal financial assistance.

Holding: Since the federal aid (grants) was given only to a group of selected students at the college, the Supreme Court stated that the college was not bound to comply with Title IX regulations. Title IX regulates only those specific programs that receive the federal aid, not the entire institution. Congress disagreed and passed a new law, the Civil Rights Restoration Act (1988), which ensured that any institution receiving federal funds could not discriminate in *any* of its programs, policies, or practices.

Note: This "Legal Landmarks" section was written by Nancy Gorenberg, an attorney and graduate of the MAT Program at American University.

SUMMARY

1. The educational history of African Americans has been marked by a long, difficult struggle. In 1896, the doctrine of "separate but equal" led to segregated school systems in many states. In 1954, under *Brown v. Board of Education of Topeka,* the "separate but equal" doctrine was abolished and many states initiated desegregation plans. These initiatives met with mixed success; the Civil Rights Act of 1964 was passed in an effort to eliminate continuing discrimination and segregation.

2. As a response to continuing segregation, magnet schools, choice plans, and voluntary metropolitan desegregation arrangements have emerged as tools to achieve desegregation.

3. Magnet schools offer special programs, including foreign language, math, science, and performing arts. Research indicates that magnet schools are successful in that they attract multiracial enrollments and result in increased achievement across racial groups.

4. Choice programs allow parents to pick three or four schools of their choice for their children; the school system then tries to place the students in the selected schools. These programs are effective in desegregation in that enrollments are controlled to meet designated goals of racial and ethnic composition.

5. Metropolitan desegregation involves desegregation plans that include both city and suburban school districts.

6. Migration to northern cities by African Americans and Latinos, combined with the flight to suburbs by white, middle-class families, has resulted in hyper-segregated big-city schools. As affluent minority families also leave the cities, they take with them skills, values, and role models that have traditionally provided the foundation of the nation's urban areas.

7. There are more than 26 million Latinos living in the United States today. The nation's Latinos comprise several groups, including Mexicans, Puerto Ricans, and Cubans. Today Latino immigration, particularly from Central American countries such as Nicaragua and El Salvador, is increasing. Students from poverty-stricken, war-torn countries often have survived traumatizing conditions. Adjustment problems, including language barriers, are just some of the reasons many Latino students are at risk.

8. Approximately 400,000 Native American students attend schools in the United States. Because of significantly different cultural backgrounds, as well as economic, health, and language problems, the dropout rate for Native American students is more than double the national average.

9. Asian/Pacific Islanders, especially new immigrants from war-ravaged nations in Indochina, face many problems, including dealing with past trauma and adjusting to a new culture and language. Other Asian Americans, such as the Japanese, are stereotyped as model minorities, a label that often masks the impact of prejudice on these children. Culture, heritage, and language differences can create difficult experiences for these minority groups in schools.

10. Women have experienced a history of inequitable treatment in schools. Even today, researchers have found that teachers interact more frequently with male students. Although female students begin school testing ahead of their male counterparts, they often end up behind.

11. Title IX of the 1972 Educational Amendments Act prohibits sex discrimination in schools that receive federal financial assistance.

12. An ongoing debate exists over whether equity and excellence in education are compatible. Some claim that efforts for equity drain resources from educational programs and subvert academic excellence. However, others claim that education cannot be excellent unless it is excellent for all.

DISCUSSION QUESTIONS AND ACTIVITIES

1. A broad overview of school bias as it applies to selected minority groups in this country has been presented. Select one of these groups for further reading and research. Analyze historical and contemporary educational developments that have affected this group, and discuss your findings with other members of your class.

2. Do research on some group not discussed in this chapter that has been or is still discriminated against in the educational process. Discuss your findings with other members of your class.

3. The next time you observe in class, do a frequency count of how many times teachers call on girls and boys. Match the amount of attention boys and girls get to their representation in the classroom. Do boys get more than their fair share of teacher attention?

4. Many of the issues we have discussed in this chapter are highly value-laden and often arouse intense emotional responses and differing opinions. How do you react to the various issues raised in this chapter? On a separate sheet of paper, complete the following sentences as honestly as you can. If you wish, share your responses with your classmates.

- When I hear the word *busing* I . . .
- I think the most important thing educators can do to achieve equal educational opportunity for all students is to . . .
- If a boy brought a favorite doll to "Show and Tell" in my first-grade classroom and the other kids laughed at him, I . . .
- If I taught in a school that in my opinion used culturally biased testing practices to track Spanish-speaking children into special education classes, I . . .
- If there were no information about members of minority groups in the social studies book assigned for my class, I . . .

5. Do you think equity and excellence in the field of education are compatible? Why or why not?[43]

NOTES

1. The discussion of the earlier educational history of African Americans, Latinos, and Native Americans is based on Meyer Weinberg, *A Chance to Learn: A History of Race and Education in the United States* (New York: Cambridge University Press, 1977).

2. Susie King Taylor, *Reminiscences of My Life in Camp with the 33rd U.S. Colored Troop Late First S. C. Volunteers* (1902; reprinted, New York: Arno Press, 1968).

3. Pauli Murray, *Proud Shoes: The Story of an American Family* (New York: Harper & Row, 1956).

4. W. E. B. Du Bois, "The United States and the Negro," *Freedomways* (1971), quoted in Weinberg, *A Chance to Learn*.

5. Fred L. Shuttlesworth, "Birmingham Revisited," *Ebony*, August 1971.

6. John Larson, *Academic Achievement Effects in Magnet Schools*. Paper presented at the American Educational Research Association, San Francisco, April 1989.

7. Jomills Henry Braddock, Robert L. Crain, and James M. McPartland, "A Long-Term View of School Desegregation: Some Recent Studies of Graduates as Adults," *Phi Delta Kappan* 66, no. 4 (December 1984): 259–264. See also Daniel Levine and Robert Havighurst, *Society and Education* (Boston: Allyn & Bacon, 1989).

8. William Julius Wilson, *The Truly Disadvantaged: The Inner City, The Underclass, and Public Policy* (Chicago: University of Chicago Press, 1987), p. 56.

9. Quoted in Gene Maeroff, "Withered Hopes, Stillborn Dreams: The Dismal Panorama of Urban Schools," *Phi Delta Kappan* 69, no. 9 (May 1988): 632–638.

10. National Advisory Commission on Civil Disorders, *Report of the National Advisory Commission on Civil Disorders* (Washington, DC: U.S. Government Printing Office, 1968), p. 369. See also Andrew Hacker, *Two Nations: Black and White, Separate, Hostile, Unequal* (New York: Charles Scribner's, 1992).

11. Levine and Havighurst, *Society and Education*. See also James Banks and Cherry McGee Banks (eds.), *Multicultural Education* (Boston: Allyn & Bacon, 1989), NEA Ethnic Report *Focus on Blacks,* February 1992.

12. Marilyn M. McMillen, Phillip Kaufman, and Summer D. Whitener, *Dropout Rates in the United States: 1993* (Washington, DC: National Center for Education Statistics, 1994).

13. James Comer, "All Our Children," *School Safety,* Winter 1989, p. 19.

14. Henry Louis Gates, Jr., *Loose Canons: Notes on the Culture Wars* (New York: Oxford, 1992).

15. NEA Ethnic Report, *Focus on Blacks,* February 1992. See also Spencer Swanson, "Policy Implications," *Education and Urban Society* 24, no. 1 (November 1991).

16. Joseph Fitzpatrick, *Puerto Rican Americans: The Meaning of Migration to the Mainland* (New York: Prentice-Hall, 1987).

17. Joan First, "Immigrant Students in U.S. Public Schools," *Phi Delta Kappan* 70, no. 3 (November 1988): 206.

18. Quoted in Laurie Olsen, "Crossing the Schoolhouse Border: Immigrant Children in California," *Phi Delta Kappan* 70, no. 3 (November 1988): 213.

19. Quoted in Weinberg, *A Chance to Learn.*

20. Quoted in Paul S. Taylor, *An American-Mexican Frontier: Nueces County, Texas* (1934; reprinted, New York: Russell & Russell, 1971).

21. NEA Ethnic Report, *Focus on Hispanics,* December 1991 and December 1995.

22. The Annie E. Casey Foundation, *Kids Count Data Book* (Washington, DC: Center for the Study of Social Policy, 1992).

23. Alfredo Castaneda, "The Educational Needs of Mexican Americans," in Alfredo Castaneda et al. (eds.), *The Educational Needs of Minority Groups* (Lincoln, NE: Professional Educators, 1974).

24. Robert S. Cotterill, *The Southern Indians: The Story of the Civilized Tribes Before Removal* (1954; reprinted, Norman: University of Oklahoma Press, 1966).

25. Quoted in Louise Udall, *Me and Mine: The Life Story of Helen Sekaquaptewa as Told to Louise Udall* (Tucson: University of Arizona Press, 1969).

26. NAACP Legal Defense and Educational Fund, in cooperation with the Center for Law and Education, Harvard University, *An Even Chance* (New York: NAACP Legal Defense and Educational Fund, 1971).

27. NEA Ethnic Report, *Focus on American Indian/Alaska Natives,* October 1991.

28. William Denmert, "Indian Education: Where and Whither?" *Education Digest* 42 (December 1976). See also Ron Holt, "Fighting for Equality: Breaking with the Past," *NEA Today,* March 1989, pp. 10–11; NEA Ethnic Report, *Focus on American Indian/Alaska Natives,* October 1991.

29. Annemarie Brewer, "On Indian Education," *Integrated Education* 15 (May-June 1977).

30. James Mahan and Mary Criger, "Culturally Oriented Instruction for Native American Students," *Integrated Education* 15 (May-June 1977). See also Lee Little Soldier, "Language Learning of Native American Students," *Educational Leadership* 46, no. 5 (February 1989): 74–75.

31. NEA Ethnic Report, *Focus on American Indian/Alaska Natives,* October 1991.

32. Much of the information on the history of Asian Americans is adapted from James Banks, *Teaching Ethnic Studies* (Boston: Allyn & Bacon, 1986).

33. Olsen, "Crossing the Schoolhouse Border."

34. Ibid.

35. Rosalind Y. Mau, "Barriers to Higher Education for Asian/Pacific-American Females," *The Urban Review* 22, no. 3 (1990): 183.

36. NEA Ethnic Report, *Focus on Asian/Pacific Islanders,* May 1992. See also Daniel Goleman, "Probing School Success of Asian-Americans, *The New York Times,* September 11, 1990, pp. C1, C10.

37. NEA Ethnic Report, *Focus on Asian/Pacific Islanders,* May 1992. See also Mau, "Barriers to Higher Education."

38. Esther Lee Yao, "Adjustment Needs of Asian American Children," *Elementary School Guidance and Counseling,* February 1985, pp. 222–227. See also Esther Lee Yao, "Working Effectively with Asian Immigrant Parents," *Phi Delta Kappan* 70, no. 3 (November 1988): 223–225.

39. Betsy West, "New Students from Southeast Asia," *Education Digest,* May 1984. See also Keith Hiroshi Osajima, *Breaking the Silence: Race and the Educational Experiences of Asian American Students.* Paper presented at the American Educational Research Association, San Francisco, 1989.

40. NEA Ethnic Report, *Focus on Asian/Pacific Islanders,* May 1992.

41. Quoted from 1989 student newspaper, Agricultural College of Pennsylvania, in Nancy Frazier and Myra Sadker, *Sexism in School and Society* (New York: Harper & Row, 1973).

42. Myra Sadker and David Sadker, "Sexism in the Classroom of the 80s," *Psychology Today,* March 1986. See also Myra Sadker, David Sadker, and Susan Klein, "The Issue of Gender in Elementary and Secondary Education," in Gerald Grant (ed.), *Review of Research in Education* (Washington, DC: American Educational Research Association, 1991), pp. 269–334; American Association of University Women, *How Schools Shortchange Girls* (Washington, DC: American Association of University Women, 1992). See also Myra and David Sadker, *Failing at Fairness: How Our Schools Cheat Girls* (New York: Touchstone Press, 1995).

43. Special thanks to Edward P. Davis for his help in revising this chapter.

CONTEMPORARY SOCIAL PROBLEMS AND CHILDREN AT RISK

OBJECTIVES

To describe the needs of single-parent families and latchkey children

To analyze the impact of television on children

To analyze problems that place children at risk, including violence, dropping out, teenage pregnancy, AIDS, substance abuse, homophobia, child abuse, youth suicide, and homelessness

To consider how school and society can respond to social issues that place children at risk

From the feminist movement to latchkey children, from single-parent families to teenage suicide, social changes have radically altered the way Americans live, think, work, and learn. The typical family structure, once a predictable model of a working father, a stay-at-home mom, and two or three or more children, is now the exception—not the rule. At-risk children may become teenage parents, abuse drugs, or execute agreements for group suicide. These are uncharted waters for educators, parents, and students.

This chapter will provide an overview of the contemporary social problems that threaten to engulf our children and our schools. The past decade was not kind to children, who now make up the poorest segment of society. Their well-being is threatened by violence, teenage pregnancy, AIDS, substance abuse, child abuse, homophobia, suicide, and homelessness. Both as a teacher and as a citizen, you will find that children need your guidance and help. As the 1992 Carnegie Council report, Fateful Choices, *makes clear, safeguarding their well-being "is not an act of charity. It is a reaffirmation of a humane society and an investment in the nation's future."*

Children at Risk

According to the 1992 Carnegie Council report, *Fateful Choices: Healthy Youth for the 21st Century,* "By age 15, about a quarter of all young adolescents are engaged in behaviors that are harmful or dangerous to themselves or others. Of 28 million adolescents between the ages of 10 and 18, approximately 7 million are at serious risk of being harmed by health- and even life-threatening activity as well as school failure. Another 7 million are at moderate risk."[1] The dropouts, the children who become parents themselves, the ones who suffer from substance abuse, the youngsters so depressed or overwhelmed they see suicide as a way out are all at risk. They need school and society to help and respond.

But according to the 1992 *Kids Count Data Book* the nation made no progress or slipped backward during the 1980s on seven of nine measures of child well-being (see Figure 15.1).[2] Today children are the poorest group in our society, and current programs and policies are woefully inadequate to meet their growing needs. Stanford's Michael Kirst sums it up this way:

> Johnny can't read because he needs glasses and breakfast and encouragement from his absent father. Maria doesn't pay attention in class because she doesn't understand English very well and she's worried about her father's drinking and she's tired from trying to sleep in her car. Dick is flunking because he's frequently absent. His mother doesn't get him to school because she's depressed because she lost her job. She missed too much work because she was sick and could not afford medical care.[3]

FIGURE 15.1

How American Children Are Doing

Kids Count *Benchmark*	*National Trends Over the 1980s*	*State Trends*
Percent of low birth weight babies	3% worse	35 states worse*
Infant mortality rate (per 1,000 live births)	22% better	51 states better*
Child death rate for ages 1–14 (per 100,000 children)	18% better	48 states better*
Teen violent death rate for ages 15–19 (per 100,000 teens)	11% worse	34 states worse*
Percent of all births that are to single teens	14% worse	42 states worse
Juvenile custody rate for ages 10–15 (per 100,000 youths)	10% worse	32 states worse*
Percent graduating high school	0% (no change)	28 states better
Percent of children in poverty	22% worse	40 states worse
Percent of children in single-parent families	13% worse	44 states worse

*Includes the District of Columbia.

Source: The Annie E. Casey Foundation, *Kids Count Data Book* (Washington, DC: Center for the Study of Social Policy, 1992).

As a teacher you will be on the front line working with youngsters who have been too long neglected. Depending on the school where you teach, you may be shocked and saddened by the condition in which the students come to school and by the way they behave. *The Condition of Teaching,* reporting the results of the largest national survey of teachers ever conducted, says that teachers are deeply concerned about the physical and emotional well-being of their students. In describing schoolchildren, they use phrases such as "emotionally needy" and "starved for attention." As one teacher said, "Children come to school sick because there is no one home to care for them, so the teacher does it."[4]

Even if you teach in schools from more affluent areas, you will find your students coping with stress, rapidly changing lifestyles, new family structures, and social problems rarely mentioned or even thought of just a few decades ago. As we noted in this book's first chapter, most people drawn to teaching want to make a difference in the lives of children. Too many of today's students are sorely in need of someone who can have that positive influence.

This chapter will highlight problems engulfing today's children and provide you with information so you can take steps to help. As the *Kids Count Data Book* warns, we have a choice, ". . . to do nothing and consign our children to rising risk and in so doing be complicit in their eclipsed futures, or to rise to the occasion and reverse these results."[5]

Young and Poor

In 1992, about 14 million children—one in five—lived in poverty, an increase of about 4 million since 1979. This figure includes disproportional levels of minority groups. For example, while white youngsters have a poverty rate of 11 percent, 40 percent of African-American and 32 percent of Hispanic children live in poverty. When one controls for inflation, the standard of living has declined for most families during the past 15 years.[6]

As has often been observed, "The rich get richer and the poor get poorer." The wealth of the richest 1 percent of the country increased from 27 percent of the total in 1973 to 42 percent in 1992. The gap between the wealthiest 20 percent of Americans and the poorest 20 percent is greater now than at any time since the nation began collecting these statistics.[7]

Most parents of poor children work, but they don't earn enough to provide their families with basic necessities—adequate food, shelter, child care, and health care. Fifteen percent of youngsters age 10 to 18 have no health insurance coverage, while one out of three poor adolescents is not covered by Medicaid.[8] And efforts to balance the federal budget often focus on reducing these services even further. When children are poor, they are more likely to drop out of school and be involved in violent crime, early sexual activity, and drugs. In short, poverty puts children at risk.

Four factors account for most of the decline in the standard of living. During the past decade, changing government policies have not been kind to children. The increasing racial and ethnic diversity of the population has also resulted in a rise in poverty. When the nation changed from a manufacturing to a service and information economy, a new group of poor was created. Without the academic skills and education necessary, this newly poor population is in danger of becoming a permanent underclass. Finally, as the next section shows, changes in family structure have hurt the financial well-being of children.

The traditional family of 35 years ago, with a father who worked in the salaried labor force and the mother in the home, is becoming a thing of the past. By the middle of the 1990s, nearly three-fourths of married women with children between 6 and 17 worked outside the home.

New Family Patterns

It was not too many years ago that the Andersons of *Father Knows Best* lived through weekly, if minor, crises on television; that Dick and Jane lived trouble-free lives with their parents and pets in America's textbooks; and that most real families contained a working dad, a stay-at-home mom, and three children confronting life's trials and tribulations as a family unit. But today's family bears little resemblance to that of the past.

Leave It to Beaver may live in rerun land forever, but Beaver Cleaver resolves the bumps and bruises of childhood in a way that by today's standards appears half a step from a fairy tale. Only three or four decades ago, a single-parent family meant one thing: a premature death. Out-of-wedlock chil-

FIGURE 15.2
Percentage of Households with Children under 18 Years Old, by Household Type, 1950 to 1990

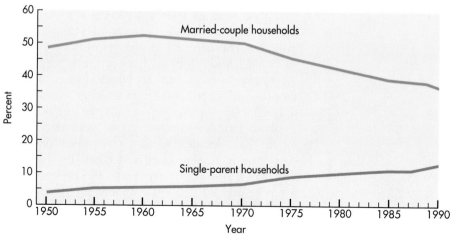

Source: U.S. Department of Commerce, Bureau of the Census, Current Population Reports, Series P-20, *Household and Family Characteristics,* various years.

dren and pregnant, unmarried teenagers were hidden from the public's attention. Divorce was rare, generally confined to movie stars and one or two acquaintances. Mothers stayed at home and fathers went to work. During the 1970s and 1980s, new family structures and roles emerged which have had a dramatic impact on schools.

Beaver Cleaver's family structure now represents fewer than 6 percent of U.S. families. The social revolution of the past decades has created a new family reality. Today approximately 13 million children—more than one in five— live in single-parent families (see Figure 15.2).[9] More than half of African-American children live with only one parent.[10] It is predicted that 60 percent of today's 5-year-olds will live in a single-parent home before they reach the age of 18.[11] Ninety percent of these will be with their mothers, a situation often representing severe loss of income. Research shows that children from single-parent families are less likely to achieve and more than twice as likely to drop out of school.[12]

Divorce

The Census Bureau predicts that a majority of women now in their twenties and thirties will experience a divorce. After a general upward trend that peaked in the late 1970s, divorce rates have now stabilized and even dropped slightly. Nevertheless, today more than 1 million children experience divorce each year.[13] (Figure 15.3 charts both the number of divorces and the number of children involved in those divorces in recent decades.) Although divorce today is common, it is hardly a routine experience. Divorced people suffer emotional and physical stress and are more likely to succumb to a variety of diseases. More than half of the couples who divorce have children. Divorced mothers with young children face particularly difficult situations as they continue to care for children while they work at new jobs and confront new financial problems.

FIGURE 15.3
Number of Divorces and Children under 18 Involved in Divorces per Year, 1950 to 1990

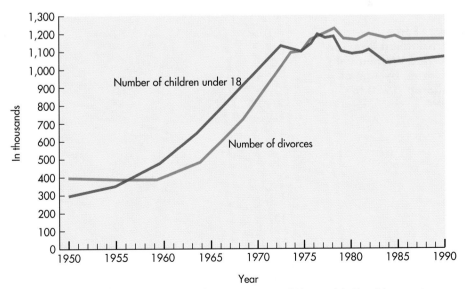

Source: U.S. Department of Commerce, Bureau of the Census, *Statistical Abstract of the United States,* various years; *Historical Statistics of the United States to 1975;* and Current Population Reports, Series P-25, nos. 311, 519, 917, and 1000; U.S. Department of Health and Human Services, National Center for Health Statistics, *Monthly Vital Statistics Report,* various years; and *Vital Statistics of the United States,* various years.

Most divorced women do not receive adequate child support from the fathers, and court financial awards to mothers are usually low and not well enforced.

Although divorce is a disruptive experience, it is the marital stress underlying divorce that is the real culprit. Divorce itself can eventually lead to a more liberating and productive life for those involved. But marital stress and the years immediately following divorce can be disruptive to the psychological, financial, and educational well-being of children. This stress can manifest itself in the classroom and present a challenge to teachers.

Children who have experienced divorce may exhibit a variety of problem behaviors, including depression, anxiety, asthma, allergies, tantrums, daydreaming, regression, aggression, frequent crying, withdrawal from relationships, and poor school performance. Often children of a divorce go through a classic mourning process similar to that experienced after a death in the family. However, most children are resilient and can rebound from the trauma of divorce, with 80 to 90 percent recovering in about a year. The classroom can be a conflict-free zone for these children, especially when teachers are aware, understanding, and tolerant of behavior change. It is important for teachers to give children the chance to express their feelings about divorce and let them know they are not alone in their experience.[14]

Wage-Earning Mothers

In 1960, 39 percent of married women with children between the ages of 6 and 17 worked; this increased to 62 percent by 1980 and to 74 percent by 1994. The rise in salaried employment for married women with children under 6 has been even more striking, jumping from 19 percent in 1960 to 62 percent in 1994.[15] (Figure 15.4 shows the tremendous increase since 1950 in the number of married mothers working outside the home.)

FIGURE 15.4
Labor Force Participation Rate for Married Women with Children, by Age of Children, 1950 to 1994

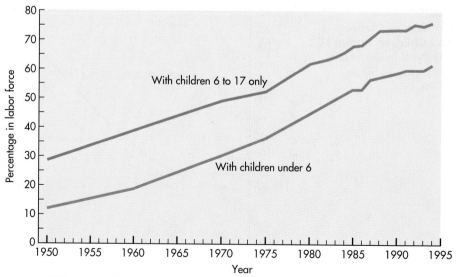

Source: U.S. Department of Commerce, Bureau of the Census, *Statistical Abstract of the United States,* various years; U.S. Department of Labor, Bureau of Labor Statistics, *Special Labor Force Reports,* nos. 13, 183, and 2163; and unpublished data.

When both parents are wage earners, the mother continues to be responsible for most housekeeping and parenting chores. Unlike family roles of the past, parenting today is more likely to be a part-time rather than a full-time activity. Mothers often feel guilty for not staying at home with their children, and they are also frustrated by inadequate child-care facilities and arrangements. Studies show that the crucial issue in parenting is not whether mothers work in the salaried labor force or work as homemakers. Rather, the most important factor is the satisfaction level of the mother. A mother who feels satisfied by her role, has adequate child-care arrangements, and does not feel guilty about working or not working outside the home is likely to have contented children.

However, it is not a search for satisfaction but economic necessity that drives most women into the labor force. Between 1979 and 1990 the real median income of families with children fell by 5 percent. But the cost of housing, transportation, health care, and education rose during this time period.[16]

For schools, wage-earning mothers represent a change from the past. Parent-teacher organizations find it more difficult to involve parents in school activities. The reservoir of volunteers for a variety of school functions has been greatly reduced, while the need for afterschool child care has increased significantly.

Stepfamilies

One in six U.S. families is a stepfamily, and about one in three children lives in a stepfamily. Stepfamilies are created when divorced or widowed parents remarry, and most do. Stepfamilies consist of biological and legal relationships with stepparents, stepsiblings, multiple sets of grandparents, and what often becomes a confusing array of relatives from old and new marriages.

Although children living in stepfamilies perform about the same in school as other children do, the stepfamily creates some special issues. Because the traditional family stereotype permeates the school curriculum, children in stepfamilies may feel discomfort about their "abnormal" lifestyle. When schools need to report student grades and involve parents in school activities, they must sort out whom to communicate with—one, two, three, or possibly more parents. Which family members should have access to the student's records? What involvement should a biological, but no longer a legal, parent have? Stepfamilies can shatter traditional school-home relationships, and not all schools have been able to adjust.

Changing family patterns have created and will continue to create a new social reality for schools. From single-parent homes or multiple-parent families, children arriving at school bring diverse home experiences and needs, and, as in the past, the schools are asked to respond. One result of changing lifestyles has been the increase in latchkey children, an issue that is of concern to teachers.

Latchkey Kids

Jennifer unlocked her door quickly, raced inside and shut it loudly behind her. She fastened the lock, threw the bolt, dropped her books on the floor, and made her way to the kitchen for her usual Twinkie. Within a few minutes Jennifer was ensconced on the sofa, the television on and her doll clutched firmly

The problems faced by latchkey children cannot be attributed to low socioeconomic or educational levels of the parents as is the case with many other student problems.

in her hand. She decided to do her homework later. Her parents would be home then and she tried not to spend too much time thinking about being lonely. She turned her attention to the television, to spend the next few hours watching talk shows.

• • •

Jennifer is a latchkey kid. More than 3 million children between 5 and 13, like Jennifer, are left to care for themselves after school.[17] Lynette and Thomas Long coined the term **latchkey kids** to describe those children who carry a key on a rope or a chain around their necks, a key to unlock their home door. (More recently, the term *self-care* has been used as an alternative label with fewer negative connotations.) Coming from single-parent homes or families with two working parents, they are products of new economic and social realities in the United States. With few extended family units (grandparents and other relatives living with or near parents) and a shortage of affordable, convenient, quality child-care facilities, many children are simply left on their own.

Latchkey kids are found in all racial and socioeconomic groups, but most are white middle-class children. The more educated the parents, the more likely they are to have a latchkey child. Although the average latchkey child is left alone 2½ hours per day, a significant number are alone much longer, more than 36 hours per week. Approximately a third of latchkey children are unable to reach either parent by phone. For these children, television is the babysitter and the telephone a lifeline.

In some cases latchkey children suffer psychological trauma and fear. The Longs estimate that as many as one in four latchkey children may be severely fearful, such as the sixth-grader who constantly checks windows and door locks and searches under beds and watches TV armed with a baseball bat. Boredom and loneliness may be these children's greatest concerns, but parents worry most about physical injury. Accidents at home, conflicts among unattended siblings, or even a criminal break-in are all potential catastrophes. If all the psychological and physical fears concerning latchkey kids could be resolved, questions about the quality of the experience would still remain. Home alone, many latchkey children watch television, talk on the telephone, or snack on a wide array of not particularly healthful foods.

When Is a Latchkey Child in Trouble?

Warning Signs for Parents

- When the parent comes home, lights are on everywhere and radios and television are at high volume.
- The child keeps some form of weapon for protection.
- The child stays in a single room, often the parent's bedroom.
- There are signs of drinking.
- The child experiences one or more of the following: nightmares, depression, significant weight change, drop in school performance.

Warning Signs for Teachers

- The child comes to school dressed inappropriately—slovenly, untidy, or in a manner that is too sexy and provocative.

- Slips that require the parent's signature are not returned to school.
- The child has neither lunch nor lunch money.
- Homework is typically not completed.
- The child hangs around the classroom after school as if reluctant to go home.
- The child exhibits more than ordinary attention-seeking behavior, unusual weight change, or significant drop in school performance.

If teachers see these warning signs, they should schedule a conference with the parent as soon as possible. It may be important for the parent to explore other child-care arrangements.

Source: Interview with Lynette Long, psychologist and expert on latchkey children, May 1992.

Latchkey children may need special attention and resources, but it is important to keep in mind that not all latchkey children are at risk. Literally millions adjust to their situations, supervising themselves in terms of homework and other decisions. But as the numbers continue to increase, it is reasonable to assume that for some, problems do develop, and there are few educational or social agencies available to respond to these needs. In fact, our lack of specific statistics on the number of latchkey children and their problems is a strong sign that we are not very informed about this group or about the work needed to ensure their safety and productivity.

For latchkey children, television is often a surrogate parent, representing company, friendship, education, or just the comforting sound of not being alone. But television may not be a productive or even a satisfactory companion.

The Impact of Television

The most popular magazine in the United States is not *People, Time,* or *Sports Illustrated;* it is *TV Guide.* Many U.S. homes have several television sets, turned on for an average of 6 hours a day, teaching and shaping those who watch. Television watching has reduced the amount of time we sleep, spend in social gatherings and leisure activities, or engage in conversation with each other. In fact, by the time the average student has reached 18 years of age, he or she will have attended 11,000 hours of school and watched 15,000 hours of television. To ignore the impact of this medium is to ignore a major educational influence on children.

Television has been blamed for an array of crises and behavior problems, from a lack of discipline and concentration to passivity, from decline in scholastic achievement to family tensions and even violence. It is unlikely that all the accusations made about the effects of television are true, but no doubt television has created problems as well as promise.

On the positive side of the ledger, the Children's Television Workshop (CTW) realized that **educational television programming,** developed along the same lines as commercial TV, could compete successfully for the time and attention of young viewers. Programs such as *Sesame Street* and *The Electric Company* effectively promote early learning skills and reading to a young audience at home. Research indicates that viewing *Sesame Street* has resulted in children's having higher verbal IQ test scores, having more positive attitudes toward school, and achieving better performance in the first grade.[18] Children who watched *The Electric Company* in school did significantly better on reading tests than did those who did not watch the program. Studies also show that children who regularly watched *Mister Rogers' Neighborhood* had greater persistence and more positive interpersonal relationships. Some dispute these findings, but most research studies show that well-crafted educational programs can result in greater educational achievement.

Although these shows have received widespread acclaim, most television programming does not consist of offerings such as *Sesame Street*. General entertainment programs and even television commercials have been criticized for promoting violence, stereotyping, and unfair and unhealthy consumer practices. A 1992 study by the American Psychological Association concluded that unregulated viewing not only robs children of both play and study time, but also leads to increases in prejudice, obesity, and aggressive behavior.[19]

The effect of television in promoting violence and aggression has created a heated debate. By the time the average child reaches age 15, he or she will have seen 13,000 murders on television. The evidence suggests that viewing this extreme violence does influence children. In one study, 9- and 10-year-old children were shown a violent episode of *The Untouchables* (a show about 1920s gangsters). A second group watched a nonviolent sports show. Both groups were then brought into a room with a box that had two buttons, labeled "help" and "hurt." The children were told that pressing the "help" button would help a child in another room to complete a game. Pushing the "hurt" button would hinder this effort. The children who watched the violent episode of *The Untouchables* pressed the "hurt" button 33 percent more often than the other children. Longitudinal data collected on television viewing and violence since 1960 presents overwhelming evidence that higher levels of viewing violence on television correlate with increased aggressive behavior, in both children and adults.[20]

Another problem is that television does not generally increase understanding and tolerance among groups. Asian Americans are often seen as servants, villains, detectives, or karate experts. Native Americans are presented without tribal distinctions and often characterized as lazy, alcoholic, and humorless. Women sell cosmetics, whereas men burn up the roads demonstrating the latest "hot" car. African-American criminals are a mainstay of many police and adventure shows. Although there are notable exceptions, ethnic, racial, and sex-role stereotyping permeate the airwaves. One study showed that characters in children's afterschool programs were overwhelmingly white. Television viewers overestimate the percentage of world population that is white and male, overestimate the number of the nation's wealthy while underestimating the number of Americans living in poverty, and overestimate the proportion of jury trials.[21]

For a number of years, television has been blamed for everything from falling test scores to violence. Clearly, television can lead to some negative, aggressive behaviors and some stereotypic perceptions of the world. But a comprehensive review of television research indicates that we may be overstating the case against TV. Daniel Anderson and Patricia Collins found that television's impact depends greatly on who is watching and their general viewing habits.[22] And the American Psychological Association found that when teachers and parents regulated television viewing, children showed gains in vocabulary, cognitive, and social skills.[23]

Billions of dollars are spent each year on television advertising, and much of it is aimed at children to promote the purchase of toys, cereals, candies, and fast food. Studies show that television is the single most important source of information about these items for children and parents.

Criticism of advertising directed at children takes several forms. Some express health concerns, complaining that the cereals, candies, and fast foods promoted are of low nutritional value. Others are worried about the entire process of conditioning children to increase their consumer desires, to want more, and, when they become adults, to purchase more. Children are more susceptible, less knowledgeable, and more naive than adults about the techniques and products promoted on television. Bombarded by 20,000 TV commercials a year, children often have trouble distinguishing advertisements from the programs themselves.[24]

Concern over the influence of television advertising is behind the controversy surrounding *Channel One,* the innovative program from Whittle Communications that brings TV to school. In more than 12,000 high schools and junior high schools across the nation, students watch 10 minutes of news and 2 minutes of commercials each day. Whittle Communications provides the programming for free and lends the monitors and a satellite dish to participating schools. Initial comparisons of students who watch *Channel One* with those who do not show that viewing students got one more item correct on a current events test than did their nonviewing counterparts. Critics charge that such minimal benefit does not warrant taking away school time to sell things to kids. However, many students and teachers in *Channel One* schools report that they are satisfied with the program.[25]

Television is a persuasive and powerful medium, one that can be used to promote education or aggression, understanding or intolerance, community projects or the purchase of sugared cereal and candy. In fact, television has done all these things. As cable and satellite programming increase, so does the capability to offer more programs to more people in more areas of the world than ever before. Although the power of television is not in dispute, the direction of television programming and advertising is in question; it will continue to be a major concern to educators in the years ahead.

Confronting Problems of Children at Risk

Dropping Out

Henry was finishing junior high school with the same resignation and despair he had felt a few years earlier at his elementary school graduation—although *graduation* did not seem to be the right word. He had just managed to squeak through Beaton Junior High with poor grades and no understanding of how this frustrating experience would help him. He wasn't good at schoolwork and felt that the classes he had to sit through were a waste of time.

Henry's father had left school after eighth grade to go to work. Although he did not make much money, he had a car and seemed to be getting along okay. Henry's mother had left high school when she became pregnant, and had never returned. Neither of Henry's parents thought school was critical, although both wanted Henry to finish. But Henry's patience was wearing thin. He wanted to end these long, boring days, get a job, and get a car. He'd had enough of school.

• • •

Henry is a good candidate to join the nation's dropouts. Although the United States has promoted the revolutionary concept of universal education, we have fallen far short of that goal. However, although we have a long way to go, the nation has made significant improvement in the rate of high school completion. In 1950, just a little over half of 25- to 29-year-olds had completed high school. By 1993, the figure had jumped to 86 percent completing high school.[26]

Gains for African Americans over the past two decades have been substantial. In 1972, about 74 percent of black students had completed high school by their early twenties. By 1993, high school completion among blacks had risen to about 84 percent. This progress is not shared by Hispanic students, whose rate of high school completion has hovered around 60 percent for the last 20 years.[27] Of course, these dropout rates vary significantly when other demographic factors such as family income level and geographic location are considered. (See Figure 15.5 for high school completion rates by race/ethnicity.)

Today, roughly one out of every nine students still does not graduate from high school. This represents not only a loss of human potential but increased future costs in welfare, unemployment benefits, and potential criminal activity. (See Figure 15.6 for information on the employment status of school dropouts.)

Students who are poor, minority, or attending school in cities are far more likely to drop out of school. Also, children are more likely to drop out if they are members of large families and if their parents are poorly educated or working in low-paying jobs, factors related to poverty. Students from low-income, low-skill, low-education family backgrounds are several times more likely to drop out of school than are students from wealthy families.

Students drop out of school for a variety of reasons: poor grades, teenage pregnancy, "school was not for me," "school was too dangerous," "couldn't get along with teachers," "didn't get into the desired program," and "was expelled or suspended."[28] Certainly many of these reasons can be attributed to the structure and size of high schools. Comprehensive high schools are designed to edu-

FIGURE 15.5
High School Completion Rates for all 29- to 30-Year-Olds, by Race/Ethnicity: 1972–1993

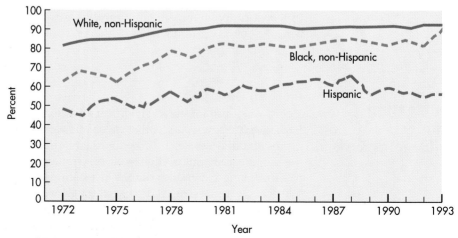

Source: U.S. Department of Commerce, Bureau of the Census, October Current Population Surveys, various years; and unpublished data.

FIGURE 15.6
Employment Rate of Recent High School Dropouts and High School Graduates Not Enrolled in College: 1960–1990

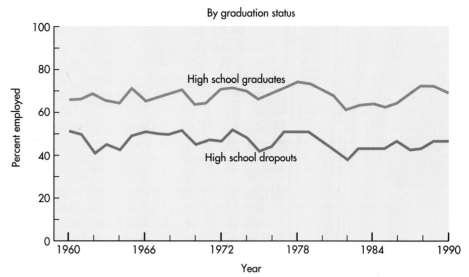

By graduation status

Source: U.S. Department of Labor, Bureau of Labor Statistics, *Labor Force Statistics Derived from the Current Population Survey: 1940–1987;* and tabulations based on the October Current Population Surveys.

cate large numbers of students at one time. Students are grouped into classes; classes are grouped into programs (academic, commercial, and so on). Learning is usually provided through a set of prescribed lessons: class discussions and lectures, reading assignments, and testing. This uniformity is undoubtedly not the most effective approach for all students. Students who learn experientially, or by practicing real-world skills, may perform less effectively than students who can function on an abstract level. Students without a support structure at home for guidance and help are faced with yet another disadvantage. And children with low self-esteem or special needs who do not fit the standard or typical student profile may not receive the individual attention they need.

There are several steps schools can take to respond to the dropout problem, including the following:

Early intervention is an important first step. Students at risk of dropping out can be targeted for special services to develop more positive school attitudes, more effective learning skills, and regular attendance patterns. Grade retention can be reduced or eliminated.

Identifying the cause for dropping out can lead to several positive developments. Counseling and special services can be utilized to respond to personal and family needs such as teenage pregnancy or parent-child conflicts. Remedial and tutorial services can be called upon to reduce academic obstacles.

Restructuring curricular and instructional practices may be necessary to reduce alienation. Changes might include ensuring student success and increasing student self-esteem; relating school work to practical, useful skills needed for adulthood; and incorporating techniques to promote motivation. Some educators believe that smaller schools and classes would reduce the dropout rate by increasing personal contacts between teachers and students. Others promote alternative schools as a solution.

Increasing the linkages between school, the family, and the community has proven to be an effective strategy. On the one hand, parents can be brought into school activities and training in order to promote home support for education. On the other hand, businesses can be encouraged to have students work part time while in school, assist in vocational education, and reserve employment openings for those who complete their education. The family and business community can become partners in keeping students in school.[29]

Most schools, although not offering a comprehensive approach to the dropout problem, do offer one or more programs to respond to the problem. Here are some typical programs currently used:

Alternative programs provide students with some unique options to traditional education. Sometimes offered as a "school within a school" or as an entirely separate **alternative school,** these programs usually include informal classes, field placement, and more flexible rules and regulations. Some alternative programs operate in storefront facilities, and are sometimes termed **street academies.**

Homebound instruction offers home instruction to students who are physically unable to attend school.

Residential treatment offers a separate facility for drug or alcohol rehabilitation that includes an educational component.

Agency services, located in penal institutions, youth wards, and detention centers, provide continuing education for students who are runaways, in criminal custody, or victims of abuse or neglect.

Experiential programs, sometimes called **schools without walls** and located in a variety of sites including businesses, government agencies, and museums, allow students to continue their education in nontraditional settings. Students learn about economics, political science, and history by participating in organizations directly involved in these activities.

These unconventional programs represent attempts to augment traditional school offerings and respond to the special needs of potential dropouts. However the staggering statistics, which show that some school systems are losing as many as one of every two students before graduation, indicate how much more needs to be done. A number of factors contribute to the high rate of dropouts, but for females the single most common cause is teenage pregnancy.

Sex Education and Teenage Pregnancy

Sex education programs in public schools have been controversial since their introduction around the turn of the century. At that time, educational reformers, including doctors and other professionals, believed that enlightened sex education for all could help banish venereal disease, prostitution, and sex outside of marriage while promoting sexual restraint. Concerned that parents could not be counted on to provide their children with sex information or to teach them about sexual restraint, the schools were charged with this responsibility.

These arguments are still controversial. Today, sex education has been thrust into a society of sexual contradictions and revolution: sexually active children and adults in conflict with religionists espousing fundamentalist tenets

When families are headed by young mothers, they are six times as likely to be in poverty.

of premarital restraint and/or abstinence; societal preaching against promiscuity within a context of sexually suggestive and explicit advertising; disputes between pro-life and pro-choice forces over the legality and morality of abortion; arguments among different groups about the appropriateness and effectiveness of the school as a place for sex education instruction. While the debate continues, the nation attempts to respond to various waves of sexual crises: spreading venereal disease, an epidemic of teenage pregnancies, and the fatal disease AIDS (acquired immune deficiency syndrome).

Although most Americans support sex education courses, they also believe that values and moral beliefs should be included in the curriculum, and of course, there are strong differences of opinion on these issues. This puts schools in a difficult position, likely to offend one group or another and trying to walk the fine line between teaching and preaching. But surveys show that the public does expect preaching; it is confused only on what the schools should preach.

Preaching morality while teaching sex education can be a dangerous, if not combustible, mixture. Research indicates that U.S. teenagers receive the message that premarital sex is wrong and, therefore, are not prepared for sex when it occurs. The nation's teenagers do not plan for something they are not supposed to be doing.

In many European countries, premarital sex is accepted and contraceptive techniques are taught. European teens use birth control techniques regularly, while fewer than 20 percent of adolescent girls in the United States use birth control during first intercourse. The result is that while European and U.S. teens experience similar rates of sexual activity, the U.S. adolescent pregnancy rate is twice as high as that of England, France, and Canada, three times as high as Sweden's and seven times as high as that of the Netherlands.[30]

Not only do people differ on the direction sex education should take, school districts differ on the content and quality of the programs they should offer. In some districts, sex education consists of a few hours of instruction on the sperm, the egg, and pregnancy. Sometimes sex education and driver education are included in the same administrative program. In other areas, sex education may be far more extensive, beginning in the early elementary grades and continuing through high school, including such topics as biology, decision making, and birth control techniques. On average, secondary schools offer only 6½ hours a year of sex education. Less than 2 hours is spent on contraception and prevention of sexually transmitted diseases.[31]

Currently there is a need to develop multicultural and linguistically appropriate sexuality education materials to meet the needs of different minority groups. Teens rely on peer networks to explain sexuality, the availability of condoms, and focus less on the biology of sex and more on how to negotiate relationships. As one young African-American woman said, "When you're in sex education class, they just tell you what goes on inside your body. They don't tell you what goes *on*."[32]

At this point we simply do not know enough about how to instruct and implement effective sex education programs. And the statistics underscore our failings. We are, in fact, in the midst of a teenage pregnancy epidemic unrivaled by any other industrialized nation.[33] Every day in the United States:

- 2,740 teenage girls become pregnant
- 1,105 teenage girls have abortions
- 369 teenage girls have miscarriages

- 1,293 teenage girls become mothers
- 7,742 teenagers become sexually active
- 623 teenagers get syphilis or gonorrhea

These statistics generate other statistics of economic, educational, and psychological devastation. Consider the following:

- More than 40 percent of teenage girls who drop out of high school do so because of pregnancy and/or marriage. In 1989, 67 percent of all teen births occurred outside marriage, compared with 30 percent in 1970. There was a 14 percent increase in the total number of births to teens during the 1980s.
- Only 14 percent of unwed mothers receive child support payments from the father.
- A teenage mother's income is approximately half of a teenage father's; teenage mothers are far less likely to graduate from high school and far more likely to be on public assistance.
- Teenage mothers and their babies are more likely to suffer medical complications and have higher mortality rates.
- Teenage mothers who marry are more than twice as likely as others to have their marriages end in divorce.
- There are approximately 1 million teenage pregnancies a year, more than half of them ending in abortion.
- This teenage pregnancy epidemic reduces the educational and economic potential of many women, while increasing their need for medical and social services. The epidemic is costly to teenage girls and their children—and to society as a whole.

While Americans debate the wisdom of sex education programs and abortion rights, the teenage pregnancy epidemic continues. And now a new threat is assaulting the fabric of U.S. society and its schools: the fear and consequences of AIDS.

AIDS: The Medical Nightmare Comes to School

For many communities, decades of opposition to sex education were unceremoniously cast aside with the emergence of the medical nightmare AIDS. Sexually active children represent a potentially major at-risk population for the disease, and sex education has become the prime weapon against the spread of the virus. In its 1992 report, *A Decade of Denial,* the House Select Committee on Children, Youth, and Families estimates that 40,000 teens each year contract the HIV virus that causes AIDS (see Figure 15.7).[34]

Federal, state, and local governments, as well as health and education organizations, have launched a major effort to educate students about the transmission and nature of this deadly threat. Now available to teachers is a wide array of recently developed curricular materials and videotapes. Many of these materials are sexually explicit when dealing with techniques that may be used to avoid contracting AIDS.

The first lesson of all AIDS programs is to decrease risk-related behaviors. Teachers are expected to be able to distinguish myth from fact concerning the disease. To test your own knowledge, try this AIDS IQ quiz.

FIGURE 15.7
Cumulative AIDS Cases Reported Among Youths, 1981–1995

Year	13–19	20–24
1981	1	6
1982	3	35
1983	11	125
1984	35	303
1985	71	645
1986	130	1,263
1987	211	2,204
1988	333	3,622
1989	401	5,063
1990	628	6,694
1991	789	8,160
1992	797	8,265
1993	1,167	10,949
1994	1,768	15,204
1995	2,184	17,745

Source: House Select Committee on Children, Youth, and Families, *A Decade of Denial: Teens and AIDS in America* (Washington, DC: Goverment Printing Office, 1992), and data from National AIDS Clearinghouse.

True or False

_____ 1. AIDS affects the body's immune system.

_____ 2. Individuals can carry the AIDS virus without contracting AIDS.

_____ 3. AIDS is confined to the homosexual community.

_____ 4. Women cannot transmit the AIDS virus.

_____ 5. You can get AIDS from donating blood.

_____ 6. Healthy-looking people can transmit the AIDS virus.

_____ 7. The AIDS virus can be transmitted by mosquitoes.

_____ 8. The AIDS virus can be transmitted by receiving a blood transfusion.

_____ 9. AIDS is the leading cause of death for 30-year-old women in New York City.

_____ 10. The higher the number of sexual partners, the higher the risk of contracting AIDS.

_____ 11. Pregnant women who are infected will not transmit the virus to their babies if they avoid nursing.

_____ 12. Condoms provide complete protection from transmitting AIDS.

_____ 13. Drugs such as AZT cure AIDS.

_____ 14. The AIDS virus is found in saliva, tears, and urine.

_____ 15. AIDS can be contracted in swimming pools.

_____ 16. The AIDS virus (HIV) can be transmitted by touch in school or work situations.

Answers

1. *True* AIDS stands for "acquired immune deficiency syndrome." Because the body is unable to defend itself against disease, AIDS victims develop a variety of life-threatening illnesses.
2. *True* AIDS is caused by the human immunodeficiency virus, or HIV. Those with HIV can spread the deadly virus, although they may not show signs of AIDS for 10 years or more. At this point, it is not clear if everyone with HIV will develop AIDS. Blood tests can tell if someone is infected with HIV.
3. *False* Although most cases of AIDS in the United States are found in gay or bisexual men, AIDS is also transmitted through sharing of drug needles and, to an increasing extent, through sexual activity in the heterosexual community.
4. *False* Heterosexual female-to-male transmission does occur. Heterosexual transmission is the leading source of AIDS in Africa.
5. *False* Donating blood in this country is safe because the needles used to extract blood are used only once and then discarded.
6. *True* Individuals can spread the AIDS virus (HIV) for years without themselves having any AIDS symptoms. An HIV blood test indicates whether a person is carrying the virus (although it may take several months after the acquisition of the virus for the blood test to reflect its presence).
7. *False* Initial reports that mosquitoes could transmit the AIDS virus have not been verified.
8. *True* There is a very small risk factor associated with receiving a blood transfusion, since the AIDS virus may not be detected in screening, especially in the early stages. Approximately 2.6 percent of AIDS patients contracted the disease through a blood transfusion.
9. *True* As the number of women with AIDS increases, so too does the number of children who contract the virus and suffer its effects.
10. *True* The disease can be transmitted during one sex act, and the risk of getting AIDS is increased as the number of sexual partners is increased.
11. *False* HIV is found in breast milk but can also be transmitted during passage through the birth canal.
12. *False* Nonlatex condoms provide little protection against acquiring HIV. Latex condoms and spermicides provide the best, but not 100 percent, protection.
13. *False* AZT (or Retrovir) inhibits the spread of infection and prolongs the life of many AIDS patients. It is not a cure.
14. *True* They have not, however, been found to be a means of transmission, as the virus concentration in these fluids is too low to pose a threat.
15. *False* There is no medical evidence establishing this connection.
16. *False* People infected with the AIDS virus cannot pass the virus to others through normal school or work activities.

The widespread publicity surrounding Ryan White, a young AIDS victim who led a courageous fight to open school doors to young AIDS patients, did much to relieve the ignorance that surrounds this deadly disease.

By 1990, AIDS-related sex education was an accepted part of some school programs, a controversial part of others, and avoided in still other communities. To many, but not all, Americans, the threat of this fatal disease was horrific enough to eliminate reservations concerning sex education programs in the schools. In 1992, in Washington, DC, schools initiated a plan whereby school nurses trained in counseling would distribute condoms. This aggressive action was taken in response to evidence that 1 in every 45 district teenagers was infected with the AIDS virus.

It is not just a question of informing students and the community about AIDS; school districts must also decide how to deal with students and teachers who contract the disease. In general, the medical community supports the proposition that the AIDS virus cannot be spread through casual contact, and there is little objective evidence for isolating AIDS victims. When the courts have entered such disputes, they have supported the rights of AIDS victims, contending that AIDS is a disability and discrimination against the disabled is illegal.

Without a clear national consensus as to the content, shape, and direction of courses and programs, conflict will undoubtedly accompany this new emphasis on sex education. Conservative religious groups and a number of parents do not believe that sex education should be taught in schools. Nevertheless, it is likely that changing mores and fears of venereal disease, AIDS, and unwanted pregnancy will continue to move sex education from the periphery to center stage in U.S. schools.

Drugs and Drinking

"I know personally kids who drink whole bottles of liquor on the weekends by themselves."

"You won't see the drug culture here unless you know what to look for. You'll get a lot of parent and school denial, but the reputation of this school is 'cocaine heaven.'"

"On an average week I gross over $2,000 dealing drugs at this school."

These personal accounts, all from high school students, support official reports indicating that the United States has the highest rate of teenage drug use of any industrialized nation in the world. This condition is often referred to as *substance abuse,* and these drugs range from alcohol and cigarettes to cocaine, LSD, and heroin.

The actual degree of alcohol abuse is difficult to assess, but it represents by far the most widespread form of substance abuse. One in 20 high school seniors reports drinking daily. According to a 1992 report released by the Surgeon General, the more teenagers drink, the more likely they are to be involved in violent crime, such as murder, rape, or robbery, either as victim or perpetrator. Justice Department figures show that alcohol or drug use is associated with more unplanned pregnancies, more sexually transmitted diseases, and more HIV infection than is any other single factor.[35]

According to annual surveys by the Institute for Social Research, illegal drug use among junior and senior high school students increased in 1993, after decreasing for several years. These results are alarming, but it is not yet clear if they mark a reversal of a 12-year downward trend seen since the 1980s. High school drug use reached its apex in 1979, when 59 percent of seniors reported using illicit drugs. This figure fell to 27 percent by 1992, but rose to 31 percent in 1993. The survey found increases in reported use of marijuana, stimulants, LSD, inhalants, and cigarettes from 1992 to 1993, while reported cocaine use remained constant.[36] (See Figure 15.8 for data on student drug and alcohol use between 1975 and 1994.)

Psychologists note that children growing up in the drug culture display symptoms similar to those shown by returning combat soldiers. These symptoms include introverted behavior, phobias, nightmares, violent outbursts, listlessness, fear of the future, and an inability to form trusting relationships. Combat veterans can be treated after they return from their traumatic environment; but psychologists worry that children need treatment while they struggle to survive in a dangerous and combatlike drug culture.

Substance abusers suffer significant school problems. Marijuana users are twice as likely as nonusers to be averaging Ds and Fs. A Philadelphia study showed that four out of five dropouts were regular drug users. Unfortunately many parents and teachers are unaware of the extent of the problem. An Emory University study found that whereas 3 percent of parents surveyed said that their children had used marijuana in the past 30 days, 28 percent of those children reported that they had actually taken the drug.[37] School and police officials confirm that parent denial, especially in the suburbs, is one of the biggest problems. "It's normal parent denial and suburban American dream denial. This isn't supposed to happen here."[38]

Some drug programs seem to be effective, while others have little impact. Richard Hawley has identified the following characteristics of effective drug education programs:[39]

1. The school must be committed to becoming drug-free.
2. Leaders must make a clear and strong commitment to a drug-free environment.
3. Preventing drug abuse is easier and more effective than remediating an existing drug problem: Early intervention for young children is essential.
4. A consensus of all school faculty, from kindergarten to grade 12, is needed in order to promote both enforcement of and education in a drug-free school environment.
5. Faculty members must not be substance abusers.
6. A drug-free environment also means an alcohol-free environment.

FIGURE 15.8
Student Drug and Alcohol Use

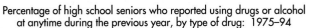

Percentage of high school seniors who reported using drugs or alcohol at anytime during the previous year, by type of drug: 1975–94

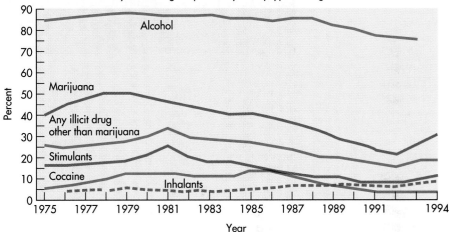

Percentage of students who had someone offer to sell them drugs at school during the first half of the school year, by grade and year and control of school: Spring 1988, 1990, and 1992

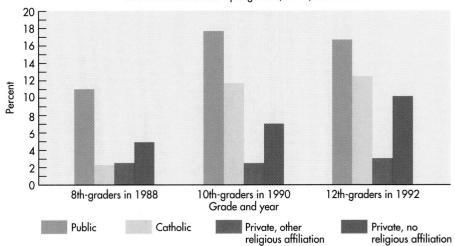

Source: U.S. Department of Education, National Center for Education Statistics, *National Education Longitudinal Study of 1988.* Base Year (1988), First Follow-up (1990), and Second Follow-up (1992) Student Surveys.

The United States has the highest rate of teenage drug use of any industrialized nation in the world.

Even after a decade of general reduction in teen substance abuse, a powder keg national problem is emerging: the increasing number of drug-damaged babies, especially those affected by crack cocaine. Pregnant women constitute a growing segment of cocaine users. Crack cocaine triggers a quick, euphoric high that wanes in about 10 minutes. To prolong the high, a user must smoke repeatedly, a pattern that can result in high levels of fetal exposure.

In 1988–1989, 10,425 infants at risk of suspected or actual substance abuse were born in Florida. In a follow-up study conducted in Palm Beach, doctors reported an extraordinary increase in drug-addicted babies. Both the medical and the education communities have been taken by surprise; they are stunned and bewildered. As one Florida educator says:

> These children have a lot of the same characteristics as children in special education classes, . . . yet behavior reinforcements that might work for other handicapped children do not necessarily work with drug-exposed children. Since 1975 educators have been trying to mainstream handicapped students into regular classes, but teachers like me are finding that just one cocaine-exposed child in a class of 30 is enough to strain the learning environment; four or five in the same classroom can be a disaster for everyone involved.[40]

As a teacher in a mainstream or special education classroom, you will be faced with growing numbers of children who were born damaged by drugs. The following warning signs will help you identify and better understand these students:[41]

- *Hyperactivity:* difficulty in controlling movements
- *Poor coordination:* difficulty in manipulating pencil and scissors
- *Attention deficit disorder:* easily distracted
- *Low tolerance level:* quickly frustrated, gives up easily

- *Unpredictable mood swings and temper tantrums*
- *Faulty memory:* trouble following three-step directions
- *Signs of home drug use*

Structure and consistency are the hallmarks of Florida preschool programs specially designed to meet the needs of drug-damaged babies. In Los Angeles, some cocaine-exposed children are separated from the mainstream; many attend the Salvin Special Education School. In this separate school, teachers can handle short attention spans and temper tantrums and offer the love and touching that seems to help. Even if drug-exposed children are mainstreamed, expensive additional services of health and education professionals will be necessary.

Many of the problems the nation's youth face—drugs, teen pregnancy, and sexually transmitted diseases, including AIDS—often take place in an environment of violence that can threaten the effectiveness and even the viability of schools.

Caught in the Crossfire: Violence at School

The United States is becoming an increasingly violent country. In 1991, the U.S. incarceration rates were the highest in the world. Between 1980 and 1990, the prison population in this country doubled. The price for prisons is increasing more rapidly than the cost for any other social services or agency—including health and education.

More than 80 percent of the 1 million U.S. prisoners did not complete high school. Ironically, increased levels of education reduce crime rates. As demographer Harold Hodgkinson says, "In Pennsylvania it is seven times more expensive to maintain someone in the state pen than it is to maintain someone at Penn State."[42] Consider the following:[43]

- Nearly 3 million crimes occur on or near school campuses each year.
- A 1993 national survey found that 23 percent of students and 11 percent of public school teachers reported being victims of violence in or around their school.
- The number of juvenile arrests for violent crimes increased by 50 percent between 1987 and 1991. Juvenile arrest rates for heroin and cocaine violations increased more than 700 percent between 1980 and 1990.
- A 1993 survey reported that 60 percent of all students in grades 6 through 12 could obtain a handgun, and 39 percent of all U.S. students know someone who was killed or wounded by gunfire.

Violence and vandalism are more likely to occur in large urban schools where students are poor and feel alienated from society. However, good schools, led by strong principals and characterized by positive and caring interactions between faculty and students, can reduce violence and create safe havens for children. Stemming the tide of violence is an educational imperative. As one Chicago school administrator, Manford Byrd, said:

The losses . . . cannot be measured in terms of dollars. No one has measured the immediate and long-term effects on the education of children resulting from the climate of fear generated by the conditions. Many hours of education are lost because of false alarms and bomb threats. Much harm is done to educational programs when classroom windows are shattered, teaching materials destroyed or stolen, and schools damaged by fire and other acts of vandalism. When students and teachers are fearful of going to school . . . a healthy environment for learning is lost.[44]

One of the most appalling forms of violence occurs when adults charged with caring for the young abuse them instead.

Child Abuse

From 1976 to 1990, reports of child maltreatment grew from 416,033 to 1,700,000 annually,[45] and most experts believe that at least 2 million more cases annually are not reported. Because teachers are often the only adults aside from family members who regularly see the children, they may represent society's best opportunity to recognize and prevent child abuse. Yet recognizing such abuse is not always easy, and stepping in to prevent it may be difficult for many teachers.

Child abuse and neglect include a range of behaviors and effects, such as the following:

- *Physical abuse:* evidenced by cuts, welts, burns, and bruises
- *Sexual molestation and exploitation*
- *Neglect:* medical, educational, or physical
- *Emotional abuse*

It is not possible for teachers who identify one or more of these problems to know for sure that child abuse and/or neglect is the cause. In fact, most teachers avoid such problems and do not report suspected incidents. The American Humane Institute reports that only 13 percent of all child abuse reports come from educators. Yet it is both the legal and moral responsibility of teachers to report abusive treatment of children. Every state requires that teachers report "suspected" cases of abuse, and failure to report such cases can lead to decertification. Most laws also protect teachers from any legal liability for reporting such cases.

Much child abuse and neglect originates with adults who were themselves abused as children. Parents who hold unrealistic expectations for their children or who are under a great deal of financial or psychological stress are also more likely to become abusers. It is important to remember that abuse and neglect rarely occur as a result of intentional actions. Rather, they usually represent moments of misplaced outrage or a lack of resources or knowledge about how to care for children.

Child abuse affects not only this generation but the next as well. As abused children grow to adulthood, they are more likely to perpetuate crime and violence. Adults who were abused as children constitute 90 percent of all violent criminals, 97 percent of hard-core juvenile offenders, 65 percent of runaways, half of female drug abusers, and 80 percent of prostitutes.[46] Preventing child abuse during the school years pays dividends for both this and the next generation.

Child Abuse: Warning Signs

Children who suffer physical abuse may:

- Exhibit signs of frequent injury—burns, black eyes, and other bruises
- Refuse to change into gym clothes; wear long sleeves even in very warm weather
- Not want to sit down
- Show unusually aggressive or unusually withdrawn behavior
- Not show emotion—no joy, pain, or anger
- Be frequently absent or tardy for no good reason
- Be unusually eager to please
- Complain about pain, beating, or other abusive treatment
- Show significant change in school attitude, behavior, or achievement

Children who suffer sexual abuse may:

- Complain of pain or itching in the genital area
- Exhibit unusual odors or signs of trauma in the genital area
- Wear bloody, torn, or stained undergarments
- Create stories or drawings of an unusually sexual nature
- Exhibit unusually sophisticated knowledge of sexual behavior
- Have difficulty in sitting or walking
- Talk about sexual involvement with an adult
- Try to run away from home
- Be extremely mature or seductive in dress and behavior
- Exhibit signs of sexually transmitted diseases
- Become pregnant

Source: Adapted from *The Abused Child Pamphlet,* Texas State Teaching Association for Instruction and Professional Development (Austin, TX: TSTA/NEA, 1984).

In *Cry Out!,* P. E. Quinn recounts the horror of his abused childhood. His story stands as a plea to teachers to become involved.

> As an adult survivor of six years of severe child abuse—both physical and emotional—I often wonder why the church did nothing to help me, my brothers, and my parents. Was it that they could not see the bruises, the cuts, scratches and abrasions covering my body? Could they not see the desperation out of which my parents lived? Or the need? Surely as I attended church school classes someone must have noticed the pain and terror in my eyes, the hopelessness with which I moved, my withdrawal into isolation, or, at least, the swelling in my hands and feet. Surely someone must have noticed me.[47]

Educators can serve as vital communication links because both child abuse and substance abuse are associated with a pervasive and frightening development in U.S. schools. Newspaper headlines in supposedly secure and comfortable communities across the country have shocked parents and citizens with reports of teenage suicide.

Youth Suicide

The closely knit New Jersey community across the Hudson River from Manhattan was viewed as a model town. The high school frequently won the state football championship, the police department won awards for its youth-assistance programs, and the town was known for the beauty of its parks and the safety of its streets.

On an early Wednesday morning in March, the citizens of Bergenfield woke up to discover that four of their teenagers had locked themselves in a garage, turned on a car engine, and left a note requesting that they be buried together. The group suicide brought the total of teen suicides in Bergenfield to eight that year.

Suicide is one of the leading causes of death among Americans aged 15 to 24. One young person commits suicide every 1 hour and 45 minutes. For every suicide there are more than 200 attempts among this age group. Ten percent of teenage boys and 18 percent of teenage girls try to kill themselves at least once.[48]

On one Wednesday evening in October, more than 300 parents and students gathered in the high school auditorium of an affluent Maryland suburb to confront the suicide issue. Within the past few months, two students, a teacher, and a parent had taken their own lives in this, one of the wealthiest communities supporting one of the best high schools in the nation. The group had come together to confront the question: What had gone wrong? The following dialogue comes from that meeting. The speaker had started a suicide prevention program in a neighboring community. Although the dialogue reflects what was said at one school meeting in one suburb, the concerns raised are heard in schools and homes across the nation.

Speaker: Although some states, like California, have classes in suicide prevention, I prefer a stress reduction program. Suicide is the result of unresolved stress and pressure. Typical stresses on young people today include divorce and separation, pressure to achieve, sex and sexuality, popularity, appearance, peer pressure, and physical changes.

Moreover, times have changed. When we went to school, a college education was more or less a guarantee of success. That's not true anymore. Many of today's children will go to college and not do as well as their parents. Because of television, fads are more rapid today. Sneakers and sweaters have brand names that are "in" one month, and "out" the next. Kids are often trying to stay "in," which is a sign of increased pressure and an increased need for money. Suburbia has also added to this money pressure. Kids need cars to be mobile. They often hang out in shopping malls and eat at fast-food restaurants. All this creates money and peer pressures that didn't exist a few years ago.

Then there are dramatic societal changes that add to this pressure. Sex has become more explicit on television, in the movies, and in magazines. Even dress styles are no longer innocent. Trying to conform to the ads in these magazines is difficult. Add this to increased drug and alcohol abuse, single-parent families, latchkey children, and even the threat of nuclear extinction, and you realize that today's children are growing up in a different world.

Parent: How do we know if our kids are thinking about suicide?

Speaker: There are signs. These include depression, loss of appetite, anxiety, listlessness, mood swings, promiscuity, severe weight loss or gain, and impulsiveness.

That last one, impulsiveness, may be particularly crucial. Kids who fly off the handle may be more likely to do something drastic without really thinking about the consequences.

One more piece of information may be helpful. The Ontario Study identifies high-risk groups for suicide. They are both the high-achieving students and the nonachievers. On opposite ends of the scale, those who are performing extremely well academically and those who are failing share a common characteristic: They are the most likely candidates for suicide.

Parent: What can we do about this problem? We have 15-year-old children killing themselves.

Speaker: For one thing, you can help kids cope by talking with them. Not on your schedule—on theirs. Avoid lectures or registering shock. Don't impress them with how well you've done. You're their parents, and despite their outside polish and sophistication, they are very vulnerable. They need time to talk with parents, with their friends, and time just to do nothing. They need to have some control over their own space and privacy.

Parent: They control their own space, and it's a mess. My kid's room looks like a bomb hit it!

Speaker: Close the door. That's their space—and they will win a power struggle on how to keep their room.

Parent: How am I to approve and communicate with my kid when she dresses so strangely? Her clothes are awful.

Speaker: Be flexible, dress and times change. Yesterday's hippy is driving a BMW today.

Student: That was my dad. How do I deal with stress? I never learned how.

Speaker: The school should establish programs for you.

Student: My class ranking is very high, and my parents keep telling everybody. It embarrasses me.

Speaker: Parents sometimes do stupid things.

Parent: How can this school deal with kids' stress?

Speaker: Mostly through talking. Parents and schools should provide these opportunities to communicate. At this school you have peer counseling. Peer groups sharing the same problems—divorce, drugs, or whatever. Peer counseling can be very helpful in reducing stress.

As in the case of child abuse, teachers can be critical in identifying potential suicide victims and preventing their self-destructive actions. But as is the rule in cases of abuse, teachers should not act alone. First, they should involve a guidance counselor, school social worker, or school psychologist. Even established medical centers working with suicidal patients employ a team of experts. Teachers should do the same. Second, teachers should confront the student in order to discuss the causes pushing the student to contemplate suicide. If the student recognizes the need for help, the family should be notified and asked to meet with appropriate mental health professionals and the school administration. Above all, the situation should be continually monitored and professionals should be in constant communication with the family. A perceptive and caring teacher can provide the critical early warning, but preventing suicide requires a coordinated effort.

What should teachers look for? Four patterns have been identified in youngsters who engage in self-destructive behaviors.

1. *Isolation:* students who passively avoid demands, whose academic performance is deteriorating, who have trouble complying with rules and are not involved in peer groups
2. *High-strung behavior:* students who have a chip on their shoulders, who are highly unstable, who push people away and prevent others from being effective

3. *Aggressiveness:* students who engage in petty crime and vandalism, delinquent or antisocial behavior, who may become involved in the juvenile justice system

4. *Immediate gratification:* students who use ineffective coping strategies and look for immediate, if inappropriate, relief (through alcohol, drugs, or thrill-seeking behaviors)[49]

These four profiles are only indicators of potential suicide, yet they are important for teachers to keep in mind. Falling grades, lack of motivation, and withdrawal are all warning signs. Impulsivity, which accounts for about one-fourth of all adolescent suicides, is particularly difficult for adults to deal with, since it may cause students to commit suicide in response to their first bout with depression. To date, teachers and parents have not been doing well in preventing youth suicide.

Gays, Lesbians, and Bisexuals: America's Invisible Students

Particularly in danger of death by suicide are gay, lesbian, and bisexual youth. They are two to three times more likely to try to kill themselves than are heterosexual youngsters. Some believe they constitute up to 10 percent of the population; but they complete 30 percent of youth suicides each year. Most of these take place before age 17. Feeling "different" and isolated from their peers, many gay, lesbian, and bisexual youngsters are subject to depression and thoughts of self-destruction from an early age. Minority gay and lesbian students are particularly at risk. For example, 36 percent of African-American lesbians, compared to 21 percent of white lesbians, and 32 percent of African-American gay males, compared to 27 percent of white gay males, attempt suicide before age 18.[50]

Closely associated with suicide are drug and alcohol abuse, especially by children younger than 14. Typical of this profile, a 14-year-old gay male describes his feelings and behavior:

> When I was 11, I started smoking dope, drinking alcohol, and snorting speed every day to make me feel better and forget I was gay. I would party with friends but get more and more depressed as the night would go on. They would always make anti-gay remarks and harass gay men while I would just stand there. Late at night after they went home, I would go down to the river and dive in—hoping I would hit my head on a rock and drown.[51]

Family problems are the most significant factor in youth suicide. Often lesbian and gay youth try to kill themselves after "coming out" and meeting rejection by their families. More than 33 percent of gay males and lesbians report verbal abuse from relatives because of their sexual orientation, and 7 percent report physical abuse as well.[52]

The *homophobia,* or fear and intolerance toward homosexuals, that characterizes most middle and high schools also causes depression and suicidal feelings. In most schools gays, lesbians, and bisexuals are treated as if they do not exist or as the objects of intense prejudice and hatred. School systems typically have no programs for these students, and most teachers and coun-

Student Sexual Diversity: Guidelines for Teachers

1. Confront directly school incidents of anti-lesbian and anti-gay prejudice—harassment, labels, jokes, put-downs, and graffiti.
2. Work to change personnel policies in order to protect students and staff from discrimination on the basis of sexual orientation.
3. Provide support groups and other resources for gay, lesbian, or bisexual students and their families.
4. Submit requests in order to improve both fiction and nonfiction library holdings on sexual diversity.
5. Include gay, lesbian, and bisexual concerns in prevention programs (pregnancy, dropout, suicide).

If a student comes to you to discuss gay, lesbian, or bisexual concerns:

- Be aware that the student may be feeling grief and emotional pain.
- Use the terms the student uses. Say "homosexual" if that is the term used, or "gay," "lesbian," or "bisexual" if the student chooses either of these terms.
- Be aware of your own feelings. Avoid making negative judgments that may cause the student even more pain.
- Respect confidentiality.
- Let the student know you appreciate his or her trust.
- Remember that gay and bisexual male students are particularly in need of information concerning protection from AIDS.

Source: Adapted from "Affording Equal Opportunity to Gay and Lesbian Students Through Teaching and Counseling" (Washington, DC: National Education Association, 1992).

selors receive little information or training in how to work with them effectively. Some schools have a climate that is actively hostile: Students and even faculty make jokes about faggots, gays, and queers; and anti-gay graffiti cover bathroom walls and school desks. At times verbal abuse turns physical, as in the case of a black male student in Ohio who was dragged into a bathroom stall. There eight boys called him a faggot, bashed his head against a toilet, and threatened to kill him. They were merely given demerits for the incident.[53]

Because homophobia is so prevalent and so virulent, most lesbian and gay students go into hiding and try to "pass" as "straight." Afraid to let other students, faculty, or even their families know, too many become painfully isolated. In *Reflections of a Rock Lobster: A Story About Growing Up Gay*, Aaron Fricke describes what it was like:

> The only goal left to me in life was to hide anything that could identify me as gay. . . . I thought that anything I did might somehow reveal my homosexuality, and my morale sank even deeper. The more I tried to safeguard myself from the outside world, the more vulnerable I felt. I withdrew from everyone and slowly formed a shell around myself. Everyone could be a potential threat to me. I resembled a crustacean with no claws; I had my shell for protection yet I would never do anything to hurt someone else. Sitting on a rock under thousands of pounds of pressure, surrounded by my enemies, the most I could hope for was that no one would cause me more harm than my shell could endure.[54]

Extraordinary signs of jeopardy and risk have finally caused some educators to respond. In 1988, the National Education Association (NEA) adopted a resolution advocating equal opportunity for students and staff regardless of sexual orientation and encouraging schools to provide counseling by trained personnel. In 1992, the NEA developed training materials and workshops on "Affording Equal Opportunity to Gay and Lesbian Students through Teaching and Counseling." School districts have also responded. San Diego, Boston, and St. Paul have issued antiharassment measures and policies designed specifically to protect homosexual students.[55] These are beginning steps, but much more must be done.

Hidden America: The Nation's Homeless

We have all seen them, and not seen them: sitting on a bench, their world's possessions arranged in a shopping cart, discarded by our society. Perhaps you have thought to yourself, "What a pity," as you walked by, avoiding eye contact. A minute later, they were out of your mind, forgotten and hidden once again from your life. But they will not go away. They are becoming more numerous and more visible.

Official government statistics, such as the Census, are unable accurately to tabulate the number of homeless in the United States. According to a 1993 estimate, anywhere from 225,000 to 500,000 American children go to sleep homeless every night. Some estimates say that up to 2 million adults and 1 million children are homeless; others say the figures are even higher. Families with children are the fastest-growing segment of the homeless population.[56]

Not since the great depression of the 1930s have so many Americans been forced to exist without homes. One of the major contributing factors to the nation's growing homeless population has been the decreasing supply of housing for those Americans living on the edge of poverty. While the income of poor Americans over the past decade has stagnated or decreased, the cost of housing has skyrocketed. The National Low-Income Housing Coalition estimates that 25 percent of families earning less than $15,000 a year must pay more than 60 percent of their income for rent. For many families, this is not possible. During the 1980s, federal aid for low-cost housing fell dramatically, while the Department of Housing and Urban Development was rocked by scandals. Few funds were earmarked for the poor; fewer funds found their way to low-cost housing programs. In its 1993 report on hunger and homelessness, the U.S. Conference of Mayors revealed that, in most major cities, requests for subsidized housing have increased. Applicants currently wait approximately 2 years before they receive assistance. The waiting period is not pleasant, and approximately one in four requests for emergency shelter goes unmet in major cities.[57]

> In Washington, D.C., a 3-year-old girl and her 5-year-old brother spend their nights with their mother, assigned to a cubicle in a school gym. The mother lost her job because of unreliable child care. Unable to meet her rent payments, she lost her apartment. Now the family is awakened at 5:30 A.M. in order to catch the 7:00 A.M. bus to a welfare hotel where breakfast is served. After breakfast, it is another bus ride to drop the 5-year-old off at a Head Start program, then back to the welfare hotel for lunch. Another bus takes them to pick up the boy from day care and then transports them to dinner back at the hotel. The final bus ride takes them to

their cubicle in the gym. The 3-year-old misses her afternoon nap on a daily basis. The mother does not have the time or means to look for a job.

The cycle continues.[58]

Nor is homelessness only an urban problem. According to the Housing Assistance Council, rural people account for almost one-quarter of those assigned to homeless shelters. In South Dakota, for example, one of the country's leading agricultural states, 90 percent of the state's 4,000 homeless people are from rural areas. America's homeless are urban and rural, white and black; it is truly a national problem.

Unfortunately, there has not been much of a national response. In 1987 Congress passed the McKinney Homeless Assistance Act, providing the homeless with emergency food services, adult literacy programs, job training, and other assistance. In 1990, the act was amended to underscore the importance of education and to facilitate the public school enrollment of homeless children. For example, the requirement of furnishing proof of immunization, a simple task for most families, was often enough to keep a homeless child out of school. The amended act reduced or eliminated many such barriers.[59] Despite this progress, funding remains inadequate to meet the educational needs of the nation's homeless children.

By the year 2000, it is likely that millions of children in the United States will have spent part or all of their childhood without a home. They pose significant problems for educators, going, as they do, from shelter to shelter, from school to school. They may be tested, counseled, assigned to a class, and then leave. They lack even rudimentary facilities for study. Frequently they arrive at school hungry and tired. In many communities, they are even denied access to school. School districts that require proof of residency or birth certificates routinely deny education to the homeless. Add to this equation the drugs, crimes, violence, and prostitution often found in shelters, and it is clear that these children are struggling uphill, against overwhelming odds, in order to get an education.

In 1989 the Johns Hopkins Institute for Policy Studies attempted for the first time to quantify the academic loss experienced by homeless children. Focusing on homeless children in New York City, the study investigated attendance records and achievement scores. Eighty-four percent of homeless children did not return to the same school for the next academic year; instead they enrolled in another district or did not enroll at all. Homeless children at the elementary level were absent almost 3 days out of every 10. At the junior high school level, the absentee rate was approximately 4 days out of 10. By high school, the typical homeless student, if still enrolled, missed 5 days out of every 10. The study also revealed significant achievement loss. Almost 72 percent of homeless children in grades 2 to 8 scored below grade level in mathematics. Almost 60 percent in grades 3 to 10 who took the standardized reading test scored below grade level. It is difficult to assess how many homeless students were not in school to even take the test.[60] Most states report that the situation is getting worse. Until more affordable housing can be made available, more effective job training is implemented, and more money expended, schools and teachers will continue to fight an uphill battle to meet the educational needs of the nation's homeless.

SUMMARY

1. One in five U.S. children lives in poverty today. This is a higher percentage than for any other developed nation.

2. The traditional family unit of the past has undergone a radical transformation as divorces, wage-earning mothers, and stepfamilies increase in number. Parents and teachers express concern about supervision of students who have become latchkey children or who watch an enormous amount of television unsupervised by adults.

3. Latchkey children are those who are left home alone for a significant portion of the day. Often latchkey children are found in white, middle-class homes with working parents. Psychologists do not share a universal view as to whether this is a harmful experience, but some express concern about possible trauma, poor nutrition, and safety.

4. Although television holds great promise, with shows such as *Sesame Street* providing an educational service for children, much of television fare is, at best, unproductive. Violence, racism, sexism, and commercialism on television provide children with negative messages. More well-designed research studies are needed in order to objectively and comprehensively evaluate television's impact on children.

5. Today 86 percent of students complete high school. Poor, minority, and urban students are more likely to drop out than are others. Reasons range from lack of motivation to teenage pregnancy. Schools are developing a number of programs to attempt to stem this tide and retain students through high school graduation.

6. The mixed messages sent to students in our society have contributed to an alarmingly high rate of teenage pregnancy. More than 1 in 10 teenage girls become pregnant, and most are destined for an early end to their educational careers and for severe deprivation of economic potential. Current school responses vary according to community norms. In some communities, sex education is a major emphasis; in others, it is minor or missing entirely.

7. Fear of AIDS has served as a catalyst for establishing sex education programs. Effective sex education programs should dispel misconceptions concerning this deadly disease. The AIDS virus, HIV, can be spread through contaminated drug needles, contaminated blood transfusions, or through sexual activity with a carrier of HIV.

8. Although substance abuse by teens has generally declined since the 1970s, reports in recent years suggest drug use may again be on the rise. Statistics on the extent of the problem are difficult to quantify and interpret, but clearly substance abuse has a devastating impact on the education and health of those involved. Drug-damaged babies will present challenges to education in the future.

9. The growing correlation between violent crimes and youth—both as perpetrators and as victims—makes violence an increasing concern for schools.

10. Nearly 2 million cases of child abuse are reported each year, with perhaps as many or more cases going unreported. Teachers can be an important force for prevention if they learn to identify the warning signs and report their suspicions. The same can be said of suicide, which is attempted by 10 percent of teenage boys and 18 percent of teenage girls.

11. Gay, lesbian, and bisexual youth are two to three times more likely to commit suicide than are heterosexual youngsters. Schools need to do much more to address the needs of these often "invisible" students.

12. The dramatic decrease in the amount of low-cost housing built and available during the 1980s and the rising cost of rent led to an increase in the need for public shelters and specific educational services for homeless children. Passage of the 1987 McKinney Homeless Assistance Act, amended in 1990, was intended to lessen the impact of this problem, but the number of homeless in the United States remains quite high.

DISCUSSION QUESTIONS AND ACTIVITIES

1. How do the following impact schools?

- Single-parent families
- High divorce rates
- Latchkey children
- Television

2. What can schools do to address each of the issues discussed in the above question?

3. What are some of the basic rules to provide a responsive school environment for latchkey children?

4. Agree or disagree: "While television does not promote understanding, it does promote capitalism. It is to a great extent a wasted educational resource."

5. Identify some of the typical programs used to prevent students from dropping out of school.

6. Describe what you would consider to be a good sex education program. Does it preach as well as teach? How might the public respond to your program?

7. What dangers confront school districts that include discussion of AIDS and teenage pregnancy in the curriculum?

8. What are some of the physical indications of child abuse? What is the teacher's role in preventing such abuse and neglect?

9. What can schools and society do to reduce teenage suicide?

10. What are some of the major barriers prohibiting the education of homeless children?

11. For each of the following issues, identify at least one problem that prevents gathering accurate statistics: latchkey kids, hours spent watching television; dropouts; drug use; teenage pregnancy; homelessness; carriers of HIV; gay and lesbian students.

NOTES

1. Fred Hechinger, *Fateful Choices: Healthy Youth for the 21st Century* (New York: Carnegie Council on Adolescent Development, 1992), p. 2.

2. The Annie E. Casey Foundation, *Kids Count Data Book* (Washington, DC: Center for the Study of Social Policy, 1992).

3. Quoted in John O'Neil, "A Generation Adrift?", *Educational Leadership* 49, no. 2 (September 1991): 4–10.

4. Quoted in the Carnegie Foundation for the Advancement of Teaching, *The Condition of Teaching* (Princeton, NJ: Carnegie Foundation, 1988).

5. The Annie E. Casey Foundation, *Kids Count*.

6. D. Stanley Eitzen, "Problem Students: The Sociocultural Roots," *Phi Delta Kappan* 73, no. 8 (April 1992): 584–590; William P. O'Hare, "Race/Ethnicity and Child Poverty: A Closer Look," *Population Today* 23, no. 3 (March 1995): 4–5.

7. Eitzen, "Problem Students"; David Francis, "New Figures Show Wider Gap Between Rich and Poor," *Christian Science Monitor,* April 21, 1995, pp. 1, 8.

8. Hechinger, *Fateful Choices.*

9. The Annie E. Casey Foundation, *Kids Count.*

10. Ibid.

11. Eitzen, "Problem Students."

12. Ibid.

13. The Annie E. Casey Foundation, *Kids Count.*

14. Candy Carlile, "Children of Divorce," *Childhood Education* 64, no. 4 (1991): 232–234.

15. U.S. Department of Education, *Youth Indicators 1991: Trends in the Well-Being of American Youth* (Washington, DC: U.S. Department of Education, 1991); U.S. Department of Labor, Bureau of Labor Statistics, unpublished data, 1996.

16. The Annie E. Casey Foundation, *Kids Count.*

17. Eitzen, "Problem Students."

18. Bruce Watkins, Althea Huston-Stein, and John Wright, "Effects of Planned Television Programming," in Edward Palmer and Aimee Dorr (eds.), *Children and the Faces of Television* (New York: Academic Press, 1980), pp. 46–49.

19. Annette Licitra, "Psychologists Spell Out Dangers of Unregulated TV Watching," *Education Daily,* February 26, 1992.

20. Jeffrey Mortimer, "How TV Violence Hits Kids," *Education Digest* 60, no. 2 (October 1994): 16–19.

21. Jack Levin, "Mapping Social Geography," *Bostonia* (March–April 1989): 64–65.

22. Daniel Anderson and Patricia Collins, *The Impact on Children's Education: Television's Influence on Cognitive Development* (Washington, DC: U.S. Department of Education, April 1988).

23. Licitra, "Psychologists Spell Out Dangers."

24. Richard P. Adler, "Children's Television Advertising: History of the Issue," in Palmer and Dorr, *Children and the Faces of Television.*

25. David Streitfeld, "Low Marks for Channel One," *Washington Post,* May 2, 1992, p. C-5; Drew Tiene, "Channel One," *International Journal of Instructional Media* 21, no. 3 (1994): 181–189; Drew Tiene, "Teens React to Channel One," *Tech Trends* 39 (April/May 1994): 17–20.

26. U.S. Department of Education, *Youth Indicators 1991;* Marilyn M. McMillen, Phillip Kaufman, and Summer D. Whitener, *Dropout Rates in the United States: 1993* (Washington, DC: National Center for Education Statistics, 1994).

27. McMillen, Kaufman, and Whitener, *Dropout Rates in the United States.*

28. Samuel Peng, "High School Dropouts: Descriptive Information from High School and Beyond," *Bulletin,* National Center for Education Statistics, November 1983.

29. S. F. Hamilton, *The Interaction of Family, Community, and Work in the Socialization of Youth* (Washington, DC: William T. Grant Foundation, Commission on Youth and America's Future, 1988).

30. Alan Guttmacher Institute, *Facts in Brief: Teenage Sexual and Reproductive Behavior* (New York: 1991).

31. Ibid.

32. Jamie Victoria Ward and Jill McLean Taylor, "Sexuality Education in a Multicultural Society," *Educational Leadership* 49, no. 1 (September 1991): 62–64.

33. The statistics that follow are derived from several sources including Alan Guttmacher Institute, *Facts in Brief;* reports from the National Center for Health Statistics; reports from the U.S. Bureau of the Census; Children's Defense Fund, *A Vision for America's Future* (Washington, DC: Children's Defense Fund, 1989); Hechinger, *Fateful Choices.*

34. House Select Committee on Children, Youth, and Families, *A Decade of Denial: Teens and AIDS in America* (Washington, DC: Goverment Printing Office, 1992).

35. Paul Taylor, "Surgeon General Links Teen Drinking to Crime, Injuries, Unsafe Sex," *The Washington Post,* April 14, 1992, p. A-1.
36. Sara Sklaroff, "Drug Use Among High Schoolers Up After Period of Decline, Study Finds," *Education Week,* February 9, 1994, p. 8.
37. *Education Update* 9, no. 4 (Fall 1986).
38. DeNeen Brown, "Fairfax Teenagers' LSD Arrests Send Parents a 'Wake-Up Call,' " *The Washington Post,* April 27, 1992, p. B-1.
39. Richard Hawley, "School Children and Drugs: The Fancy That Has Not Passed," *Phi Delta Kappan* 68, no. 9 (May 1987).
40. Lameece Atallah Gregorchik, "The Cocaine-Exposed Children Are Here," *Phi Delta Kappan* 73, no. 9 (May 1992): 710.
41. Ibid., pp. 709–711.
42. Harold Hodgkinson, "Reform Versus Reality," *Phi Delta Kappan* 73, no. 1 (September 1991): 9–16.
43. Jeffrey Coben, Harold Weiss, Edward Mulvey, and Stephen Dearwater, "A Primer on School Violence Prevention," *Journal of School Health* 64, no. 8 (October 1994): 309–313; "Dealing with Aggressive and Violent Students," *Preventing School Failure* 38, no. 3 (Spring 1994): 5–6; Brenda Smith Myles and Richard L. Simpson, "Understanding and Preventing Acts of Aggression and Violence in School-Age Children and Youth," *Preventing School Failure* 38, no. 3 (Spring 1994): 40–46.
44. U.S. Senate Subcommittee to Investigate Juvenile Delinquency, *Challenge for the Third Century in a Safe Environment—Final Report on the Prevention of School Violence and Vandalism* (Washington, DC: U.S. Government Printing Office, 1977), p. 17.
45. Hechinger, *Fateful Choices.*
46. Jan English and Anthony Papalia, "The Responsibility of Educators in Cases of Child Abuse and Neglect," *Chronicle Guidance* (January 1988): 88–89.
47. P. E. Quinn, *Cry Out!* (Nashville, TN: Abingdon Press, 1984).
48. John O'Neil, "A Generation Adrift?" See also Sidney Barish, "Responding to Adolescent Suicide: A Multi-Faceted Plan," *NASSP Bulletin* 75, no. 538 (November 1991): 98–103.
49. Jack Frymier, "Understanding and Preventing Teen Suicide: An Interview with Barry Garfinkle," *Phi Delta Kappan* 70, no. 4 (December 1988): 290–293.
50. Paul Gibson, "Gay Male and Lesbian Youth Suicide," in Marcia Feinleib (ed.), *Report of the Secretary's Task Force on Youth Suicide* (Washington, DC: U.S. Department of Health and Human Services, January 1989), pp. 3-110–3-142. See also James Sears, "Helping Students Understand and Accept Sexual Diversity," *Educational Leadership* 49, no. 1 (September 1991): 54–56.
51. Quoted in Gibson, "Gay Male and Lesbian Youth Suicide."
52. Ibid.
53. Jesse Green, "This School Is Out," *The New York Times Magazine,* October 13, 1991, pp. 32–36, 59, 68.
54. Aaron Fricke, *Reflections of a Rock Lobster: A Story About Growing Up Gay* (Boston: Alyson, 1981).
55. Jessica Portner, "Districts Adopting Policies to Protect Gay Students' Rights," *Education Week,* October 5, 1994, p. 8.
56. Laura DeKoven Waxman and Lilia M. Reyes, *A Status Report on Hunger and Homelessness in America's Cities: 1990* (Washington, DC: U.S. Conference of Mayors, December 1990); George E. Pawlas, "Homeless Students at the School Door," *Educational Leadership* 51 (May 1994): 79–82.
57. Rick Fantasia and Maurice Isserman, *Homelessness: A Sourcebook* (New York: Facts on File, 1994), pp. 113–114.
58. This anecdote is based on information in Children's Defense Fund, *A Vision for America's Future,* pp. 27–36.
59. Fantasia and Isserman, *Homelessness.*
60. Lisa Jennings, "Report Documents Effects of Homelessness on Education," *Education Week,* May 3, 1989, p. 7. See also Michelle Fryt Linehan, "Children Who Are Homeless: Educational Strategies for School Personnel," *Phi Delta Kappan* 74, no. 1 (September 1992).

16

TOMORROW'S SCHOOLS

OBJECTIVES

To assess innovations for rewarding effective teaching

To describe curricular innovations for fostering students' intellectual and moral growth

To analyze the impact of computers, the Internet, and other technological innovations on life in schools

To analyze the significance of global education for curriculum and instruction

To assess the positive and negative aspects of today's testing movement

To explore the home school movement

To describe why much of the criticism about U.S. schools might be a "manufactured crisis"

A *sage once said that "nothing endures but change," and this paradox is an apt characterization of the teaching profession. The elementary and secondary schools that you attended have already changed since your graduation. To be a successful teacher, you will need to adapt to innovations in education. Although it is difficult to forecast the precise nature of future change, it is helpful to begin thinking about it now. By examining the impact of the reform movement, educational innovations, technological breakthroughs, and global trends, you can gain insight into the changes you will face in the years ahead.*

As a beginning teacher on the cusp of the twenty-first century, you are likely to encounter more changes in U.S. education than have ever before been faced. Many forces are converging on education: reform efforts of the 1980s and 1990s; increasing demands from teachers for professional respect and salary levels; charges from the public for greater accountability from schools; rapid technological advances; and a national economy interdependent with the rest of the world and hungry for well-educated, thoughtful workers. One example of such a change was the establishment in 1991 of the New American Schools Development Corporation, which attempted to develop 535 "break-the-mold" schools throughout the nation.

As you enter the field of teaching for the first time, awareness of the possibilities for change and a willingness to look ahead are two of the most important attributes you can possess. Take a moment to imagine the kind of school where you might like to teach 20 years from now. What kind of innovations do you foresee?

- A computer on your desk that allows you to take attendance and lunch counts, or contact other teachers and do research, via electronic mail
- Committees of teachers that share the responsibility for all the decisions made in a school
- Students completing video portfolios of their work instead of taking examinations
- The abolishment of all grade distinctions between kindergarten and third grade
- The location of social service agencies within a school dealing with such issues as health, housing, job training, and recreation

Sound exciting? Well, don't be surprised, because all of these innovations are in place or being developed for schools across the United States.[1] For teachers, one of the most significant developments is the new concern with professionalism demonstrated by the formation of a national board to certify teachers. Can such a board, or any other kind of initiative, grant to teachers the recognition they deserve? The next section explores this question.

Teacher Recognition

Ironically, one of the most controversial arenas of education reform has been teacher recognition. How can good teachers best be professionally recognized for their dedication and excellence? Many teachers face the constant frustration of knowing they are giving their profession their best efforts without receiving much in return. Third-grade teacher Patricia Adams expresses this viewpoint:

> How would I describe my teaching? Well, let me put it this way—I work hard. Free time is a thing of the past. My students are really important to me, and I'm willing to go the extra mile to give them feedback, organize field trips and projects, meet with them or their parents, give them a stimulating classroom. In fact, most Saturdays I'm working on grades or new projects. And I think it pays off—my kids are blossoming! That's a great feeling. But sometimes I wonder if it's all worth it. Is anyone ever going to notice my hard work? Brad down the hall just comes in and does his job without a second thought, and his paycheck looks just like mine. It

doesn't seem fair. Teachers who deserve it should be able to earn something more—more money, more respect.

Though a fictitious character, Patricia Adams could represent any of the thousands of teachers struggling for professional recognition. Working hard in a demanding profession, teachers often do not feel valued or appreciated, and many leave the field each year as a result. National reform efforts have identified this problem and are working on solutions. Three possible solutions that we will discuss in this section are the National Board for Professional Teaching Standards, merit pay, and career ladders. The *National Board for Professional Teaching Standards* is establishing higher standards for teaching and grants special certification to teachers who qualify. *Merit pay* is a plan to give additional financial compensation to teachers who demonstrate excellence, though different plans define *excellence* differently. *Career ladders* allow teachers to take on additional responsibilities along with their teaching as a way of advancing in the field. Each of these solutions has its drawbacks as well as advantages. Nevertheless, all three influence how teachers are recognized.

The National Board for Professional Teaching Standards

In *A Nation Prepared: Teachers for the 21st Century,* the Carnegie Foundation addressed the need for improved teacher preparation. This reform report resulted in the establishment of a national board to evaluate and certify outstanding teachers. For the first time in history, a board (the National Board for Professional Teaching Standards) defines what every classroom teacher should know and do to be considered a true professional.

Many political leaders believe the plan has considerable merit. According to former North Carolina governor James Hunt, Jr.:

> For once in this country, we are working out standards for measuring excellence rather than minimum competency. The certification process has the potential to transform the current educational system, leverage current investment in teaching, and build a national consensus for increased support of schools.[2]

Board certification should not be confused with obtaining your license to teach. When you complete your teacher education program, you will apply to a state for a teacher's license. When you receive your license, it is recognition by the state that you have met the minimum state requirements and can be hired as a teacher. Board certification goes beyond this license to teach and provides a higher level of professional recognition.[3] Imagine yourself with the responsibility of determining what skills and behaviors should be evaluated in order to determine those teachers who are truly excellent. How would you begin? The board has identified five general areas that serve as criteria for board certification:

1. *Teachers are committed to students and their learning.* Board-certified teachers should know about research in the psychology of learning, exhibit positive expectations for student abilities, demonstrate equitable treatment of students, and effectively individualize instruction.

Part of the drive to assess, train, and reward qualified teachers involves direct observation of classroom teaching performance.

2. *Teachers know the subjects they teach and how to teach those subjects to students.* Board-certified teachers are expected not only to have mastered their subject but also to have mastered strategies and techniques for conveying the subject to students.

3. *Teachers are responsible for managing and monitoring student learning.* Board-certified teachers are competent in using motivational techniques, establishing appropriate class norms, and employing a variety of techniques to measure student performance.

4. *Teachers think systematically about their practice and learn from experience.* Board-certified teachers model what they teach and exemplify such traits as openness, curiosity, tolerance, and the ability to critically examine their own performance.

5. *Teachers are members of learning communities.* This area includes such behaviors as collaborative work on curriculum, policy, staff training, and other efforts to improve the school and community.

Lee Schulman and his colleagues at Stanford University have developed a comprehensive evaluation:

- *Portfolios.* Teachers provide documentary evidence and examples of their performance, such as lesson plans, videotapes of teaching, and writing samples.
- *Observations.* Qualified observers view and assess teacher performance in the classroom.

- *Assessment centers.* At special centers located throughout the nation, teachers participate in simulations and interviews dealing with a variety of professional skills, such as lesson planning and textbook selection.
- *Written examination.* A comprehensive test assesses mastery of subject matter and knowledge of developments and research in education.[4]

Testing is not the only problem confronting the national certification board. Funds are in short supply, and without enough money, board-certification of teachers may be an unrewarded "honor." In some districts, board-certified teachers have been the object of scorn and derision from their colleagues. As the president of the San Francisco affiliate of the American Federation of Teachers (AFT) put it, "Unless board certification really means something, I'm not sure teachers will find it worth their while to subject themselves to what is likely to be an anxiety-ridden process."[5]

As you enter the teaching profession, you will want to stay abreast of the activities concerning the national board and determine where you stand on this issue. Will you become a board-certified teacher?

Merit Pay and Career Ladders

National Board certification may be an important step toward improving teacher professionalism and giving recognition to good teachers, but many people consider it insufficient. While board certification might stimulate increased compensation for quality teachers, a plan such as merit pay would ensure tangible compensation. Merit pay is designed to link teacher performance directly to teacher salary and thus make teaching more accountable, as well as more financially rewarding. Many groups support merit pay, including the National Science Board, the National Association of Secondary School Principals, the American Association of School Administrators, the National Association of Elementary School Principals, and the National Commission on Excellence in Education. The NEA and many teachers oppose it, however.[6]

Why would anyone oppose merit pay? What makes a plan that proposes to pay teachers more money so controversial? Let's listen in on a faculty meeting to see what merit pay really involves for teachers.

Dr. Moore faced her staff and began, "You know our district has been given the go-ahead to develop a merit pay proposal. I'd like to outline some of the different plans and then open the floor for your reactions." You watch intently as she lays a transparency on the overhead projector to illustrate the different plans.

"Basically, there are four different types of merit pay:

"Merit pay based on student performance. This rewards teachers whose students make gains on standardized tests. It implies that a good teacher will help students achieve in the content areas.

"Merit pay based on teacher performance. Under this program, the district would develop criteria to measure your teaching effectiveness, and you would receive raises based on evaluations by outside observers.

"Merit pay based on individualized productivity plan. Do you remember the personal goals each of you wrote for this school year? This plan would ask you to write a more detailed set of goals for what you would

like to accomplish this year. Once they are approved, you would receive financial bonuses based on how much you accomplish.

"Merit pay based on the teaching assignment. With this plan, you could receive compensation according to how difficult or how much in demand your teaching position is. Our math, science, and special education teachers would probably receive the greatest bonuses if we adopted this plan."

You think this sounds very interesting. There seem to be mixed feelings among the teachers, however. You overhear a number of different opinions.

"This sounds great! I can finally get that bonus I deserve for all my extra hours."

"I wonder how this can work. After all, does the teacher with all the smart kids really deserve a raise if they do well on tests?"

"I don't think I'd feel comfortable if other people found out I was getting merit pay. Teaching is supposed to mean working as a team, not competing for bonuses."

"Only the people who are in good with the supervisors will get merit pay. How can that be fair?"

"I think we need some sort of merit pay system in teaching that will give all of us something to work for."

Obviously, there are many ways to look at merit pay. Many teachers fear the competition or the methods for objectively judging who deserves merit pay, while others are excited about the possibility of a higher salary. Nevertheless, a few merit pay programs have succeeded in pleasing their districts, and the rest of the country can learn from their experience. The Granite School District in Salt Lake City, Utah, developed both criteria for excellence in teaching and a comprehensive evaluation process. The district instituted an optional program where a bonus can be earned each year, and where performance evaluation is linked to in-service training and development.[7] More experience is still needed to shape universally successful merit pay programs, but progress in individual school systems is being made.

Career ladder programs are another alternative to the teacher recognition dilemma. The career ladder is designed to create different levels for teachers by creating a "ladder" that one can climb to receive increased pay through increased work responsibility and status.[8] By the beginning of the 1990s more than half the states had some form of career ladder or incentive program with state assistance in place. Some critics argue that career ladder programs have the same drawbacks as merit pay—a lack of clear standards or appropriate evaluation tools—but others claim that career ladders can be more effective because they are rooted in career development and professionalism. The distinguishing characteristic of the career ladder is the increased responsibility given to the teacher. The Rochester, New York, Career in Teaching plan is a good example. Here, an outstanding teacher such as Patricia Adams has the opportunity to become a "master" or "mentor teacher," write curricula, select textbooks, or plan staff development programs while continuing to teach in the classroom.[9] Thus, good teachers are not removed from the classroom, yet they receive an increase in responsibility and in salary.

All teacher recognition plans share the common goal of making the teaching profession more attractive and more rewarding, whether through official certification, financial compensation, or increased professional responsibility. In

---

Teacher Recognition at a Glance

- ***National Board for Professional Teaching Standards.*** This board recognizes superior performance.
  Advantage: Higher standards set for teaching
  Disadvantage: Fear that teacher status, pay, and respect would not be affected

- ***Merit pay.*** Teachers who meet specified criteria for excellence receive financial bonuses.
  Advantage: Higher pay available to teachers, making the profession more attractive

  Disadvantage: Difficult to define criteria for excellence

- ***Career ladders.*** Teachers who meet criteria for excellence and experience receive increased responsibility.
  Advantage: Opportunities for advancement in the field while continuing to teach
  Disadvantage: Difficult to define criteria for excellence

---

what other ways might teachers be able to earn more respect or more money? As you enter the teaching profession, you will want to be aware of what kinds of incentives are available and what kinds you would like to see instituted.

Is U.S. Education Going Test Crazy?

Like teacher recognition, testing is an issue that finds itself more and more in the public eye. Reform's emphasis on higher achievement has sparked national and local efforts to assess whether U.S. students are measuring up. As one critic grumbled, "If it moves, test it."

It is one thing to discuss test taking; it is quite another to take a test. Assume that you have just applied to Cabin Cove Schools—a place where you have always wanted to teach. To ensure that teachers are "culturally literate" the school board now requires that all teacher candidates take a basic knowledge exam—you know, to be sure each has received an education in the basics, the things we all should know.

Try your hand at the following baker's dozen multiple-choice questions and get a first-hand "feel" for the testing issue.

History

1. Thomas Jefferson authored:
   a. The Bill of Rights
   b. The Declaration of Independence
   c. The U.S. Constitution
   d. The Emancipation Proclamation
2. The *Federalist Papers* were designed to:
   a. Win popular support for the American Revolution
   b. Establish freedom of speech
   c. Win support for the U.S. Constitution
   d. Free and enfranchise slaves
3. Senator Joseph McCarthy was associated with:
   a. Government corruption
   b. Civil rights
   c. Education funding
   d. Communist hunting

A byproduct of the recent calls for educational reform has been the explosion of student (and teacher) testing to ensure that revised school goals are being met.

4. The Cherokee syllabary was developed by:
   a. Sitting Bull
   b. Maria Tallchief
   c. Geronimo
   d. Sequoyah

Literature

5. The novel *1984* concerns:
   a. Time travel
   b. Government-imposed conformity
   c. A hoax about an invasion from Mars
   d. World War III
6. Stratford-on-Avon is associated with:
   a. Shakespeare
   b. Wollstonecraft
   c. Chaucer
   d. Shelley
7. Jane Austen wrote about the Bennett family's five daughters in:
   a. *10 Downing Street*
   b. *Pride and Prejudice*
   c. *Midliothian Tales*
   d. *Clarissa*

Geography

8. List the states that touch on the Pacific Ocean.
9. List as many countries as you can that border the former Soviet Union.
10. Where is Mount St. Helens?

Science

11. Coal, gas, and oil shortages may result in an increased dependence on electricity. What is your evaluation of this idea?
    a. The economy cannot be changed that quickly.
    b. Electric automotive technology will simply not match gasoline engines.
    c. Electricity is generally produced from coal, gas, and oil, so it cannot replace them.
    d. The current cost of electricity is much higher than that of coal or gas, and somewhat higher than that of gasoline, so it is a very expensive and unlikely eventuality.
12. What is the approximate distance between the earth and the sun?
    a. 90,000 miles
    b. 900,000 miles
    c. 9,000,000 miles
    d. 90,000,000 miles
13. What is the major cause of urban pollution?
    a. Automobiles
    b. Factories
    c. Open incineration of garbage
    d. Heat inversion causing smog

Here are the answers to the quiz. Take a moment and see how you did.

1. b; 2. c; 3. d; 4. d; 5. b; 6. a; 7. b; 8. Hawaii, Alaska, Oregon, Washington, and California; 9. Afghanistan, China, Czechoslovakia, Finland, Hungary, Iran, Mongolia, North Korea, Norway, Poland, Rumania, and Turkey (if you identified at least seven of these countries give yourself full credit); 10. Washington state, 11. c; 12. d; 13. a.

Add up your correct responses and compare your results to the following score card.

Cabin Cove Teacher Assessment Scale

9–13 correct: You have demonstrated an adequate level of general knowledge. You are culturally literate. Welcome to the Cabin Cove School District.

6–8 correct: You have qualified for probationary status. If you agree to enroll in a number of courses at Cabin Cove College, you will be allowed to teach in the public schools.

Fewer than 6 correct: You have failed the teacher assessment test and will not be offered a position in this community.

How do you feel about the use of a test such as this one to determine your future? Do you think that it is unfair to measure your teaching skills and abilities according to this single dimension, or do you feel that it is reasonable to assume all teachers should be expected to demonstrate a minimal level of general knowledge and cultural literacy? Perhaps you feel that all teachers should be literate in the abstract but have a problem when this kind of test is applied to you. After all, if you failed this test, maybe it is not your fault at all; maybe it simply reflects a limited high school or college curriculum. Perhaps your schools did not prepare you for the test, and so it is unfair to insist that you be able to pass it.

All these arguments and more have emerged in the last few years as the United States becomes concerned—some say obsessed—with testing.

The National Commission on Testing and Public Policy estimated that 127 million tests are given to elementary and secondary students each year.[10] In an extreme case, all students in Newark, New Jersey, including first-graders, were tested nine times a year.[11] Nor does the testing craze start only at the first grade. About half of all 4- and 5-year-olds will also be tested to determine kindergarten and prekindergarten placement.[12] In fact, by law 42 states require regularly scheduled **achievement tests,** starting in the first grade.

Tests are used to answer a growing list of educational questions: Who is "ready" to begin kindergarten? Who should be promoted or retained? Who should be given "special" educational services? Who should be placed in the advanced track? Who should be allowed to graduate? Who should be admitted to prestigious schools or colleges?

More and more it is not only students who are tested but educators and schools as well. Beginning teachers may be asked to take the Praxis series of tests (see Chapter 3 and Appendix 2) or a state or local equivalent in order to obtain a position. Teachers, principals, and superintendents may have their job security determined by how well or poorly their students score on standardized tests. Poor test results may lead to reprimands or termination as communities rely more and more on test scores to determine the quality of their schools. In fact, test scores have been tied to the economic prosperity or poverty of a community. The value of real estate or the attraction of business to a community is related to test scores. Does this seem far-fetched? Consider the following dialogues:

Real estate agent to prospective home owner: "Of course, this house costs more than similar houses in other neighborhoods. This is in the Whitmore School District. These are the best schools in the area, with the highest SAT scores. Houses here cost more."

Mayor to corporate executive: "If you move your corporate headquarters to our city, you will get more than special tax breaks. Your managers will be able to send their children to one of the finest school districts in the state, a school district with test scores in the top 10 percent nationally. I can't think of a more attractive enticement for relocating to our city. Your employees will love it here—and so will their spouses and children."

Testing, like the textbook industry, has become big business. The two largest firms producing and marketing the nation's standardized tests are Educational Testing Services (ETS) and American College Testing Program (ACT). Some firms that produce and market such tests, such as Harcourt Brace Jovanovich, also publish textbooks. Literally hundreds of millions of dollars are spent in testing, and these test companies have a great deal invested in maintaining, if not increasing, the level of test taking in the United States.[13]

The testing companies are not alone in their desire to increase testing. Across the country, many advocates of testing seek greater accountability in the nation's schools. Proponents of nationwide testing believe that it will force schools to be accountable for student performance and will lead educators to define standards for education more clearly across the nation. At its best, testing not only measures academic performance but also provides direction for school improvement. Weak practices will be eliminated, incompetent teachers and administrators replaced, superior educators rewarded, and schools made more responsive to the needs of students and society.

However, many argue that testing is far from perfect. Standardized tests are criticized for their assumption that a child's competence can be measured by her or his ability to recognize and choose correct responses from given lists. Such tests, critics insist, undermine the critical-thinking, creative problem-solving, and cooperative skills that teachers are trying to build.[14] Furthermore, standardized tests limit a school's curriculum, since many teachers feel obligated to "teach to the test." Yet the tests themselves yield little insight for individualizing or enriching instruction, since they give little feedback about student strengths and weaknesses. Edward B. Fiske speaks for many educators in his criticism of standardized tests: "They measure the wrong things in the wrong way for the wrong reasons."[15]

Standardized testing is also charged with bias against females and minorities. Researcher Phyllis Rosser finds that girls receive poorer scores than boys, in part because of bias in test construction. For example, 15 percent more males than females responded correctly to the following analogy item (and as you might suspect, such a question may also be particularly challenging to poorer and minority students):[16]

Dividends : Stockholders:
(A) investments : corporations
(B) purchase : customers
(C) royalties : authors
(D) tapes : workers
(E) mortgages : homeowners

For a summary of the pros and cons of standardized testing, see the accompanying balance sheet. And if you are curious, the correct answer to the item above is (C).

Tomorrow's Schools Balance Sheet 1
Standardized Tests

Are Essential Because . . .

We must be able to objectively measure programs. The public and educators need to use standardized test scores to determine how well students are performing and whether programs are effective (that is, should the program be kept, modified, or discarded?).

They allow us to assess individual as well as group performance and to determine if the nation is providing quality education to all its students, regardless of race, ethnicity, creed, national origin, or gender.

Without a national curriculum, the thousands of individual school districts are free to offer a diversity of educational experiences. Standardized tests en-

Are Ineffective and Potentially Dangerous Because . . .

Teachers and administrators do not want their schools and students to look bad, so they teach to the test. Areas to be tested are taught, while other areas are ignored.

Multiple-choice responses are emphasized and taught while other forms of measuring student learning, such as essays, are ignored. Learning becomes choppy and disconnected.

Higher-order skills and concepts are replaced by simpler, discrete segments of information that are easier to test. The test results mislead the public because they reflect test-wise skills, not real learning.

able us to use a national norm to ensure that all geographic areas are providing students with an appropriate education.

They enable Americans to compare our educational efforts with those of past generations as well as other nations. Standardized tests enable us to maintain national accountability for our schools.

Our teachers can be assessed as well as our students, and the nation can ensure that teachers possess fundamental knowledge and skills.

Females, minorities, and the poor are often victims of test bias. The SAT, for example, often underestimates the potential of these groups to do college work. As a result, admission to college and awards of financial aid based on SATs favor white males.

Test-driven instruction tends to deprofessionalize teaching. Many talented teachers will choose to leave the classroom rather than teach to the test.

Test bias became a legal issue in New York in the early 1990s when a group including the American Civil Liberties Union, the National Organization for Women, and the Girls Clubs of America, now called Girls, Inc., sued the Educational Testing Services, claiming that the Scholastic Assessment Test (SAT) and PSAT (a standardized test similar to the SAT) exams discriminated against females. Since New York State scholarship awards were based on these scores, the alleged sex bias had direct financial ramifications. In fact, males had regularly gotten higher PSAT and SAT scores and received about twice as many scholarships as females. The judge agreed with the plaintiffs, finding, among other problems, that these exams consistently underestimated female performance in school. New York State was ordered to find another means for awarding its college scholarships.

This ruling, referred to as the *Walker* case (after Judge Walker) has implications for other state and national scholarship programs. The best known of these may be the National Merit Scholarships, distributed based on PSAT scores. Another similarity to the New York case is that here, too, boys score consistently higher than girls and receive about twice the number of scholarships. Legal challenges of this and other scholarship programs are sure to fill courtrooms in the years ahead.

The latest reform in testing is the creation of tests that are grounded more firmly in classroom performance. These are often referred to as *alternative, performance-based,* or **authentic assessment**—implying that tests are truer when based on what students actually do in school. Authentic assessment represents actual performance, encourages students to reflect on their own work, and is integrated into the student's whole learning process. Such tests usually require students to synthesize knowledge from different areas and use that knowledge actively.[17] Teaching to an authentic test is encouraged, for in such a test, the student must actually perform what he is expected to know. Comparisons are often made to sports, where participants are expected to demonstrate in a game what they learned in practice. A tennis player works on her backhand so that she can demonstrate mastery of it in a game; similarly, when students know that they will be called on to demonstrate and use their knowledge, they are more motivated to practice their academic skills.

Most states are exploring new (and more authentic) methods of assessment. The most popular method is the writing sample.[18] While this can be an effective means of judging children's writing, critics caution against evaluating a timed writing sample, since such a sample does not allow students time to demonstrate the mastery of the writing process, including revising and editing.

Some of the best examples of authentic assessment come from the Coalition of Essential Schools, led by prominent educator Theodore Sizer. The coalition encourages schools to define their own model for successful reform, guided by nine basic principles that emphasize the personalization of learning. These principles include the requirement that students complete "exhibitions," tasks that call on them to exhibit their knowledge concretely. The high school curriculum is structured around these demanding, creative tasks, which may include:

- Completing a federal Internal Revenue Service Form 1040 for a family whose records you receive, working with other students in a group to ensure that everyone's IRS forms are correct, and auditing a return filed by a student in a different group
- Designing a nutritious and attractive lunch menu for the cafeteria within a specified budget, and defending your definitions of *nutritious* and *attractive*
- Designing and building a wind instrument from metal pipes, then composing and performing a piece of music for that instrument
- Choosing one human emotion to define in an essay, through examples from literature and history, and in at least three other ways (through drawing, painting, or sculpture; through film, photographs, or video; through music; through pantomime or dance; through a story or play that you create)

These examples come from Theodore Sizer's book *Horace's School: Redesigning the American High School,* and represent the new tests teachers are designing to challenge students to prove their knowledge in different ways.[19]

The future of testing in the United States promises to shape education in many ways. If national tests become a reality, then a national curriculum may follow—such a curriculum has been heralded by some as vital to maintaining consistent quality across the nation, and is dreaded by others as marking the end of individuality and autonomy in teaching. The persistence of traditional standardized testing may prompt continued emphasis on the memorization of discrete facts. On the other hand, an increase in authentic testing may contribute to a greater classroom focus on higher-level processes such as critical thinking and moral development.

Trends in Critical Thinking and Moral Development

During the past decade, several new developments have emerged in schools. Two of these focus on critical thinking and moral education. It is interesting that neither of these trends—one cognitive, the other affective—is really new; rather each is a traditional educational goal that has been reawakened and renewed in this time of flux and transition. Each is an attempt to respond to intellectual or moral challenges of a new era. There is a good chance that as you begin teaching, you will encounter one or both of these programs.

Critical Thinking

The extraordinary pace of change has sparked renewed interest in the teaching of critical thinking. Technological developments have shifted the focus of the U.S. economy from the production of goods (industrial) to an emphasis on

Educators today believe that higher level thinking skills, like competency in writing, can be taught directly.

information processing (postindustrial). Traditional employment patterns are being altered as new careers in technology, computers, and communications emerge. This accelerated rate of change has created not only an unpredictable future but an uncertain school curriculum as well. The current curricular focus on transmitting content, generally referred to as *factual knowledge,* rather than teaching the flexibility and skill needed in the new information society has been criticized as inappropriate to the current needs of the country. Books such as John Naisbitt's *Megatrends,* Alvin Toffler's *The Third Wave* and *In Search of Excellence* by Thomas Peters and Robert Waterman alerted Americans to the increasing pressures placed on the U.S. economy by international competition and the tremendous knowledge explosion that has produced more information than schools can teach. Critics believe that schools need to turn away from the traditional curriculum and to focus on critical-thinking skills required in this information age.

Educators today believe that critical-thinking skills, like competency in playing a clarinet or skiing or writing clear sentences, must be taught directly. Several different approaches have been developed to teach critical thinking.

One of the pioneering works, *Teaching for Thinking: Theory and Application,* by Louis Raths and others, identified "thinking operations" for school instruction, including comparing, interpreting, observing, summarizing, classifying, decision making, creating, and criticizing. Raths promoted the notion of incorporating these thinking operations in regular course offerings. Specific classroom activities in history or mathematics could be shaped so that students would analyze and evaluate information. Raths recommended that teachers encourage higher-order thinking by asking higher-order questions. Several research studies supported this approach, indicating that students not only could learn these critical-thinking skills, but that their knowledge of content also increased when they applied critical-thinking skills in the classroom.[20]

Many different programs and approaches have emerged since Rath's approach, ranging from courses designed to teach thinking skills to techniques for infusing critical thinking into ongoing course work.[21]

- David Perkins of Harvard University's *Project Zero* emphasizes "thinking frames." Using this approach students develop a framework to acquire information, internalize practices, and transfer information.
- Reuven Feuerstein's *instrumental enrichment* curriculum stresses the development of mental processes such as comparing, classifying, and predicting. This Israeli psychologist has developed learning activities to help students adjust to and succeed in new environments.
- Edward de Bono attempts to teach thinking skills directly by helping students restate and diagram problems, break them into smaller parts, and compare them to similar problems that have already been solved.
- Matthew Lipman's *philosophy for children* program offers classroom activities and a teacher education approach that emphasizes reasoning by means of language skills and philosophy techniques.
- Arthur Whimby and J. Lochhead have developed procedures to help students be more systematic in their thinking. These exercises encourage students to work in pairs and externalize their thinking, or think aloud, so that errors and problems can be identified.
- Joseph Hester developed *Teaching for Thinking* as a comprehensive program to improve schools by infusing critical-thinking techniques throughout the school curriculum and encouraging the school faculty to make use of them as well.

One of the more widely known approaches, developed by Robert Marzano and his colleagues, identifies five dimensions of thinking:

1. *Metacognition.* **Metacognition** is awareness of our own thinking as we perform various tasks and operations. Metacognition enables students to monitor and control their commitment, attitudes, and attention during the learning process.
2. *Critical and creative thinking.* Critical thinking enables students to become objective, committed to accuracy and clarity. Creative thinking helps students form new combinations of ideas that lead to creative output or results. According to Marzano, critical and creative thinking are closely related.
3. *Thinking processes.* Thinking processes refers to mental operations such as concept formation, principle formation, comprehension, problem solving, decision making, research, composition, and oral discourse.
4. *Core thinking skills.* Core thinking skills are essential to the functioning of the broader dimensions of thinking. For example, the core thinking skill of goal setting can assist in the larger dimension of metacognition.
5. *The relationship of content-area knowledge to thinking.* Educators frequently debate the question: Can thinking be taught in isolation, or should it be taught as part of the academic subject areas? Most researchers conclude that instruction in thinking should be strongly linked with content instruction. Therefore, content specialists need to identify important models and modes of instruction in their academic disciplines and relate these to the dimensions of thinking.[22]

More recently, Marzano identified the productive habits of mind that foster critical and creative thinking. For critical thinking, these include open-mindedness, sensitivity to the feelings and knowledge of others, an emphasis on clarity and accuracy, and a willingness to take a stand on an issue when necessary. Important habits for creative thinking include the ability to push one's own limits, the willingness to look at situations in new ways, and a capability for focusing intensely on tasks. If these habits are instilled in students, they will be independent learners for the rest of their lives—one of the goals of the critical thinking movement.[23]

Moral Education: Teaching Right and Wrong

Few people argue with the importance of improving critical-thinking skills in subjects such as mathematics, English, or history. Yet what about applying these same skills to other questions. For example, "should Americans always be loyal?" "Is it ever right to disobey a law?" "What are the limits, if any, to 'Honor thy mother and father'?" In short, should society's traditional values be accepted and indoctrinated, or critically analyzed and possibly changed in the future?

Some citizens think that the most important issue that will face U.S. schools in the near future is the shaping of children's views of right and wrong. For these parents and community members, moral education is as important as, or even more important than, whether a student can speak a second language or solve an algebraic equation. A 1994 survey by the Public Agenda Foundation found that 95 percent of Americans want schools to teach basic values such as honesty and respect, but a Gallup survey in the same year revealed that only half of the public supports school programs that directly promote more specific values.[24] How can our diverse society agree on which values—if any— are appropriate to teach? Can we teach moral values without entangling public schools in religious issues?

During the early part of the American experience, schools had no trouble accepting and transmitting a common set of values: the Protestant ethic. Diligence, hard work, punctuality, neatness, conformity, and respect for authority were all elements of this commonly accepted ethic. Those few individuals who received a college education during the eighteenth and nineteenth centuries received an education that was above all an experience in character development. The most important course in the college curriculum was moral philosophy, required of all students and often taught by the college president. Even those receiving a minimal education got a heavy dose of morality, perhaps illustrated best by McGuffey's readers, reading texts replete with tales and poems of moral elevation.

The role of schools as the transmitter of society's code of ethics has changed dramatically as the nature of the United States itself changed. Throughout this century, two primary approaches to moral education have emerged: *traditional inculcation* and *individual analysis*. In the traditional approach, a set of values is identified and promoted directly through the curriculum and school practices. In the analytic approach, students are encouraged to consider the moral implications of past and present events and to formulate a set of values based on their analyses. The accompanying balance sheet compares these two approaches.

Shifts in the prevalent approach to moral education can be linked to trends in U.S. society. For example, the tremendous influx of immigrants in the early part of this century prompted a resurgence of the traditional approach to moral education. Classrooms were viewed as the tools for melding an increasingly diverse society through direct teaching of core U.S. values and democratic principles. During the social and political uncertainty of the 1960s and 1970s, a more analytical and individual approach to moral education was preferred by most schools. The pendulum now appears to be swinging back to the traditional model of moral education, as more schools seek to transmit specified core values to their students.

Today, school districts usually choose one of three approaches: (1) teaching traditional values, (2) adopting a program of analyzing and developing individual value systems, or (3) avoiding the issue entirely and not instituting special programs that teach moral development. For those schools that teach values directly, several approaches are available. Three of the most widely known are values clarification, character education, and moral stages of development.

Tomorrow's Schools Balance Sheet 2
Two Approaches to Moral Education

Traditional

Societies not only have the right to inculcate values, it is their historical obligation to teach these values to younger generations in order to promote unity, cultural traditions, and national purpose.

Recent problems such as alienation, teenage pregnancy, and suicide are the result of schools not teaching traditional values. Most Americans want greater discipline, clear values, and character development to be taught and practiced in school.

Without effective moral development, human beings are likely to engage in selfish, self-serving activities. The sacrifice and community spirit necessary for the general good may be lost without the inculcation of a moral code.

We can all agree on a common code of values for our society. American values include tolerance, patriotism, justice, moderation, and parental respect, to name but a few. These represent commonly accepted virtues that are needed for any culture to survive and thrive.

Children are unable to make wise moral decisions and need adult guidance and supervision.

Analytical

We are at a new and more complex stage of human development, and the historical practices of the past are no longer appropriate for the complexities and individual development needed in contemporary society.

Inculcating traditional values is ineffective in eliminating these problems. Adolescent problems are not reduced by promoting values that are not critically understood and that receive at best only a superficial commitment from students.

Individuals need to develop a code of behavior that they themselves form, with thought and personal commitment. Selfishness is not a natural state, and students who critically develop values will undoubtedly exhibit a moral code that reflects sensitivity to others.

Our pluralistic society makes the inculcation of a single set of values impossible. For example, we can now extend "life" for brain-dead parents through artificial means. Does "honor your parents" mean this is the wisest course? Other issues, such as "pro-life" or "pro-choice" also defy national consensus. We are beyond the era of a single value system applicable to all.

Children can be taught to make their own moral decisions and to abide by them.

Source: Adapted from "The School's Role in Developing Character," *Educational Leadership* 43, no. 4 (December 1985–January 1986).

Values Clarification

The controversial, yet widely used, series of classroom activities called **values clarification** is designed to help students develop and eventually act on their values. For example, students might be asked to describe their preferences (select the 10 things you most enjoy doing), analyze behavior (when did you last do each of these activities?), analyze reasons (what appeals to you about each of these activities?), and develop action plans (how can you schedule more time to do what you enjoy?). These strategies, developed by Louis Raths, Sidney Simon, and others, in several books, including *Values and Teaching,* are attractive to teachers because they are easy to use, touch upon issues usually omitted from the curriculum, and are engaging to students. Students begin to bring values, often kept in private, to a public level where they can be considered, analyzed, and acted upon. But critics believe that in values clarification, all values are treated equally, and there is no guarantee that good and constructive values will be promoted or that negative values will be condemned.

Character Education

Character education programs—currently employed in some form by an estimated 20 percent of all public school districts[25]—assume that there are core attributes of a moral individual that children should be directly taught in school. While still a form of moral inculcation, character education programs are less didactic and more analytic than are previous traditional approaches.[26] Character education programs promote specified core values—such as trustworthiness, respect, responsibility, fairness, caring, and good citizenship—through the school culture, conduct codes, curriculum, and community service.[27] Younger students may be asked to find examples of these qualities in literature and history, while older students may consider these values through ethical reasoning exercises. Opponents of this approach believe that such activities are generally ineffective and superficial, artificially forcing a diverse student population into a simplistic and narrow set of unexamined values.

Moral Stages

Based on the work of Jean Piaget, the psychologist who identified stages of intellectual development (see "Hall of Fame" in Chapter 9), this schema, proposed by Lawrence Kohlberg, identifies moral stages of development. The earliest stages focus on simple rewards and punishments. Young children are taught "right" and "wrong" by learning to avoid spankings and to strive for rewards. Most adults function at a middle, or conventional, stage where they obey society's laws, even laws that may be unjust. At the highest level, individuals act on principles, such as civil rights or pacifism, that may violate conventional laws. Kohlberg believes that teachers can facilitate student growth to higher stages of morality.

Critics express concern that traditional (what Kohlberg calls "conventional") values are attacked. Others point out that Kohlberg's theory was developed on an all-male population and that females may go through different stages of moral reasoning. Harvard professor Carol Gilligan, for example, found that women and men react differently when responding to moral dilemmas. Finally, Kohlberg's stages are intellectually based and do not focus on behavior, yet behavior is the real measure of one's morality.

These approaches need not be exclusive. Howard Kirschenbaum suggests that both values clarification and traditional inculcation have important lessons for children. His model, called Comprehensive Values Education, insists that traditional values, such as honesty, caring, and responsibility, should be taught and demonstrated directly. However, since other values are less straightforward, such as favoring or rejecting the death penalty, students should be taught the analytical skills that will help them to make wise decisions. There is an appropriate place in the school curriculum for each approach, Kirschenbaum insists, and many teachers instinctively apply multiple approaches.[28]

Confronting Values Teaching

Regardless of your opinion of these approaches to moral education, the simple fact is that schools are always teaching values. Students are rewarded for some behaviors and punished for others, and in this process they acquire a clear picture of what is acceptable and what is inappropriate. Certainly punctuality is valued, as is completing assignments on time. Hard work and good grades are rewarded, and misbehavior is punished. Perhaps the most persuasive and pervasive moral lessons being taught in schools every day come from teachers' behavior. The values that teachers model—daily compassion or insensitivity, equity or favoritism, caring or sarcasm—all send clear messages.

Yet for many educators and parents, values are too important to be dealt with only in the hidden curriculum. Statistics on crime, violence, and neglect in our society and in our schools have prompted many people to conclude that schools can no longer afford to be bystanders in students' moral development. Indeed, if our society does not confront the issue of morality satisfactorily, we risk becoming a technologically advanced society without an ethical compass.

Global Education: Emerging Curricular Trend

In the early part of the twentieth century, social studies educators developed a curriculum called *expanding horizons*. The idea behind this curriculum was that children know best those ideas and events that are closest to them. As students progressed from kindergarten to sixth grade, their social studies curriculum expanded each year from the home, to the community, to the nation, and finally the world. In short, the horizons of the curriculum expanded. You probably participated in this curriculum when you went to school. Do you remember "community helpers"? How about your state map on which you recorded the products and resources of your state? And your first encounter with U.S. history probably occurred during the fifth or sixth grade, toward the end of your expanding horizons curriculum.

Today our environment and our horizons vary dramatically from the early part of the century. Our world has been called a "global village." Satellite communication makes possible television, telephone, and document transmittal (facsimile, or fax) across thousands of miles in a thousandth of a second. Five-year-olds can view on television warfare in Latin America, famine in Africa, and industrial pollution in Europe. Economic or political disruptions in one part of the planet rapidly ripple to our country and our community. Today's young children have new, broader horizons never dreamed of by those who developed the original expanding horizons curriculum.

A number of educators are attempting to construct a more contemporary curriculum, responsive to the concept of a global village. One aspect of this

Technological break-throughs in satellite communication and increasing international trade make it likely that global education will become a reality in the years ahead.

revision is the increased use of technology in the classroom. Another dimension is the incorporation of the changing reality of our world's society. If you were to design a curriculum for the future, what issues, concepts, and skills would you include? Perhaps conflict-resolution strategies, to avoid a potentially cataclysmic nuclear war? Or problem-solving strategies for such ecological issues as global warming, deforestation, and toxic waste disposal? Perhaps you would include strategies to increase tolerance and understanding of the various cultural, ethnic, and racial groups who populate our planet. These and other topics fall into a new area of the curriculum called **global education.**

In an age of multiple reforms, global education has remained a low priority for many school systems. However, in the years ahead it is likely that many of the topics and skills included in global education will be incorporated into the curriculum of our schools. Global education has a variety of goals, ranging from increased knowledge about the peoples of the world to resolutions of global problems; from increased fluency in foreign languages to the development of more tolerant attitudes toward other cultures and peoples. Those committed to global education see many of today's challenges as transcending national borders. The depletion of the ozone layer and the planet's natural resources, for example, are planetary problems. The impact of regional wars and conflicts transcends national boundaries. Global education targets these and other issues as important focal points for curricula in the twenty-first century. This shift in emphasis to a world view represents an innovative departure from the traditional social science courses of the past.[29]

There are a number of emerging curriculum designs for global education. William Kniep suggests four domains of student inquiry:

1. *Human values.* The universal values shared by humanity as well as the diverse values of various groups

2. *Global systems.* Emphasis on global systems and an interdependent world, including economy, ecology, politics, and technology
3. *Global issues and problems.* Investigating worldwide concerns and challenges, including peace and security, environmental issues, and human rights
4. *Global history.* Including the evolution of universal and diverse human values, the history of global systems, and the roots of global problems[30]

Schools around the country provide examples of global education in action.

- In Seattle, Washington, Kimball Elementary School instituted a program for its first graders to communicate with and visit first graders in other countries. Exchange programs at all levels provide students with rich experiences in other cultures.[31]
- Middle school students in Massachusetts ended a unit on environmental science with a live teleconference with students from Karlsruhe, Germany. Computer and telecommunications technology enabled students to communicate and learn from each other throughout the year and encouraged cross-cultural communication of all kinds.[32]
- Fourth-grade students in Rhode Island studied the drawings of their peers from Africa, Asia, and Latin America, thereby learning a great deal about how life in other parts of the world compares with their own.[33]

While some teachers and students may long for the more traditional curriculum of the past—one in which expanding horizons have distinct geographic limits, almost all futurists predict increasing globalization in the decades ahead. Global education emerges as the school's response to the need to "educate children for the world they are entering rather than the world they are leaving behind."[34]

Home Schools: Home Teachers

Thirteen-year old Taylor is working at the kitchen table, sorting out mathematical exponents. At 10, Travis is absorbed with *The Story of Jackie Robinson,* while his brother Henry is practicing Beethoven's Minuet in G on his acoustical guitar. The week before, the brothers had attended a local performance of a musical comedy, attended a seminar on marine life and participated in a lively debate about news reports concerning corporal punishment in Singapore. These boys are part of a growing number of students being educated at home. What makes their story somewhat unusual is that their father is unable to participate in their education as much as he might like, because he must spend time at his own work: teaching English at a local public high school.[35]

Why would a schoolteacher choose to educate his own children outside of school? It is ironic that while some educators view the world as a classroom, others see education as a cottage industry. Today between half a million and one and a half million children in the United States are believed to participate in home schooling; 20 years earlier, only 12,500 students were home-schooled.[36] Why the huge increase? Most people credit the explosion in the number of home-schooled children to the growth of fundamentalist Christianity, whose adherents often choose to educate their children at home. While religious motivation is the reason that most families choose home schooling, it is not the only reason.[37]

Some historical perspective might be helpful. Home schooling is not new; it predates schools and has always been around in one form or another. As recently as the 1970s, "romantic" critics—such as John Holt, Ivan Illich, and Jonathan Kozol—were advocating home schooling as a way to avoid the oppressive, dehumanizing practices that they believed characterize public schools. It is fascinating that home schooling appeals to liberals, who view schools as too conservative, as well as to conservatives, who view schools as too liberal. But conservatives, liberals, or middle-of-the-roaders can be drawn to home schooling for a number of reasons.

Van Galen has analyzed this movement and divides home schoolers into two groups: ideologues and pedagogues. *Ideologues* are rigid in their approach, viewing the home as a school setting where they choose the curricula, create the rules, and enforce the schedules. Religiously motivated home schoolers fall into the "ideologue" category. *Pedagogues* tend to be far less rigid, interested not in recreating the school according to their own image of it, but in redefining it. Pedagogues are humanistic, and the learner is central. Intrinsic motivation rather than external schedules guides instruction; individual interests and experiential activities are emphasized. The ideologues and the pedagogues share a dissatisfaction with schools, but they agree on little else.[38]

In urban areas, the lack of school safety may motivate some pedagogues to educate their children in the security of their own homes, away from the dangers of guns and violence. Other parents are disenchanted with the quality and lack of responsiveness of schools, and home schooling provides them with a base from which to launch their ideas about education, and to test their own teaching skills, in an intimate and nurturing environment. Economics can play a role as well. In some two-parent working families, the income earned by one parent is consumed by the high cost of child care. In such cases, one parent can readily give up the "outside" job to become a home teacher—and the family may not lose any real income. But not all home schools are initiated for positive motivations. Sometimes racism, antisemitism, or some other hateful reason can inspire an ideologue to withdraw his or her children from a public school and initiate a home school.

As home schools' philosophies vary, so does their quality. Some parents are incredibly talented and dedicated teachers, while others are less than competent. But even when parents may fall short of teaching excellence, individualized instruction is powerful. This may be one reason why home-schooled children generally score quite well on standardized tests, averaging between the sixty-fifth and eightieth percentiles.[39] A number of home-schooled children have even achieved national acclaim. Grant Colfax was taught by his parents, and never attended elementary or secondary school. He won admission to Harvard, graduated *magna cum laude,* became a Fulbright scholar, and eventually was graduated from Harvard Medical School. His home-schooled brothers enjoyed similar success—all endorsements of home schooling.

Home-schooling critics are more concerned with potential abuses than with success stories like that of the Colfax family. Do children educated in isolation from their peers suffer any consequences? What is lost by not working and learning with other children of diverse beliefs and backgrounds? Since

Home-Schooled—and Proud of It

Home schooling was more the norm than the exception in times past. Among wealthier British and U.S. families in the seventeenth and eighteenth centuries, parents and home tutors were the educators of choice. Home-schooling traditions exist in different cultures as well. In many Native American cultures, for example, the elders served—and often still serve—as teachers. Contemporary advocates often dip into the well of history to claim the success of home-schooled people such as:

- Woodrow Wilson
- Margaret Mead
- Florence Nightingale
- John Quincy Adams
- Franklin Roosevelt
- Thomas Edison
- The Wright Brothers
- Andrew Carnegie

- Abraham Lincoln
- Pearl Buck
- Agatha Christie
- Benjamin Franklin

These success stories indicate that home schooling can be effective. But then again, the student's needs and the teacher's talents—at home or at school—are more important than any list of home-schooled achievers.

Source: R. S. Moore and D. N. Moore "Better Late Than Early: A New Approach to Your Child's Education" (New York: Reader's Digest Press) 1975; Gary Knowles, James A. Muchmore, and Holly W. Spaulding, "Home Education as an Alternative to Institutionalized Education," *The Education Forum* 58 (Spring 1994): 238–243; telephone conversation with staff of *Growing Without Schooling* magazine.

Americans were originally motivated to build schools in order to promote Americanization, to meld a single nation, it is logical to wonder: Will home schooling adversely affect our national cohesion?

Home-schooling families hold different views as to the importance of socialization. Some point out that much of what passes for socialization in school is negative, including everything from unhealthy competition to gang violence. They believe that, in the final analysis, their children come out ahead by remaining at home. Other home-school families believe that socialization is important, and create their own social groups, such as book clubs, with like-minded others. Still others forge a relationship with local school districts so that their children, although instructed at home, can participate in district schools' sports or other extracurricular activities. School districts vary in their receptivity to such "dual" enrollments. In Virginia, for example, home schoolers are allowed to participate only "unofficially" in afterschool sports activities, and their sports accomplishments cannot be taken into account when they are considered for college scholarships. In Ames, Iowa, on the other hand, home schoolers participate in sports events equally, have access to school textbooks and standardized tests, and even receive "enrichment" classes designed specifically for them. While some districts view home schooling as a competing educational approach, others view the relationship more as a partnership.[40] Litigation has often resulted in opening public school resources to home schoolers.[41]

Advances in technology have been a catalyst for the home-schooling movement, particularly the proliferation of personal computers and the increase in Internet subscribers. America Online, for example, offers a home-schooling forum complete with lesson plans, tutoring, legislative updates, and the capability for networking with others interested in group work. New multimedia curriculum can now be brought into the home. In Michigan, the Noah Web-

A World without Schools

Even the decision to have schools reflects a value. In *Deschooling Society,* Ivan Illich likens schools to the church during medieval times.[a] He views schools as institutions that perform a political rather than an educational function. To Illich, the diplomas and degrees issued by schools reflect a certification role rather than an educational one. Schools provide society's "stamp of approval," announcing who shall succeed, who shall be awarded status, and who shall remain in poverty. In addition, by compelling students to attend, by judging and labeling them, by confining them, and by discriminating among them, Illich believes that schools are actually harming children. He would replace our traditional schools with a variety of learning "networks" that would be both lifelong and compulsory. To Illich, the notion of waking up to a world without schools is not an outlandish proposition. It is a dream fulfilled.

[a]Ivan Illich, *Deschooling Society* (New York: Harper & Row, 1973).

ster charter school offers a "school-less school," one that connects children and parents to teachers and curriculum through telephone lines and terminals. The children are "schooled" at home via their computer terminals. Students and parents have ready access to the Noah Webster faculty, who evaluate each student's progress. Technology is radically altering education, and the school of the future may be less a place than a password onto the information superhighway. In the future, home schooling may be far less exotic and far more prevalent.[42]

Tomorrow's Technology

By the middle of the twentieth century there was a growing realization that the face of education had been changed forever. Human beings serving as teachers, the core of schooling for centuries if not millennia, were being made obsolete by the advances of technology. The new invention would work its way into affluent schools and eventually all schools, slowly but surely replacing the classroom teacher. These new machines could take students where they had never been before, do things no human could do, and share an unlimited reservoir of information. Clearly this new breakthrough had the potential to teach more effectively at a far lower cost than human teachers. Predictions varied from the replacement of all teachers to the replacement of most teachers. Some even predicted the replacement of schools themselves.

The advent of computer technology has led some individuals to foresee revolutionary changes in education, but the machines described above do not refer to computers. They refer to televisions, and the revolutionary changes were predicted more than 30 years ago. Futurists then were predicting that educational television would make teachers obsolete.

We can and have overestimated the impact of technology. Or have we underestimated the inertia and stability of schools? Either way, foreseeing the impact of the latest technology—computers and the Internet—is a forecasting task that is fraught with danger. In fact, the first decade of computers in education has brought far fewer changes than originally predicted. Yet the feeling persists that, at some point, technology will revolutionize schools.

The History of Computers

- Computers first became popular for military uses during World War II. When the British captured Enigma, the German cipher machine used to code secret Nazi messages, it was the computer developed to decode those messages that helped defeat Germany.
- American campuses used computers during the 1940s for war-related research. The University of Pennsylvania was the first to develop ENIAC, a computer that used vacuum tubes. However, the vacuum tubes often overheated and burnt out and required a great deal of electricity. When the university turned on its new computer, the lights of North Philadelphia dimmed.
- A 1945 computer, dependent on the vacuum tube and capable only of the same level of calculations as today's tabletop home computers, would have had to be the size of New York City and would have required more electricity than New York's subway system.[a]

- Bell Laboratories in New Jersey developed a second generation of computers in 1947, replacing the large, costly vacuum tube with the transistor. The transistor required less power, generated less heat, and performed calculations far more quickly.
- Computers soon replaced transistors with circuits printed on silicon chips. A vacuum tube could be held in one hand; a transistor could be held on a fingertip; a silicon chip was so tiny it could pass through the eye of a needle. This miniaturization of computers made them faster, more powerful, more dependable, portable, and less expensive.
- If a Rolls-Royce had benefited from the same cost efficiency as has the microprocessor during the past decade, it would now cost $3.[b]

[a]Harold Shane, "The Silicon Age and Education," *Phi Delta Kappan* 63, no. 5 (January 1982): 303–308.
[b]Ibid.

Perhaps the biggest obstacle to realizing the potential of computers in the classroom is the traditional vision of education that persists. Few schools perceive computers as an integral part of instruction. Too many school systems purchase computers because they are expected to, without thinking about how they are to be used, and then provide little or no guidance for the teachers who must use them. This is one reason why not all teachers have enlisted in the "computer brigade." In fact, surveys suggest that a significant number of the nation's teachers simply do not use computers at all. And those who do use computers in the classrooms do not always use them effectively. Intimidated by these machines and ignorant of their possibilities, many teachers use them in the least threatening ways possible: for drill and practice exercises, simple programming skills, or educational games. Instead of being used to create new educational realities, computers are made to conform to existing ones.

Other obstacles exist as well. Many classrooms lack relevant software for their curricula, and few teachers have designed or know how to use appropriate assessment tools for computer work. Computers are also a financial burden, requiring expensive equipment and maintenance. Many old school buildings lack the electrical and communications wiring needed to support today's technology, particularly the Internet. This often leads to the inequitable distribution of computers among poor and wealthy schools, with the latter having greater access not only to computers but to the rich resources of the Internet. White children are more likely to work with computers than are minority children both at school and at home.[43] Furthermore, boys seem to enjoy greater access to this new technology than do girls. The availability and use of the computer has been shaped and limited by the wealth or poverty of local districts and by sexism in school.[44]

Nevertheless, the impact of computers in the classroom will probably be substantial, and even revolutionary. Computers have found their way into the vast majority of the nation's schools, according to Jay Becker of Johns Hopkins University.[45] The barriers to equal access will continue to fall as technological advances decrease costs. In addition, educational software companies are flourishing as they develop better and more relevant curricular materials and the Internet is opening a new world of possibility. The biggest question is, how will computers reshape tomorrow's classrooms?

The Apple Classrooms of Tomorrow (ACOT) project has yielded insight into the stages teachers go through when dealing with technology in their classrooms. Initially, most of the teachers that participated in the project experienced uncertainty and frustration with the introduction of computers. Eventually they incorporated computers in their classroom routines, using them as tools to support traditional methods of instruction. The key turning point came when teachers were able to feel mastery over the technology—and began to change instruction to suit the possibilities of the computers. Impressed by the potential of desktop publishing, one teacher said, "Now we can simulate a newspaper company. Eventually students will work in groups, each with their own task, some for art, business graphs, articles, and the editing group." Learning became more interactive as the teachers and students felt empowered to use technology together. The final stage the ACOT researchers perceived was that of invention: where teachers began to revamp all their classroom practices. Another teacher explained, "As you work into using the computer in the classroom, you start questioning everything you have done in the past and wonder how you can adapt it to the computer. Then, you start questioning the whole concept of what you originally did." Computer technology, according to these teachers, can be the gateway to a whole new process of learning and teaching.[46]

Indeed, the pioneers of educational technology are not actually the computer or software companies: They are the teachers who are experimenting to find the most innovative and appropriate uses for them. For example, some teachers are organizing information into databases so that students will have the equivalent of an electronic encyclopedia at their fingertips. Other teachers are simulating biology experiments such as dissections or other projects too dangerous or difficult for a high school lab.[47] The students of Foxboro Middle School, Massachusetts, established contact with students in Kindersley, Saskatchewan, and learned through direct computer discussion about realities of life in Canada.[48] Kathleen Duplantier, an elementary teacher in Louisiana, used the Apple Macintosh Hypercard program to create the Hypertext Folklife Curriculum, where students research and record their various cultural backgrounds.[49] Often these creative teachers must pursue their own sources of funding, but their perseverance leads to a new and richer view of education.

While individual teachers explore classroom innovations that incorporate computer use, the Internet is bringing down classroom walls in dramatic and unanticipated ways. The impact of the Internet can be compared to the impact of computers themselves, as the number of Internet users has been increasing dramatically. Students may now communicate with teachers who are hundreds or thousands of miles away. As they talk to each other, students do not lean over their desks, they lean over the boundaries of cities, states, or countries. For research projects, Internet users tap into data sources far beyond the limits of their local libraries. The Internet not only redefines distance, it also

Going Global: Teaching and the Internet

Ready or not, the Internet will probably be a part of your classroom within the next few years. As school systems invest in the hardware and software required to join the global network, teachers wonder if the Internet will be as earthshaking as the media and political hype seem to indicate. Current trends suggest that the Internet will indeed have a significant impact on your life as a teacher. If you are new to the Internet or have never thought about its classroom applications, here is a primer you should find useful.

What Is the Internet?

The Internet is a name given to the network of computers all over the world that are linked not only to each other but to a massive amount of information on an endless array of topics. For teachers, the key is learning how to access and use this information in and beyond the classroom.

What Will I Need to Get Connected?

The easiest way to access the Internet is through the World Wide Web (WWW). In order to see the Web, your computer needs an Internet connection and Web browser software. This browser software tells the computer how to find and display WWW pages. The good news is that Web browser software is often provided free of charge. The bad news is that net access is rarely free. If your school does not have a direct connection and the appropriate wiring, you will need to get your own account on a commercial Internet service. These services usually charge by the hour for the amount of time users are connected. (Some states sponsor Internet access for teachers—check with your teacher education program for information.) An additional requirement is adequate phone line support, which can be a problem, especially in older buildings. If the school budget comes up short, businesses, universities, or service organizations can sometimes help a school to get connected. If you can't afford a connection that supports graphics, sound, and other more exotic features, you can still use many of the most powerful tools available on the Web, especially E-mail.

E-Mail

One of the first tools available on the Internet was electronic mail, E-mail for short. As the name suggests, E-mail is very similar to traditional mail service (haughtily called "snail mail" by Internet users) but usually takes just minutes to be delivered. One user types in a message on the terminal, hits a key and the message is electronically delivered to another terminal a few feet, or a few thousand miles, away. If you have an E-mail account, you will have an Internet "address" made up of two parts, a userid (pronounced "user-I-D") and a domain name. Your userid is the part of your address that is specific to you (think of it as the name and street address on a standard envelope). Your domain name indicates what part of the Internet your account is located in (think of it as the city and state lines of your snail mail address). Your userid and your domain name together, separated by an "@" sign, are your Internet address. For example, if the user Horace Mann has an E-mail account at Fictional University, his E-mail address might be: "hmann@fictional.edu."

One of the most significant advantages of E-mail (and many other Internet tools) is that it is basically free. If you use a telephone and modem to connect to the Internet, you only pay the charge for a local telephone call to your Internet mainframe, even if you send a message to the other side of the country—or the other side of the world. For example, a user who accesses a commercial Internet provider with a local telephone call can send free messages to friends, colleagues, and students all over the world. The user pays only for the call to the provider for the time that she is connected. Once the message is sent, it travels free of charge.

The World Wide Web

You probably have heard a great deal about the World Wide Web. Whenever you see an address that starts with "http://" (they often appear on television or radio) you are seeing a location on the World Wide Web.

World Wide Web information is presented on "homepages." These pages range from the IRS's official page giving tips on how to fill out your tax return, to personal pages with long lists of the author's favorite movies or songs, to files containing classic literature or paintings, to information on how to join some bizarre extremist groups. Many universities have homepages that feature scholarly information or documents. Everything from literary classics to astronomical pictures from NASA spacecraft are available. While the WWW contains a huge volume of information, there is no guarantee that all of it will be useful, or even accurate, or that educators will want to make it all available to students. The WWW makes critical reading and understanding of author motives more vital than ever.

Using the World Wide Web

There are several ways of weaving your way through the Web. One is a subject list—a set of topics from which users choose their area of interest. As the user chooses new categories of information, the lists become more and more detailed. A user seeking the website of a particular school might choose "Education" from a list of general topics, then choose "K-12" from a list of different topics within education, and finally choose the desired page from a list of different school districts. Due to the hierarchical nature of subject lists, users may have to go down through many levels of subdirectories before finding the desired topic.

Another popular information-finding tool is an Internet search. The user goes to a special homepage, sometimes known as a "search engine," which allows them to type in "key words." Key words are the words the user hopes to find in a homepage. The words are sent to a computer that contains a database of most homepages available on the Web. When the computer finds a homepage containing the words, it sends a message to the user, telling them which homepages they should visit. It is important to be as specific as possible with this type of searching. Otherwise, a teacher looking for lesson plans for a reading unit might get a list containing the homepage of the Reading, Pennsylvania, Chamber of Commerce.

Writing the World Wide Web

Perhaps the most educationally exciting use for the WWW is the opportunity it affords students to connect with other users around the world. Although the technology that makes homepages visible around the world is very complex, the programming language Web authors use is relatively simple. Students could easily write their own homepages and bring the outside world into the classroom. Examples of projects in which students could incorporate include:

- Student-created surveys that Internet users answer. Responses could come from users throughout the world, through a hyperlink connected to a class E-mail address
- A social studies project in which students collaborate with a class in another part of the country, or the world, to trade information about their lives, customs, and culture
- An ESL class might create a homepage listing and celebrating each of their respective cultures, including links to homepages in their own countries
- A reading and writing class could build a creative writing homepage filled with student work. With the collaboration of another classroom linked to the Web, students could run a virtual creative writing workshop
- Math students and teachers could create a mathphobia homepage, featuring step-by-step approaches to solving problems for and by students, while reducing math anxiety
- Foreign language students can converse with native speakers on other continents by E-mail, or using advanced Internet tools that allow for transmission of video and sound through the computers. Conversely, your class can help others touch up on their English
- Students can participate in an on-line science fair, presenting science projects using text and graphics
- Electronic student publications: school yearbooks, newspapers, and literary magazines can be (and already are being) made accessible to the rest of the world
- Students interested in science can browse the pictures uploaded by NASA, along with resources from almost every major science or health organization
- Students applying to colleges can browse the homepages set up by different colleges and universities

You may have noticed from this list that many of these projects sound very much like projects you might already be doing or planning to do in your classroom. But unlike the typical projects, the global scope of the network is what really sets it apart. The Internet is creating classrooms without walls and even without national boundaries.

Examples of Internet Sites for Educators

In this list, you will find several locations on the Web that you may find helpful. The list is by no

(Box continues on next page.)

means inclusive. (Each item is followed by its Internet address.)

Yahoo! One of the first and largest subject directories on the Web. Look for the information you want in an easy-to-understand subject-based list.

http://www.yahoo.com/

Web66 A site dedicated to the introduction of the Internet to schools on the K-12 level. Web66 features many resources, including a registry of schools on the Web, step-by-step instructions for setting up a Web server, and HTML (Hypertext Markup Language) pages that you can download and use on your own Internet server.

http://web66.coled.umn.edu/

NCSS Online The website created and maintained by the National Council for the Social Studies, the professional organization for teachers of social studies from elementary school through college. Valuable resources include: information about conferences, membership, and the NCSS standards document for the social studies.

http://www.ncss.org/online/

Virtual Frog Dissection Kit Biology teachers can take their students to learn about amphibian anatomy without formaldehyde or scalpels. Users choose which of the frog's internal organs are shown, and the angle at which they are presented. For advanced users, movies show the frog being virtually rotated.

http://george.lbl.gov/ITG.hm.pg.docs/dissect/info.html

The English Server Based at Carnegie-Mellon University, this site contains many resources valuable to English teachers, including the complete text of many literary works that have entered the public domain. Also located here are journals, lists of other Internet resources, and literary criticism on topics from gender issues to technical writing.

http://english-www.hss.cmu.edu/

The AskEric Virtual Library The Educational Resources Information Center features all kinds of information for teachers at all levels. The resources here include lesson plans and the AskEric Q&A service, which answers questions submitted by users via E-mail.

http://ericir.syr.edu/

Dave's ESL Cafe on the Web ESL students and teachers will find plenty to occupy them at this site. Students can practice their English with quizzes, E-mail pen pals, a graffiti wall, and many other activities. Teachers can also take advantage of the E-mail pen pals or message exchange features and can check out the ESL Teacher Links section as well.

http://www.pacificnet.net/~sperling/eslcafe.html

Of course there are thousands more homepages out there than could be listed here. By looking at these pages, you can get an idea of the sort of resources and possibilities that the Web provides.

Note: The section on teaching and the Internet was written by Paul Degnan. Paul Degnan graduated from the MAT program at the American University School of Education in the Spring of 1996.

creates a different learning dynamic. Large-group interactions in class are replaced by interactions between individuals or smaller groups working at terminals. For quieter students, whose learning style may be submerged and lost in large classroom discussions, the Internet offers a more intimate, if more technical, way to communicate and to learn. The same is true of disabled students whose disabilities may all but vanish when they work on the Internet. Discussion groups and e-mail (electronic mail) replace schoolyard conversations

Typically, computers have been used for drill and practice, simple programming, and educational games.

and physical bulletin boards. Internet adds an entirely new dimension to computers; it impacts the classroom in ways still being explored by teachers and students who are becoming "Internauts."[50]

With increased teacher education and the commitment to using computers more fully, the obstacles to the success of computers as educational tools may be overcome. Many challenges remain for the years ahead, but the potential for reshaping education is exciting. Consider the following possibilities:

- Mathematics education could be reshaped to eliminate the teaching of mechanics (division, square roots, and so on), which can be accomplished by inexpensive calculators. Instead, math instruction could focus on the theory and meaning of numbers, becoming more conceptual and less mechanical.
- Gifted students, students with learning disabilities, or students with other special characteristics could be provided with personal tutors in the shape of specially designed programs to meet their unique needs.
- Voice-activated computers could provide foreign language instruction or even give voice lessons to singers on a one-to-one basis. Computers are already aiding students to overcome auditory-processing difficulties.
- As discussed in the previous section on home-schooling, "electronic cottages," described by Toffler in *The Third Wave*, may become a reality. Education will be (and in some cases, is being) transported beyond schools to homes.
- A number of Third World educators confronting staggering illiteracy rates in their developing countries have suggested that computers can help

them to "leapfrog" this problem. By focusing on "electronic literacy," an unprecedented approach to learning may be created that actually bypasses reading entirely.

- The long gaps between the discovery of new information and its appearance in the curriculum could be eliminated. Rather than waiting years for new scientific breakthroughs and other advances to appear in textbooks, by combining computer and video technologies, educators could eliminate this lag time and current events and breakthroughs could be incorporated instantly into the school curriculum.
- By using computers with access to the Internet, students could surmount the national barriers that inhibit schools from focusing on global problems. World population growth, dwindling resources, even war and peace could be explored by students in countries around the world. New technology may truly create a "global village," enabling youngsters and adults to confront the problems that threaten our existence on this planet.

The possibilities seem endless. The new technology has the potential to dramatically reshape our current perception of education. The direction of the next breakthrough is an important ingredient in forecasting the future: What will the next generation of computers be like? Will they continue the trend toward less expensive and smaller machines so that all of us can carry a powerful computer in our pockets? Will the next generation of computers converse with us, eliminating the need for keyboard skills and programming? In such a scenario, we could talk directly to the computer, printing letters and papers by speaking—or perhaps skipping printing entirely and simply instructing our computer to transmit information to the computers of others. Perhaps the next breakthrough will be true artificial intelligence, computers that can counsel us on our professional and personal lives, becoming mechanical advisers and friends. If the pace and direction of computer technology continue, whatever shape the next generation of computers takes will undoubtedly have a profound impact on our lives within and beyond the classroom.

America's Schools: Better Than We Think

Everyone is aware today that our educational system has been allowed to deteriorate. It has been going downhill for some years without anything really constructive having been done to arrest the decline, still less to reverse its course. We thus have a chronic crisis: an unsolved problem as grave as any that faces our country today. Unless this problem is dealt with promptly and effectively, the machinery that sustains our level of material prosperity and political power will begin to slow down.[51]

Sound familiar? As though you just read it in today's newspaper? Actually, this was written in the 1950s by Admiral Hyman Rickover, a frequent critic of U.S. schools. And that's the point that a growing number of educators are making: School bashing is nothing new, it is as American as apple pie, an old tradition that has reached a new peak in recent years. In fact, these educators believe that the current crescendo of criticism is not only old hat, it is terribly misguided, because today's schools are doing as well as they ever have—and maybe, just maybe, they are doing better.

Relatively low performance by U.S. students on international tests has frequently been cited as "evidence" that the nation's schools are in terrible shape.

But school advocates point out that this is a classic case of misinterpreting test data. What the tests may reflect are cultural and curricular differences, not necessarily problems with our educational system. Consider the comparison between Japanese and U.S. middle school students on algebra tests. Japanese students score significantly higher, but that is not too surprising when one realizes that most Japanese students take algebra a year or two earlier than U.S. students do. Comparing algebra scores of those who took an algebra course with those who did not is something quite less than a fair comparison of educational systems. Moreover, most Japanese children go to private academies, called *Juku* schools, attending classes after regular school hours and on weekends. By 16 years of age, the typical Japanese student will have attended 2 or more years of classes than a U.S. student will have done, another reason why such comparisons are misleading. In fact, because of the greater comparative effectiveness of U.S. colleges in relation to Japanese colleges, many of these differences evaporate on later tests. Perhaps there are two lessons here: (1) U.S. students should spend more time in school and (2) the Japanese need to improve the quality of their colleges.

Student selection also affects test scores. In the United States, the full range of students are included in test populations, strong students and weak students, English-speaking and non-English-speaking. In other countries, students who do not speak the dominant language are routinely excluded. In still other nations, only a small percentage of the most talented students are selected or encouraged to continue their education and go on to high school. As one might imagine, this highly selective population does quite well on international tests. Comparing all of America's students to the best of another nation's is a biased comparison.

Cultural differences affect not only student selection, but test performance as well. Americans value a comprehensive education, one in which students are involved in a wide array of activities, from theater to sports to working part-time jobs. The U.S. public typically values spontaneity, social responsibility, a degree of independence in their children, values that are not assessed in international tests. Where the United States values the breadth of education, some other cultures have emphasized a focused, more narrow education stressing competitive testing. In a number of European and Asian countries, a student's entire future may hinge on a single critical test. Only the few students who are successful "test takers" are allowed to go on to academic high schools and college or to take international tests. This "test-well-or-perish" syndrome affects their approach to international tests. Consider the way a South Korean teacher identifies the students selected for the International Assessment of Educational Progress (IAEP):

> The math teacher . . . calls the names of the 13-year-olds in the room who have been selected as part of the IAEP sample. As each name is called, the student stands at attention at his or her desk until the list is complete. Then, to the supportive and encouraging applause of their colleagues, the chosen ones leave to [take the assessment test].[52]

U.S. students selected to take international exams do not engender cheers from their classmates, and do not view such tests as a matter of national honor, as do the South Korean students. Quite the contrary, they are more likely to view such exams as an inconvenience. Too often our culture belittles "intellectuals" and mocks the gifted student.

School Matters

A massive study of schools, the 1966 Coleman report declared that schools were not important in determining the academic success of students. James Coleman found that the most critical factor in determining a child's academic performance was the social and educational background of his or her family. The second most critical factor was the social and educational background of other children in the school. The influence of the policies and practices of the schools themselves came in a distant third.

Christopher Jencks found that schools had minimal impact on intellectual performance, on future income of students, or on reducing the gap between rich and poor. Again, the Jencks research pointed to family background as the most critical factor in student success.

These disheartening findings of the late 1960s and early 1970s pointed to the educational impotence of schools. However, they have been disproved by more recent research showing that schools can make a difference. For example, during the 1970s educators focused on improving the achievement of disadvantaged students. The following statistics show the results of these efforts:

- During the 1970s, historically low-scoring students markedly improved their reading scores as measured by the National Assessment of Educational Progress (NAEP).
- By 1990, average SAT scores of African-American, Asian-American, and Puerto Rican students had

all increased from the average scores registered in 1975.
- In 1950, only 25 percent of African-American students graduated from high school. By 1979, 75 percent of African-American students graduated, and by 1993, the figure had reached 84 percent.

Coleman and Jencks had been too pessimistic. Schools could and did make a difference. At least some schools made a difference. The challenge now was to find out why some schools succeeded while others failed.

Sources: James Coleman et al., *Equality of Educational Opportunity* (Washington, DC: U.S. Government Printing Office, 1966); Christopher Jencks et al., *Inequality: A Reassessment of the Effect of Family and Schooling in America* (New York: Basic Books, 1972); Roy Forbes, "Academic Achievement of Historically Lower-Achieving Students During the Seventies," *Phi Delta Kappan* 6, no. 8 (April 1985): 542–544; Archie Lapointe, "The Good News about American Education," *Phi Delta Kappan* 65, no. 10 (June 1984): 663–667; Tommy Tomlinson and Christopher Cross, "Student Effort: The Key to High Standards," *Educational Leadership* 49, no. 1 (September 1991): 69–73; Michael Kirst, "The Need to Broaden Our Perspective Concerning America's Educational Attainment," *Phi Delta Kappan* 73, no. 2 (October 1991): 118–120; Gerald Bracey, "Why Can't They Be Like We Were?" *Phi Delta Kappan* 73, no. 2 (October 1991): 104–117. Marilyn M. McMillen, Phillip Kaufman and Summer D. Whitener, *Dropout Rates in the United States: 1993* (Washington, DC: National Center for Education Statistics, 1994).

Poverty in the United States also depresses U.S. test scores. About one in five children in the United States lives in poverty; a reality that is lost on most middle- and upper-class Americans. The United States has by far the largest proportion of poor children when compared to other developed nations participating in these exams. These students bring precious few resources to schools or to tests. Facing such problems as malnutrition, inadequate housing, and family instability, these poverty-stricken students would lower the average score of any nation. As if extensive poverty of families and their children were not enough of a handicap, school funding practices amplify the problem. Americans tolerate enormous inequities in school funding levels, and typically schools in the poorest neighborhoods need to struggle the most for adequate funding. Other Western nations distribute school funds more equitably, avoiding the extremes of wealth and poverty that characterize U.S. education. Funding inequities and high levels of poverty are factors few commentators mention when discussing test scores of U.S. students.

Despite all these obstacles, on several key tests, the nation's students are doing quite well. For example, by the mid-1990s American students had the second-highest average score among 31 nations on international comparisons of reading. On the National Assessment of Educational Progress (NAEP), students attained all-time high scores in seven of the nine areas, including reading, math, and science. The proportion of students scoring above 650 on the SAT mathematics tests has reached an all-time high. The number of students taking Advanced Placement (AP) tests soared from 98,000 in 1978 to 448,000 in 1994. Similar improvements have been documented on the California Achievement Test, the Iowa Test of Basic Skills, and the Metropolitan Achievement Test, tests used across the nation to measure student learning. One of the most encouraging signs in improving test scores has been the performance of minority students, whose scores have risen dramatically. Among 17-year-old African-American students, average reading scores on the NAEP tests rose two grade levels between 1971 and 1992, an impressive improvement.[53] Decades ago, these students probably would not have even been in school, much less taking tests. In 1940, the overall high school graduation rate in the United States was only 38 percent; by the early 1990s, it was approaching 90 percent. Other indicators reflect that students are not only staying in school longer, they are also enrolling in more advanced math and science classes. Beyond the test controversy, it is evident that U.S. schools are teaching more students, that students are staying in school for longer periods of time, and that children are studying more challenging courses than ever before. Then why the national upheaval about education? Why all the furor about our failing schools, and why the demands for radical school reform?

Educators have advanced a number of possible explanations:

- School bashing is a traditional U.S. pastime, so the current criticism is not a new behavior. Journals and politicians have been critiquing schools since the nation began.
- The nation's schools have always been described as having been better "back then." Adults tend to romanticize what schools were like when they attended as children, for they always studied harder and learned more than their children do (and when they went to school, they had to walk through 4 feet of snow, uphill, in both directions).
- Americans are also unrealistic in their expectations about schools. They expect schools to conquer all sorts of social and academic ills, from illiteracy to teenage pregnancy, from the difficulty of advanced math to AIDS prevention. Since today's social problems of crime, violence, divorce, and poverty are growing, schools must be failing.
- Today's schools are being challenged as never before. Schools today work with tremendous numbers of poor students, non-English-speaking children, minorities, and special education students who just a few years ago would not be attending school as long, or in some cases, would not be attending school at all. If progress has been slower than desired, perhaps part of the reason is that the challenge is greater than ever before.
- Many Americans confuse "real" schools with "ideal" schools, and hold unrealistic visions of what schools should be like. While all schools can be improved, unrealistic, idealized images of schools can never be realized.

"The Millennium Is at Hand"

"The millennium is at hand. Man has invented everything that can be invented. He has done all he can do."

So spoke the bishop at an 1870 church gathering. But the presiding officer suggested that more great inventions were just over the horizon. The bishop took issue and asked him to name an invention yet to be created.

"I think man will learn to fly," responded the presiding officer.

"Don't you know that flight is reserved to the angels?" responded the bishop, upset with the blasphemy he had just heard.

The bishop who considered human flight blasphemy was Milton Wright. Thirty-seven years later two of his children, Orville and Wilbur, invented the airplane.

Source: Cream of the Kappan, 1956–1981, Stanley Elam, ed. (Bloomington: Phi Delta Kappan Educational Foundation, 1981), p. 397.

- By the 1990s, Americans expressed dissatisfaction with many institutions, from government bureaucracies to labor unions to journalists. The perception of schools has been colored by this general feeling of discontent.
- In *The Manufactured Crisis,* David Berliner and Bruce Biddle put much of the blame for the current criticism on neoconservative politicians who arrived in Washington with presidents Reagan and Bush, and whose perspectives and clout were reinforced by the conservative Republican Congress elected in 1994. Their political agenda supporting private schools, business interests, and vouchers marked the beginning of a major assault on public education, on federal involvement in schools, and on equal educational programs targeted at minority groups and women. The result has been a loss of confidence in the performance of public schools, an emphasis on alternative forms of education, and the rapid growth of "for-profit" educational companies.
- Along with a political change of climate, Berliner and Biddle also finger the press, which has been all too willing to publish negative stories about schools—stories based on questionable sources. From uncritically accepting the idea that campuses are characterized by "political correctness" gone to extremes, to publishing selective test scores that reflect negatively on U.S. education, sloppy, biased reporting has damaged the public's perception of schools.

These are only some of the possible reasons underlying the current criticism of education, but they provide perspective. To keep one's perspective broad, it is helpful to remember two points: First, criticism can be fruitful. If additional attention and even criticism help to shape stronger schools, then at least some of the current furor will have a positive impact. Second, there are countless students in all parts of the country who every day work diligently and perform with excellence. The United States continues to produce leaders in fields as diverse as medicine and sports, business and entertainment. To a great extent, these untold success stories are also the stories of talented and dedicated teachers. Although their quiet daily contributions rarely reach the headlines, they do make a difference. You represent the next generation of teachers who will weather difficult times and sometimes adverse circumstances to touch the lives of students, and to shape a better America.[54]

SUMMARY

1. As we approach the twenty-first century, U.S. education faces many changes. Reforms and other forces are eliciting innovations in areas from technology to testing, and beginning teachers should be aware of the new developments.

2. One of the more controversial reform recommendations established a professional board to identify and assess superior teachers, termed *board-certified teachers*. This is one of several efforts designed to increase the professional status of teaching.

3. Merit pay and career ladders are two other such efforts. Merit pay offers teachers more money based on different criteria, including gains in student performance, typically measured by standardized tests; teacher performance, as measured by outside evaluators; individualized plans, in which teachers have a voice in setting their own goals; and the nature of the teaching assignment. Each of these approaches is controversial. Career ladders, on the other hand, offer teachers increases in salary by developing different levels for advancement and increasing responsibility. Some argue that the problems of this approach mirror those of merit pay, while others insist that career ladder programs offer room for true professional development.

4. Testing has indicated that U.S. students are not scoring as well as students from other developed countries. These poor scores provided one catalyst for the reform movement. But before long, the tests themselves became an issue. Critics voiced concern about the negative impact of teaching to the test, giving students too many tests, racism and sexism in standardized test questions, and the low level of thinking required by such examinations. Test advocates stressed the need for objective measures of our students, programs, and schools.

5. The latest development in testing is authentic assessment, which calls for testing to represent real performance. An authentic assessment demands that students synthesize what they have learned in different areas to complete a challenging, creative task. Accomplishing something real is motivating for students, and teachers can learn a great deal about how to adjust instruction from student performances, which they seldom can with standardized tests. In *Horace's School,* Theodore Sizer presents many examples of authentic assessment tasks, which he refers to as "exhibitions."

6. New curricular trends include the development of critical-thinking skills, approaches to teaching ethics and values, and the creation of a global perspective. These curricular innovations have received increased attention with the growth of the information age and the sophisticated technological developments of the past decades. Although not entirely new curricular ideas, these areas may become important chapters in tomorrow's textbooks.

7. While home schooling is far from being a new phenomenon, the number of parents educating their children at home has grown dramatically in recent years. Home-schooling parents can be divided into two groups: Ideologues, often including religiously motivated parents, view the home school as an opportunity to indoctrinate their rules, curricula, and beliefs. Pedagogues tend to be more learner-centered than are most schools, and depend on intrinsic motivation, student interests, and experiential learning activities. Technological advances, including the use of the Internet, have opened the possibility of converting education into a "cottage industry."

8. The technological advances of the past decade have not only brought computers into homes and schools but also raised the potential of profoundly changing where and how children learn. Although computers and the Internet have yet to radically alter schools, revolutionary technological advances offer the promise of restructuring education as we know it.

9. Americans have a long tradition of criticizing schools, but in recent years these criticisms have intensified. Several educators have countered this popular perception of failing schools with the contrary view that schools are, in fact, doing very well. They point to the large numbers of diverse students, many from poor backgrounds, who are staying in school longer and enrolling in more challenging courses than ever before. According to these school advocates, a number of critical test scores and studies indicate that the nation's schools—despite economic deprivations, disheartening inequities, and political opposition—continue to do a remarkable job in educating U.S. children.

DISCUSSION QUESTIONS AND ACTIVITIES

1. Choose one type of merit pay that you believe could be effective. Draw up a proposal for a school system in which you explain in detail how your type of merit pay would be distributed and what the benefits would be to the school system.

2. Consider how people in other professions are recognized, and apply your insights to teaching. How could good teachers be recognized more effectively? How could your ideas for teacher recognition be implemented?

3. Support the statement "More testing is good for U.S. education." Now refute it.

4. "Critical thinking has always been a silent partner in the curriculum." Do you agree or disagree?

5. "Moral education is not a new focus of the curriculum, but a newly identified need." Why?

6. Which of the three approaches to moral education (values clarification, moral development, or character education) appeals to you most? Why?

7. Collect newspaper articles concerning home schools. Decide whether the home schooling described in the articles falls into the "ideologue" or the "pedagogue" category. Are the stories generally objective, or can you detect a bias for or against home schools?

8. Does your local public school district have an official (or unofficial) policy concerning home schooling? Do home-school students participate in any school activities, or do they receive any school resources? How do you feel about these (un)official policies?

9. Choose a subject you may be teaching and explain how the computer or the Internet can facilitate learning.

10. Identify four dangers of using computers in schools.

11. Do you think it is important to include global education in the curriculum? Why or why not? What are some dangers inherent in a global education curriculum?

12. Organize a class debate on the following topic: "U.S. schools are better than ever."

13. Describe authentic assessment. If the majority of classroom testing were to become authentic, how would this affect curriculum and instruction? Identify the advantages and disadvantages of such a change.

14. How accurate and objective is the information regarding U.S. schools that reaches the public? Analyze and evaluate newspaper accounts, tapes of radio or television reports, or statements made by politicians and other community leaders about the effectiveness of the nation's schools. What is the impact of these messages on public beliefs about schools?

NOTES

1. Edward B. Fiske, *Smart Schools, Smart Kids* (New York: Simon & Schuster, 1991).
2. Quoted in "Forging a Profession," *Teacher* (September/October 1989): 12, 16.
3. "National Certification Picks Up Steam," *American Teacher* 76, no. 6 (May/June 1992): 3.
4. Lee S. Schulman, "A Union of Insufficiencies: Strategies for Teacher Assessment in a Period of Educational Reform," *Educational Leadership* 46, no. 3 (November 1988): 36–39.
5. Quoted in "Forging a Profession," p. 16.
6. Briant Farnsworth, Jerry Debenham, and Gerald Smith, "Designing and Implementing a Successful Merit Pay Program for Teachers," *Phi Delta Kappan* 73, no. 4 (December 1991): 320–325.
7. Ibid.
8. *Is "Paying for Performance" Changing Schools?*, The SREB Career Ladder Clearinghouse Report 1988 (Atlanta, GA: Southern Regional Education Board), p. 8.
9. Adam Urbanski, "The Rochester Contract: A Status Report," *Educational Leadership* 40, no. 3 (November 1988): 48–52.
10. Fiske, *Smart Schools, Smart Kids,* p. 122.
11. Carin Rubenstein, "Surviving the Dreaded Kindergarten Exam," *Working Mother,* August 1989, p. 76.
12. Ibid., p. 75.
13. Joel Spring, *Conflict of Interests: The Politics of American Education* (New York: Longman, 1988), pp. 139–143.
14. Vito Perrone, "On Standardized Testing," *Childhood Education* 67, no. 3 (Spring 1991): 132–142.
15. Fiske, *Smart Schools, Smart Kids,* p. 117.
16. "Recent SAT Questions," *Fair Test Examiner* 3, no. 3 (Summer 1989): 4.
17. Grant Wiggins, "Teaching to the (Authentic) Test," *Educational Leadership* 46, no. 7 (April 1989): 41–47. See also Rieneke Zessoules and Howard Gardner, "Authentic Assessment: Beyond the Buzzword and into the Classroom," in Vito Perrone (ed.), *Expanding Student Assessment* (Alexandria, VA: Association for Supervision and Curriculum Development, 1991).
18. Gene I. Maeroff, "Assessing Alternative Assessment," *Phi Delta Kappan* 73, no. 4 (December 1991): 272–281.
19. Theodore Sizer, *Horace's School: Redesigning the American High School* (New York: Houghton Mifflin, 1992).
20. Louis Raths, Selma Wasserman, Arthur Jones, and Arnold Rothstein, *Teaching for Thinking: Theory and Application* (Columbus, OH: Merrill, 1966). See also Selma Wasserman, "Teaching for Thinking: Louis E. Raths Revisited," *Phi Delta Kappan* 68, no. 6 (February 1987): 460–466.
21. Summaries of these approaches are found in Barbara Presseisen, *Thinking Skills: Research and Practice* (Washington, DC: National Education Association, 1986). See also R. Feuerstein, *Instrumental Enrichment: An Intervention Program for Cognitive Modifiability* (Baltimore: University Park Press, 1980); A. H. Schoenfeld, "Measures of Problem-Solving Instruction," *Journal for Research in Mathematics Education* 13 (1982); E. de Bono, "The Cognitive Research Trust (CORT) Thinking Program," in W. Maxwell (ed.), *Thinking: The Expanding Frontier* (Hillsdale, NJ: Erlbaum, 1983); Joseph Hester, *Teaching for Thinking: A Program for School Improvement Through Teaching Critical Thinking Across the Curriculum* (Durham, NC: Carolina Academic Press, 1994), pp. 1–23.

22. Robert J. Marzano, Ronald Brandt, Carolyn Hughes, Beau Fly Jones, Barbara Presseisen, Stuart Rarkin, and Charles Suhor, *Dimensions of Thinking* (Alexandria, VA: Association for Supervision and Curriculum Development, 1988).

23. Robert J. Marzano, *A Different Kind of Classroom: Teaching with Dimensions of Learning* (Alexandria, VA: Association for Supervision and Curriculum Development, 1992).

24. Stephen Bates, "A Textbook of Virtues," *The New York Times,* January 8, 1995, education supplement p. EL-16+.

25. Philip Cohen, "The Content of Their Character: Educators Find New Ways to Tackle Values and Morality," *Association for Supervision and Curriculum Development Curriculum Update,* Spring 1995, p. 1.

26. Bates, "A Textbook of Virtues."

27. James Leming, "In Search of Effective Character Education," *Educational Leadership* 51, no. 3 (November 1993): 63–70.

28. Howard Kirschenbaum, "A Comprehensive Model for Values Education and Moral Education," *Phi Delta Kappan* 73, no. 10 (June 1992): 771–776.

29. Barbara Benham Tye and Kenneth Tye, *Global Education: A Study of School Change* (Albany: State University of New York Press, 1992) pp. 1–13.

30. Andrew F. Smith, "A Brief History of Pre-collegiate Global and International Studies Education," in John Fonte and Andre Ryerson, *Education for America's Role in World Affairs* (New York: University Press of America, 1994), p. 15.

31. Jane McLane, "From Seattle to Novosibirsk: A 1st Grade Exchange," *Educational Leadership* 48, no. 7 (April 1991): 58–60.

32. John LeBaron and Rebecca Warshawsky, "Satellite Teleconferencing between Massachusetts and Germany," *Educational Leadership* 48, no. 7 (April 1991): 61–64.

33. Meg Little Warren, "Educating for Global Citizenship Through Children's Art," *Educational Leadership* 48, no. 7 (April 1991): 53–57.

34. William Kniep, "Global Education as School Reform," *Educational Leadership* 47, no. 1 (September 1989): 45.

35. "Live and Learn," *Harper's Bazaar* 127 (September 1994): 268–270.

36. P. M. Lines, "Home Schooling," *Eric Digest* 95 (1995): 1–3; J. Natale, "Home, But Not Alone," *The American School Board Journal* 182, no. 7: 34–36; Home School Legal Defense Association, *Answers to Commonly Asked Questions About Home Schooling,* 1996, available from Home School Legal Defense Association, P.O. Box 159, Paeonian Springs, VA 22129.

37. M. Mayberry, "Characteristics and Attitudes of Families Who Home School," *Education and Urban Society* 21, 1988, pp. 32–41; M. Mayberry, "Home-based Education in the United States: Demographics, Motivations, and Educational Implications," *Educational Review* 41, no. 2 (1989): 171–180.

38. J. A. Van Galen, "Schooling in Private: A Study of Home Education," doctoral dissertation, University of North Carolina, Chapel Hill, 1986.

39. Nancy Gibbs, *Time,* October 31, 1994, pp. 62–63.

40. "Home-Taught Students Miss School Activities," *The Washington Post,* November 26, 1995, pp. B-1, B-5; Chris Jeub, "Why Parents Choose Home Schooling," *Educational Leadership* 52, no. 1 (September 1994): 50–52.

41. Gary Knowles, James A. Muchmore, and Holly W. Spaulding, "Home Education as an Alternative to Institutionalized Education," *The Education Forum* 58 (Spring 1994): 238–243.

42. "Charter 'Profit': Will Michigan Heap Money on an Electronic Charter School?" *The American School Board Journal* 181, no. 9 (September 1994): 27–28; "The Dawn of Home Schooling," *Newsweek* 124 (October 10, 1994): 67.

43. Lyn Nell Hancock, "The Haves and the Have-Nots," *Newsweek,* February 27, 1995, pp. 50–53.

44. Emily Nye, "Computers and Gender: Noticing What Perpetuates Inequality," *English Journal* 80, no. 3 (March 1991): 94–95; see also John Lipkin and David Sadker, "Sex Bias in Mathematics, Computer Science and Technology: Report Card 3" (Washington, DC: Mid-Atlantic Center for Sex Equity, American University, 1984);

Thomas Gilman, "Changes in Public Education: A Technological Perspective," series no. 1 (Eugene, OR: ERIC Clearinghouse on Educational Management, 1989).

45. Fiske, *Smart Schools, Smart Kids,* p. 147.

46. David C. Dwyer, Cathy Ringstaff, and Judy H. Sandholtz, "Changes in Teachers' Beliefs and Practices in Technology-Rich Classrooms," *Educational Leadership* 48, no. 8 (May 1991): 45–52.

47. Jeff Meade, "Tuning In, Logging On," *Teacher* 2, no. 4 (January 1991): 30–31.

48. Bruce Watson, "The Wired Classroom: American Education Goes On-Line," *Phi Delta Kappan* 72, no. 2 (October 1990): 109–112.

49. Lisa Wolcott, Debra Ladestro, and Sharon Williams, "Something for Everyone," *Teacher* 2, no. 4 (January 1991): 40–43.

50. Carla Schutte, "Going Global," *Electronic School,* February 1995, pp. A39–A40; Elaine K. Bailey and Morton Cotlar, "Teaching Via the Internet," *Communication Education* 43 (April 1994): 184–193; Carol S. Holzberg, "Technology in Special Education," *Technology and Learning* 15 (February 1995): 18–20+.

51. David C. Berliner and Bruce J. Biddle, *The Manufactured Crisis* (Reading, MA: Addison-Wesley, 1995), p. 146.

52. Lapointe quoted in Gerald W. Bracey, "The Second Bracey Report on the Condition of Public Education," *Phi Delta Kappan,* October 1992, pp. 104–117, cited in Berliner and Biddle, *The Manufactured Crisis,* p. 54.

53. Gerald W. Bracey, "U.S. Students: Better Than Ever," *The Washington Post,* December 22, 1995, p. A-9; Robert J. Samuelson, "Three Cheers for Schools," *Newsweek,* December 4, 1995, p. 61; see also Berliner and Biddle, *The Manufactured Crisis,* pp. 13–64.

54. Kathryn McNerney assisted with the revision of this chapter.

Appendix 1

OBSERVATION MANUAL

*M*any education courses now require or recommend field observation activities. This manual will help you sharpen and focus your field observation skills. Accurate data collection and thoughtful reflection about what you see can give you new insights into life in the classroom and the process of teaching.

UNITS

General Observation Guidelines

While the field experience is an integral part of virtually all teacher preparation programs, the specific design and approach of school observation varies greatly. In some teacher education programs, the field experience is a component of the introduction to teaching course or the foundations of education course; in others, it is a separate course. And, in still others, it has become a continuous strand that serves to link most, if not all, education courses.

Whatever approach your college or university provides, this experience, if used well, can offer rich insight into the real world of teaching and schools and can help answer your concerns and questions about teaching as a career. Unfortunately, poorly structured school visits quickly deteriorate into a vacuous waste of time. This manual provides the structure and focus to ensure accurate observation and thoughtful reflection about the information you gather. But that is only half—perhaps less than half—of the formula needed for successful school observation. The other central ingredient is you. How you approach the experience, and what you do or do not do with the information you gather, ultimately will determine how well your field experience will work for you.

John Dewey, perhaps America's most famous educator, wrote extensively about *reflective thinking,* which he defined as avoiding "routine" and "impulsive" behaviors in favor of taking the time to give "serious . . . consideration" to our actions. According to Dewey, the intelligent person thinks before he or she acts, and action becomes deliberate and intentional. If you want to glean knowledge and insight from your field experience, your observations must be careful, analytical, and deliberate. Once your observations have been made, you will need to consider carefully what you have seen before you formulate conclusions about life in schools.

The reflective field experience structured in this manual will encourage you not only to see what schools do but also to consider what they might do differently. As a teacher, you may wish to adopt teaching styles and procedures that you observe, but you should also begin to devise new teaching ideas. Just visiting schools is no guarantee of a worthwhile experience; however, thinking reflectively about what you have observed can help you grow personally and professionally. Once you begin this reflective process, it should continue throughout your professional preparation and your teaching career.

This manual includes several strategies that will help you give careful reflection to your field experience. In this unit, you are asked to consider your goals and concerns before beginning your field experience. Then, general techniques and strategies for observation are outlined. Units 2 through 5 focus on four areas of the schooling experience that apply to all the subjects and grade levels you might be exploring. These areas are the setting (school and community), the teacher, the student, and the curriculum. For each of these areas, you are provided with specific directions and activities to help you gather objective data. Unit 6 gives you strategies to assess the effectiveness of schools you might visit. In Unit 7, a series of questions and activities encourages you to think about what you have seen and how you can use that information in planning for your own career in education. These activities and questions are intended to help develop the reflective thinking essential to professionalism as a teacher.

Identifying Your Goals and Concerns

Each student approaches the field experience with a unique personal history and set of expectations. It is useful to think about and prioritize these perceptions and concerns before you begin. Take a minute and, on a separate sheet of paper or in your journal or notebook, write a brief list of your goals as you prepare for your field experience. In short, what information and insight do you want to get out of your field experience? After you have written down your goals, consider the following questions.

Are your goals clear or do you need to give them more thought? Are some of these goals more important than others? (You may want to rank them in order of priority.) Do your goals fall into one or two broad categories, or are they more diverse? As indicated previously, this manual structures your field experiences into several categories: the setting, the teacher, the student, and the curriculum. Some field activities are related to the research on effective schools. Have you considered all these areas in your goals—or, like most beginning teachers, have you omitted one or more? Which areas have you omitted? Why? Since these are the key areas your field experience should emphasize, take a few moments before you arrive at your observation site and consider what you want to learn about the following components.

> *Setting.* While setting can be interpreted very broadly, for purposes of this field experience you are asked to focus on the physical and social environment of the community, the school, and the classroom. This area includes questions such as the following: What is the socioeconomic status of the community? What are the community's values concerning education generally and the schools in particular? Are parents involved in the schools? What is the academic and social culture of the school? What is important in this community and in this school? How would you describe the physical environment of the community, the school, and the classroom? How are the classrooms organized to promote learning?
>
> Identify those aspects of the *setting* you would like to emphasize, and take this opportunity to record them.
>
> *Teaching.* The area of teaching includes topics such as the following: Why do people enter teaching? What do they like about teaching? Why do people leave teaching? What are the responsibilities of teachers? How do you become an effective teacher? What successful teaching skills are used in this school? What needs to be improved? Do I like teaching? Am I good at it? How can I apply what I learn in my education courses to my own teaching?
>
> What aspects of *teaching* would you like to focus on in your field experience? List them on a sheet of paper, in your field observation notebook, or in your journal. You will need to reconsider them at the end of your experience.
>
> *Students.* As you prepare for a teaching career, your concerns and interests are naturally focused on the teaching aspect of the classroom and whether you will like teaching and be good at it. But teaching does not exist in isolation; key to the context of teaching are the students. Who are the learners and what are their interests? What motivates students to learn? What are the barriers? How can work be individualized?

How can discipline problems be handled? Avoided? Which age group and which type of students do you prefer to work with?

These and other issues concerning learners provide a critical dimension in teaching success. Take a moment to consider and record *student*-related questions you would like to address during your field experience.

Curriculum. Students spend approximately 90 percent of their academic time involved in reading textbooks and other curricular materials. Curricular issues that could be addressed in the field experience include the following: What is taught in your school? Is breadth or depth emphasized? Are students responsible for problem solving and critical thinking? Or is drill and rote memorization emphasized? Is adequate time provided for each subject? Is there bias in the curriculum? Which topics are emphasized? Omitted? Is the curriculum interesting and motivating? What is the school's policy concerning a core curriculum? Has your college work prepared you to teach the curriculum? How might you present the curriculum differently?

After considering these and other *curricular* questions, indicate in your notebook or other appropriate place those curricular issues you would like to explore more fully during your school observation.

Effective Schools. While Gertrude Stein could write "A rose is a rose is a rose," she might hesitate before extending this notion to schools. Schools differ dramatically. Some schools glisten with modern equipment and the latest facilities while others are incredibly old, serving students since the 1800s. Beyond these obvious differences, schools also differ in their effectiveness. Research suggests that the quality of school leadership, a sense of physical safety, and a clear school mission are several factors related to overall effectiveness. How does the school you are visiting measure up in these areas? Do teachers monitor student progress? Do they hold high expectations for their students? These are additional factors related to school effectiveness. The activities in this section will help you to focus on school effectiveness characteristics and to realize that teachers do not work in insulated classroom environments.

This manual will investigate each of these areas, providing you with activities to ensure that you get the most out of your field experience. Working with your instructor and colleagues, you may want to develop and use other data collection activities as well. In Unit 7, you will return to your initial perceptions and goals, and by reflecting on these, assess how your experience has changed or confirmed your interests. Before you begin, here are some useful observation strategies for you to keep in mind.

Learning How to Observe

Students preparing to be teachers suffer from the handicap of too much familiarity with school. Consequently, they may block out valid and useful insights. Thousands of hours spent behind students' desks inure many to the subtle and not-so-subtle aspects of schooling in the United States. In order to become an effective teacher, you need to erase this past conditioning and reawaken yourself to the realities of school and classroom life. The development of observation skills will not only sensitize you to these realities but will enable you to compare and contrast the effectiveness of the various instructional and management practices that teachers and administrators employ in dealing with them.

> I sat in class for days wondering what there was to observe. Teachers taught, reprimanded, rewarded while pupils sat at desks squirming, whispering, reading, writing, staring into space, as they had in my own grade school experience, in my practice teaching in a teacher training program, and in the two years of public school teaching I had done before World War II.[1]

So wrote George Spindler, the researcher who is credited with developing educational anthropology as a legitimate field of scholarship. His problem was one that faces any serious observer in an environment that is too familiar. Everything seems trivial and obvious. As Margaret Mead said, "If a fish were to become an anthropologist, the last thing that it would discover would be the water."[2]

Spindler became so frustrated with viewing the commonplace that he almost gave up his research. Education majors who are asked to observe in local elementary and secondary schools face similar problems. Because they find the environment as comfortable and everyday as a worn shoe, they often miss subtle incidents and the underlying significance of events.

Fortunately, Spindler did not give up school-based observations. He interviewed the target teacher he was observing, as well as supervisors and students. He collected autobiographical and psychological information from the teacher, analyzed the teacher's evaluations of his students, and conducted sociograms (i.e., recording popular and isolated students, as well as cliques) to determine students' attitudes toward one another. As a result of careful data collection, Spindler discovered that the target teacher, who at casual glance seemed to treat all students similarly, actually favored white middle- and upper-class students. The teacher was completely unaware of this differential treatment, but the students were readily able to identify the teacher's favorites. If the teacher had known how to observe subtle classroom dynamics, he would have been aware of this disability. Without the skills of observation, interpretation, and reflection, the teacher remained ignorant of important elements of the classroom social structure.[3]

Classrooms and schools are complex intellectual, social, personal, and physical environments where the average teacher has more than 1,000 interactions a day, each with different levels and nuances of meaning. In this multifaceted, fast-paced, confusing culture called *school,* it is all too easy to miss much of what you think you "see." But if you immerse yourself in this culture, observe and record your experiences systematically, and then reflect on and interpret what you have seen, you can gain greater insight into how and why teachers and students behave the way they do.

There are many sources for collecting objective data. These include direct observation; document analysis of school mission statements, discipline codes, textbooks, and lesson plans; and interviews with key participants, such as teachers, students, administrators, and parents. Observation followed by reflection will provide crucial data about the realities, frustrations, and rewards of classroom life—information that will help you become a better teacher.

Observation Techniques

This manual provides you with a variety of **observation techniques** to collect information. You and your instructor may determine to use only a few of these methods—or all six.

Interviewing

Depending on the role they play in school, various participants may have different interpretations of and opinions about events. For example, a student's feelings about a pep rally may differ from those of the school principal. Interviews are an excellent method for bringing to light these different perspectives and points of view. Your interviewing protocol may consist of very specific questions ("How many years have you taught in this school?") or questions that are broad and open-ended ("How does this school differ from other elementary schools where you have taught?").

Asking questions that draw the subject out is a challenging skill to master. For example, during an interview you may ask, "Do you enjoy teaching?" If you get a simple "yes" or "yes" or "no," you will need to ask follow-up, or probing, questions to get more detailed information. Assuring the interviewee that answers will be kept confidential may be helpful in obtaining frank and comprehensive responses.

Whenever possible, take notes during the interview, perhaps just jotting down key phrases if you do not have time to record complete sentences. Later you may find it difficult to remember exactly what the interviewee said, or you may inadvertently distort or rephrase what was said to fit your own preconceived notions of people and events. Although most of us like to think we are completely objective, our past experiences and our perspectives may interfere with clear vision.

Questionnaires

Interviews are a good strategy for gathering in-depth information, but time constraints will limit the number of people you can reach. Questionnaires provide the opportunity to gather information from a much larger sample of faculty, staff, or students. You will need to decide what you want to ask and how you want participants to respond. For example, you can ask an open-ended question:

> How would you describe the audiovisual equipment in this
> school? _____

Or you might want to structure your questions so that a particular type of response is generated:

> Audiovisual equipment is used frequently.
> Agree Strongly ____ Agree ____ Disagree ____ Disagree Strongly ____

You will also need to decide whether you wish respondents to identify themselves or whether questionnaires should be anonymous. Although questionnaires are not stressed in the data collection activities in this manual, they are a good source of information. If you are interested in this method of data collection, discuss how to develop and distribute questionnaires with your course instructor.

Observation Data

A much-utilized technique for capturing, comparing, and analyzing human behavior of all kinds is the *structured observation system.* Community life, school activities, and classroom behaviors can be recorded and evaluated through a coherent set of questions or more sophisticated coding techniques. In fact, a number of these structured observation systems were originally designed for educational research, but they have now found their way into everyday school practice. These instruments measure everything from the kinds of questions teachers ask to the nature of peer-group interaction. One of the earlier and more influential observation instruments is the Flanders Interaction Analysis, which is summarized briefly in Figure 1.

Typically, standardized observation instruments are developed by researchers over an extended period of time, and sometimes observers require training so that they can use these tools accurately and reliably. Several books listed at the end of this manual contain collections of different standardized observation instruments. Your instructor will indicate whether you should use any of these instruments during your observations and whether training is necessary for accurate and reliable data collection using these tools.

Document Analysis

By analyzing the documents, written records, and other materials of classroom and school, you can gain important information about how the school works and what is emphasized. For example, does your school have a philosophy or mission statement in which goals are set forward? What policies govern staff and student behavior? Is there a disciplinary policy for students, and are they aware of it? What kinds of textbooks are used, and do teachers supplement texts with additional materials? What kind of report card or evaluation system is in use? What do newspapers and yearbooks tell you about the social system of the school? The written records of the school should provide an important complement to the data you collect from observing and interviewing.

Note Taking

Note taking, a technique borrowed from cultural anthropologists, is one of the most commonly used methods for gathering data. When you first begin observing and taking notes on what you see, you may try to record everything. But in the hectic, multifaceted school and classroom environment, you will soon discover that it is impossible to capture accurately so many different stimuli at one time. You will need to narrow your focus and target specific aspects of the environment for your data collection and note-taking activities. For example, you may choose to focus on how curriculum is developed or the nature of leadership exerted by the principal. You may target your activities to record the frequency and quality of teacher questions or the way discipline is handled in the school. In order to select the most important information, you will need to come into the environment with a series of *focusing questions.*

FIGURE 1
Flanders Interaction Analysis: An Early and Influential Coding System

Originally developed as a research tool, Flanders Interaction Analysis became a widely used coding system to analyze and improve teaching skills. This observation system was designed to categorize the type and quantity of verbal dialogue in the classroom and to plot the information on a matrix so that it could be analyzed. The result gave a picture of who was talking in a classroom and the kind of talking that was taking place.

As a result of research with his coding instrument, Flanders uncovered the **two-thirds rule:** About two-thirds of classroom time is devoted to talking. About two-thirds of this time the person talking is the teacher, and two-thirds of the teacher's talk is "direct" (that is, lecturing, giving directions, and controlling students). The two-thirds rule is actually three related two-thirds rules and serves to substantiate that, typically, teachers verbally dominate classrooms.

Some people feel that Flanders' work has underscored the fact that a teacher's verbal domination of the classroom conditions students to become passive and to be dependent on the teacher. It is claimed that this dependency has an adverse effect on student attitudes toward school and student performance in school. Interestingly, Flanders found that when teachers are trained in his observation technique and become aware of the importance of language in the classroom, their verbal monopoly decreases.

To use the Flanders Interaction Analysis, one codes the verbal interaction in 1 of 10 categories, plots the coded data onto a matrix, and analyzes the matrix. Following are the 10 categories in the Flanders Interaction Analysis Coding Instrument.

Summary of Categories for Interaction Analysis

Indirect Teacher Talk

1. *Accepts feeling*
   Acknowledges student-expressed emotions (feelings) in a nonthreatening manner
2. *Praises or encourages*
   Provides positive reinforcement of student contributions
3. *Accepts or uses ideas of students*
   Clarifies, develops, or refers to student contribution, often nonevaluatively
4. *Asks questions*
   Solicits information or opinion (not rhetorically)

Direct Teacher Talk

5. *Lectures*
   Presents information, opinion, or orientation; perhaps includes rhetorical questions
6. *Gives directions*
   Supplies direction or suggestion with which a student is expected to comply
7. *Criticizes or justifies authority*
   Offers negative evaluation of student contributions or places emphasis on teacher's authoritative position

Student Talk

8. *Student talk—response*
   Gives a response to the teacher's question, usually a predictable answer
9. *Student talk—initiation*
   Initiates a response that is unpredictable or creative in content
10. *Silence or confusion*
    Leaves periods of silence or inaudible verbalization lasting more than 3 seconds

Several such focusing questions are included in the data collection activities in the next section; or you may wish to work with your peers and instructor on developing your own focusing questions. These will guide your observations and interviews and help you organize the field notes you record.

It is wise to keep your notes in a looseleaf notebook (such as the one you may have already begun using to record your observation goals and priorities). This gives you the advantage of being able to move and shift your notes around into different organizational formats. As you spend more time in field observation and collect increasing amounts of data, this ability to reorganize notes without losing them will be extremely helpful.

Sometimes it is impossible to take notes during observations and interviews. There may not be time, or you may sense that the interviewee will "clam up" if you whip out your notepad and pencil. In cases such as these, you will need to summarize your notes later. Whether you take notes during observations and interviews or make summary observations, you should record when and where each data collection activity took place. The more detailed dialogue and clearly defined images you include in your notes, the more useful they will be. Thorough and complete notes, filled with anecdotes and details, are called "rich data" and will help you reach the most insightful interpretations of events and behavior.

Logs and Journals

Many teacher education programs require or recommend that you maintain a log or journal during your field experience. Some programs specify a particular format, while others allow a more open-ended approach. In either case, the log or journal is intended to help you document and reflect on your observations. As you write your account, you will be giving thought both to the field experience and to its impact on you. Over time, you will detect growth and possibly significant change in what you believe about teaching and schools. When your field experience is completed, you will have a written account of your activities and changing views during this formative period of your professional preparation.

In your log, you should also describe incidents observed or activities participated in as objectively as possible. This log should be kept on a daily basis, because time erases memories and feelings. Each day your log should include one or two events that are particularly meaningful to you. An event may be significant because it impresses you (for example, a terrific teaching technique), because it is educationally important (such as a successful strategy for classroom management), because it disturbs you (for example, a poorly executed activity, a negative interaction you have), or because it challenges or confirms your beliefs and ideas. These events, whether positive or negative, should be selected and described because they are critical incidents for learning. The descriptions should be objective and detailed. Later you should set time aside, mull them over, and interpret what you learned. This part of the log is akin to a professional diary. If you have trouble analyzing any of these significant events, your instructor or other students may be able to assist. Identifying what events are most significant to you is a key step both in keeping a journal and developing a reflective and professional approach to teaching. If your field experience does not have a specific log or journal format, here is one that you may find useful:

Sample Log Format

Location: _____ Name: _____

Date: _____

Time: _____ Activities: _____

_____	_____
_____	_____
_____	_____
_____	_____
_____	_____
_____	_____
_____	_____
_____	_____
_____	_____
_____	_____
_____	_____

Significant event: _____

Description:

Analysis:

Other significant events, if appropriate:

_____

In the log, as well as in your observation activities, it is useful to distinguish between description and judgment. It is also helpful to recognize some basic rules for observing. The next two sections focus on these issues.

Becoming Accepted as an Observer

A principal once told a story of an observer who became so involved in a teacher's lesson that he was soon raising his hand, responding to the teacher's questions, inserting personal anecdotes, and monopolizing classroom interaction. By the end of the class, the observer and the teacher were engaged in an animated dialogue, and the students had become passive onlookers. The observer had completely disrupted the classroom activities he was there to study. Such a complete role reversal is uncommon, but the following guidelines are offered as an antidote to the potentially disruptive effect posed by any classroom observer.

As an observer, you can generally avoid such direct verbal involvement as was described above, but the more subtle challenge is to avoid nonverbal intrusion. What do you do when children engage you in nonverbal conversation consisting only of eye contact and facial expressions? Do you smile back, wink, and establish an unspoken kinship? Or, for fear of disturbing the class routine, do you ignore the students and possibly alienate them?

Although hard-and-fast rules are difficult to come by, it is clear that your presence in the classroom is not intended either to win friends and influence people or to alienate others. You must learn to accept students' nonverbal messages yet avoid prolonging these interactions. Ignoring all eye contact can be just as disruptive as encouraging such contact can be. With experience, you will be able to accept these subtle forms of communication without amplifying them. In this way, you can demonstrate that, although you are not insensitive to the interest and curiosity of students, your purpose in the classroom is to observe, not to alter, classroom life.

A primary goal is to observe the most and intrude the least. For most observations, this means positioning yourself in the back of the room, where you are behind the students but have a clear view of the teacher. It is also useful to conduct some observations from the side of the room, so that you can see the children's faces and nonverbal cues. The expressions, comments, and activities of the students will give valuable insights about student-teacher relationships and the nature of classroom life. In some cases, you may have to change your location while a lesson is in progress (for example, moving among various groups of students to observe their activities). Whatever your location, it is important to avoid coming between people who wish to communicate.

To some extent, our society consists of a series of minisocieties, each with its values and rules of order. Schools are examples of such minisocieties, with each level (elementary, secondary, college) having its own unique set of norms. As an observer in schools, you will be judged by students and staff alike on the basis of their norms, not on the basis of those you have become accustomed to in college. You will probably be expected to dress rather formally, to arrive early or notify the school if you will be late, and to conform to the school's rules and regulations. Your college supervisor will probably inform you of the prevailing norms.

Confidentiality of Records

As you observe and collect data, you must make certain that your actions do not invade the privacy of or, in any other way harm, those you are observing. Most schools require anonymity in your observations and confidentiality in the data you collect. Individual teachers, students, or others should not risk inconvenience, embarrassment, or harm as a result of your field experience.

Each school has its own norms and rules regarding what observers can and cannot do. Some require a signed release from school officials and/or from students (informed consent), while others are less formal. You should share your observation plan and data-gathering activities with your instructor to make certain that you are following the appropriate procedures. Your cooperating teacher and/or the principal in the school where you will be observing may also need to be informed. In cases where permission is not granted, you will need to find another setting.

All data that you collect should remain absolutely confidential. The importance of this point cannot be stressed too much. You may wish to use code names or numbers for people you describe, and you should never discuss observations with any members of the school community. For example, if you tell teachers some information you have learned about students, you run the risk of losing trust and credibility and possibly harming some member of the school community. Your records should be stored away from the field school, in a location that is both safe and private. In this way you can ensure that the confidentiality of your subjects will be protected.

Distinguishing between Description and Interpretation

As you collect data, your information should be recorded—at least initially—in a descriptive rather than a judgmental manner. As a student, your observations about school were probably casual, resulting in the formation of opinions, such as Teacher A is "interesting," School B is "the pits," or geometry is "hard." These interpretations, although colorful and useful, are personal in nature and would have been likely to evoke disagreement from some of your fellow students.

A better approach for an observer is first to gather descriptive data regarding some aspect of school or classroom life, interpret the data, and, when appropriate, form conclusions and judgments. Rather than saying that Teacher A is "good" (an interpretation), you might count the number of questions Teacher A asks, or the amount of time Teacher A spends helping students, or even the number of advanced degrees Teacher A holds. All these findings provide objective, descriptive data. Although some of your descriptive data may not be useful, other notes may be crucial to your final interpretations and insights.

Data collection activities presented in this manual frequently ask you to record descriptive details and, after reflection, to interpret the information. The following examples will help you distinguish between description and interpretation:

Description:	The teacher asked 23 questions in 7 minutes.
Interpretation:	The teacher asked too many questions.
Description:	The teacher scolded Henry 10 times during the morning.
Interpretation:	The teacher picked on Henry.
Description:	The student yawned twice and spent 8 minutes looking out the window.
Interpretation:	The student was bored.
Description:	The building was constructed in 1940.
Interpretation:	The building is old.
Description:	This school consists of 121 elementary school classrooms.
Interpretation:	The school is too big.
Description:	Twenty-five out of 27 students volunteered answers during math class.
Interpretation:	The students are interested in math.

This ability to separate fact from opinion is a crucial skill that can prevent you from jumping to erroneous conclusions. Most of us like to think that "seeing is believing," but sometimes "believing may be seeing." In other words, each of us brings to any observation a set of biases and perspectives through which events may be colored or distorted. The way to guard against reaching inaccurate interpretations is first to make a careful record of what you see. Judgmental comments can also be made, but they should be kept separate from your descriptive observations. Some observers insert interpretations and questions into their records, but they separate them from their descriptive notes with parentheses.

Interpreting the Data

After you have collected your data, you will need to interpret and make sense of a vast amount of information. To do this, it will be helpful to look for words, patterns, phrases, and topics that keep recurring in your records. If competency testing is being used in your school, for example, you may find that the teachers talk about these exit exams in many classes and spend a great deal of time preparing students for them. After analyzing your notes from patterns, you may reach the conclusion that competency testing is exerting too great an influence on what is taught. As you form impressions and interpretations, it is a good idea to check these with participants in the environment. For example, you might ask the teachers: "I've noticed that your students will take competency exams this year. What influences do you think these exams have in the school?" You can also check your interpretations by searching for instances of contrary behavior. In this hypothetical situation, say, you have found that many teachers spend a great deal of time teaching for the competency tests. However, it is also important to look for counterinstances, teachers who devote little time or attention to the competency tests. If you find several teachers in this category, your initial impressions may not be accurate. After all your notes have been recorded and analyzed, the final product is often an ethnographic report or case study. How insightful your report is will depend on the richness of detail in your notes and how thoughtfully you have interpreted the data. Typically, an ethnographic report comprises two sections: (1) a descriptive summary of the data you observed and (2) an interpretation or evaluation section that sets forth your conclusions. Your instructor can help you determine the particular form your final report should take.

In Units 2 to 7, you will find 31 specific data collection activities that can help you sort through the fast-paced and multilayered climate in schools and classrooms in order to understand the nature of learning and the process of teaching. Study these data collection activities carefully, and, with your instructor, determine which ones will be most helpful for you to use at your observation site.

UNIT 2 | Data Collection Activities: The Setting

No student or teacher functions in isolation. As you think about your future life in the classroom, you must also consider the general community, the school building, and even the physical environment of the classroom. Students arrive at school after years of being taught the unofficial curriculum of parents, friends, and neighbors; their previously learned values and skills can help or hinder their efforts in the classroom. Understanding community attitudes and actions can be pivotal to enhancing your teaching effectiveness, as well as the classroom performance of your students. The physical qualities of the school building and the quantity and quality of classroom resources also will shape your life in the classroom. This unit provides strategies for analyzing the school and community setting and classroom milieu.

The Community

Activity 1: Neighborhood Visit   Take a walk through the neighborhood around the school where you are doing your field experience. Stop by a restaurant or store and listen to the conversations. If you feel comfortable, join in. See if you can find out the community's values. What goals and issues are important to community members? If you can, guide the conversation toward education in general and the school system in particular. (You may want to tell people you will be working in the school.) But whether or not you are able to engage in these conversations, you should observe and describe the community. The following categories may be useful in recording your observations.

Guidelines: Neighborhood Visit

Housing (type, economic levels, physical condition, other)
Business (type, condition, other)
Economic base (where people work, approximate income level, other)
Demographics (national, racial, and religious backgrounds; family size; young or older community; other)
Attitudes and values (political and social values of the community, attitudes toward the schools and education, other)

Activity 2: Community Meeting   In the local community or school system newspaper, you can often find announcements for public meetings. The school can also tell you when various organizations, such as the parents' association, meet. Choose one or two of these groups (school-related might be best) and attend one or more meetings. Try to gauge the community's interests and values from this experience. Here are some categories into which you might organize your thoughts:

Guidelines: Community Meeting

Agenda (What topics or issues appear important?)
Attendance (Is there a large, moderate, or small turnout?)
Comments (Take notes on the meeting. What issues emerge as concerns of the group?)
Values and attitudes (Can you determine the group's view of education or the school system? Are these participants likely to support educational efforts in the community?)

Activity 3: Local Newspaper   Most communities have a local newspaper or are covered in a section of a large-circulation newspaper that focuses on community affairs. If your school library or the public library carries back issues of these publications, read those for the last several months. In addition, keep up with local news coverage for that community. From your analysis of the news stories, editorials, advertisements, and letters to the editor, how would you answer the following?

Guidelines: Local Newspaper

What are the major community concerns?

What are the school's major projects? Are there any school-community partnerships to accomplish education-related goals?

Which aspect of school life receives the most coverage (athletics, academics, cultural activities, and so on)?

How does the community react to standardized test scores, financial needs, new facilities, and other educational concerns?

Analysis and Synthesis: The Community

1. If you were able to accomplish two or all three of these activities, you might want to compare your findings. Do they complement each other, or do they conflict? How do you explain any contradictions? Do you think that you have an adequate picture of the community, or do you need more information?

2. If you were able to develop a narrative about this community, what would be the major points of your description? Would you like to live in this community?

3. Based on the information you have so far, predict what life in this community's schools would be like. What are the likely goals and behavior norms? What do you suppose faculty morale is like?

4. As a teacher in this community, what educational projects will most likely generate community support? What activities is the public less likely to support—or likely to oppose?

5. Complete the following: "As a result of my experience observing this community, I have learned that . . ."

The School

Winston Churchill once pointed out that, although people initially shape buildings, over the long haul the buildings shape the people. For example, an ultramodern building of glass, concrete, and steel shapes the attitudes and behavior of its inhabitants in quite a different manner than does a 100-year-old Victorian edifice of wood and stone. Open spaces with brightly colored walls affect people differently than do buildings with small rooms painted "never-can-tell-whether-it's-dirty-or-clean" institutional yellow-grayish brown. The physical structure of buildings helps shape the feelings people have about their work, and schools vary greatly in their physical structure.

Historically, researchers have not spent much time studying the physical environment of schools. Within recent years, however, *proxemics*—the study of the relationship between physical space and human behavior—has received increasing attention. For example, studies show that discussion is improved when students sit in a circle rather than in rows, a clear demonstration of the power of space over behavior. During the late 1960s and early 1970s, the importance of proxemics could be seen in the rise and fall of the open school movement. During that time, in many schools walls were torn down and barriers removed so that a child-centered, flexible, open space was created. The teacher became a facilitator, and the emphasis was on educating the student as an individual rather than on large-group instruction.

In creating these child-centered classrooms where students had the freedom to take charge of their own learning, insufficient attention was paid to the impact of the physical environment. Noise disrupted learning, and students were distracted by so much activity and interaction around them. While open space created great opportunity for freedom, at the same time it deprived students and teachers of privacy.[4] Today the walls have been erected once again, and open classrooms are an experiment that failed, because the innovation did not give sufficient weight to the importance of the physical environment. The following data collection activities are designed to help you reflect on the nature of a school's environment and its potential effect on students and teachers.

Activity 4: School Physical Environment   Although public schools are social institutions, not all provide bland and sterile environments. Some are, in fact, harsh and cold, but others are vibrant and warm. Some schools look as if they were built to withstand a nuclear attack (or even worse, a student attack), while others resemble country clubs. The physical structure of private schools can also convey messages, from stern military discipline to bucolic charm. What message does the school where you are observing send? Respond to the following questions about the external and internal school environment.

Guidelines: School Physical Environment

External. As you approach the building:

How are the school grounds arranged (lawns, play areas, parking lots, concrete school yards, locked fences, and so on)?

Describe the outer structure of the building. Note the size and shape; construction material; windows; architectural aspects; the inclusion of any bars, locks, or other restrictive devices; age; and any unique aesthetic features.

Does the building appear to be part of the community or isolated from it? Provide a rationale for your answer.

Do students have sufficient space for recess and for physical and athletic activities? Do all students have equal access to this space? Be specific in your responses.

Internal. As you enter the building:

Do you have to circle the building in order to find an open door, or are all of the doors to the school unlocked?

What do you see when you first enter the building? Are there signs to guide you to offices and classrooms?

What are the walls made of (plaster, tile, or another material)? What colors are the walls? Are they decorated? List and describe the kinds of bulletin boards or exhibits displayed.

How old is the school building? How did you find out? Does the school show signs of deterioration? Have efforts been made to keep the school building in good condition?

Does the school serve a hot lunch? Are the students provided with a choice of lunch items, or is the same lunch served to everyone? How much does the lunch cost? Is it well-balanced and nutritious?

Does the school have special facilities—gym, music rooms, art rooms, theater? Does the school provide for any special areas of instruction—aesthetic education, new media facilities, special learning laboratories, and so on?

Does the school have a library? How many books are in the library? Is the library centrally located? How are the books arranged and displayed?

Does the school have computers? How many? Where are they located? How do students gain access to them? Do all students seem to have equal access to computers? Are the computers and software up-to-date, or antiquated?

How would you describe the noise level? Are the noises from laughter, disruptive activities, yelling, lecturing, discussion, games, or other sources (describe)?

Activity 5: The Faculty Room A visit to the faculty room can teach you a great deal in a short time about the faculty, how they are treated, and their level of professionalism. Here is an outline to assist you in this activity:

Guidelines: The Faculty Room

Describe the size of the room and its furnishings.

Is coffee available? Food? What kind? Who is responsible for making coffee and bringing in food?

Are the chairs comfortable? Are there desks? Tables? Are they clean? Who is responsible for cleaning the faculty room?

Is there a professional library? What journals are available? Are they recent? How are they displayed? Do faculty read them, or are these magazines ignored?

Are many faculty present? At what time of day is the faculty room most heavily used? Do the faculty talk about topics related to education? Do they discuss the students? What other kinds of conversations take place?

Activity 6: The Principal Interview While the physical characteristics of a building establish the tone, or flavor, of the school, research indicates that the principal is very influential in creating a school's climate. If you have the opportunity to formally interview or informally talk with the principal, here are some questions to guide your discussion.

Guidelines: The Principal Interview

What aspects of the school are you most proud of?

What are the greatest challenges?

How are disciplinary problems handled? How much of a problem is discipline? What are the major discipline infractions?

How would you describe your role and responsibilities?

How would you describe the relationship between the school and the community?

What is your leadership style?

Activity 7: Unobtrusive Measures *Unobtrusive measurement* is a way of assessing a situation without altering it.[5] For example, if you ask students what they think of a school, they may guard their comments and share only part of their real feelings. They do not know you or what you might do with the information. Just by asking such questions, you decrease the accuracy of the information you receive. Obtrusive methods, such as asking questions directly, frequently contaminate the findings.

As a student, you probably experience a similar phenomenon when you take exams. Before answering the questions, you may consider the attitudes and values of the teacher and tailor your responses accordingly. You may try to answer the questions not only correctly but also in a way that pleases the teacher. Have you ever changed the response you gave in order to fit your teacher's expectations? This strategy may improve your grade, but it denies the teacher an accurate insight into your attitudes and perspective.

One famous experiment in unobtrusive measures attempted to determine which exhibit in a museum was attracting the most visitors. An obtrusive measure (direct questioning) had previously indicated that a prestigious work of art was the most popular. However, an examination of the wear and tear on the floors, of the number of fingerprints on the protective glass, and of other unobtrusive data indicated that an incubator with hatching chickens was the most frequently visited exhibit. This contradiction between verbal and nonverbal responses was probably the result of the patrons' belief that visiting a work of art was more intellectually appropriate than watching chickens hatch. In short, the obtrusive interview technique distorted the responses and was therefore less effective than was the unobtrusive measure (that is, assessing the amount of dirt and the wear and tear on carpets and windows).

As these examples illustrate, unobtrusive measures are intentionally indirect in order to avoid contaminating the evidence. In the data collection activity that follows, you will be using unobtrusive procedures. Answer each question with descriptive data. Then think abut the information you have gathered and consider what interpretations or judgments to make.

Guidelines: Unobtrusive Measures

Record the graffiti written on walls, desks, and, especially, in bathrooms.

Examine the exhibits and bulletin boards to determine if they are student-made, teacher-made, or commercially produced. Do they appear to have been there a long time, or do they seem to be changed regularly? As the students pass by, do they stop and look at them?

Ask the librarian if you may look at information about books that were checked out during the last 2 weeks. How many were checked out, and what were they about? Examine some books. Are they in good condition? Are they badly worn? Defaced?

Check the lunchroom after lunch has been served. Are the trash cans filled with normal debris—or uneaten lunches?

Examine the floors for wear and tear. What floor spaces in the school and in the classrooms seem to be most worn? What is located in these areas? What areas of the school seem to be getting the least traffic? What is located in these areas?

Visit the main office and keep a tally of the conversations held by the school secretary. Who is scheduled to meet with the principal? How many of these visitors are students? Faculty? Parents? Others?

Whom does the principal visit? How often does he or she leave the office to interact with teachers and students?

Analysis and Synthesis: The School

1. If you were able to accomplish two, three, or all four of these activities, you might want to compare your findings. Do they reinforce each other, or do they conflict? (That is, do the internal and external school environments send the same message? Do the principal's comments mesh with your observations?) Do you have adequate information, or do you need more data?
2. Identify the salient aspects of the school by carefully choosing three or four adjectives that describe this school.
3. How does your description of the community in the previous section predict or contradict your description of the school?
4. Would you describe the school environment as warm or as institutional? Does it provide an atmosphere of intellectual stimulation for students?
5. How would you describe the faculty room? Is it a refuge? A place for professional growth? A room that is frequently used? How does the faculty room reflect or contrast with the school and community environments? As a teacher in this school, do you think that you would be spending much time in the faculty room? Why or why not?
6. How do the unobtrusive measures confirm or contradict your other observations?
7. Complete the following: "As a result of my experience in this school, I have learned that . . ."

The Classroom

Activity 8: The Classroom   The structure of the school affects the physical structure of the classroom. The wealth and commitment to education reflected by the community are also manifested in most classrooms. But a third element, the teacher's influence, further shapes the classroom and can create a unique learning environment. Once you are assigned to a specific classroom, you should describe and analyze the classroom climate.

Guidelines: The Classroom

What is posted on the classroom walls? Are these exhibits student- or teacher-made, or are they commercially produced? What color are the walls? Are there rugs or carpets on the floor?

How is the furniture arranged? Does it promote individual or group work, cooperative or competitive student learning? Do all seats have a clear view of the board and other main instructional areas?

Does the room contain any specialized resources (computers, library, learning centers, exhibits, and so on)? Are these resources accessible to the students? Are these used? Is the room clean?

Describe the classroom in terms of lighting, acoustics, temperature, internal and external noise, ventilation, and other physical conditions.

Does the classroom have windows? What do the windows face? Are the windows clean? Are they decorated? Are any of the windows broken?

You may want to draw a diagram of the classroom in order to help you in your analysis. Include doors, windows, desks, storage areas, special equipment, sinks, adjoining rooms and halls, resource areas, chalkboards, and the like.

Does your diagram bring to light any important information that was previously neglected in your observation?

Analysis and Synthesis: The Classroom

1. How would you characterize the classroom environment? Select five adjectives that best describe it.
2. In what ways does the classroom environment reflect the community, school, teacher, student, and other influences?
3. What aspects of the classroom do you like? What changes might you make?
4. Is the classroom environment in keeping with other aspects of the school and community, or does it represent a break from the larger environment?
5. How does the classroom represent the teacher's approach to instruction and learning?

UNIT 3   Data Collection Activities: The Teacher

As you approach your field experience, your primary concerns may well be focused on teaching. Will you like it? Will you be good at it? Will the teacher you work with be helpful? What, precisely, is "good teaching"? During your teacher education program, and even during your initial years as a teacher, you will, in all likelihood, continue to focus on questions relating to teachers and teaching.

Activity 9: Teacher Interview   If you are assigned to a specific classroom, conduct an interview with the teacher. Here are some questions to help guide the interview:

Guidelines: Teacher Interview

How long have you been teaching?
What do you enjoy most about teaching?
What is the most difficult aspect of teaching for you?
Is discipline a problem? If so, how do you handle classroom management problems?
How much freedom do you have in deciding what to teach? How to teach?
In what ways do parents and the community participate in school-sponsored educational activities?
What decision-making activities are students involved in?

What advice would you give to a beginning teacher?

What are the most important changes—either good or bad—that you have seen in the teaching profession?

The activities in this unit are based on a structured approach to classroom observation. Taken together, they will help you assess the equity and effectiveness of classroom interaction. All of these activities rely on a similar data collection approach, and the use of a class seating chart.

The research on teacher effectiveness (Chapter 2) discusses the importance of active student interaction in promoting learning and positive attitudes toward school. Unfortunately, teachers do not distribute their attention evenly; rather, they ask many questions of some students and none of others. Teachers may direct questions more to children of one gender or race than to those of another. Attention, questions, and praise may be distributed on the basis of which students the teacher likes, or even on the basis of where the students happen to be seated in the classroom. One very common form of bias is for teachers to direct most of their questions to the better students, because their replies are more likely to be on target and, therefore, satisfying. Whatever the bias, the result is imbalanced classroom interaction, with some students getting an inordinate amount of attention and others being left out of the discussion.[6] Both the quantity and quality of teacher attention have an impact on student achievement.

In the following series of activities, you will need to construct a seating chart. (Perhaps the teacher has one that you can use.) But, unlike the teacher's, your chart should include the name, gender, and, when possible, race of each student. (A sample seating chart is provided in Figure 2.)

To begin, on your seating chart, you will record who the teacher interacts with in the classroom. There are two types of teacher-student interactions to be recorded: (1) those that depend on voluntary responses offered by the students and (2) those responses that are involuntary. Voluntary student responses occur when students:

- Raise their hands to respond
- Call out an answer
- Voluntarily respond to the teacher through any established classroom procedure

Involuntary student responses occur when the teacher initiates or requests a response from a student who has not expressed any desire to communicate. The student, in this case, has not raised a hand, called out an answer, or in any other way indicated an interest in answering. It is because of the teacher's initiative and desire that the student is expected to respond.

Each time a teacher elicits a response, the observer records a V or an N for that student directly on the classroom seating chart. V, representing a volunteer, indicates that the teacher is investing time in a student who is volunteering to respond. N, representing a nonvolunteer, indicates that the teacher is intentionally soliciting a response from a nonvolunteering student. (NOTE: A student calling out or in some other way responding who is not recognized by the teacher does not receive a code. The teacher has ignored this volunteer and not invested any time in this student.)

Teacher's name _____ Date _____

Observer's name _____ Time begin _____

Time end _____

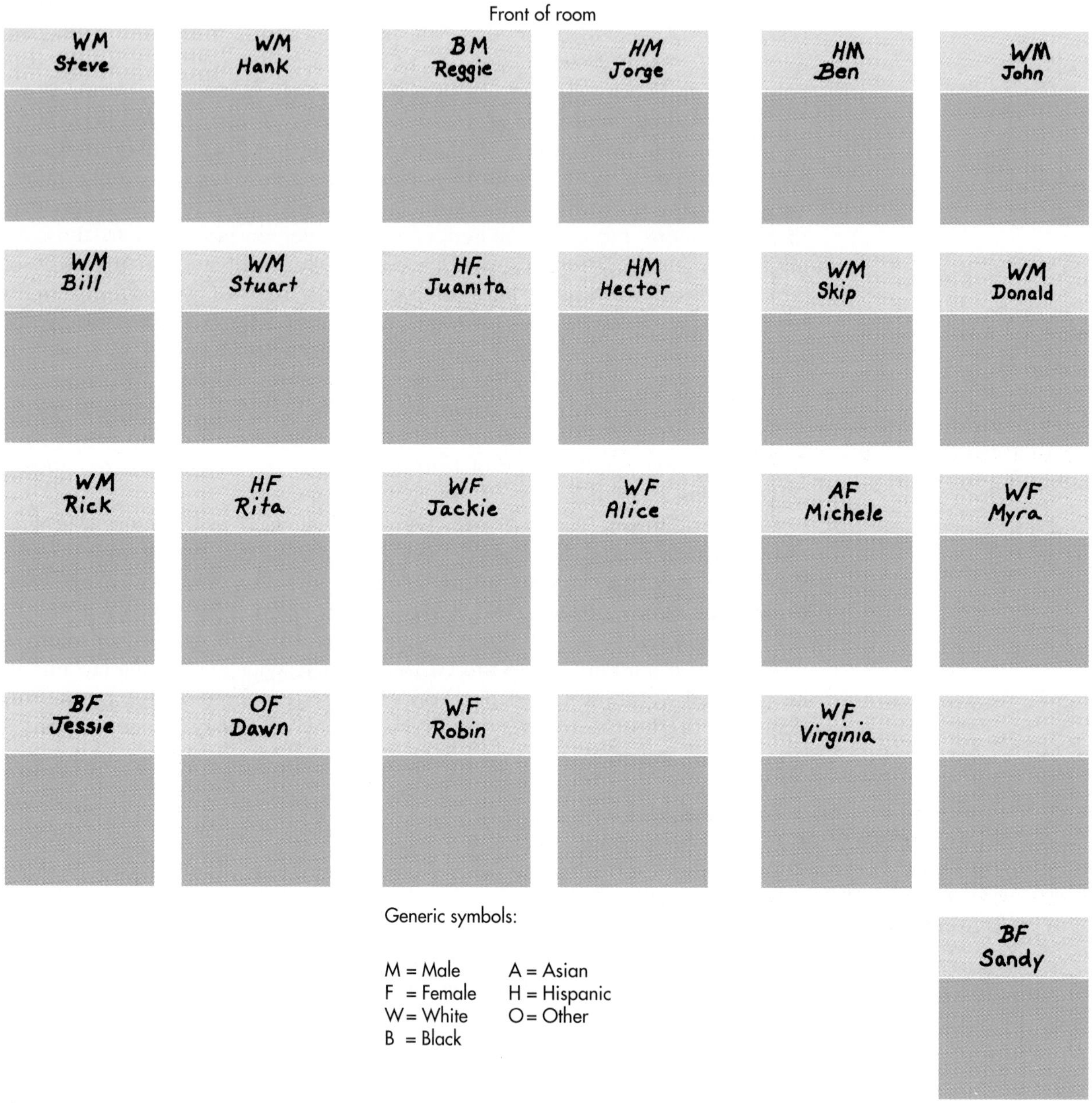

Front of room

WM Steve	WM Hank	BM Reggie	HM Jorge		HM Ben	WM John
WM Bill	WM Stuart	HF Juanita	HM Hector		WM Skip	WM Donald
WM Rick	HF Rita	WF Jackie	WF Alice		AF Michele	WF Myra
BF Jessie	OF Dawn	WF Robin			WF Virginia	

Generic symbols:

M = Male   A = Asian
F = Female   H = Hispanic
W = White   O = Other
B = Black

BF Sandy

FIGURE 2
Sample Seating Chart 1

FIGURE 3
Sample Classroom Dialogue

	Dialogue	*Action*	*Code*
Teacher:	"Who can answer question number three?"	Hank raises hand.	
Teacher:	"Hank."		Mark *V* for Hank.
Hank:	"Twenty-two."		
Teacher:	"No. That's not correct. Maria?"	Maria not volunteering.	Mark *N* for Maria.
Maria:	"Twenty."		
Teacher:	"Correct."		
Steve:	"I thought the answer was 18."	Steve calling out.	
Teacher:	"Let's look at the next question."		No mark. Steve was not recognized.
Teacher:	"Rita?"	Rita not volunteering.	Mark *N* for Rita.
Rita:	(*no response*)		
Teacher:	"Apply the formula, Rita."	Rita still not volunteering.	Mark *N* for Rita.
Rita:	"Oh, I see. Is it seven?"		
Teacher:	"Good. That's it. Why is it seven, Rita?"	Rita not volunteering.	Mark *N* for Rita.
Rita:	"You add the two sides."		
Teacher:	"Terrific."		

Figure 3 is a sample classroom dialogue demonstrating how this coding system works. This description of classroom interaction is coded on the sample seating chart in Figure 4.

Once the observation data have been collected, several activities and levels of analysis are possible. Analyses such as those that follow provide important insights into the distribution of teacher attention.

Activity 10: Classroom Geography   Simply examining the pattern of teacher questions directly from the seating chart provides you with an immediate, visual impression of those areas in the classroom that receive a great deal of interaction, as well as those areas that are interaction-poor. Some students may very well be involved in no interaction at all; others may take part in a number of interactions. Some students may only have one or two N's, while others may have a great number of V's. You may want to circle the areas of the classroom that are rich with teacher attention, as well as those areas that are interaction-poor.

Guidelines: Classroom Geography

Are the more interactive areas closer to the teacher? Is there a pattern you can detect regarding what classroom areas are receiving significant or minimal teacher attention?

Teacher's name _____   Date _____

Observer's name _____   Time begin _____

                                                                    Time end _____

Front of room

WM Steve	WM Hank	BM Reggie	HM Jorge	HM Ben	WM John
	V			N	

WM Bill	WM Stuart	HF Juanita	HM Hector	WM Skip	WM Donald

WM Rick	HF Rita	WF Jackie	WF Alice	AF Michele	WF Myra
	N,N,N				

BF Jessie	OF Dawn	WF Robin		WF Virginia	

Symbols for this observation:

N = Nonvolunteering student
V = Volunteering student

Generic symbols:

M = Male   A = Asian
F = Female   H = Hispanic
W = White   O = Other
B = Black

BF Sandy

FIGURE 4
Sample Seating Chart 2

If you trace on your seating chart the teacher's movements through the room, are there areas that the teacher rarely goes to? Are there areas in which the teacher usually can be found? How do the teacher's travel patterns relate to the areas in which the students receive a lot of attention or are ignored?

Are most of the interactions V's, or are they N's? Who is making the most frequent decisions about classroom interaction—the teacher (N's) or the students (V's)—or are they evenly shared?

How many students in the class were silent (no interactions)?

Are there some students—one or two—who monopolize classroom interaction?

Activity 11: Detecting Racial Bias Although educators as a group are firmly committed to educational equality, subtle and often unintentional biases can nonetheless emerge.[7] Teachers often unknowingly give more attention to students of one race than to those of another, or give different kinds of attention to one group than they give to another. Detecting these subtle biases is a matter of recording data on your seating chart. It is best to record several sessions of classroom interaction in order to obtain an accurate measure of potential racial bias. The procedure then becomes one of simple mathematics. First, identify the expected number of interactions or questions (that is, a fair share) for each race. If, for instance, a class consists of 40 percent minority students, then a fair share would mean that minority students receive 40 percent of the teacher's questions. If the minority students receive fewer than 40 percent, they are not getting their fair share. For the second step, determine the actual number of interactions that each race receives. Finally, compare the figures. Here is how you would do the computations:

Sample Classroom Data

Class attendance   5 minority students
                   10 majority students
                   ─────────────────────
                   15 total students in the class

Teacher questions 15 to minority students
                   45 to majority students
                   ─────────────────────
                   60 total interactions

Step 1

Determine expected or fair share of questions, by race:

$$\text{Minority fair share} = \frac{\text{minority attendance}}{\text{total attendance}} = \frac{5}{15} = 33\%$$

$$\text{Majority fair share} = \frac{\text{majority attendance}}{\text{total attendance}} = \frac{10}{15} = 67\%$$

Step 2

Determine actual share of interaction, by race:

Percentage minority interactions = number of interactions with minority ÷ total interactions

$$\frac{\text{Minority interactions}}{\text{Total interactions}} = \frac{15}{60} = 25\%$$

Percentage majority interactions = number of interactions with majority ÷ total interactions

$$\frac{\text{Majority interactions}}{\text{Total interactions}} = \frac{45}{60} = 75\%$$

Step 3

Determine the difference between expected (or fair share) and actual distribution of interactions:

Minority actual share	=	25%
Minority fair share	=	33%
Difference	=	−8% (8% fewer interactions than a fair share)

Majority actual share	=	75%
Majority fair share	=	67%
Difference	=	+8% (8% more interactions than a fair share)

Minorities received approximately 8 percent fewer questions than would be their fair share, or the amount that would be expected based on their representation in the class. Majority students received approximately 8 percent more than their fair share, or the amount that would be expected based on their attendance in class. Subtle bias exists in this sample classroom interaction.

Activity 12: Detecting Gender Bias The same procedure can be used to determine gender bias.[8] After several observations using your seating charts, tally your results and follow the same steps. An example, similar to that given for detecting racial bias, follows.

Sample Classroom Data

Class attendance	15 females
	10 males
	25 total students in the class

Teacher questions	15 to females
	15 to males
	30 total interactions

Step 1

Determine expected or fair share of questions, by gender:

$$\text{Female fair share} = \frac{\text{female attendance}}{\text{total attendance}} = \frac{15}{25} = 60\%$$

$$\text{Male fair share} = \frac{\text{male attendance}}{\text{total attendance}} = \frac{10}{25} = 40\%$$

Step 2

Determine actual share of interactions, by gender:

Percentage female interactions = number of interactions with females ÷ total interactions

$$\frac{\text{Female interactions}}{\text{Total interactions}} = \frac{15}{30} = 50\%$$

Percentage male interactions = number of interactions with males ÷ total interactions

$$\frac{\text{Male interactions}}{\text{Total interactions}} = \frac{15}{30} = 50\%$$

Step 3

Determine the difference between expected (or fair share) and actual distribution of interactions:

Female actual share	=	50%
Female fair share	=	60%
Difference	=	−10% (10% fewer interactions than a fair share)
Male actual share	=	50%
Majority fair share	=	40%
Difference	=	+10% (10% more interactions than a fair share)

Females received 10 percent fewer questions than would be their fair share, or the amount that would be expected based on their representation in the classroom. Males received 10 percent more than their fair share, or the amount that would be expected based on their representation in the classroom. Subtle gender bias exists in this sample classroom interaction.

Activity 13: Questioning Level John Dewey was one of many noted educators who believed that questioning is central not only to education but to the process of thinking itself. Unfortunately, research indicates that most teachers do not use effective questioning techniques. Not only is the distribution of questions often inequitable, but teachers rarely use challenging classroom questions. Instead, they tend to rely on lower-order, or memory, questions. This observation activity focuses on the problem of too much emphasis on lower-order questions.

Lower-order questions are those that deal with the memorization and recall of factual information. The student is not required to manipulate (that is, apply, analyze, synthesize, or evaluate) information. There is nothing inherently wrong with asking memory questions, such as "When did the American Revolution begin?" or "Identify one poem written by Robert Frost." However, a heavy reliance on such questions reduces the opportunity for students to develop higher-order thinking.

Conversely, higher-order questions are those that require students to apply, analyze, synthesize, or evaluate information. They encourage students to think creatively. When a teacher asks, "What is your opinion of this poem by Robert Frost, and what evidence can you cite to support your opinion?" that teacher is asking a higher-order question. Only 10 percent of most teachers' questions fall into this higher-order category.

To help you distinguish between lower-order (memory) questions and higher-order (thought) questions, here are some examples of each:

Lower-Order Questions

- Who founded abstract art?
- Name three Romantic authors.
- Whose signatures appear on the Declaration of Independence?

- In what year did the war begin?
- Who wrote your text?

Higher-Order Questions

- What conclusions can you reach concerning the images Shakespeare uses to portray death?
- What forces motivated Romantic authors?
- Why did no females or African Americans sign the Declaration of Independence?
- Was this a good idea? Why or why not?
- What does this poem mean to you?
- What would you say in a letter to the President of the United States?

To record lower-order and higher-order questioning, use the following procedure. When a lower-order question is asked, record an L on your seating chart. When a higher-order question is asked, record an H on the seating chart. The sample coding form in Figure 5 illustrates the use of this approach. Each student who is asked a question receives an H or an L (to denote higher- and lower-order questions). On Sample Seating Chart 3 in Figure 5, recording a hypothetical classroom discussion, the preponderance of lower-order questions is evident, as well as several patterns of bias. Can you detect some of these patterns? Take a minute to analyze the teacher's level and distribution of questions and jot down any problems you detect. Then compare your analysis to the one that follows.

Problems Reflected on Sample Seating Chart 3

- Preponderance of lower-order questions
- More questions asked to males
- More questions asked to majority than to minority students
- Left side of the room and back of the room ignored

Try this in a classroom that you are observing. After constructing a seating chart, choose a 20- or 30-minute segment of teacher-student interaction. Record the number of higher-order and lower-order questions asked of each student in the class by noting H's and L's, as called for, on your seating chart. Then analyze the questioning pattern, using the following questions as a guide.

Guidelines: Questioning Level and Race and Gender Bias

How many questions were asked? What was the average number of questions per minute (total questions divided by minutes observed)?

What was the ratio of lower- to higher-order questions?

What were the areas of the class that received a greater number of higher-order questions?

Do you detect any patterns of racial or gender bias in the distribution of questions in general and of higher-order questions in particular?

Activity 14: Wait Time and Student Questions   *Wait time* is the period of silence that occurs between the end of a teacher question and the beginning of a student response. It is the quiet time in which a student is allowed to

Teacher's name _____ Date _____

Observer's name _____ Time begin _____

Time end _____

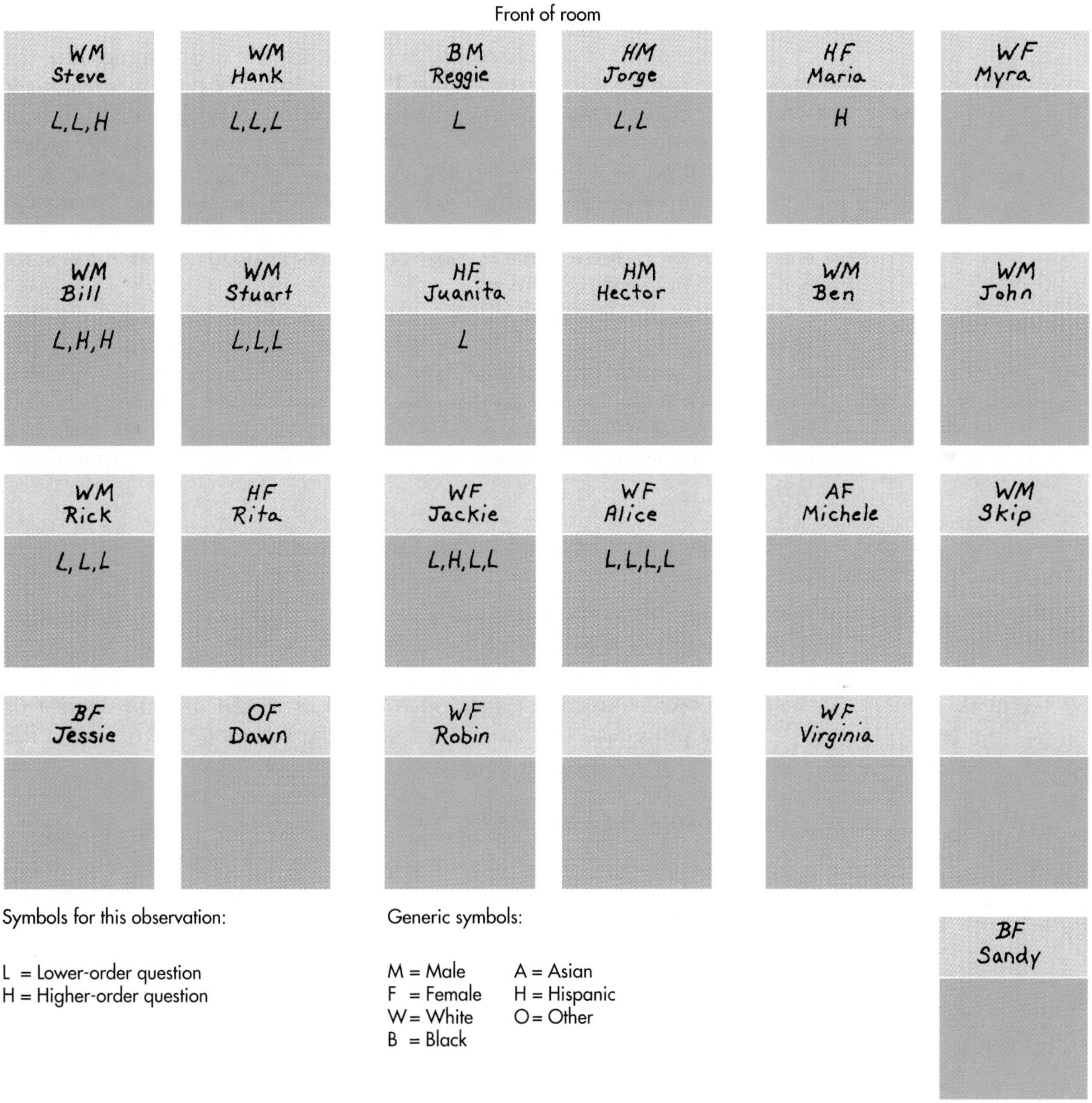

Front of room

WM Steve L,L,H	WM Hank L,L,L		BM Reggie L	HM Jorge L,L		HF Maria H	WF Myra
WM Bill L,H,H	WM Stuart L,L,L		HF Juanita L	HM Hector		WM Ben	WM John
WM Rick L,L,L	HF Rita		WF Jackie L,H,L,L	WF Alice L,L,L,L		AF Michele	WM Skip
BF Jessie	OF Dawn		WF Robin			WF Virginia	

Symbols for this observation:

L = Lower-order question
H = Higher-order question

Generic symbols:

M = Male   A = Asian
F = Female   H = Hispanic
W = White   O = Other
B = Black

| BF
Sandy |

FIGURE 5
Sample Seating Chart 3

think about the question and answer it properly. Studies show that the average length of time after a teacher asks a question (wait time) is less than 1 second. If a student is unable to think quickly enough, the teacher moves on by giving the answer, repeating or rephrasing the question, or calling on a different student. Very little time is provided for a student to develop a coherent and thoughtful answer.

This phenomenon of split-second wait time usually occurs again after the student's response. In less than 1 second, most teachers reward or correct their student's responses, ask another question, or call on another student. Student answers are often interrupted. Once again, the students are denied the opportunity to pursue their line of thought to completion. When teachers increase wait time from less than a second to 3–5 seconds, students responses become longer, more accurate, and reflect higher-order thought processes. Other benefits include an increase in the number of students responding and in the number of student-initiated questions.

Most teachers ask a tremendous number of questions, almost 400 per day, according to one study, but the typical student asks only one question per month. This statistic suggests that most schools are failing to develop rational inquiry skills in students or to encourage student curiosity. Although the following activities will test your reflexes (and your timepiece), try to determine how long the teacher's wait time is. Use a stopwatch or a watch with a second hand.

Guidelines: Wait Time and Student Questions

Select a 20- or 30-minute interaction period and determine the average length of time the teacher waits (1) after asking a question and (2) after a student's response.

Select a 20- to 30-minute interactive period and see if any students ask a question. If a student question is asked, is it related to the content or is it procedural (such as "Can I go to the bathroom?") Who asked the question—a frequent participant or a quiet student?

Analysis and Synthesis: The Teacher

1. If you were to answer the interview questions in Activity 9, how would your answers differ from the teacher's? What did you learn from the teacher's responses? Did anything surprise you?
2. Did the teacher's responses fit into your perception of the school, the classroom, and the community?
3. How would you characterize the teacher in terms of the following areas?

   - Interaction patterns
   - Ability to generate student participation
   - Biases (intentional or unintentional) toward any student or group of students
   - Level of questions
   - Length of wait time

4. What did you find most interesting about the nature of teacher-student interaction? What did you learn?
5. What effective teaching techniques did you see during your observations? What practices will you try to avoid?

6. As a result of your observations, what skills and information related to teaching would you like to develop further?

UNIT 4

Data Collection Activities: The Students

Although the students in any school constitute the reason for everything else—the building, the curriculum, the teachers—their interests are sometimes overlooked. You can learn a great deal about the school milieu, the community, and the kind of teaching students prefer by including an analysis of learners in your field experience. This section focuses on students and the social system in which they live and learn.

It is easy to lose sight of the fact that schools are created and maintained by the larger society for the express purpose of socializing its young into the roles of the prevailing culture.[9] To the casual observer this socializing function is not apparent. The school seems to be an isolated and self-contained subculture accountable to no one. By collecting data on the school and classroom social system, the links between school and society will emerge with greater clarity and you will be able to interpret their significance.

Since most of us are so accustomed to the norms, values, and beliefs that constitute our culture, we have difficulty detecting their influence all about us. We are much more alert to things that are new and different. Consequently, the data collection activities in this section are designed to help you perceive with fresh meaning and significance events that are so routine that you may no longer even see them.

To gain new insights from the commonplace, researcher Seymour Saranson recommends that you take the perspective of a visitor from outer space, who will be more alert to both blatant and subtle patterns of the school as a social system.[10] For example, an important aspect of our schools, but one not usually thought about, is that they must provide custody and control of youngsters for a major part of the work week. Housing a large group of children and adolescents in a small space for many hours a day has a major impact on the classroom social system. "Only in school do 30 or more people spend several hours a day literally side by side. Once we leave the classroom, we seldom again are required to have contact with so many people for so long a time."[11] In these crowded conditions students and teachers often clash, because their purposes may be vastly different. The teacher is there to socialize the young and help them learn. Grade school students are often in class to play and have fun, whereas adolescent goals may involve developing social and sexual relationships.

In the densely populated classroom, the teacher functions as a supply sergeant (giving out paper, books, and so on), as a timekeeper (determining how long the class will spend on given activities), and as a gatekeeper to class discussion (deciding who will talk and for how long).[12] While the teacher is busy filling all these roles, students are left to wait and do nothing. They stand in lines, they sit with their hands raised, they wait for other students to finish so that they can go on to other activities. Sitting still and remaining silent are denials of their natural instincts.

Frustrated by this densely populated and artificial situation, students often rebel, pitting their own group power against the authority of the teacher. Sometimes this power struggle is subtle, with sizing up and testing of the teacher its only visible signs (for example, by not handing in homework on time, cajoling to get an assignment lessened or postponed). At other times the power struggle erupts to the surface of the social system as students openly flout or disregard adult authority. Observing these overt signs of the power struggle is easy. Picking up the subtle rituals and patterns of the social system that underlie these disruptions is a more challenging task.

Use the data collection activities that follow as if you were a visitor from another culture or planet. Although it is extremely difficult to abandon one's habitual way of viewing the world to look at events from a completely fresh and detached point of view, that is precisely what social scientists attempt to do. By adopting their attitudes and approaches, you will gain a better insight into the school's role in society and the teacher's role as a leader of the classroom social system.

Activity 15: Student Observation   As you visit your school, spend some time observing students before and after school begins, in the cafeteria, during free periods, in the halls, and on the school grounds. Then try to gather data to complete the information requested on the observation sheet at the end of this unit.

Guidelines: Student Observation

How are the students dressed? Are different groups distinguishable by their dress?

Do students group together on the basis of race, sex, economic class, or other factors? Are there identifiable cliques?

How does students' classroom language and behavior compare with the students' language and behavior outside the classroom?

Do different groups claim different territorial areas? Where? Are some students left out of groups? Where do they go?

Can you hear any of the students' conversations? What topics do they talk about? What emotions do you hear in their voices?

Do any school groups appear more powerful than others? Are there conflicts between the groups? What is the source of each group's power? What are the reasons for the conflicts?

Activity 16: Student Interviews   If you have the opportunity, try to talk to one, two, or a group of students. Make sure they understand that you are not an "official" of the school, but rather a future teacher who wants to learn more about the school, and that what they say will be "off the record." Be sure, however, that your interview does not degenerate into gossip about individual teachers or students. Below are some interview questions you may want to pursue; you may need to change the vocabulary used, depending on the age of the student.

Guidelines: Student Interviews

What advice would you give to a new student about how to get along in this school?

What are the different cliques or groups in this school? Describe them.

In what ways is the school like the community? In what ways is it different?

What are your plans after graduation? What do most students do after they graduate?

Who is your favorite teacher? Why? What makes a good teacher? What characteristics lead to ineffective teaching?

What are the important extracurricular activities in this school? Why?

What makes certain students popular? Unpopular? Why?

How do parents view school? How involved are they with school activities? Homework?

What do students do after school? How many students work? What transportation do students use to get to and from places?

What are the biggest problems students face in the school? Is drug and alcohol abuse a problem? What are other problems?

What do you like or dislike most about school in general and this school in particular?

Activity 17: Student Groups Social status is a powerful force in school, and groups and cliques are often officially or unofficially labeled. The race, gender, national origin, social class, or ability level of a group's members may affect how it is labeled. The following activity will focus on the treatment of these special groups. Some of these data can be collected through observation; in other cases, information can best be gathered through interviews. Answer as many of the following as you can to glean insight into the special world of students.

Guidelines: Student Groups

Do students form groups or cliques based on such characteristics as race, gender, religion, national origin, achievement level, or social class?

Do these groups occupy ("hang out" around) certain school areas? Do they sit together in class?

What are the values and priorities of such groups? How do they differ from other social groups?

Do school displays and classroom bulletin boards reflect all groups (females, minorities, disabled, and so on) or mainly white males? Do these displays promote stereotypic or nonstereotypic perceptions?

Do students from these different groups actively and equitably participate in classroom interaction? In extracurricular activities?

How does the school reflect community values in its treatment of females, minorities, the disabled, and so on? How does the school environment differ from that of the community?

What special education needs are represented by exceptional children in the school? If physically disabled children are present, are there physical barriers within the school that restrict their access to facilities?

To what degree are students with special needs mainstreamed? To what degree are they provided with segregated special education?

Are students in the school "tracked"? If so, what generalizations can you make about the students in each track?

What provisions are made for students whose native language is not English? How does this affect their adjustment to the school?

Activity 18: Teachers' Views of Students Try to talk to three or four teachers to assess their perceptions of the students who attend the school. The following teacher interview questions will enable you to learn about each teacher's perception of the students' social system, as well as the norms and rules they establish for classroom management.

Guidelines: Teachers' Views of Students

What are your classroom norms and rules for appropriate behavior?

What are the penalties for students who violate the rules?

What was the worst discipline problem you ever had to handle?

What advice would you give a new teacher about classroom management?

How many different cliques are there in your classroom? Are there isolates, students who do not seem to belong to any social group?

Is there race or class segregation in work or play groups? Who does the segregating? Are there any penalties for students who try to integrate these groups?

How are the needs of special education students met? What is done to meet the needs of the gifted?

What social or interpersonal aspects of the class have given you the greatest pleasure during the past year? The greatest problem?

Analysis and Synthesis: The Students

1. Because of the sheer size of institutions such as schools, people frequently form subgroups or subcultures. List what you consider to be the most distinguishing characteristics of each of the following subgroups. Describe how these subgroups are treated by other students.

Observation Sheet

Term to Describe Subgroup	Characteristics and/or Function	Treatment by Other Students
A. "Popular" "Innies"	_____	_____
B. "Nerds" "Geeks" "Brains"	_____	_____
C. "Dorks" "Townies" "Blue-collar kids"	_____	_____
D. "Jocks"	_____	_____
E. "Preppies"	_____	_____
F. "Skinheads"	_____	_____
(Other labels used in your school)		
G. "Dopers"	_____	_____
H. "Ropers"	_____	_____
I. "_____"	_____	_____
J. "_____"	_____	_____
K. "_____"	_____	_____
L. "_____"	_____	_____

How does membership in these subgroups prepare (or fail to prepare) students for participation in adult society?

2. Based on student interviews and observations, what conclusions can you make about student attitudes toward themselves and toward one another in the school where you are observing?

3. How aware is the teacher of the subtle dynamics of the classroom social system? In what ways does this social system affect his or her teaching?

4. What conclusions can you reach about the treatment of the following groups in the school where you are observing?

- Minorities
- Females and males
- Special education students
- Lower and upper socioeconomic class
- Gifted and talented
- Athletes
- Other groups that you included in your response to the first item in this section

5. School publications often reflect the social system. See if you can locate the last five school yearbooks. What values are reflected? Based on your reading and the data you collected, how would you characterize the social system of the school? Do the yearbooks reflect this? How does the school prepare students for roles in adult society? Has this changed during the past 5 years?

6. How might your behavior as a teacher be affected by the student social system in the school?

7. How does the school social system mirror or reflect the community's social system and values?

UNIT 5

Data Collection Activities: The Curriculum

In the midst of a worldwide knowledge explosion, it has become impossible to teach or learn all the information and skills now known. Moreover, every year more and more knowledge becomes available. Clearly, decisions need to be made about what to teach and what to learn. Although states and local school districts are pivotal in shaping the curriculum that you will be teaching, you have some decisions to make, as well. You need to consider your own ability in the subject or subjects you are to teach. Do you need to take additional academic courses to improve your own preparation? Once assigned a curriculum, how do you decide what to emphasize? What are the most important things for your students to learn?

The nature and direction of the school curriculum are explored in several chapters in this text, but it is useful for you to consider these and other curricular issues during your field experience. The activities in this section will start you on a career-long investigation of what you should teach and what is worth knowing.

Activity 19: Self-Inventory Think back to your own years in elementary and high school, as well as in college, and to the different subjects you took. Identify five courses that you consider most valuable, courses that were significant to you and that made a difference in your education.

As you reflect on these courses, identify those factors that played a role in your choice. The following characteristics have frequently been cited in identifying important courses. Are any of these reasons similar to yours?

- The quality of the instructor teaching the course
- Personal interest in the area
- Related to your career choice
- Provided you with important skills
- Motivated you to continue your studies
- General usefulness
- Related to your age development or interest at the time

As you examine your most valuable courses, do you detect some commonality among your choices? Now look at the other side of the coin. Take a moment and repeat this exercise, only this time identify the five courses that were least valuable to you. As you examine your list, do you uncover common reasons that certain courses were of little value to you? What are these reasons?

As you might suspect, students differ in their course selections and their reasons. In fact, courses that some students find most important, others find least valuable. If you have the opportunity, you may want to share your choices and reasons with others in your class. Your choices in course selection, like your choices in so many things, are in part a function of your personal history. Perhaps you have selected a certain grade level or subject specialization to teach as a result of the courses you have selected and your own life experiences. The next activity will assist you in reflecting on the ways your personal history has influenced your view of the curriculum.

Activity 20: People and Experiences Take a moment to think about how your individual experiences have led to your unique outlook on the curriculum. Next to the people and experiences listed below, indicate which have influenced your view of subject matter and the curriculum. (Note at least three people and three experiences and indicate how each has influenced your view.)

People
Family: _____

Relatives:_____

Teachers:_____

Friends: _____

Others: _____

Events
Trips: _____

Volunteer work: _____

Salaried employment:_____

Personal successes: _____

Personal failures: _____

Other: _____

Your personal life experiences, in conjunction with your school classes, have shaped and directed your view of subject matter and the curriculum. Your background also contributes to your philosophy of teaching and learning. Examine your answers to the last two activities and complete the following statement:

I believe that some of the most important reasons to study my subject (or, if in elementary school, the subjects at my grade level) include: _____

_____

Activity 21: The School Curriculum Most schools or school districts have a published curriculum for each subject at the secondary level, or for specific grades at the elementary level, and teachers are provided with a copy of this curriculum. Although the specifics vary from one district to another, these curricular units frequently contain objectives, content, teacher guides, and at times even specific lesson plans. Ask your cooperating teacher for a copy of the school curriculum, and respond to the following questions.

Guidelines: The School Curriculum

What are some of the primary skills and areas of knowledge that students are expected to acquire?

Can you tell who developed these objectives and goals?

How are these objectives and goals evaluated?

Are ample resources provided by the school in order to achieve these goals and objectives?

Activity 22: Teacher Interview If you have the opportunity, take a few minutes to interview the teacher about the curriculum. The following questions can help guide your interview.

Guidelines: Teacher Interview

What are the strengths and weaknesses of the curriculum?

What changes, if any, would you recommend for the curriculum?

How much flexibility do you have in implementing the curriculum? What kind of changes, if any, would you make?

How do the students and the community react to the curriculum?

Who developed the curriculum? (Are teachers involved?)

Do you think there should be a core curriculum? If so, what should it include?

How are textbooks selected in your school? Do you have any voice in the books you use to teach?

Have there been any attempts to censor books in your school? Which books were challenged? Were the attempts successful?

Activity 23: Textbook Analysis Review a textbook used in your school. In your analysis, look carefully at narrative and pictures. The following questions should guide your textbook review.

Guidelines: Textbook Analysis

How recent is the textbook edition? What is the copyright date?

How would you characterize the quality of the writing? Is it stilted and dull or rich and interesting? Give examples to support your point of view.

Is the textbook guilty of "mentioning"—providing facts and figures without adequate context and explanation? Give examples to support your point of view.

Does the text include adequate representation of males, females, majority and minority group members? Count the number of males, females, majority and minority group members in order to reach your conclusions.

What kind of supplementary materials accompany the textbook? Is there a workbook, a teacher's manual, or other supplementary materials? Do these supplementary materials treat the teacher as a professional—or are the directions so specific that the teacher becomes little more than a technician?

Activity 24: Student Interview Interview several students concerning their views of the curriculum. The following questions can provide a guide for the interview. Obviously, the vocabulary used in the questions may need to be changed, depending on the age of the students interviewed.

Guidelines: Student Interview

What is your favorite subject? Why? What subject do you dislike the most? Why?

What is your opinion of your textbooks? How could they be made more interesting?

Are there any subjects that are not taught in school that you think should be? Which ones? Why?

Which subjects should be dropped from the curriculum? Why?

Are all the students in your school exposed to the same curriculum? Or are there tracks or ability groups in which students study different curricula depending on their ability?

Do you think changing the curriculum to suit student ability is a good idea? Why or why not?

Analysis and Synthesis: The Curriculum

1. How does your view of the curriculum mesh with the official approach taken by the school?
2. Are there areas in the curriculum that you feel unprepared to teach? If so, what coursework, or other efforts, should you undertake to remedy this deficiency?
3. Do you have ideas or approaches that you are considering in teaching the curriculum? What are they?
4. How does the school curriculum reflect the community? The needs of the learner? In what ways does the curriculum fail to reflect these needs?
5. What changes, if any, would you suggest in the curriculum (additions, deletions, modifications)?
6. Do you think bias is reflected in the curriculum? If so, how?
7. Do you think there should be a core curriculum? Why or why not?
8. What is your overall assessment of the textbooks used in your school?

Data Collection Activities: Effective Schools

This unit provides observation and interview strategies that will help you assess the effectiveness of schools that you might visit and offers sets of questions and categories that will help you focus on the characteristics of effective schools. As you complete each set of data collection activities, you will have another lens through which to observe and interpret the school environment.

Activity 25: Looking at Leadership Strong leadership by the principal is at the heart of a good school. But how can you tell if such leadership is being provided? Before you can make judgments, it is necessary to collect data. Following are some data collection activities that will help you to determine whether effective leadership is being provided.

1. Schedule an interview with the principal and ask questions about leadership style. (If you cannot get an interview, this also says a lot about style and accessibility.) How often does the principal go into classrooms to observe teachers? How important does the principal think this is? What is the principal's concept of effective teaching? Does the principal get involved in curriculum development? If so, how?

2. If possible, "shadow" the principal for a day. How does he or she spend time? Is the principal based mainly in the office, completing paperwork and talking on the telephone? Or does the principal travel the school extensively, walking the halls, the classrooms, the teachers' room, the lunchroom? How many daily interactions does the principal have with teachers? Students? Parents? Other members of the community? How often do students or teachers get to see the principal? What are the main problems the principal faces?

3. Ask to see the observation form the principal uses to supervise teachers. Does this form reflect current research on effective teaching? (See Chapter 6.)

4. What is the principal's office like? Is it similar to an office you might find in a business or corporation, or is it filled with children's paraphernalia and objects? (We have even seen principals' offices that are filled with stuffed animals and have a corner where children can sit and talk.)

5. Where is the school secretary based in relationship to the principal? How many daily interactions do the secretary and principal have? Describe the secretary's role in relation to the principal.

6. Analyze the information you gained from interviews, as well as observations of the principal's activities and the setting where she or he works. What themes or patterns emerge that will help you determine the nature and style of leadership the principal exerts?

Activity 26: The School Mission A clearly articulated school mission shared by all members of the educational community is a key component of an effective school. The following guidelines and data collection strategies will enable you to determine what the school's mission is and how clearly and widely it is communicated.

1. Interview the principal and ask what the mission or key goals of the school are. Then interview teachers and ask them the same question. Are the responses of the principal and the teachers similar or are they different? If they are different, what are the points of divergence? Are the teachers working as a team to accomplish the school mission? If so, how? Ask for specific examples of actions, behaviors, and events.

2. Interview students at different grade levels and ask them what they think the mission or the major purpose of the school is. If possible, interview parents about the mission of the school. How do student and parent responses compare to those of the teachers and principal? Are parents working actively with teachers to accomplish the school mission? If so, how? Ask for examples of specific actions rather than vague and general statements.

3. Is the school mission or philosophy written down? If so, obtain a copy. Is this written statement similar to the interview responses you obtained? Why or why not? How many members of the educational community know that the written policy exists and how to obtain it?

4. Analyze the written mission statement, as well as your interview responses. What themes emerge? Is the school philosophy or mission primarily cognitive or is it affective? Is the emphasis on "back to basics" or on creativity and the arts? Is any mention made of vocational or career education? Is concern for equity expressed? Is there any mention of the achievement of minority children and female students? Is there any emphasis on the partnership between parents and school? Are steps delineated by which the school community can accomplish its mission?

Activity 27: A Safe and Orderly Climate A safe and orderly climate is a necessary condition for learning. Here are some guidelines and data collection strategies to determine whether that climate exists in the school where you are observing.

1. As you approach the school, what is the physical environment like? Are the building and grounds clean and well kept, or are graffiti, broken windows, and other signs of neglect evident? Are there graffiti on desks and bathroom walls? Do students write hostile statements about the school and its staff? Are there expressions of fear?

2. Observe in the halls and on playgrounds, especially between classes and before and after school begins. Do students behave in an orderly way, or is disruptive conduct and language apparent? If so, how frequent are these incidents? Describe them. Is there evidence of gangs or of hostility between different racial or ethnic groups?

3. Interview students and teachers. Do they think the school environment is safe and orderly? Are there any areas in the school that are less safe than others? Which ones? Are students' possessions in lockers and desks safe, or is theft prevalent? Is student conduct in classrooms orderly? If there are disruptions, are teachers assisted in reestablishing order by the administration? If so, how?

4. Is there a written discipline code or policy? If so, obtain a copy. Who wrote it? Is it specific in its definition of misbehavior? Is the discipline policy disseminated widely and available to parents, students, and teachers?

5. Interview the administration to see what the procedures are when students are absent from school. Is the student's home notified to make sure parents or guardians are aware of the absence? What other strategies does the school use to make sure that absences are justified?

6. Again, examine the data you have collected from observations, interviews, and analysis of documents. What patterns emerge, and what conclusions can you reach concerning the safety level of the school?

Activity 28: Monitoring Student Progress Providing evaluation of student work, as well as feedback to students about their progress, is an integral component of effective schools. The following guidelines and data collection tasks will help you determine whether this occurs in your school.

1. Find out what records are kept concerning progress as students move from grade to grade. If permission is given, analyze these records. How are students performing on norm-referenced tests such as the California Achievement Test (CAT) or the Scholastic Assessment Test (SAT)? Are minority students performing as well as majority students are? Are there sex differences in student achievement? If so, what are they?

2. Interview teachers and ask them how they monitor student progress. How often are major tests given? Quizzes? How often do students have writing assignments? Do teachers write comments on themes and compositions? How often are report cards given? Do teachers just assign a letter grade, or do they write comments as well? What other mechanisms do teachers use to communicate with parents about their children's progress? Do teachers think that students have a clear sense of their strengths, as well as the areas where improvement is needed?

3. Interview students and ask them similar questions about how progress is monitored. Are their responses similar to those of the teachers, or are there areas of difference?

4. Find out whether students keep a record of their own progress. If you have permission, look in their notebooks or folders to see how these records are kept.

5. Look at the walls of classrooms and hallways to see whether records of student progress are posted. Keep a frequency count to see whether students check these records of progress daily, weekly, or not at all.

6. Seek to identify patterns in the information you collect from student and teacher records, interviews, and observations. What interpretations and evaluations can you extract from your data concerning how student progress is monitored?

Activity 29: Teacher Expectations A school climate characterized by high expectations for both students and teachers is a key characteristic of effective schools. The following strategies will help you assess the school climate and the level of expectations in the school where you observe.

1. Some schools have mottos or slogans, such as "Be all you can be," that encourage student effort and achievement. See whether your school has a motto and, if so, how many of the teachers and students know it.

2. Examine the walls in classrooms and hallways. Are there murals, posters, statements, or other materials encouraging students or rewarding them

for good work? If so, describe them. Are there awards or other forms of recognition given for various kinds of student achievement in academics, athletics, or the arts? Do students and teachers seem to know what these forms of recognition are?

3. Observe in classrooms to see whether teachers exhibit high expectations for students. For each class you observe, draw a seating chart and record the number of academic contacts made with each student. Are all students called on, or are some ignored? When students do not know answers, do teachers ask probing questions to assist them? Do teachers make attributions to effort or ability, such as "I know you can do this"? Record the attributions teachers make.

4. Interview students. Do they feel positive and confident about their ability to do schoolwork, or do they express a sense of academic futility?

5. Find out whether there is ability grouping or tracking in the school where you are observing. Are students aware of the different groups and tracks? If you have permission, ask them how they feel about their placement in different ability groups.

6. Interview teachers to determine whether they have high expectations of their own performance. Do teachers recognize which members of the faculty are talented instructors? Is there envy and jealousy, or are quality teachers acknowledged and respected?

7. Identification of patterns from your interviews, observations, and analysis of documents should enable you to analyze and evaluate what kind of expectations teachers and other participants in the school environment hold.

In order to analyze the school you are observing in terms of all five data collection categories, look for events, words, and phrases that occur repeatedly. Analyze how these different events and settings are similar. How do they differ? Always be alert for what is unexpected and surprising.

When you write up the information generated by the data collection categories, start with description—the what, when, where, and who of your observations. After your objective description, you can seek to determine the why and how of what you saw in your school.

Reflection: Looking Back on Your Field Observations

Your field experience is an exciting part of your professional preparation, bridging all your past experiences as a student with your future career as a teacher. After you have completed the field experience, you may find it particularly useful to consider what you have learned and how you have grown from this experience. This final unit provides you with strategies to reflect productively on your experience.

Activity 30: Reassessing Your Goals and Concerns   The initial exercises in this manual asked you to identify your general goals and concerns, as well as specific goals within the categories of the setting, teaching, students, curriculum, and effective schools. As a result of your field experience, some of your prior beliefs may have been confirmed, while others may have been altered.

Review your goals and concerns (identified in Unit 1 of this manual) and respond to the following questions.

1. Have your goals been met and your concerns addressed in your field experience? Which ones remain unresolved?
2. What were the most important or surprising insights that you gained from your field experience in each of the following areas?
   a. Setting
   b. Teachers
   c. Students
   d. Curriculum
   e. Effective schools
3. As a result of your field experience, you may have identified areas that you need to improve upon or learn more about:
   a. Setting (for example, areas of community life you need to learn more about, other kinds of schools or communities you may want to visit, more effective community–school cooperative activities)
   b. Teaching (for example, skills to be worked on, new grade levels to consider)
   c. Students (for example, strategies for motivating students, additional study or work with special student populations such as at-risk students, more detailed observation of the school's social system)
   d. Curriculum (for example, areas of the school curriculum where you may need additional coursework or preparation, other curricular areas you might like to teach, or new skills to develop, such as assessing textbooks)
   e. Effective schools (for example, how a school leader's sense of a school mission or your colleagues' views of students' abilities may impact your life in the classroom)
4. How would you describe the greatest benefits that you derived from your field experience? What was your most significant insight during the experience?

Activity 31: Field Experience Report If you have a journal or log, refer to it as you respond to this final activity in which you will develop your field experience report. If you did not keep a journal, look over your responses to the prior activities as you record your reactions to this activity. The following outline is suggested as a framework for your report. Your instructor may either ask you to follow this format or may modify or replace it to better meet the course goals and specifics of your field experience.

Outline: Field Experience Report

Summary. In several paragraphs, describe the setting, teachers, students, curriculum, and effective schools you encountered in your field experience.

Goals and concerns. Refer to the summary of your major goals and objectives in Unit 1. Include any changes or additions to these that may have occurred as a result of your field experience.

Insights. Identify the major insights that you gained from this experience. What did you learn about effective or ineffective teaching and curriculum, about students and about school–community relationships?

Critical event or incident. Identify the single event or incident that was most critical during your field experience. Why does this stand out? What did you learn from this event?

Professional impact. Although it is useful, even essential, to consider the specifics of your field experience, it is also important not to miss the forest for the trees. Considering your experiences, what did you learn that has general application to teaching and learning? What major insight did you gain that you believe will affect your development as a professional in the field of education?

The 31 data collection activities included in this manual provide you with a framework for approaching and analyzing your field experience.

All of these activities only touch upon the hundreds and hundreds of techniques that have been developed to analyze school life. This myriad of observation instruments attests to the importance of understanding the complex world of the school. The activities in this manual provide you with opportunities for experience and reflection. These forge a critical link between your current role as a student and your future role as a professional in the field of education. The more expert you become in observing and reflecting on school life, the more insight and understanding you will gain about the nature and challenges of teaching.

NOTES

1. George Spindler, *Doing the Ethnography of Schooling: Educational Anthropology in Action* (New York: Holt, Rinehart & Winston, 1982), p. 24.
2. Quoted in Spindler, *Doing the Ethnography of Schooling,* p. 24.
3. Marilyn Cohn, Robert Kottkamp, and Eugene Provanzo, Jr., *To Be a Teacher: Cases, Concepts, Observation Guides* (New York: Random House, 1987).
4. L. Smith and P. Keith, *Anatomy of an Educational Innovation* (New York: Wiley, 1971).
5. Eugene J. Webb, Donald Campbell, Richard Schwartz, and Lee Sechrest, *Unobtrusive Measures* (Skokie, IL: Rand McNally, 1966).
6. Myra Sadker and David Sadker, "Questioning Skills," in James M. Cooper (ed.), *Classroom Teaching Skills: A Handbook* (Lexington, MA: D. C. Heath, 1989).
7. Hugh B. Price, "Multiculturalism: Myths and Realities," *Phi Delta Kappan* 74, no. 3 (November 1992): 208–213.
8. Myra Sadker and David Sadker, "Sexism in the Classroom: From Grade School to Graduate School," *Phi Delta Kappan* 67, no. 7 (April 1986): 512–528.
9. Joseph Grannis, "The School as a Model of Society," *Harvard Graduate School of Education Association Bulletin* 21 (1967). See also Jules Henry, *Culture Against Man* (New York: Random House, 1963); Seymour Sarason, *The Culture of the School and the Problem of Change* (Boston: Allyn & Bacon, 1971); George D. Spindler (ed.), *Education and Culture: Anthropological Approaches* (New York: Holt, Rinehart & Winston, 1963); Talcott Parsons, "The School as a Social System: Some of Its Functions in American Society," in Robert J. Havighurst, Bernice L. Neugarten, and Jacqueline M. Falk (eds.), *Society and Education* (Boston: Allyn & Bacon, 1967).
10. Sarason, *The Culture of the School and the Problem of Change.*
11. Philip Jackson, *Life in Classrooms* (New York: Holt, Rinehart & Winston, 1968).
12. Jackson, *Life in Classrooms.*

Appendix 2

Just what is the Praxis Series? Developed by Educational Testing Service (ETS), the Praxis Series: Professional Assessments for Beginning Teachers assesses competence in three broad areas: Praxis I tests foundation skills (reading, writing, and mathematics), Praxis II assesses subject area knowledge, and Praxis III judges teaching skill in the classroom.

- Praxis I, the three-component academic skills assessment, tests reading, mathematics, and writing skills. It is offered in two formats: a paper-and-pencil version and a computer-based assessment. The Pre-Professional Skills Tests (PPST) are administered in the standard paper-and-pencil format at set times throughout the year. They feature multiple-choice questions and, in the writing test, a 30-minute essay. The Computer-Based Tests (CBT) are offered year-round by appointment at a network of Sylvan Technology Centers, ETS field offices, and selected colleges and universities. Taken on an IBM-compatible computer (with mouse), the CBT is an adaptive test: correct responses trigger harder questions, whereas incorrect answers generate easier questions. Question types may include multiple-choice response, highlighting, fill-ins, and reordering. The essay portion of the writing test may be answered in longhand or on the computer. Unlike the scoring of the paper-and-pencil format of the PPST, the scoring of the CBT is performed immediately for the reading and mathematics tests. The essay is sent to ETS for scoring and the score is typically received by the test taker within 2 to 4 weeks.

- Praxis II assessments, offered at set times throughout the year, measure content-area knowledge in a wide array of subjects, from accounting to world and U.S. history. For some subjects you may find not only a multiple-choice format that tests core knowledge, but also modules that offer constructed-response questions. For instance, the Mathematics Assessment might offer a 2-hour multiple-choice core, along with a constructed-response module that tests the candidate's ability to construct proofs. Also included in Praxis II is the set of tests known as the *National Teacher's Examination* (NTE) *Core Battery*. These measure general knowledge, communication skills, and professional knowledge. Finally, you may find that some states require either the Multiple Subjects Assessment for Teachers (MSAT), developed jointly by ETS and the California Commission on Teacher Credentialing, or the Principles of Learning and Teaching (PLT) for grades K–6 or 7–12; these also are offered as part of Praxis II.

- As yet, the Classroom Performance Assessment, Praxis III, does not seem to be widely adopted. You might be interested, however, in the general format. The assessment is designed for first-year teachers; but, under special circum-stances, it may be administered during a teacher's second year. Trained local observers, using a common framework of criteria, evaluate the skills of teachers in their own classrooms. A combination of in-class assessment, documentation, and pre- and postobservation interviews yields the overall classroom performance assessment score.

Think of the Praxis Series as a "menu" of tests from which states select the assessments that will best support their licensing requirements. As you pursue certification, you will find that different states require different combinations of tests offered by ETS under the auspices of the Praxis Series. You will need to do some legwork in order to determine which assessments are required by the states in which you would like to be certified. To help you, we have provided a sample User's Chart that shows the assessments required by various states (and the District of Columbia) as of 1995. Please note that the requirements are revised from time to time. Your best bet is to check directly with the state certification offices (see Appendix 3 for a listing of state certification office addresses and phone numbers).

Demonstrating your competence in general, professional, and subject-specific knowledge does not come cheap. Considering it an investment in your chosen profession may help motivate you to undertake this effort and expense. In past years, fees for individual Praxis Series tests have ranged from $25 to $85. The reading, mathematics, and writing components of the PPST cost $25 each, and the general knowledge, communication skills, and professional knowledge sections of the NTE Core Battery cost $30 each. Subject area tests generally cost $40 or $55, with the most expensive (the MSAT Content Area Exercises) costing $85. The CBT (which encompasses reading, mathematics, and writing tests) costs $65 for one test, $85 for two tests, and $105 for all three.

ETS makes available a series of booklets called *Tests at a Glance,* which you may find useful as you look into which Praxis Series assessments you will need for certification. The *Tests at a Glance* booklets include sample questions in each content area, test-taking strategies, and short descriptions of topics covered in the exams. You should be able to find these free booklets, along with a registration bulletin for the Praxis Series, at your local college or university. ETS offers study guides (for a fee) for the PPST, NTE Core Battery tests, and selected subject area tests. The Praxis Series registration bulletin contains more information about how to order these study guides. If you would like to contact ETS, you may call 1-800-772-9476 or 609-771-7395, or write:

The Praxis Series
ETS
P.O Box 6051
Princeton, NJ 08541-6051

THE PRAXIS SERIES USERS' CHART (as of April 15, 1995)

The Praxis Series is responsible for the development, administration, scoring, and reporting of its tests. Policies regarding their use or the setting of qualifying scores are established by the score users or score recipients. Questions about the development and administration of The Praxis Series tests should be addressed to The Praxis Series office. **Questions regarding admission, certification, or other requirements should be addressed to the appropriate state agency, association, or organization office.** Please note that the requirements are periodically revised. The requirements of individual colleges and school districts may differ from state requirements. The Praxis Series is not responsible for incorrect information that examinees may receive from agencies that require its tests.

	AR	CA	CT	DE	DC	FL	HI	ID	IN	KS	KY	LA	ME	MD	MN
NTE CORE BATTERY TESTS															
General Knowledge (10510)								•	•		•	•	•	•	
Communication Skills (20500)								•	•		•	•	•	•	
Professional Knowledge (30520)	•					*		•	•	•	•	•	•	•	
PRINCIPLES OF LEARNING AND TEACHING															
PLT: Grades K-6 (30522)							•								
PLT: Grades 7-12 (30524)							•								
MULTIPLE SUBJECTS ASSESSMENT FOR TEACHERS															
Content Knowledge (10140)		•													
Content Area Exercises (20151)		•													
PRAXIS I: ACADEMIC SKILLS ASSESSMENTS															
Pre-Professional Skills Tests: Mathematics (10730)	•			•	•	*	•			•			•		•
Pre-Professional Skills Tests: Reading (10710)	•			•	•	*	•			•			•		•
Pre-Professional Skills Tests: Writing (20720)	•			•	•	*	•			•			•		•
Computer-Based Test: Mathematics	X	•		X	X	*	X						X		X
Computer-Based Test: Reading	X	•		X	X	*	X						X		X
Computer-Based Test: Writing	X	•		X	X	*	X						X		X
PRAXIS II: SUBJECT ASSESSMENTS & NTE SPECIALTY AREA TESTS															
Accounting (PA) (10791)															
Agriculture (10700)											•				
Agriculture (CA) (10900)		•													
Agriculture (PA) (10780)			•												
Art: Content Knowledge (10133)							•								
Art: Content, Traditions, Criticism, & Aesthetics (20132)		•	•				•								
Art Education (10130)	•		•						•		•			•	
Art Making (20131)		•	•												
Audiology (10340)															
Biology (10230)			•						•					•	
Biology: Content Essays (30233)		•		*			*				*				
Biology: Content Knowledge, Part 1 (20231)				*	•		•				*				
Biology: Content Knowledge, Part 2 (20232)					•		*								
Biology: Pedagogy (30234)				*	•		*								
Biology & General Science (10030)	•								•		•	•		•	
Business Education (10100)	•	•	•				•				•	•		•	
Chemistry (10240)			•						•					•	
Chemistry: Content Essays (30242)		•	•	*											
Chemistry: Content Knowledge (20241)				*	•		*				*				
Chemistry, Physics, & General Science (10070)	•										•	•		•	
Communication (10800)															
Computer Literacy/Data Processing (10650)															
Cooperative Education (10810)															
Data Processing (PA) (10792)															
Early Childhood Education (10020)	•				•	*			•		•	•		•	
Earth Science: Content Knowledge (20571)															

Reprinted by permission of Educational Testing Service, the copyright owner.

KEY:
- ● — Test is in use.
- ★ — Under consideration; verify with state.
- X — Alternative option to the PPST.
- □ — May no longer be required; verify with state.

- **ASHA** — American Speech-Language-Hearing Association
- **CAE** — The Council for Academic Excellence in Ohio Schools
- **DODDS** — Department of Defense Dependents Schools
- **NASP** — National Association of School Psychologists
- **NASW** — National Association of Social Workers

MS	MO	MT	NE	NV	NJ	NM	NY	NC	OH	OK	OR	PA	RI	SC	TN	VA	WV	WI	ASHA	CAE	DODDS	NASP	NASW
●		●		●		●	□		●			●	●		●	●				●			
●		●				●	□					●	●		●	●				●	●		
●	●	●		●		●	□	●	●	●		●	●	●	●	●					●		
											★												
											★												
											●												
											★												
★			●	●		●		●	●		●					●				●	●		
★			●	●		●		●	●		●					●				●	●		
★			●	●		●		●	●		●					●				●	●		
★			X	X		X		X	X		X					X				X			
★			X	X		X		X	X		X					X				X			
★			X	X		X		X	X		X					X				X			
											●												
	●														●								
								●															
											●												
											★												
											★												
●	●				●	●		●			●	●	●	●	●	●							
											★												
●								●	●									●					
●	●					●					●	●			□	●							
								●			●				★								
		★						●			●				★								
			●					●			●												
		★						●			●				★								
●			●		●							●		●		●							
●	●		●	●		●		●			●	●		●	●	●							
●	●					●						●			□	●							
								●			●				★								
								●			●				★								
●			●			●						●	●			●							
											●												
●																							
											●												
	●							●	●		●		●	●	●								

PRAXIS II: SUBJECT ASSESSMENTS & NTE SPECIALTY AREA TESTS	AR	CA	CT	DE	DC	FL	HI	ID	IN	KS	KY	LA	ME	MD	MN
Earth/Space Science (20570)			•	*					•						
Economics (20910)									•						
Education in the Elementary School (20010)	•					*			•		•	•		•	
Education of Students with Mental Retardation (10320)						*			•			•			
Educational Leadership: Administration & Supervision (10410)	•										•	•			
Elementary Educ: Content Area Exercises (20012)				*	•		*								
Elementary Educ: Curriculum, Instruction, and Assessment (10011)				*	•	*	•								
English Language & Literature (10040)	•								•		•	•		•	
English Language, Lit., & Composition: Content Knowledge (10041)			•	*	•	*	•				*				
English Language, Literature, & Composition: Essays (20042)		•	•	*							*				
English Language, Literature, & Composition: Pedagogy (30043)				*	•		•								
Environmental Education (10830)															
Foreign Language Pedagogy (10840)															
French (10170)	•		•			•			•		•	•		•	
French: Content Knowledge (10173)							•								
French: Linguistic, Literary, & Cultural Analysis (30172)		•													
French: Productive Language Skills (20171)		•	•				•								
General Science (10430)		•							•						
General Science: Content Essays (30433)		•		*			*								
General Science: Content Knowledge, Part 1 (10431)					•		•								
General Science: Content Knowledge, Part 2 (10432)				*	•		*				*				
Geography (20920)									•						
German (20180)		•	•				•		•		•	•		•	
German: Content Knowledge (20181)															
Government/Political Science (20930)									•						
Health & Physical Education (10850)															
Health Education (10550)	•		•						•						
Home Economics Education (10120)	•	•	•				•		•		•	•		•	
Introduction to the Teaching of Reading (10200)	•	•		*					•						
Italian (10620)			•												
Japanese (10660)															
Latin (10600)			•												
Library Media Specialist (10310)	•						•		•		•	•		•	
Marketing Education (10560)	•														
Marketing (PA) (10793)															
Mathematics (10060)	•		•			*			•		•	•		•	
Mathematics: Content Knowledge (10061)				*	•		•				*				
Mathematics: Pedagogy (20065)				*	•		•								
Mathematics: Proofs, Models, and Problems, Part 1 (20063)		•		*	•						*				
Mathematics: Proofs, Models, and Problems, Part 2 (30064)		•													
Music Education (10110)	•		•						•		•	•		•	
Music: Analysis (20112)		•													
Music: Concepts & Processes (30111)		•					•								
Music: Content Knowledge (10113)							•								
Office Technology (10980)															
Office Technology (PA) (10794)															
Physical Education (10090)	•					*			•		•	•		•	
Physical Education: Content Knowledge (10091)		•					•				*				
Physical Education: Movement Forms-Analysis & Design (30092)		•	•				•				*				
Physical Education: Movement Forms-Video Evaluation (20093)			•												
Physical Science: Content Essays (20482)		•		*			*								

MS	MO	MT	NE	NV	NJ	NM	NY	NC	OH	OK	OR	PA	RI	SC	TN	VA	WV	WI	ASHA	CAE	DODDS	NASP	NASW
	•							•				•			•	•							
															•								
•	•							•	•			•		•	•	•							
•								•	•		•			•		•							
•				•	•			•	•		•			•	•								
				•																			
				•																			
•	•													•	□	•							
					•			•			•	•			*								
				•				•			•				*								
				•				•							*								
											•												
											•												
•	•			•	•			•	•		•			•	•	•							
											*												
											*												
											*												
				•					•														
				*				•			•				*								
				*	•			•			•				*								
				*	•			•			•				*								
															•								
•	•				•			•			•					•							
											*												
															•								
											•												
	•			•				•	•		•	•		•	•	•							
•	•			•	•			•	•		•	•		•	•	•							
				•	•			•	•		•			•									
											•												
															•								
•								•	•		•	•		•	•								
•	•							•	•		•	•		•	•	•							
											•												
•	•							•	•		•			•	□	•							
				•	•			•			•				*								
				•				•			•				*								
				•							•												
											•												
•	•				•			•			•	•		•	•	•							
											*												
											*												
											*												
															•								
											•												
•	•					•								•	□	•							
				•	•			•			•				*								
				•				•			•				*								
											•												
				*																			

PRAXIS II: SUBJECT ASSESSMENTS & NTE SPECIALTY AREA TESTS	AR	CA	CT	DE	DC	FL	HI	ID	IN	KS	KY	LA	ME	MD	MN
Physical Science: Content Knowledge (20481)				*	•		•								
Physical Science: Pedagogy (30483)				*	•		*								
Physics (10260)			•						•					•	
Physics: Content Essays (30262)		•	•	*											
Physics: Content Knowledge (10261)				*			*				*				
Pre-Kindergarten Education (10530)									•						
Psychology (20390)									•						
Reading Specialist (10300)	•														
Safety/Driver Education (10860)															
School Food Service Supervisor (10970)															
School Guidance & Counseling (20420)	•					*	•								
School Psychologist (10400)	•										•				
School Social Worker (10210)						*									
Secretarial (PA) (10795)															
Social Studies (10080)	•					*			•		•	•		•	
Social Studies: Analytical Essays (20082)		•		*											
Social Studies: Content Knowledge (10081)					•	*	•	*	•			*			
Social Studies: Interpretation of Materials (20083)		•										*			
Social Studies: Pedagogy (30084)				*	•		•								
Sociology (20950)									•						
Spanish (10190)	•								•		•	•		•	
Spanish: Content Knowledge (10191)			•		•		•				*				
Spanish: Linguistic, Literary, & Cultural Analysis (30193)		•													
Spanish: Pedagogy (30194)					•		*								
Spanish: Productive Language Skills (20192)		•	•		•		*				*				
Special Education (10350)	•		•		•	*	•				•			•	
Special Education: Application of Core Principles Across Categories of Disability (10352)															
Special Education: Knowledge-based Core Principles (10351)							*								
Special Education: Preschool/Early Childhood (10690)															
Special Education: Teaching Students with Behavioral Disorders/Emotional Disturbances (20371)					*										
Special Education: Teaching Students with Learning Disabilities (20381)															
Special Education: Teaching Students with Mental Retardation (20321)															
Speech Communication (10220)	•								•		•			•	
Speech-Language Pathology (10330)	•														
Teaching Deaf and Hard of Hearing Students (10270)	•								•						
Teaching English as a Second Language (20360)					•		•								
Teaching Speech to Students with Language Impairments (10880)															
Teaching Students with Emotional Disturbance (10370)						*			•						
Teaching Students with Learning Disabilities (10380)						*			•						
Teaching Students with Orthopedic Impairments (10290)															
Teaching Students with Physical and Mental Disabilities (10870)															
Teaching Students with Visual Impairments (10280)	•														
Technology Education (10050)	•	•	•				•		•		•			•	
Theatre (10640)															
Vocational General Knowledge (10890)															
World & U.S. History (10940)															

MS	MO	MT	NE	NV	NJ	NM	NY	NC	OH	OK	OR	PA	RI	SC	TN	VA	WV	WI	ASHA	CAE	DODDS	NASP	NASW
				*				•							*								
•	•							•				•			□	•							
											•				*								
					•						•				*								
				•										•	•								
								•			•	•											
											•												
															•								
•				•				•	•		•			•	•								
•						•		•	•		•			•	•							•	
															•								•
											•												
•	•								•		•			•	•								
				•				•			•												
				•	•			•			•												
								•			•												
															•								
•	•								•					•	□	•							
				•	•			•			•				*								
				•				•			•				*								
•	•			•				•			•			•	•								
											*												
											*												
				*							•				•								
•	•			•	•			•			•				•	•							
•	•			•	•			•	•		•			•	*			•					
•								•			•	•		•									
								•	•														
				*								•											
•								•	•					•	•								
								•	•					•	•								
														•									
												•											
								•	•		•	•		•	•								
•	•				•			•			•	•		•	•	•							
															•								
												•											
				•											•								

Appendix 3

ALABAMA
State Department of Education
Teacher Certification Office
5201 Gordon Persons Bldg.
PO Box 302101
Montgomery, AL 36130-2101
(334) 242-9977

ALASKA
Department of Education
Teacher Education and Certification
801 W. 10th Street, Ste. 200
Juneau, AK 99811-0500
(907) 465-2831

ARIZONA
Teacher Certification Unit
PO Box 25609
1535 West Jefferson
Phoenix, AZ 85002
(602) 542-4368

ARKANSAS
Teacher Education and Certification
Department of Education
4 Capitol Mall
Little Rock, AR 72201-1071
(501) 682-4342

CALIFORNIA
Commission on Teacher Credentialing
1812 9th Street
Sacramento, CA 95814
(916) 445-7254

COLORADO
Teacher Certification
Department of Education
201 E. Colfax Avenue
Denver, CO 80203
(303) 866-6628

CONNECTICUT
Bureau of Certification and
Accreditation
State Department of Education
PO Box 2219
Hartford, CT 06145
(203) 566-5201

DELAWARE
Teacher Certification
Department of Public Instruction
PO Box 1402
Dover, DE 19903
(302) 739-4688

DISTRICT OF COLUMBIA
Division of Teacher Services
415 12th Street N.W.
Room 1013
Washington, DC 20004
(202) 724-4246

FLORIDA
Department of Teacher Certification
325 W. Gaines, Rm. 201
Tallahassee, FL 32399
(904) 488-5724

GEORGIA
Division of Teacher Certification
State Department of Education
1452 Twin Towers East
Atlanta, GA 30334-5070
(404) 656-2406

HAWAII
State Department of Education
Office of Personnel Services
PO Box 2360
Honolulu, HI 96804
(808) 586-3420

IDAHO
State Department of Education
Teacher Education and Certification
L. B. Jordan Office Building
PO Box 83720
Boise, ID 83720
(208) 334-3475

ILLINOIS
State Teacher Certification Board
100 N. First Street
Springfield, IL 62777
(217) 782-2805

INDIANA
Professional Standards Board
Center for Professional Development
Rm. 229, State House
Indianapolis, IN 46204-2798
(317) 232-9010

IOWA
Board of Educational Examiners
Practitional Preparation and Licensure
Bureau
Grimes State Office Building
Des Moines, IA 50319
(515) 281-3245

KANSAS
State Department of Education
Certification Office
120 S.E. 10th Street
Topeka, KS 66612-1103
(913) 296-2288

KENTUCKY
State Department of Education
Division of Certification
18th Floor—Capital Plaza Tower
500 Mero Street
Frankfort, KY 40601
(502) 564-4606

LOUISIANA
State Department of Education
Bureau of Higher Education and
Teacher Certification
PO Box 94064
Baton Rouge, LA 70804-9064
(504) 342-3490

MAINE
Department of Education
Division of Certification and
Placement
23 State House Station
Augusta, ME 04333
(207) 289-5944

MARYLAND
State Department of Education
Division of Certification and
Accreditation
200 West Baltimore Street
Baltimore, MD 21201
(410) 767-0412

MASSACHUSETTS
State Department of Education
Division of Educational Personnel
Teacher Certification
350 Melden Street
Quincy, MA 02148
(617) 388-3300

MICHIGAN
Teacher Preparation and Certification
Michigan Department of Education
PO Box 30008
Lansing, MI 48909
(517) 373-3310

MINNESOTA
State Department of Education
Personnel Licensing
Capitol Square Building
550 Cedar Street
St. Paul, MN 55101
(612) 296-2046

MISSISSIPPI
State Department of Education
Division of Teacher Certification
PO Box 771
Jackson, MS 39205-0771
(601) 359-3483

MISSOURI
Teacher Certification Office
Department of Elementary and
Secondary Education
PO Box 480
Jefferson City, MO 65102
(314) 751-3486

MONTANA
Office of Public Instruction
Teacher Education and Certification
State Capitol
PO Box 202501
Helena, MT 59620
(406) 444-3150

NEBRASKA
Department of Education
Teacher Education and Certification
301 Centennial Mall South
Box 94987
Lincoln, NE 68509-4987
(402) 471-2496

NEVADA
Department of Education
State Mail Room
1850 E. Sahara, Rm. 207
Las Vegas, NV 89158
(702) 486-6546

NEW HAMPSHIRE
State Department of Education
Bureau of Credentialing
State Office Park South
101 Pleasant Street
Concord, NH 03301
(603) 271-2407

NEW JERSEY
Department of Education
Division of Professional Development
240 West State Street, CN 500
Trenton, NJ 08625
(609) 984-1216

NEW MEXICO
State Department of Education
Professional Licensure Unit
Education Building
Santa Fe, NM 87501-2786
(505) 827-6587

NEW YORK
State Department of Education
Office of Teaching
Cultural Education Center
Empire State Plaza
Albany, NY 12230
(518) 474-3901

NORTH CAROLINA
Department of Public Instruction
Certification Section
361 N. Wilmington Street
Raleigh, NC 27601-2825
(919) 733-0377

NORTH DAKOTA
Educational Standards and Practices
Board
Teacher Certification
600 East Boulevard Avenue
Bismarck, ND 58505
(701) 328-2264

OHIO
Department of Education
Division of Teacher Education and
Certification
65 South Front Street
Columbus, OH 43215
(614) 466-3593

OKLAHOMA
Department of Education
Professional Standards
Hodge Education Building
2500 N. Lincoln Blvd., Rm. 211
Oklahoma City, OK 73105
(405) 521-3337

OREGON
Teacher Standards and Practices
Commission
255 Capitol Street N.E., Rm. 105
Salem, OR 97310
(503) 378-3586

PENNSYLVANIA
State Department of Education
Bureau of Teacher Preparation and
Certification
333 Market Street, 3rd Fl.
Harrisburg, PA 17126-0333
(717) 787-2967

RHODE ISLAND
Department of Education
Teacher Education and Certification
Roger Williams Building
22 Hayes Street
Providence, RI 02908
(401) 277-2675

SOUTH CAROLINA
State Department of Education
The Office of Education Professions
1429 Senate Street
Rm. 1015, Rutledge Building
Columbia, SC 29201
(803) 734-8466

SOUTH DAKOTA
Division of Education and Cultural
Affairs
Teacher Certification
700 Governor's Drive
Pierre, SD 57501
(605) 773-3553

TENNESSEE
State Department of Education
Teacher Licensing and Career Ladder
Certification
5th Fl., Gateway Plaza
710 James Robertson Parkway
Nashville, TN 37243
(615) 532-4885

TEXAS
Texas Education Agency
Teacher Certification
1701 North Congress Avenue
Austin, TX 78701-1494
(512) 463-8976

UTAH
State Office of Education
Certification and Personnel
Development
250 East 500 South Street
Salt Lake City, UT 84111
(801) 538-7741

VERMONT
State Department of Education
Educational Licensing Office
120 State Street
Montpelier, VT 05602-2703
(802) 828-2444

VIRGINIA
Department of Education
Teacher Certification
PO Box 2120
Richmond, VA 23216
(804) 225-2094

WASHINGTON
Professional Education and
Certification Office
Superintendent of Public Instruction
PO Box 47200
Olympia, WA 98504-7200
(360) 753-6773

WEST VIRGINIA
Department of Education
Office of Professional Preparation
Capitol Complex, Rm. B-337, Bldg. 6
Charleston, WV 25305
(800) 982-2378

WISCONSIN
Department of Public Instruction
Teacher Education, Licensing and
Placement
Teacher Certification
PO Box 7841
Madison, WI 53707-7841
(608) 266-1027

WYOMING
State Department of Education
Professional Teaching Standards
Board
Hathaway Bldg., 2nd Fl.
2300 Capital Drive
Cheyenne, WY 82002
(307) 777-6261

PUERTO RICO
Department of Education
Certification Office
PO Box 190759
San Juan, PR 00919
(809) 759-2000

U.S. Department of Defense
Overseas Dependent Section
Certification Unit
4040 N. Fairfax Drive
Arlington, VA 22203-1634
(703) 696-3081

VIRGIN ISLANDS
ST. THOMAS/ST. JOHNS DISTRICT
Educational Personnel Services
Department of Education
44-46 Kongens Gade
St. Thomas, VI 00802
(809) 774-5240

VIRGIN ISLANDS
ST. CROIX DISTRICT
Department of Education
Educational Personnel Services
21-23 Hospital Street
St. Croix, VI 00820
(809) 773-5844

Source: 1996 ASCUS Annual (Evanston, IL: Association for School, College and University Staffing, Inc., 1995).

Appendix 4

A SUMMARY OF SELECTED REPORTS ON EDUCATION REFORM

Title	Source	Data
The Paideia Proposal (1982)	Mortimer Adler for the Paideia Group	22 members contributed to a philosophical analysis of educational needs.
A Nation at Risk: The Imperative for Educational Reform (1983)	The National Commission on Excellence in Education—U.S. Department of Education	18 political and educational leaders commissioned papers and reviewed available materials, including national and international test scores.
America's Competitive Challenge: The Need for a Response (1983)	Business–Higher Education Forum	16 representatives of business and higher education reviewed expert opinions and past surveys.
Action for Excellence: A Comprehensive Plan to Improve Our Nation's Schools (1983)	Task Force of the Education Commission of the States, chaired by Governor James Hunt	41 governors, legislators, labor leaders, business leaders, and school board members collected data and interpreted results.
Academic Preparation for College: What Students Need to Know and Be Able to Do (1983)	Education Equality Project—The College Board	200 high school and college teachers and college board members collected and interpreted test results.
Making the Grade (1983)	Twentieth-Century Fund Task Force on Federal Elementary and Secondary Education Policy	11 members of state, local, and higher education organizations reviewed research studies.
Educating Americans for the 21st Century: A Report to the American People and the National Science Board (1983)	National Science Board Commission on Pre-College Education in Mathematics, Science and Technology	Commission members and others reviewed a number of professional association, business, and other education programs.
The Good High School: Portraits of Character and Culture (1983)	Sara Lawrence Lightfoot	Field study of six private and public schools.

Recommendations

The book urges a radical reorganization to focus on three areas: (1) the development of personal, mental, moral, and spiritual growth; (2) citizenship; and (3) basic skills. Teaching methods and subject areas would be revised, and there would be a core curriculum for all students from elementary through secondary education.

The report's powerful rhetoric, such as the "rising tide of mediocrity" and "a nation at risk," galvanized public attention regarding school reform. The report suggests that poor school performance threatens our nation's economic health. It emphasizes rigorous courses, a core curriculum, recruiting of talented teachers, and thorough assessment of student and teacher competence.

The report indicates that a major reason for U.S. economic problems and falling productivity is the inadequate education of the nation's workers, who need more schooling in mathematics, science, critical-thinking skills, and verbal expression.

The report urges state leadership to develop action plans for improving education, including more community involvement, additional funds, better preparation and pay for teachers, stronger curricular offerings, greater accountability, more effective principals, and better programs for poorly achieving students.

More rigorous preparation for college is called for, including better-trained teachers, more demanding elementary and secondary curricula, and higher expectations of students. Colleges should also provide remedial help for ill-prepared students and should work more closely with high schools in preparing students for college.

The report states that the criticism of U.S. schools is exaggerated and that schools are fundamentally doing their job. Suggestions for improvement include federal aid for schools, a clearer focus on educational quality, a continued commitment to educational equality, and support for local decision making.

Emphasizing a strong mathematics and science curriculum, the report highlights the need to attract individuals with these skills into teaching.

Although this is not technically a reform report, the author's observations of four public and two private high schools provide valuable insights into effective and ineffective school practices.

Title	Source	Data
High School: A Report on Secondary Education in America (1983)	The Carnegie Foundation for the Advancement of Teaching	Ernest Boyer chaired a national panel of educators and citizens who reviewed past research and undertook field studies in public high schools.
A Place Called School (1983)	John Goodlad	Presents observations of and results of questionnaires administered in schools over an 8-year period.
Horace's Compromise: The Dilemma of the American High School (1984)	Theodore Sizer	Interviews and observations in the 15 schools in the report *A Study of High Schools*.
The Shopping Mall High School (1985)	Arthur Powell, Eleanor Farrar, and David Cohen	One of three efforts in *A Study of High Schools,* this field analysis of 15 schools used comprehensive interviews and classroom observation.
The Last Citadel (1986)	Robert Hempel	Four of the 15 schools visited in *A Study of High Schools* were examined historically through oral histories, published and unpublished records, and historical files of a variety of educational institutions.
A Nation Prepared: Teachers for the 21st Century (1986)	Task Force on Teaching as a Profession, Carnegie Forum on Education and the Economy	14-member panel of educators, policy makers, politicians, and others analyzed existing data.
Tomorrow's Teachers (Holmes Report, 1986)	Deans of selected teacher education colleges	13 education deans and one college president formulate their professional and philosophical views.
Time for Results (1986)	National Governors Association	Lamar Alexander chaired the governor's task force that reviewed research and existing reports.
First Lessons (1986)	U.S. Department of Education	William Bennett and 21 other distinguished citizens summarize critical findings concerning more effective elementary education.

Recommendations

The report recommends a heavy emphasis on English (particularly writing) and a strong academic core for all students. It suggests elimination of the vocational track and advocates a 5-year teacher education program.

This report recommends making the principal a manager and creating a "head teacher" to focus on instructional improvement. Goodlad also calls for grouping students in clusters rather than by grade level. The book highlights the need for a greater variety of teaching methods to deal with student diversity.

Dramatizing the difficult working conditions facing teachers, Sizer emphasizes the need to develop close teacher-student relationships, high student motivation, and a less fragmented curriculum.

To ensure effective reform, the authors recommend an informed public, involved parents, high expectations and outstanding teachers, and more time in study and preparation of lessons, as well as greater standards of professionalism for teachers.

Hempel offers a study of the alteration of the U.S. high school since the 1940s, noting that academic subjects have remained intact and schedules and routines are virtually unchanged. The book highlights the need to deal sensitively with multiple priorities and recommends that more emphasis be placed on orderly thinking than on orderly discipline.

The report calls for the establishment of a National Board of Professional Teaching Standards to test and certify all teachers, as well as testing for and issuing an advanced teaching certificate. It recommends that all teachers take a 5-year teacher education program, including 4 years of liberal arts and science.

Expressing their personal and professional views, these educators call for reforming teacher education by requiring that all teachers receive a bachelor's degree in an academic field and a master's degree in education. The report recommends greater recognition of teaching and improvement of teachers' working conditions.

The governors placed themselves on the cutting edge of school reform by producing numerous recommendations, including parental choice in school selection, career ladders, state takeovers of poorly performing school districts, programs to prevent students from dropping out, and emphasis on technology in teacher preparation.

The former secretary of education calls for elementary students to be taught a rigorous regime of reading and other basic skills, including foreign language and computer skills.

Title	Source	Data
James Madison High (1986)	U.S. Department of Education	William Bennett provides his ideas for a high school curriculum, based on research and practice in secondary schools.
Turning Points: Preparing American Youth for the 21st Century (1989)	Carnegie Foundation Task Force on Education of Young Adolescents	David Hornbeck chaired the 18-member task force of educators, government officials, and others who, through analysis of interviews and commission studies, collected relevant data.
America 2000: An Education Strategy (1991) **Goals 2000: Educate America Act (1994)**	President Bush and governors; continued and modified by the Clinton administration	Administration-led political effort to respond to educational needs cited in numerous reports, international test scores, etc.

Recommendations

The former secretary of education recommends a traditional high school curriculum with few electives; 4 years of literature; a senior research paper; 3 years of math, science, and social studies with a U.S. and Western focus; and emphasis on foreign language.

This is an unusual report in that it focuses on the junior high, or middle school, a period of significant physical, social, and psychological change for young adolescents. Recommendations include creating small learning communities within large schools, a core curriculum that is academically demanding, elimination of tracking, empowering teachers and principals by giving them more authority, improving school–community–parent relationships, and promoting student self-esteem.

A political consensus identified a number of national goals: among others, a 90 percent or higher high school graduation rate, number one ranking for U.S. students in math and science, 100 percent adult literacy, parental involvement, and teacher development.

GLOSSARY

ability grouping The assignment of pupils to homogeneous groups according to intellectual ability or level, for instructional purposes.

academic freedom The opportunity for teachers and students to learn, teach, study, research, and question without censorship, coercion, or external political and other restrictive influences.

academic learning time The time a student is actively engaged with the subject matter and experiencing a high success rate.

academies The private or semipublic secondary schools in the United States from 1830 through 1870 that stressed practical subjects.

accelerated program The more rapid promotion of gifted students through school.

accountability Holding schools and teachers responsible for student performance.

accreditation Certifying an education program or school that has met professional standards of an outside agency.

achievement tests Examinations of the knowledge and skills acquired, usually as a result of specific instruction.

adult education Courses and programs offered to high school graduates by colleges, business, industry, and governmental and private organizations that lead to academic degrees, occupational preparation, and the like.

advanced placement Courses and programs in which younger students can earn college credit.

aesthetics The branch of philosophy that examines the nature of beauty and judgments about it.

affective domain The area of learning that involves attitudes, values, and emotions.

affirmative action A plan by which personnel policies and hiring practices reflect positive steps in recruiting and hiring women and members of minority groups.

allocated time The amount of time a school or an individual teacher schedules for a subject.

alternative school A private or public school that provides religious, academic, or other alternatives to the regular public school.

American Federation of Teachers (AFT) A national organization of teachers that is primarily concerned with improving educational conditions and protecting teachers' rights.

authentic assessment A type of evaluation that represents actual performance, encourages students to reflect on their own work, and is integrated into the student's whole learning process. Such tests usually require that students synthesize knowledge from different areas and use that knowledge actively.

back to basics During the 1980s, a revival of the back to basics movement evolved out of concern for declining test scores in math, science, reading, and other areas. Although there is not a precise definition of back to basics, many consider it to include increased emphasis on reading, writing, and arithmetic, fewer electives, and more rigorous grading.

behavioral objective A specific statement of what a learner must accomplish in order to demonstrate mastery.

behavior modification A strategy to alter behavior in a desired direction through the use of rewards.

bilingual education Educational programs in which students of limited or no English-speaking ability attend classes taught in English, as well as in their native language. There is great variability in these programs in terms of goals, instructional opportunity, and balance between English and a student's native language.

board certification Recognition of advanced teaching competence, awarded to teachers who demonstrate high levels of knowledge, commitment, and professionalism through a competitive review process administered by the National Board for Professional Teaching Standards.

board of education Constituted at the state and local levels, this agency is responsible for formulating educational policy. Members are sometimes appointed but, more frequently, they are elected at the local level.

busing A method for remedying segregation by transporting students to schools that have been racially or ethnically unbalanced. It should be noted that before busing and desegregation were linked, busing was not a controversial issue, and in fact, the vast majority of students riding school buses are not involved in desegregation programs.

career education A program to teach elementary and secondary students about the world of work by integrating career awareness and exploration into the school curriculum.

career ladder A system designed to create different status levels for teachers by developing steps one can climb to receive increased pay through increased responsibility or experience.

Carnegie unit A credit awarded to a student for successfully completing a high school course. It is used in determining graduation requirements and college admissions.

categorical grant Financial aid to local school districts from state or federal agencies for specific purposes.

certification State government evaluation and approval that results in an applicant's being provided with a license to teach.

character education A model comprised of various strategies that promote a defined set of core values to students.

charter school A group of teachers, parents, and even businesses may petition a local school board, or state government, to form a charter school which is exempt from many state and local regulations. Designed to promote creative new schools, the charter represents legal permission to try new approaches to educate students. First charter legislation was passed in Minnesota in 1991.

chief state school officer The executive head of a state department of education. The chief state school officer is responsible for carrying out the mandates of the state board of education and enforcing educational laws and regulations. This position is also referred to as *state superintendent.*

child advocacy movement A movement dedicated to defining and protecting the rights of children. Child advocates recognize that children are not yet ready to assume all the rights and privileges of adults, but they are firmly committed to expanding the rights currently enjoyed by children and to no longer treating children as objects or as the property of others.

child-centered instruction Instruction that is designed to meet the interests and needs of individual students. It is also referred to as **individualized instruction.**

classroom climate A term that refers to the physical, emotional, and aesthetic characteristics, as well as the learning resources, of a school classroom.

cognitive domain The area of learning that involves knowledge, information, and intellectual skills.

Coleman report A study commissioned by President Johnson (1964) to analyze the factors that influence the academic achievement of students. One of the major findings of James Coleman's report was that schools in general have relatively little impact on learning. Family and peers were found to have more impact on a child's education than the school itself did.

collective bargaining A negotiating procedure between employer and employees for resolving disagreements on salaries, work schedules, and other conditions of employment. In collective bargaining, all teachers in a school system bargain as one group through chosen representives.

common school Refers to a public, tax-supported school. First established in Massachusetts, the school's purpose was to create a common basis of knowledge for children. It usually refers to a public elementary school.

community schools Schools connected with a local community to provide for the educational needs of that community.

compensatory education Educational experiences and opportunities designed to overcome or compensate difficulties associated with a student's disadvantaged background.

competency The ability to perform a particular skill or to demonstrate a specified level of knowledge.

competency-based teacher education (CBTE) A teacher preparation approach in which knowledge and skills requisite for successful teaching performance are specified and teacher candidates are held responsible for mastering these competencies. It is also referred to as *performance-based teacher education* (PBTE).

comprehensive high school A public secondary school that offers a variety of curricula, including vocational, academic, and general education programs.

compulsory attendance A state law requiring that children and adolescents attend school until reaching a specified age.

computer-assisted instruction (CAI) Individualized instruction between a student and programmed instructional material stored in a computer.

computer-managed instruction (CMI) A record-keeping procedure for tracking student performance using a computer.

consolidation The trend toward combining small or rural school districts into larger ones.

cooperative learning In classrooms using cooperative learning, students work on activities in small groups, and they receive rewards based on the overall group performance.

core curriculum Refers to a central body of knowledge that schools require all students to study.

corporal punishment Disciplining students through physical punishment by a school employee.

cultural literacy Refers to student knowledge of those people, places, events, and concepts central to knowledge of the standard literate culture.

cultural pluralism Acceptance and encouragement of cultural diversity.

curriculum Planned content of instruction that enables the school to meet its aims.

curriculum development The processes of assessing needs, formulating objectives, and developing instructional opportunities and evaluation.

dame schools Primary schools in colonial and other early periods in which students were taught by untrained women in the women's own homes.

day care centers Facilities charged with caring for children. The quality of care varies dramatically and may range from well-planned educational programs to little more than custodial supervision.

decentralization The trend of dividing large school districts into smaller and, it is hoped, more responsive units.

deductive reasoning Working from a general rule to identify particular examples and applications to that rule.

de facto segregation The segregation of racial or other groups resulting from circumstances such as housing patterns rather than from official policy or law.

de jure segregation The segregation of racial or other groups on the basis of law, policy, or a practice designed to accomplish such separation.

Department of Education (ED) U.S. cabinet-level department in charge of federal educational policy and the promotion of programs to carry out policies.

descriptive data Refers to the collection and categorization of information to provide an objective depiction of various aspects of school or classroom life.

desegregation The process of correcting past practices of racial or other illegal segregation.

direct teaching A model of instruction in which the teacher is a strong leader who structures the classroom and sequences subject matter to reflect a clear academic focus. This model emphasizes the importance of a structured lesson in which presentation of new information is followed by student practice and teacher feedback.

disabled See **handicapped.**

dual-track system The European traditional practice of separate primary schools for most children and secondary schools for the upper class.

due process Refers to the procedural requirements that must be followed in such areas as student and teacher discipline and placement in special educational programs. Due process exists to safeguard individuals from arbitrary, capricious, or unreasonable policies, practices or actions. The essential elements of due process are (1) a notice of the charge or actions to be taken, (2) the opportunity to be heard, (3) and the right to a defense that reflects the particular circumstances and nature of the case.

early childhood education Learning undertaken by young children in the home, in nursery schools, and in kindergartens.

eclecticism In this text, refers to drawing on elements from several educational philosophies or methods.

educable child A mentally retarded child who is capable of achieving only a limited basic learning and usually must be instructed in a special class.

educational malpractice A new experimental line of litigation similar to the concept of medical malpractice. Educational malpractice is concerned with assessing liability for students who graduate from school without fundamental skills. Unlike medical malpractice, many courts have rejected the notion that schools or educators be held liable for this problem.

educational park A large, campuslike facility often including many grade levels and several schools and often surrounded by a variety of cultural resources.

educational television programming Refers to those television programs that are educational.

educational vouchers A flat grant or payment representing the cost of educating a student at a school. Awarded to the parent or child to enable free choice of a school—public or private—the voucher payment is made to the school that accepts the child.

elementary school An educational institution for children in grades 1 to 6 or 1 to 8, often including kindergarten.

emergency certificate A substandard certificate that recognizes teachers who have not met all the requirements for certification. It is issued on a temporary basis to meet the needs of communities that do not have certified teachers available.

emotional intelligence (EQ) Personality characteristics, such as persistence, can be measured as part of a new human dimension referred to as EQ. Some believe that EQ scores may be better predictors of future success than IQ scores.

empiricism The philosophy that maintains that sensory experiences such as seeing, hearing, and touching are the ultimate sources of all human knowledge. Empiricists believe that we experience the external world by sensory perception; then, through reflection, we conceptualize ideas that help us interpret the world.

enculturation The process of acquiring a culture; a child's acquisition of the cultural heritage through both formal and informal educational means.

engaged time The part of time that a teacher schedules for a subject in which the students are actively involved with academic subject matter. Listening to a lecture, participating in a class discussion, and working on math problems all constitute engaged time.

English grammar school The demand for a more practical education in eighteenth-century America led to the creation of these private schools that taught commerce, navigation, engineering, and other vocational skills.

environmental education The study and analysis of the conditions and causes of pollution, overpopulation, and waste of natural resources, and of the ways to preserve Earth's intricate ecology.

epistemology The branch of philosophy that examines the nature of knowledge and learning.

equal educational opportunity Refers to giving every student the educational opportunity to develop fully whatever talents, interests, and abilities he or she may have, without regard to race, color, national origin, sex, disability, or economic status.

equity Refers to educational policy and practice that is just, fair, and free from bias and discrimination.

essentialism An educational philosophy that emphasizes basic skills of reading, writing, mathematics, science, history, geography, and language.

establishment clause A section of the First Amendment of the U.S. Constitution that says that Congress shall make no law respecting the establishment of religion. This clause prohibits nonparochial schools from teaching religion.

ethics The branch of philosophy that examines questions of right and wrong and good and bad.

ethnic group A group of people with a distinctive culture and history.

evaluation Assessment of learning and instruction.

exceptional learners Students who require special education and related services in order to realize their full potential. Categories of exceptionality include retarded, gifted, learning disabled, emotionally disturbed, and physically disabled.

existentialism A philosophy that emphasizes the ability of an individual to determine the course and nature of her or his life and the importance of personal decision making.

expulsion Dismissal of a student from school for a lengthy period, ranging from one semester to permanently.

extracurriculum The part of school life that comprises activities such as sports, academic and social clubs, band, chorus, orchestra, and theater. Many educators think that the extracurriculum develops important skills and values, including leadership, teamwork, creativity, and diligence.

fair use A legal principle allowing limited use of copyrighted materials. Teachers must observe three criteria: brevity, spontaneity, and cumulative effect.

Flanders Interaction Analysis An instrument developed by Ned Flanders for categorizing student and teacher verbal behavior, it is used to interpret the nature of classroom verbal interaction.

flexible scheduling A technique for organizing time more effectively in order to meet the needs of instruction by dividing the school day into smaller time modules that can be combined to fit a task.

foundation program Program for distribution of state funds designed to guarantee a specified minimum level of educational support for each child.

future shock Term coined by Alvin Toffler. It refers to the extraordinarily accelerated rate of change and the disorientation of those unable to adapt to rapidly altered norms, institutions, and values.

futurism In this book, focused forecasting and planning for future developments in education.

gifted learner There is great variance in definitions and categorizations of the "gifted." The term is most frequently applied to those with exceptional intellectual ability, but it may also refer to learners with outstanding ability in athletics, leadership, music, creativity, and so forth.

global education Because economics, politics, scientific innovation, and societal developments in different countries have an enormous impact on children in the United States, the goals of global education include increased knowledge about the peoples of the world, resolutions of global problems, increased fluency in foreign languages, and the development of more tolerant attitudes toward other cultures and peoples.

handicapped A learning or physical condition, a behavior, or an emotional problem that impedes education. Educators now prefer to speak of "students with disabilites," not "handicapped students," emphasizing the person, not the disability.

Head Start Federally funded pre-elementary school program to provide learning opportunities for disadvantaged students.

heterogeneous grouping A group or class consisting of students who show normal variation in ability or performance. It differs from *homogeneous grouping,* in which criteria such as grades or scores on standardized tests are used to group students similar in ability or achievement.

hidden curriculum What students learn, other than academic content, from what they do or are expected to do in school; incidental learnings.

hidden government The unofficial power structure within a school. It cannot be identified by the official title, position, or functions of individuals. For example, it reflects the potential influence of a school secretary or custodian.

higher-order questions Questions that require students to go beyond memory in formulating a response. These questions require students to analyze, synthesize, evaluate, and so on.

home schooling A growing trend (but a longtime practice) of parents educating their children at home, for religious or philosophical reasons.

homogeneous grouping The classification of pupils for the purpose of forming instructional groups having a relatively high degree of intellectual similarity.

hornbook A single sheet of parchment containing the Lord's Prayer and letters of the alphabet. It was protected by a thin sheath from the flattened horn of a cow and fastened to a wooden board, hence, the name. It was used during the colonial era in primary schools.

humanistic education A curriculum that stresses personal student growth; self-actualizing, moral, and esthetic issues are explored.

idealism A doctrine holding that knowledge is derived from ideas and emphasizing moral and spiritual reality as a preeminent source of explanation.

independent school A nonpublic school unaffiliated with any church or other agency.

individualized education program (IEP) The mechanism through which a disabled child's special needs are identified, objectives and services are described, and evaluation is designed.

individualized instruction Curriculum content and instructional materials, media, and activities designed for individual learning. The pace, interests, and abilities of the learner determine the curriculum.

inductive reasoning Drawing generalizations based on the observation of specific examples.

infrastructure A substructure of underlying foundation; especially, the basic installations and facilities on which the continuance and growth of a community depend.

in loco parentis Latin term meaning "in place of the parents"; that is, a teacher or school administrator assumes the duties and responsibilities of the parents during the hours the child attends school.

instruction The process of implementing a curriculum.

integration The process of developing positive interracial contacts and improving the performance of low-achieving minority students.

interest centers Usually associated with an open classroom, such centers provide independent student activities related to a specific subject.

junior high school A 2- or 3-year school between elementary and high shool for students in their early adolescent years, commonly grades 7 and 8 or 7 to 9.

kindergarten A preschool, early childhood educational environment first designed by Froebel in the mid-nineteenth century.

labeling Refers to categorizing or classifying students for the purposes of educational placement. One unfortunate consequence may be that of stigmatizing students and inhibiting them from reaching their full potential.

laboratory schools Schools often associated with a teacher preparation institution for practice teaching, demonstration, research, or innovation.

land grant colleges State colleges or universities offering agricultural and mechanical curricula, funded originally by the Morrill Act of 1862.

latchkey kids A term used to describe those children who come home after school to an empty house; their parents or guardians are usually working and not home.

Latin grammar school A classical secondary school with a Latin and Greek curriculum preparing students for college.

learning centers See **interest centers**.

learning disability An educationally significant language and/or learning deficit.

least restrictive environment Refers to the program best suited to meeting a disabled student's special needs without segregating the student from the regular educational program.

limited English proficiency (LEP) A student who has a limited ability to understand, speak, or read English and who has a native language other than English.

logic The branch of philosophy that deals with reasoning. Logic defines the rules of reasoning, focuses on how to move from one set of assumptions to valid conclusions, and examines the rules of inference that enable us to frame our propositions and arguments.

lower-order questions Questions that require the retrieval of memorized information and do not require more complex intellectual processes.

magnet school A specialized school open to all students in a district on a competitive or lottery basis. It provides a method of drawing children away from segregated neighborhood schools while affording unique educational specialties, such as science, math, and the performing arts.

mainstreaming The inclusion of special education students in the regular education program. The nature and extent of this inclusion should be based on meeting the special needs of the child.

malfeasance Deliberately acting improperly and causing harm to someone.

mastery learning An educational practice in which an individual demonstrates mastery of one task before moving on to the next.

merit pay A salary system that periodically evaluates teacher performance and uses these evaluations in determining salary.

metacognition Self-awareness of our thinking process as we perform various tasks and operations. For example, when students articulate how they think about academic tasks, it enhances their thinking and enables teachers to target assistance and remediation.

metaphysics The area of philosophy that examines the nature of reality.

microteaching A clinical approach to teacher training in which the teacher candidate teaches a small group of students for a brief time while concentrating on a specific teaching skill.

middle schools Two- to four-year schools of the middle grades, commonly grades 5 through 8, between elementary school and high school.

minimum competency tests Exit-level tests designed to ascertain whether students have achieved basic levels of performance in areas such as reading, writing, and computation. Some states require that a secondary student pass a minimum competency test in order to receive a high school diploma.

misfeasance Failure to act in a proper manner to prevent harm.

multicultural education Refers to educational policies and practices that not only recognize but also affirm human differences and similarities associated with gender, race, ethnicity, nationality, disability, and class.

multiple intelligences A theory developed by Howard Gardner to expand the concept of human intelligence to include areas, such as logical-mathematical, linguistic, bodily-kinesthetic, musical, spatial, interpersonal, and intrapersonal.

National Assessment of Educational Progress (NAEP) Program to ascertain the effectiveness of U.S. schools and student achievement.

National Association of State Directors of Teacher Education and Certification (NASDTEC) An organization comprising participating state departments of education that evaluates teacher education programs in higher education.

National Council for the Accreditation of Teacher Education (NCATE) An organization that evaluates teacher education programs in many colleges and universities. Programs approved by the NCATE have assured approval of applications for teacher certification in over half the states.

National Education Association (NEA) The largest organization of educators, the NEA is concerned with the overall improvement of education and of the conditions of educators. It is organized at the national, state, and local levels.

nonfeasance Failure to exercise appropriate responsibility that results in someone's being harmed.

nongraded school A school organization in which grade lines are eliminated for 2 or more years.

nonverbal communication The act of transmitting and/or receiving messages through means not having to do with oral or written language, such as eye contact, facial expressions, or body language.

normal school A 2-year teacher education institution popular in the nineteenth century that frequently was expanded to become today's state colleges and universities.

norm-referenced tests Tests that compare individual students to others in a designated norm group.

objective The purpose of a lesson expressed in a statement.

objective-referenced tests Tests that measure whether students have mastered a designated body of knowledge rather than how they compare to other students in a norm group.

observation techniques Structured methods for observing various aspects of school or classroom activities.

open classroom Based on the British model, it refers not only to an informal classroom environment but also to a philosophy of education. Students pursue individual interests with the guidance and support of the teacher; interest centers are created to promote this individualized instruction. Students may also have a significant influence in determining the nature and sequence of the curriculum. It is sometimes referred to as *open education*.

open enrollment The practice of permitting students to attend the school of their choice within their school system. It is sometimes associated with magnet schools and desegregation efforts.

open-space school Refers to a school building without interior walls. Although it may be designed to promote the concept of the open classroom, the open-space school is an architectural concept rather than an educational one.

paraprofessional A lay person who serves as an aide, assisting the teacher in the classroom.

parochial school An institution operated and controlled by a religious denomination.

peace studies The study and analysis of the conditions of and need for peace, the causes of war, and the mechanisms for the nonviolent resolution of conflict. It is also referred to as *peace education*.

pedagogical cycle A system of teacher-student interaction that includes four steps: structure—teacher introduces the topic; question—teacher asks questions; respond—student answers or tries to answer questions; and react—teacher reacts to student's answers and provides feedback.

pedagogy The science of teaching.

perennialism The philosophy that emphasizes rationality as the major purpose of education. It asserts that the essential truths are recurring and universally true; it stresses Great Books.

permanent certificate Although there is some variation from state to state, a permanent certificate is issued after a candidate has completed all the requirements for full recognition as a teacher. Requirements may include a specified number of courses beyond the bachelor's degree or a specified number of years of teaching experience.

political philosophy An approach to analyzing how past and present societies are arranged and governed and how better societies may be created in the future.

portfolio Compilations of student work (such as papers, projects, videotapes, etc.) assembled to demonstrate student progress, creativity, and competence. Often advocated as a more comprehensive assessment than test scores.

Praxis series of tests Developed by ETS to assess teachers' competence in various areas: reading, writing, math, professional and subject area knowledge. Praxis test requirements differ among states. (Appendix 2)

primary school A separately organized and administered elementary school for students in the lower elementary grades, usually grades 1 through 3, and sometimes including preprimary years.

private school A school controlled by an individual or agency other than the government, usually supported by other than public funds.

probationary teaching period A specified period of time in which a newly hired teacher must demonstrate teaching competence. This period is usually 3 years for public school teachers and 6 years for college professors. Generally, upon satisfactory completion of the probationary period, a teacher is granted **tenure.**

progressive education An educational philosophy emphasizing democracy, student needs, practical activities, and school-community relationships.

project-based instruction An approach that builds curriculum around intriguing real-life problems and asks students to work cooperatively to develop and demonstrate their solutions.

provisional certificate Also referred to as a *probationary certificate,* a provisional certificate is frequently issued to beginning teachers. It may mean that a person has completed most, but not all, of the state requirements for permanent certification. Or, it may mean that the state requires several years of teaching experience before it will qualify the teacher for higher certification.

racial discrimination Actions that limit or deny a person or group any privileges, roles, or rewards on the basis of race.

racism Attitudes, beliefs, and behavior based on the notion that one race is superior to other races.

rationalism The philosophy that emphasizes the power of reason and the principles of logic to derive statements about the world. Rationalists encourage schools to emphasize teaching mathematics, because mathematics involves reason and logic.

readability formulas Formulas that use objective, quantitative measures to determine the reading level of textbooks.

reflective teaching Predicated on a broad and in-depth understanding of what is happening in the classroom, reflective teaching promotes thoughtful consideration and dialogue about classroom events.

revenue sharing The distribution of federal money to state and local governments to use as they decide.

romantic critics Critics such as Paul Goodman, Herbert Kohl, John Holt, and so on, who believed that schools were stifling the cognitive and affective development of children. Individual critics stressed different problems or solutions, but they all agreed that schools were producing alienated, uncreative, and unfulfilled students.

sabbatical A leave usually granted with full or partial pay after a teacher has taught for a specified period of time (for example, 6 years). Typically, it is to encourage research and professional development.

school-based management The recent trend in education reform that stresses decision making on the school level. In the past, school policies were set by the state and the districts. Now there is a trend towards individual schools' making their own decisions and policies.

school bonds A method of financing a substantial, one-time education expenditure, such as a new school building. School bonds are typically brought before the public to be approved or disapproved, for they usually require a tax increase.

school financing Refers to the ways in which monies are raised and allocated to schools. The methods differ widely from state to state, and many challenges are being made in courts today because of the unequal distribution of funds within a state or among states.

school infrastructure The basic facilities and structures that underpin a school plant, such as plumbing, sewage, heat, electricity, roof, masonry, and carpentry.

school superintendent The chief administrator of a school system, responsible for implementing and enforcing the school board's policies, rules, and regulations, as well as state and federal requirements. The superintendent is directly responsible to the school board and is the formal representative of the school community to outside individuals and agencies.

schools without walls An alternative education program that stressed involving the total community as a learning resource.

secular humanism The belief that people can live ethically without faith in a supernatural or supreme being. Some critics have alleged the secular humanism is a form of religion and that publishers are promoting secular humanism in their books.

separate but equal A legal doctrine that holds that equality of treatment is accorded when the races are provided substantially equal facilities, even though those facilities are separate. This doctrine was ruled unconstitutional in regard to race.

sex bias The degree to which an individual's beliefs and behavior are prejudiced on the basis of sex.

sex discrimination Any action that limits or denies a person or group of persons opportunities, privileges, roles, or rewards on the basis of sex.

sexism The collection of attitudes, beliefs, and behavior that results from the assumption that one sex is superior to the other.

sex-role stereotyping Attributing behavior, abilities, interests, values, and roles to a person or group of persons on the basis of sex. This process ignores individual differences.

simulation A role-playing technique in which students take part in re-created real-life situations.

Socratic method An educational strategy attributed to Socrates by which a teacher encourages a student's discovery of truth by questions.

special certificate A non-teaching license that is designed for specialized educational careers, such as counseling, library science, and administration.

special education Programs and instruction for children with physical, mental, emotional, or learning disabilities or gifted students who need special educational services in order to achieve at their ability level.

state adoption The process by which members of a textbook adoption committee review and select the books used throughout a state. Advocates of this process say that it results in a common statewide curriculum that unites educators on similar issues and makes school life easier for students who move within the state. Critics charge that it gives too much influence to large states and results in a "dumbed down" curriculum.

state board of education The state education agency that regulates policies necessary to implement legislative acts related to education.

state department of education An agency that operates under the direction of the state board of education, accrediting schools, certifying teachers, appropriating state school funds, and so on.

street academies Alternative schools designed to bring dropouts and potential dropouts, often inner-city youths, back into the educational mainstream.

superintendent of schools The executive officer of the local school district.

taxonomy A classification system of organizing information and translating aims into instructional objectives.

teacher centers Sites to provide training to improve teaching skills, inform teachers of current educational research, and develop new curricular programs.

teacher flexibility Adapting a variety of skills, abilities, characteristics, and approaches, according to the demands of each situation and the needs of each student.

tenure A system of employment in which teachers, having served a probationary period, acquire an expectancy of continued employment. The majority of states have tenure laws.

tracking The method of placing students according to their ability level in homogeneous classes or learning experiences. Once a student is placed, it may be very difficult to move up from one track to another. The placements may reflect racism or sexism.

transitional bilingual education Teaching students in their own language until they can learn in the national language.

tuition tax credits Tax reductions for parents or guardians of children attending public or private schools.

unobtrusive measurement A method of observing a situation without altering it.

values clarification A model, comprising various strategies, that encourages students to express and clarify their values on different topics.

vouchers A voucher is like a coupon, and represents money targeted for schools. In a voucher system, parents would take educational vouchers and "shop" for a school. Schools would receive part or all of their per-pupil funding from these vouchers. In theory, good schools would thrive and poor ones would close for lack of students.

wait time The amount of time a teacher waits for a student's response after a question is asked. Also, the amount of time following a student's response before the teacher reacts.

zero reject The principle that no child with disabilities may be denied a free and appropriate public education.

PHOTO CREDITS

INDEX

Numbers in **boldface** indicate where a term is defined in the text.